Cisco Networking Academy Program

CCNA 1 and 2 Companion Guide
Revised Third Edition

Cisco Press

800 East 96th Street

Indianapolis, Indiana 46240 USA

www.ciscopress.com

Cisco Networking Academy Program

CCNA 1 and 2 Companion Guide
Revised Third Edition

Cisco Systems, Inc.
Cisco Networking Academy Program
Copyright © 2005 Cisco Systems, Inc.

Published by:
Cisco Press
800 East 96th Street
Indianapolis, Indiana 46240 USA

All rights reserved. No part of this book may be reproduced or transmitted in any form or by any means, electronic or mechanical, including photocopying, recording, or by any information storage and retrieval system, without written permission from the publisher, except for the inclusion of brief quotations in a review.

ISBN: 1-58713-150-1

Library of Congress Cataloging-in-Publication Number: 2004101985

Printed in the United States of America   1 2 3 4 5 6 7 8 9 0

First Printing   August 2004

Trademark Acknowledgments

All terms mentioned in this book that are known to be trademarks or service marks have been appropriately capitalized. Cisco Press or Cisco Systems, Inc., cannot attest to the accuracy of this information. Use of a term in this book should not be regarded as affecting the validity of any trademark or service mark.

Warning and Disclaimer

This book is designed to provide information about CCNA 1: Networking Basics and CCNA 2: Routers and Routing Basics of the Cisco Networking Academy Program CCNA curriculum. Every effort has been made to make this book as complete and as accurate as possible, but no warranty or fitness is implied.

The information is provided on an "as is" basis. The author, Cisco Press, and Cisco Systems, Inc., shall have neither liability nor responsibility to any person or entity with respect to any loss or damages arising from the information contained in this book or from the use of the discs or programs that may accompany it.

The opinions expressed in this book belong to the author and are not necessarily those of Cisco Systems, Inc.

This book is part of the Cisco Networking Academy® Program series from Cisco Press. The products in this series support and complement the Cisco Networking Academy Program curriculum. If you are using this book outside the Networking Academy program, then you are not preparing with a Cisco trained and authorized Networking Academy provider.

For information on the Cisco Networking Academy Program or to locate a Networking Academy, please visit www.cisco.com/edu.

Corporate and Government Sales

Cisco Press offers excellent discounts on this book when ordered in quantity for bulk purchases or special sales.

For more information please contact: U.S. Corporate and Government Sales 1-800-382-3419
corpsales@pearsontechgroup.com

For sales outside the U.S. please contact: International Sales international@pearsoned.com

Feedback Information

At Cisco Press, our goal is to create in-depth technical books of the highest quality and value. Each book is crafted with care and precision, undergoing rigorous development that involves the unique expertise of members from the professional technical community.

Readers' feedback is a natural continuation of this process. If you have any comments regarding how we could improve the quality of this book or otherwise alter it to better suit your needs, you can contact us through e-mail at networkingacademy@ciscopress.com. Please make sure to include the book title and ISBN in your message.

We greatly appreciate your assistance.

Publisher	John Wait
Editor-in-Chief	John Kane
Executive Editor	Mary Beth Ray
Cisco Representative	Anthony Wolfenden
Cisco Press Program Manager	Nannette M. Noble
Production Manager	Patrick Kanouse
Senior Development Editor	Chris Cleveland
Senior Editor	Sheri Cain
Revised Edition Technical Editors	Bill Chapman, Rick Graziani, Elaine Horn, Allan Johnson, Andrew Large, and Tony Rufi
Third Edition Technical Editors	Jhun DeLeon, Ralph Duffy, Jim Lorenz, Arthur Tucker
Assistant Editor	Tammi Barnett
Designer	Louisa Adair
Composition	Mark Shirar, Octal Publishing, Inc.
Indexer	Tim Wright
Proofreader	Marcia Ellett

Corporate Headquarters
Cisco Systems, Inc.
170 West Tasman Drive
San Jose, CA 95134-1706
USA
www.cisco.com
Tel: 408 526-4000
      800 553-NETS (6387)
Fax: 408 526-4100

European Headquarters
Cisco Systems International BV
Haarlerbergpark
Haarlerbergweg 13-19
1101 CH Amsterdam
The Netherlands
www-europe.cisco.com
Tel: 31 0 20 357 1000
Fax: 31 0 20 357 1100

Americas Headquarters
Cisco Systems, Inc.
170 West Tasman Drive
San Jose, CA 95134-1706
USA
www.cisco.com
Tel: 408 526-7660
Fax: 408 527-0883

Asia Pacific Headquarters
Cisco Systems, Inc.
Capital Tower
168 Robinson Road
#22-01 to #29-01
Singapore 068912
www.cisco.com
Tel: +65 6317 7777
Fax: +65 6317 7799

Cisco Systems has more than 200 offices in the following countries and regions. Addresses, phone numbers, and fax numbers are listed on the
Cisco.com Web site at www.cisco.com/go/offices.

Argentina • Australia • Austria • Belgium • Brazil • Bulgaria • Canada • Chile • China PRC • Colombia • Costa Rica • Croatia • Czech Republic
Denmark • Dubai, UAE • Finland • France • Germany • Greece • Hong Kong SAR • Hungary • India • Indonesia • Ireland • Israel • Italy
Japan • Korea • Luxembourg • Malaysia • Mexico • The Netherlands • New Zealand • Norway • Peru • Philippines • Poland • Portugal
Puerto Rico • Romania • Russia • Saudi Arabia • Scotland • Singapore • Slovakia • Slovenia • South Africa • Spain • Sweden
Switzerland • Taiwan • Thailand • Turkey • Ukraine • United Kingdom • United States • Venezuela • Vietnam • Zimbabwe

Copyright © 2003 Cisco Systems, Inc. All rights reserved. CCIP, CCSP, the Cisco Arrow logo, the Cisco *Powered* Network mark, the Cisco Systems Verified logo, Cisco Unity, Follow Me Browsing, FormShare, iQ Net Readiness Scorecard, Networking Academy, and ScriptShare are trademarks of Cisco Systems, Inc.; Changing the Way We Work, Live, Play, and Learn, The Fastest Way to Increase Your Internet Quotient, and iQuick Study are service marks of Cisco Systems, Inc.; and Aironet, ASIST, BPX, Catalyst, CCDA, CCDP, CCIE, CCNA, CCNP, Cisco, the Cisco Certified Internetwork Expert logo, Cisco IOS, the Cisco IOS logo, Cisco Press, Cisco Systems, Cisco Systems Capital, the Cisco Systems logo, Empowering the Internet Generation, Enterprise/Solver, EtherChannel, EtherSwitch, Fast Step, GigaStack, Internet Quotient, IOS, IP/TV, iQ Expertise, the iQ logo, LightStream, MGX, MICA, the Networkers logo, Network Registrar, *Packet*, PIX, Post-Routing, Pre-Routing, RateMUX, Registrar, SlideCast, SMARTnet, StrataView Plus, Stratm, SwitchProbe, TeleRouter, TransPath, and VCO are registered trademarks of Cisco Systems, Inc. and/or its affiliates in the U.S. and certain other countries.

All other trademarks mentioned in this document or Web site are the property of their respective owners. The use of the word partner does not imply a partnership relationship between Cisco and any other company. (0303R)

Printed in the USA

About the Technical Reviewers

Bill Chapman : Currently, Bill Chapman is a computer-science teacher at Arcadia High School, teaching computer applications, C++, Java, CCNA, and CompTia A+ certifications. Bill serves as a member of the Academic Mentor Planning Committee, Emergency Planning Committee, and as a Certified District Technology Instructor for the staff. Bill also teaches part time for Pasadena City College in the Computer Information Department and serves on the advisory committees on A+ and Cisco curricular issues for the Los Angeles County Regional Occupational Program. Bill has given presentations on teaching the Cisco Networking Academy Program curriculum at the annual California Industrial Technology Education Association state conference. Bill is certified as a Networking Academy instructor for the CCNA courses and holds CompTia A+, Network+, and i-net+ certifications.

Allan Johnson : A business owner/operator for 10 years, Allan Johnson entered the teaching field in 1999 to dedicate his time and effort to training adolescents and adults. Allan has two master's degrees from Texas A&M-Corpus Christi: an MBA and a master's degree in Occupational Training and Development. Currently, he is an information technology instructor at Mary Carroll High School and Del Mar College in Corpus Christi, Texas. In addition, Allan dedicates some of his spare time to the CCNA/CCNP Instructional Support and Services team at Cisco.

Rick Graziani has worked in the networking and computer technology area for more than 20 years. He is currently a computer science/networking instructor at Cabrillo College in Aptos, California. He holds a BA degree from Loyola Marymount University and a MA degree in computer science and systems theory from California State University Monterey Bay. His primary area of interest is in routing protocols, specifically OSPFv3 and MANET (Mobile Ad-hoc Networks). He would like to thank his friends and colleagues Mark Boolootian, Dave Barnett, Jim Warner, and Fred Baker for all of their assistance over the years, and especially his wife, Teri, for all of her support. Rick holds CCNP and CCAI certifications.

Elaine Horn has been a CATC/Regional Networking Academy instructor since 1998. She has a BS and MA degree in Mathematics Education from Ohio State University. Elaine has worked in the educational field for 27 years. Currently, she works at Tri-Rivers Educational Computer Association (the Ohio Cisco Academy Training Center [CATC]) supporting and training Cisco Networking Academy instructors in Kentucky, Michigan, and Ohio. Elaine holds CCNA, CCDA, and CCAI certifications.

Andrew Large has been a Regional Networking Academy instructor since 1998. He has a BA, M.Ed, and an Educational Specialist Degree from the University of South Alabama. Andrew has worked in the educational field for 13 years and had trained instructors worldwide for Cisco Systems. Currently, he runs his own network consulting business and is a Local/Regional Academy Instructor for the Cisco Networking Academy Program. Andrew holds CCNA, CCNP, and CCAI certifications.

Antoon W. Rufi is a networking professional who retired from the United States Air Force in June 2000. During his 29 years in the Air Force, Tony worked on systems that varied from the Titan II Intercontinental Ballistic Missile systems to current state-of-the-art Meteorological and Navigational networks. Since retirement, Tony has worked for ECPI College of Technology, a Virginia-based for-profit college. He is currently the Director of Continuing Education at the Newport News Campus of ECPI.

Tony holds an AS degree from the Community College of the Air Force in electronic engineering technology. He has a BS degree from Southern Illinois University in industrial technology and a MS degree from University of Maryland, University College in information technology. Tony is a certified CCNA, holds the CompTIA network + certification, and has passed the Advanced Routing and Remote Access certifications toward the CCNP certification.

Overview

Table of Contents

Cisco Systems Networking Icon Legend

Cisco Systems uses a standardized set of icons to represent devices in network topology illustrations. The following icon legend shows the most commonly used icons that you might encounter throughout this book.

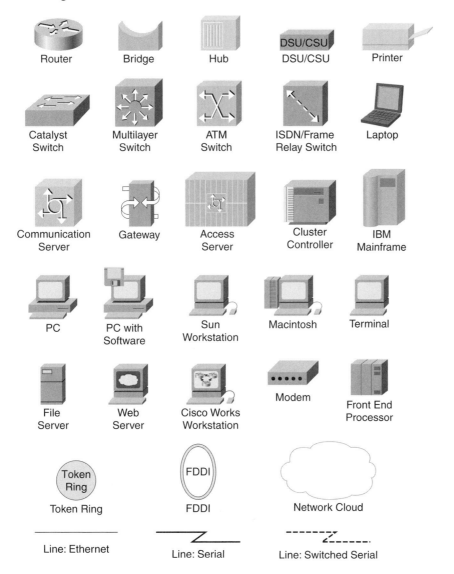

Command Syntax Conventions

The conventions used to present command syntax in this book are the same conventions used in the Cisco IOS Software Command Reference. The Command Reference describes these conventions as follows:

- Vertical bars (l) separate alternative, mutually exclusive elements.

- Square brackets ([ ]) indicate optional elements.

- Braces ({ }) indicate a required choice.

- Braces within brackets ([{ }]) indicate a required choice within an optional element.

- **Boldface** indicates commands and keywords that are entered exactly as shown.

- *Italic* indicates arguments for which you supply values.

Foreword

Throughout the world, the Internet has brought tremendous new opportunities for individuals and their employers. Companies and other organizations are seeing dramatic increases in productivity by investing in robust networking capabilities. Some studies have shown measurable productivity improvements in entire economies. The promise of enhanced efficiency, profitability, and standard of living is real and growing.

Such productivity gains aren't achieved by simply purchasing networking equipment. Skilled professionals are needed to plan, design, install, deploy, configure, operate, maintain, and troubleshoot today's networks. Network managers must assure that they have planned for network security and for continued operation. They need to design for the required performance level in their organization. They must implement new capabilities as the demands of their organization, and its reliance on the network, expands.

To meet the many educational needs of the internetworking community, Cisco Systems established the Cisco Networking Academy Program. The Networking Academy is a comprehensive learning program that provides students with the Internet technology skills essential in a global economy. The Networking Academy integrates face-to-face teaching, web-based content, online assessment, student performance tracking, hands-on labs, instructor training and support, and preparation for industry-standard certifications.

The Networking Academy continually raises the bar on blended learning and educational processes. The Internet-based assessment and instructor support systems are some of the most extensive and validated ever developed, including a 24/7 customer service system for Networking Academy instructors. Through community feedback and electronic assessment, the Networking Academy adapts the curriculum to improve outcomes and student achievement. The Cisco Global Learning Network infrastructure designed for the Networking Academy delivers a rich, interactive, and personalized curriculum to students worldwide. The Internet has the power to change the way people work, live, play, and learn, and the Cisco Networking Academy Program is in the forefront of this transformation.

This Cisco Press title is one of a series of best-selling companion titles for the Cisco Networking Academy Program. Designed by Cisco Worldwide Education and Cisco Press, these books provide integrated support for the online learning content that is made available to Academies all over the world. These Cisco Press books are the only authorized books for the Networking Academy by Cisco Systems, and provide print and CD-ROM materials that ensure the greatest possible learning experience for Networking Academy students.

I hope you are successful as you embark on your learning path with Cisco Systems and the Internet. I also hope that you will choose to continue your learning after you complete the Networking Academy curriculum. In addition to its Cisco Networking Academy Program titles, Cisco Press also publishes an extensive list of networking technology and certification publications that provide a wide range of resources. Cisco Systems has also established a network of professional training companies—the Cisco Learning Partners—who provide a full range of Cisco training courses. They offer training in many formats, including e-learning, self-paced, and instructor-led classes. Their instructors are Cisco certified, and Cisco creates their materials. When you are ready, please visit the Learning & Events area on Cisco.com to learn about all the educational support that Cisco and its partners have to offer.

Thank you for choosing this book and the Cisco Networking Academy Program.

Kevin Warner
Senior Director, Marketing
Worldwide Education
Cisco Systems, Inc.

Introduction

The *Cisco Networking Academy Program CCNA 1 and 2 Companion Guide,* Revised Third Edition, supplements your classroom and laboratory experience with version 3.1 of the CCNA curriculum within the Cisco Networking Academy Program.

Successful completion of the course results in a basic understanding of networking, routers, and routing and begins your preparation toward the Cisco Certified Network Associate (CCNA) certification exam. This textbook closely follows the style and format that Cisco Systems has incorporated into the Cisco Networking Academy Program curriculum.

This material extends your knowledge and practical experience with the design, configuration, and maintenance of local-area networks (LANs). The concepts covered in this book enable you to develop experience in cabling, routing, IP addressing, routing protocols, and network troubleshooting. This book introduces the OSI model, and discusses collisions and segmentations, Ethernet technologies, and Ethernet switching. This *Companion Guide* also features enhanced chapters on IOS, TCP/IP, and access control lists.

In addition to the CCNA Certification exam objectives, this book covers several topics to enhance your overall understanding of the networking industry. These topics are listed at the beginning of each chapter as "Additional Topics of Interest" and are generally set apart as sidebars within the chapter noted as "More Information." This additional material covers important topics that are relevant to career success in the information technology industry and should be considered no less important to anyone learning about the networking field than any of the other sections pertaining to the CCNA exam.

Goal of This Book

The goal of this book is to educate you about Cisco supported networking technologies, and to help you understand how to design and build networks and to configure Cisco routers. It is designed for use in conjunction with the Cisco Networking Academy Program online curriculum.

Audience for This Book

This book's main audience is students interested in networking technologies. In particular, it is targeted toward students in the Cisco Networking Academy Program. In the classroom, this book can serve as a supplement to the online curriculum.

This book is also appropriate for corporate training faculty and staff members, as well as general users. The book's user-friendly, nontechnical approach is ideal for readers who prefer to stay away from technical manuals.

Book Features

Many of this book's features help facilitate a full understanding of the networking and routing covered in this book:

- **Objectives** —Each chapter starts with a list of objectives that should be mastered by the end of the chapter. The objectives provide a reference of the concepts covered in the chapter and generally correlate to the CCNA exam objectives covered in that chapter. Formatted as questions, the chapter objectives can also serve as guide to approach the material in the chapter to learn the answers.

- **Key terms** —Each chapter includes a list of defined key terms that will be covered in the chapter. The key terms are then highlighted in color throughout the chapter where they are used in context. Definitions are provided in a comprehensive glossary to serve as a study aid to help you understand the chapter material before you move on to new concepts.

- **Figures, examples, and tables** —This book contains figures, examples, and tables that explain theories, concepts, commands, and setup sequences by helping you to visualize the content covered in the chapter.

- **Chapter summaries** —At the end of each chapter is a summary of the concepts covered in the chapter. It provides a synopsis of the chapter and serves as a study aid focusing on the key objectives.

- **Check Your Understanding questions** —Review questions, presented at the end of each chapter, serve as an assessment and help test your understanding before you move on to new chapters. The answers are provided in an appendix.

- **Lab Activity references** —Throughout this book are references to lab activities that can be found in *Cisco Networking Academy Program CCNA 1 and 2 Lab Companion*, Revised Third Edition. These labs help you make a connection between theory and practice. References to the labs are marked with the following icon:

- **CD Activity references** —Throughout this book are references to Interactive Media Activities, PhotoZooms, and Videos found on this book's accompanying CD-ROM. These activities supplement the material found within this book to solidify your understanding of hardware components and networking concepts. References to these activities are marked with the following icon:

How This Book Is Organized

This book is divided into 22 chapters, 11 each for the CCNA 1 and CCNA 2 material, as well as 3 appendixes.

CCNA 1 Material

- **Chapter 1, "Introduction to Networking,"** presents the basics of connecting to the Internet. It also introduces different number systems and the processes used to convert a number from one number system to another.

- **Chapter 2, "Networking Fundamentals,"** introduces some of the terminology used by networking professionals and various types of computer networks. It also describes how the OSI reference model networking scheme supports networking standards. In addition, this chapter describes the basic functions that occur at each layer of the OSI model. Finally, this chapter describes various network devices and networking topologies.

- **Chapter 3, "Networking Media,"** introduces the basic theory of electricity, which provides a foundation for understanding networking at the physical layer of the OSI model. This chapter also discusses different types of networking media that are used at the physical layer, including shielded twisted-pair cable, unshielded twisted-pair cable, coaxial cable, and fiber-optic cable, as well as wireless media.

- **Chapter 4, "Cable Testing,"** describes issues related to the testing of media used for physical layer connectivity in local-area networks (LANs). Networking media is literally and physically the backbone of a network. Inferior quality of network cabling results in network failures and in networks with unreliable performance. The equipment used to perform these tests involves certain electrical and mathematical concepts and terms, such as signal, wave, frequency, and noise. Understanding this vocabulary is helpful when learning about networking, cabling, and cable testing.

- **Chapter 5, "Cabling LANs and WANs,"** describes issues related to cabling a WAN and cabling a LAN. Although each LAN is unique, many design aspects are common to all LANs. For example, most LANs follow the same standards and the same components. This chapter presents information on elements of Ethernet LANs and common LAN devices. Several WAN connections are available today. They range from dialup to broadband access, and differ in bandwidth, cost, and required equipment. This chapter presents information on the various types of WAN connections.

- **Chapter 6, "Ethernet Fundamentals,"** discusses the operation of Ethernet, Ethernet framing, error handling, and the different type of the collisions on Ethernet networks. In addition, this chapter introduces the collision domains and broadcast domains. Finally, this chapter describes segmentation and the devices used to create the network segments.

- **Chapter 7, "Ethernet Technologies,"** introduces Layer 2 bridging and switching techniques. It introduces the Spanning-Tree Protocol (STP), tells how STP works, and covers the STP switch port states. This chapter provides details about the most important types of Ethernet. The goal is to help you understand what is common to all forms of Ethernet. This chapter also covers the standards for Gigabit Ethernet, which has emerged in only 3 years. An even faster Ethernet version—10-Gigabit Ethernet—is now widely available, and still faster versions are being developed.

- **Chapter 8, "Ethernet Switching,"** introduces the concepts related to Ethernet switching. Bridges were developed to help correct performance problems that arose from increased collisions. Switches evolved from bridges to become the main technology in modern Ethernet LANs. This chapter also explores the effects of collisions and broadcasts on network traffic and then describes how bridges/switches and routers are used to segment networks for improved performance.

- **Chapter 9, "TCP/IP Protocol Suite and IP Addressing,"** presents an overview of the TCP/IP protocol suite. It starts with the history and future of TCP/IP, compares the TCP/IP protocol model to the OSI model, and identifies and describes each layer of the TCP/IP protocol suite.

- **Chapter 10, "Routing Fundamentals and Subnets,"** covers the topics related to the Internet Protocol (IP). This chapter also discusses the difference between routing and routed protocols, and tells how routers track distance between locations. Finally, this chapter introduces the distance vector, link-state, and hybrid routing approaches, as well as how each resolves common routing problems.

- **Chapter 11, "TCP/IP Transport and Application Layers,"** covers the issues related to the transport layer and how it uses the services provided by the network layer, such as best path selection and logical addressing, to provide end-to-end communication between source and destination. This chapter describes how the transport layer regulates the flow of information from source to destination reliably and accurately.

CCNA 2 Material

- **Chapter 1, "WANs and Routers,"** introduces WAN devices, technologies, and standards. In addition, it discusses the function of a router in a WAN.

- **Chapter 2, "Introduction to Routers,"** describes how to start a router for the first time by using the correct commands and startup sequence to do an initial configuration of the router. This chapter also explains the startup sequence of a router and the setup dialog that the router uses to create an initial configuration file using current versions of Cisco IOS Software.

- **Chapter 3, "Configuring a Router,"** discusses the router modes and configuration methods for updating a router's configuration file. It is important that a firm understand Cisco IOS Software and know the procedures for starting a router. In addition, this chapter describes the tasks necessary for password recovery.

- **Chapter 4, "Learning About Other Devices,"** covers how to implement, monitor, and maintain Cisco Discovery Protocol by using the correct router commands. In addition, this chapter explains the three most used commands.

- **Chapter 5, "Managing Cisco IOS Software,"** examines the stages of the router boot sequence. It also covers how to use a variety of Cisco IOS Software source options, execute commands to load Cisco IOS Software onto the router, maintain backup files, and upgrade Cisco IOS Software. In addition, this chapter discusses the functions of the configuration register and tells how to determine the version of the IOS file. Finally, this chapter describes how to use a TFTP server as a software source.

- **Chapter 6, "Routing and Routing Protocols,"** covers the router's use and operations in performing the key internetworking function of the Open System Interconnection (OSI) reference model's network layer, Layer 3. In addition, this chapter discusses the difference between routing and routed protocols and tells how routers track distance between locations. Finally, this chapter introduces distance vector, link-state, and hybrid routing approaches and details how each resolves common routing problems.

- **Chapter 7, "Distance Vector Routing Protocols,"** covers the initial configuration of the router to enable the Routing Information Protocol (RIP) and the Interior Gateway Routing Protocol (IGRP). In addition, this chapter describes how to monitor IP routing protocols.

- **Chapter 8, "TCP/IP Suite Error and Control Messages,"** covers ICMP, the ICMP message format, ICMP error message types, potential causes of specific ICMP error messages, a variety of ICMP control messages used in networks today, and the causes for ICMP control messages.

- **Chapter 9, "Basic Router Troubleshooting,"** provides an introduction to network testing. It emphasizes the necessity of using a structured approach to troubleshooting. Finally, this chapter describers the fundamentals of troubleshooting routers.

- **Chapter 10, "Intermediate TCP/IP,"** describes TCP/IP operation to ensure communication across any set of interconnected networks. In addition, this chapter covers the TCP/IP protocol stack components, such as protocols to support file transfer, e-mail, remote login, and other applications. This chapter also introduces reliable and unreliable transport layer protocols and details connectionless datagram (packet) delivery at the network layer. Finally, it explains how ARP and RARP work.

- **Chapter 11, "Access Control Lists (ACLs),"** includes tips, considerations, recommendations, and general guidelines on how to use ACLs, and includes the commands and configurations needed to create ACLs. Finally, this chapter provides examples of standard and extended ACLs and tells how to apply ACLs to router interfaces.

Appendixes

- **Appendix A, "Structured Cabling,"** includes coverage of structured cabling systems, standards, and codes. In addition, this appendix provides coverage of cabling safety, tools of the trade, installation process, finish phase, overview of the cabling business. This appendix also provides a cabling case study that covers how to apply all of the information in this chapter to a real-world scenario. This appendix provides some valuable information that you will need to know as a CCNA.

- **Appendix B, "Check Your Understanding Answer Key,"** provides the answers to the Check Your Understanding questions that you find at the end of each chapter.

- **Appendix C, "Glossary of Key Terms,"** provides a compiled list of all the key terms that appear throughout this book.

About the CD-ROM

A CD-ROM accompanies this book to further enhance your learning experience. The CD contains a test engine with CCNA practice exam questions, Interactive Media Activities, PhotoZooms of networking equipment and hardware, and instructional Videos and animations that highlight potentially difficult concepts. These materials support self-directed study by allowing you to engage in learning and skill building exercises outside of the classroom. The CD-ROM also contains Packet Tracer 3.1, a standalone, medium-fidelity simulation environment for students and instructors to design, configure, and troubleshoot CCNA-level networks.

CHAPTER 1

Introduction to Networking

Objectives

Upon completion of this chapter, you should be able to answer the following questions:

- What are the requirements for an Internet connection?
- What are the major components of a personal computer (PC)?
- What are the functions of a network interface card (NIC)?
- Which components are needed for NIC installation?
- What is TCP/IP?
- What are the functions of the `ping` command?
- What are the features of a web browser?
- Which units measure the size of digital data?

- What is the Base 10 number system?
- What is the Base 2 number system?
- How do you convert a decimal number to a binary number?
- How do you convert a binary number to a decimal number?
- How do you convert a hexadecimal number to a binary number?
- How do you convert a binary number to a hexadecimal number?
- What is Boolean or binary logic?
- What are IP addresses?

Additional Topics of Interest

In addition to the core objective areas, this chapter introduces you to the following topics of interest to networkers:

- Desktops versus laptops
- The Base 16 number system

Key Terms

The following is a list of key terms introduced in this chapter. For your reference, a definition for each term can be found at the end of this chapter.

Internet   page 5

physical connection   page 6

logical connection   page 6

protocol   page 6

Transmission Control Protocol/Internet Protocol (TCP/IP)   page 6

applications   page 6

web browser   page 6

File Transfer Protocol (FTP)   page 6

backplane   page 7

memory chips   page 7

This chapter presents the basics of computers and connection to the Internet. It also introduces different number systems and the processes used to convert a number from one number system to another.

Please be sure to look at this chapter's associated Interactive Media Activities and Photo-Zooms that you will find on the CD-ROM accompanying this book. These CD elements are designed to supplement the material and reinforce the concepts introduced in this chapter.

Connecting to the Internet

The Internet is a valuable resource, and connection to it is essential for business, industry, and education. Building a network that will connect to the Internet requires careful planning. Even for the individual user, some planning and decisions are necessary. The computer itself must be considered, as well as the device itself that makes the connection to the local-area network (LAN), such as the network interface card (NIC) or modem. The correct protocol must be configured so that the computer can connect to the Internet. Proper selection of a web browser is also important. This section discusses these features.

Requirements for Internet Connection

To understand the role that computers play in a networking system, consider the *Internet*. The Internet can be thought of as a tree with computers as leaves. Computers are the sources and receivers of information by way of the Internet. Computers can function without the Internet, but the Internet cannot exist without computers. The Internet is growing rapidly, and users are becoming increasingly dependent on it for many services.

Computers, along with being an integral part of a network, also play a vital role in the world of work. Businesses use their computers for a variety of purposes, but they also use them in some common ways. They use servers to store important data to manage customer and employee accounts. They use spreadsheet software to organize financial information, word processor software to maintain records and correspondence, and browsers to access internal and external websites.

High-speed accesses to the Internet, such as cable modem and DSL services, are now available to the home and small office, which is increasing the demand for support services. No longer satisfied with a single computer connected to the Internet, the consumer needs the tools to be able to share the connection.

The Internet is the largest data network in the world. The Internet consists of millions of interconnected networks, both large and small. At the edge of this giant network is the individual consumer computer.

Connection to the Internet can be broken down into the following components:

- *Physical connection*—A physical connection to a network is made by inserting a specialized expansion card, such as a modem or a network interface card (NIC), in the computer. A cable will be used to connect from the PC to the network. The physical connection is used to transfer signals between PCs in the local network and remote devices on the Internet.

- *Logical connection*—A logical connection uses standards called protocols. A *protocol* is a formal description of a set of rules and conventions that govern how devices on a network communicate. Connections to the Internet may use multiple protocols. The *Transmission Control Protocol/Internet Protocol (TCP/ IP)* suite is the primary protocol used on the Internet. TCP/IP is a suite of protocols that work together to send and receive data. You learn more about TCP/IP in Chapter 9, "TCP/IP Protocol Suite and IP Addressing."

- *Applications*—The application that interprets the data and displays the information in an understandable format is the last part of the connection. Applications work with protocols to send and receive data across the Internet. A *web browser* displays HTML as a web page. *File Transfer Protocol (FTP)* is used to download files and programs from the Internet. Web browsers also use proprietary plug-in applications to display special data types such as video, audio, and animation.

This introductory view might make the Internet seem like an overly simple process. However, as this topic is explored in greater depth later in this book, it becomes apparent that sending data across the Internet is a complicated task.

PC Basics

NOTE

This chapter does not explain the components and concepts in detail. If you are new to the field of computer technology, you may want to read or take the IT Essentials book/course to learn more about these topics.

Because computers are important building blocks in a network, it is important to be able to recognize and name the major components of a PC. Think of the internal components of a PC as a network of devices, all attached to the system bus. In a sense, a PC is a small computer network.

Many networking devices, such as routers and switches, are special-purpose computers and have many of the same parts as normal PCs. For a computer to be a reliable means of obtaining information, it must be in good working order. You should be able to recognize, name, and state the purpose of the PC components (this information pertains to laptops as well) described in the following sections.

Small, Discrete Components

Electronic components are unique in that they are designed to conduct or transmit data or signals in electronic form. Most electronic components are found on the motherboard and expansion cards that plug into the motherboard. Here are some of the parts that commonly are found on electronic components:

- **Transistor**—A device that amplifies a signal or opens and closes a circuit. Microprocessors can have millions of transistors.

- **Integrated circuit (IC)**—A device made of semiconductor material. It contains many transistors and performs a specific task.

- **Resistor**—A device that is made of material that opposes the flow of electric current.

- **Capacitor**—An electronic component that stores energy in the form of an electrostatic field. It consists of two conducting metal plates separated by an insulating material.

- **Connector**—A port or interface that a cable plugs into. Examples include serial, parallel, USB, and disk drive interfaces.

- **Light emitting diode (LED)**—A semiconductor device that emits light when a current passes through it. These are commonly used as indicator lights.

NOTE

Some computers have a network card, sound card, video card, and other cards integrated into the motherboard.

Backplane Components

The motherboard is the computer's main circuit board. It is crucial because it is the nerve center of the computer system. Everything else in the system plugs into it, is controlled by it, and depends on it to communicate with other devices in the system.

The following list describes the motherboard's various components:

- *Backplane*—A large circuit board that contains sockets for expansion cards.

- *Memory chips*—RAM chips on memory cards plug into the motherboard.

- *Network interface card (NIC)*—An expansion board that provides a network communication connection to and from a PC. Many newer desktop and laptop computers have an Ethernet NIC built into the motherboard.

- *Video card*—A board that plugs into a PC to give it display capabilities. Video cards typically include onboard microprocessors and additional memory to speed up and enhance graphics display.

- *Sound card*—An expansion board that handles all sound functions.

- *Parallel port*—An interface that can transfer more than 1 bit at a time. It connects external devices, such as printers.

- *Serial port*—An interface used for serial communication in which only 1 bit is transmitted at a time. The serial port can connect to an external modem, plotter, or serial printer. It can also be used to connect to networking devices, such as routers and switches, as a console connection.

- *Mouse port*—A port designed for connecting a mouse to a PC.

- *Keyboard port*—A port designed to connect a keyboard to a PC.

- *Power cord*—A cord that connects an electrical device to an electrical outlet to provide power to the device.

■ *Universal Serial Bus (USB) port*—This interface lets peripheral devices such as mice, modems, keyboards, scanners, and printers be plugged in and unplugged without resetting the system. USB ports eventually might replace serial and parallel ports.

Lab 1.1.2 PC Hardware

This lab helps you become familiar with the basic peripheral components of a PC system and their connections, including network attachment. You examine the internal PC configuration and identify major components. You also observe the boot process for the Windows operating system and use the Control Panel to find out information about the PC hardware.

More Information: Personal Computer Subsystems

PC components are typically thought of as packaged or add-on parts that provide additional functionality to a PC. This is in contrast to vital electronic components that are necessary in every PC. These include things such as media drives, memory, hard drives, processors, and the power supply. Here are some of the most common PC components:

Printed circuit board (PCB)—A thin plate on which chips (integrated circuits) and other electronic components are placed. Examples include the motherboard and various expansion adapters.

CD-ROM drive—An optical drive that can read information from a CD-ROM. This can also be a CD-RW (compact disk read-write) drive or a DVD (digital video disk) drive or a combination of all three in one drive.

Central processing unit (CPU)—The "brain" of the computer, where most of the calculations take place (see Figure 1-1).

Floppy disk drive—The device that can read and write to floppy disks (see Figure 1-2).

Hard disk drive—A device that reads and writes data on a hard disk. The primary storage device in the computer.

Figure 1-1 Central Processing Unit

More Information: Personal Computer Subsystems (Continued)

Figure 1-2 Floppy Disk Drive

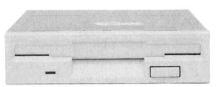

Microprocessor—A silicon chip that contains a CPU. A typical PC has a number of microprocessors, including the main CPU.

Motherboard—The computer's main circuit board (see Figure 1-3). The motherboard is crucial because it is the computer's nerve center. Everything else in the system plugs into it, is controlled by it, and depends on it to communicate with other devices in the system.

Bus—A collection of circuits through which data is transmitted from one part of a computer to another. The bus connects all the internal computer components to the CPU. The Industry-Standard Architecture (ISA) and the peripheral component inter-connect (PCI) are two types of buses.

Random-access memory (RAM)—Also known as read-write memory, RAM can have new data written to it and can have stored data read from it. RAM is the main working area, or temporary storage, used by the CPU for most processing and operations. A drawback of RAM is that it requires electrical power to maintain data storage. If the computer is turned off or loses power, all data stored in RAM is lost unless the data was previously saved to disk. Memory boards with RAM chips plug into the motherboard.

Figure 1-3 Motherboard

More Information: Personal Computer Subsystems (Continued)

Read-only memory (ROM)—A type of computer memory in which data has been prerecorded. After data has been written onto a ROM chip, it cannot be removed and can only be read. A version of ROM known as EEPROM (electronically erasable programmable read-only memory) can be written to. It is called Flash memory or firmware. The basic input/output system (BIOS) in most PCs is stored in EEPROM.

Expansion slot—An opening in a computer, usually on the motherboard, where an expansion card can be inserted to add new capabilities to the computer (see Figure 1-4).

System unit—The main component of the PC system. It includes the case, chassis, power supply, microprocessor, main memory, bus, expansion cards, disk drives (floppy, CD hard disk, and so on), and ports. The system unit does not include the keyboard, the monitor, or any other external devices connected to the computer.

Power supply—The component that supplies power to a computer by taking alternating current (AC) and converting it to 5 to 12 volts direct current (DC) to power the computer.

Figure 1-4 Expansion Slot

Desktop Versus Laptop

Laptop and notebook computers are popular. Laptop components are smaller than those found in desktop PCs. Laptops offer more mobility and portability. The expansion slots are called *Personal Computer Memory Card International Association (PCMCIA) card* slots or PC card slots in laptop computers. The PC card slots are where devices such as NICs, modems, hard drives, and other useful devices (usually the size of a thick credit card) are connected. Figure 1-5 shows a PC card adapter for a wireless local-area network (WLAN).

More Information: Personal Computer Subsystems (Continued)

Figure 1-5 PC Card

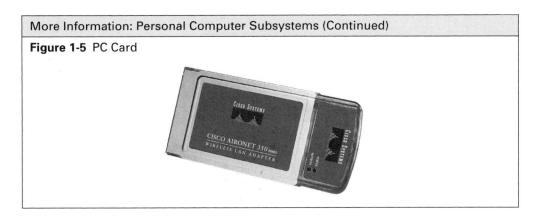

Network Interface Card

As shown in Figure 1-6, a NIC is a printed circuit board that provides network communication capabilities to and from a PC. Also called a LAN adapter, a NIC plugs into a motherboard and provides a port for connecting to the network. The NIC connects the computer to the LAN.

Figure 1-6 Network Interface Card

NOTE

If you are new to the field of computer technology, it is recommended that you take the HP IT Essentials course or read the *HP IT Essentials I: PC Hardware and Software Companion Guide*, Second Edition, to learn more information and gain a better understanding of the details of interrupt requests (IRQs), input/output (I/O) addresses, CPUs, and the functions of an operating system.

The NIC communicates with the network through a cable (or radio waves for wireless NICs) and with the computer via an expansion slot. When a NIC is installed in a computer, it requires an **interrupt request** (IRQ) for service from the CPU, as well as an input/output (I/O) address, a memory space for the operating system (such as Linux or Windows), and drivers to perform its function. An IRQ is a signal that informs a CPU that an event needing its attention has occurred. An IRQ is sent over a hardware line to the microprocessor. An example of an interrupt being issued is a key being pressed on the keyboard. The CPU must move the character from the keyboard to RAM. An I/O address is a location in memory used to enter data into or retrieve data from a computer using an auxiliary device.

When selecting a NIC for a network, consider the following:

- **Type of network**—Different types of networks use different types of NICs. For example, Ethernet NICs are designed for Ethernet LANs. Some other types of networks include Token Ring and Fiber Distributed Data Interface (FDDI). Ethernet is by far the most common.

- **Type of medium**—The type of port or connector used by the NIC for network connection is specific to the medium type, such as twisted-pair, coaxial, fiber-optic, or wireless. Coaxial is becoming increasingly rare.

- **Type of system bus**—There are different types of system buses, such as PCI and ISA. Because PCI slots are faster than ISA slots (and they plug and play better), the latter are being phased out.

PhotoZoom   Network Interface Card

In this PhotoZoom, you view a network interface card.

NIC and Modem Installation

Connectivity to the Internet requires an adapter card, which might be a modem or NIC.

A *modem* is an electronic device that is used for computer communications through telephone lines. It allows data transfer between one computer and another over the Public Switched Telephone Network (PSTN). Figure 1-7 shows an example of an external modem. Typically, modems send data in blocks of bytes. After each block, basic math is performed to analyze the block, and the computer on the receiving end is asked whether it agrees with the results. If any differences appear, the block is sent again. The modems convert digital data to analog signals for transmission over the Public Switched Telephone Network (PSTN) and then convert analog signals back to digital data on the receiving end.

Figure 1-7 External Modem

The term *modem* derives from the function of this device. Digital signals from the computer are converted to analog signals before they are sent over the telephone line, and then converted from analog back to digital when they are received over the telephone line. This process is called *modulation/demodulation* (hence the term *modem*). Modems can be installed internally or attached to the computer via a serial or USB interface externally. Modems connect a computer to the network by dialing the telephone number of another computer's modem, typically that of the Internet service provider (ISP). Modems have relatively slow transmission speeds, with a theoretical maximum speed of 56 kbps, and an actual maximum speed of 53 kbps. Keep in mind that cable modems and DSL modems provide much higher speeds than dialup modems, which are described here.

The NIC lets hosts connect to the LAN with typical connection speeds of 10 Mbps or 100 Mbps. Multiple computers on the LAN can then be connected to the Internet using a typical modem, DSL modem, cable modem, or other networking device depending on the type of connection between the LAN and the ISP. The NIC is considered a key component. NICs are available in different types, depending on the individual device configuration. Notebook computers can have a built-in interface or use a PCMCIA card. Desktop systems can use a built-in or adapter card-type NIC.

Situations that require NIC installation include the following:

- Adding a NIC to a PC that does not already have one

- Replacing a bad or damaged NIC

- Upgrading from a 10-Mbps NIC to a 10/100-Mbps NIC

To install a NIC, as shown in Figure 1-8, you need the following resources:

- Knowledge of how the adapter is configured, including jumpers and plug-and-play software. Most modern NICs do not require jumpers and are plug-and-play, requiring little or no configuration. They can be configured using software that comes with the NIC, if necessary.

- Use of network card diagnostics, including the vendor-supplied diagnostics and loopback test (see the card's documentation).

- The ability to resolve hardware resource conflicts, including IRQ, I/O base address, and direct memory address (DMA), which transfers data from RAM to a device without going through the CPU.

Figure 1-8 Installing a NIC

Overview of High-Speed and Dialup Connectivity

In the early 1960s, modems were introduced to provide data communications connectivity for dumb terminals to a centrally based computer, typically a mainframe or minicomputer. Many companies rented computer time because owning an onsite system was cost-prohibitive. The connection rate was very slow—300 bits per second (bps), which translates to about 30 characters per second.

As PCs became affordable in the 1970s, Bulletin Board Systems (BBSs) appeared, allowing users to connect and post or read messages on a discussion board. Running at 300 bps was acceptable because the information was text-based, and this also exceeded the speed at which most people can read or type. BBSs did not become widely used until the early 1980s, and the transfer of files and graphics began to be desirable. The 300 bps speed quickly became intolerable, and modem speeds started to increase. By the 1990s, modems were running at 9600 bps. They reached the current standard of 56 kbps (56,000 bps) by 1998.

Inevitably, with the evolution of the Internet the high-speed services used in the corporate environment, such as digital subscriber line (DSL) and cable modem access, migrated to the consumer market. These services no longer required expensive equipment or a second phone line. They are also *always-on* services and therefore provide instant access that does not require a connection to be established for each session. This results in greater reliability and flexibility. It has also led to the ease of Internet connection sharing and small office and home networks.

TCP/IP Description and Configuration

TCP/IP is a set of protocols or rules developed to allow cooperating computers to share resources across a network. A computer must be running the TCP/IP protocol suite to access the Internet. To enable TCP/IP on the workstation, it must be configured using the operating system tools. The PC requires an IP address, subnet mask, default gateway, Domain Name System (DNS) information. These can be assigned manually or obtained from a Dynamic Host Configuration Protocol (DHCP) server. The information necessary to configure TCP/IP on a computer is typically obtained from a network administrator or an ISP. The process is similar whether you're using a Windows or Apple Macintosh operating system. TCP/IP, DHCP, and DNS are covered in subsequent chapters.

Lab 1.1.6   PC Network TCP/IP Configuration

This lab introduces you to the methods of discovering your computer's network connection, host name, MAC (Layer 2) address, and network (Layer 3) address.

Testing Connectivity with Ping

Ping is a program that is useful for verifying a successful TCP/IP installation. It is named after the sonar operation used to locate and determine the distance to an underwater object. Ping stands for Packet Internet Groper.

The **ping** command works by sending Internet Control Message Protocol (ICMP) datagrams to request a reply. The output response for a ping contains the success ratio and round-trip time to the destination. From this information, you can determine if there is connectivity to a destination. The **ping** command is used to test the NIC transmit/receive function, the TCP/IP configuration, and network connectivity. The following are some usages of the **ping** command:

- **ping 127.0.0.1** (internal loopback test)— Because no packets are transmitted, pinging the loopback interface tests basic TCP/IP network configuration. Figure 1-9 shows the **ping 127.0.0.1** test.

- **ping** *IP address of host computer*—Verifies the TCP/IP address configuration for the local host.

- **ping** *default-gateway IP address*—Verifies whether the router that connects the local network to other networks can be accessed.

- **ping** *remote destination IP address*—Verifies connectivity to a remote host.

Ping is covered in more detail in subsequent chapters.

Figure 1-9 ping 127.0.0.1

```
C:\WINNT\System32\command.com                              _ |□| x|
Microsoft(R) Windows DOS
(C)Copyright Microsoft Corp 1990-1999.

C:\DOCUME~1\UCLEUCH\DESKTOP>ping 127.0.0.1

Pinging 127.0.0.1 with 32 bytes of data:

Reply from 127.0.0.1: bytes=32 time<10ms TTL=128
Reply from 127.0.0.1: bytes=32 time<10ms TTL=128
Reply from 127.0.0.1: bytes=32 time<10ms TTL=128
Reply from 127.0.0.1: bytes=32 time<10ms TTL=128

Ping statistics for 127.0.0.1:
    Packets: Sent = 4, Received = 4, Lost = 0 (0% loss),
Approximate round trip times in milli-seconds:
    Minimum = 0ms, Maximum =  0ms, Average =  0ms

C:\DOCUME~1\UCLEUCH\DESKTOP>
```

Lab 1.1.7   Using **ping** and **tracert** from a Workstation

In this lab, you learn to use the TCP/IP **ping** and **traceroute** commands to test connectivity in a network. In the process, you see name resolution occur.

Web Browser and Plug-Ins

A web browser acts on a user's behalf by

- Contacting a web server
- Requesting information
- Receiving information
- Displaying the results on the screen

A web browser is software that interprets *Hypertext Markup Language (HTML)*, one of the languages used to code web page content. Other markup languages, such as SGML and XML, provide more advanced features for creating dynamic and interactive web pages than does HTML. HTML, the most common markup language, can display graphics and play sound, movies, and other multimedia files. *Hyperlinks* are computer-program commands that point to other HTML files on a web server or other places in the same documents, which provide shortcuts to other web pages and files.

Two of the most popular web browsers are Internet Explorer (IE) and Netscape Navigator. Although they are identical in the task they perform, there are differences between them. Some websites might not support the use of one or the other, so it can be beneficial to have both programs installed on the computer.

Table 1-1 compares the characteristics of these two web browsers.

Table 1-1 Microsoft Internet Explorer Versus Netscape Communicator

IE	Communicator
Integrated with other Microsoft products	First popular browser
Takes up more disk space	Takes up less disk space
Displays HTML files and performs e-mail, file transfers, and other functions	Displays HTML files and performs e-mail, file transfers, and other functions

Standard web browsers cannot display many special, or proprietary, file types. To view these files, the browser must be configured to use *plug-in* applications. These applications work in conjunction with the browser to launch the program required to view the special files. Here are some of the more popular proprietary plug-ins:

- **Flash Player/Shockwave Player**—A plug-in that plays multimedia files created by Macromedia Flash.

- **Adobe Acrobat Reader**—A software program that allows the user to view and print Adobe Portable Document Format (PDF) files.

- **Windows Media Player**—A software program that allows the user to play audio and video files.

- **Quicktime**—A software program created by Apple that allows the user to play video and audio files.

- **Real Player**—A software program that allows the user to play audio files.

 Lab 1.1.8 Web Browser Basics

In this lab, you learn how to use a web browser to access Internet sites, become familiar with the concept of a URL, and use a search engine to locate information on the Internet. You access selected websites to learn the definitions of networking terms and use hyperlinks to jump from the current website to other websites.

More Information: Other Common Computer Applications

Computers perform many other useful tasks. In business, employees regularly use a set of applications that come in the form of an *office suite,* such as Microsoft Office or Lotus Smart Suite. Office applications typically include the following:

Spreadsheet software—An application that lets users construct spreadsheets consisting of columns and rows. It is often used with formulas to process and analyze data.

A word processor—An application that lets users create and edit text documents. Modern word processors allow the user to create sophisticated documents that include graphics and richly formatted text.

Database software—An application that lets users store, maintain, organize, sort, and filter records. A *record* is a collection of information identified by a common theme, such as a customer name.

Presentation software—An application that lets users design and develop presentations to deliver at meetings, classes, or sales presentations.

Personal information managers—Applications that can include features such as e-mail, contact lists, a calendar, and a to-do list.

Troubleshooting Internet Connection Problems

These are the steps for the PC/network troubleshooting process:

Step 1   Define the problem.

Step 2   Gather the facts.

Step 3   Consider the possibility.

Step 4   Create an action plan.

Step 5   Implement the plan.

Step 6   Observe the results.

Step 7 Document the results.

Step 8 Introduce problems and troubleshoot.

 Lab 1.1.9 Basic PC/Network Troubleshooting Process

In this lab, you apply the basic troubleshooting model to simple and common network problems. You also become familiar with the more common hardware and software problems.

Network Math

This section introduces the way in which data is represented inside a computer and the form in which it is transmitted across a network. You also learn about the various number systems and logic used with computers.

Binary Presentation of Data

Computers are electromechanical devices made up of electronic switches. At the lowest levels of computation, computers depend on these electronic switches to make decisions. As such, computers react only to electrical impulses. These impulses are understood by the computer as either *on* or *off* states (1s or 0s).

Computers work with and store data using electronic switches that are either on or off. Computers can only understand and use data that is in this two-state (binary) format. 1 represents an on state, and 0 represents an off state. These 1s and 0s represent the two possible states of an electronic component in a computer. These 1s and 0s are called binary digits or *bits*.

The *American Standard Code for Information Interchange (ASCII)*, the most commonly used code for representing alphanumeric data in a computer, uses binary digits to represent the symbols typed on the keyboard. When computers send on/off states over a network, electricity, light, or radio waves represent the 1s and 0s. Each character has a unique pattern of eight binary digits assigned to represent the character.

Bits and Bytes

Bits are binary digits. They are either 0s or 1s. In a computer, they are represented by on/off switches or the presence or absence of electrical charges, light pulses, or radio waves.

For example:

A binary 0 might be represented by 0 volts of electricity (0 = 0 volts).

A binary 1 might be represented by +5 volts of electricity (1 = +5 volts).

Computers are designed to use groupings of 8 bits. This grouping of 8 bits is called a *byte*. In a computer, 1 byte represents a single addressable storage location. These storage locations represent a value or a single character of data, such as an ASCII code. The total number of combinations of the eight switches being turned on and off is 256 (or 2^8). The value range of a byte is from 0 to 255. So, a byte is an important concept to understand when working with computers and networks.

Most computer coding schemes use 8 bits to represent each number, letter, or symbol. A series of 8 bits is called a byte; 1 byte represents a single addressable storage location (see Table 1-2).

It is common to confuse KB with Kb and MB with Mb. Remember to do the proper calculations when comparing transmission speeds that are measured in KB with those measured in Kb. For example, modem software usually shows the connection speed in kilo*bits* per second (for example, 45 kbps). However, popular browsers display file download speeds in kilo*bytes* per second. This means that with a 45-kbps connection, the download speed would be a maximum of 5.76 kBps. In practice, this download speed cannot be reached because of other factors that consume bandwidth at the same time. Also, file sizes are typically expressed in bytes, whereas LAN bandwidth and WAN links are typically expressed in kilobits per second (kbps) or Megabits per second (Mbps). You must multiply the number of bytes in the file by 8 to determine the amount of bandwidth consumed in bps.

Table 1-2 Units of Information

Unit	Bytes[*]	Bits[*]
Bit (b)	1/8 byte	1 bit
Byte (B)	1 byte	8 bits
Kilobyte (KB)	1000 bytes	8000 bits
Megabyte (MB)	1 million bytes	8 million bits
Gigabyte (GB)	1 billion bytes	8 billion bits
Terabyte (TB)	1 trillion bytes	8 trillion bits

[*]Common or approximate bytes or bits

The following are commonly used computer measurement terms:

- *Bit*—The smallest unit of data in a computer. A bit equals 1 or 0, and it is the binary format in which data is processed, stored, and transmitted by computers.

- *Byte*—A unit of measure used to describe the size of a data file, the amount of space on a disk or another storage medium, or the amount of data being sent over a network. 1 byte equals 8 bits of data.

- *Kb (kilobit)*—Approximately 1000 bits.

- *KB (kilobyte)*—Approximately 1000 bytes (1024 bytes exactly).

- *Mb (megabit)*—Approximately 1 million bits.

- *MB (megabyte)*—Approximately 1 million bytes (1,048,576 bytes exactly). A megabyte is sometimes called a "meg." The amount of RAM in most PCs is typically measured in MB. Large files are often some number of MB in size.

- *GB (gigabyte)*—Approximately 1 billion bytes. A gigabyte is sometimes called a "gig." Hard drive capacity on most PCs is typically measured in GB.

- *TB (terabyte)*—Approximately 1 trillion bytes. Hard drive capacity on some high-end computers is measured in TB.

- *kbps (kilobits per second)*—One thousand bits per second. This is a standard measurement of the amount of data transferred over a network connection.

- *kBps (kilobytes per second)*—One thousand bytes per second. This is a standard measurement of the amount of data transferred over a network connection.

- *Mbps (megabits per second)*—One million bits per second. This is a standard measurement of the amount of data transferred over a network connection. Basic Ethernet operates at 10 Mbps.

- *MBps (megabytes per second)*—One million bytes per second. This is a standard measurement of the amount of data transferred over a network connection.

- *Gbps (gigabits per second)*—One billion bits per second. This is a standard measurement of the amount of data transferred over a network connection. 10G or 10 Gigabit Ethernet operates at 10 Gbps.

- *Tbps (terabits per second)*—One trillion bits per second. This is a standard measurement of the amount of data transferred over a network connection.

- **Hz (hertz)**—A unit of frequency. It is the rate of change in the state or cycle in a sound wave, alternating current, or other cyclical waveform. It represents one cycle per second.

NOTE

PC processors are getting faster all the time. The microprocessors used in PCs in the 1980s typically ran at less than 10 MHz (the original IBM PC was 4.77 MHz). Currently, PC processors are pushing speeds up to 3 GHz, with faster processors being developed for the future. This is covered in more detail in subsequent chapters.

- **MHz (megahertz)**—One million (1,000,000) cycles per second. This is a common measurement of the speed of a processing chip, such as a computer microprocessor. Some cordless phones operate in this range (for example, 900 MHz).

- **GHz (gigahertz)**—One billion (1,000,000,000) cycles per second. This is a common measurement of the speed of a processing chip, such as a computer microprocessor. Some cordless phones and wireless LANs operate in this range (for example, 802.11b at 2.4 GHz). Some cordless phones also operate in the 2.4-GHz range.

Because computers are designed to work with on/off switches, binary digits and binary numbers are natural to them. However, humans use the decimal number system in their daily lives. It is hard to remember the long series of 1s and 0s that computers use. Therefore, the computer's binary numbers need to be converted to decimal numbers.

Sometimes, binary numbers need to be converted to hexadecimal (hex) numbers. This is done because hex numbers can represent a long string of binary digits with just a few hexadecimal digits. This makes it easier to remember and work with the numbers.

Base 10 Number System

A number system consists of symbols and rules for using those symbols. Many number systems exist. The number system used most frequently is the decimal, or Base 10, number system. It is called Base 10 because it uses ten symbols. These ten symbols are the digits 0, 1, 2, 3, 4, 5, 6, 7, 8, and 9. Combinations of these digits can represent all possible numeric values, as documented in Table 1-3.

Table 1-3 Base 10 Number System

Number of Symbols	Ten			
Symbols	0, 1, 2, 3, 4, 5, 6, 7, 8, 9			
Base Exponent	10^3	10^2	10^1	10^0
Place Value	1000	100	10	1
Example: 2,134	$2*10^3$	$1*10^2$	$3*10^1$	$4*10^0$

The decimal number system is based on powers of 10. The value of each column position from right to left is multiplied by the number 10 (the base number) raised to a power (exponent). The power that 10 is raised to depends on its position to the left of the decimal point. When a decimal number is read from right to left, the first (rightmost) position represents 10^0 (1), and the second position represents 10^1 ($10 * 1 = 10$). The third position represents 10^2 ($10 * 10 = 100$). The seventh position to the left represents 10^6 ($10 * 10 * 10 * 10 * 10 * 10 = 1,000,000$). This is true no matter how many columns the number has. (Note: You must start counting from right to left at 10^0.)

For example:

$$2134 = (2 * 10^3) + (1 * 10^2) + (3 * 10^1) + (4 * 10^0)$$

There is a 4 in the ones position, a 3 in the tens position, a 1 in the hundreds position, and a 2 in the thousands position. This example seems obvious when the decimal number system is used. Seeing exactly how the decimal system works is important, because it is needed for you to understand two other number systems, binary (Base 2) and hexadecimal (Base 16). These systems use the same methods as the decimal system. Human-readable IP addresses are expressed in Base 10 (decimal). The IP address 172.16.14.188 is made up of four decimal numbers separated by dots or periods. However, computer and networking devices see the IP address as a series of 32 bits, 32 0s and 1s, with each of the four decimal numbers in the address using 8 bits. This is demonstrated later in the following sections.

Base 2 Number System

Computers recognize and process data using the *binary*, or Base2, number system. The binary number system uses only two symbols (0 and 1) instead of the ten symbols used in the decimal, or Base10, number system. The position, or place, of each digit represents the number 2 (the base number) raised to a power (exponent) based on its position (2^0, 2^1, 2^2, 2^3, 2^4, and so on), as documented in Table 1-4.

Table 1-4 Base 2 Number System

Number of Symbols	Two							
Symbols	0, 1							
Base Exponent	2^7	2^6	2^5	2^4	2^3	2^2	2^1	2^0
Place Value	128	64	32	16	8	4	2	1
Example: 10110	0	0	0	1	0	1	1	0

Example:

$$10110 = (1 * 2^4 = 16) + (0 * 2^3 = 0) + (1 * 2^2 = 4) + (1 * 2^1 = 2) + (0 * 2^0 = 0)$$
$$= (16 + 0 + 4 + 2 + 0) = 22$$

If the binary number (00010110) is read from left to right, there is a 0 in the 128s position, a 0 in the 64s position, a 0 in the 32s position, a 1 in the 16s position, a 0 in the 8s position, a 1 in the 4s position, a 1 in the 2s position, and a 0 in the 1s position, which adds up to decimal number 22. Machine-readable IP addresses are expressed as a string of 32 bits (binary).

More Information: Base 16 Number System

The Base16, or hexadecimal (hex), number system is another number system that is used frequently when working with computers because it can represent binary numbers in a more readable form. The computer performs computations in binary, but there are several instances in which a computer's binary output is expressed in hexadecimal form to make it easier to read.

The hexadecimal number system uses 16 symbols. Combinations of these symbols can represent all possible numbers. Because only ten symbols represent digits (0, 1, 2, 3, 4, 5, 6, 7, 8, and 9) and because Base16 requires six more symbols, the extra symbols are the letters A, B, C, D, E, and F. The A represents the decimal number 10, B represents 11, C represents 12, D represents 13, E represents 14, and F represents 15, as shown in Table 1-5.

More Information: Base 16 Number System (Continued)

The position of each symbol (digit) in a hex number represents the base number 16 raised to a power (exponent) based on its position. Moving from right to left, the first position represents 16^0 (or 1), the second position represents 16^1 (or 16), the third position represents 16^2 (or 256), and so on. Network adapter or NIC addresses are expressed as a string of 12 hexadecimal characters.

Table 1-5 Base 16 Number System

Number of Symbols	Two							
Symbol	0,1							
Base Exponent	2^7	2^6	2^5	2^4	2^3	2^2	2^1	2^0
Place Value	128	64	32	16	8	4	2	1
Example 10110	0	0	0	1	0	1	1	0

Example:

$1A2C = (1 * 16^3 = 4096) + (10(A) * 16^2 = 2560) + (2 * 16^1 = 32) + (12 * 16^0 = 12) = (4096 + 2560 + 32 + 12) = 6700$

Converting Decimal Numbers to 8-Bit Binary Numbers

You can convert decimal numbers to binary numbers in many different ways. The flowchart shown in Figure 1-10 describes one method. This process involves trying to figure out which values of the power of 2 are added together to get the decimal number being converted. This is one of several methods used for conversion. It is best to select one method and practice with it until it always produces the correct answer.

Here's an example:

These steps convert the decimal number 168 to binary:

Step 1   128 fits into 168, so the leftmost bit in the binary number is a 1.

168 – 128 = 40

Step 2   64 does not fit into 40, so the second bit from the left is a 0.

Step 3   32 fits into 40, so the third bit from the left is a 1.

40 – 32 = 8

Step 4   16 does not fit into 8, so the fourth bit from the left is a 0.

Step 5   8 fits into 8, so the fifth bit from the left is a 1.

8 – 8 = 0, so the remaining bits to the right are all 0s.

Step 6   As a result, the binary equivalent of the decimal value 168 is 10101000.

For more practice, try converting decimal 255 to binary. The answer should be 11111111.

Figure 1-10 Decimal-to-Binary Conversion Process

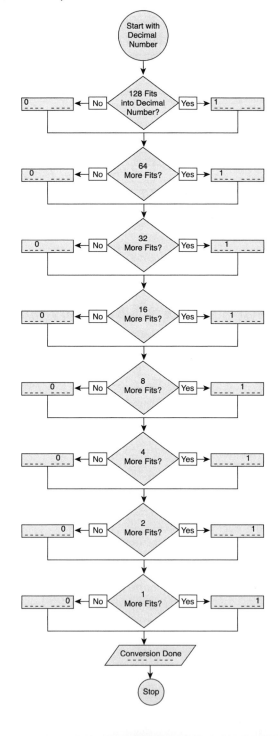

This flowchart works for decimal numbers of 255 or less. It yields an eight-digit binary number. This is appropriate for translating decimal IP addresses. Larger numbers can be converted by starting with the highest power of 2 that fits. For example, the number 650 can be converted by first subtracting 512. This yields a ten-digit binary number.

 Lab 1.2.5   Decimal to Binary Conversion

In this lab, you practice converting decimal values to binary values.

Converting 8-Bit Binary Numbers to Decimal Numbers

As with decimal-to-binary conversion, there is usually more than one way to solve the conversion. The flowchart in Figure 1-11 shows one example.

Binary numbers can also be converted to decimal numbers by multiplying the binary digits by the base number of the system (Base2) raised to the exponent of its position.

Here's an example:

Work from right to left. Remember that anything raised to the 0 power is 1; therefore, $2^0 = 1$.

Convert the binary number 01110000 to a decimal number.

$$* 2^0 = 0$$

$$+$$

$$0 * 2^1 = 0$$

$$+$$

$$0 * 2^2 = 0$$

$$+$$

$$0 * 2^3 = 0$$

$$+$$

$$1 * 2^4 = 16$$

$$+$$

$$1 * 2^5 = 32$$

$$+$$

$$1 * 2^6 = 64$$

$$+$$

$$0 * 2^7 = 0$$

$$112$$

(The sum of the powers of 2 that have a 1 in their position)

Figure 1-11 Binary-to-Decimal Conversion Process

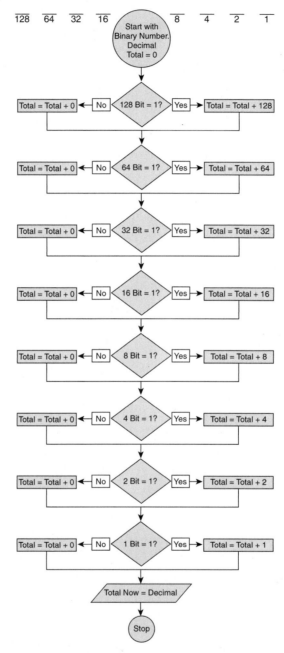

As with the flowchart shown in Figure 1-10, the flowchart shown in Figure 1-11 also works for decimal numbers of 255 or less that start with an eight-digit binary number. Larger binary numbers can be converted by increasing the power of 2 for each bit on the right. For example, if you have a 10-digit binary number, the tenth digit is worth 512, and the ninth is worth 256 if they are turned on (have a value of 1).

 Lab 1.2.6   Binary to Decimal Conversion

In this lab, you learn and practice the process of converting binary values to decimal values.

Four-Octet Dotted-Decimal Representation of a 32-Bit Binary Number

Currently, addresses assigned to computers on networks that use TCP/IP have IP addresses that are 32-bit binary numbers. Any device that wants to communicate using the Internet must have an IP address. To make it easier to work with these addresses, the 32-bit binary number is broken into a series of decimal numbers. To do this, split the binary number into four groups of eight binary digits. Then, convert each group of 8 bits (an octet) into its decimal equivalent. Do this conversion exactly as was shown in the section, "Converting 8-Bit Binary Numbers to Decimal Numbers."

IP addresses are discussed in detail in subsequent chapters. The information provided here demonstrates only the conversion between the dotted-decimal notation and its binary representation.

When written, the complete decimal number is represented as four groups of decimal digits separated by periods, such as 10.15.129.201. This is called *dotted-decimal notation* and provides a compact, easy-to-remember way of referring to 32-bit addresses. This representation is used frequently later in this course, so be sure to understand it. When converting to binary from dotted decimal, remember that each group of one to three decimal digits represents a group of eight binary digits. If the decimal number you are converting is less than 128, you need to add 0s to the left of the equivalent binary number until you have a total of 8 bits.

For example, to convert the dotted-decimal value 10.15.129.201 to its binary equivalent, you should write the number as 00001010.00001111.10000001.11001001:

> 10 = 00001010
>
> 15 = 00001111
>
> 129 = 10000001
>
> 201 = 11001001

Hexadecimal

Converting a hexadecimal number to binary form and vice versa is a common task when dealing with the configuration register in Cisco routers. Cisco routers have a configuration

NOTE

MAC addresses are discussed in subsequent chapters. The information provided here demonstrates only the conversion between the hexadecimal and binary number systems.

register that is 16 bits long. That 16-bit binary number can be represented as a four-digit hexadecimal number. For example, 0010000100000010 in binary equals 2102 in hex.

Layer 2 *Media Access Control (MAC) addresses* are typically written in hex.

For Ethernet and Token Ring, these MAC addresses are 48 bits, or six *octets* (one octet is 8 bits). ("Oct" comes from the Greek word for eight.) Because these addresses consist of six distinct octets, they can be expressed as 12 hex numbers instead. Every 4 bits is a hex digit ($2^4 = 16$), as you will see in Table 1-6.

Instead of writing

    10101010.11110000.11000001.11100010.01110111.01010001

you can write the much-shorter hex equivalent:

    AA.F0.C1.E2.77.51.

    A = 1010

    A = 1010

    F = 1111

    0 = 0000

    C = 1100

    1 = 0001

    E = 1110

    2 = 0010

    7 = 0111

    7 = 0111

    5 = 0101

    1 = 0001

To make handling hex versions of MAC addresses even easier, the dots are placed only after every four hex digits, as in AAF0.C1E2.7751.

The most common way for computers and software to express hexadecimal output is by using 0x in front of the hexadecimal number. Thus, whenever you see 0x, you know that the number that follows is a hexadecimal number. For example, 0x1234 means 1234 in base 16.

Like the binary and decimal number systems, the hexadecimal system is based on the use of symbols, powers, and positions. The symbols that hex uses are 0 through 9 and A through F. Table 1-6 shows the binary and decimal equivalents of hex digits.

Table 1-6 Binary and Decimal Equivalents of Hexadecimal Digits

Binary	Hexadecimal	Decimal
0000	0	0
0001	1	1
0010	2	2
0011	3	3
0100	4	4
0101	5	5
0110	6	6
0111	7	7
1000	8	8
1001	9	9
1010	A	10
1011	B	11
1100	C	12
1101	D	13
1110	E	14
1111	F	15

To convert from hexadecimal to binary, convert every hex digit into 4 bits. For example, to convert hex AC (0xAC) to binary, you first convert hex A, which is 1010 binary, and then you convert hex C, which is 1100 binary. So hex AC is 10101100 in binary.

Notice that all possible combinations of four binary digits have only one hexadecimal symbol, whereas two symbols are required for decimal. The reason why hex is used is that two hexadecimal digits can efficiently represent any combination of eight binary digits (as opposed to decimal, which would require up to four digits). In allowing two decimal digits to represent 4 bits, using decimal could also cause confusion in reading a value. For example, the eight bit binary number 01110011 would be 115 if converted to decimal digits. Does this represent 11-5 or 1-15? If 11-5 is used, the binary number would be 10110101, which is not the number originally converted. Using hexadecimal, the conversion is 1F, which always converts back to 00011111.

The best way to think about hexadecimal is to think of it as a shorthand way of reading binary. It reduces an 8-bit number to just two hex digits. This reduces the confusion of reading long strings of binary numbers and the amount of space it takes to write them. Remember that hexadecimal is sometimes abbreviated as 0x, so hex 5D might be written as 0x5D.

To convert from hex to binary, simply expand each hex digit into its 4-bit binary equivalent.

Lab 1.2.8   Hexadecimal Conversions

In this lab, you learn the process to convert hexadecimal values to decimal and binary values.

Boolean or Binary Logic

Boolean logic is based on digital circuitry that accepts one or two incoming voltages and, based on these input voltages, generates an output voltage. For the purpose of computers, the voltage difference is associated with two states, on and off. These two states are in turn represented by a 1 or a 0, which are the two digits in the binary number system.

Boolean logic is a binary logic that allows two numbers to be compared, and then a choice based on those two numbers is generated. These choices are the logical AND, OR, and NOT. With the exception of the NOT, Boolean operations have the same function. They accept two numbers (1 or 0) and generate a result based on the logic rule.

This section presents the operations, starting with the NOT operation. The next section provides an example of directly applying Boolean logic in networking—network masking. This example covers the AND operation.

The NOT operation, as shown in Table 1-7, simply takes whatever value is presented (0 or 1) and inverts it. A 1 becomes a 0, and a 0 becomes a 1. Remember that the logic gates are electronic devices built specifically for this purpose. This is the logic rule that they follow; whatever is input, the opposite is output.

Table 1-7 NOT Operation

Input	Output
0	1
1	0

The AND operation, as shown in Table 1-8, takes two input values. If both values are 1, the logic gate generates a 1 output; otherwise, it outputs a 0. There are four combinations of input values. Three combinations generate a 0, and one combination generates a 1. The AND operation is used extensively with IP addressing and subnet masks.

Table 1-8 AND Operation

AND	0	1
0	0	0
1	0	1

The OR operation, as shown in Table 1-9, also takes two input values. If one value is 1 or both values are 1, the output is 1. Just like the AND operation, there are four combinations of input values. However, in an OR operation, three of the combinations generate a 1 output, and one combination generates a 0 output.

Table 1-9 OR Operation

OR	0	1
0	0	1
1	1	1

The two networking operations that use Boolean logic are subnetwork masking and wildcard masking. Masking operations provide a way to filter addresses. The addresses identify the devices on the network. Masking allows the addresses to be grouped or controlled by other network operations.

IP Addresses and Network Masks

The 32-bit binary addresses used on the Internet are called *Internet Protocol (IP)* addresses. This section covers the relationship between IP addresses and network masks. You learn more about IP addresses in Chapter 9, "TCP/IP Protocol Suite and IP Addressing." The purpose of this section is to become familiar with using binary numbers and the AND operation.

When IP addresses are assigned to computers, some of the bits on the left side of the 32-bit IP number are used to represent a network. In classful networks, the number of bits designated depends on the address class. The bits left over in the 32-bit IP address identify a particular computer on the network. A computer is called a host. So a computer's IP address usually consists of a network portion and a host portion that represents a particular computer on a particular network. Classful and classless networks are covered in subsequent chapters.

For the computer to know how the 32-bit IP address has been split, a second 32-bit number called a *subnetwork mask* is used. This mask is a guide that indicates how the IP address should be interpreted by identifying how many of the bits identify the computer's network. The network mask sequentially fills in the 1s from the left side of the mask. A subnetwork mask is always all 1s until the network address is identified. Then it is all 0s from there to the rightmost bit of the mask. The bits in the IP address that are 0 identify the computer (host) on that network. Again, at this point, it is not important to understand how subnet masks are used or what importance they play in networks. This section's purpose is only to demonstrate how subnet masks are represented in dotted-decimal notation and how the AND operation functions.

Some examples of subnet masks follow.

Example 1:

11111111.00000000.00000000.00000000 written in dotted decimal is 255.0.0.0.

Example 2:

11111111.11111111.00000000.00000000 written in dotted decimal is 255.255.0.0.

In the first example, the first 8 bits from the left are the network address, and the last 24 bits are the host address. In the second example, the first 16 bits are the network address, and the last 16 bits are the host address.

Converting the IP address 10.34.23.134 to binary results in the following:

00001010.00100010.00010111.10000110

To determine the network portion of the IP address, compare the subnet mask bits to all 32 bits of the IP address 1 bit at a time, using the AND process, and record the result. The combination of a 0 IP address bit and a 0 mask bit is a 0. The combination of a 0 and a 1 is a 0. The combination of a 1 and a 1 is a 1. To better demonstrate, consider the following examples:

Example 1. Using the first mask (255.0.0.0):

00001010.00100010.00010111.10000110: IP address

11111111.00000000.00000000.00000000: network mask

00001010.00000000.00000000.00000000: network address

Then, the AND operation is performed on the IP address and its relative network mask bit, which results in the bit for the network address. 00001010.00000000.00000000.00000000 is the resulting network part of the address. In dotted-decimal format, 10.0.0.0 is the network portion of the IP address.

Example 2. Using the second mask (255.255.0.0):

00001010.00100010.00010111.10000110: IP address

11111111.11111111.00000000.00000000: network mask

00001010.00100010.00000000.00000000 is the network part of the address. In dotted-decimal format, 10.34.0.0 is the network portion of the IP address.

The importance of subnetwork masking becomes clearer as you work more with IP addresses. For now, it is only important that you understand the concept of the AND operations between the IP address and the network mask.

Summary

In this chapter, you learned the following key points:

- Computers are vital components of every network. The more you know about computers, the easier it is to understand networks.

- Knowledge about how a computer functions makes it easier to understand networks.

- TCP/IP is the protocol of the Internet.

- The **ping** command is a simple way to test connectivity.

- Software allows the user to interface with the hardware. In networking, web browsers and e-mail are the most commonly used software programs.

- The ability to troubleshoot PCs is a necessary skill for people who work on networks.

- It is important to be familiar with the components of a computer and to understand the functions of a NIC. It is also important to be able to install a NIC.

- Bits are binary digits. Eight bits equals one byte.

- Computers use the binary number system to recognize and process data. The binary number system is made up of 0s and 1s.

- The hexadecimal number system is used frequently at higher levels of computation. The hexadecimal number system uses 16 symbols: 0, 1, 2, 3, 4, 5, 6, 7, 8, 9, A, B, C, D, E, and F.

- Boolean logic is a binary logic that allows two numbers to be compared. An operation is created based on the two numbers. Three common Boolean logic operators are NOT, AND, and OR.

- IP addresses are the 32-bit binary addresses used on the Internet.

To supplement all that you have learned in this chapter, refer to the chapter-specific Interactive Media Activities and PhotoZooms that you will find on the CD-ROM accompanying this book.

Key Terms

American Standard Code for Information Interchange (ASCII)   The most commonly used code for representing alphanumeric data in a computer. Uses binary digits (bits) to represent the symbols typed on the keyboard.

application   Interprets the data and displays the information in a comprehensible format as the last part of an Internet connection. Applications work with protocols to send and receive data across the Internet.

backplane   A large circuit board that contains sockets for expansion cards.

binary   A number system characterized by 1s and 0s (1 = on, and 0 = off).

bit   The smallest unit of data in a computer. A bit equals 1 or 0. It is the binary format in which data is processed, stored, and transmitted by computers. In a computer, bits are represented by on/off switches or the presence or absence of electrical charges, light pulses, or radio waves.

Boolean logic   In computer operation with binary values, Boolean logic can describe electromagnetically charged memory locations or circuit states that are either charged (1 or true) or not charged (0 or false). The computer can use an AND gate or an OR gate operation to obtain a result that can be used for further processing.

bus   A collection of circuits through which data is transmitted from one part of a computer to another.

byte   A unit of measure that describes the size of a data file, the amount of space on a disk or another storage medium, or the amount of data being sent over a network. 1 byte equals 8 bits of data.

CD-ROM drive   An optical drive that can read information from a CD-ROM.

central processing unit (CPU)   The computer's "brain," where most of the calculations take place.

dotted-decimal notation   A syntactic representation for a 32-bit integer that consists of four 8-bit numbers written in base 10 with periods (dots) separating them. Used to represent IP addresses on the Internet, as in 192.67.67.20.

expansion slot   An opening in a computer, usually on the motherboard, where an expansion card can be inserted to add new capabilities to the computer.

File Transfer Protocol (FTP)   An application protocol, part of the TCP/IP protocol suite, used to transfer files between network hosts.

floppy disk drive   Reads and writes to floppy disks.

GB (gigabyte)   Approximately 1 billion bytes. Sometimes called a "gig." Hard drive capacity on most PCs is typically measured in GB.

Gbps (gigabits per second)   One billion bits per second. A standard measurement of the amount of data transferred over a network connection. 10G or 10 Gigabit Ethernet operates at 10 Gbps.

hard disk drive   Reads and writes data on a hard disk. The primary storage device in the computer.

hyperlink   A computer program command that points to other HTML files on a web server or other places on the same documents. Provides shortcuts to other web pages and files.

Hypertext Markup Language (HTML)   A simple hypertext document-formatting language that uses tags to indicate how a given part of a document should be interpreted by a viewing application, such as a web browser.

Internet   The largest global internetwork, connecting tens of thousands of networks world-wide and having a culture that focuses on research and standardization based on real-life use.

Internet Control Message Protocol (ICMP)   Network layer Internet protocol that reports errors and provides other information relevant to IP packet processing.

Internet Protocol (IP)   A network layer protocol in the TCP/IP protocol suite offering a connectionless internetwork service.

Kb (kilobit)   Approximately 1000 bits.

KB (kilobyte)   Approximately 1000 bytes (1024 bytes exactly).

kbps (kilobits per second)   One thousand bits per second. A standard measurement of the amount of data transferred over a network connection.

kBps (kilobytes per second)   One thousand bytes per second. A standard measurement of the amount of data transferred over a network connection.

keyboard port   Connects a keyboard to a PC.

logical connection   Uses standards called protocols.

Mb (megabit)   Approximately 1 million bits.

MB (megabyte)   Approximately 1 million bytes (1,048,576 bytes exactly). A megabyte is sometimes called a "meg." The amount of RAM in most PCs is typically measured in MB. Large files are typically some number of MB in size.

Mbps (megabits per second)   One million bits per second. A standard measurement of the amount of data transferred over a network connection. Basic Ethernet operates at 10 Mbps.

MBps (megabytes per second)   One million bytes per second. A standard measurement of the amount of data transferred over a network connection.

Media Access Control (MAC) address   A standardized data link layer address that is required for every port of devices that connect to a LAN. Other devices in the network use these addresses to locate specific ports in the network and to create and update routing tables and data structures. MAC addresses are 6 bytes long and are controlled by the IEEE.

memory chips   RAM chips on memory cards plug into the motherboard.

microprocessor   A silicon chip that contains a CPU.

modem   A device that converts digital and analog signals. At the source, a modem converts digital signals to a form suitable for transmission over analog communication facilities. At the destination, the analog signals are returned to their digital form.

motherboard   A computer's main circuit board.

mouse port   Connects a mouse to a PC.

network interface card (NIC)   A printed circuit board that provides network communication capabilities to and from a PC.

octet   Eight bits. In networking, the term octet often is used (rather than byte) because some machine architectures employ bytes that are not 8 bits long.

parallel port   An interface that can transfer more than 1 bit simultaneously. It connects external devices, such as printers.

Personal Computer Memory Card International Association (PCMCIA)   An organization that has developed a standard for small credit card-sized devices called PCMCIA cards (or PC cards). Originally designed to add memory to portable computers, the PCMCIA standard has been expanded several times and is now suitable for many types of devices.

physical connection   A connection to a network that is made by connecting a specialized expansion card, such as a modem or NIC, from a PC with a cable to a network.

ping   Stands for Packet Internet Groper. Often used in IP networks to test the reachability of a network device.

plug-in   Software or a program that can easily be installed and used as part of a web browser.

power cord   Connects an electrical device to an electrical outlet to provide power to the device.

power supply   Supplies power to a computer.

printed circuit board (PCB)   A thin plate on which chips (integrated circuits) and other electronic components are placed.

protocol   A formal description of a set of rules and conventions that govern how devices on a network exchange information.

random-access memory (RAM)   Also known as read-write memory. Can have new data written to it as well as stored data read from it.

read-only memory (ROM)   A type of computer memory in which data has been prerecorded.

serial port   Can be used for serial communication in which only 1 bit is transmitted at a time.

sound card   An expansion board that handles all sound functions.

subnetwork mask   A 32-bit address mask used in IP to indicate the bits of an IP address that are being used for the subnet address.

system unit   The main component of a PC system.

TB (terabyte)   Approximately 1 trillion bytes. Hard drive capacity on some high-end computers is measured in TB.

Tbps (terabits per second)   One trillion bits per second. A standard measurement of the amount of data transferred over a network connection.

Transmission Control Protocol/Internet Protocol (TCP/IP)   A common name for the suite of protocols developed by the U.S. DoD in the 1970s to support the construction of worldwide internetworks. TCP and IP are the two best-known protocols in the suite.

universal serial bus (USB) port   Lets peripheral devices such as mice, modems, keyboards, scanners, and printers be plugged in and unplugged without resetting the system.

video card   A board that plugs into a PC to give it display capabilities.

web browser   A graphical user interface (GUI)-based hypertext client application, such as Internet Explorer or Netscape Navigator, used to access hypertext documents and other services located on remote servers throughout the WWW and the Internet.

Check Your Understanding

Complete all the review questions to test your understanding of the topics and concepts in this chapter. Answers are listed in Appendix B, "Check Your Understanding Answer Key."

1. The connection to the Internet can be broken down into which of the following?

   A. Physical connection

   B. Logical connection

   C. Applications

   D. All of the above

2. What is the main circuit board of a computer?

   A. PC subsystem

   B. Motherboard

   C. Backplane

   D. Computer memory

3. What are PCMCIA slots?

   A. Slots used primarily in laptops for expansion cards

   B. Slots used as expansion slots primarily in PCs

   C. Expansion slots for a NIC

   D. Slots for certain specialized devices

4. What is a NIC?

   A. A WAN adapter

   B. A printed circuit board that provides network communication

   C. A card used only for Ethernet networks

   D. A standardized data link layer address

5. Which of the following is/are the resource(s) you need before you install a NIC?

   A. Knowledge of how the network card is configured

   B. Knowledge of how to use the network card diagnostics

   C. Capability to resolve hardware resource conflicts

   D. All of the above

6. Which number system is based on powers of 2?

   A. Octal

   B. Hexadecimal

   C. Binary

   D. ASCII

7. Match the following terms with their definitions.

Bit	The smallest unit of data in a computer
Byte	A standard measurement of the rate at which data is transferred over a network connection
kbps	A unit of frequency; the rate of change in the state or cycle in a sound wave, alternating current, or another cyclical waveform
MHz	A unit of measure that describes the size of a data file, the amount of space on a disk or another storage medium, or the amount of data being transferred over a network

8. What is the largest decimal value that can be stored in 1 byte?

   A. 254

   B. 256

   C. 255

   D. 257

9. What is the decimal number 151 in binary?

   A. 10100111

   B. 10010111

   C. 10101011

   D. 10010011

10. What is the binary number 11011010 in decimal?

   A. 186

   B. 202

   C. 218

   D. 222

11. What is the binary number 0010000100000000 in hexadecimal?

   A. 0x2100

   B. 0x2142

   C. 0x0082

   D. 0x0012

12. What is the hexadecimal number 0x2101 in binary?

   A. 0010 0001 0000 0001

   B. 0001 0000 0001 0010

   C. 0100 1000 0000 1000

   D. 1000 0000 1000 0100

13. Which of the following statements is true of ping?

   A. The **ping** command is used to test a device's network connectivity.

   B. Ping stands for packet Internet groper.

   C. The **ping 127.0.0.1** command is used to verify the operation of the TCP/IP stack
   and the NIC transmit/receive function.

   D. All of the above

CHAPTER 2

Networking Fundamentals

Objectives

Upon completion of this chapter, you should be able to answer the following questions:

- How did data networks develop?

- What are some common networking devices and at what layer of the OSI model do they operate?

- What are the bus, star, extended-star, ring, hierarchy, mesh, and partial-mesh topologies?

- What are the differences between physical and logical topologies?

- What are network protocols?

- What are the features of a LAN, WAN, MAN, SAN, and data center?

- What are the functions, benefits, and technologies of VPNs?

- What are intranets and extranets?

- What is the importance of bandwidth?

- What are the units used to measure bandwidth?

- What are the maximum lengths and limitations of bandwidth?

- What is throughput?

- How are data transfers calculated?

- What are the differences between digital and analog?

- What is the process of layer communication?

- What are the benefits of the OSI reference model?

- What are the functions of each of the seven layers of the OSI reference model?

- What is the basic process of communication that is used among the layers of the OSI reference model?

- What are the names of the TCP/IP protocol model layers?

- What is data encapsulation and de-encapsulation?

Additional Topics of Interest

In addition to the core objective areas, this chapter introduces you to the following topics of interest to networkers:

- Functions of a repeater, hub, NIC, bridge, switch, and router

- Functions of a voice gateway, DSLAM, CMTS, and optical platform

- Functions of a firewall, AAA server, and VPN concentrator

- Functions of a wireless adapter, wireless access point, and wireless bridge

Key Terms

The following is a list of key terms introduced in this chapter. For your reference, a definition for each term can be found at the end of the chapter.

local-area network (LAN)   page 45

metropolitan-area network (MAN)   page 45

wide-area network (WAN)   page 45

network interface card (NIC)   page 49

repeater   page 49

hub   page 49

collision   page 51

collision domain   page 51

Media Access Control (MAC)   page 51

bridge   page 51

flooding   page 53

broadcast   page 53

broadcast domain   page 53

switches   page 53

microsegmentation   page 54

router   page 55

firewall   page 58

bus topology   page 63

star topology   page 64

extended-star topology   page 64

ring topology   page 65

hierarchical topology   page 67

full-mesh topology   page 67

partial-mesh topology   page 68

token passing   page 68

protocol suites   page 69

protocol   page 69

storage-area network (SAN)   page 73

data center   page 74

virtual private network (VPN)   page 75

intranet   page 77

extranet   page 77

bandwidth   page 78

throughput   page 83

OSI reference model   page 89

application layer   page 90

presentation layer   page 90

session layer   page 90

transport layer   page 91

network layer   page 91

data link layer   page

physical layer   page 91

peer-to-peer communication   page 92

segment   page 92

packet   page 92

frame   page 92

encapsulation   page 94

de-encapsulation   page 96

This chapter introduces some of the terminology used by networking professionals and various types of computer networks. It explains how standards ensure greater compatibility and interoperability among various types of network technologies. It also describes how the OSI reference model networking scheme supports networking standards. In addition, this chapter describes the basic functions that occur at each layer of the OSI model. As you work through this chapter, you learn about the basic functions that take place at each layer of the OSI model, which will serve as a foundation as you begin to design, build, and troubleshoot networks.

Finally, this chapter describes various network devices as well as cabling physical and logical layouts.

Be sure to look at this chapter's associated Interactive Media Activities, PhotoZooms, and Videos, which you can find on the CD-ROM accompanying this book. These CD elements are designed to supplement the material and reinforce the concepts introduced in this chapter.

Networking Terminology

This section introduces the concept and history of the data network. It also discusses the basic features of the following types of networks:

- Local-area networks (LANs)
- Wide-area networks (WANs)
- Metropolitan-area networks (MANs)
- Storage-area networks (SANs)
- Data centers
- Intranets
- Extranets
- Virtual private networks (VPNs)

Data Networks

Data networks developed as a result of businesses and government agencies needing to exchange electronic information across long distances. At the time, microcomputers were not connected as mainframe computer terminals were, so there was no efficient way of sharing data between multiple microcomputers. Figure 2-1 illustrates a company with many microcomputers without a network connection.

NOTE

In the early days, a company invested in computers as standalone devices that sometimes had printers attached. When employees who didn't have a printer needed to print documents, they had to copy a file to a floppy disk and load it on to a coworker's PC that was connected to a printer, and print it from there. This rather crude version of a network became known as *sneakernet* (see Figure 2-2).

Figure 2-1 Company with Many Standalone Computers

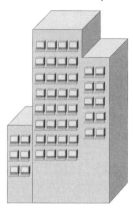

Figure 2-2 Sneakernet

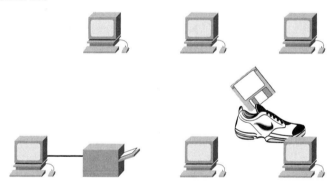

It became apparent that sharing data through the use of floppy disks was not an efficient or cost-effective manner in which to conduct business. Each time a file was modified, it had to be shared again with all the other people who needed it. If two people modified the file and then tried to share it, one of the sets of changes would be lost.

Businesses needed a solution that would address the following concerns:

- How to avoid duplication of equipment and resources
- How to communicate efficiently
- How to set up and manage a network

Businesses realized that networking technology could increase productivity while saving money. Networks were added and expanded almost as rapidly as new network technologies and products were introduced. In the early 1980s, networking saw a tremendous expansion, even though the early development of networking was chaotic.

The network technologies that emerged in the mid-1980s were created with a variety of hardware and software. Each company that created network hardware and software used its own company standards that were developed because of competition with other companies. Consequently, many new network technologies were incompatible with each other. It became increasingly difficult for networks that used different specifications to communicate with each other. This often required the old network equipment to be removed to implement the new equipment.

One early solution was the creation of *local-area network (LAN)* standards. Because LAN standards provided an open set of guidelines for creating network hardware and software, the capability to mix and match different equipment manufactured by different companies facilitated stability in LAN implementation. Figure 2-3 shows a simple LAN.

As the use of computers in businesses grew, it soon became obvious that even LANs were insufficient. In a LAN system, each department or company is a kind of electronic island, as shown in Figure 2-4.

Before LANs were created, there was a need for information to move efficiently and quickly—not only within a company, but also from one business to another. The solution was the creation of *metropolitan-area networks (MANs)* and *wide-area networks (WANs)*. Because WANs could connect user networks over large geographic areas, they made it possible for businesses to communicate with each other across great distances, as shown in Figure 2-5.

Figure 2-3 A Simple LAN

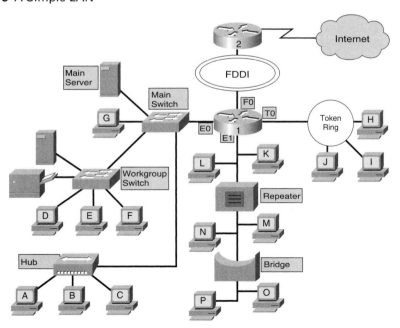

Figure 2-4 LAN

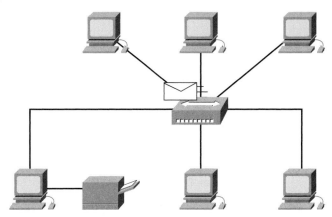

Figure 2-5 WAN

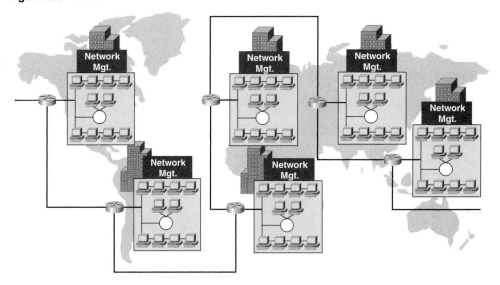

Network History

The history of computer networking is complex, involving many people from all over the world over the past 35 years. Table 2-1 presents a simplified view of how the Internet evolved. The processes of invention and commercialization are far more complicated, but it is helpful to look at the fundamental development.

Table 2-1 Microcomputer Development Timeline

Time Period	Development
Early 1940s	Large electromechanical devices that were prone to failure.
1947	The invention of the semiconductor transistor opened up many possibilities for making smaller, more reliable computers.
1950s	The integrated circuit was invented. It combined several—and then many, and now millions—of transistors on one small piece of semiconductor.
1960s	Mainframes with terminals were commonplace, and integrated circuits were widely used.
Late 1960s and 1970s	Smaller computers called minicomputers came into existence.
1977	Apple Computer introduced the microcomputer, also called the personal computer (PC).
1981	IBM introduced its first PC.
Mid-1980s	Computer users using standalone computers started sharing data (files) through the use of modems connected to another computer. This was called point-to-point or dialup communication.

In the 1940s, computers were large electromechanical devices that were prone to failure. In 1947, the invention of a semiconductor transistor opened up many possibilities for making smaller, more-reliable computers. In the 1950s, mainframe computers, run by punched-card programs, began to be used by large institutions. In the late 1950s, the integrated circuit was invented. It combined several—and then many, and now millions—of transistors on one small piece of semiconductor. Through the 1960s, mainframes with terminals were commonplace, and integrated circuits were widely used.

In the late 1960s and 1970s, smaller computers called minicomputers (even though they were still very large by today's standards) came into existence. In 1975, Micro Instrumentation Telemetry Systems (MITS) introduced the first microcomputer for consumers: the Altair 8800. In 1977, Apple Computer introduced its microcomputer: the Apple II. In 1981, IBM entered the market with its first microcomputer: the IBM PC (personal computer). The user-friendly Apple Macintosh, the open-architecture IBM PC, and the further microminiaturization of integrated circuits led to widespread use of PCs in businesses and homes.

In the mid-1980s, computer users using standalone computers started sharing data (files) through the use of a modem connected to another computer. This was called *point-to-point* or *dialup* communication. This concept was expanded by the use of computers that were the central point of communication in a dialup connection. These computers were called *bulletin boards*. Users would connect to the bulletin board, leave and pick up messages, and upload and download files. The drawback of this type of system was that there was very little, if any, direct communication, and then only with those who knew about the bulletin board. Another limitation was that the bulletin board computer required one modem per connection. If five people connected simultaneously, five modems connected to five separate phone lines were required. Imagine if 500 people wanted to connect at the same time!

In 1957, as a result of the USSR launching the first satellite, Sputnik, the U.S. Department of Defense (DoD) formed the Defense Advanced Research Projects Agency (DARPA) to help maintain U.S. technological superiority. DARPA began developing the first packet-switched networks over wide-area networks, using the first routers called Interface Message Processors (IMPs). This network was known as the Arpanet. This technology was different from the point-to-point communication used in bulletin boards. It allowed multiple computers to be connected using many different paths. The network itself determined how to move data from one computer to another. Instead of being able to communicate with only one other computer at a time, networking made it possible for a computer to reach many computers using the same connection. Arpanet eventually became the Internet.

Networking Devices

Equipment that connects directly to a network segment is called a *device*. These devices are broken into two classifications:

- **End user devices**—Includes computers, printers, scanners, and other devices that provide services directly to the user.

- **Network devices**—Includes all devices that connect the end-user devices to allow them to communicate.

End-user devices that provide users with a connection to the network are also called *hosts*. Figure 2-6 shows an example of an end-user device—a workstation.

Figure 2-6 End-User Device: Workstation

These devices allow users to share, create, and obtain information. Host devices can exist without a network, but without a network, host capabilities are greatly reduced. Host devices are physically connected to the network media using a ***network interface card (NIC)***. They use this connection to perform the tasks of sending e-mails, printing reports, scanning pictures, or accessing databases. A NIC is a printed circuit board that fits into the expansion slot of a bus on a computer motherboard, or it can be a peripheral device. It is also called a network adapter. Laptop or notebook computer NICs are usually the size of a PCMCIA card.

Each NIC carries a unique code called a MAC address. As the name implies, the NIC controls host access to the networking medium. The details of MAC addresses are covered in later chapters.

There are no standardized symbols for end-user devices in the networking industry. They bear a resemblance to the real device to allow for quick recognition.

Network devices provide transport for the data that needs to be transferred between end-user devices. Network devices extend cable connections, concentrate connections, convert data formats, and manage data transfers. Examples of devices that perform these functions are repeaters, hubs, bridges, switches, and routers. The following sections provide an overview of some common networking devices.

Repeaters

Repeaters are networking devices that exist at Layer 1, the physical layer, of the OSI reference model. To understand how a repeater works, it is important to understand that as data leaves a source and goes out over the network, it is transformed into either electrical or light pulses that pass along the networking medium. These pulses are called *signals*. When signals leave a transmitting station, they are clean and easily recognizable. However, the longer the cable length, the weaker and more deteriorated the signals become as they pass along the networking medium. The purpose of a repeater is to regenerate and retime network signals at the bit level, allowing them to travel a longer distance on the medium.

The term *repeater* originally meant a single port "in" device and a single port "out" device. Today multiple-port repeaters also exist. Repeaters are classified as Layer 1 devices in the OSI model because they act only on the bit level and look at no other information.

Hubs

The purpose of a ***hub*** is to regenerate and retime network signals. The characteristics of a hub are similar to those of a repeater. A hub is a common connection point for devices in a network, as shown in Figure 2-7. Hubs commonly connect segments of a LAN. A hub contains multiple ports. When a packet arrives at one port, it is copied to the other ports so that all the LAN segments can see all the packets.

Figure 2-7 Hub

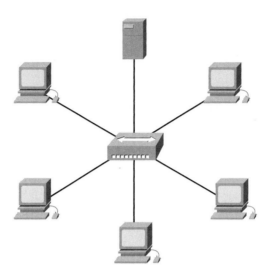

Because hubs and repeaters have similar characteristics, a hub is also called a *multiport repeater*. The difference between a repeater and a hub is the number of cables that connect to the device. Whereas a repeater typically has only two ports, a hub generally has from four to 20 or more ports, as shown in Figure 2-8. Whereas a repeater receives on one port and repeats on the other, a hub receives on one port and transmits on all the other ports.

Figure 2-8 Hubs Have Several Ports

The following are the most important properties of hubs:

- Hubs amplify signals.

- Hubs propagate signals through the network.

- Hubs do not require filtering.

- Hubs do not require path determination or switching.

- Hubs are used as network-concentration points.

Hubs are commonly used in Ethernet 10BASE-T or 100BASE-T networks. (You learn more about Ethernet networks in Chapter 7, "Ethernet Technologies.") Hubs create a central connection point for the wiring medium. They also increase the network's reliability by allowing any single cable to fail without disrupting the entire network. This feature differs from the bus topology, in which the failure of one cable disrupts the entire network. (Network topology is discussed later in this chapter.) Hubs are considered Layer 1 devices because they only regenerate the signal and repeat it out all their ports (network connections).

In Ethernet networks, all the hosts are connected to the same physical medium. Signals that are sent out across the common medium are received by all devices. A *collision* is a situation that can occur when 2 bits propagate at the same time on the same network. The area within the network from where the data packets originate and collide is called a *collision domain*. You learn more about collision domains in Chapter 6, "Ethernet Fundamentals."

As you will learn later in the OSI model and OSI layer sections in this chapter, the function of a Layer 1 device, such as a hub in this case, is simply to facilitate the transmission of signals. The hub does not recognize any information patterns in the signals, addresses, or data.

Network Interface Cards

Network interface cards (NICs) are considered Layer 2 devices because each NIC throughout the world carries a unique code, called a *Media Access Control (MAC)* address. This address controls data communication for the host on the LAN. The NIC controls the access of the host to the medium. Figure 2-9 shows a NIC.

Figure 2-9 Network Interface Card

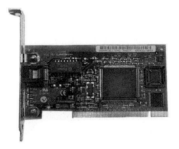

Bridges

A *bridge* is a Layer 2 device designed to create two or more LAN segments, each of which is a separate collision domain. In other words, bridges were designed to create more usable bandwidth. The purpose of a bridge is to filter traffic on a LAN to keep local traffic local yet allow connectivity to other parts (segments) of the LAN for traffic that is directed there. Every networking device has a unique MAC address on the NIC. The bridge keeps track of which MAC addresses are on each side of the bridge and makes forwarding decisions based on this MAC address list.

Bridges learn about devices by examining the source MAC address and filter network traffic by looking only at the destination MAC address. Therefore, they can rapidly forward traffic representing any network layer protocol. Because bridges look only at MAC addresses, they are not concerned with network layer protocols. Consequently, bridges are concerned only with passing or not passing frames, based on their destination MAC addresses. The following are the important properties of bridges:

- Bridges are more "intelligent" than hubs. Bridges operate at Layer 2 only, that is, they can analyze incoming frames and forward (or drop) them based addressing information.

- Bridges collect and pass packets between two or more LAN segments.

- Bridges create more collision domains, allowing more than one device to transmit simultaneously without causing a collision.

- Bridges maintain MAC address tables known as bridge tables.

Figure 2-10 shows how a bridge is used. The appearances of bridges vary greatly, depending on the type.

Figure 2-10 Bridge

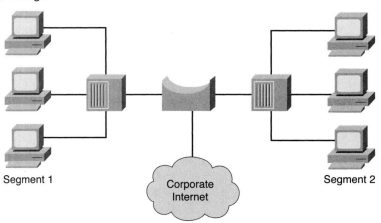

Segment 1   Corporate Internet   Segment 2

What defines a bridge is its Layer 2 filtering of frames and how this is accomplished. To filter or selectively deliver network traffic, bridges build tables of all MAC addresses located on a network segment and other networks and then map them to associated ports. The process is as follows:

Step 1   When a device first transmits a frame, the bridge learns the source MAC address and copies it to the bridge's MAC address table or bridge table.

Step 2   If data comes along the network medium, a bridge compares the destination MAC address carried by the data to MAC addresses contained in its tables.

Step 3   If the bridge determines that the data's destination MAC address is from the same network segment as the source, it does not forward the data to other segments of the network. This process is known as *filtering*. By performing this process, bridges can significantly reduce the amount of traffic between network segments by eliminating unnecessary traffic.

Step 4   If the bridge determines that the data's destination MAC address is not from the same network segment as the source, it forwards the data to the appropriate segment.

Step 5   If the destination MAC address is unknown to the bridge, the bridge transmits the data out all interfaces on a bridge except the one on which it was received. This process is known as *flooding*.

Step 6   The bridge learns where devices are by examining the source MAC address of each frame. If the source MAC address of the data—the frame—is not in the bridge's table, the bridge adds the source MAC address to the table. In the case of switches—which act as multiport bridges—if the MAC address is in the table, but listed as being on a different interface than the one on which the frame was received, the switch updates its table to reflect the new location of the device.

A *broadcast* is a data packet that is sent to all nodes on a network. A *broadcast domain* consists of all the devices connected to a network that receive the data packet broadcast by a node to all other nodes on the same network. Bridges always forward broadcast because they cannot learn the broadcast MAC address of FF.FF.FF.FF.FF.FF, and bridges will always forward them. Therefore, all segments in a bridged environment are considered to be in the same broadcast domain.

> **NOTE**
>
> These same steps and concepts also refer to multiport bridges known as switches.

As was the case in the repeater/hub combination, another device, called a switch, is a multiport bridge. The next section discusses switches in greater detail.

Layer 2 Switches

Layer 2 switches, also called LAN switches or workgroup switches, often replace shared hubs and work with existing cable infrastructures to ensure that the switches are installed with minimal disruption of existing networks. Figure 2-11 shows a switch.

Figure 2-11 Switch

Like bridges, switches connect LAN segments, use a table of MAC addresses to determine the segment on which a frame needs to be transmitted, and reduce traffic. Switches operate at much higher speeds than bridges.

Switches are data link layer devices that, like bridges, let multiple physical LAN segments be interconnected into single larger networks. Similar to bridges, switches forward and flood traffic based on MAC addresses. Because switching is performed in hardware, it is significantly faster than the switching function performed by a bridge using software. Think of each switch port as a microbridge. Each switch port acts as a separate bridge and gives each host the medium's full bandwidth. This process is called microsegmentation.

Microsegmentation allows the creation of private or dedicated segments—one host per segment. Each host receives instant access to the full bandwidth and does not have to compete for available bandwidth with other hosts. In full-duplex switches, because only one device is connected to each switch port, collisions do not occur.

However, as with a bridge, a switch forwards a broadcast message to all the segments on the switch. All segments in a switched environment are therefore considered to be in the same broadcast domain.

Some switches, such as high-end and enterprise-level switches, perform multilayer functioning. This means that in addition to providing Layer 2 functions, the switches also perform some Layer 3 functions. The Cisco Catalyst 8500, as shown in Figure 2-12, is an example of a higher-end enterprise-level switch that can perform Layer 3 functions, such as ATM switching. Keep in mind that these multilayer-functioning switches are beyond the scope of the CCNA course. Furthermore, for the purposes of the CCNA course, only Layer 2 switches are covered.

Figure 2-12 Cisco Catalyst 8500 Switch

Routers

A *router*, as shown in Figure 2-13, is a type of internetworking device that passes data packets between networks based on Layer 3 addresses. A router can make decisions regarding the best path for delivery of data on the network because routers forward data based on network address. In other words, unlike switches or bridges, routers know the location of where to send the data.

Working at Layer 3 allows the router to make decisions based on network addresses instead of individual Layer 2 MAC addresses. Routers also can connect different Layer 2 technologies, such as Ethernet, Token Ring, and Fiber Distributed Data Interface (FDDI). Routers also commonly connect Asynchronous Transfer Mode (ATM) and serial connections. However, because of their capability to route packets based on Layer 3 information, routers have become the backbone of the Internet and run the IP protocol.

Figure 2-13 Router

The purpose of a router is to examine incoming packets (Layer 3 data), choose the best path for them through the network, and then switch them to the proper outgoing port. Routers are the most important traffic-regulating devices on large networks. Routers let virtually any type of computer communicate with any other computer anywhere in the world.

Routers and Layer 3 functions are explained in more detail in subsequent chapters.

Voice, DSL, Cable Modem, and Optical Devices

Recent networking demands of voice and data network integration and fast data transmission for end users and network backbones have resulted in the development of the following new networking devices:

- Voice gateways for handling converged packetized voice and data traffic
- Digital subscriber line access multiplexers (DSLAMs) used at the service provider's central office for concentrating DSL modem connections from hundreds of homes
- Cable Modem Termination System (CMTS) used at a cable operator's headend or central location to concentrate connections from many cable modem subscribers
- Optical platforms for sending and receiving data over fiber-optic cable, providing high-speed connection

These technologies are explained in more detail in CCNA 2.

More Information: Voice Gateway

A *gateway* is a special-purpose device that converts information from one protocol stack to another. The Cisco AS5400 Series Universal Access Server provides cost-effective platforms that combine routing, remote access, voice gateway, firewall, and digital modem functionality. Figure 2-14 shows a Cisco AS5400 Series Universal Gateway, which offers voice, wireless, and fax services on any port at any time.

Figure 2-14 Cisco AS5400 Series Universal Gateway

DSLAM

A DSLAM is a device used in a variety of DSL technologies. A DSLAM serves as the interface point between a number of subscriber premises and the carrier network. Figure 2-15 shows a Cisco 6100 Series Advanced DSL Access Multiplexer.

Figure 2-15 Cisco 6100 Series DSLAM

More Information: Voice Gateway (Continued)

CMTS

Cable operators use a Cable Modem Termination System (CMTS) at various concentration points or nodes in the cable network to provide high-speed Internet access, voice, and other networking services to home and business subscribers. The Cisco uBR7100 (Universal Broadband Router) CMTS series is designed for multitenant units (MTUs) such as apartment buildings and hotels. High-capacity models such as the uBR10012 series, shown in Figure 2-16, can handle thousands of subscribers.

Figure 2-16 Cisco CMTS uBR10012

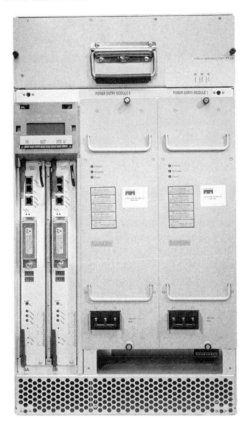

Optical Platforms

Several optical platforms are available for optical networking, which is primarily a backbone, wide-area technology. Figure 2-17 shows a Cisco ONS 15454 dense wavelength division multiplexing (DWDM) optical network system (ONS). The Cisco ONS 15454 provides the functions of multiple network elements in a single platform.

More Information: Voice Gateway (Continued)

Figure 2-17 Optical Platform—The Cisco ONS 15454 DWDM Optical Network System

Security Devices

Because of increased Internet and extranet connections, as well as more telecommuters and mobile users accessing enterprise networks from remote sites, the importance of network security increases. Firewalls, AAA servers, and VPN concentrators are components or devices related to network security.

Firewalls

The term *firewall* refers to either a firewall program running on a router or server or a special standalone hardware component of a network. A firewall protects a private network's resources from users in other networks.

Working closely with a router program, a firewall examines each network packet to determine whether to forward it to its destination. Using a firewall is like using a traffic officer to ensure that only valid traffic can enter or leave certain networks. Figure 2-18 shows a Cisco PIX Firewall 535 series, which is a dedicated network device.

Figure 2-18 Cisco PIX Firewall

More Information: Voice Gateway (Continued)

AAA Servers

A *AAA server* is a server program that handles user requests for access to computer and network resources. A AAA server provides authentication, authorization, and accounting services for an enterprise. The AAA server ensures that only authentic users can get into the network (authentication), that the users are allowed access only to the resources they need (authorization), and that records are kept of everything they do after they are allowed entry (accounting).

A AAA server is like the credit card system. To put charges on a credit card, the merchant must verify that the credit card actually belongs to the person using it (authentication). The merchant must also check that the credit card has enough credit left for the requested charge amount (authorization), and then the merchant must record the charge to the user's account (accounting). Figure 2-19 shows an example of where a AAA server is used.

Figure 2-19 AAA Server

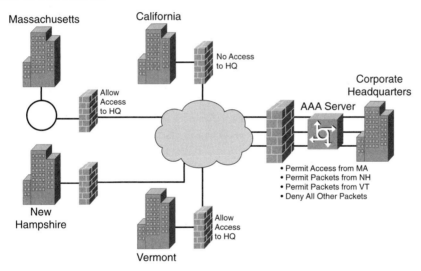

VPN Concentrators

A VPN concentrator offers powerful remote access and site-to-site VPN capability, an easy-to-use management interface, and a VPN client. The Cisco VPN 3000 Concentrator Series is a family of purpose-built, remote-access VPN platforms and client software that incorporates high availability, high performance, and scalability with the most advanced encryption and authentication techniques available today. Figure 2-20 shows a VPN 3000 Concentrator.

More Information: Voice Gateway (Continued)

Figure 2-20 Cisco VPN 3000 Concentrator

Wireless Devices

A wireless LAN (WLAN) provides all the features and benefits of traditional LAN technologies, such as Ethernet, without the limitations of wire or cables. Some common wireless networking devices include wireless NICs, wireless access points, and wireless bridges. The following sections briefly describe these wireless networking devices.

Wireless NICs

Each wireless client requires a wireless NIC or client adapter. These are available as PCMCIA and PCI cards to provide wireless connectivity for both laptop and desktop workstations. Laptops or notebook PCs, with wireless NICs, can move freely throughout a campus environment while maintaining connectivity to the network. Wireless PCI and ISA adapters (for desktop workstations) allow end stations to be added to the LAN quickly, easily, and inexpensively without the need for additional cabling. All adapters feature antennas—the PCMCIA card with a built-in antenna and the PCI card with an external antenna. The antennas provide the range required for data transmission and reception. Figure 2-21 shows wireless adapters.

Figure 2-21 Wireless Adapters

More Information: Voice Gateway (Continued)

Wireless Access Points

The access point (AP) or base station (see Figure 2-22) is a wireless LAN transceiver that can act as a hub—the center point of a standalone wireless network—or as a bridge—the connection point between wireless and wired networks. Multiple APs can provide roaming functionality, allowing wireless users freedom to roam throughout a facility while maintaining uninterrupted connectivity to the network.

Figure 2-22 Wireless Access Point

Wireless Bridges

A wireless bridge, shown in Figure 2-23, provides high-speed (11 Mbps), long-range (up to 25 miles), line-of-sight wireless connectivity between Ethernet networks. Any Cisco AP can be used as a repeater (extension point) for the wireless network.

Figure 2-23 Wireless Bridge

PhotoZoom   Cisco 1503 Micro Hub

In this PhotoZoom, you view a Cisco 1503 hub.

PhotoZoom   Cisco Catalyst 1924 Switch

In this PhotoZoom, you view a Cisco Catalyst 1924 switch.

PhotoZoom   Cisco 2621 Router

In this PhotoZoom, you view a Cisco 2621 router.

Network Topology

A network topology defines how computers, printers, network devices, and other devices are connected. In other words, a network topology describes the layout of the wire and devices as well as the paths used by data transmissions. The topology greatly influences how the network works.

Networks can have both a physical and a logical topology. *Physical topology* refers to the physical layout of the devices and media. Physical topologies that are commonly used are

- Bus
- Ring
- Star
- Extended star
- Hierarchical
- Mesh

Figure 2-24 illustrates the different physical topologies.

Figure 2-24 Physical Topologies

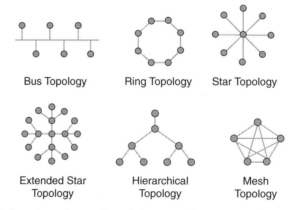

Logical topology defines how the medium is accessed by the hosts for sending data. The following sections describe different types of physical and logical topologies.

Figure 2-25 shows many different topologies connected by networking devices. It shows a network of moderate complexity that is typical of a school or small business.

Figure 2-25 Networking Topologies

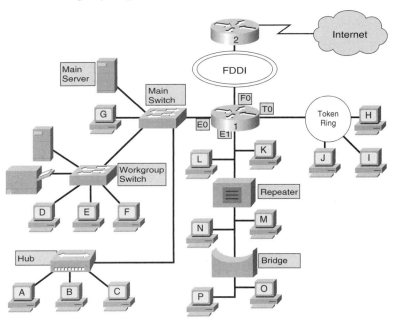

The following sections describe the different networking topologies in more detail.

Bus Topology

Commonly called a linear bus, a ***bus topology*** connects all the devices using a single cable (see Figure 2-26). This cable proceeds from one computer to the next like a bus line going through a city.

Figure 2-26 Bus Topology

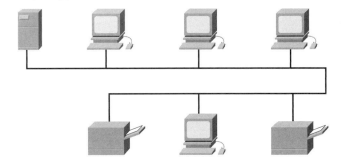

With a physical bus topology, the main cable segment must end with a terminator that absorbs the signal when it reaches the end of the line or wire. If there is no terminator, the electrical signal representing the data bounces back at the end of the wire, causing errors in the network.

Bus topologies were common in the early days of LANs that used a single coaxial cable to connect multiple PCs and printers.

Star and Extended-Star Topologies

The *star topology*, shown in Figure 2-27, is the most commonly used physical topology in Ethernet LANs. When installed, the star topology resembles spokes in a bicycle wheel. The star topology is made up of a central connection point that is a device such as a hub, switch, or router, where all the cabling segments meet. Each host in the network is connected to the central device with its own cable.

Although a physical star topology costs more to implement than the physical bus topology, the advantages of a star topology make it worth the additional cost. Because each host is connected to the central device with its own cable, when that cable has a problem, only that host is affected; the rest of the network remains operational. This benefit is extremely important and is why virtually every newly designed Ethernet LAN has a physical star topology.

A central connection point might be desirable for security or restricted access, but this is also a main disadvantage of a star topology. If the central device fails, the whole network becomes disconnected.

Figure 2-27 Star Topology

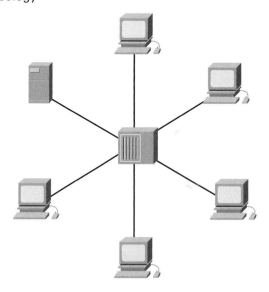

When a star network is expanded to include an additional networking device that is connected to the main networking device, it is called an *extended-star topology*, as shown in Figure 2-28.

Figure 2-28 Extended-Star Topology

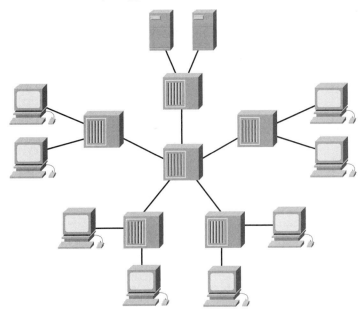

Star topologies and extended-star topologies become more apparent in later chapters when switches and routers are discussed in more detail.

Ring Topology

The logical *ring topology* is another important topology in LAN connectivity. As the name implies, hosts are connected in the form of a ring or circle. Unlike the physical bus topology, the ring topology has no beginning or end that needs to be terminated. Data is transmitted in a way unlike the logical bus topology. A frame travels around the ring, stopping at each node. If a node wants to transmit data, it is permitted to add that data as well as the destination address to the frame. The frame then continues around the ring until it finds the destination node, which takes the data out of the frame. The advantage of using this type of method is that there are no collisions of data frames.

Two types of rings exist:

- Single ring
- Dual ring

In a single ring, as shown in Figure 2-29, all the devices on the network share a single cable, and the data travels in one direction only. Each device waits its turn to send data over the network. Most single-ring topologies are actually wired as a star. Token Ring networks use single ring topologies. Token Ring is becoming less common as it gets replaced by Ethernet star and extended-star topology networks.

Figure 2-29 Ring Topology

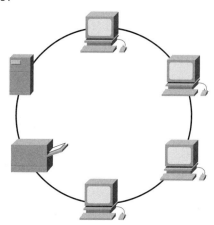

In a dual ring, two rings allow data to be sent in both directions, as shown in Figure 2-30. This setup creates redundancy (fault tolerance), meaning that if one ring fails, data can be transmitted on the other ring. Also, if both rings fail, a "wrap" at the fault can heal the topology back into a ring. Fiber Distributed Data Interface (FDDI) is an example of a technology that uses the dual-ring topology. Like Token Ring, FDDI is also becoming a lesser-used technology.

Figure 2-30 Dual-Ring Topology

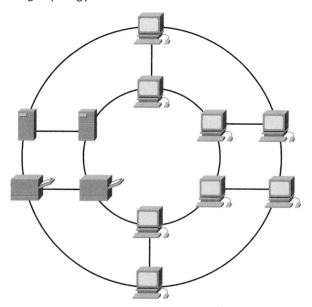

Hierarchical Topology

A *hierarchical topology* is created similarly to an extended-star topology. The primary difference is that it does not use a central node. Instead, it uses a trunk node from which it branches to other nodes, as shown in Figure 2-31.

Figure 2-31 Hierarchical Topology

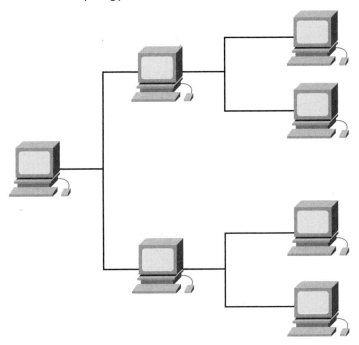

Full-Mesh and Partial-Mesh Topologies

The *full-mesh topology* connects all devices (nodes) to each other for redundancy and fault tolerance, as shown in Figure 2-32. The wiring in a full-mesh topology has very distinct advantages and disadvantages. The advantage is that every node is connected physically to every other node, which creates a redundant connection. If any link fails, information can flow through many other links to reach its destination. The primary disadvantage is that for anything more than a small number of nodes, the amount of media for the links and the number of the connections on the lines becomes overwhelming. Implementing a full-mesh topology is expensive and difficult. The full-mesh topology is usually implemented in WANs between routers.

Figure 2-32 Full-Mesh Topology

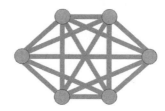

In a *partial-mesh topology*, at least one device maintains multiple connections to others without being fully meshed, as shown in Figure 2-33. A partial-mesh topology still provides redundancy by having several alternative routes. If one route cannot be used, the data takes another route, even if it is longer. The partial-mesh topology is used for many telecommunications backbones, as well as the Internet.

Figure 2-33 Partial-Mesh Topology

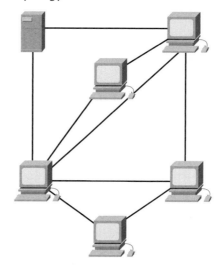

Logical Topology

A network's logical topology is how the hosts communicate across the medium. The two most common types of logical topology are broadcast and *token passing*.

Broadcast topology simply means that each host addresses its data to a particular NIC, to a multicast address, or to a broadcast address on the network medium. There is no order that the stations must follow to use the network. It is first come, first serve. Ethernet also works this way, as explained later in this book.

The second logical topology is token passing. Token passing controls network access by passing an electronic token sequentially to each host. When a host receives the token, it can send data on the network. If the host has no data to send, it passes the token to the next host, and the process repeats itself. Two examples of networks that use token passing are Token Ring and FDDI, both of which are examples of token passing on a physical ring topology.

Network Protocols

Protocol suites are collections of protocols that enable network communication from one host through the network to another host. A *protocol* is a formal description of a set of rules and conventions that govern a particular aspect of how devices on a network communicate. Protocols determine the format, timing, sequencing, and error control in data communication. Without protocols, the computer cannot create or rebuild the stream of incoming bits from another computer into the original data.

Protocols control all aspects of data communication. They determine how the physical network is built, how computers connect to the network, how the data is formatted for transmission, and how that data is sent. These network rules are created and maintained by many different organizations and committees:

- Institute of Electrical and Electronic Engineers (IEEE)

- American National Standards Institute (ANSI)

- Telecommunications Industry Association (TIA)

- Electronic Industries Alliance (EIA)

- International Telecommunications Union (ITU), formerly known as the CCITT (Comité Consultatif International Téléphonique et Télégraphique)

Local-Area Networks (LANs)

LANs consist of computers, network interface cards, peripheral devices, networking media, and network devices. Figure 2-34 illustrates a LAN.

LANs make it possible for businesses that use computer technology to locally share files and printers efficiently and make internal communications possible, such as e-mail. LANs tie together data, local communications, and computing equipment.

Figure 2-34 LAN

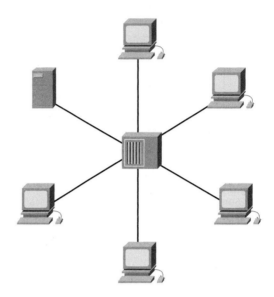

LANs are designed to do the following:

- Operate within a limited geographic area
- Allow many users to access high-bandwidth media
- Provide full-time connectivity to local services
- Connect physically adjacent devices

Some common LAN technologies are

- Ethernet
- Token Ring
- FDDI

Wide-Area Networks (WANs)

WANs interconnect LANS. WANs provide LANs access to computer or file servers in other locations. Because WANs connect user networks over a large geographic area, as shown in Figure 2-35, they make it possible for businesses to communicate across great distances.

Figure 2-35 WAN

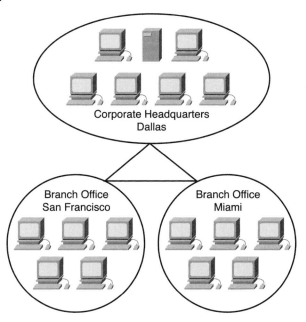

Using WANs allows computers, printers, and other devices on a LAN to share and be shared with distant locations. WANs provide instant communications across large geographic areas. The ability to send an instant message (IM) to someone anywhere in the world provides the same communication capabilities that used to be possible only if people were in the same physical office. Collaboration software provides access to real-time information and resources that allow meetings to be held remotely instead of in person. Wide-area networking has also created a new class of workers called *telecommuters*—people who never have to leave home to go to work.

WANs are designed to do the following:

- Operate over large, geographically separated areas
- Allow users to engage in real-time communication with other users
- Provide full-time remote resources connected to local services
- Provide e-mail, World Wide Web, file transfer, and e-commerce services

Here are some common WAN technologies:

- Modems (Asynchronous dial-up)
- Integrated Services Digital Network (ISDN)
- Digital subscriber line (DSL)
- Frame Relay

- T1 or E1 leased lines—T1, E1, T3, E3, and so on

- Synchronous Optical Network (SONET)—Synchronous Transport Signal level 1 (STS-1) (Optical Carrier [OC]-1), STS-3 (OC-3), and so on

---

More Information: Emerging Home Networking Applications

People now design and build their homes to be Internet homes, wiring them for Ethernet connectivity. People integrate their computer(s) with their phone system, security system, home theater system, heating and air conditioning, lighting, and other electronic components to be able to control them all with the click of a mouse or even via a voice command.

Service providers have built cellular- and satellite-based carrier networks that offer sophisticated services, such as wireless Internet access. Local exchange carriers (LECs) (commonly known as local telephone companies) are implementing high-speed services for data transfer, such as DSL services, at a cost low enough to market to home users. Many cable operators, in addition to cable TV, now provide high-speed Internet access that can be shared among networked home computers. Cisco products support the latest wireless, DSL, and cable technologies.

People also are integrating PC, telephone, and fax capabilities, allowing for automatic answering and message storage and retrieval via computer. In addition, the Internet phone, which uses IP telephony technology and Voice over IP (VoIP), allows people to bypass telephone lines entirely with an Internet connection through cable, wireless, or some other medium to make long distance calls without paying long distance charges.

Metropolitan-Area Networks (MANs)

A MAN is a network that spans a metropolitan area, such as a city or a suburban area. MANs are networks that connect LANs separated by distance and that are located within a common geographic area, as shown in Figure 2-36. For example, a bank with multiple branches might use a MAN. Typically, a service provider connects two or more LAN sites using private communication lines or optical services. A MAN also can be created using wireless bridge technology by beaming signals across public areas. The higher optical bandwidths that are currently available make MANs a more functional and economically feasible option than in the past.

The following features differentiate MANs from LANs and WANs:

- MANs interconnect users in a geographic area or region larger than that covered by a LAN but smaller than the area covered by a WAN.

- MANs connect networks in a city into a single larger network (which can then also offer efficient connection to a WAN).

- MANs also are used to interconnect several LANs by bridging them with backbone lines.

Figure 2-36 MAN

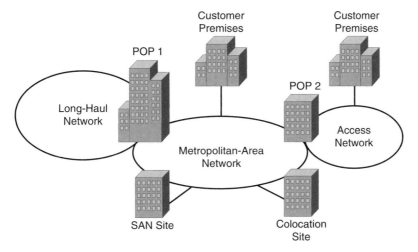

More Information: Specialized Networks Located Within the LAN

There are times when smaller and more specialized networks might reside within the LAN. Most notably, these specialized networks are used for access to storage systems, data center technology systems and devices, intranets or extranets, and VPNs. These various specialized networks are covered in this section.

Storage-Area Networks (SANs)

A *storage-area network (SAN)* is a dedicated, high-performance network that moves data between servers and storage resources. Because it is a separate dedicated network, it avoids any traffic conflict between clients and servers, as shown in Figure 2-37.

SAN technology allows high-speed server-to-storage, storage-to-storage, or server-to- server connectivity. This method uses a separate network infrastructure that relieves any problems associated with existing network connectivity.

SANs offer the following features:

- **Performance**—SANs enable concurrent access to disk or tape arrays by two or more servers at high speeds, providing enhanced system performance.

- **Availability**—SANs have disaster tolerance built in, because data can be mirrored using a SAN up to 10 kilometers (km) (6.2 miles) away.

- **Scalability**—Like a LAN/WAN, a SAN can use a variety of technologies. This allows easy relocation of backup data operations, file migration, and data replication between systems.

Figure 2-37 SAN

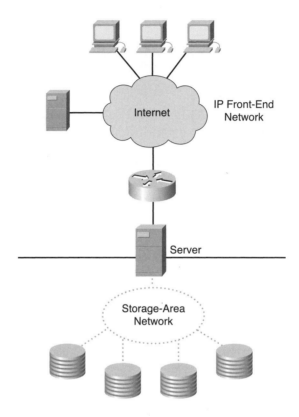

More Information: Data Center Technology

A *data center*, as shown in Figure 2-38, is a globally coordinated network of devices designed to accelerate the delivery of information over the Internet infrastructure. By taking advantage of services in the core IP network, enterprises and service providers can accelerate and improve the use of rich content such as broadband streaming media. Data center technology improves network performance and eliminates the need to stream media on the infrastructure.

A data center bypasses potential sources of congestion by distributing the load across a collection of content engines that are located close to the viewing audience. Rich web and multimedia content is copied to the content engines, and users are routed to an optimally located content engine.

More Information: Data Center Technology (Continued)

Figure 2-38 Data Center

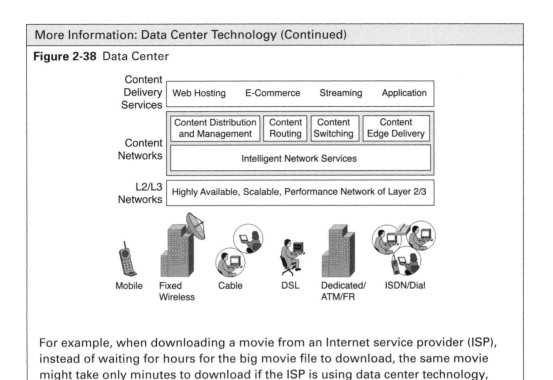

For example, when downloading a movie from an Internet service provider (ISP), instead of waiting for hours for the big movie file to download, the same movie might take only minutes to download if the ISP is using data center technology, because a data center can accelerate the delivery of information.

Virtual Private Network (VPN)

A *virtual private network (VPN)* is a private network that is constructed within a public network infrastructure such as the global Internet. For example, using a VPN, a telecommuter can access the company headquarters' network through the Internet by building a secure tunnel between the telecommuter's PC and a VPN router in the headquarters.

Benefits of VPNs

Cisco products support the latest in VPN technology. A VPN is a service that offers secure, reliable connectivity over a shared public network infrastructure such as the Internet. VPNs maintain the same security and management policies as a private network. They are the most cost-effective method of establishing a point-to-point connection between remote users and an enterprise customer's network. Three main types of VPNs exist, as shown in Figure 2-39.

Figure 2-39 VPN Technologies

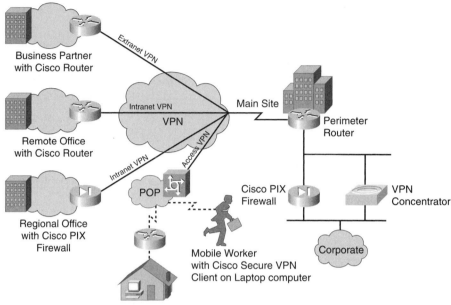

- **Access VPNs** provide remote access for a mobile worker and small office/home office (SOHO) to the headquarters' intranet or extranet over a shared infrastructure. Access VPNs use analog dialup, ISDN, DSL, mobile IP, and cable technologies to securely connect mobile users, telecommuters, and branch offices.

- **Intranet VPNs** link regional and remote offices to the headquarters' internal network over a shared infrastructure using dedicated connections. Intranet VPNs differ from extranet VPNs in that they allow access only to the enterprise customer's employees.

- **Extranet VPNs** link business partners to the headquarters' network over a shared infrastructure using dedicated connections. Extranet VPNs differ from intranet VPNs in that they allow access to users outside the enterprise.

VPNs have the following advantages:

- A single VPN technology can provide privacy for multiple TCP/IP applications. Providing privacy for multiple TCP/IP applications is especially important in environments in which you want to provide secure access for partners or telecommuters.

- Encryption services can be provided for all TCP/IP communications between the trusted client and the VPN server. This scenario has the advantage of being transparent to the end user. Because encryption is turned on, the server can enforce it.

- VPN provides mobility to employees and allows employees to access the corporate network securely.

Intranets and Extranets

One common configuration of a LAN is an *intranet*. Intranet web servers differ from public web servers in that the public does not have access to an organization's intranet without the proper permissions and passwords. Intranets are designed to be accessed by users who have access privileges to an organization's internal LAN. Within an intranet, web servers are installed in the network, and browser technology is used as the common front end to access information such as financial data or graphical, text-based data stored on those servers.

An *extranet* is an intranet that is partially accessible to authorized outsiders. Whereas an intranet resides behind a firewall and is accessible only to people who are members of the same company or organization, an extranet provides various levels of accessibility to outsiders. You can access an extranet only if you have a valid username and password, and your identity determines which parts of the extranet you can view. Extranets help extend the reach of applications and services that are intranet-based but that employ extended, secure access to external users or enterprises. This access is usually accomplished through passwords, user IDs, and other application-level security. Therefore, an extranet is the extension of two or more intranet strategies with a secure interaction between participant enterprises and their respective intranets. The extranet maintains control of access to the intranets within each enterprise in the deployment. Extranets link customers, suppliers, partners, or communities of interest to a corporate intranet over a shared infrastructure using dedicated connections.

Figure 2-40 illustrates an intranet and an extranet.

Figure 2-40 Intranet and Extranet

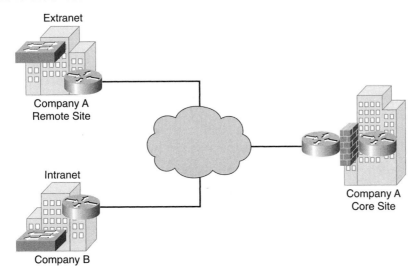

Bandwidth

LANs and WANs have always had one thing in common: the use of the term *bandwidth* to describe their capabilities. This term is essential to understanding networks, but it can be confusing at first. The following sections take a detailed look at this concept before delving too far into networking.

Importance of Bandwidth

Bandwidth is defined as the amount of information that can flow through a network connection in a given period of time. This definition might seem simple, but you must understand the concept of bandwidth when studying networking. Why is it so important to understand bandwidth?

- **Bandwidth is finite**—Regardless of the medium used to build the network, there are limits on the capacity of the network to carry information. Bandwidth is limited both by the laws of physics and by the technologies employed to place information on the medium. For example, a conventional modem bandwidth is limited to about 56 kilobits per second (kbps) by both the physical properties of twisted-pair phone wires and by voice modem technology. The technologies employed by DSL also use the same twisted-pair phone wires, yet DSL uses much greater bandwidth than is available with conventional modems. The frequency range (bandwidth) that DSL uses is much wider than the frequency range used for voice (and used by the POTS modem). That is why you can send more bits per second (bps) over DSL. Optical fiber has the physical potential to provide virtually limitless bandwidth. Even so, the bandwidth of optical fiber cannot be fully realized until technologies are developed to take full advantage of its potential.

- **Bandwidth is not free**—It is possible to buy equipment for a LAN that will provide nearly unlimited bandwidth over a long period of time. For WAN connections, it is almost always necessary to buy bandwidth from a service provider. In either case, an understanding of bandwidth, and changes in demand for bandwidth over a given time, can save an individual or business a significant amount of money. A network manager needs to make the right decisions about the kinds of equipment and services to buy.

- **Bandwidth is a key factor in analyzing network performance, designing new networks, and understanding the Internet**—A networking professional must understand the tremendous impact of bandwidth and throughput on network performance and design. Information flows as a string of bits from computer to computer throughout the world. The Internet is trillions upon trillions of bits, representing massive amounts of information flowing back and forth across the globe in seconds or less. In a sense, it might be appropriate to say that the Internet is bandwidth.

- **The demand for bandwidth is ever-increasing**—As soon as new network technologies and infrastructures are built to provide greater bandwidth, new applications are created to take advantage of the greater capacity. The delivery over the network of rich media content, including streaming video and audio, requires tremendous amounts of bandwidth. IP telephony systems are now commonly installed in place of traditional voice systems, adding further to the need for bandwidth. The successful networking professional must anticipate the need for increased bandwidth and plan accordingly.

Analogies

The idea that information flows suggests two analogies that might make it easier to visualize bandwidth in a network. Because both water and traffic are said to *flow,* consider the following:

- **Bandwidth is like the width of a pipe, as shown in Figure 2-41**—A network of pipes brings fresh water to homes and businesses and carries wastewater away. This water network is made up of pipes with different diameters. A city's main water pipe might be 2 meters in diameter, whereas a kitchen faucet might have a diameter of only 2 centimeters. The width of the pipe determines the pipe's water-carrying capacity. Thus, the water is analogous to data, and pipe width is analogous to bandwidth. Many networking experts say they need to "put in bigger pipes" when they want to add more information-carrying capacity.

- **Bandwidth is like the number of lanes on a highway, as shown in Figure 2-42**—A network of roads serves every city or town. Large highways with many traffic lanes are joined by smaller roads with fewer traffic lanes. These roads lead to even smaller, narrower roads, and eventually to the driveways of homes and businesses. When very few automobiles use the highway system, each vehicle can move freely. When more traffic is added, each vehicle moves more slowly, especially on roads with fewer lanes for the cars to occupy. Eventually, as even more traffic enters the highway system, even multi-lane highways become congested and slow. A data network is much like the highway system, with data packets analogous to automobiles, and bandwidth analogous to the number of lanes on the highway. When a data network is viewed as a system of highways, it is easy to see how low-bandwidth connections can cause traffic to become congested all over the network.

Figure 2-41 Pipe Analogy for Bandwidth

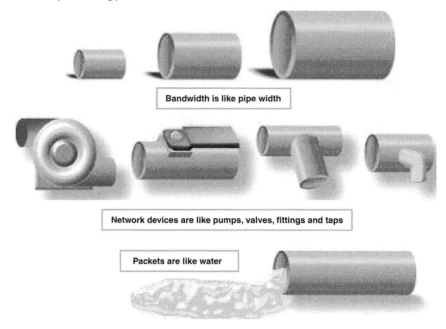

Figure 2-42 Highway Analogy for Bandwidth

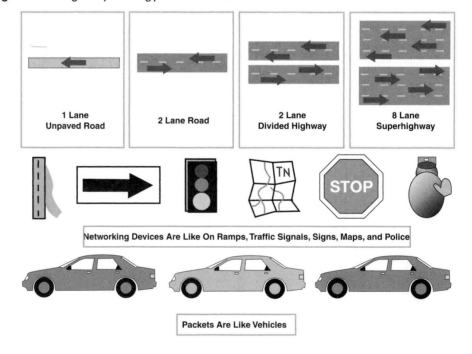

Keep in mind that the true, actual meaning of bandwidth, in this context, is the maximum number of bits that theoretically can pass through a given area of space in a specified amount of time (under the given conditions). These analogies are only to make it easier to understand the concept of bandwidth.

Measurement

In digital systems, the basic unit of bandwidth is bits per second (bps). Bandwidth is the measure of how much information, or bits, can flow from one place to another in a given amount of time, or seconds. Although bandwidth can be described in bits per second, usually some multiple of bits per second is used. In other words, network bandwidth is typically described as thousands of bits per second, millions of bits per second, and even billions of bits per second.

Although the terms *bandwidth* and *speed* are often used interchangeably, they are not exactly the same thing. You might say, for example, that a T3 connection at 45 megabits per second (Mbps) operates at a higher speed than a T1 connection at 1.544 Mbps. The actual bits for both T3 and T1 travel near the speed of light, so the actual speed of the bit does not change. Bandwidth refers to how many bits per second are transmitted over the link, not how fast the bits actually travel. However, if only a small amount of their data-carrying capacity is being used, each of these connection types carries data at roughly the same speed, just as a small amount of water flows at the same rate through a small pipe as through a large pipe. Therefore, it is usually more accurate to say that a T3 connection has greater bandwidth than a T1, because it can carry more information in the same period of time, not because it has a higher speed.

Table 2-2 summarizes the various units of bandwidth.

Table 2-2 Units of Bandwidth

Unit of Bandwidth	Abbreviation	Equivalent
Bits per second	bps	1 bps = fundamental unit of bandwidth
Kilobits per second	kbps	1 kbps = 1000 bps = 10^3 bps
Megabits per second	Mbps	1 Mbps = 1,000,000 bps = 10^6 bps
Gigabits per second	Gbps	1 Gbps = 1,000,000,000 bps = 10^9 bps

Limitations

Bandwidth varies depending on the type of medium as well as the LAN and WAN technologies used. The physics of the medium account for some of the difference. Physical differences in the ways signals travel through twisted-pair copper wire, coaxial cable, optical fiber, and even air result in fundamental limitations on the information-carrying capacity of a given medium. However, a network's actual bandwidth is determined by a combination of the physical medium and the technologies chosen for signaling and detecting network signals.

For example, current understanding of the physics of unshielded twisted-pair (UTP) copper cable puts the theoretical bandwidth limit at more than 1 Gbps. But in actual practice, the bandwidth is determined by the use of a particular technology, such as 10BASE-T, 100BASE-TX, or 1000BASE-TX Ethernet. Bandwidth is also determined by other varying factors, such as the number of users in the network, the equipment being used, applications, the amount of broadcast, and so on. In other words, the actual bandwidth is determined not by the limitation of the medium, but by the signaling methods, NICs, and other items of network equipment that are chosen.

Table 2-3 lists some common networking media types, along with their limits on distance and bandwidth.

Table 2-3 Maximum Bandwidths and Length Limitations

Medium	Maximum Theoretical Bandwidth	Maximum Physical Distance
50-ohm coaxial cable (10BASE2 Ethernet, Thinnet)	10 Mbps	185 m
50-ohm coaxial cable (10BASE5 Ethernet, Thicknet)	10 Mbps	500 m
Category 5 UTP (10BASE-T Ethernet)	10 Mbps	100 m
Category 5 UTP (100BASE-TX Ethernet)	100 Mbps	100 m
Category 5 UTP (1000BASE-TX Ethernet)	1000 Mbps	100 m
Multimode optical fiber (62.5/125 μm) (100BASE-FX Ethernet)	100 Mbps	2000 m
Multimode optical fiber (62.5/125 μm) (1000BASE-SX Ethernet)	1000 Mbps	220 m
Multimode optical fiber (50/125 μm) (1000BASE-SX Ethernet)	1000 Mbps	550 m
Single-mode optical fiber (9/125 μm) (1000BASE-LX Ethernet)	1000 Mbps	5000 m

Table 2-4 summarizes common WAN services and the bandwidth associated with each.

Table 2-4 WAN Services and Bandwidths

WAN Service	Typical User	Bandwidth
Modem	Individuals	56 kbps = 0.056 Mbps
DSL	Individuals, telecommuters, and small businesses	128 kbps to 6.1 Mbps = 0.128 Mbps to 6.1 Mbps
ISDN	Telecommuters and small businesses	128 kbps = 0.128 Mbps
Frame Relay	Small institutions (schools) and medium-sized businesses	56 kbps to 44.736 Mbps (U.S.) or 34.368 Mbps (Europe) = 0.056 Mbps to 44.736 Mbps (U.S.) or 34.368 Mbps (Europe)
T1	Larger entities	1.544 Mbps
T3	Larger entities	44.736 Mbps
STS-1 (OC-1)	Phone companies, data-comm company backbones	51.840 Mbps
STS-3 (OC-3)	Phone companies, data-comm company backbones	155.251 Mbps
STS-48 (OC-48)	Phone companies, data-comm company backbones	2.488 Gbps

Throughput

Bandwidth is the measure of the amount of information that can move through the network in a given period of time. Therefore, the amount of available bandwidth is a critical part of the network's specification. A typical LAN might be built to provide 100 Mbps to every desktop workstation, but this does not mean that each user can actually move one hundred megabits of data through the network for every second of use. This is true only under the most ideal circumstances. The concept of throughput can help explain why this is so.

Throughput refers to actual measured bandwidth at a specific time of day, using specific Internet routes, and while a specific set of data is transmitted on the network. Unfortunately, for many reasons, throughput is often far less than the maximum possible digital bandwidth of the medium that is being used. The following are some of the factors that determine throughput:

- Internetworking devices
- Type of data being transferred

- Network topology

- Number of users on the network

- User's computer

- Server computer

- Power conditions

- Congestion

The theoretical bandwidth of a network is an important consideration in network design, because network bandwidth is never greater than the limits imposed by the chosen medium and networking technologies. Figure 2-43 lists some of the variables that affect throughput. However, it is just as important for a network designer and administrator to consider the factors that might affect actual throughput. By measuring throughput on a regular basis, a network administrator will be aware of changes in network performance and changes in the needs of network users. The network can then be adjusted accordingly.

Figure 2-43 Throughput Variables

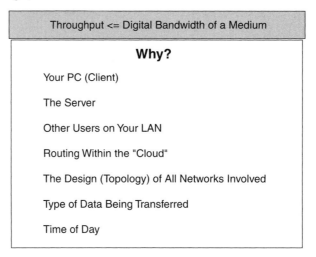

> Throughput <= Digital Bandwidth of a Medium
>
> **Why?**
>
> Your PC (Client)
>
> The Server
>
> Other Users on Your LAN
>
> Routing Within the "Cloud"
>
> The Design (Topology) of All Networks Involved
>
> Type of Data Being Transferred
>
> Time of Day

Data Transfer Calculation

Network designers and administrators are often called on to make decisions regarding bandwidth. Should the size of the WAN connection be increased to accommodate a new database? Is the current LAN backbone of sufficient bandwidth for a streaming-video training program? The answers to questions like these are not always easy to find, but one place to start is with a simple data transfer calculation.

Using the formula $T = S / BW$ (transfer time = size of file / bandwidth) lets a network administrator estimate several of the important components of network performance. If the typical file size for a given application is known, dividing the file size by the network bandwidth yields an estimate of the fastest time that the file can be transferred.

Two important points should be considered when doing this calculation:

- The result is an estimate only, because the file size does not include any overhead added by the process that takes place to prepare data to be transferred over the network. This process is called encapsulation. Encapsulation is covered in more detail in later chapters.

- The result is likely to be a best-case transfer time, because available bandwidth is almost never at the theoretical maximum for the network type. (A more accurate estimate can be attained if throughput is substituted for bandwidth in the equation.)

Although the data transfer calculation is quite simple, it can be tricky if you are not careful to use the same units throughout the equation. In other words, if the bandwidth is measured in Mbps, the file size must be in megabits (Mb), not megabytes (MB). Because file sizes are typically given in megabytes, you might need to multiply the number of megabytes by 8 to convert to megabits.

Try to answer the following question using the formula $T = S / BW$. (Be sure to convert units of measurement as necessary.)

Would it take less time to send the contents of a floppy disk full of data (1.44 MB) over an ISDN line or to send the contents of a 10-GB hard drive full of data over an OC-48 line?

Figure 2-44 summarizes a simple formula for file transfer time calculations.

Figure 2-44 File Transfer Time Calculation

Best Download $T = \dfrac{S}{BW}$		Typical Download $T = \dfrac{S}{P}$
BW =		Maximum theoretical bandwidth of the "slowest link" between the source host and the destination host (measured in bits per second).
P =		Actual throughput at the moment of transfer (measured in bits per second).
T =		Time for file transfer to occur (measured in seconds).
S =		File size in bits.

Digital Versus Analog

Until recently, radio, television, and telephone transmissions were sent through the air and over wires using electromagnetic waves. These waves are called *analog* because they have the same shapes as the light and sound waves produced by the transmitters. As light and sound waves change size and shape, the electrical signal that carries the transmission changes proportionately. In other words, the electromagnetic waves are *analogous* to the light and sound waves.

Analog bandwidth is measured by how much of the electromagnetic spectrum is occupied by each signal. The basic unit of analog bandwidth is *hertz* (Hz), or cycles per second. Typically, multiples of this basic unit of analog bandwidth are used, just as with digital bandwidth. Units of measurement that are commonly seen are kilohertz (kHz), megahertz (MHz), and gigahertz (GHz). These are the units used to describe the frequency of cordless telephones (which usually operate at either 900 MHz or 2.4 GHz). 802.11a and 802.11b wireless network frequencies usually operate at 5 GHz and 2.4 GHz.

Although analog signals can carry a variety of information, they have some significant disadvantages compared to digital transmissions. The analog video signal that requires a wide frequency range for transmission cannot be squeezed into a smaller band. Therefore, if the necessary analog bandwidth is unavailable, the signal cannot be sent. The same goes for digital bandwidth; however, it is less common for digital bandwidth to experience this because of its much-larger bandwidth capabilities.

In digital signaling, all information is sent as bits, regardless of the kind of information it is. Voice, video, and data all become streams of bits when they are prepared for transmission over digital media, which gives digital bandwidth an important advantage over analog bandwidth. Unlimited amounts of information can be sent over the smallest (lowest-bandwidth) digital channel. Regardless of how long it takes, when the digital information arrives at its destination and is reassembled, it can be viewed, listened to, read, or processed in its original form.

It is important to understand the differences and similarities between digital and analog bandwidth. Both types of bandwidth are regularly encountered in the field of information technology. However, because this book is concerned primarily with digital networking, the term *bandwidth* refers to digital bandwidth.

Networking Models

Learning about networking is easier when you start with theory and concepts and then move on to the more concrete aspects of implementation. As a network professional, you need to learn the theory of how networks communicate before you design, build, and maintain networks. Learning the concept of layers can help you understand the action that occurs during communication from one computer to another.

This section covers the concepts of layering and how it applies specifically to communication models. Two specific models, OSI and TCP/IP, are described, as well as peer- to-peer layer communication and encapsulation.

Using Layers to Analyze Problems in a Flow of Materials

The concept of layers helps you understand the action that occurs during communication from one computer to another. The following questions involve the movement of physical objects, such as highway traffic or electronic data:

- What is flowing?

- What are the different forms of the object that is flowing?

- What rules govern flow?

- Where does the flow occur?

This motion of objects, whether physical or logical, is called *flow*. Layers help describe the details of the flow process. Examples of systems that flow are the public water system, the highway system, the postal system, and the telephone system.

Now examine Table 2-5. What network is being examined? What is flowing? What are the different forms of the object that is flowing? What are the rules for flow? Where does the flow occur? The networks listed in this chart give analogies to help you understand data flow in computer networks.

Table 2-5 Network Comparisons

Network	What Is Flowing	Different Forms	Rules	Where
Water	Water	Hot, cold, drink-able, wastewater/sewer	Access rules (turning taps), flushing, not putting certain things in drains	Pipes
Highway	Vehicles	Trucks, cars, cycles	Traffic laws and common courtesy	Roads and highways
Postal	Objects	Letters (written information), packages	Rules for packaging and attaching postage	Postal service boxes, offices, trucks, planes, delivery people
Telephone	Information	Spoken languages	Rules for accessing phone and rules for politeness	Phone system wires, EM waves, and so on

The network communication process is complex. The data, in the form of electronic signals, must travel across media to the correct destination computer and then be converted back into its original form to be read by the recipient. Several steps are involved in this process. For this reason, the most efficient way to implement network communications is a layered process. In a layered communication process, each layer performs a specific task.

In the next few sections, you see how the network communication process is broken down using a layered model. You'll also see how data is sent over the network and how it reaches its intended destination. As you learn about the network communication process, it is important for you to understand the various steps, components, and protocols of the network communication process. This understanding provides you with valuable troubleshooting information when the communications process does not proceed smoothly.

Using Layers to Describe Data Communication

The difficulty in dealing with network communications is that it is a very complex process. It would be extremely difficult for someone to understand this process if he or she looked only at network communication as a whole. The solution to this issue was to break down the total network communication system into a series of layers. Each layer is responsible for a specific part of network communication. These layers interact with the layer above and below them only. This interaction very narrowly defines the purpose of a layer. The two common network models that use layers are the Open System Interconnection (OSI) reference model and the TCP/IP reference model.

OSI Model

The early development of LANs, MANs, and WANs was chaotic in many ways. The early 1980s saw tremendous increases in the number and size of networks. As companies realized the money they could save and the productivity they could gain by using networking technology, they added networks and expanded existing networks almost as rapidly as new network technologies and products were introduced.

By the mid-1980s, these companies began to experience difficulties from all the implemented expansions. It became more difficult for networks that used different specifications and implementations to communicate with each other. These companies realized that they needed to move away from *proprietary* networking systems. Proprietary systems are privately developed, owned, and controlled. In the computer industry, proprietary is the opposite of open. Proprietary means that one company or a small group of companies controls all usage of the technology. *Open* means that free usage of the technology is available to the public.

To address the problem of network incompatibility and the inability to communicate with one another, the International Organization for Standardization (ISO) researched different network schemes, such as DECnet, Systems Network Architecture (SNA), and TCP/IP, to find a set of rules. As a result of this research, the ISO created a network model that would help vendors create networks that would be compatible and operate with other networks.

The process of breaking down complex communications into smaller discrete tasks can be compared to the process of building an automobile. When taken as a whole, the design, manufacture, and assembly of an automobile is a highly complex process. It is unlikely that a

NOTE

These layers are introduced in this section but can be difficult to understand until you learn more about the devices and protocols that operate at these layers. As you read subsequent chapters, you will become more familiar with the OSI layers and the differences between them. If the OSI model and the seven layers are not clear after reading this section, they will be after you read later chapters.

single person would know how to perform all the required tasks to build a car from scratch. This is why mechanical engineers design the car, manufacturing engineers design the molds to make the parts, and assembly technicians each assemble a part of the car.

The *OSI reference model*, released in 1984, was the descriptive scheme that the ISO created. This reference model provided vendors with a set of standards that ensured greater compatibility and interoperability among the various types of network technologies that were produced by many companies around the world.

The OSI reference model is the primary model used as a guideline for network communications. Although other models exist, most network vendors today relate their products to the OSI reference model, especially when they want to educate users on the use of their products. The OSI reference model is considered the best tool available for teaching people about sending and receiving data on a network.

The OSI reference model defines the network functions that occur at each layer. More importantly, it is a framework that facilitates an understanding of how information travels throughout a network. In addition, the OSI reference model describes how information, or data packets, travels from application programs (such as spreadsheets and documents) through a network medium (such as wires) to another application program that is located in another computer on a network, even if the sender and receiver have different types of network media.

The OSI reference model has seven numbered layers, each of which illustrates a particular network function:

- **Layer 7**—Application layer
- **Layer 6**—Presentation layer
- **Layer 5**—Session layer
- **Layer 4**—Transport layer
- **Layer 3**—Network layer
- **Layer 2**—Data link layer
- **Layer 1**—Physical layer

This separation of networking functions is called *layering*. Dividing the network into seven layers provides the following advantages:

- It standardizes network components to allow multiple-vendor development and support.
- It allows different types of network hardware and software to communicate.
- It prevents changes in one layer from affecting the other layers so that they can be developed more quickly.
- It breaks network communication into smaller components to make learning easier.

By working through the layers of the OSI reference model, you will understand how data packets travel through a network and what devices operate at each layer. As a result, you will understand how to troubleshoot network problems if they occur during data packet flow.

 Interactive Media Activity   Checkbox: Benefits of the OSI Model

After completing this activity, you will be able to identify the benefits of the OSI model.

OSI Layers

Each OSI layer has a set of functions that it must perform for data packets to travel from a source to a destination on a network. The following sections briefly describe each layer in the OSI reference model.

Layer 7: The Application Layer

The *application layer* is the OSI layer that is closest to the user. It provides network services to the user's applications. It differs from the other layers in that it does not provide services to any other OSI layer; instead, it provides services only to applications outside the OSI model. Examples of such applications are spreadsheet programs and word-processing programs. The application layer establishes the availability of intended communication partners and also synchronizes and establishes agreement on procedures for error recovery and control of data integrity. Examples of the Layer 7 applications include Telnet and HTTP.

Layer 6: The Presentation Layer

The *presentation layer* ensures that the information that the application layer of one system sends out can be read by the application layer of another system. If necessary, the presentation layer translates among multiple data formats by using a common format. One of the more important tasks of this layer is encryption and decryption. The common Layer 6 graphic standards are PICT, TIFF, and JPEG. Examples of Layer 6 standards that guide the presentation of sound and movies are MIDI and MPEG.

Layer 5: The Session Layer

As its name implies, the *session layer* establishes, manages, and terminates sessions between two communicating hosts. The session layer provides its services to the presentation layer. It also synchronizes dialogue between the two hosts' presentation layers and manages their data exchange. In addition to handling session regulation, the session layer offers provisions for efficient data transfer, class of service, and exception reporting of session layer, presentation layer, and application layer problems. Examples of Layer 5 protocols are the Network File System (NFS), X-Window System, and AppleTalk Session Protocol (ASP).

Layer 4: The Transport Layer

The *transport layer* segments data from the sending host's system and reassembles it into a data stream on the receiving host's system. The boundary between the transport layer and the session layer can be thought of as the boundary between application protocols and data-flow protocols. Whereas the application, presentation, and session layers are concerned with application issues, the lowest four layers are concerned with data-transport issues.

The transport layer attempts to provide a data-transport service that shields the upper layers from transport-implementation details. Specifically, issues such as reliability of transport between two hosts are the concern of the transport layer. In providing communication service, the transport layer establishes, maintains, and properly terminates virtual circuits. Transport error detection and recovery and information flow control are used to provide reliable service. Examples of Layer 4 protocols are Transmission Control Protocol (TCP), User Datagram Protocol (UDP), and Sequenced Packet Exchange (SPX).

Layer 3: The Network Layer

The *network layer* is a complex layer that provides connectivity and path selection between two host systems that might be located on geographically separated networks. Additionally, the network layer is concerned with logical addressing. Examples of Layer 3 protocols are Internet Protocol (IP), Internetwork Packet Exchange (IPX), and AppleTalk.

Layer 2: The Data Link Layer

The *data link layer* provides reliable transit of data across a physical link. In so doing, the data link layer is concerned with physical (as opposed to logical) addressing, network topology, network access, error notification, ordered delivery of frames, and flow control. Examples of Layer 2 protocols include Ethernet, Token Ring, ISDN, PPP, and Frame Relay.

Layer 1: The Physical Layer

The *physical layer* defines the electrical, mechanical, procedural, and functional specifications for activating, maintaining, and deactivating the physical link between end systems. Such characteristics as voltage levels, timing of voltage changes, physical data rates, maximum transmission distances, physical connectors, and other similar attributes are defined by physical layer specifications.

 Interactive Media Activity   Drag and Drop: The Seven Layers of the OSI Model

After completing this activity, you will be able to identify some of the functions of the seven OSI layers.

Video and Animation   OSI Layers

In this video, you learn how data is transmitted via the OSI layers.

Peer-to-Peer Communications

For data packets to travel from the source to the destination, each layer of the OSI model at the source must communicate with its peer layer at the destination. This form of communication is called *peer-to-peer communication*. During this process, the protocols at each layer exchange information, called *protocol data units (PDUs),* between peer layers. Each layer of communication on the source computer communicates with a layer-specific PDU and with its peer layer on the destination computer, as shown in Figure 2-45.

Figure 2-45 Peer-to-Peer Communication

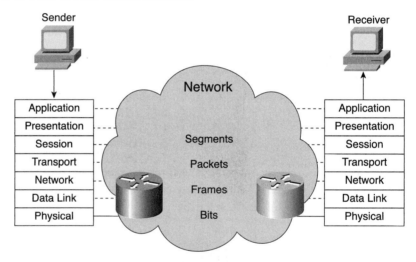

Data packets on a network originate at a source and then travel to a destination. Each layer depends on the service function of the OSI layer below it. To provide this service, the lower layer uses encapsulation to put the PDU from the upper layer into its data field. Each layer then adds whatever headers it needs to perform its function. As the data moves through the layers of the OSI model, additional headers are added. The grouping of data at the Layer 4 PDU is called a *segment*.

The network layer provides a service to the transport layer. The network layer moves the data through the internetwork by encapsulating the data and attaching a header to create a *packet* (the Layer 3 PDU). The header contains information required to complete the transfer, such as source and destination logical addresses.

The data link layer provides a service to the network layer. It encapsulates the network layer information in a *frame* (the Layer 2 PDU). The frame header contains the physical addresses required to complete the data link functions, and the frame trailer contains the frame check sequence (FCS), which is used by the receiver to detect whether the data is in error. This then becomes the data that is passed down to the physical layer.

The physical layer provides a service to the data link layer. The physical layer encodes the data link frame into a pattern of 1s and 0s (bits) for transmission on the medium (usually a wire) at Layer 1.

Network devices such as hubs, switches, and routers work at the lowest three layers. Hubs operate at Layer 1, switches operate at Layer 2, and routers at Layer 3. The first layer that deals with the end-to-end transport between end users is the transport layer (Layer 4).

TCP/IP Model

Although the OSI reference model is universally recognized, the historical and technical open standard of the Internet is Transmission Control Protocol/Internet Protocol (TCP/IP). The TCP/IP reference model and the TCP/IP protocol suite make data communication possible between any two computers anywhere in the world at nearly the speed of light. The TCP/IP model has historical importance, just like the standards that allowed the telephone, electrical power, railroad, television, and videotape industries to flourish.

The U.S. DoD provided funding for the invention of the TCP/IP reference model because it wanted a network that could survive any conditions, even a nuclear war. To illustrate further, imagine a world at war, criss-crossed by different kinds of connections, including wires, microwaves, optical fibers, and satellite links. Then imagine that information/data (in the form of packets) must flow, regardless of the condition of any particular node or network on the internetwork (which, in this case, might have been destroyed by the war). The DoD wants its packets to get through every time, under any conditions, from any one point to any other point. This very difficult design problem brought about the creation of the TCP/IP model, which has since become the standard on which the Internet has grown.

When reading about the TCP/IP model layers, remember the original intent of the Internet; it helps explain why certain things are as they are. The TCP/IP model, as shown in Figure 2-46, has four layers:

- The application layer
- The transport layer
- The Internet layer
- The network access layer

Figure 2-46 The TCP/IP Model

OSI	TCP/IP
Application (Layer 7)	Application
Presentation (Layer 6)	Application
Session (Layer 5)	Application
Transport (Layer 4)	Transport
Network (Layer 3)	Internet
Data Link (Layer 2)	Network Access
Physical (Layer 1)	Network Access

It is important to note that some of the layers in the TCP/IP model have the same names as layers in the OSI model. However, do not confuse the layers of the two models. Even with the same name, most of the layers have the same functions in each model, but some do not.

 Lab 2.3.6   OSI Model and TCP/IP Model

In this exercise, you describe and compare the layers of the OSI and TCP/IP models. You also name the TCP/IP protocols and utilities that operate at each layer.

Detailed Encapsulation Process

All communications on a network originate at a source and are sent to a destination. The information that is sent on a network is called data or data packets. If one computer (Host A) wants to send data to another computer (Host B), the data must first be packaged by a process called *encapsulation*.

NOTE

The word *header* means that information was added to the front of the packet, just as trailers are added to the end. In addition, an address is an important piece of information that gets added.

Encapsulation

Encapsulation wraps data with the necessary protocol information before network transit. Therefore, as the data moves down through the layers of the OSI model, each OSI layer adds a header (and also a trailer at Layer 2) to the data before passing it down to a lower layer. The headers and trailers contain control information for the network devices and receiver, to ensure proper delivery of the data and to ensure that the receiver can properly interpret the data. For example, think of a header as an address on an envelope. An address is required on the envelope so that the letter inside the envelope can be delivered to the desired recipient.

To see how encapsulation occurs, examine the manner in which data travels through the layers, as illustrated in Figure 2-47. After the data is sent from the source, it travels through the application layer down through the other layers. The packaging and flow of the data that is exchanged go through changes as the layers perform their services for end users.

The data, in the form of electronic signals, must travel across a cable to the correct destination computer and then be converted to its original form to be read by the recipient. As you can imagine, several steps are involved in this process. For this reason, developers of hardware, software, and protocols recognized that the most efficient way to implement network communications would be as a layered process.

Figure 2-47 Encapsulation

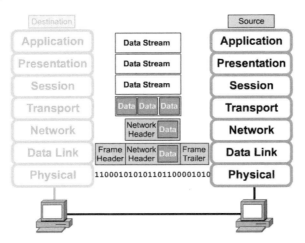

As illustrated in Figure 2-48, networks must perform the following five conversion steps to encapsulate data:

Step 1   **Build the data**—As a user sends an e-mail message, its alphanumeric characters are converted to data that can travel across the internetwork.

Step 2   **Package the data for end-to-end transport**—The data is packaged for internetwork transport. By using segments, the transport function ensures that the message hosts at both ends of the e-mail system can communicate reliably.

Step 3   **Append (add) the network address to the header**—The data is put into a packet or datagram that contains a network header with source and destination logical addresses. These addresses help network devices send the packets across the network along a chosen path.

Step 4   **Append (add) the local address to the data link header**—Each network device must put the packet into a frame. The frame allows connection to the next directly connected network device on the link. Each device in the chosen network path requires framing to be connected to the next device.

Step 5   **Convert to bits for transmission**—A clocking function lets the devices distinguish these bits as they travel across the medium. The medium on the physical internetwork can vary along the path used. For example, the e-mail message can originate on a LAN, cross a campus backbone, and go out a WAN link until it reaches its destination on another remote LAN. Headers and trailers are added as data moves down through the layers of the OSI model.

Figure 2-48 Data Encapsulation Process

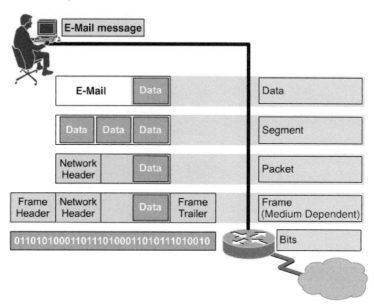

De-Encapsulation

When the remote device receives a sequence of bits, the physical layer at the remote device passes the bits to the data link layer for manipulation. The data link layer does the following:

Step 1 Verifies that the MAC destination address matches this station's address or is an Ethernet broadcast. If neither of these situations is true, the frame is discarded.

Step 2 If the data is in error, it can be discarded, and the data link layer might ask for the data to be retransmitted. If the data is not in error, the data link layer reads and interprets the control information in the data link header.

Step 3 The data link layer strips the data link header and trailer and then passes the remaining data up to the network layer based on the control information in the data link header.

This process is called *de-encapsulation*. Each subsequent layer performs a similar de-encapsulation process. Think of the de-encapsulation process as the process of reading the address on a letter to see if it is for you and then removing the letter from the envelope if the letter is addressed to you.

> **More Information: Cyclical Redundancy Check**
>
> Each data packet has information added to the raw data itself, in the form of packet headers. The headers contain addressing information so that the packets reach the correct destination. They also contain sequencing information so the data can be reassembled accurately when all packets reach the receiving computer.
>
> Header information is placed at the head of the packet, in front of the original data. Packets also can include trailer information, which is appended to the back of the packet, following the original data.
>
> The error-checking component in the trailer is called a cyclical redundancy check (CRC). The CRC performs calculations on the packet before it leaves the source computer and again when it reaches the destination. If the results of these calculations are different, the data has changed. This can occur because of a disruption of the electrical signals that represent the 0s and 1s making up the data. If a discrepancy is found, that packet can be resent.

Lab 2.3.7 OSI Model Characteristics and Devices

In this lab, you learn the seven layers of the OSI model and the characteristics, functions, and keywords relating to each layer.

Interactive Media Activity Drag and Drop: Encapsulation Process Flowchart

In this lab, you complete the encapsulation process flowchart.

Summary

In this chapter, you learned the following key points:

- Networking devices are products that connect networks. Hubs, switches, and routers interconnect devices within LANs, MANs, and WANs. Networking devices function at different layers of the OSI model.

- A physical topology describes the plan that is used to wire the physical devices. A logical topology describes how information flows through a network.

- In a physical bus topology, a single cable connects all the devices.

- The most commonly used architecture in Ethernet LANs is the physical star topology. In a star topology, each host in the network is connected to the central device with its own cable. When a star network is expanded to include additional networking devices that are connected to the main networking device, it is called an extended-star topology.

- In a ring topology, all the hosts are connected in the form of a ring or circle.

- A full-mesh topology connects all devices to each other.

- A LAN consists of computers, NICs, peripheral devices, networking media, and network devices.

- A WAN consists of two or more LANs that span two or more geographically separate areas.

- A MAN spans a metropolitan area, such as a city or a suburban area.

- A SAN provides enhanced system performance, is scalable, and has disaster tolerance built in.

- Intranets are designed to be accessed by users who have access privileges to the internal network of an organization. Extranets are designed to deliver applications and services that are intranet-based but that employ extended, secured access to external users or enterprises.

- A VPN is a private network that is constructed within a public network infrastructure. Three main types of VPNs are access, intranet, and extranet.

- Bandwidth and throughput are measures of the speed or capacity of a network.

- Bandwidth is measured in bps, kbps, Mbps, or Gbps.

- Limitations on bandwidth include type of media used, LAN and WAN technologies, and network equipment.

- Throughput refers to actual measured bandwidth, which is affected by factors such as the number of users on a network, networking devices, the type of data, computers, and the server.

- The formula T=S/BW, or transfer time, equals size of file divided by bandwidth, can be used to calculate data-transfer time.

- Analog bandwidth is measured by how much of the electromagnetic spectrum is occupied by each signal.

- In digital signaling, all information is sent as bits, regardless of the kind of information it is.

- A complex problem should be broken into smaller units to help you understand the larger problem.

- Communication is a complex problem that can be broken into a series of layers. Multiple systems can be used for the breakdown.

- The ISO created and released the OSI model in 1984 to provide vendors with a set of standards to ensure greater compatibility and interoperability among various types of network technologies.

- The OSI reference model is a descriptive network scheme with standards that ensure greater compatibility and interoperability between various types of network technologies.

- Each OSI layer has a specific function and protocols to support it. The seven layers of the OSI model are application, presentation, session, transport, network, data link, and physical.

- Each layer in the communication protocol of a device that sends data communicates with its peer layer in the device that receives data.

- The four layers of the TCP/IP model are application, transport, Internet, and network access.

- All communications on a network originate at a source and are sent to a destination. The encapsulation wraps data with the necessary protocol information before network transit.

To supplement all that you have learned in this chapter, refer to the chapter-specific Interactive Media Activities, PhotoZooms, and Videos on the CD-ROM that accompanies this book.

Key Terms

application layer   Layer 7 of the OSI reference model. This layer provides services to application processes (such as e-mail, file transfer, and terminal emulation) that are outside the OSI reference model.

bandwidth   The amount of information that can flow through a network connection in a given period of time.

bridge   A Layer 2 device designed to create two or more LAN segments, each of which is a separate collision domain.

broadcast   A data packets that is sent to all nodes on a network. Broadcasts are identified by a broadcast address.

broadcast domain   The set of all devices that receive broadcast frames originating from any device in the set.

bus topology   Commonly called a linear bus, this topology connects all the devices with a single cable. This cable proceeds from one computer to the next like a bus line going through a city.

collision   In Ethernet, the result of two nodes transmitting simultaneously. The frames from each device impact and are damaged when they meet on the physical medium.

collision domain   In Ethernet, the network area within which frames that have collided are propagated. Repeaters and hubs propagate collisions; LAN switches, bridges, and routers do not.

data center   A globally coordinated network of devices designed to accelerate the delivery of information over the Internet infrastructure.

data link layer   Layer 2 of the OSI reference model. Provides transit of data across a physical link. The data link layer is concerned with physical addressing, network topology, line discipline, error notification, ordered delivery of frames, and flow control.

de-encapsulation   Unwrapping data in a particular protocol header.

encapsulation   Wrapping data in a particular protocol header.

extended-star topology   A network in which a star network is expanded to include an additional networking device that is connected to the main networking device.

extranet   Intranet-based applications and services that employ extended, secure access to external users or enterprises.

firewall   A router or access server designated as a buffer between any connected public networks and a private network.

flooding   A traffic-passing technique used by switches and bridges in which traffic received on an interface is sent out all that device's interfaces except the interface on which the information was received originally.

frame   A logical grouping of information sent as a data link layer unit over a transmission medium.

full-mesh topology   Connects all devices (nodes) to each other for redundancy and fault tolerance.

hierarchical topology   Created similarly to an extended-star topology. The primary difference is that it does not use a central node. Instead, it uses a trunk node from which it branches to other nodes.

hub   A common connection point for devices in a network. Hubs commonly connect segments of a LAN. A hub contains multiple ports. When a packet arrives at one port, it is copied to the other ports so that all the segments of the LAN can see all the packets.

intranet   A common LAN configuration. Intranets are designed to be accessed by users who have access privileges to an organization's internal LAN.

local-area network (LAN)   A high-speed, low-error data network covering a relatively small geographic area (up to a few thousand meters). LANs connect workstations, peripherals, terminals, and other devices in a single building or another geographically limited area.

Media Access Control (MAC)   A hardware address that uniquely identifies each node of a network. This address controls data communication for the host on the network.

metropolitan-area network (MAN)   A network that spans a metropolitan area. Generally, a MAN spans a larger geographic area than a LAN but a smaller geographic area than a WAN.

microsegmentation   Allows the creation of private or dedicated segments—one host per segment. Each host receives instant access to the full bandwidth and does not have to compete for available bandwidth with other hosts.

network interface card (NIC)   A printed circuit board that fits into the expansion slot of a bus on a computer motherboard. Also can be a peripheral device.

network layer   Layer 3 of the OSI reference model. This layer provides connectivity and path selection between two end systems. The network layer is the layer at which routing occurs.

Open System Interconnection (OSI) reference model   A network architectural model developed by the ISO. This model consists of seven layers, each of which specifies particular network functions, such as addressing, flow control, error control, encapsulation, and reliable message transfer. The OSI reference model is used universally as a method for teaching and understanding network functionality.

packet   A logical grouping of information that includes a header containing control information and (usually) user data. Packets most often refer to network layer units of data.

partial-mesh topology   At least one device maintains multiple connections to others without being fully meshed. A partial-mesh topology still provides redundancy by having several alternative routes.

peer-to-peer communication   A form of communication in which each layer of the OSI model at the source must communicate with its peer layer at the destination.

physical layer   Layer 1 of the OSI reference model. The physical layer defines the electrical, mechanical, procedural, and functional specifications for activating, maintaining, and deactivating the physical link between end systems.

presentation layer   Layer 6 of the OSI reference model. This layer ensures that information sent by the application layer of one system can be read by the application layer of another.

protocol   A formal description of a set of rules and conventions that govern how devices on a network exchange information.

protocol suite   A set of related communications protocols that operate together and, as a group, address communication at some or all of the seven layers of the OSI reference model. Not every protocol stack covers each layer of the model, and often a single protocol in the suite addresses a number of layers at once. TCP/IP is a typical protocol suite.

repeater   A networking device that exists at Layer 1, the physical layer, of the OSI reference model. The purpose of a repeater is to regenerate and retime network signals at the bit level, allowing them to travel a longer distance on the medium.

ring topology   A topology in which hosts are connected in the form of a ring or circle. Unlike the physical bus topology, the ring topology has no beginning or end that needs to be terminated.

router   A type of internetworking device that passes data packets between networks based on Layer 3 addresses. A router can make decisions regarding the best path for delivery of data on the network.

segment   In the TCP specification, a logical information group at transport layers of the OSI reference model.

session layer   Layer 5 of the OSI reference model. This layer establishes, manages, and terminates sessions between applications and manages data exchange between presentation layer entities.

star topology   The most commonly used physical topology in Ethernet LANs. The star topology is made up of a central connection point that is a device such as a hub, switch, or router, where all the cabling segments meet.

storage-area network (SAN)   A dedicated, high-performance network that moves data between servers and storage resources.

switch   A device that connects LAN segments, uses a table of MAC addresses to determine the segment on which a frame needs to be transmitted, and reduces traffic. Switches operate at much higher speeds than bridges.

throughput   The rate of information arriving at or passing through a particular point in a network system.

token passing   An access method by which network devices access the physical medium in an orderly fashion based on possession of a small frame called a token.

transport layer   Layer 4 of the OSI reference model. This layer is responsible for reliable network communication between end nodes. The transport layer provides mechanisms to establish, maintain, and terminate virtual circuits, transport fault detection and recovery, and information flow control.

virtual private network (VPN)   A private network constructed within a public network infrastructure such as the global Internet.

wide-area network (WAN)   A data communications network that serves users across a broad geographic area and often uses transmission devices provided by common carriers.

Check Your Understanding

Complete all the review questions to test your understanding of the topics and concepts in this chapter. Answers are listed in Appendix B, "Check Your Understanding Answer Key."

1. What was the first type of microcomputer network to be implemented?

   A. MAN

   B. WAN

   C. LAN

   D. PAN

2. Using modem connections, how many modems would it take to allow connections from ten individual computers within the same location?

   A. One

   B. Five

   C. Ten

   D. Fifteen

3. What is the information that is "burned in" to a network interface card?

   A. NIC

   B. MAC address

   C. Hub

   D. LAN

4. Which topology has all its nodes connected directly to one center point and has no other connections between nodes?

   A. Bus

   B. Ring

   C. Star

   D. Mesh

5. What do TIA and EIA stand for?

   A. Television Industry Association, Electronic Industries Association

   B. Telecommunications Industry Association, Electronic Industries Alliance

   C. Telecommunications Industry Alliance, Electronic Industries Association

   D. Téléphonique International Association, Elégraphique Industries Alliance

6. LANs are designed to do which of the following? (Select all that apply.)

   A. Operate within a limited geographic area

   B. Allow many users to access high-bandwidth media

   C. Connect to the Internet

   D. Provide full-time connectivity to local services

7. Which of the following statements best describes a WAN?

   A. It connects LANs that are separated by a large geographic area.

   B. It connects workstations, terminals, and other devices in a metropolitan area.

   C. It connects LANs within a large building.

   D. It connects workstations, terminals, and other devices within a building.

8. Which of the following statements correctly describes a MAN?

   A. A MAN is a network that connects workstations, peripherals, terminals, and other devices in a single building.

   B. A MAN is a network that serves users across a broad geographic area. It often uses transmission devices provided by common carriers.

   C. A MAN is a network that spans a metropolitan area such as a city or suburban area.

   D. A MAN is a network that is interconnected by routers and other devices and that functions as a single network.

9. Which of the following is *not* one of the features of a SAN?

   A. SANs enable concurrent access of disk or tape arrays, providing enhanced system performance.

   B. SANs provide a reliable disaster recovery solution.

   C. SANs are scalable.

   D. SANs minimize system and data availability.

10. What service offers secure, reliable connectivity over a shared public network infrastructure?

   A. Internet

   B. Virtual private network

   C. Virtual public network

   D. WAN

11. What links enterprise customer headquarters, remote offices, and branch offices to an internal network over a shared infrastructure?

   A. Access VPN

   B. Intranet VPN

   C. Extranet VPN

   D. Internet VPN

12. What is the name of the part of a company's LAN that is made available to select parties such as employees, customers, and partners?

   A. The Internet

   B. The extranet

   C. The intranet

   D. The LAN

13. What is the movement of data through layers?

   A. Wrapping

   B. Encapsulation

   C. Traveling

   D. Transmission

14. The OSI model has how many layers?

    A. Four

    B. Five

    C. Six

    D. Seven

15. What is the OSI model?

    A. A conceptual framework that specifies how information travels through networks

    B. A model that describes how data makes its way from one application program to another throughout a network

    C. A conceptual framework that specifies which network functions occur at each layer

    D. All of the above

16. Which of the following is the correct order of the network layers?

    A.

    1: Physical

    2: Data link

    3: Transport

    4: Network

    5: Presentation

    6: Session

    7: Application

    B.

    1: Physical

    2: Data link

    3: Network

    4: Transport

    5: Session

    6: Presentation

    7: Application

    C.

    1: Physical

    2: Data link

3: Network

4: Session

5: Transport

6: Application

7: Presentation

D.

1: Physical

2: Network

3: Session

4: Data link

5: Transport

6: Application

7: Presentation

17. Which layer of the OSI model handles physical addressing, network topology, network access, and flow control?

   A. The physical layer

   B. The data link layer

   C. The transport layer

   D. The network layer

18. Which of the following best defines encapsulation?

   A. Segmenting data so that it flows uninterrupted through the network

   B. Compressing data so that it moves faster

   C. Moving data in groups so that it stays together

   D. Wrapping data in a particular protocol header

19. An e-mail message is sent from Host A to Host B on a LAN. Before this message can be sent, the data must be encapsulated. Which of the following best describes what happens after a packet is constructed?

   A. The packet is transmitted along the medium.

   B. The packet is encapsulated into a frame.

   C. The packet is segmented into frames.

   D. The packet is converted to binary format.

20. In the TCP/IP model, which layer deals with reliability, flow control, and error correction?

    A. Application

    B. Transport

    C. Internet

    D. Network access

21. Repeaters can provide a simple solution for what problem?

    A. Too many types of incompatible equipment on the network

    B. Too much traffic on a network

    C. Too-slow convergence rates

    D. Too much distance between nodes or not enough cable

22. Which of the following is true of a bridge and its forwarding decisions?

    A. Bridges operate at OSI Layer 2 and use IP addresses to make decisions.

    B. Bridges operate at OSI Layer 3 and use IP addresses to make decisions.

    C. Bridges operate at OSI Layer 2 and use MAC addresses to make decisions.

    D. Bridges operate at OSI Layer 3 and use MAC addresses to make decisions.

23. Which of the following is true of a switch's function?

    A. Switches increase the size of collision domains.

    B. Switches combine the connectivity of a hub with the capability to filter or flood traffic based on the destination MAC address of the frame.

    C. Switches combine the connectivity of a hub with the traffic direction of a router.

    D. Switches perform Layer 4 path selection.

24. What does a router route?

    A. Layer 1 bits

    B. Layer 2 frames

    C. Layer 3 packets

    D. Layer 4 segments

25. What is/are the function(s) of a AAA server? (Select all that apply.)

    A. To ensure that only authenticated users can get into the network

    B. To ensure that the users are allowed access to only the resources they need

    C. To ensure that records are kept of everything the authentic users do after they are allowed entry

    D. All of the above

CHAPTER 3

Networking Media

Objectives

Upon completion of this chapter, you should be able to answer the following questions:

- What are the main parts of an atom?
- Which terms measure electricity?
- What is resistance and impedance?
- What is current?
- What are circuits?
- What are the different cable specifications and expectations for performance?
- What are the primary types and uses of coaxial cables?

- What are the primary types and uses of twisted-pair cables?
- What is the electromagnetic spectrum?
- What is multimode fiber?
- Which organizations develop standards for wired and wireless networks?
- What are the primary devices and topologies of wireless media?

Additional Topics of Interest

In addition to the core objective areas, this chapter introduces you to the following topics of interest to networkers:

- Electrical properties of matter
- Reflection
- Refraction
- Primary types and uses of fiber-optic cables
- Signals and noise in optical fiber
- How wireless LANs communicate
- Authentication and association

- Different modulation techniques
- Radio frequency modulation
- Benefits of spread-spectrum technology
- Frequency-hopping spread spectrum and direct-sequence spread spectrum
- Importance of encryption and security in a wireless environment

Key Terms

The following is a list of key terms introduced in this chapter. For your reference, a definition for each term can be found at the end of this chapter.

coaxial cable   page 111

resistance   page 115

impedance   page 115

standards   page 119

Institute of Electrical and Electronic Engineers (IEEE)   page 119

Telecommunications Industry Association (TIA)   page 119

Electronic Industries Association (EIA)   page 119

patch panel   page 120

backbone   page 122

thicknet   page 122

thinnet   page 122

crosstalk   page 123

shielded twisted-pair (STP)   page 124

unshielded twisted-pair (UTP)   page 125

media   page 125

electromagnetic interference (EMI)   page 128

radio frequency interference (RFI)   page 128

wavelength   page 129

reflection   page 132

angle of incidence   page 132

angle of reflection   page 133

refraction   page 134

fiber-optic cable   page 136

multimode   page 138

single-mode   page 138

modal dispersion   page 139

noise   page 143

attenuation   page 144

dispersion   page 144

amplitude modulation (AM)   page 150

frequency modulation (FM)   page 150

phase modulation (PM)   page 150

spread spectrum (SS)   page 152

frequency-hopping spread spectrum (FHSS)   page 153

direct-sequence spread spectrum (DSSS)   page 153

wired equivalent privacy (WEP)   page 162

The function of the physical layer is to transmit data by defining the electrical, wireless, or light specifications between the source and destination. After it reaches a building, low-voltage electricity is carried to workstations, servers, and network devices via wires concealed in walls, floors, and ceilings. Data, which can consist of such things as text, pictures, audio, or video, travels through the wires and is represented by the presence of either electrical pulses on copper conducting wires or light pulses in optical fibers.

This chapter introduces the basic theory of electricity, which provides a foundation for understanding networking at the physical layer of the OSI model. This chapter also discusses different types of networking media that are used at the physical layer, including shielded twisted-pair cable, unshielded twisted-pair cable, coaxial cable, and fiber-optic cable, as well as wireless media.

Copper Media

This section discusses the basic theory of electricity, which provides a foundation for understanding networking at the physical layer (Layer 1) of the OSI reference model.

Copper is the most common medium for signal wiring. Copper wires carry the signals from the source computer to the destination computer. Copper has several important properties that make it well suited for electronic cabling:

- **Conductivity**—Copper is perhaps best known for its ability to conduct electric current. Copper is also an excellent conductor of heat. This property makes it useful as a material in cooking utensils, radiators, and refrigerators.

- **Corrosion resistance**—Copper does not rust and is fairly resistant to corrosion. Copper corrodes as copper oxide at a slower pace than other metals.

- **Ductility**—Copper possesses great ductility, which is the ability to be drawn into thin wires without breaking. For example, a copper rod that is 1 centimeter (cm) in diameter can be heated, rolled, and drawn into a wire that is thinner than a human hair.

- **Malleability**—Pure copper is highly malleable (easy to shape). It does not crack when hammered, stamped, forged, or spun into unusual shapes. Copper can be worked (shaped) when it is hot or cold.

- **Strength**—Cold-rolled copper has a tensile strength 3500 to 4900 kilograms per square centimeter. Copper keeps its strength and toughness up to about 400° Fahrenheit (204° Celsius [C]).

This section focuses on two types of copper cable used for networks:

- **Twisted-pair**—Twisted-pair cables are composed of one or more pairs of copper wires. Most data and voice networks use twisted-pair cabling.

- **Coaxial**—*Coaxial cable* has one center conductor of either solid or stranded copper wire. Coaxial cable, once the choice for local-area network (LAN) cabling, is now used primarily for video connections, high-speed connections such as T1/T3 or E1/E3 lines, and cable television.

Atoms and Electrons

The basic unit of all matter in the universe is the atom. The atom is made of three tiny parts: protons, neutrons, and electrons. The protons and neutrons make up the nucleus, which is the center part of an atom. The electrons flow freely around the nucleus. The Periodic Table of Elements, as shown in Figure 3-1, lists all known types of atoms and their properties:

- **Protons**—Particles that have a positive charge

- **Neutrons**—Particles that have no charge

- **Electrons**—Particles that have a negative charge

Figure 3-1 Periodic Table of Elements

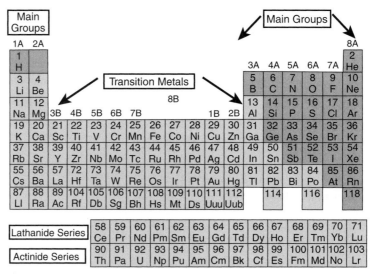

Atoms normally have equal numbers of protons and electrons. Because the positive and negative charges are equal, atoms have no net charge.

Niels Bohr, a Danish physicist, developed a simplified model to illustrate atoms, as shown in Figure 3-2. This illustration shows the Bohr model for a helium atom, which has two protons, two neutrons, and two electrons. The protons and neutrons form the nucleus at the center of the atom, and the electrons are shown in orbit around the nucleus. The diagram is not drawn to scale, but if the protons and neutrons of this atom were the size of soccer balls in the middle of a soccer field, the electrons would be the size of cherries, and would be orbiting near the outer-most seats of the stadium. The electrons are quite small compared to the nucleus, and the orbit is quite large compared to the size of the particles, even though the atoms themselves are microscopic.

Figure 3-2 Bohr Model of a Helium Atom

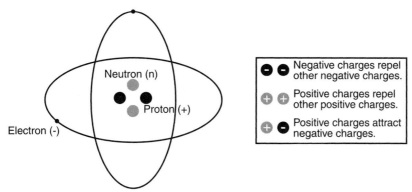

Atoms bond together in different combinations to form molecules of various types of matter. For example, hydrogen and oxygen atoms bond to form water molecules.

Electrical Properties of Matter

The nucleus of an atom is bound together by a very powerful force. Electrons are bound to their orbit around the nucleus by a much weaker force. Electrons in certain atoms can be pulled away from their orbit and go into orbit around nearby atoms. This movement of electrons is defined as electric current.

If an atom loses or gains an electron, it no longer has the same number of electrons and protons. Such an atom is called an ion, and it has a net charge since the number of protons and electrons is not equal. The charge of an ion exerts a force on nearby atoms that can cause them to lose or gain electrons. Thus, as electrons of nearby atoms move, current flows through a material.

Atoms and molecules can be classified as belonging to one of three groups, depending on how easily electrons are pulled out of their orbit. These three groups are insulators, conductors, and semiconductors. See Table 3-1 for a summary.

Electrical Insulators

Insulators are materials made of atoms or molecules that require a great deal of force to remove their electrons from orbit. Examples of electrical insulators include plastic, glass, air, dry wood, paper, rubber, helium gas, and pure water (whose atoms are not ions).

Table 3-1 Summary of the Three Main Types of Electrical Materials

Material	Flow	Examples
Insulators	Electrons flow poorly.	Plastic, paper, rubber, dry wood, air, pure water, and glass.
Conductors	Electrons flow well.	Copper (Cu), silver (Ag), gold (Au), solder, water with ions, and the human body.
Semiconductors	Electrons flow can be controlled precisely.	Carbon , germanium (Ge), gallium arsenide (GaAs), and silicon (Si).

Electrical Conductors

Conductors are materials made of atoms or molecules with electrons that are bound very loosely to the nucleus and require little force to remove them from orbit. The Periodic Table categorizes groups of atoms, listing them by columns. The best conductors are located in one particular column of Table 3-1: copper (Cu), silver (Ag), and gold (Au). Other conductors include lead solder, which is a mixture of lead (Pb) and tin (Sn), and water in which some atoms are ions. Because the human body is made of approximately 70 percent ionized water, it is also a conductor.

Electrical Semiconductors

Semiconductors are materials made of atoms or molecules with electrons whose movement can be precisely controlled. The most important semiconductor is silicon (Si). Other examples from the same column of the Periodic Table include carbon and germanium (Ge). Gallium arsenide (GaAs), a molecule, is also a common semiconductor.

Silicon is common and can be found in sand, glass, and many types of rocks. The region around San Jose, California, is known as Silicon Valley because the computer industry, which depends on silicon microchips, started in that area. The switches, or gates, inside a microprocessor are made up of semiconductors.

Lab 3.1.1 Safe Handling and Use of a Multimeter

In this lab, you learn how to use or handle a multimeter correctly.

Voltage

As with any other physical process or concept, you need to be able to measure electricity to make use of it. You can measure electricity in numerous ways, but in this section and those that follow, you focus on voltage, current, resistance, and impedance.

Because electrons and protons have opposite charges, they are attracted to each other with a force similar to the attractive force of the north and south poles of two magnets. When the charges are separated, this separation creates an attractive force or pressure field between the charges. This force is voltage. The force that is created pulls toward the opposite charge and pushes away from the like charge. This process occurs in a battery, where chemical action causes electrons to be freed from the battery's negative terminal and to travel to the opposite, or positive, terminal through an external circuit—not through the battery itself. The separation of charges results in voltage. Voltage can also be created by friction (static electricity), by magnetism (electric generator), or by solar energy.

Voltage is represented by the letter V. The unit of measurement for voltage is the volt, and it is also represented with the letter V (for example, 12 V = 12 volts).

Two kinds of voltage exist:

- **Direct-current (DC) voltage**—A battery is an example of a DC voltage source. The movement of electrons in a DC circuit is always in the same direction, from negative to positive.

- **Alternating-current (AC) voltage**—In an AC circuit, the positive and negative terminals of the AC voltage source regularly change to negative and positive and back again, as shown in Figure 3-3. This change makes the direction of electron movement change, or alternate, with respect to time.

Figure 3-3 Alternating Current

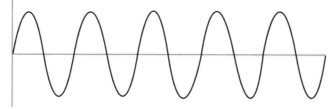

 Lab 3.1.2   Voltage Measurement

In this lab, you demonstrate the ability to measure voltage with the multimeter.

Resistance and Impedance

Conductors exchange electrons very easily, so it does not take much voltage to cause electrons to move through them. Conversely, the electrons in insulators are bound to their orbits much more tightly, so they oppose the movement of electrons. *Resistance* is the property of a material that resists electron movement. Conductors have low resistance, and insulators have high resistance.

Resistance is represented by the letter R. The unit of measurement for resistance is the ohm, and it is represented by the Greek letter omega (Ω), because omega sounds like ohm.

The term *resistance* is generally used when referring to DC circuits. The resistance to the movement of electrons in an AC circuit is called *impedance*. Impedance is represented by the letter Z. Like resistance, its unit of measurement is the ohm, represented by Ω. The term *attenuation* is important when learning about networks. *Attenuation* refers to the resistance to the flow of electrons, and why a signal becomes degraded as it travels along the conduit.

 Lab 3.1.3   Resistance Measurement

In this lab, you demonstrate the ability to measure resistance and continuity with the multimeter.

Current

Electrical current is the flow of charges that is created when electrons move. When voltage (electrical pressure) is applied and a path for the current exists, electrons move from the negative terminal (which repels them), along the path, to the positive terminal (which attracts them).

Current is represented by the letter I. The unit of measurement for current is the ampere, and it is represented by the letter A, or by the abbreviation amp. An amp is defined as the number of charges per second that pass by a point along a path. It can be thought of as the amount of electron traffic that is flowing through a circuit. The more electrons that pass by any given point in a circuit, the higher the current will be.

Current that results from DC voltage always flows in the same direction, from negative to positive. Current that results from AC voltage flows in one direction, then changes direction, and then alternates back to the original direction, and so on.

Wattage

If amperage or current can be thought of as the amount or volume of electron traffic that is flowing, then voltage can be thought of as the speed of the electron traffic. The combination of amperage (quantity of electrons past a given point) and voltage (pressure or speed of electrons) equals *wattage* or electrical power. A watt (W) is the basic unit of electrical power or work done by electricity. Wattage equals voltage times amperage ($W = V \cdot I$).

Electrical devices such as light bulbs, motors, and computer power supplies are rated in terms of watts, which is how much power they consume or produce. It is the current or amperage in an electrical circuit that really does the work. As an example, static electricity has very high voltage, so much that it can jump a gap of an inch or more. However, it has very low amperage and, as a result, can create a shock but not injure someone. The starter motor in an automobile operates at a relatively low 12 volts but requires very high amperage to generate enough energy to turn over the engine. Lightning has very high voltage and high amperage and can cause severe damage or injury.

Circuits

Current flows in closed loops are called circuits. Circuits must be composed of conducting materials, and must have sources of voltage. *Voltage* causes current to flow, while resistance and impedance oppose it. Current consists of electrons flowing away from negative terminals and toward positive terminals. Knowing these facts allows people to control a current flow.

Electricity will naturally flow to the earth if there is a path. Current also flows along the path of least resistance. If a human body provides the path of least resistance, the current will flow through it. When an electric appliance has a plug with three prongs, one of the three prongs serves as the ground, or zero volts. The ground provides a conducting path for the electrons to flow to the earth because the resistance traveling through the body would be greater than the resistance flowing directly to the ground. *Ground* typically means the zero volts level (when making electrical measurements). Voltage is created by the separation of charges, which means that voltage measurements must be made between two points.

Electrons move best through conductive materials. Although air in a dry climate can be conductive, as noticed through shocks of static electricity, electrons cannot jump across air from a battery to an unconnected, nearby piece of copper wire. Current, or electron movement, occurs only in circuits that form complete loops. These circuits are known as closed circuits.

Figure 3-4 shows a simple circuit, typical of a lantern-style flashlight. The switch is like two ends of a single wire that can be opened (or broken) and then closed (or shorted) to prevent or allow current.

Figure 3-4 Serial Circuit—Flashlight

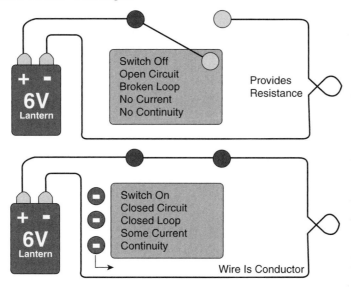

The top of Figure 3-4 illustrates the flashlight with its switch turned off. The chemical processes in the battery cause charges to be separated, which provides voltage. However, because no complete path for electron movement exists, there is no current, and the bulb will not be lit.

As shown in the bottom of Figure 3-4, the switch is turned on, and a complete path of conductive wire for current exists. The bulb provides resistance to the flow of electrons, causing the current to release energy in the form of light.

The circuits involved in networking use the same concepts as this very simple circuit, but networking circuits are much more complex. When you are learning a new concept, it is often helpful to relate the concept to a familiar example. The circuit discussed previously can be compared to a water circuit, as illustrated in Figure 3-5. The pressure that causes water flow comes from the weight of the water in the tank. The tap can be compared with the switch in the previous example. When the tap is turned off, it blocks water from moving. When the tap is turned on, it allows water to move and also provides resistance to the flow of water, because a small tap will allow a lesser flow than a large tap. Finally, the pipe provides a closed path for the flow of water to cycle back into the tank.

Figure 3-5 Water Circuit Analogy for Flowing Electrons

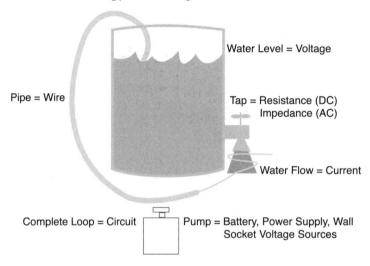

The relationship among voltage, resistance, and current is voltage (V) = current (I) multiplied by resistance (R). In other words, $V = I * R$. This is *Ohm's law*; it was named after the scientist who explored these issues.

Two ways in which current flows are alternating current (AC) and direct current (DC). Alternating current (AC) and voltages vary over time by changing their polarity (direction). AC flows in one direction, then reverses its direction and flows in the other direction, and then repeats the process. AC voltage is positive at one terminal, and negative at the other. Then, the AC voltage reverses its polarity so that the positive terminal becomes negative, and the negative terminal becomes positive. This process continuously repeats itself.

DC always flows in the same direction, and DC voltages always have the same polarity. One terminal is always positive, and the other is always negative. They do not change or reverse. Power lines carry electricity in the form of AC because it can be delivered efficiently over large distances. DC can be found in flashlights and batteries, and as power for the microchips on the motherboard of a computer, where it needs only to go a short distance.

For AC and DC electrical systems, the flow of electrons is always from a negatively charged source to a positively charged source. However, for the controlled flow of electrons to occur, a complete circuit is required. Remember, electrical current follows the path of least resistance.

 Lab 3.1.5   Series Circuits

In this lab, you build and explore the basic properties of series circuits.

Cable Specifications

Specifications, or *standards*, are sets of rules or procedures that are widely used and serve as the accepted method of performing a task. For example, the OSI reference model standards help ensure that networking devices around the world are compatible and can work together. Many specifications exist for cabling to ensure interoperability, safety, and performance.

The *Institute of Electrical and Electronic Engineers (IEEE)* has outlined LAN cabling specifications. IEEE 802.3 is a standard for Ethernet networks, and IEEE 802.5 is a Token Ring network standard. The Underwriters Laboratories issues standards that are primarily concerned with safety.

The *Telecommunications Industry Association (TIA)* and the *Electronic Industries Association (EIA)* have jointly issued cabling standards often called TIA/EIA standards. The list that follows describes some of the TIA/EIA standards:

- **TIA/EIA-568-B**—This is a commercial building telecommunication cabling standard.

- **TIA/EIA-569-B**—Formerly the TIA/EIA-568-A standard. This is a commercial building standard for telecommunications pathways and spaces.

- **TIA/EIA-570-A**—This is a residential and light commercial telecommunications wiring standard.

- **TIA/EIA-606**—This is an administration standard for the telecommunications infrastructure of commercial buildings.

- **TIA/EIA-607**—This is a commercial building grounding and bonding requirement for telecommunications.

The specifications created by this organization have had the greatest impact on networking media standards and include standards for horizontal and backbone (vertical) cabling, wiring closets and equipment rooms, work areas, and entrance facilities. The TIA/EIA standards allow for the planning and installation of LAN equipment in a way that allows network designers the freedom to choose the devices needed while assuring the operability of the LAN design.

The TIA/EIA-568-B standard focuses on horizontal cabling, which is cabling that runs from a wall outlet at a work area to a wiring closet. There are five historic categories for cable (CAT 1 through CAT 5), and of these, only CAT 3, CAT 4, and CAT 5 meet the TIA/EIA-568-B standard. CAT 5 cable is the most frequently installed. Recent standards have been developed for CAT 5e and CAT 6, and a new standard for CAT 7 cabling is also underway. These new standards offer improvements to CAT 5 and are becoming more common.

TIA/EIA-568-B calls for two cables to each work area outlet:

- A telephone cable for voice
- A network cable for data

The voice cable must be a two-pair UTP cable with its correct connectors, or terminators. The network cable must be one of the following and must include the correct connectors, or terminators:

- 150 ohm STP two-pair cable (Token Ring LANs)
- 100 ohm UTP four-pair cable (Ethernet LANs)
- 62.5/125 μ fiber-optic cable (Ethernet LANs)
- Coaxial cable (rarely used for new installations and expected to be removed from this list the next time the standard is updated)

Although not part of the standard, if desired, a coaxial 75 ohm RG-6 cable can also be run for cable TV connection in addition to the minimum voice and data connections.

The standard also specifies the maximum length of each cabling run from the wall outlet to the wiring closet connections for UTP cabling. A 3-meter patch cord is specified from the workstation to the wall outlet. A 90-meter cable run is allowed from the wall outlet to the *patch panel* in the wiring closet. A 6-meter patch cord is permitted from the patch panel to the horizontal cross connect in the wiring closet. This standard ensures that the entire cable run does not exceed 100 meters.

Some other examples of cable specifications that relate to Ethernet cable include the following:

- 10BASE-T
- 10BASE5
- 10BASE2

10BASE-T refers to the speed of transmission at 10 Mbps. The type of transmission is baseband (digitally interpreted). The T stands for twisted pair.

10BASE5 refers to the speed of transmission at 10 Mbps. The type of transmission is baseband. The 5 represents the capability of the cable to allow the signal to travel for approximately 500 meters before attenuation could disrupt the ability of the receiver to appropriately interpret the signal being received. 10BASE5 is often referred to as Thicknet. Thicknet is actually a type of network, while 10BASE5 is the cabling used in that network.

10BASE2 refers to the speed of transmission at 10 Mbps. The type of transmission is baseband. The 2 in 10BASE2 represents the ability of the cable to allow the signal to travel for approximately 200 meters before attenuation could disrupt the ability of the receiver to appropriately interpret the signal being received. 10BASE2 is often referred to as Thinnet. Thinnet is actually a type of network, while 10BASE2 is the cabling used in that network.

Coaxial Cable

Coaxial cable, as shown in Figure 3-6, consists of four main parts:

- Copper conductor
- Plastic insulation
- Braided copper shielding
- Outer jacket

At the center of the cable is a solid copper conductor. Surrounding that conductor is a layer of flexible plastic insulation. A woven copper braid or metallic foil is wrapped around the insulation. This layer acts as the second wire in the cable. It also acts as a shield for the inner conductor and helps reduce the amount of outside interference. Covering this shield is the outer cable jacket. The connector used on coaxial cable is called a BNC, short for British Naval Connector or Bayonet Neill Concelman, connector.

Figure 3-6 Coaxial Cable

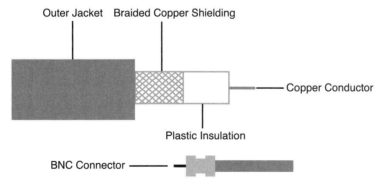

Coaxial cable was a popular choice with LANs in the past. It offered several advantages. It can be run with fewer boosts from repeaters for longer distances between network nodes than either shielded twisted pair (STP) or unshielded twisted pair (UTP). Although more expensive than UTP, coaxial cable is less expensive than fiber-optic cable. The technology is well known, because it has been used for many years in various types of data communication. For example, coaxial cable is commonly used in homes to deliver cable television signals and high-speed Internet access. For cable TV, RG-59 is commonly used inside the home and has a center conductor of 20 AWG. RG-6 is most often used from the street pedestal to the home due to heavier shielding and a larger center conductor of 18 AWG. RG-11 cable is heavier still with a center conductor of 14 AWG and is used to bring cable into neighborhoods.

When working with cable, consider its size. As the diameter of the cable increases, so does the difficulty in working with it because cable must be pulled through existing conduits that are limited in size. Coaxial cable comes in several sizes. The largest diameter (1 cm) was once specified for use as Ethernet **backbone** cable because it had a greater transmission length and better noise rejection characteristics than other types of cable. This type of coaxial cable is frequently referred to as **thicknet**, as shown in Figure 3-7. As its nickname suggests, thicknet cable can be too rigid to install easily in some situations because of its thickness. The general rule is that the more difficult the network medium is to install, the more expensive it is to install. Coaxial cable is more expensive to install than twisted-pair cable. Thicknet cable is almost never used except for special-purpose installations.

Figure 3-7 Coaxial Cable—Thicknet

Coaxial cable with a diameter of 0.35 cm, sometimes referred to as **thinnet**, was also frequently used in Ethernet networks at one time. Thinnet, as shown in Figure 3-8, was especially useful for cable installations that required the cable to make many twists and turns. Because it was easier to install, it was also cheaper to install. Thus, it was sometimes referred to as *Cheapernet*.

However, in both types of coaxial cable, the outer conductor must be carefully and properly grounded, which increases the complexity of the installation. It is for this reason that, despite its advantages, coaxial cable is no longer commonly used in Ethernet networks.

Although many bus topology networks still utilize coaxial cable, the IEEE no longer recommends coaxial cable as a standard for use with Ethernet. Nearly all new LANs use Ethernet extended star topology and a combination of UTP and fiber.

The following summarizes the features of coaxial cables:

- Speed and throughput—10 to 100 Mbps
- Average cost per node—Inexpensive
- Media and connector size—Medium
- Maximum cable length—500 m (medium)

Figure 3-8 Coaxial Cable—Thinnet

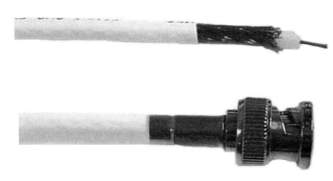

More Information: Plenum Cable

Plenum cable is the cable that runs in plenum spaces of a building. In building construction, a plenum (pronounced PLEH-nuhm, from Latin meaning "full") is a separate space to provide air circulation for heating, ventilation, and air-conditioning (sometimes referred to as HVAC), typically in the space between the structural ceiling and a drop-down ceiling. In buildings with computer installations, the plenum space often is used to house connecting communication cables. Because ordinary cable introduces a toxic hazard in the event of fire, special plenum cabling is required in plenum areas.

Plenum cable sheathing is often made of Teflon and is more expensive than ordinary cabling and does not act as a wick. Its outer material is more resistant to flames and, when burning, produces less smoke than ordinary cabling. Both twisted-pair and coaxial cable are made in plenum cable versions.

More Information: American Wire Gauge System

The diameter of cable wires or conductors is commonly measured using the American wire gauge (AWG) system. AWG is a U.S. standard for measuring the diameter of primarily copper and aluminum cable. Typical residential wiring is AWG 12 or 14. The conductor or wire size used in the UTP in most telephone local loops (from the central office to a home or residence) is between 19 and 26 AWG. Most newer telephone wire is from 22 to 26 gauge with 24 gauge being the most common. The lower the gauge number the thicker the wire. Thicker wire has less resistance and can carry more current resulting in a better signal over longer distances. A wire with an AWG size of 24 would be 1/24th of an inch in diameter.

Twisted-Pair Cable

Twisted-pair cable is a type of cabling that is used for telephone communications and most modern Ethernet networks. A pair of wires forms a circuit that can transmit data. The pairs are twisted to provide protection against *crosstalk*, the noise generated by adjacent pairs.

> **More Information: American Wire Gauge System (Continued)**
>
> The wire pairs are twisted for two reasons. First, when a wire is carrying a current, that current creates a magnetic field around the wire. This field can interfere with signals on nearby wires. To combat this, pairs of wires carry signals in opposite directions, so that the two magnetic fields also occur in opposite directions and cancel each other out. This process is known as *cancellation*. Twisting the pairs holds the two wires closer together and helps to ensure effective cancellation within the cable.
>
> Second, network data is sent using two wires in a twisted pair. One copy of the data is sent on each wire, and the two copies are mirror images of each other. These signals are called *differential signals*. If the two wires are twisted together, noise seen on one wire is also seen on the other wire. When the data is received, one copy is inverted, and the two signals are then compared. In this manner the receiver can filter out noise because the noise signals cancel each other.
>
> Two basic types of twisted-pair cable exist: shielded twisted-pair (STP) and unshielded twisted-pair (UTP). The following sections discuss UTP and STP cable in more detail.

STP Cable

Shielded twisted-pair (STP) cable contains four pairs of thin, copper wires covered in color-coded plastic insulation that are twisted together. Each pair is wrapped in metallic foil, and then the four pairs are collectively wrapped in another layer of metallic braid or foil. This layer is wrapped with a plastic outer jacket. Figure 3-9 illustrates an example of STP.

Figure 3-9 Shielded Twisted-Pair Cable

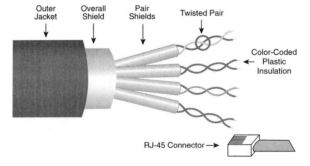

Screened twisted-pair (ScTP), also known as foil twisted-pair (FTP), is a variation of STP. ScTP is essentially STP with just one layer of foil shielding around the set of all four-wire pairs, as shown in Figure 3-10. The shielding in both STP and ScTP reduces unwanted electrical noise. This noise reduction provides a major advantage of STP over unshielded cable.

Figure 3-10 Screened Twisted-Pair Cable

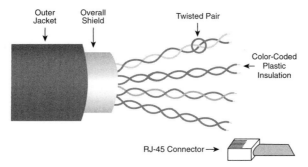

However, shielded cable is more difficult to install than unshielded cable because the metallic shielding needs to be grounded. If improperly installed, STP and ScTP become very susceptible to noise problems because an ungrounded shield acts like an antenna, picking up unwanted signals. STP and ScTP cable cannot be run as far as coaxial and fiber-optic cable without the use of repeaters. The insulation and shielding considerably increase the size, weight, and cost of the cable. Despite these disadvantages, shielded copper cable is still used as networking media today, especially in Europe.

The following summarizes the features of STP cable:

- Speed and throughput—10 to 100 Mbps

- Average cost per node—Moderately expensive

- Media and connector size—Medium to large

- Maximum cable length—100 meters (m) (short)

UTP Cable

Unshielded twisted-pair (UTP) cable is a common networking *media*. It consists of four pairs of thin, copper wires covered in color-coded plastic insulation that are twisted together, as shown in Figure 3-11. The wire pairs are then covered with a plastic outer jacket. The connector used on a UTP cable is called a registered jack 45 (RJ-45) connector, as shown in Figure 3-12.

Figure 3-11 Unshielded Twisted-Pair Cable

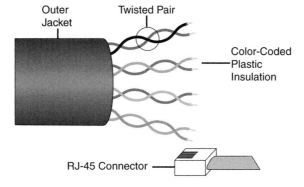

Figure 3-12 RJ-45 Connector

UTP cable has many advantages. It has a small diameter and does not require grounding, so it is the easiest type of cable to install. Its size provides an additional advantage because more UTP cable can fit in a given area than other copper media. It is also the least expensive type of networking media, and the connector is the easiest to build. It supports the same data speeds as other copper media.

The primary disadvantage to UTP is that it is more susceptible to electrical noise and interference than any other type of networking media. Because it has no shielding, it relies solely on the cancellation and differential signals to reduce the effects of noise. The other main disadvantage is that its maximum run length is less than that allowed for coaxial and fiber-optic cables.

Although UTP was once considered to be slower at transmitting data than other types of cable, this is no longer true. In fact, UTP is considered the fastest copper-based medium today. The following summarizes the features of UTP cable:

- Speed and throughput—10 to 1000 Mbps
- Average cost per node—Least expensive
- Media and connector size—Small
- Maximum cable length—100 m (short)

Commonly used types of UTP cabling are as follows:

- **Category 1 (CAT 1)**—Used for telephone communications. Not suitable for transmitting data.
- **Category 2 (CAT 2)**—Capable of transmitting data at speeds up to 4 Mbps.
- **Category 3 (CAT 3)**—Used in 10BASET Ethernet networks. Can transmit data at speeds up to 10 Mbps.
- **Category 4 (CAT 4)**—Used in Token Ring networks. Can transmit data at speeds up to 16 Mbps.
- **Category 5 (CAT 5)**—Can transmit data at speeds up to 100 Mbps. Used in Fast Ethernet networks.

- **Category 5e (CAT 5e)**—Used in networks running at speeds up to 1000 Mbps (1 Gbps). Used in Gigabit Ethernet (GigE) networks.

- **Category 6 (CAT 6)**—The specification for CAT 6 is new, was released on February 3, 2003, and is currently available for installation and use. Used in Gigabit Ethernet (GigE) networks.

Typically, CAT 5 and higher network cable consists of four pairs of 24 AWG multistrand copper wires. Older cabling installations run CAT 3 for voice and CAT 5 for data. Most new installations run a minimum of CAT 5e for voice and data. Although CAT 5e costs a little more, it is worth it in the long run.

When comparing UTP and STP, keep the following points in mind:

- The speed of both types of cable is usually satisfactory for local-area distances.

- These are the least-expensive media for data communication. UTP is less expensive than STP.

- Because most buildings are already wired with UTP, many transmission standards are adapted to use it to avoid costly rewiring with an alternative cable type. You must take care to ensure that the category level of the cable is adequate to handle the bandwidth desired. As an example, a building wired with CAT 3 cable cannot support Fast Ethernet, which requires at least CAT 5.

Lab 3.1.9a   Communications Circuits

In this lab, you build series circuits and explore their basic properties.

Lab 3.1.9b   Fluke 620 Basic Cable Testing

In this lab, you use a simple cable tester to verify whether a straight-through or crossover cable is good or bad. You also use the Fluke 620 advanced cable tester to test cables for length and connectivity.

Lab 3.1.9c   Straight-Through Cable Construction

In this lab, you build a CAT 5 or CAT 5e UTP Ethernet network patch cable (or patch cord). You also test the cable for good connections (continuity) and correct pinouts (correct color of wire on the right pin).

Lab 3.1.9d Rollover Cable Construction

In this lab, you build a CAT 5 or CAT 5e UTP console rollover cable. You also test the cable for good connections (continuity) and correct pinouts (correct wire on the right pin).

Lab 3.1.9e Crossover Cable Construction

In this lab, you build a CAT 5 or CAT 5e UTP Ethernet crossover cable to TIA-568-B and TIA-568-A standards. You also test the cable for good connections (continuity) and correct pinouts (correct wire on the right pin).

Lab 3.1.9f UTP Cable Purchase

In this lab, you are introduced to the variety and prices of network cabling and related components in the market. This lab looks specifically at patch cables and bulk cable.

Optical Media

Optical fiber is the most frequently used medium for the longer, high-bandwidth, point-to-point transmissions required on LAN backbones and on wide-area networks (WANs). Very good reasons exist for the popularity of fiber.

Optical fiber is used in networks because

- Fiber is not susceptible to lightning, *electromagnetic interference (EMI)*, or *radio frequency interference (RFI)*, and it does not generate EMI or RFI.

- Fiber has much greater bandwidth capabilities than other media.

- Fiber allows significantly greater transmission distances and excellent signal quality because very little signal attenuation occurs.

- Fiber is more secure than other media because it is difficult to tap into a fiber and easy to detect someone's placing a tap on the fiber.

- Current fiber transmitter and receiver technologies can be replaced by newer, faster devices as they are developed so that greater transmission speeds can be achieved over existing fiber links with no need to replace the fiber.

- Fiber costs less than copper for long-distance applications.

- The raw material that fiber is made from is sand, a plentiful substance.

- With fiber, you have no grounding concerns as you have when signaling using electricity.

- Fiber is light in weight and easily installed.

- Fiber has better resistance to environmental factors, like water, than copper wire.

- Lengths of fiber can easily be spliced together for very long cable runs.

For these reasons, when very large numbers of bits need to be sent over distances greater than 100 meters, fiber-optic fiber is often used.

This section explains the basics of fiber-optic cable. You learn about how fibers can guide light for long distances. You also learn about the types of cable used, how fiber is installed, the type of connectors and equipment used with fiber-optic cable, and how fiber is tested to ensure that it functions properly.

The Electromagnetic Spectrum

The light used in optical fiber networks is one type of electromagnetic energy. When an electric charge moves back and forth, or accelerates, a type of energy called electromagnetic energy is produced. This energy, in the form of waves, can travel through a vacuum, the air, and through some materials like glass. An important property of any energy wave is its *wavelength*, as shown in Figure 3-13.

Figure 3-13 Wavelength

To human beings, radio, microwaves, radar, visible light, X rays, and gamma rays seem to be very different things, but they are all types of electromagnetic energy. If all the types of electromagnetic waves are arranged in order from waves with the longest wavelength down to those waves with the shortest wavelength, it creates a continuum called the *Electromagnetic Spectrum*, as shown in Figure 3-14.

Figure 3-14 Electromagnetic Spectrum

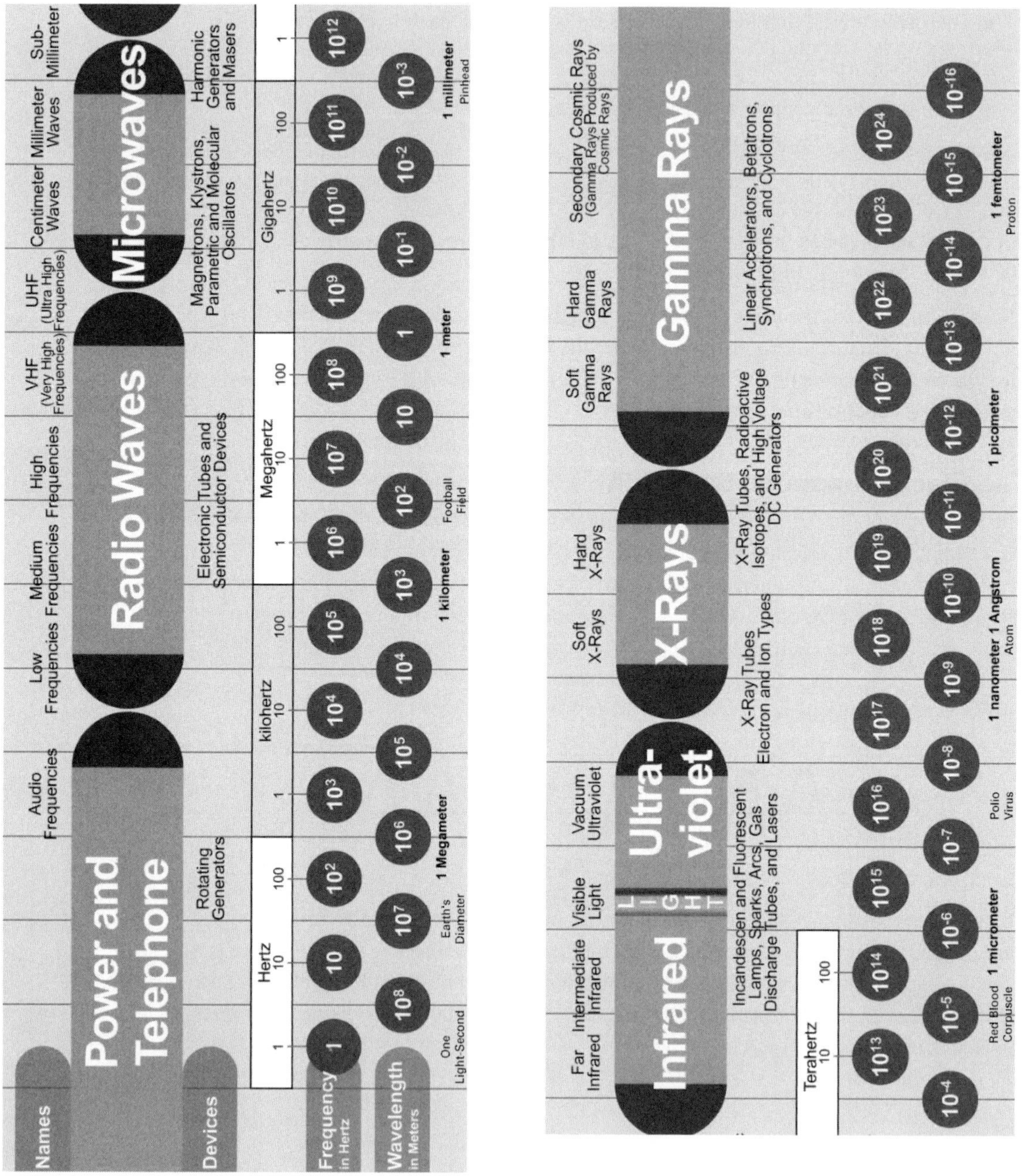

The wavelength of an electromagnetic wave is determined by how frequently the electric charge that generates the wave moves back and forth. For example, if the charge moves back and forth slowly, it generates a long wavelength. Visualize the movement of the electric charge as like that of a stick in a pool of water. If the stick is moved back and forth slowly, it generates ripples in the water with a long wavelength between the tops of the ripples. If the stick is moved back and forth more rapidly, the ripples have a shorter wavelength.

Because electromagnetic waves are all generated in the same way, all electromagnetic waves share many of the same properties. For example, they all travel at the same rate of speed through a vacuum, about 300,000 kilometers per second or 186,000 miles per second, the speed of light.

Human eyes can sense electromagnetic energy only with wavelengths between 700 nanometers and about 400 nanometers. A nanometer is one billionth of a meter (0.000000001 m) in length and is abbreviated nm. Electromagnetic energy with wavelengths between 700 nm and 400 nm is called *visible light*. The longer wavelengths of light (those around 700 nm) are seen as the color red. The shortest wavelengths (around 400 nm) appear as the color violet. This part of the electromagnetic spectrum is seen as the colors in a rainbow.

To transmit data over optical fiber, wavelengths that are not visible to the human eye are used. These wavelengths are slightly longer than red light and are called *infrared light*. Infrared light is used in TV remote controls. The wavelength of the light in optical fiber is one of the following wavelengths:

- 850 nm

- 1310 nm

- 1550 nm

These wavelengths were selected because they travel better through optical fiber than other wavelengths.

Ray Model of Light

When electromagnetic waves, including light, travel out from the source, they travel in straight lines. These straight lines pointing out from the source are called *rays*.

Think of light rays as narrow beams of light like those produced by lasers. In the vacuum of empty space, light travels continuously in a straight line at 300,000 kilometers per second. However, light travels at different, slower speeds through other materials like air, water, and glass. When a light ray (called the *incident ray*) crosses the boundary from one material (air, for example) to another (glass, for example), some of the light energy in the ray is reflected back. That is why you can see yourself in a mirror. The light that is reflected back is called the *reflected ray*.

The light energy in the incident ray that is not reflected enters the glass. The entering ray is usually bent at an angle from its original path. This ray is called the *refracted ray*. How much the incident light ray is bent depends on two factors:

- The angle at which the incident ray strikes the surface of the glass

- The different rates of speed at which light travels through the two substances (air and glass in this example)

The bending of light rays at the boundary of two substances is the reason why light rays are able to travel through an optical fiber even if the fiber curves in a circle.

How much rays of light in glass bend is determined by the optical density of the glass. Optical density refers to how much a light ray is slowed down by passing through a substance. The greater the optical density of a material, the more it slows light down from its speed in a vacuum. The ratio of the speed of light in a material to the speed of light in a vacuum is called the material's index of refraction (IR) and is expressed as follows:

Index of Refraction = n = Speed of Light in Vaccum / Speed of Light in material

Therefore, the measure of a material's optical density is that material's index of refraction. A material with a large index of refraction is more optically dense and slows light down more than a material with a smaller index of refraction.

Table 3-2 shows the IR of air, glass, diamond, and water.

Table 3-2 Index of Refraction

Substance	Index of Refraction
Air	1.000
Glass	1.523
Diamond	2.419
Water	1.333

For a substance like glass, the index of refraction (the optical density) can be made larger by adding chemicals to the glass. The index of refraction can be made smaller by making the glass very pure.

In the next two sections, you learn more about the *reflection* and refraction that help you to understand the design and operation of optical fibers.

Reflection

When light travels through a medium like air and strikes another medium like glass, the light either reflects off the surface or passes into or through the second medium, as shown in Figure 3-15. It depends on the angle it strikes the surface. The angle between the incident ray and a line perpendicular to the surface of the glass at the point where the incident ray strikes the glass is called the *angle of incidence*. When this angle of incidence reaches a certain point, called the critical angle, all the light is reflected back into the original medium, as illustrated in Figure 3-16.

Figure 3-15 Reflection

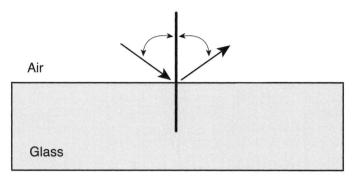

Figure 3-16 Critical Angle

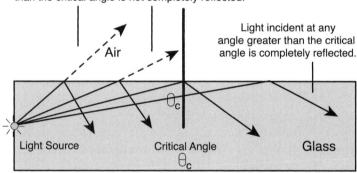

The perpendicular line is called the *normal*. It is not a light ray but a tool to allow the measurement of angles. The angle between the reflected ray and the normal is called the angle of reflection. The Law of Reflection states that the ***angle of reflection*** of a light ray is equal to its angle of incidence. In other words, the angle at which a light ray strikes a reflective surface determines the angle that the ray reflects off the surface.

Refraction

When light strikes the interface between two transparent materials like air and glass, the light divides into two parts. Part of the light ray is reflected back into the first substance (the air), with the angle of reflection equaling the angle of incidence. The remaining energy in the light ray crosses the interface and enters into the second substance (the glass).

If the incident ray strikes the glass surface at exactly a 90-degree angle, the ray goes straight into the glass. The ray is not bent. But, if the angle of incidence is not exactly 90 degrees, then the ray that enters the glass (the transmitted ray) is bent. We call this bending of the entering ray *refraction*. How much the ray is bent (refracted) depends on the index of refraction of the two transparent materials. If the light ray travels from a substance whose index of refraction is smaller into a substance where the index of refraction is larger, the refracted ray is bent towards the normal. If the light ray travels from a substance where the index of refraction is larger into a substance where the index of refraction is smaller, the refracted ray is bent away from the normal. Figure 3-17 illustrates an example of refraction.

Figure 3-17 Refraction

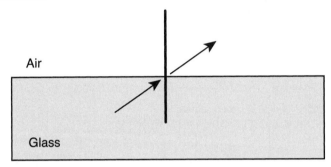

For example, consider a light ray moving at some angle other than 90 degrees through the boundary between glass and a diamond, as shown in Figure 3-18. The glass has an index of refraction of about 1.523. The diamond has an index of refraction of about 2.419. Therefore, the ray that continues into the diamond is bent towards the normal. When that light ray crosses the boundary between the diamond and the air at some angle other than 90 degrees, it is bent away from the normal. The reason for this is that air has a lower index of refraction (about 1.000) than does the diamond.

Figure 3-18 Refraction Example

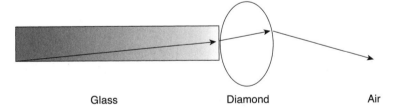

Glass   Diamond   Air

Total Internal Reflection

A light ray that is being turned on and off to send data 1s and 0s into an optical fiber must stay inside the fiber until it reaches the far end. The ray must not refract into the material wrapped around the outside of the fiber because such refraction causes the loss of part of the ray's light energy. A design for the fiber that makes the outside surface of the fiber act like a mirror to the light ray moving through the fiber must be achieved. If any light ray that tries to move out through the side of the fiber is reflected back into the fiber at an angle that sends it towards the far end of the fiber, this is a good *pipe* or *wave guide* for the light waves, as illustrated in Figure 3-19.

Figure 3-19 Total Internal Reflection

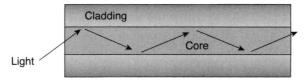

The laws of reflection and refraction tell how to design a fiber that guides the light waves through the fiber with a minimum energy loss. Two conditions are needed to cause light rays in a fiber to be reflected back into the fiber without any loss due to refraction. These two conditions are as follows:

- The core (the inside) of the optical fiber has to have a larger (a higher) index of refraction than the material that surrounds it. The material that surrounds the core of the fiber is called the cladding.

- The angle of incidence of the light ray is greater than the critical angle for the core and its cladding.

When both of these conditions are met, all the incident light in the fiber is reflected back inside the fiber. This condition is called *total internal reflection*, which is the foundation on which optical fiber is constructed. Total internal reflection causes the light rays in the fiber to bounce off the core-cladding boundary and continue their journey toward the far end of the fiber. The light follows something of a zigzag path through the core of the fiber.

A fiber that meets the first condition (a core with a higher index of refraction than the cladding) can be easily created. Also, the angle of incidence of the light rays that enter the core can be controlled. Restricting two factors controls the angle of incidence:

- The numerical aperture of the fiber. The numerical aperture of a core is the range of angles of incident light rays entering the fiber that are totally internally reflected, as illustrated in Figure 3-20.

- The paths (called the modes) that a light ray can follow when traveling down a fiber.

Figure 3-20 Numerical Aperture

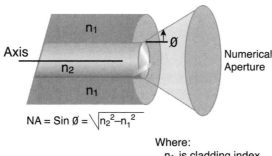

$$NA = \sin \emptyset = \sqrt{n_2^2 - n_1^2}$$

Where:
n_1 is cladding index
n_2 is core index

Controlling conditions 1 and 2 creates a fiber with total internal reflection, consequently giving a light wave path that can be used for data communications, as shown in Figure 3-21.

Figure 3-21 Light Wave Path

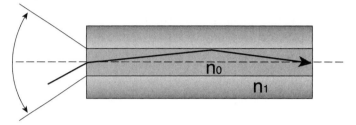

Light must fall inside this angle
to be guided in the fiber core.

n_0

n_1

Fiber-Optic Cables

Fiber-optic cable is a networking medium that uses modulated light for data transmissions through thin strands of glass. Signals that represent data bits are converted into beams of light. It is important to recognize that while electricity is required to generate and interpret the fiber-optic signals at the end devices, no electricity is in the cable itself as there is with copper media. In fact, fiber-optic cable components are very good insulators. Many characteristics of fiber-optic media are superior to copper.

Every fiber-optic cable used for networking consists of two glass fibers encased in separate sheaths. One fiber carries transmitted data from device A to device B; the second fiber carries data from device B to device A. A fiber for data goes in each direction, similar to two one-way streets going in opposite directions. This arrangement provides a full-duplex communication link. Just as copper twisted-pair uses separate wire pairs to transmit (Tx) and receive (Rx), fiber-optic circuits use one fiber strand to transmit and one to receive, as illustrated in Figure 3-22. Typically, these two fiber cables are in a single outer jacket until they reach the point at which connectors are attached.

Figure 3-22 Duplex Fiber

Tx   Rx

Rx   Tx

At this point, the two fiber cables are separated. No need for twisting or shielding exists because no light escapes when it is inside a fiber, which means no crosstalk issues exist with fiber. It is common to see multiple fiber pairs encased in the same cable. This arrangement allows a single cable to be run between data closets, floors, or buildings. One cable can contain 2, 4, 8, 12, 24, 48, or more separate fibers. With copper, one UTP cable has to be pulled for each circuit. Fiber can carry many more bits per second and carry them farther than copper can.

Fiber-Optic Cables (Continued)

As illustrated in Figure 3-23 and Figure 3-24, five parts typically make up each fiber-optic cable:

- The core
- The cladding
- A buffer
- A strengthening material
- An outer jacket

Figure 3-23 Five Elements of a Fiber-Optic Cable

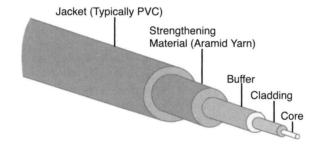

Figure 3-24 Cross Section Showing the Five Elements of a Fiber-Optic Cable

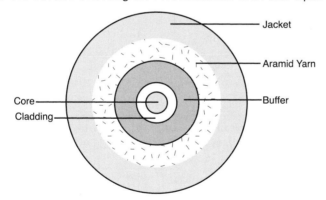

The core is the light transmission element at the center of the optical fiber, and all the light signals travel through the core. This core is typically glass made from a combination of silica (silicon dioxide) and other elements. Surrounding the core is the cladding, also made of silica but with a lower index of refraction than the core. Light rays traveling through the fiber core reflect off this core-to-cladding interface where the core and cladding meet, which keeps light in the core as it travels down the fiber.

Surrounding the cladding is a buffer material, usually plastic, that helps shield the core and cladding from damage.

Fiber-Optic Cables (Continued)

The strengthening material surrounds the buffer, preventing the fiber cable from being stretched when installers pull it. The material used is often Kevlar, the same material used to produce bulletproof vests. The final element, the outer jacket, surrounds the cable to protect the fiber against abrasion, solvents, and other contaminants. This outer jacket composition can vary depending on the cable usage.

The part of an optical fiber through which light rays travel is called the *core* of the fiber. Light rays cannot enter the core of an optical fiber at all angles. The rays can enter the core only if their angle is inside the fiber's numerical aperture. Likewise, once the rays have entered the fiber's core, a limited number of optical paths exist that a light ray can follow through the fiber. These optical paths are called modes. If the diameter of a fiber's core is large enough so that many paths exist that light can take as it passes through the fiber, the fiber is called *multimode* fiber. *Single-mode* fiber has a much smaller core that allows light rays to travel along only one path (one mode) inside the fiber. Figure 3-25 illustrates the differences between multimode and single-mode fibers.

Figure 3-25 Single-Mode Versus Multimode

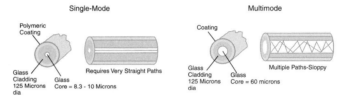

Table 3-3 compares the features of single-mode and multimode fiber.

Table 3-3 Features of Single-Mode and Multimode Fiber

	Single-Mode Fiber	Multimode Fiber
Core Features	Small core (10 microns or less)	Larger core than single-mode cable (50 or 62.5 microns or greater)
Dispersion Characteristics	Less dispersion	Allows greater dispersion and, therefore, loss of signal
Distance Characteristics	Suited for long-distance applications (up to 3 kilometers [9842 feet])	Used for long-distance applications, but shorter than single-mode (up to 2 kilometers [6560 feet])
Light Source	Uses lasers as the light source often within campus backbones for distances of several thousand meters	Uses LEDs as the light source, often within LANs or distances of a couple hundred meters within a campus network

The next two sections cover the two basic types of optical fiber, multimode and single-mode, in more detail.

Multimode Fiber

Multimode fiber allows multiple modes (paths) of light to propagate through the fiber-optic core, as compared to single-mode fiber, which allows only one mode. Multiple modes of light propagating through fiber might travel different distances, depending on their entry angles. This angle causes them to arrive at the destination (receiving end of the cable) at slightly different times—a phenomenon called *modal dispersion*. Multimode uses a type of glass, called *graded index glass*, which has a lower index of refraction towards the outer edge of the core. This glass causes the light to slow down when passing through the center of the core and accelerate when passing through the outer areas of the core, ensuring that all modes of light reach the end at approximately the same time. This design is used because a light ray following a mode that goes straight down the center of the core does not have to go as far as a ray following a mode that bounces around in the fiber. All rays should arrive at the end of the fiber together. Then, the receiver at the end of the fiber receives a strong flash of light rather than a long, dim pulse.

A standard multimode fiber-optic cable (the most common type of fiber-optic cable used in LANs) uses an optical fiber with either a 62.5- or a 50-micron core and a 125-micron diameter cladding. This cable is commonly designated as 62.5/125 or 50/125 micron optical fiber. A micron is one millionth of a meter. Because the diameter of the cladding is considerably larger than the wavelength of the light being transmitted, the light bounces around (reflects) inside the core as it is propagated along the transmission line.

Infrared light emitting diodes (LEDs) or vertical cavity surface emitting lasers (VCSELs) are usually the light source used with multimode fiber. LEDs are a little cheaper to build and require somewhat less safety concerns than lasers. However, LEDs cannot transmit light over cable as far as the lasers. Multimode fiber (62.5/125) can carry data distances of up to 2000 meters (6560 feet). Multimode fiber is mainly used in LAN applications including backbone cabling.

Single-Mode Fiber

Be aware that the laser light used with single-mode has a longer wavelength than can be seen, and it is so strong that it can seriously damage eyes. Never look at the end of a fiber that is connected to a device at its far end. Never look into the transmit port on a NIC, switch, or router. There is nothing that can be seen anyway. Remember to keep protective covers over the ends of fiber and inserted into the fiber-optic ports of switches and routers. Be very careful!

Single-mode fiber uses only one mode of light to propagate through the fiber-optic core. In single-mode fiber-optic cabling, the core is much smaller than in multimode. The single-mode core is 8 to 10 microns in diameter. Nine micron cores are the most common. A 9/125 marking on a single-mode fiber's jacket indicates that the core fiber has a diameter of 9 microns and the surrounding cladding is 125 microns in diameter.

The size of the core in single-mode fiber leaves very little room for light to bounce around. Furthermore, a very focused infrared laser is used as the light source in single-mode fiber. The ray of light it generates enters the core at a 90-degree angle. As a result, the data carrying light ray pulses in single-mode fiber are essentially transmitted in a straight line right down the middle of the core, as shown in Figure 3-26. This greatly increases both the speed and the distance that data can be transmitted.

Figure 3-26 Single-Mode Fiber

Because of its design, single-mode fiber is capable of higher rates of data transmission (bandwidth) and greater cable run distances than multimode fiber. Single-mode fiber can carry LAN data up to 3000 meters. Multimode is only capable of up to 2000 meters. Lasers and single-mode fibers are more expensive than LEDs and multimode fiber. Because of these characteristics, single-mode fiber is often used for interbuilding connectivity or WANs (for example, telephone company network connections).

Figure 3-27 compares the relative sizes of the core and cladding for both types of fiber-optic cable in different sectional views. The much smaller and more refined fiber core in single-mode fiber, although it entails more manufacturing costs, is the reason single-mode has a higher bandwidth and cable run distance than multimode fiber.

Figure 3-27 Single-Mode and Multimode Fiber

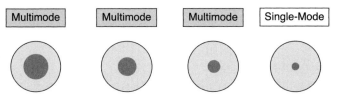

The following summarizes the features of fiber-optic cables:

- **Speed and throughput**—More than 1 Gbps

- **Average cost per node**—Expensive

- **Media and connector size**—Small

- **Maximum cable length**—More than 15 kilometers (km) for single-mode; up to 2 km for multimode

Cable Designs

As illustrated in Figure 3-28, two basic cable designs exist:

■ Loose-tube

■ Tight-buffered

Figure 3-28 Loose-Tube Versus Tight-Buffer Construction

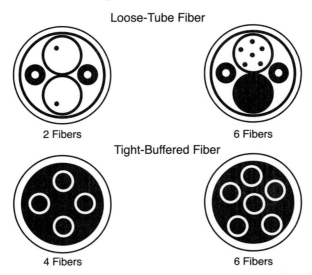

Loose-Tube Fiber

2 Fibers   6 Fibers

Tight-Buffered Fiber

4 Fibers   6 Fibers

Tight-buffered cables have the buffering material that surrounds the cladding in direct contact with the cladding. The main practical difference between the two designs is the applications for which they are used. Loose-tube cable is primarily used for outside-building installations, while tight-buffered cable is used inside buildings. Most of the fiber used in LANs is tight-buffered multimode cable.

Other Optical Components

Most of the data sent over a LAN is in the form of electrical signals. But, optical fiber links use light to send data. So, something is needed to convert the electricity to light and, at the other end of the fiber, convert the light back to electricity. This situation means that two devices are always required: a transmitter and a receiver.

In addition to transmitters and receivers, this section also discusses different types of fiber-optic cable connectors as well as devices used in optical networking.

Transmitters

The transmitter receives data to be transmitted from switches and routers. This data is in the form of electrical signals. The transmitter converts the electronic signals into their equivalent light pulses. Two types of light sources encode and transmit the data through the cable. These two sources are

- **Light emitting diodes (LEDs)**—An LED produces infrared light with wavelengths of either 850 or 1310 nm. These are used with multimode fiber in LANs. Lenses are used to focus the infrared light on the end of the fiber. LEDs have fewer safety concerns.

- **Light amplification by stimulated emission radiation (Laser)**—Laser is a light source producing a thin beam of intense infrared light usually with wavelengths of 1310 or 1550 nm. Lasers are used with single-mode fiber over the longer distances involved in WANs or campus backbones. Exercise extra care to prevent eye injury.

Each light source can be lighted and darkened quickly to send data 1s and 0s at a high number of bits per second.

Receiver

At the other end of the optical fiber from the transmitter is the receiver. It functions something like the photoelectric cell in a solar-powered calculator. When light strikes the receiver, it produces electricity. The first job of the receiver is to detect a light pulse that arrives from the fiber. Then the receiver converts the light pulse back into the original electrical signal that first entered the transmitter at the far end of the fiber. Now the signal is again in the form of voltage changes. The signal is ready to be sent over copper wire into any receiving electronic device such as a computer, switch, or router. The semiconductor devices that are usually used as receivers with fiber-optic links are called p-intrinsic-n diodes (PIN photodiodes).

PIN photodiodes are manufactured to be sensitive to the particular wavelength of light (850, 1310, or 1550 nm) generated by the transmitter at the far end of the fiber. When struck by a pulse of light at the proper wavelength, the PIN photodiode quickly produces an electric current of the proper voltage for the network. It instantly stops producing the voltage when no light strikes the PIN photodiode. This process generates the voltage changes that represent the data 1s and 0s on a copper cable.

Connectors

Connectors are attached to the fiber ends so that the fibers can be connected to the ports on the transmitter and receiver. A common type of connector used with multimode fiber is the subscriber connector (SC), as shown in Figure 3-29. On single-mode fiber, the straight tip (ST) connector, as shown in Figure 3-30, is frequently used. With SC and ST, there is one connector for each fiber. Newer connectors combine the send and receive fibers into one modular connector, comparable in size to an RJ-45, to save space.

Figure 3-29 SC Connector

Figure 3-30 Figure 3-30ST Connector

Optical Amplifiers and Fiber Patch Panels

In addition to the transmitters, receivers, connectors, and fibers that are always required on an optical network, you can sometimes see several other devices on an optical fiber network.

Repeaters are optical amplifiers that receive attenuating light pulses traveling long distances and restore them to their original shapes, strengths, and timings. Then the restored signals can be sent on along the journey to the receiver at the far end of the fiber.

Fiber-optic patch panels, as shown in Figure 3-31, are similar to the patch panels used with copper cable. These panels increase the flexibility of an optical network by allowing quick changes to the connection of devices like switches or routers with various available fiber runs (cable links).

Figure 3-31 Fiber-Optic Patch Panels

 Lab 3.2.8   Fiber-Optic Cable Purchase

In this lab, you are introduced to the variety and prices of network cabling and related components in the market. This lab looks specifically at fiber-optic patch cables and bulk fiber cable.

Signals and Noise in Optical Fibers

Fiber-optic cable is not affected by the sources of external *noise* that cause problems on copper media. Why? Because external light cannot enter the fiber except at the transmitter end. The cladding is covered by a buffer and an outer jacket that stops light from entering or leaving the cable.

Furthermore, the transmission of light on one fiber in a cable does not generate interference that disturbs transmission on any other fiber, which means that fiber does not have the problem with crosstalk that copper media does. In fact, the quality of fiber-optic links is so good that the recent standards for Gigabit and 10-Gigabit Ethernet specify transmission distances that far exceed the traditional 2-kilometer reach of the original Ethernet. (You learn more about the Ethernet technologies in Chapter 7, "Ethernet Technologies," and Chapter 8, "Ethernet Switching.") Fiber-optic transmission allows the Ethernet protocol to be used on metropolitan-area networks (MANs) and WANs.

Although fiber is the best of all the transmission media at carrying large amounts of data over long distances, fiber is not without problems. When light travels through fiber, some of the light energy is lost. The farther a light signal travels through a fiber, the more it loses strength. This **attenuation** of the signal is due to several factors involving the nature of fiber itself. The most important factor is *scattering*. The scattering of light in a fiber is caused by microscopic non-uniformity (distortions) in the fiber that reflects and scatters some of the light energy, as shown in Figure 3-32.

Figure 3-32 Scattering

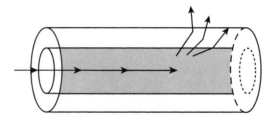

Absorption is another cause of light energy loss. When a light ray strikes some types of chemical impurities in a fiber, the impurities absorb part of the ray's energy. This light energy is converted to a small amount of heat energy. Absorption makes the light signal a little dimmer.

Another factor that causes attenuation of the light signal is manufacturing irregularities or roughness in the core-to-cladding boundary. Power is lost from the light signal as a result of the less than perfect total internal reflection in that rough area of the fiber. If there are any microscopic imperfections in the thickness or symmetry of the fiber, it cuts down on total internal reflection, and some light energy is absorbed by the cladding.

Dispersion of a light flash limits transmission distances on a fiber. Dispersion is the technical term for the spreading of pulses of light as they travel down the fiber, as shown in Figure 3-33.

Figure 3-33 Dispersion

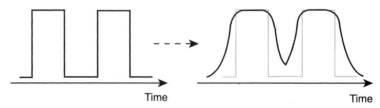

Graded index multimode fiber is designed to compensate for the different distances the various modes of light have to travel in the large diameter core. Single-mode fiber does not have the problem of multiple paths that the light signal can follow. Chromatic dispersion, however, is a characteristic of both multimode and single-mode fiber. Some wavelengths of light travel at slightly different speeds through glass than do other wavelengths. This discrepancy causes chromatic dispersion. That is why a prism separates the wavelengths of light. Ideally, an LED or laser light source emits light of just one frequency. Then, chromatic dispersion is not a problem.

Unfortunately, lasers and, especially, LEDs generate a range of wavelengths so chromatic dispersion limits the distance you can transmit on a fiber. If you try to transmit a signal too far, what started as a bright pulse of light energy is spread out, separated, and dim when it reaches the receiver. The receiver is not able to distinguish a 1 from a 0.

Installation, Care, and Testing of Optical Fiber

A major cause of too much attenuation in fiber-optic cable is improper installation. If the fiber is stretched or curved too tightly, it can cause tiny fissures (cracks) in the core that scatter the light rays. Bending the fiber in too tight a curve can change the incident angle of light rays striking the core-to-cladding boundary. Then, the ray's incident angle becomes less than the critical angle for total internal reflection. Instead of reflecting around the bend, some light rays refract into the cladding and are lost.

There are two types of bending:

- **Macrobending**—A macrobend is a bend you can see. When you bend fiber, you can cause some of the light rays to exceed the critical angle, allowing light to leak out of the core and into the cladding. When light is in the cladding, it cannot easily get back into the core; it then leaks out through the buffer, as shown in Figure 3-34.

- **Microbending**—Microbending produces the same effect as macrobending; it causes the light to exceed the critical angle and leak out of the core, as shown in Figure 3-34. It occurs on a microscopic scale and is not visible to the eye.

Microbending can also be caused by extreme temperature swings in installed cable when the different materials in the cable structure expand and contract at different rates. This expansion and contraction causes the fiber to be squeezed or stretched, which causes microbending.

To prevent fiber bends that are too sharp, fiber is usually pulled through a type of installed pipe called *interducting*. The interducting is much stiffer than fiber and cannot be bent so sharply that the fiber inside the interducting has too tight a curve. The interducting protects the fiber, makes it easier to pull the fiber, and ensures that the bending radius (curve limit) of the fiber is not exceeded.

When the fiber has been pulled, the ends of the fiber must be cleaved (cut) and properly polished to ensure that the ends are smooth. Figure 3-35 illustrates the problems with improper fiber end face finishes, and Figure 3-36 illustrates the proper fiber end face polishing techniques.

Figure 3-34 Macrobending and Microbending

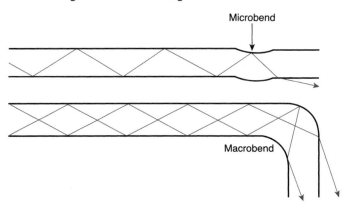

Figure 3-35 Fiber End Face Finishes

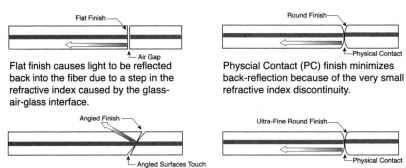

Flat finish causes light to be reflected back into the fiber due to a step in the refractive index caused by the glass-air-glass interface.

Physcial Contact (PC) finish minimizes back-reflection because of the very small refractive index discontinuity.

Angle polish connectors cause the reflection to exit the core and dissipate in the cladding.

Ultra polish connector finish uses several grades of polishing film to achieve an ultra-smooth surface.

Figure 3-36 Fiber End Face Polishing Techniques

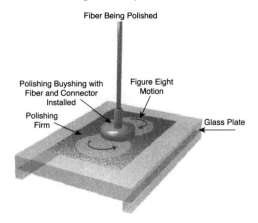

A microscope or test instrument with a built-in magnifier is used to examine the end of the fiber and verify that it is properly polished and shaped. Then, the connector is carefully attached to the fiber end. Improperly installed connectors, improper splices, or the splicing of two cables with different core sizes dramatically reduces the strength of a light signal. Figure 3-37 illustrates the splicing of a 62.5 micron fiber to a 50 micron fiber.

Figure 3-37 Splicing of Different Types of Fiber

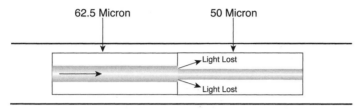

After the fiber-optic cable and connectors are installed, the connectors and the ends of the fibers must be kept spotlessly clean. The ends of the fibers should be covered with protective covers to prevent damage to the fiber ends. When these covers are removed prior to connecting the fiber to a port on a switch or router, the fiber ends must be cleaned. Clean the fiber ends with lint-free lens tissue moistened with pure isopropyl alcohol. The fiber ports on a switch or router should also be kept covered when not in use and cleaned with lens tissue and isopropyl alcohol before a connection is made. Dirty ends on a fiber cause a big drop in the amount of light that reaches the receiver.

All these factors, scattering, absorption, dispersion, improper installation, and dirty fiber ends, diminish the strength of the light signal and are referred to as fiber noise. Before using a fiber-optic cable, it must be tested to ensure that enough light actually reaches the receiver for it to detect the 0s (off) and 1s (on) in the signal.

When a fiber-optic link is being planned, the amount of signal power loss that can be tolerated must be calculated. This tolerance is referred to as the *optical link loss budget*. It is like your monthly financial budget. After all your expenses (attenuations) are subtracted from your initial income, enough money must be left to get you through the month.

The decibel (dB) is the unit used to measure the amount of power loss. It tells what percent of the power that leaves the transmitter actually enters the receiver.

Testing fiber links is extremely important, and records of the results of these tests must be kept. Several types of fiber-optic test equipment are used. Two of the most important instruments are Optical Loss Meters and Optical Time Domain Reflectometers (OTDRs).

These meters both test optical cable to ensure that the cable meets the TIA standards for fiber. They also test to verify that the link power loss does not fall below the optical link loss budget. OTDRs can provide a lot of detailed diagnostic information about a fiber link and can be used to troubleshoot a link when problems occur.

More Information: Wireless Communications

Wireless signals are electromagnetic waves that can travel through the vacuum of outer space or through a medium such as air. No physical copper-based or fiber-optic medium is necessary for wireless signals, which makes utilizing wireless signals a very versatile way to build a network. Wireless transmissions can cover large distances by using high-frequency signals. Each signal uses a different frequency measured in hertz so that they remain unique from one another.

Wireless technologies have been around for many years. Satellite TV, AM/FM radio, cellular phones, remote-control devices, radar, alarm systems, weather radios, cordless phones, and retail scanners are integrated into everyday life. Today, wireless technologies are a fundamental part of business and personal life.

Wireless Data Communications

The radio spectrum is the part of the electromagnetic spectrum used to transmit voice, video, and data. It uses frequencies from 3 kilohertz (kHz) to 300 gigahertz (GHz). This section considers only the part of the radio spectrum that supports wireless data transmission.

Many different types of wireless data communications exist, as illustrated in Figure 3-38.

Figure 3-38 Wireless Data Networks

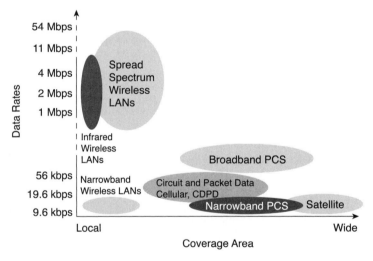

Each type of wireless data communication has its advantages and drawbacks, as follows:

- **Infrared (IR)**—Very high data rates and lower cost, but very short distance.

- **Narrowband**—Low data rates and medium cost. Requires a license and covers a limited distance.

- **Spread spectrum**—Medium cost and high data rates. Limited to campus coverage. Cisco Aironet products are spread spectrum.

More Information: Wireless Communications (Continued)

- **Broadband personal communications service (PCS)**—Low data rates, medium cost, and citywide coverage. Sprint is an exception; Sprint PCS provides nationwide and international coverage.

- **Circuit and packet data (cellular data and Cellular Digital Packet Data [CDPD])**—Low data rates, high packet fees, and national coverage.

- **Satellite**—Variable data rates depending on type of service, high cost, and nationwide or worldwide coverage.

Wireless Signal

When a signal is transmitted in a data format, you must consider the following three parameters:

- **How fast**—What data rate can be achieved?

- **How far**—How far can wireless LAN (WLAN) units be placed apart and still get the maximum data rate?

- **How many**—How many users can exist without slowing the data rate?

These parameters all relate to the ability to receive a good signal as far away as possible. Increasing the amount of data requires the use of more frequency spectra or a different method of placing the data on the radio frequency (RF) signal.

RF efficiency is affected by the following three factors, as shown in Figure 3-39:

- **Type of modulation used**—More complex modulation techniques provide greater throughput.

- **Distance**—The farther the signal must be transmitted, the weaker the signal becomes.

- **Noise**—Electronic noise and barriers negatively affect RF.

Figure 3-39 Factors Affecting RF Efficiency

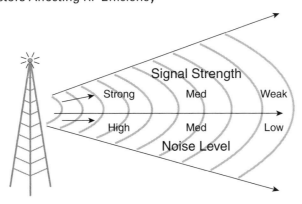

The following sections discuss these three factors in greater detail.

More Information: Wireless Communications (Continued)

Modulation

Modulation is the process by which the amplitude, frequency, or phase of an RF or light wave is altered to transmit data. The characteristics of the carrier wave instantaneously are varied by another modulating waveform. Modulation blends a data signal (text, voice, and so on) into a carrier for transmission over a network.

The most common methods of modulation are as follows (see Figure 3-40):

- *Amplitude modulation (AM)*—Modulates the height of the carrier wave
- *Frequency modulation (FM)*—Modulates the frequency of the wave
- *Phase modulation (PM)*—Modulates the polarity (phase) of the wave

Figure 3-40 Modulation

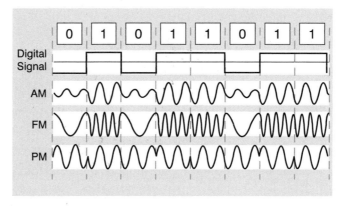

Effects of Distance on a Signal

As a receiver moves farther from a transmitter, the signal gets weaker, and the difference between the signal and noise becomes less. Eventually, the signal cannot be distinguished from the noise, and loss of communication occurs. The amount of compression (or modulation scheme) at which the signal is transmitted determines the amount of signal needed to be heard through the noise. As transmission, or modulation schemes (compression), becomes more complex and data rates increase, immunity to noise lessens. Therefore, the distance is reduced.

Effects of Noise on a Signal

To be received correctly, complex modulation schemes require optimal signal-to-noise ratios (more signal with less noise). If there is noise on the channel, the line speed is reduced. Noise, speed, and distance are all interrelated.

Electronic noise and barriers negatively affect RF efficiency. An exact transmission distance for WLAN products cannot be provided without going to the site and actually testing the environment. Walls with internal metal structures, for example, greatly limit RF transmission range.

More Information: Wireless Communications (Continued)

Radio Frequency Bands

Most radio frequencies are licensed by government agencies, such as the Federal Communications Commission (FCC) in the United States. To broadcast over these frequencies, you need to have a license and to pay a fee.

Unlicensed frequency bands are easier to implement and cost less over time because they do not require licenses. Three unlicensed bands exist, as illustrated in Figure 3-41:

- **900 megahertz (MHz)**—The 900-MHz band carries cordless and cellular phones.

- **2.4 gigahertz (GHz)**—The 802.11g and 802.11b standard, the most widely deployed wireless standard, operates in the 2.4-GHz unlicensed radio band, delivering a maximum data rate of 11 Mbps.

- **5 GHz**—Recently, the FCC opened up the 5-GHz band for unlicensed use by high-speed data communications devices. Cisco has acquired 5-GHz technology and uses this frequency in new products, such as the Cisco Aironet 1200 series, which is dual band, delivering support for both 2.4 GHz (802.11b) and 5 GHz (802.11a) standards. The 802.11a standard can deliver a maximum data rate of 54 Mbps.

Figure 3-41 Unlicensed Frequency Bands

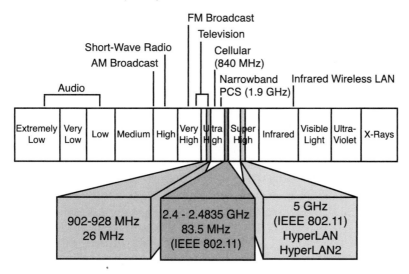

A relationship exists between the frequency and the amount of data that can be sent. The concept is like that of a pipe. The wider the bandwidth is, the more frequencies are available. The wider the spectrum is, the higher the data rate can be transmitted. The amount of spectrum available determines the data rate.

More Information: Wireless Communications (Continued)

Because the 900-MHz band supports cellular phones and other consumer products, the band has become overcrowded. As a result, users often experience interference or cannot access the network. As a benefit, 900 MHz offers longer range (for the same gain antennas) than 2.4 GHz. The drawback of 900 MHz is that the fastest, most reliable data rate is only 1 Mbps because of its limited frequency range.

The 2.4-GHz frequency range is much wider than 900 MHz, allowing higher data rates with a reliable range of up to 25 miles. The Cisco Aironet 340 Wireless LAN Series can deliver 11-Mbps throughput because it operates in the 2.4-GHz frequency.

Cisco has acquired 5-GHz technology and will deliver products for the 5-GHz frequency range because its wider bandwidth allows for faster throughput of data. The Cisco Aironet 5 GHz 54 Mbps Wireless LAN client adapter is an IEEE 802.11a-compliant CardBus adapter that operates in the UNII-1 and UNII-2 bands. The client adapter complements the Cisco Aironet 1200 Series 802.11a Access Point, providing a solution that combines performance and mobility with the security and manageability that enterprises require. It will be possible to achieve data rates of greater than 20 Mbps in this frequency range. The drawback of the 5-GHz frequency, however, is its limited range. The typical range for 5 GHz inside is about 50 feet; outside poses a limitation of approximately 2500 feet.

Spread-Spectrum Technology

Narrowband interference occurs when two signals are broadcasting at the same frequency in the same geographic area. The term *band* refers to a grouping of frequencies; narrowband would mean a relatively smaller range of frequencies. Narrowband noise might disrupt certain channels or spread-spectrum components.

Just as the radio in your car has AM and FM bands, other radios use certain bands, frequencies, and types of modulation. *Spread spectrum (SS)* is a modulation technique developed in the 1940s that spreads a transmission signal over a broad band of radio frequencies. The term *spread spectrum* describes a modulation technique that sacrifices bandwidth to gain signal-to-noise performance. This technique is ideal for data communications because it is less susceptible to radio noise and creates little interference.

Spread spectrum, as illustrated in Figure 3-42, is a system in which the transmitted signal is spread over a frequency much wider than the minimum bandwidth required to send the signal. The fundamental premise is that in channels with narrowband interference, increasing the transmitted signal bandwidth results in an increased probability that the received information is correct.

Figure 3-42 Spread-Spectrum Technology

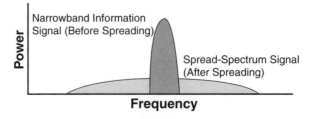

More Information: Wireless Communications (Continued)

To use the unlicensed radio bands, you have to use spread-spectrum techniques. *Frequency-hopping spread spectrum (FHSS)* and *direct-sequence spread spectrum (DSSS)* are two ways of doing spread spectrum. These spread-spectrum techniques spread the RF energy over the available band. The next sections describe FHSS and DSSS in more detail.

FHSS Versus DSSS

As modulation techniques, both FHSS and DSSS have advantages and limitations.

With FHSS technology, transmissions hop from one frequency to another in random patterns. Figure 3-43 illustrates an example of an FHSS. In this example, the transmission hops from C (2.42 GHz), to A (2.40 GHz), to D (2.43 GHz), then to B (2.41 GHz), and finally to E (2.44 GHz). This technique enables the transmissions to hop around narrowband interference, resulting in a clearer signal and higher reliability of the transmission. However, FHSS technology is slower, and the receiver must use the same pattern to decode.

Figure 3-43 Frequency-Hopping Spread Spectrum

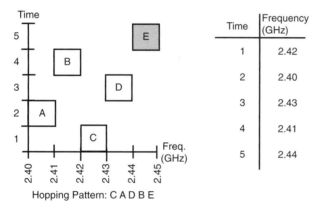

Time	Frequency (GHz)
1	2.42
2	2.40
3	2.43
4	2.41
5	2.44

Hopping Pattern: C A D B E

DSSS technology transmissions, as illustrated in Figure 3-44, are more reliable because each bit (1 or 0) is represented by a string of 1s and 0s called a *chipping sequence*. Even if up to 40 percent of the string is lost, the original transmission can be reconstructed. DSSS technology also enables high throughput of data and longer-range access.

More Information: Wireless Communications (Continued)

Figure 3-44 Direct-Sequence Spread Spectrum

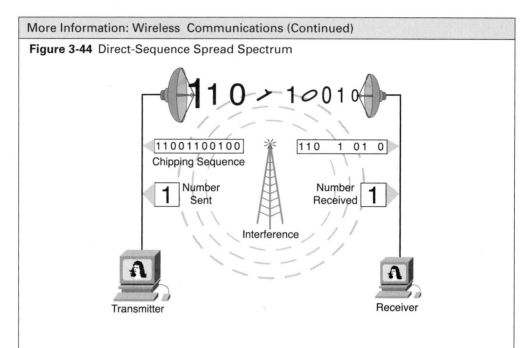

Limited to a 2-Mbps data-transfer rate, FHSS is recommended for only very specific applications, such as for certain types of watercraft. For all other wireless LAN applications, DSSS is the better choice. The recently released evolution of the IEEE standard, 802.11b, provides for a full Ethernet-like data rate of 11 Mbps over DSSS. FHSS does not support data rates greater than 2 Mbps.

Wireless Media

When the computer was first introduced to the world, it was affordable by only large corporations, governments, and universities. From the first building-sized devices with minimal computing power to those that fit in the palm of a person's hand, huge leaps in technology have occurred. The same is true on the connectivity side of the industry.

The various types of networking discussed earlier in this chapter have all involved physical connectivity. The advantages are speed, reliability, and to a certain extent, convenience. Physical connectivity allows an increase in productivity by allowing the sharing of printers, servers, and software. However, networked systems require that the workstation remain stationary, permitting moves only within the limits of the media and office area.

The introduction of wireless technology removes these restraints and brings true portability to the computing world. While the current state of wireless technology does not provide the high-speed transfers of cabled networks nor the security and uptime reliability, the flexibility justifies the trade off.

When considering the installation of a network in an existing facility, wireless is at the top of many an administrator's lists of options. A simple wireless network can be up and running in just a few minutes after the workstations are turned on. Connectivity to the Internet is provided through a wired connection, router, cable modem, or Digital Subscriber Line (DSL) modem, and a wireless access point that acts as a hub for the wireless nodes. In a residential or small office environment these devices might be combined into a single unit.

Wireless LAN Organization and Standards

An understanding of the regulations and standards that apply to wireless technology ensures that deployed networks are interoperable and in compliance. Just as in cabled networks, IEEE is the prime issuer of standards for wireless networks. The standards have been created within the framework of the regulations set forth by the FCC.

A key technology contained within the IEEE 802.11 standard is Direct Sequence Spread Spectrum (DSSS) . DSSS applies to wireless devices operating within a 1- to 2-Mbps range. A DSSS system can operate at up to 11 Mbps but is not considered compliant above 2 Mbps. The next standard approved was IEEE 802.11b, which increased transmission capabilities to 11 Mbps. Even though DSSS WLANs are able to interoperate with the FHSS WLANs, problems developed prompting design changes by the manufacturers. In this case, IEEE's task was simply to create a standard that matched the manufacturer's solution.

IEEE 802.11b, called Wi-Fi or high-speed wireless, refers to DSSS systems that operate at 1, 2, 5.5, and 11 Mbps. All 802.11b systems are backward-compliant in that they also support 802.11 for 1- and 2-Mbps data rates for DSSS only. This backward compatibility is extremely important because it allows upgrading of the wireless network without replacing the network interface cards (NICs) or access points.

IEEE 802.11b devices achieve the higher data throughput rate by using a different coding technique from 802.11, allowing for a greater amount of data to be transferred in the same time frame. The majority of 802.11b devices still fail to match the 10-Mbps throughput of wired Ethernet, and generally function in the 2- to 4-Mbps range.

802.11a covers WLAN devices operating in the 5-GHz transmission band. Using the 5-GHz range disallows interoperability of 802.11b devices as they operate within 2.4 GHz. 802.11a is capable of supplying data throughput of 54 Mpbs and, with proprietary technology known as *rate doubling*, has achieved 108 Mbps. In production networks a more standard rating is 20 to 26 Mbps.

802.11g provides the same throughput as 802.11a but with backwards compatibility for 802.11g devices using Orthogonal Frequency Division Multiplexing (OFDM) modulation technology. Cisco has developed an access point that permits 802.11b and 802.11a devices to coexist on the same WLAN. The access point supplies gateway services allowing these otherwise incompatible devices to communicate.

Wireless Devices and Topologies

A wireless network can consist of as few as two devices, two nodes with wireless NICs. Figure 3-45 shows an internal wireless NIC, and Figure 3-46 shows an external USB wireless NIC. The nodes can be desktop workstations or notebook computers. Equipped with wireless NICs, an *ad hoc* network can be established that equates to a peer-to-peer wired network. Both devices act as servers and clients in this environment, and although it does provide connectivity, security is at a minimum along with throughput. Another problem with this type of network is compatibility; oftentimes, NICs from different manufacturers do not interoperate.

Figure 3-45 Internal Wireless NIC

Figure 3-46 External USB Wireless NIC

More commonly, an access point (AP), as shown in Figure 3-47, is installed, acting as a central hub for the WLAN *infrastructure mode*. The AP is hard wired to the cabled LAN to provide Internet access and connectivity to the wired network. APs are equipped with antennae and provide wireless connectivity over a specified area referred to as a cell.

Figure 3-47 Access Point

Depending on the structural composition of the location in which the AP is installed and the size and gain of the antennae, the size of the cell can range from a few dozen feet to 25 miles. More commonly, the range is from 300 to 500 feet. To service larger areas, multiple APs can be installed with a degree of overlap, permitting *roaming* between cells, as illustrated in Figure 3-48. This roaming is very similar to the services provided by cellular phone companies. Overlap on multiple AP networks is critical to allow for movement of devices within the WLAN, and although it is not addressed in the IEEE standards, a 20–30 percent overlap is desirable. This rate of overlap permits roaming between cells, allowing for the disconnect/reconnect activity to occur seamlessly without service interruption.

When a client is activated within the WLAN, it starts listening for a compatible device with which to associate. This process is referred to as *scanning* and can be active or passive.

Active scanning causes a probe request to be sent from the wireless node seeking to join the network. The probe request contains the Service Set Identifier (SSID) of the network it wants to join. When an AP with the same SSID is found, the AP issues a probe response, and the authentication and association steps are completed.

Figure 3-48 Roaming

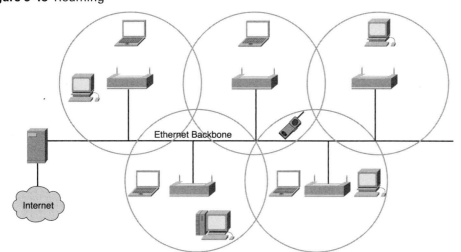

Passive scanning nodes listen for beacon management frames (beacons), which are transmitted by the AP (infrastructure mode) or peer nodes (ad hoc). When a node receives a beacon that contains the SSID of the network it is trying to join, an attempt is made to join the network. Passive scanning is a continuous process, and nodes can associate or disassociate with APs as signal strength changes.

How Wireless LANs Communicate

After establishing connectivity to the WLAN, a node passes frames similarly to any other 802 network. WLANs do not use a standard 802.3 frame. Therefore, using the term *wireless Ethernet* is misleading. There are three types of frames: control, management, and data. The following lists the frames that are included in each type of frame:

- Management frames
  - Association request frame
  - Association response frame
  - Probe request frame
  - Probe response frame
  - Beacon frame
  - Authentication frame
- Control frames
  - Request to send (RTS)
  - Clear to send (CTS)
  - Acknowledgment
- Data frames

Only the data frame type is similar to 802.3 frames. However, the payload of wireless and 802.3 frames is 1500 bytes, and an Ethernet frame cannot exceed 1518 bytes. On the other hand, a wireless frame can be as large as 2346 bytes. Usually, the WLAN frame size is limited to 1518 bytes because it is most commonly connected to a wired Ethernet network.

Because RF is a shared medium, collisions can occur just as they do on wired shared medium. The significant difference is that there is no method by which the source node is able to detect that a collision has occurred. In view of this, WLANs use carrier sense multiple access with collision avoidance (CSMA/CA). This feature is somewhat like Ethernet carrier sense multiple access collision detect (CSMA/CD). Chapter 6, "Ethernet Fundamentals," discusses CSMA/CD in greater detail.

When a source node sends a frame, the receiving node returns a positive acknowledgment (ACK), which can consequently cause consumption of 50 percent of the available bandwidth. This overhead, when combined with the collision avoidance protocol overhead, reduces the actual data throughput to a maximum of 5.0 to 5.5 Mbps on an IEEE 802.11b wireless LAN rated at 11 Mbps.

Performance of the network will also be affected by signal strength and degradation in signal quality due to distance or interference. As the signal becomes weaker, Adaptive Rate Selection (ARS) can be invoked, and the transmitting unit drops the data rate from 11 Mbps to 5.5 Mbps, from 5.5 Mbps to 2 Mbps, or 2 Mbps to 1 Mbps, as illustrated in Figure 3-49.

Authentication and Association

WLAN authentication occurs at Layer 2 and is the process of authenticating the device, not the user. This point is a critical one to remember when considering WLAN security, troubleshooting, and overall management.

Authentication might be a null process, as in the case of a new AP and NIC with default configurations in place. The client sends an authentication request frame to the AP, and the frame is accepted or rejected by the AP. The client is notified of either course of action via an authentication response frame. The AP might also be configured to hand off the authentication task to an authentication server, which performs a more thorough credentialing process.

Figure 3-49 Adaptive Rate Selection

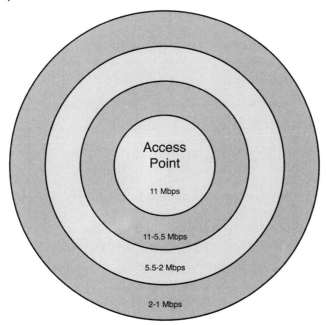

Association, performed after authentication, is the state that permits a client to use the AP's services to transfer data.

Authentication and Association Types

The authentication and association types are as follows:

- **Unauthenticated and unassociated**—The node is disconnected from the network and not associated to an access point.

- **Authenticated and unassociated**—The node has been authenticated on the network but has not yet associated with the access point.

- **Authenticated and associated**—The node is connected to the network and able to transmit and receive data through the access point.

Methods of Authentication

IEEE 802.11 lists two types of authentication processes:

- **Open system**—This process is an open connectivity standard in which only the SSID must match. It can be used in a secure or non-secure environment, although the ability of low-level network sniffers to ascertain the SSID of the WLAN is fairly high.

- **Shared key**—This process requires the use of Wired Equivalent Privacy (WEP) encryption. WEP is a fairly simple algorithm using 64- and 128-bit keys. The AP is configured with an encrypted key, and nodes attempting to access the network through the AP must have a matching key. Statically assigned WEP keys provide a higher level of security than the open system but are definitely not hack proof.

The susceptibility to unauthorized entry into WLANs is being addressed by a number of emerging security solution technologies.

The Radiowave and Microwave Spectrums

Computers send data signals electronically. Radio transmitters convert these electrical signals to radio waves. The radio waves are generated by changing electric currents in a transmitter's antenna. These radio waves radiate out in straight lines from the antenna. However, radio waves weaken (attenuate) as they move out from the transmitting antenna. In a WLAN, a radio signal measured at a distance of just 10 meters (30 feet) from the transmitting antenna is only 1/1000th of its original strength. Like light, radio waves can be absorbed by some materials and reflected by others. When passing from one material, like air, into another material, like a plaster wall, radio waves are refracted (bent). Radio waves are also scattered and absorbed by water droplets in the air.

These qualities of radio waves are important to remember when a WLAN is being planned for a building or for a campus. The process of evaluating a location for the installation of a WLAN is called making a site survey.

Because radio signals weaken as they travel away from the transmitter, the receiver must also be equipped with an antenna. When radio waves hit a receiver's antenna, weak electric currents are generated in that antenna. These electric currents, caused by the received radio waves, are equal to the currents that originally generated the radio waves in the transmitter's antenna. The receiver amplifies the strength of these weak electrical signals.

In a transmitter, the electrical (data) signals from a computer or a LAN are not sent directly into the transmitter's antenna. Rather these data signals are used to alter a second, strong signal called the carrier signal.

A receiver demodulates the carrier signal that arrives from its antenna. The receiver interprets the phase changes of the carrier signal and reconstructs from it the original electrical data signal.

Signals and Noise on a WLAN

On a wired Ethernet network, it is usually a fairly simple process to diagnose the cause of interference. When using RF technology, you must take into account many kinds of interference:

- **Narrowband**—This is the opposite of spread-spectrum technology. As the name implies, narrowband does not affect the entire frequency spectrum of the wireless signal. One solution to a narrowband interference problem is simply changing the channel that the AP is using. Actually, diagnosing the cause of narrowband interference can be a costly and time-consuming experience. To identify the source requires a spectrum analyzer and even a low-cost model can cost $3000 to $4000 in the U.S. Examples of narrowband interference include CB radios and ham radios.

- **All band**—All band interference affects the entire spectrum range. Bluetooth technologies hop across the entire 2.4 GHz many times per second and can cause significant interference on an 802.11b network. It is not uncommon to see signs in facilities that use wireless networks requesting that all Bluetooth devices be shut down before entering. In homes and offices, a device that is often overlooked as causing interference is the standard microwave oven. Leakage from a microwave of as little as 1 watt into the RF spectrum can cause major network disruption. Wireless phones operating in the 2.4-GHz spectrum can also cause network degradation.

- **Weather**—Generally, the RF signal is not affected by even the most extreme weather conditions. However, fog or very high moisture conditions can and do affect wireless networks. Lightning can also charge the atmosphere and alter the path of a transmitted signal.

The first and most obvious source of a signal problem is the transmitting station and antenna type. A higher output station transmits the signal further, and a parabolic dish antenna that concentrates the signal increases the transmission range.

In a small office, home office (SOHO) environment, most access points utilize twin omnidirectional antennae that transmit the signal in all directions, thereby reducing the range of communication. Figure 3-50 illustrates an omnidirectional antenna.

Figure 3-50 Omnidirectional Antenna

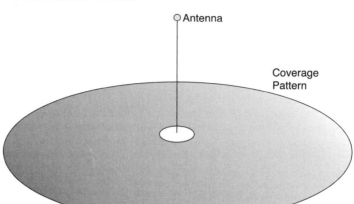

Wireless Security

The exponential growth of networking, including wireless technologies, has led to increased security risks. Increasing the security means increasing the time spent managing the system.

The first level of security in a wireless LAN consists of protecting the radio frequency waveform itself. Wireless access points radiate radio waves over a large area that is not contained in a physical building, which makes the radio waves accessible to eavesdroppers and increases vulnerability. The radio waves of wireless bridges are concentrated in a beam. An eavesdropper must get into the beam path to intercept the communication. Therefore, wireless access points usually require better security than wireless bridges.

WEP

Wired equivalent privacy (WEP) is a security mechanism, defined within the 802.11 standard, that is designed to protect the over-the-air transmission between wireless LAN access points and NICs. The IEEE 802.11b requires 40-bit encryption keys. However, many vendors, such as Cisco, support the optional 128-bit standard.

The main goals with WEP follow:

- Deny access to the network by unauthorized users who do not possess the appropriate WEP key

- Prevent the decoding of captured WLAN traffic that is WEP-encrypted without the possession of the WEP key

WEP uses the RC4 stream cipher that was invented by Ron Rivest of RSA Data Security, Inc., (RSADSI) for encryption. The RC4 encryption algorithm is a symmetric-stream cipher that supports a variable-length key. A symmetric cipher uses the same key for both encryption and decryption. The key is the one piece of information that must be shared by both the encrypting and decrypting endpoints.

Recently, encryption analysts have reported weaknesses in the authentication and WEP encryption schemes in the IEEE 802.11 WLAN standard. Improvements on WEP have been developed to address the weaknesses found by encryption analysts. However, it is not recommended to use WEP as a sole security mechanism for a WLAN. WEP should be supplemented with additional higher-level security mechanisms, such as a VPN or firewalls.

VPN, EAP, and LEAP

A number of new security solutions and protocols, such as Virtual Private Network (VPN) and Extensible Authentication Protocol (EAP) are evolving. Using EAP, the access point does not provide authentication to the client but passes the duties to a more sophisticated server designed for that purpose. Using an integrated VPN server, VPN technology creates a tunnel on top of an existing protocol such as IP. This tunnel is a Layer 3 connection as opposed to the Layer 2 connection between the AP and the sending node.

The following list briefly describes EAP and LEAP:

- **EAP-MD5 Challenge**—EAP is the earliest authentication type, which is very similar to Challenge Handshake Authentication Protocol (CHAP) password protection on a wired network. EAP allows wireless client adapters that can support different authentication types to communicate with different back end servers, such as Remote Authentication Dial-In User Service (RADIUS).

- **Lightweight Extensible Authentication Protocol (LEAP)**—Cisco has developed a derivation of EAP based on mutual authentication called LEAP. Mutual authentication means that both the user and the access point to which the user is attempting to connect must be authenticated before access onto the corporate network is allowed. Mutual authentication protects enterprises from unauthorized APs serving as a potential entrance into the network. LEAP is the type of authentication primarily used on Cisco WLAN access points. LEAP provides security during credential exchange, encrypts using dynamic WEP keys, and supports mutual authentication.

VPN security levels include the following:

- **User authentication**—Allows only authorized users to connect, send, and receive data over the wireless network.

- **Encryption**—Provides encryption services, further protecting the data from intruders.

- **Data authentication**—Ensures the integrity of the data, authenticating source, and destination devices.

VPN technology effectively closes the wireless network because an unrestricted WLAN automatically forwards traffic between nodes that appear to be on the same wireless network. WLANS often extend outside the perimeter of the home or office in which they are installed, and without security, intruders can infiltrate the network with little effort. Conversely, it takes minimal effort on the part of the network administrator to provide low-level security to the WLAN.

Summary

In this chapter, you learned the following key points:

- All matter is composed of atoms. The three main parts of an atom are protons, neutrons, and electrons. The protons and neutrons are located in the center part of the atom (nucleus).

- Electrostatic discharge (ESD) can create serious problems for sensitive electronic equipment.

- Attenuation refers to the resistance to the flow of electrons, and why a signal becomes degraded as it travels.

- Currents flow in closed loops called circuits, which must be composed of conducting materials and must have sources of voltage.

- A multimeter measures voltage, current, resistance, and other electrical quantities expressed in numeric form.

- Three types of copper cables used in networking are straight-through, crossover, and rollover.

- Coaxial cable consists of a hollow outer cylindrical conductor that surrounds a single inner wire conductor.

- UTP cable is a four-pair wire medium used in a variety of networks.

- STP cable combines the techniques of shielding, cancellation, and twisting of wires.

- Optical fiber is a good transmission medium when it is properly installed, tested, and maintained.

- Light energy, a type of electromagnetic energy wave, is used to transmit large amounts of data securely over relatively long distances.

- The light signal carried by a fiber is produced by a transmitter that converts an electrical signal into a light signal.

- The receiver converts light that arrives at the far end of the cable back to the original electrical signal.

- Fibers are used in pairs to provide full-duplex communications.

- Light rays obey the laws of reflection and refraction as they travel through a glass fiber. This allows fibers with the property of total internal reflection to be manufactured.

- Total internal reflection makes light signals stay inside the fiber, even if the fiber is not straight.

- Attenuation of a light signal becomes a problem over long cables, especially if sections of cable are connected at patch panels or spliced.

- Cables and connectors must be properly installed and thoroughly tested with high-quality optical-test equipment before being used.

- Cable links must be tested periodically with high-quality optical test equipment to check whether the link has deteriorated in any way.

- Always take care to protect your eyes when intense light sources, such as lasers, are used.

- Understanding the regulations and standards that apply to wireless technology ensures that deployed networks will be interoperable.

- Compatibility problems with NICs are solved by installing an access point (AP) to act as a central hub for the WLAN.

- Three types of frames are used in wireless communication: control, management, and data.

- WLANs use carrier sense multiple access/collision avoidance (CSMA/CA).

- WLAN authentication authenticates the device, not the user.

- Wireless standards include IEEE 802.11, IEEE 802.11a, IEEE 802.11b, and IEEE 802.11g.

- Wireless devices include PCMCIA NICs for laptops, external USB wireless NICs, access points, and wireless LANs.

Key Terms

AM (amplitude modulation)   Modulates the height of the carrier wave.

angle of incidence   The angle at which the ray hits the glass surface.

angle of reflection   The angle between the reflected ray and the normal.

attenuation   Loss of communication signal energy.

backbone   The part of a network that acts as the primary path for traffic that is most often sourced from, and destined for, other networks.

coaxial cable   A cable consisting of a hollow outer cylindrical conductor that surrounds a single inner wire conductor.

crosstalk   The unwanted reception of electromagnetic signals on a wire from a nearby wire.

dispersion   The broadening of light signals along the length of the fiber.

DSSS (direct-sequence spread spectrum)   A technology in which transmissions are more reliable because each bit (1 or 0) is represented by a string of 1s and 0s, called a chipping sequence.

EIA (Electronic Industries Association)   A group that specifies electrical transmission standards. The EIA and TIA have developed numerous well-known communication standards.

EMI (electromagnetic interference)   An electromagnetic field that has the potential to disrupt the operation of electronic components, devices, and systems in its vicinity.

FHSS (frequency-hopping spread spectrum)   A technology in which transmissions hop from one frequency to another in random patterns. This feature enables the transmissions to hop around narrowband interference, resulting in a clearer signal and higher reliability of the transmission.

fiber-optic cable   A physical medium capable of conducting modulated light transmission. Compared with other transmission media, fiber-optic cable is more expensive but is not susceptible to electromagnetic interference. Sometimes called optical fiber.

FM (frequency modulation)   Modulates the frequency of the wave.

IEEE (Institute of Electrical and Electronic Engineers)   A professional organization whose activities include the development of communications and network standards. IEEE LAN standards are the predominant LAN standards.

impedance   The resistance to the movement of electrons in an AC circuit.

media   The plural of medium. Media refers to various physical environments through which transmission signals pass. Common network media include twisted-pair, coaxial, fiber-optic cable, and the atmosphere (through which microwave, laser, and infrared transmission occurs).

modal dispersion   When multiple modes of light propagating through fiber travel different distances, depending on their entry angles, which causes them to arrive at the destination (receiving end of the cable) at slightly different times.

multimode   A type of fiber-optic cable that transmits more than one light path.

noise   An unwanted electrical signal on a wire that interferes with the quality of the signal by altering its shape.

patch panel   An assembly of pin locations and ports that can be mounted on a rack or wall bracket in the wiring closet. Patch panels act like switchboards that connect workstations' cables to each other and to the outside.

PM (phase modulation)   Modulates the polarity (phase) of the wave.

reflection   The photons of light striking a surface and leaving that surface in an equal but opposite direction.

refraction   The change in direction of a beam of light when it enters another medium.

resistance   The property of a material that resists electron movement.

RFI (radio frequency interference)   The noise on wires caused by radio signals.

single-mode   An optical fiber that has only one mode of light transmission. Contrast with multimode.

SS (spread spectrum)   A modulation technique developed in the 1940s that spreads a transmission signal over a broad band of radio frequencies. The term spread spectrum describes a modulation technique that sacrifices bandwidth to gain signal-to-noise performance.

standard   A set of rules or procedures that are either widely used or officially specified.

STP (shielded twisted-pair)   A two-pair wiring medium used in a variety of network implementations. STP cabling has a layer of shielded insulation to reduce EMI.

thicknet   An early form of coaxial cable using 10BASE5 for networking. Thicknet was once desirable because it could carry signals up to 500 meters.

thinnet   A simple, thin, coaxial network cable for the 10BASE2 system. Thinnet can carry a signal only 185 meters, but was much easier to work with than thicknet.

TIA (Telecommunications Industry Association)   A standards association that publishes standards for telecommunications.

UTP (unshielded twisted-pair)   A four-pair wire medium used in a variety of networks.

wavelength   The length of a wave measured from any point on one wave to the corresponding point on the next wave. The wavelength of light is usually measured in nanometers (nm).

WEP (wired equivalent privacy)   A security mechanism, defined within the 802.11 standard, that is designed to protect the over-the-air transmission between wireless LAN APs and NICs.

Check Your Understanding

Complete all the review questions to test your understanding of the topics and concepts in this chapter. Answers are listed in Appendix B, "Check Your Understanding Answer Key."

1. Match the columns:

   1) Neutrons   A) Particles that have a negative charge

   2) Protons   B) Particles that have no charge (neutral)

   3) Electrons   C) Particles that have a positive charge

   A. 1-C, 2-B, 3-A

   B. 1-A, 2-C, 3-B

   C. 1-B, 2-C, 3-A

   D. 1-B, 2-A, 3-C

2. Which of the following regarding electricity is untrue?

   A. Opposite charges react to each other with a force that causes them to be attracted to each other.

   B. Like charges react to each other with a force that causes them to repel each other.

   C. In the case of opposite and like charges, the force increases as the charges move closer to each other.

   D. None of the above.

3. Match the following to their respective units of measurement:

   1) Voltage   A) Ohm

   2) Current   B) Ampere

   3) Resistance   C) Volt

   A. 1-C, 2-B, 3-A

   B. 1-B, 2-C, 3-A

   C. 1-A, 2-C, 3-B

   D. 1-C, 2-B, 3-A

4. Electrons flow in _____ loops called _____.

   A. Open; voltage

   B. Closed; voltage

   C. Open; circuits

   D. Closed, circuits

5. What is the maximum cable length for STP?

   A. 100 feet

   B. 150 feet

   C. 10 meters

   D. 100 meters

6. How many pairs of wires make up a UTP cable?

   A. 2

   B. 4

   C. 6

   D. 8

7. Which connector does UTP use?

   A. STP

   B. BNC

   C. RJ-45

   D. RJ-69

8. What is an advantage that coaxial cable has over STP or UTP?

   A. It is capable of achieving 10 Mbps to 100 Mbps.

   B. It is inexpensive.

   C. It can run for a longer distance unboosted.

   D. None of the above.

9. What does the twisting of the wires do in a twisted-pair cable?

   A. It makes it thinner.

   B. It makes it less expensive.

   C. It reduces noise problems.

   D. It allows six pairs to fit in the space of four pairs.

10. What is the importance of the EIA/TIA standards? Select all that apply.

   A. They provide a framework for the implementation of the OSI reference model.

   B. They provide guidelines for manufacturers to follow to ensure compatibility.

   C. They provide the minimum media requirements for multiproduct and multivendor environments.

   D. None of the above.

11. A fiber-optic cable transmits multiple streams of LED-generated light.

   A. Multimode

   B. Multichannel

   C. Multiphase

   D. None of the above

12. What is one advantage of using fiber optic cable in networks?

   A. It is inexpensive.

   B. It is easy to install.

   C. It is an industry standard and is available at any electronics store.

   D. It is capable of higher data rates than either coaxial or twisted-pair cable.

CHAPTER 4

Cabling Testing

Objectives

Upon completion of this chapter, you should be able to answer the following questions:

- What are the differences between sine waves and square waves?

- How do analog signals vary with time and frequency?

- What are the two types of basic copper cable?

- How does fiber-optic cable transmit data signals?

- What is attenuation?

- What are some sources of noise on copper media?

- What are the three types of crosstalk?

- What are the ten primary cable-testing parameters used to meet the TIA/EIA standards?

Additional Topics of Interest

In addition to the core objective areas, this chapter introduces you to the following topics of interest to networkers:

- Exponents and logarithms

- Decibels

- Signals viewed in time and frequency

- Noise in time and frequency

- The units of analog and digital bandwidth

- Time-based parameters

- How optical fiber is tested

- The Category 6 standard

Key Terms

The following is a list of key terms introduced in this chapter. For your reference, a definition for each term can be found at the end of the chapter.

wave   page 173

frequency   page 173

amplitude   page 173

hertz   page 173

pulse   page 174

sine waves   page 174

square waves   page 175

logarithms   page 176

decibel   page 176

oscilloscope   page 178

spectrum analyzer   page 178

noise   page 179

thermal noise   page 179

radio frequency interference (RFI)   page 179

electromagnetic interference (EMI)   page 179

white noise   page 179

narrowband interference   page 179

analog bandwidth   page 180

digital bandwidth   page 180

attenuation   page 184

impedance   page 185

jitter   page 185

crosstalk   page 185

alien crosstalk   page 185

near-end crosstalk (NEXT)   page 186

far-end crosstalk (FEXT)   page 187

power sum near-end crosstalk (PSNEXT)   page 187

TIA/EIA-568-B standard   page 188

insertion loss   page 190

equal-level far-end crosstalk (ELFEXT)   page 190

power sum equal-level far-end crosstalk (PSELFEXT)   page 190

propagation delay   page 190

delay skew   page 191

This chapter describes issues relating to the testing of media used for physical layer connectivity in local-area networks (LANs). In order for the LAN or WAN to function properly, the physical layer medium must meet the industry standards specified for the data rate used to transmit signals over Ethernet (10, 100, 1000, or 10,000 Mbps). The use of *signals* in this text refers to the data signals that move from the transmitter to the receiver. The signals weaken (attenuate) traveling over the physical media; however, the receiver must still be able to clearly determine the state of each bit of the data (1 or 0). Otherwise, the error rate on the network will be too high for the LAN or WAN connections to be useful.

Networking media is literally and physically the backbone of a network. Inferior-quality network cabling results in network failures and in networks with unreliable performance. All three categories of networking media (copper-based, optical fiber, and wireless) require testing and measurement to determine their quality, and this testing is the primary subject of this chapter.

Frequency-Based Cable Testing

The equipment used to perform quality testing and measurement of copper-based, optical fiber, and wireless networking media involves certain electrical and mathematical concepts and terms, such as signal, wave, frequency, and noise. Understanding this vocabulary is helpful when learning about networking, cabling, and cable testing.

Waves

A *wave* is energy traveling from one place to another. Many types of waves exist, but all can be described with similar vocabulary.

It is helpful to think of waves as disturbances. A bucket of water that is completely still, with no disturbances, does not have waves. Conversely, the ocean always has some sort of detectable waves due to disturbances such as wind and tide.

Ocean waves can be described in terms of their height, or amplitude, which can be measured in meters. They can also be described in terms of how frequently the waves reach the shore. This feature can be described in two similar ways: period and frequency. The period of the waves is the amount of time between each wave and is measured in seconds. The *frequency* is the number of waves that reach the shore each second.

The *amplitude* of an electrical signal represents its height just as in ocean waves, but it is measured in volts instead of meters. If the signal repeats itself regularly, then the period of the signal is the amount of time to complete one cycle of the signal. The period is measured in seconds, just as the period of ocean waves is the amount of time for one wave to complete. The frequency of an electrical signal is the number of complete cycles (or waves) per second and is measured in *hertz*.

If a disturbance is deliberately caused and involves a fixed, predictable duration, it is called a *pulse*. Pulses are important in electrical signals because they determine the value of the data being transmitted.

Figure 4-1 shows a representation of the concepts of amplitude and frequency.

Networking professionals are interested in specific types of waves:

- Voltage waves on copper media

- Light waves in optical fiber

- Alternating electric and magnetic fields called electromagnetic waves used in the wireless environment

Figure 4-1 Amplitude and Frequency

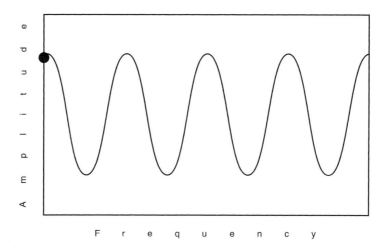

Sine Waves and Square Waves

Sine waves, or sinusoids, are graphs of mathematical functions, as shown in Figure 4-2.

Sine waves have certain characteristics:

- They are periodic (which means that they repeat the same pattern at regular intervals).

- They are continuously varying (which means that no two adjacent points on the graph have the same value).

Sine waves are graphical representations of many natural occurrences that change regularly over time, such as the distance from the earth to the sun, the distance from the ground while riding a Ferris wheel, and the time of day that the sun rises. Since sine waves are continuously varying, they are examples of analog waves.

Figure 4-2 Analog Signals

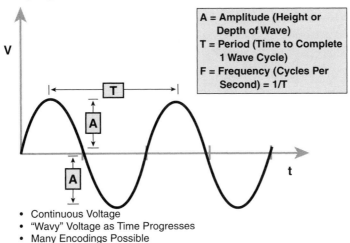

- Continuous Voltage
- "Wavy" Voltage as Time Progresses
- Many Encodings Possible

Square waves, like sine waves, are periodic. However, square wave graphs do not continuously vary with time. The values remain the same for some time, then suddenly change, then remain the same, and then suddenly return to the initial value, as shown in Figure 4-3. Square waves represent digital signals, or pulses. Square waves, like all waves, can be described in terms of amplitude, period, and frequency.

Figure 4-3 Digital Signals

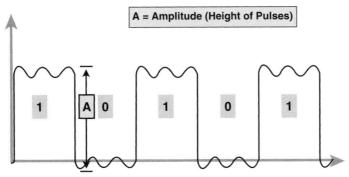

- Discrete Pulses (Not Continuous)
- Can Only Have One of Two States (1/0, On/Off)
- Voltage Jumps Between Levels

Exponents and Logarithms

As discussed in Chapter 1, "Introduction to Networking," in networking, it is important to remember the following three important number systems:

- Base 2 (binary)

- Base 10 (decimal)

- Base 16 (hexadecimal)

Recall that the base of a number system refers to the number of different symbols that can occupy one place. For example, binary– numbers have only two different placeholders (the numbers 0 and 1), decimal numbers have 10 different place holders (the numbers 0–9), and hexadecimal numbers have 16 different placeholders (the numbers 0–9 and the letters A–F).

Remember that 10 * 10 can be written as 10^2 (10 "squared," or 10 raised to the second power, or 10 multiplied by itself 2 times). 10 * 10 * 10 can be written as 10^3 (ten "cubed," or 10 raised to the third power, or 10 multiplied by itself 3 times). When written this way, you say that 10 is the base of the number and 2 or 3 is the exponent of the number. The following example demonstrates the preceding concepts.

$y = 10^x$	$y = 10^x$
x: 2	x: 3
y: 100	y: 1000

The base of a number system also refers to the value of each digit. The least significant digit has a value of $base^0$ (base raised to the zero power), or one. The next digit has a value of $base^1$. This is equal to 2 for binary numbers, 10 for decimal numbers, and 16 for hexadecimal numbers.

Numbers with exponents are used to more easily represent very large numbers. It is much easier and less error prone to represent one billion numerically as 10^9 than as 1,000,000,000. Many calculations involved in cable testing involve numbers that are very large, so exponents are the preferred format.

One way to work with the very large and very small numbers that occur in networking is to transform the numbers according to the rule, or mathematical function, known as the logarithm. *Logarithms* are referenced to the base of the number system being used. For example, base 10 logarithms are often abbreviated as log.

To take the "log" of a number, use a calculator. For example, log (10^9) equals 9, log (10^{-3}) = -3. You can also take the logarithm of numbers that are not powers of 10, but you cannot take the logarithm of a negative number. While the study of logarithms is beyond the scope of this course, the terminology is used commonly in calculating decibels, which is a way of measuring signals on copper, optical, and wireless media.

Decibels

An important way of describing networking signals is a unit of measure called the *decibel* (dB). The decibel is related to the exponents and logarithms described in prior sections. The formulas for calculating decibels are as follows:

Power Formula: $dB = 10 \log_{10} (P_{final} / P_{ref})$

or

Voltage Formula: $dB = 20 \log_{10} (V_{final} / V_{reference})$

Typically, light waves on optical fiber and radio waves in the air are measured using the power formula, and electromagnetic waves on copper cables are measured using the voltage formula. In these formulas,

- dB measures the loss or gain of the power of a wave. Decibels are usually negative numbers representing a loss in power as the wave travels, but can also be positive values representing a gain in power if the signal is amplified.

- $\log_{10}$ indicates that the number in parenthesis is transformed using the base 10 logarithm rule.

- P_{final} is the delivered power measured in watts.

- P_{ref} is the original power measured in watts.

- V_{final} is the delivered voltage measured in volts.

- V_{ref} is the original voltage measured in volts.

The following example illustrates how the dB value is calculated:

$$P_{final} = P_{\mathbf{ref}} * 10^{(\mathbf{dB/10})}$$

$$dB = 20$$

$$P_{ref} = 2 \text{ kilowatts}$$

$$P_{final} = 200 \text{ kilowatts}$$

When you enter values for dB and Pref, the resulting power changes. This calculation can be used to see how much power is left in a radio wave after it has traveled over a distance, through different materials, and through various stages of electronic systems such as a radio. To explore decibels further, try the following examples:

- If Pfinal is 1 microWatt ($1 * 10^{-6}$ watts) and Pref is 1 milliWatt ($1 * 10^{-3}$ watts), what is the gain or loss in decibels? Is this value positive or negative? Does the value represent a gain or a loss in power?

- If the total loss of a fiber link is -84 dB, and the source power of the original laser (Pref) is 1 milliWatt ($1 * 10^{-3}$ watts), how much power is delivered?

- If 2 microVolts ($2 * 10^{-6}$ volts) are measured at the end of a cable and the source voltage was 1 volt, what is the gain or loss in decibels? Is this value positive or negative? Does the value represent a gain or a loss in voltage?

Time and Frequency of Signals

One of the most important facts of the "information age" is that data symbolizing characters, words, pictures, video, or music can be represented electrically by voltage patterns on wires and in electronic devices. The data represented by these voltage patterns can be converted to light waves or radio waves and back to voltage waves. Consider the example of an analog telephone. The sound waves of the caller's voice enter a microphone in the telephone. The microphone converts the patterns of sound energy into voltage patterns of electrical energy that represent the voice.

If the voltage patterns are graphed over time, the distinct patterns representing the voice are displayed. An *oscilloscope* is an important electronic device used to view electrical signals, such as voltage waves and pulses. The x-axis on the display represents time, and the y-axis represents voltage or current. There are usually two y-axis inputs, so two waves can be observed and measured at the same time.

Analyzing signals using an oscilloscope is called time-domain analysis because the x-axis or domain of the mathematical function represents time. Engineers also use frequency-domain analysis to study signals. In frequency-domain analysis, the x-axis represents frequency. An electronic device called a *spectrum analyzer* creates graphs for frequency-domain analysis. Figure 4-4 illustrates several signals of how the output looks on both the oscilloscope and the spectrum analyzer.

Figure 4-4 Fourier Synthesis

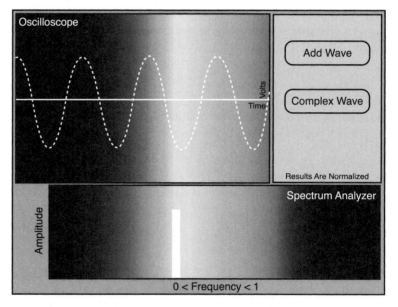

Electromagnetic signals use different frequencies for transmission so that different signals do not interfere with each other. For example, frequency modulation (FM) radio signals use frequencies that are different than television or satellite signals. When listeners change the station on a radio, they are changing the frequency that the radio is receiving.

Analog and Digital Signals

To understand the complexities of networking signals and cable testing, examine how analog signals vary with time and with frequency. First, consider a single-frequency electrical sine wave, whose frequency can be detected by the human ear. If this signal is transmitted to a speaker, a tone can be heard. How would a spectrum analyzer display this pure tone?

Next, imagine the combination of several sine waves. The resulting wave is more complex than a pure sine wave. Several tones would be heard. How would a spectrum analyzer display this? The graph of several tones shows several individual lines corresponding to the frequency of each tone. Finally, imagine a complex signal, such as a voice or a musical instrument. What would its spectrum analyzer graph look like? If many different tones are present, a continuous spectrum of individual tones would be represented.

Noise in Time and Frequency

An important concept in communications systems, including LANs, is *noise*, as shown in Figure 4-5. Although noise usually signifies undesirable sounds, the definition of noise that is related to communications is undesirable signals. Noise can originate from natural and technological sources and is added to the data signals in communications systems.

All communications systems have noise. Even though noise cannot be completely eliminated, its effects can be minimized if the sources of the noise are understood. Sources of noise include the following:

- Nearby cables that carry data signals
- *Thermal noise*, which is noise generated by thermal agitation of electrons in a conductor
- *Radio frequency interference (RFI)*, which is noise from other signals being transmitted nearby
- *Electromagnetic interference (EMI)*, which is noise from nearby sources such as motors and lights
- Laser noise at the transmitter or receiver of an optical signal

Noise that affects all transmission frequencies equally is called *white noise*. Noise that affects only small ranges of frequencies is called *narrowband interference*. When detected on a radio receiver, white noise interferes with all radio stations, while narrowband interference affects only a few stations whose frequencies are close together. When detected on a LAN, white noise affects all data transmissions, but narrowband interference might disrupt only certain signals. However, if the band of frequencies affected by the narrowband interference included all frequencies transmitted on the LAN, the performance of the entire LAN is compromised.

Figure 4-5 Recognizing and Defining Noise

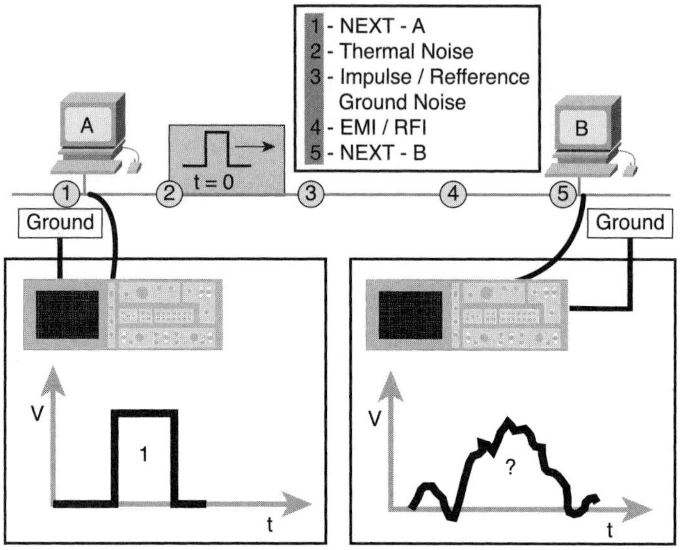

Bandwidth

Bandwidth is an extremely important concept in communications systems. For your study of LANs, two ways of considering bandwidth are important: analog bandwidth and digital bandwidth.

Analog bandwidth typically refers to the frequency range of an analog electronic system. Analog bandwidth can be used to describe the range of frequencies transmitted by a radio station or an electronic amplifier. The units of analog bandwidth are the units of frequency, cycles per second, or hertz. Examples of analog bandwidth values are 3 kilohertz (kHz) for telephony, 20 kHz for audible signals, 5 kHz for AM radio stations, and 200 kHz for FM radio stations.

Digital bandwidth measures how much information can flow from one place to another in a given amount of time. The fundamental unit of measurement for digital bandwidth is bits per second (bps). However, because LANs are capable of speeds of millions of bits per second, the unit is often expressed in kilobits per second (kbps) or megabits per second (Mbps), as shown in Table 4-1. Bandwidth is limited by physical media, current technologies, and the laws of physics.

During cable testing, analog bandwidth is used to determine the digital bandwidth of a copper cable. Analog frequencies are transmitted from one end and received on the opposite end. The two signals are then compared, and the amount of attenuation of the signal is calculated. In general, media that supports higher analog bandwidths without high degrees of attenuation will also support higher digital bandwidths.

Table 4-1 Units of Digital Bandwidth

Digital Units of Bandwidth	Abbreviation	Equivalence
Bits per second	bps	1 bps = fundamental unit of bandwidth
Kilobits per second	kbps	1 kbps = 1000 bps = 10^3 bps
Megabits per second	Mbps	1 Mbps = 1,000,000 bps = 10^6 bps
Gigabits per second	Gbps	1 Gbps = 1,000,000,000 bps = 10^9 bps

Signals and Noise

Noise refers to any interference on the physical medium that makes it difficult for the receiver to detect the data signal. Copper cabling is susceptible to many sources of noise, but far fewer sources of noise are possible when optical fiber is used as the transmission medium. Some level of noise on the medium is inevitable, but that acceptable level of noise must be kept as low as possible. Just as it is difficult to carry on a conversation when the background noise of the room is high compared to the volume of the participants' voices, data signals can be overwhelmed by the strength of noise to the point that the desired signal cannot be interpreted.

Proper cable installation techniques and proper attachment of connectors at both ends of a cable are vital. If standards are followed, the data signal experiences less attenuation, and noise levels are kept at a minimum.

Once the cable has been installed, it must be tested and meet the specifications of the Telecommunications Industry Association/Electronics Industries Alliance TIA/EIA-568-B standards. Problems must be identified and corrected prior to further installation of network hardware. Installed cable should also be tested periodically after the installation to determine if it still meets specifications. Cable and connectors experience wear and deterioration over a period of time, and potential problems must be identified and corrected to ensure reliable network operation. For all cable testing and troubleshooting, quality cable testers must be properly used.

Signaling Over Copper and Fiber-Optic Cabling

On copper cable, the data signals are represented by voltage changes that depict binary 1s and 0s. At the transmitter and receiver, the voltage levels are measured with respect to the signal ground. The signal ground provides a reference level of zero volts. The transmitting and receiving device must be properly grounded so that this zero volt reference point is accurate.

For the LAN to operate properly, the receiving device must be able to accurately interpret the binary 1s and 0s transmitted as voltage levels. The signals use very low voltages, less than 5 volts. Because current Ethernet technology supports data rates of billions of bits per second, each bit must be recognized even though its duration is very small. Therefore, as much of the original signal strength as possible must be retained as the signal moves through the cable and passes through the connectors. In anticipation of ever-faster Ethernet protocols, new cable installations should be made with the best available Category 5 (CAT 5) unshielded twisted-pair (UTP) or higher rated cable, connectors, and interconnect devices such as, punch-down blocks and patch panels.

Two basic types of copper cable exist, shielded and unshielded. In shielded cable, some types of shielding protect the data signal from external sources of noise. Other types of shielding protect one pair of wires in a cable from noise generated by electrical signals on another pair of wires within the same cable.

Coaxial cable is a type of shielded cable, as shown in Figure 4-6. It consists of a solid copper conductor surrounded, first, by an insulating material and, then, by a braided conductive shielding. In LAN applications, the braided shielding is electrically grounded, protecting the inner conductor from external electrical noise. The shielding also helps eliminate signal loss by keeping the transmitted signal confined to the cable, which helps make coaxial cable less "noisy" than twisted-pair. Coaxial cable is also more expensive. The need to ground the shielding and the bulky size of coaxial cable also make it more difficult to install than other types of copper cabling.

Figure 4-6 Coaxial Cable

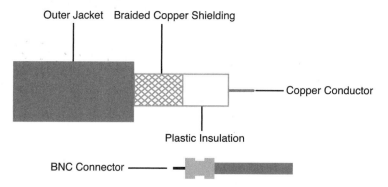

There are two types of twisted-pair cable:

- Shielded twisted-pair (STP) (see Figure 4-7)
- Unshielded twisted-pair (UTP) (see Figure 4-8)

Figure 4-7 Shielded Twisted-Pair Cable

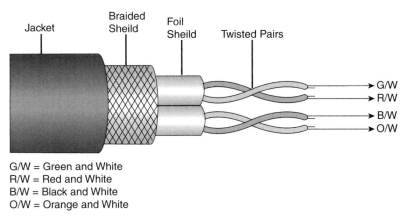

G/W = Green and White
R/W = Red and White
B/W = Black and White
O/W = Orange and White

STP cable, which can also be referred to as screened twisted-pair (ScTP) or foil twisted-pair (FTP), contains an outer conductive shield that is electrically grounded to insulate the signals from external electrical noise. STP also uses inner foil shields to protect each wire pair from noise generated by the other pairs. STP cable is more expensive, more difficult to install, and less frequently used than UTP. UTP contains no shielding and is the noisiest copper cabling, but it is the most frequently used because it is inexpensive and easier to install.

Figure 4-8 Unshielded Twisted-Pair Cable

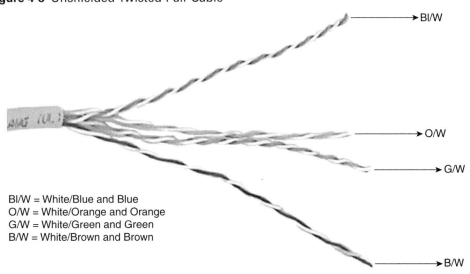

Bl/W = White/Blue and Blue
O/W = White/Orange and Orange
G/W = White/Green and Green
B/W = White/Brown and Brown

Fiber-optic cable, shown in Figures 4-9 and 4-10, transmits data signals by increasing and decreasing the intensity of light to represent binary 1s and 0s. The strength of a light signal does not diminish like the strength of an electrical signal does over an identical run length. Optical signals are not affected by electrical noise, and optical fiber does not need to be grounded. Therefore, optical fiber is often used between buildings and between floors within the building. As costs decrease and demand for speed increases, optical fiber may become a more commonly used LAN media.

Figure 4-9 Fiber Connector

Figure 4-10 Fiber-Optic Cable

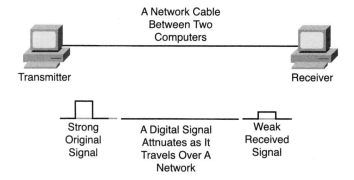

Attenuation and Insertion Loss on Copper Media

Attenuation is the decrease in signal amplitude over the length of a link, as shown in Figure 4-11. Long cable lengths and high signal frequencies contribute to greater signal attenuation. For this reason, attenuation on a cable is measured by a cable tester using the highest frequencies that the cable is rated to support.

Figure 4-11 Attenuation

Attenuation is expressed in decibels (dB) using negative numbers. Smaller negative dB values are an indication of better link performance.

Several factors contribute to attenuation:

- The resistance of the copper cable converts some of the electrical energy of the signal to heat.

- Signal energy is also lost when it leaks through the insulation of the cable and by impedance caused by defective connectors.

Impedance is a measurement of the resistance of the cable to alternating current (AC) and is measured in ohms. The normal (characteristic) impedance of a CAT 5 cable is 100 ohms. If a connector is improperly installed on CAT 5, it has a different impedance value than the cable. This difference is called an *impedance discontinuity* or an *impedance mismatch*.

Impedance discontinuities cause attenuation because a portion of a transmitted signal is reflected back to the transmitting device rather than continuing to the receiver, much like an echo. This effect is compounded if multiple discontinuities cause additional portions of the remaining signal to be reflected back to the transmitter. When this returning reflection strikes the first discontinuity, some of the signal rebounds in the direction of the original signal, creating multiple echo effects. The echoes strike the receiver at different intervals making it difficult for the receiver to accurately detect data values on the signal. This effect is called jitter and results in data errors. *Jitter* is defined as the slight movement of a transmission signal in time or phase that can introduce errors and loss of synchronization. More jitter is encountered with longer cables, cables with higher attenuation, and signals at higher data rates.

The combination of the effects of signal attenuation and impedance discontinuities on a communications link is called *insertion loss*. Proper network operation depends on constant characteristic impedance in all cables and connectors, with no impedance discontinuities in the entire cable system.

Sources of Noise on Copper Media

Noise is any electrical energy on the transmission cable that makes it more difficult for a receiver to interpret the data sent from the transmitter. TIA/EIA-568-B certification of a cable now requires testing for a variety of types of noise. UTP does not have any shielding from internal or external sources. Examples of external sources of noise would be nearby motors or fluorescent lights.

Crosstalk involves the transmission of signals from one wire pair to nearby pairs. When voltages change on one pair of wires, electromagnetic energy is generated. This energy radiates outward from the transmitting wire pair like a radio signal from a transmitter. Adjacent wire pairs in the cable act like antennas generating a weaker but similar electrical signal onto the nearby wire pairs. Crosstalk can cause interference with data that might be present on the adjacent wires. Crosstalk can also be caused by signals from a completely separate nearby cable. When crosstalk is caused by a signal on another cable, it is called *alien crosstalk*. Crosstalk is more destructive at higher transmission frequencies.

Cable testing instruments measure crosstalk by first applying a test signal to one wire pair. The cable tester then measures the amplitude of the unwanted crosstalk signals induced on the other wire pairs in the cable. At higher transmission frequencies, crosstalk increases and is more destructive to data signals.

Undesired crosstalk occurs when the wire pairs are untwisted and thus subject to data crosstalk from another wire pair, as shown in Figure 4-12. Therefore, crosstalk can be minimized by twisting the wire pairs. The higher the category of UTP, the more twists in the cable are necessary to minimize crosstalk even at high transmission frequencies. To ensure reliable LAN communications, the untwisting of wire pairs must be kept to an absolute minimum. This point is especially important to remember when attaching connectors to the ends of UTP cable.

Figure 4-12 Connector Vulnerable to Crosstalk

Bad Connector. Wires are untwisted for too great a length.

Good Connector. Wires are only untwisted to the extent necessary to attach the connector.

Types of Crosstalk

There are three distinct types of crosstalk:

- Near-end crosstalk (NEXT)

- Far-end crosstalk (FEXT)

- Power sum near-end crosstalk (PSNEXT)

Near-end crosstalk (NEXT), shown in Figure 4-13, is computed as the ratio in voltage amplitude between the test signal and the crosstalk signal when measured from the same end of the link. This difference is expressed in a negative value of decibels (dB). Low negative numbers indicate more noise, and large negative numbers indicate less noise, just as a larger number (less crosstalk) is more desirable than a smaller number (more crosstalk). By tradition, cable testers do not show the minus sign indicating the negative NEXT values. A NEXT reading of 30 dB (really -30) indicates less NEXT noise and a better cable than does a NEXT reading of 10 dB (really -10.)

Figure 4-13 Near-End Crosstalk (NEXT)

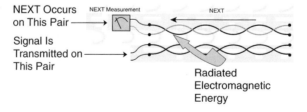

NEXT needs to be measured from every pair to every other pair in a UTP link and from both ends of the link. To shorten test times, some cable test instruments allow the user to test the NEXT performance of a link by using larger frequency step sizes than specified by the TIA/ EIA standard. The resulting measurements might not comply with TIA/EIA-568-B and might overlook link faults. To verify proper link performance, NEXT should be measured from both ends of the link with a high-quality test instrument. This verification is also a requirement for complete compliance with high-speed cable specifications.

Because of attenuation, crosstalk occurring further away from the transmitter (*far-end crosstalk [FEXT]*) creates less noise on a cable than NEXT, as shown in Figure 4-14. The noise caused by FEXT still travels back to the source, but the noise is attenuated as it returns. Thus, FEXT is not as significant a problem as NEXT.

Figure 4-14 Far-End Crosstalk (FEXT)

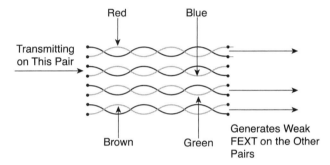

Power sum near-end crosstalk (PSNEXT), shown in Figure 4-15, measures the cumulative effect of NEXT from all wire pairs in the cable. For each wire pair in the four-pair cable, PSNEXT is computed from three pair-to-pair NEXT test results. The combined effect of crosstalk from multiple simultaneous transmission sources can be very detrimental to the signal. TIA/ EIA-568-B certification now requires this PSNEXT test.

Figure 4-15 Power Sum Near-End Crosstalk (PSNEXT)

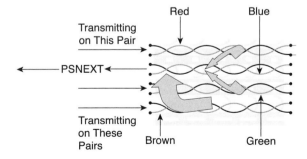

Some Ethernet standards, such as 10BASE-T and 100BASE-TX, receive data from only one wire pair in each direction. However, for newer technologies, such as 1000BASE-T, that receive data simultaneously from multiple pairs in the same direction, power sum measurements are important tests.

Cable Testing Standards

The *TIA/EIA-568-B* standard specifies ten tests that a copper cable must pass if it is to be used for modern, high-speed Ethernet LANs. All cable links should be tested to the maximum rating that applies for the category of cable being installed.

The primary test parameters that must be verified for a cable link to meet TIA/EIA-568-B standards are as follows:

- Wire map
- Insertion loss
- Near-end crosstalk (NEXT)
- Power sum near-end crosstalk (PSNEXT)
- Equal-level far-end crosstalk (ELFEXT)
- Power sum equal-level far-end crosstalk (PSELFEXT)
- Return loss
- Propagation delay
- Cable length
- Delay skew

The Ethernet standard specifies that each of the pins on an RJ-45 connector has a particular purpose, as shown in Figure 4-16. A network interface card (NIC) transmits signals on pins 1 and 2, and it receives signals on pins 3 and 6. The wires in UTP cable must be connected to the proper pins at each end of a cable. The wire map test insures that no open or short circuits exist in the cable. An open circuit occurs if the wire does not attach properly at the connector. A short circuit occurs if two wires are connected to each other.

The wire map test also verifies that all eight wires are connected to the correct pins on both ends of the cable. The wire map test can detect several different wiring faults. The reversed-pair fault occurs when a wire pair is correctly installed on one connector, but reversed on the other connector. If the orange striped wire is on pin 1 and the orange wire is on pin 2 at one end, but the orange striped wire is on pin 2 and the orange wire is on pin 1 at the other end, then the cable has a reversed-pair fault, as demonstrated in Figure 4-17.

Figure 4-16 Ethernet Standards for RJ-45 Connectors

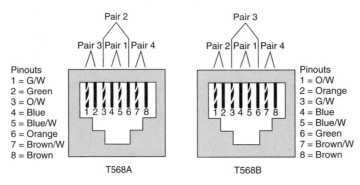

Figure 4-17 Cable Wire Map Problems

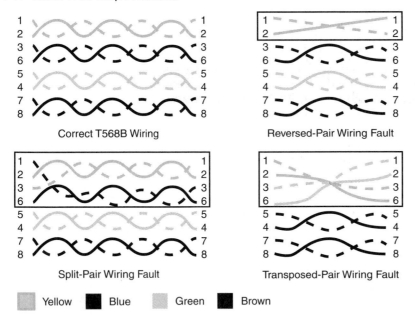

A split-pair wiring fault occurs when two wires from different wire pairs are connected to the wrong pins on both ends of the cable. Look carefully at the pin numbers in Figure 4-17 to detect the wiring fault. A split pair creates two transmit or receive pairs each with two wires that are not twisted together.

Transposed-pair wiring faults occur when a wire pair is connected to completely different pins at both ends. Contrast this with a reversed-pair where the same pair of pins is used at both ends. Transposed pairs also occur when two different colors codes on punch-down blocks (representing T568A and T568B) are used at different locations on the same link.

Other Test Parameters

The combination of the effects of signal attenuation and impedance discontinuities on a communications link is called insertion loss. *Insertion loss* increases as data transmission speeds and frequencies increase. Insertion loss is measured in decibels. The TIA/EIA-568-B standard requires that a cable and its connectors pass an insertion loss test before the cable can be used as a communications link in a LAN.

Crosstalk is measured in four separate tests:

- NEXT
- ELFEXT
- PSELFEXT
- Return loss

A cable tester measures NEXT by applying a test signal to one cable pair and measuring the amplitude of the crosstalk signals received by the other cable pairs. The NEXT value, expressed in decibels, is computed as the difference in amplitude between the test signal and the crosstalk signal measured at the same end of the cable. Remember, because the number of decibels that the tester displays is a negative number, the larger the number, the lower the NEXT on the wire pair.

The *equal-level far-end crosstalk (ELFEXT)* test measures FEXT. Pair-to-pair ELFEXT is expressed in dB as the difference between the measured FEXT and the insertion loss of the wire pair whose signal is disturbed by the FEXT. ELFEXT is an important measurement in Ethernet networks using 1000BASE-T technologies.

Power sum equal-level far-end crosstalk (PSELFEXT) is the combined effect of ELFEXT from all wire pairs.

Return loss is a measure in decibels of reflections that are caused by the impedance discontinuities at all locations along the link. Recall that the main impact of return loss is not on loss of signal strength. The significant problem is that signal echoes caused by the reflections from the impedance discontinuities strike the receiver at different intervals causing signal jitter.

Time-Based Parameters

Propagation delay is a simple measurement of how long it takes for a signal to travel along the cable being tested. The delay in a wire pair depends on its length, twist rate, and electrical properties. Delays are measured in the hundredths of nanoseconds (one nanosecond is one-billionth of a second, or 0.000000001 second). The TIA/EIA-568-B standard sets a limit for propagation delay for the various categories of UTP.

Propagation delay measurements are the basis of the cable length measurement. TIA/EIA-568-B-1 specifies that the physical length of the link is calculated using the wire pair with the shortest electrical delay. Testers measure the length of the wire based on the electrical delay

as measured by a Time Domain Reflectometry (TDR) test, not the physical length of the cable jacket. Because the wires inside the cable are twisted, signals actually travel farther than the physical length of the cable. When a cable tester makes a TDR measurement it sends a pulse signal down a wire pair and measures the amount of time required for the pulse to return on the same wire pair.

The TDR test is used not only to determine length, but also to identify the distance to wiring faults such as shorts and opens. When the pulse encounters an open, short, or poor connection, all or part of the pulse energy is reflected back to the tester, which can calculate the approximate distance to the wiring fault. This calculation can be helpful in locating a faulty connection point, such as a wall jack, along a cable run.

The propagation delays of different wire pairs in a single cable can differ slightly because of differences in the number of twists and electrical properties of each wire pair. The delay difference between pairs is called ***delay skew***. Delay skew is a critical parameter for high-speed networks in which data is simultaneously transmitted over multiple wire pairs, such as 1000BASE-T Ethernet. If the delay skew between the pairs is too great, the bits arrive at different times, and the data cannot be properly reassembled. Even though a cable link might not be intended for this type of data transmission, testing for delay skew helps ensure that the link supports future upgrades to high-speed networks.

All cable links in a LAN must pass all of the tests covered in the preceding text as specified in the TIA/EIA-568-B standard to ensure that they function reliably at high speeds and frequencies. Perform cable tests when the cable is installed, and afterward on a regular basis to ensure that LAN cabling meets industry standards. Use high-quality cable test instruments correctly to ensure that the tests are accurate. Carefully document test results.

Testing Optical Fiber

A fiber link consists of two separate glass fibers functioning as separate and independent data pathways. One fiber carries transmitted signals in one direction, while the second carries signals in the opposite direction. Each glass fiber is surrounded by a sheath that light cannot pass through, so no crosstalk problems exist on fiber-optic cable. The jacket, external EMI or noise has no affect on fiber cabling. Attenuation does occur on fiber links, but to a lesser extent than on copper cabling.

Fiber links are subject to the optical equivalent of UTP impedance discontinuities. When light encounters an optical discontinuity, some of the light signal is reflected back in the opposite direction with only a fraction of the original light signal continuing down the fiber towards the receiver. This results in a reduced amount of light energy arriving at the receiver making signal recognition more difficult. Just as with UTP cable, improperly installed connectors are the main cause of light reflection and signal strength loss in optical fiber.

Because noise is not an issue when transmitting on optical fiber, the main concern with a fiber link is the strength of the light signal that arrives at the receiver. If attenuation weakens the light signal at the receiver, then data errors result. Testing fiber-optic cable primarily involves shining a light down the fiber and measuring whether a sufficient amount of light reaches the receiver.

On a fiber-optic link, the acceptable amount of signal power loss that can occur without dropping below the requirements of the receiver must be calculated. This calculation is referred to as the optical link loss budget. Today's optical-fiber attenuation ranges from 0.5dB/km to 1000dB/hm, depending on the optical fiber used. Attenuation limits are based on intended application. A fiber test instrument checks whether the optical link loss budget has been exceeded. If the fiber fails the test, the cable test instrument indicates where the optical discontinuities occur along the length of the cable link. Usually, the problem is one or more improperly attached connectors. The cable test instrument indicates the location of the faulty connections that must be replaced. When the faults are corrected, the cable must be retested.

A New Standard

On June 20, 2002, the Category 6 (CAT 6) addition to the TIA-568 standard was published. The official title of the standard is ANSI/TIA/EIA-568-B.2-1. This new standard specifies the original set of ten tests for Ethernet cabling and the passing scores for each of these tests. Cables certified as CAT 6 cable must pass all ten tests.

Although the CAT 6 tests are essentially the same as the CAT 5 standard specifies, CAT 6 cable must pass the tests with higher scores to be certified. CAT 6 cable must be capable of carrying frequencies up to 250 MHz and must have lower levels of crosstalk and return loss.

A quality cable tester similar to the Fluke DSP-4000 series or Fluke OMNIScanner2 can perform all the test measurements required for CAT 5, CAT 5e, and CAT 6 cable certifications of both permanent links and channel links.

Lab 4.2.9a   Fluke 620 Cable Tester: Wire Map

In this lab, you learn the wire mapping features of the Fluke 620 LAN CableMeter.

Lab 4.2.9b   Fluke 620 Cable Tester: Faults

In this lab, you learn the Cable Fault Test—Pass/Fail features of the Fluke 620 LAN CableMeter.

Lab 4.2.9c   Fluke 620 Cable Tester: Length

In this lab, you learn the cable length feature of the Fluke 620 LAN CableMeter.

Lab 4.2.9d   Fluke LinkRunner: LAN Tests

In this lab, you use the Fluke LinkRunner to determine whether a cable drop is active and identify its speed, duplex capabilities, and service type. You also verify network layer connectivity with **ping**.

Lab 4.2.9e   Fluke LinkRunner: Cable and NIC Tests

In this lab, you use the Fluke LinkRunner to verify cable length and integrity and determine where a cable terminates. You also verify PC NIC functionality.

Summary

In this chapter, you learned the following key points:

- Waves are energy traveling from one place to another, and are created by disturbances. All waves have similar attributes such as amplitude, period, and frequency.

- Sine waves are periodic, continuously varying functions. Analog signals look like sine waves.

- Square waves are periodic functions whose values remain constant for a period of time and then change abruptly. Digital signals look like square waves.

- Exponents are used to represent very large or very small numbers. The base of a number raised to a positive exponent is equal to the base multiplied by itself exponent times. For example, $10^3 = 10 \times 10 \times 10 = 1000$.

- Logarithms are similar to exponents. A logarithm to the base of 10 of a number equals the exponent to which 10 would have to be raised in order to equal the number. For example, $\log_{10} 1000 = 3$ because $10^3 = 1000$.

- Decibels are measurements of a gain or loss in the power of a signal. Negative values represent losses and positive values represent gains.

- Time-domain analysis is the graphing of voltage or current with respect to time using an oscilloscope. Frequency-domain analysis is the graphing of voltage or power with respect to frequency using a spectrum analyzer.

- Undesirable signals in a communications system are called noise. Noise originates from other cables, RFI, and EMI. White noise affects all frequencies, while narrowband interference affects only a certain subset of frequencies.

- Analog bandwidth is the frequency range that is associated with certain analog transmission, such as television or FM radio.

- Digital bandwidth measures how much information can flow from one place to another in a given amount of time. Its units are in various multiples of bits per second.

- Most LAN problems occur at the physical layer. The only way to prevent or trouble-shoot many of these problems is through the use of cable testers.

- Proper cable installation, according to standards, increases LAN reliability and performance.

- Copper media is available in shielded and unshielded forms. Unshielded cable is more susceptible to noise.

- Signal degradation is caused by various factors, such as noise, attenuation, impedance mismatch, and several types of crosstalk. These factors decrease network performance.

- The TIA/EIA-568-B standard specifies ten tests that a copper cable must pass if it will be used for modern, high-speed Ethernet LANs.

- Optical fiber must also be tested according to networking standards.

- Category 6 cable must meet more rigorous frequency testing standards than Category 5 cable.

Key Terms

alien crosstalk   When crosstalk is caused by a signal from outside the cable.

amplitude   The amplitude of an electrical signal represents its height, but it is measured in volts instead of meters.

analog bandwidth   Typically refers to the frequency range of an analog electronic system. Analog bandwidth can be used to describe the range of frequencies transmitted by a radio station or an electronic amplifier.

attenuation   The decrease in signal amplitude over the length of a link.

crosstalk   The transmission of signals from one wire pair to nearby pairs. Adjacent wire pairs in the cable act like antennas generating a weaker but similar electrical signal onto the nearby wire pairs. This crosstalk causes interference with data that might be present on the adjacent wires.

decibel   An important way of describing networking signals as a unit that measures the loss or gain of the power of a wave. Decibels are usually negative numbers representing a loss in power as the wave travels, but can also be positive values representing a gain in power if the signal is amplified.

delay skew   The propagation delays of different wire pairs in a single cable can differ slightly because of differences in the number of twists and electrical properties of each wire pair. Delay skew is the delay difference between pairs.

digital bandwidth   Measures how much information can flow from one place to another in a given amount of time.

ELFEXT (equal-level far-end crosstalk)   A test that measures FEXT.

EMI (electromagnetic interference)   Noise from nearby sources such as motors and lights.

FEXT (far-end crosstalk)   Crosstalk that occurs when signals on one twisted pair are coupled to another pair as they arrive at the far end of a multipair cable system.

frequency   The amount of time between each wave.

hertz   The unit of measure for the frequency of an electrical signal in the number of complete cycles per second.

impedance   A measurement of the resistance of the cable to AC and is measured in ohms.

insertion loss   The combination of the effects of signal attenuation and impedance discontinuities on a communications link.

jitter   The slight movement of a transmission signal in time or phase that can introduce errors and loss of synchronization. More jitter will be encountered with longer cables, cables with higher attenuation, and signals at higher data rates.

logarithms Equals the exponent that a given number has to be raised to in order to generate a certain value.

narrowband interference Noise that only affects small ranges of frequencies.

NEXT (near-end crosstalk) Computed as the ratio in voltage amplitude between the test signal and the crosstalk signal when measured from the same end of the link.

noise As related to communications, noise refers to undesirable signals. Noise can originate from natural and technological sources and is added to the data signals in communications systems.

oscilloscope An important electronic device used to view electrical signals such as voltage waves and pulses.

propagation delay A simple measurement of how long it takes for a signal to travel along the cable being tested.

PSELFEXT (power sum equal-level far-end crosstalk) The combined effect of ELFEXT from all wire pairs.

PSNEXT (power sum near-end crosstalk) Measures the cumulative effect of NEXT from all wire pairs in the cable.

pulse Determines the value of the data being transmitted. If a disturbance is deliberately caused and involves a fixed, predictable duration, it is called a pulse.

RFI (radio frequency interference) Noise from other signals being transmitted nearby.

sine waves Graphs of mathematical functions of many natural occurrences that change regularly over time, such as the distance from the earth to the sun, the distance from the ground while riding a Ferris wheel, and the time of day that the sun rises.

spectrum analyzer An electronic device that creates graphs for frequency-domain analysis. Engineers also use frequency-domain analysis to study signals.

square waves Graphs that do not continuously vary with time. The values remain the same for some time, then suddenly change, then remain the same, and then suddenly return to the initial value.

TIA/EIA-568-B standard Specifies ten tests that a copper cable must pass if it is used for modern, high-speed Ethernet LANs.

wave Energy traveling from one place to another.

white noise Noise that affects all transmission frequencies equally.

Check Your Understanding

Complete all the review questions to test your understanding of the topics and concepts in this chapter. Answers are listed in Appendix B, "Check Your Understanding Answer Key."

1. Which of the following is a characteristic of fiber-optic cable?

    A. It uses an intense incandescent light.

    B. Its core is made of highly reflective Kevlar.

    C. It relies on total internal cancellation to guide light for long distances.

    D. It is capable of higher data rates than other types of networking media.

2. Which of the following describes attenuation?

    A. A loss of signal strength

    B. An increase in signal amplitude

    C. The delay experienced during signal travel

    D. The time it takes a signal to reach its destination

3. Which of the following is a cause of crosstalk?

    A. Poorly terminated network cabling

    B. The loss of a signal's ground reference

    C. AC line noise coming from a nearby video monitor or hard disk drive

    D. FM radio signals, TV signals, various types of office equipment

4. Which of the following are tests specified by the TIA/EIA-B standard for copper cable? (Select all that apply.)

    A. Signal harmonics

    B. Conductive response

    C. Wire map

    D. Signal absorption

    E. Insertion loss

    F. Propagation delay

5. What are three distinct kinds of crosstalk?

   A. NEXT

   B. FEXT

   C. ANEXT

   D. SPNEXT

   E. PSNEXT

6. In designing a network, what would be used to calculate an optical link loss budget?

   A. Amount of data lost during impedence mismatch events

   B. Amount of attenuation signal loss that can occur before data becomes corrupt

   C. Amount of signal power loss that can occur without dropping below receiver requirements

   D. Total amount of data that can be lost before regeneration of signal

7. Which numbering system uses 2 as its base?

   A. Octal

   B. Hexidecimal

   C. Binary

   D. ASCII

8. Which of the following describes a common function of a cable-testing device?

   A. TDR tests and detects faulty virtual circuits.

   B. TDR tests provide information about the location of a cabling run.

   C. Wire maps provide information about the distance to a cabling fault.

   D. Cable testers can detect open circuits in existing cabling installations.

9. Which electronic device is used to view electrical signals such as voltage waves and pulses?

   A. Multileter

   B. Autocollimator

   C. Spectrum analyzer

   D. Oscilloscope

   E. Spectroscope

   F. Spectophotometer

10. Through wire testing, electrical interference and signal loss can be measured. Match the names on the left column with the definitions on the right column.

A. Near-end crosstalk	Decrease in signal amplitude over the length of a link
B. Far-end crosstalk	Crosstalk occuring further away from the transmitter
C. Power sum near-end crosstalk	Measures the cumulative effect of NEXT
D. Attenuation	Crosstalk signal measured from the same end of the link
E. Insertion loss	Ensures that no open or short circuits exist in the cable
F. Wire map	Combination of impedance discontinuities on a communications link and signal attenuation

CHAPTER 5

Cabling LANs and WANs

Objectives

Upon completion of this chapter, you should be able to answer the following questions:

- What media can be used at the physical layer of a LAN? What are the advantages and disadvantages of media that can be used at the physical layer of a LAN? How can Ethernet technologies be used in a campus network?

- What are the connector requirements for the different types of Ethernet media?

- What different connection types are used by each physical layer implementation?

- What is the purpose of an RJ-45 connector? Which wiring situations require straight-through cables? Which wiring situations require crossover cables?

- Which situations require rollover cables?

- What are repeaters?

- What is a hub? Name the three types of hubs.

- What are some common applications of wireless data communications?

- What are the two most common wireless technologies that are used for networking?

- What is the main function of a bridge?

- What are the similarities and differences between switches and bridges?

- What are the benefits of switches?

- What is the main function of a NIC?

- Why are NICs considered to be Layer 2 devices?

- What is a peer-to-peer network? How does it function?

- What is a client/server network?

- What are the types of WAN physical layer implementations?

- What is the main function of the CSU/DSU?

- What are DTE and DCE?

- How are interfaces on routers named?

- How do you set up a console connection?

Additional Topics of Interest

In addition to the core objective areas, this chapter introduces you to the following topics of interest to networkers:

- Routers and ISDN BRI connections

- Routers and DSL connections

- Routers and cable connections

Key Terms

The following is a list of key terms introduced in this chapter. For your reference, a definition for each term can be found at the end of this chapter.

Although each local-area network (LAN) is unique, many design aspects are common to all LANs. For example, most LANs follow the same standards and the same components. This chapter presents information on elements of Ethernet LANs and common LAN devices.

Several wide-area network (WAN) connections are available today. They range from dialup to broadband access, and differ in bandwidth, cost, and required equipment. This chapter presents information on the various types of WAN connections.

Be sure to look at this chapter's associated Interactive Media Activity and PhotoZooms, which you can find on the CD-ROM accompanying this book. These CD elements are designed to supplement the material and reinforce the concepts introduced in this chapter.

Cabling LANs

The cabling aspect of the LAN exists at Layer 1 of the OSI reference model. To understand the types of cabling used in networking devices, you need to understand the LAN physical layer implementation of Ethernet. Ethernet is a LAN technology that is specified at the data link layer.

It is important that you can identify the usages of different types of cable and differentiate among the types of connectors that connect Ethernet.

This section addresses the LAN physical layer implementation and the main principle of implementing Ethernet in a campus LAN. This chapter also discusses the different types of connectors specified for Ethernet use as well as the UTP wiring standards.

LAN Physical Layer

Ethernet is the most widely used LAN technology. Ethernet was first implemented by a group called DIX (Digital, Intel, and Xerox). DIX created and implemented the first Ethernet LAN specification, which was used as the basis for the Institute of Electrical and Electronics Engineer (IEEE) 802.3 specification released in 1980. Later, the IEEE extended the 802.3 committee to new committees known as 802.3u (Fast Ethernet), 802.3z (Gigabit Ethernet over Fiber), 802.3ab (Gigabit Ethernet over UTP), and 802.3ae (10 Gigabit Ethernet).

The cabling aspect of the LAN exists at Layer 1 of the Open System Interconnection (OSI) reference model. Many topologies support LANs, as well as different physical media. Figure 5-1 shows a subset of physical layer implementations that you can deploy to support Ethernet.

Figure 5-1 FLAN Physical Layer Implementation

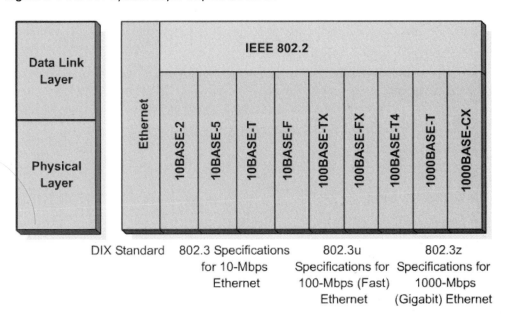

The symbols for media vary. For example, the symbol for a serial line looks like an elongated letter z or a lighting bolt. The Ethernet symbol is typically a straight line with perpendicular lines projecting from it. The Token Ring network symbol is a circle with hosts attached to it. For FDDI, the symbol is two concentric circles with attached devices, as shown in Figure 5-2.

Figure 5-2 LAN Physical Layer Media Symbols

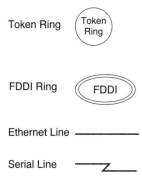

The basic functions of media are to carry a flow of information, in the form of bits and bytes, through a LAN. Other than wireless LANs (that use the atmosphere, or space, as the medium), networking media confines network signals to a wire, cable, or fiber. Networking media are considered Layer 1 components of LANs.

Computer networks can be built with many different media types. Each media has advantages and disadvantages. What is an advantage for one media (CAT 5 cost) might be a disadvantage for another (fiber-optic cost). The primary advantage and disadvantage comparison categories are as follows:

- Cable length

- Cost

- Ease of installation

- Susceptibility to interference

Coaxial cable, optical fiber, and even free space can carry network signals. However, the principal medium that is studied is called Category 5 unshielded twisted-pair cable (CAT 5 UTP).

Ethernet in the Campus

Given the variety of Ethernet speeds that you can deploy in the campus, you need to determine when, if, and where to upgrade to faster Ethernet implementations. With the correct hardware and cabling infrastructure, 10- or 100-Mbps Ethernet can be run anywhere in the network. As noted in Table 5-1, 10-Mbps Ethernet typically is implemented at the end-user level to connect to desktops, and faster technologies are used to interconnect to servers and network devices, such as routers and switches.

Table 5-1 Ethernet Connectivity Recommendations

	Ethernet 10BASE-T Position	**Fast Ethernet Position**	**Gigabit Ethernet Position**
End-User Level (End-user device to workgroup device)	Provides connectivity between the end-user device and the user-level switch.	Gives high-performance PC work stations 100-Mbps access to the server.	Not typically used at this level.
Workgroup Level (Workgroup device to backbone)	Not typically used at this level.	Provides connectivity between the end user and workgroups. Provides connectivity from the workgroup to backbone. Provides connectivity from the server block to the backbone.	Provides high-performance connectivity from the workgroup to backbone. Provides high-performance connectivity to the enterprise server block.
Backbone Level	Not typically used at this level.	Provides connectivity for low- to medium-volume applications.	Provides high-speed backbone and network device connectivity.

In today's installations, although customers are providing Gigabit Ethernet from the backbone to the end user, costs for cabling and switch ports can make this prohibitive. Before making this decision, you must determine network requirements. For example, a network running at traditional Ethernet speeds of 10 Mbps can be easily overwhelmed with the new generation of multimedia, imaging, and database products.

In general, you can use Ethernet technologies in a campus LAN in several different ways:

- An Ethernet speed of Fast Ethernet can be used at the user level to provide good performance. Also, Fast Ethernet or Gigabit Ethernet can be used for clients or servers that consume high bandwidth.

- Fast Ethernet is often used as the link between the user-level and network devices, supporting the aggregate traffic from each Ethernet segment on the access link.

- Many client/server networks suffer from too many clients trying to access the same server, creating a bottleneck where the server attaches to the LAN. To enhance client/server performance across the campus LAN and avoid bottlenecks at the server, you can use Fast Ethernet or Gigabit Ethernet links to connect enterprise servers. Fast Ethernet or Gigabit Ethernet creates an effective solution for avoiding slow networks.

- You also can use Fast Ethernet links to provide the connection between the workgroup level and the backbone. Because the campus LAN model supports dual links between each workgroup router and backbone switch, you can load balance the aggregate traffic from multiple-access switches across the links.

- You can use Fast Ethernet (or Gigabit Ethernet) between switches and the backbone. Implement the fastest medium affordable between backbone switches.

Ethernet Media and Connector Requirements

In addition to network need, and before selecting an Ethernet implementation, you must consider the media and connector requirements for each implementation. The cables and connector specifications used to support Ethernet implementations are derived from the Electronic Industries Alliance and (newer) Telecommunications Industry Association (EIA/TIA) standards. The categories of cabling defined for the Ethernet are derived from the EIA/ TIA-568 (SP-2840) Commercial Building Telecommunications Wiring Standards. The EIA/ TIA specifies an **RJ-45** connector for UTP cable. The letters *RJ* stand for *registered jack*, and the number 45 refers to the physical connector that has eight conductors.

Table 5-2 compares the cable and connector specifications for the most popular Ethernet implementations. The important difference to note is the medium used for 10-Mbps Ethernet versus 100-Mbps and 1000-Mbps Ethernet. In today's networks, in which you see a mix of 10- and 1000-Mbps requirements, you must be aware of the need to change over to UTP CAT 5 to support Fast Ethernet or Gigabit Ethernet

Table 5-2 Comparing Ethernet Media Requirements

	Media	Maximum Segment Length	Topology	Connector
10BASE2	50-ohm coaxial (thinnet)	185 m (606.94 feet)	Bus	British Naval Connector (BNC)
10BASE5	50-ohm coaxial (thicknet)	500 m (1640.4 feet)	Bus	Attachment unit interface (AUI)
10BASE-T	EIA/TIA CAT 3, 4, 5 UTP, two pair	100 m (328 feet)	Star	ISO 8877 (RJ-45)
100BASE-TX	EIA/TIA CAT 5 UTP, two pair	100 m (328 feet)	Star	ISO 8877 (RJ-45)

Table 5-2 Comparing Ethernet Media Requirements (Continued)

	Media	Maximum Segment Length	Topology	Connector
100BASE-FX	62.5/125 multi-mode fiber	400 m (1312.3 feet)	Star	Duplex media interface connector (MIC), straight tip (ST) connector, or subscriber connector (SC)
1000BASE-CX	STP	25 m (82 feet)	Star	ISO 8877 (RJ-45)
1000BASE-T	EIA/TIA CAT 5 UTP, four pair	100 m (328 feet)	Star	ISO 8877 (RJ-45)
1000BASE-SX	62.5/50 micro multimode fiber	275 m (853 feet) for 62.5 micro fiber; 550 m (1804.5 feet) for 50 micro fiber	Star	SC
1000BASE-LX	62.5/50 micro multimode fiber; 9-micron single-mode fiber	440 m (1443.6 feet) for 62.5 micro fiber; 550 m (1804.5 feet) for 50 micro fiber; 3 to 10 km (1.86 to 6.2 miles) on single-mode fiber	Star	SC

Figure 5-3 illustrates some of the different connection types used by the physical layer implementation.

Figure 5-3 Differentiating Among Connections

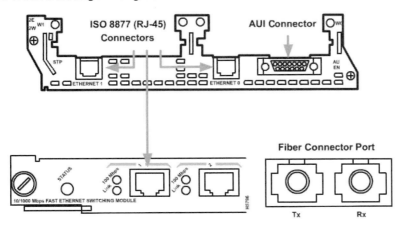

Connection Media

This section briefly discusses the connection types used by physical layer implementation and an interface device, Gigabit Interface Converter (GBIC), used between the Ethernet and fiber-optic systems. This section covers the following topics:

- **RJ-45**—A connector commonly used for finishing a twisted-pair cable

- **AUI**—A connector that interfaces between a computer's NIC or router interface and an Ethernet cable

- **GBIC**—A device used as an interface between the Ethernet and fiber-optic systems

RJ-45

The RJ-45 connector and jack are the most prevalent. RJ-45 connectors are discussed in more detail in the section, "UTP Implementation" later in this chapter.

Attachment Unit Interface

In some cases, the type of connector on a NIC does not match the type of media that it needs to connect to. An interface exists for the AUI connector. The *attachment unit interface (AUI)* is the 15-pin physical connector interface between a computer's NIC and Ethernet cable. On 10BASE5 (thicknet) Ethernet, a short cable is used to connect the AUI on the computer with a transceiver on the main cable. In 10BASE2 (thinnet) Ethernet networks, the NIC connects directly to the Ethernet coaxial cable at the back of the computer.

More Information: Gigabit Interface Converter

A *Gigabit Interface Converter (GBIC)* is a hot-swappable input/output device that plugs into a Gigabit Ethernet port. A key benefit of using a GBIC is that GBICs are interchangeable. This feature gives users the flexibility to deploy other 1000BASE-X technology without needing to change the physical interface/module on the router or switch.

The fiber-optic GBIC is a transceiver that converts serial electric currents to optical signals and that also coverts optical signals to digital electric currents. Some of the optical GBICs include the following:

- Short wavelength (1000BASE-SX)

- Long wavelength/long haul (1000BASE-LX/LH)

- Extended distance (1000BASE-ZX)

Typically, the GBIC is used as an interface between the Ethernet and fiber-optic systems, such as Fiber Channel and Gigabit Ethernet. Figure 5-4 shows a GBIC, and Figure 5-5 shows a Cisco WS-X2931 Gigabit Ethernet Module with the GBIC out.

More Information: Gigabit Interface Converter (Continued)

Figure 5-4 Gigabit Interface Converter (GBIC)

Figure 5-5 Cisco WS-X2931 Gigabit Ethernet Module with GBIC Out

UTP Implementation

If you look at the RJ-45 transparent end connector, you can see eight colored wires. These wires are twisted into four pairs. Four of the wires (two pairs) carry the positive, or true, voltage and are considered "tip" (T1 through T4); the other four wires carry the inverse, or false, voltage grounded and are called "ring" (R1 through R4). Tip and ring are terms that originated in the early days of the telephone. Today, these terms refer to the positive and the negative wire in a pair. The wires in the first pair in a cable or a connector are designated as T1 and R1, the second pair is T2 and R2, and so on.

The RJ-45 plug is the male component, crimped at the end of the cable. As you look at the male connector from the front, with the clip facing down, the pin locations are numbered from 8 on the left down to 1 on the right, as shown in Figure 5-6. The jack, shown in Figure

5-7, is the female component in a network device, wall or cubicle partition outlet, or patch panel. As you look at the device port, the corresponding female pin locations are 1 on the left up to 8 on the right.

Figure 5-6 Pin Locations on the RJ-45 Connector

Figure 5-7 RJ-45 Jack and Wire Order

For electricity to run between the connector and the jack, the order of the wires must follow EIA/TIA-568-A and EIA/TIA-568-B standards.

In addition to identifying the correct EIA/TIA category of cable to use for a connecting device (which depends on what standard is being used by the jack on the network device), you need to determine which of the following to use:

- A *straight-through cable* — A cable that maintains the pin connection all the way through the cable. Thus, the wire connected to pin 1 is the same on both ends of the cable.

- A *crossover cable* — A cable that crosses the critical pair to properly align, transmit, and receive signals on the device with line connections.

If the two RJ-45 ends of a cable are held side by side in the same orientation, the colored wires (or strips or pins) are seen at each connector end. If the order of the colored wires is the same at each end, the cable is straight-through. Figure 5-8 illustrates that the RJ-45 connectors on both ends show all the wires in the same order.

Figure 5-8 UTP Implementation: Straight-Through Cable

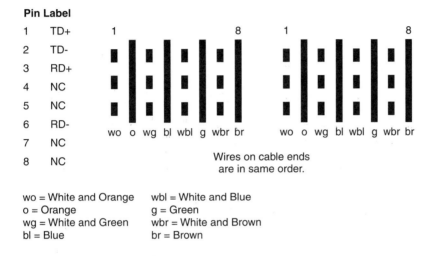

Pin Label

Pin	Label
1	TD+
2	TD-
3	RD+
4	NC
5	NC
6	RD-
7	NC
8	NC

Wires on cable ends are in same order.

wo = White and Orange
o = Orange
wg = White and Green
bl = Blue

wbl = White and Blue
g = Green
wbr = White and Brown
br = Brown

Specified for Ethernet, in a CAT 5 UTP cable, only wires 1, 2, 3, and 6 are used for transmit (TD) and receive (RD) signals. The other four wires are not used. As shown on the left of Figure 5-8, in a straight-through cable, the RJ-45 pins 1, 2, 3, and 6 at one end are connected to pins 1, 2, 3, and 6 at the other end of the connection. Gigabit Ethernet, however, uses all eight wires.

You can use a straight-through cable to connect devices such as PCs or routers to other devices used as hubs or switches. As Figure 5-9 shows, you should use straight-through when only one port is designated with an x.

Figure 5-9 Interconnecting Devices Using Straight-Through Cable

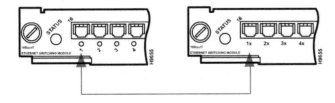

With a crossover cable, the RJ-45 connectors on both ends show that some of the wires on one side of the cable are crossed to a different pin on the other side of the cable. Specifically

for Ethernet, pin 1 at one RJ-45 end should connect to pin 3 at the other end. Pin 2 at one end should connect to pin 6 at the other end, as shown in Figure 5-10.

Figure 5-10 UTP Implementation—Crossover

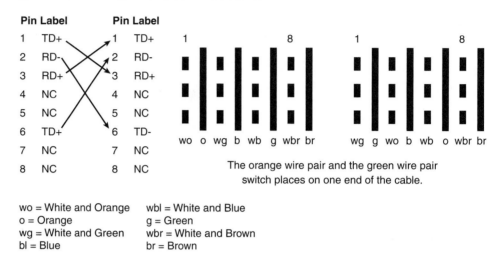

Pin	Label		Pin	Label
1	TD+		1	TD+
2	RD-		2	RD-
3	RD+		3	RD+
4	NC		4	NC
5	NC		5	NC
6	TD+		6	TD-
7	NC		7	NC
8	NC		8	NC

wo o wg b wb g wbr br   wg g wo b wb o wbr br

The orange wire pair and the green wire pair switch places on one end of the cable.

wo = White and Orange   wbl = White and Blue
o = Orange   g = Green
wg = White and Green   wbr = White and Brown
bl = Blue   br = Brown

You can use a crossover cable to connect similar devices, switch to switch or switch to hub. Figure 5-11 shows that you use a crossover cable when both ports are designated with an x or when neither port is designated with an x.

Figure 5-11 Interconnecting Devices Using Crossover Cable

The following are the guidelines for the type of cable to use when interconnecting networking devices.

Use straight-through cables for the following cabling:

- Switch to router
- Switch to PC or server
- Hub to PC or server

Use crossover cables for the following cabling:

- Switch to switch
- Switch to hub
- Hub to hub
- Router to router
- PC to PC
- Router to PC

PhotoZoom   Straight-Through Cable

In this PhotoZoom, you view a straight-through cable.

PhotoZoom   Crossover Cable

In this PhotoZoom, you view a crossover cable.

Lab 5.1.5   RJ-45 Jack Punch Down

In this lab, you learn the correct process for teminating or punching down an RJ-45 jack and learn the correct procedure for installing the jack in a wall plate.

Repeaters

Many types of devices are connected to make up a LAN. These are called the LAN hardware components. This section discusses some of the common hardware components that are used in a LAN environment. LAN devices can include repeaters, hubs, bridges, switches, and routers, with switches being the most prevalent device in modern LANs.

As mentioned in the section, "LAN Physical Layer," many types of media exist, and each one has advantages and disadvantages. One of the primary disadvantages of CAT 5 UTP cable is the maximum length. The maximum length for UTP cable in a network is 100 meters (approximately 333 feet). If you have to expand the network beyond that limit, you need to add a repeater. In most Ethernet networks this repeater normally takes the form of a hub, which is a multiport repeater, or a newer technology switch.

The term *repeater* comes from the early days of visual communication when a person situated on a hill would repeat the signal that was just received from the person on the previous hill to communicate the signal to the person on the next hill. Telegraph, telephone, microwave, and optical communications all use repeaters to strengthen their signals over long distances.

The purpose of a repeater, shown in Figures 5-12 and 5-13, is to regenerate and retime network signals at the bit level to allow them to travel a longer distance on the media. Repeaters are commonly used if too many network nodes exist or the number of cables is insufficient. The Four Repeater Rule for 10-Mbps bus-based Ethernet, also known as the 5-4-3 Rule, is used as a standard when extending LAN segments. This rule states that no more than five network segments can be connected end-to-end using four repeaters, but only three segments can have hosts (computers) on them. Although the 5-4-3 rule is important when applied to bus-based networks, it does not have much validity with switches and extended star topologies.

Figure 5-12 Repeaters

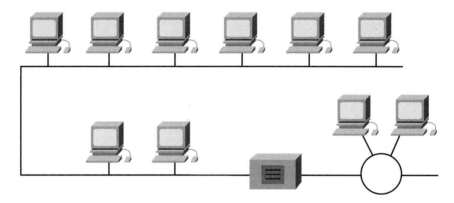

Figure 5-13 Repeaters Connect Two End Nodes

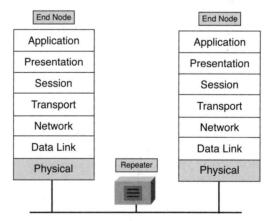

Hubs

Hubs are actually multiport repeaters. In many cases, the difference between the two devices is the number of ports that each provides. While a typical repeater has just 2 ports, a hub generally has from 4 to 24 ports, as shown in Figure 5-14. Additionally, hubs are most commonly used in Ethernet 10BASE-T or 100BASE-T networks, although other network architectures use them as well.

Figure 5-14 Eight-Port Hub

Using a hub changes the network topology from a linear bus, where each device plugs directly into the wire, to a star. With hubs, data arriving over the cables to a hub port is electrically repeated on all the other ports connected to the same network segment, except for the port on which the data was sent.

Hubs come in three basic types:

- **Active**—An *active hub* must be plugged into an electrical outlet because it needs power to amplify the incoming signal before passing it out to the other ports.

- **Intelligent**—*Intelligent hubs* are sometimes called *smart hubs*. These devices basically function as active hubs, but also include a microprocessor chip and diagnostic capabilities. They are more expensive than active hubs, but are useful in troubleshooting situations.

- **Passive**—A passive hub serves as a physical connection point only. It does not manipulate or view the traffic that crosses it. It does not boost or clean the signal. A passive hub is used only to share the physical media. As such, the passive hub does not need electrical power.

All devices that are attached to a hub hear all traffic. Therefore, hubs maintain a single collision domain. A collision is a situation where two end stations send data over the network wire at the same time.

Sometimes, hubs are called concentrators because they serve as a central connection point for an Ethernet LAN.

Lab 5.1.7 Hub and NIC Purchase

This lab introduces you to various network components and their prices. This lab looks specifically at Ethernet hubs and NICs.

Wireless

A wireless network is an alternative method for connecting a LAN. You don't need to run any cables, and you can easily move computers. Wireless networks use radio frequency (RF), laser, infrared (IR), or satellite/microwaves to carry signals from one computer to another without a permanent cable connection. Wireless signals are electromagnetic waves that travel through the air. No physical medium is necessary for wireless signals, which makes them a versatile way to build a network.

A common application of wireless data communication is for mobile use. Some examples of mobile use include commuters, airplanes, satellites, remote space probes, space shuttles, and space stations.

At the core of wireless communication are devices called transmitters and receivers. The source interacts with the transmitter that converts data to electromagnetic (EM) waves that are received by the receiver. The receiver then converts these electromagnetic waves back into data for the destination. For two-way communication, each device requires a transmitter and a receiver. Many networking device manufacturers build the transmitter and receiver into a single unit called a transceiver or wireless network card. All devices in wireless LANs (WLANs) must have the appropriate wireless network card installed.

The two most common wireless technologies used for networking are infrared (IR) and radio frequency (RF). IR technology has its weaknesses. Workstations and digital devices must be in the line of sight of the transmitter to operate. An IR-based network suits environments where all the digital devices that require network connectivity are in one room. IR networking technology can be installed quickly, but the data signals can be weakened or obstructed by people walking across the room or by moisture in the air. However, new IR technologies that can work out of sight are being developed.

RF technology allows devices to be in different rooms or even buildings. The limited range of the radio signals still restricts the use of this kind of network. RF technology can be on single or multiple frequencies. A single radio frequency is subject to outside interference and geographic obstructions. Furthermore, a single frequency is easily monitored by others, which makes the transmissions of data insecure. Spread spectrum avoids the problem of insecure data transmission by using multiple frequencies to increase the immunity to noise and to make it difficult for outsiders to intercept data transmissions.

Bridges

At times, you need to break up a large LAN into smaller, more easily managed segments. This strategy decreases the amount of traffic on a single LAN and can extend the geographical area past what a single LAN can support, as shown in Figure 5-15. The devices that are used to connect network segments together include bridges, switches, routers, and gateways.

Switches and bridges operate at the data link layer of the OSI model. The function of the bridge is to make intelligent decisions about whether or not to pass signals on to the next segment of a network. Bridges can also be used to connect dissimilar protocols and media as with wireless bridges interconnecting Ethernet LANs in a metropolitan area.

Figure 5-15 Bridges Segmenting a Network

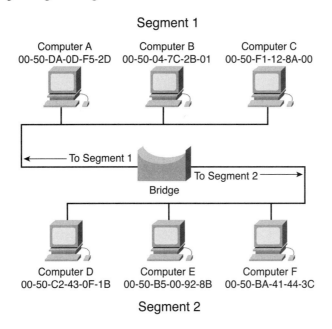

When a bridge receives a frame on the network, the destination MAC address is looked up in the bridge table to determine whether to filter, flood, or copy the frame onto another segment. This decision process occurs as follows:

- If the destination device is on the same segment as the frame, the bridge blocks the frame from going on to other segments, as shown in Figure 5-16. This process is known as *filtering*.

- If the destination device is on a different segment, the bridge forwards the frame to the appropriate segment, as shown in Figure 5-17.

- If the destination address is unknown to the bridge, the bridge forwards the frame to all segments except the one on which it was received. This process is known as *flooding*.

If placed strategically, a bridge greatly improves network performance.

Figure 5-16 Bridges Segmenting a Network: Filtering

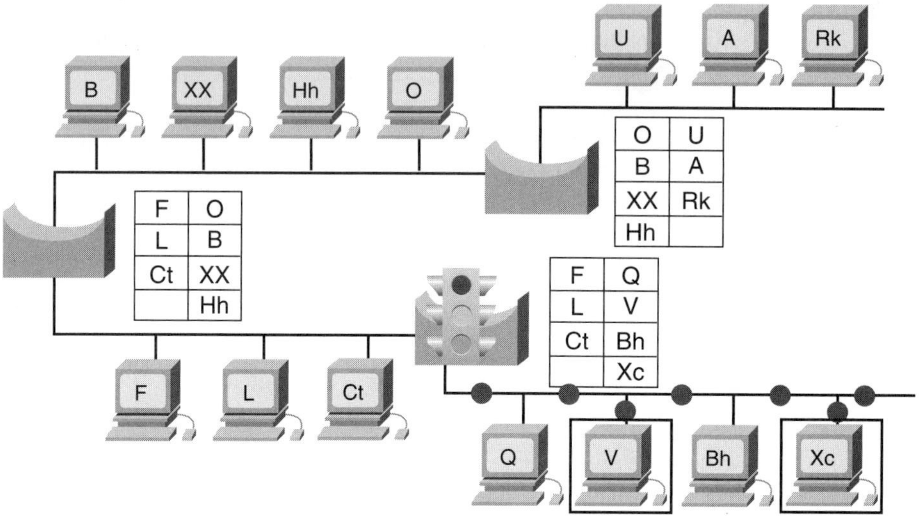

In this example, a data packet originates from Computer V and its destination is Computer Xc. The packet reaches its final destination and is not broadcast to other segments of the network.

Figure 5-17 Bridges Segmenting a Network: Forwarding

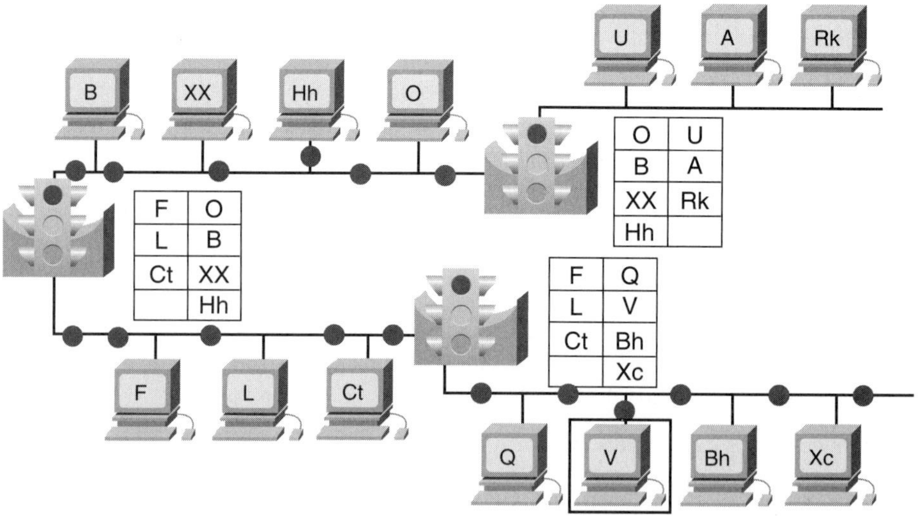

In this example, a data packet originates from Computer V and its destination is Computer Hh. The bridge checks its table to determine whether or not to allow the signal to continue to other segments of the network.

Switches

A *switch* is sometimes described as a multiport bridge. While a typical bridge might have just two ports (linking two network segments), the switch can have multiple ports depending on how many network segments are to be linked. Like bridges, switches learn certain information about the data packets that they receive from various computers on the network. They use this information to build forwarding tables to determine the destination of data being sent by one computer to another computer on the network, as demonstrated in Figure 5-18.

Figure 5-18 Switching Table

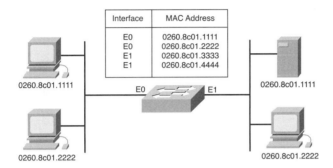

Interface	MAC Address
E0	0260.8c01.1111
E0	0260.8c01.2222
E1	0260.8c01.3333
E1	0260.8c01.4444

Although some similarities exist between the two, a switch is a more sophisticated device than a bridge. A bridge determines whether the frame is forwarded to the other network segment based on the destination MAC address. A switch has many ports with many network segments connected to them. A switch chooses the port to which the destination device or workstation is connected. Ethernet switches are becoming popular connectivity solutions because, like bridges, they improve network performance (speed and bandwidth).

Switching is a technology that alleviates congestion in Ethernet LANs by reducing traffic and increasing bandwidth. Switches often replace shared hubs because they work with existing cable infrastructures, which improves performance with a minimum of intrusion into an existing network.

Today, in data communications, all switching equipment performs two basic operations:

- **Switching data frames**—The process by which a frame is received on an input medium and then transmitted to an output medium.

- **Maintenance of switching operations**—Switches build and maintain switching tables and search for loops.

Switches operate at much higher speeds than bridges and can support other functionality, such as virtual LANs.

An Ethernet switch has many benefits, such as allowing many users to communicate in parallel through the use of virtual circuits and dedicated network segments in a virtually collision-free environment, as shown in Figure 5-19. This arrangement maximizes the bandwidth available on the shared medium. Another benefit is that moving to a switched LAN environment is very cost effective because existing hardware and cabling can be reused. Switches are also capable of physically connecting the transmit and receive pair of one port to the receive and transmit pair of another port. This creates a collision-free environment, and allows for full use of the bandwidth between them.

Figure 5-19 Microsegmentation of the Network via Switches

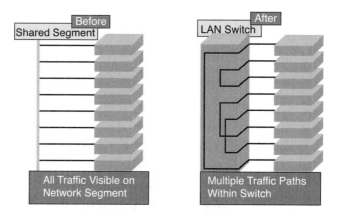

Lab 5.1.10 Purchasing LAN Switches

This lab introduces you to various network components and the prices of these components. This lab looks specifically at Ethernet switches and NICs.

Host Connectivity

In terms of appearance, a NIC, shown in Figures 5-20 and 5-21, is a printed circuit board that fits into the expansion slot of a bus on a computer's motherboard or peripheral device. It is also called a network adapter. On laptop/notebook computers, NICs are usually the size of a credit card. Its function is to connect the host device to the network medium.

NICs operate at both Layer 1 and Layer 2 of the OSI model. NICs are considered Layer 2 devices because each individual NIC throughout the world carries a unique code, called a Media Access Control (MAC) address. This address controls data communication for the host on the network. Layer 2 devices, such as a bridge or switch, use each individual NIC's MAC address. This MAC address controls data communication for the host on the network. You will learn more about the MAC address in later chapters. As its name implies, the NIC controls the host's access to the medium. For this reason, a NIC also works at Layer 1 because it looks only at bits and not at any address information or higher-level protocols. NICs typically have the transceiver built in.

Figure 5-20 Network Interface Card (Circuit Board)

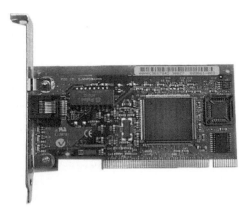

Figure 5-21 Network Interface Card (Media Connection)

In some cases, the type of connector on the NIC does not match the type of media that needs to be connected to it. A good example is a Cisco 2500 router. On the router, the Ethernet interface is an AUI connector, and that connector needs to connect to a UTP CAT 5 Ethernet cable. To do this, a transceiver (transmitter/receiver) is used. The Ethernet transceiver provides the transmit/receive function (because none is built into the Ethernet interface) and, at the same time, converts one type of signal or connector to another (for example, to connect a 15-pin AUI interface to an RJ-45 jack).

In diagrams, NICs have no standardized symbol. It is implied that, when networking devices are attached to network media, a NIC or NIC-like device is present. Wherever a dot is seen on a topology map, it represents either a NIC or an interface (port), which acts like a NIC.

Peer-to-Peer

By using LAN and WAN technologies, many computers are interconnected to provide services to their users. To accomplish this, networked computers take on different roles or functions in relation to each other. Some types of applications require computers to function as equal partners. Other types of applications distribute their work so that one computer functions to serve a number of others in an unequal relationship. In either case, two computers typically communicate with each other by using request/response protocols. One computer issues a request for a service, and a second computer receives and responds to that request. The requestor takes on the role of a client, and the responder takes on the role of a server.

In a *peer-to-peer network*, the networked computers act as equal partners, or peers, to each other. Peer-to-peer networks are also referred to as workgroups. As peers, each computer can take on the client function or the server function. At one time, for example, computer A might make a request for a file from computer B, which responds by serving the file to computer A. Computer A functions as client, while B functions as the server. At a later time, computers A and B can reverse roles. B, as client, makes a print request of A, which has a shared printer attached, and A, as server, responds to the request from B. A and B stand in a reciprocal or peer relationship to each other.

In a peer-to-peer network, individual users control their own resources. They can decide to share certain files with other users, as shown in Figure 5-22 and Figure 5-23. They might also require passwords before they allow others to access their resources. Because individual users make these decisions, no central point of control or administration exists in the network. In addition, individual users must back up their own systems to be able to recover from data loss in case of failures. When a computer acts as a server, the user of that machine might experience reduced performance as the machine serves the requests made by other systems.

Peer-to-peer networks are relatively easy to install and operate. No additional equipment is necessary beyond a suitable operating system installed on each computer. Most modern desktop operating systems provide support for peer-to-peer networking. Because users control their own resources, no dedicated administrators are needed.

A peer-to-peer network works well with a small number of computers, perhaps ten or fewer. As networks grow, peer-to-peer relationships become increasingly difficult to coordinate and manage. Because they do not scale well, their efficiency decreases rapidly as the number of computers on the network increases. Also, individual users control access to the resources on their computers, which means security might be difficult to maintain. The client/server model of network can be used to overcome the limitations of the peer-to-peer network.

Figure 5-22 Sharing Files

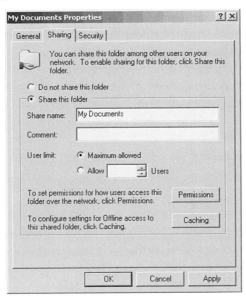

Figure 5-23 Shared File

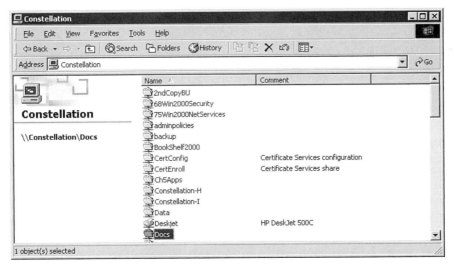

Lab 5.1.12   Building a Peer-to-Peer Network

In this lab, you create a simple peer-to-peer network between two PCs. You identify and locate the proper cable, configure workstation IP addresses, and test connectivity using the **ping** command. You also share a folder on one PC and access it with the other.

Client/Server

In a client/server arrangement, network services are located on a dedicated computer called a server, which responds to the requests of clients, as shown in Figure 5-24. The server is a central computer that is continuously available to respond to a client's requests for file, print, application, and other services. Most network operating systems (NOS) adopt the form of client-server relationships. Typically, desktop computers function as clients and one or more computers with additional processing power, memory, and specialized software function as servers.

Figure 5-24 Client-Server Model

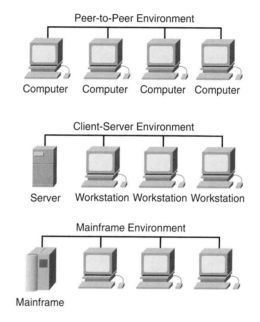

Servers are designed to handle requests from many clients simultaneously, as shown in Figure 5-25. Before a client can access the server resources, the user must be identified and be authorized to use the resource. You handle this authorization by assigning each user an account name and password that is verified by an authentication service acting as a sentry to guard access to the network. By centralizing user accounts, security, and access control, server-based networks simplify the work of network administration.

The concentration of network resources, such as files, printers, and applications on servers, also makes the data they generate easier to back up and maintain. Rather than having these resources spread around individual machines, they can be located on specialized, dedicated servers for easier access. Most client-server systems also include facilities for enhancing the network by adding new services that extend the usefulness of the network.

Figure 5-25 Server Resources

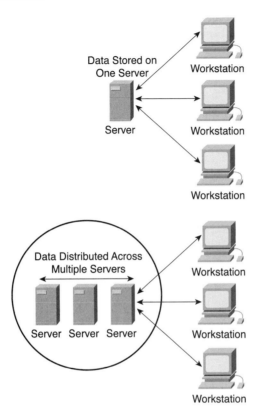

The distribution of functions in client-server networks brings substantial advantages, but it also incurs some costs. Although the aggregation of resources on server systems brings greater security, simpler access, and coordinated control, the server introduces a single point of failure into the network. Without an operational server, the network cannot function at all. Servers require a trained, expert staff to administer and maintain. This requirement increases the expense of running the network. Server systems also require additional hardware and specialized software that add to the cost.

Tables 5-3 and 5-4 summarize the advantages and disadvantages of peer-to-peer versus client-server.

Table 5-3 Peer-to-Peer/Client-Server Advantages

Advantages of a Peer-to-Peer Network	Advantages of a Client-Server Network
Less expensive to implement.	Provides for better security and scalability.
Does not require NOS server software.	Easier to administer when the network is large because administration is centralized.
Does not require a dedicated network administrator.	All data can be backed up on one central location.

Table 5-4 Peer-to-Peer/Client-Server Disadvantages

Disadvantages of a Peer-to-Peer Network	Disadvantages of a Client-Server Network
Does not scale well to large networks and administration becomes unmanageable.	Requires NOS software such as in Windows 2000/2003, Novell NetWare, Linux, or UNIX.
Each user must be trained to perform administrative tasks.	Requires expensive, more powerful hardware for the server machine.
Less secure.	Requires a professional administrator.
All machines sharing the resources negatively impact the performance.	Has a single point of failure if there is only one server, and user's data can be unavailable if the server is down.

Lab 5.1.13a   Building a Hub-Based Network

In this lab, you create a simple network between two PCs using an Ethernet hub. You identify and locate the proper cables, configure workstation IP addresses, and test connectivity using the **ping** command.

Lab 5.1.13b   Building a Switch-Based Network

In this lab, you create a simple network between two PCs using an Ethernet switch. You identify and locate the proper cables, configure workstation IP addresses, and test connectivity using the **ping** command.

Cabling WANs

To connect one network to other remote networks, it is sometimes necessary to utilize wide-area network (WAN) services. WAN services provide different connection methods, and the cabling standards differ from those of LANs. Therefore, it is important for you to understand the types of cabling needed to connect to these services.

This section explains the cabling and connectors that are used to interconnect switches and routers in a LAN or WAN. This section also discusses how to cable routers for serial connection, Integrated Services Digital Network Basic Rate Interface (ISDN BRI) connection, digital subscriber line (DSL) connection, and cable connection, as well as how to set up a console connection.

WAN Physical Layer

Many physical implementations carry traffic across the WAN. Needs vary, depending on the distance of the equipment from the services, the speed, and the actual service itself. Figure 5-26 lists a subset of data link and physical implementations that support some of the more prominent WAN solutions today. The type of physical layer you choose depends on the distance, speed, the type of interface you need to connect, and availablility in your area.

Figure 5-26 WAN Physical Layer Implementations

Cisco High-level Data Link Control (HDLC)	PPP	Frame Relay	ISDN BRI (with PPP)	DSL Modem	Cable Modem
EIA/TIA-232 EIA/TIA-449 X.21 V.24 V.35			RJ -45 *Note:* ISDN BRI Cable Pinouts Are Different than the Pinouts for Ethernet	RJ -11 *Note:* Works over Telephone Line	F *Note:* Works over Cable TV Line

Serial connections are used to support WAN services such as dedicated leased lines that run the Point-to-Point Protocol (PPP) or Frame Relay. The speed of these connections ranges from 2400 bps to T1 (1.544 Mbps).

Other WAN services, such as the ISDN, offer dial-on-demand connections or dial-backup services. An ISDN BRI is composed of two 64-kbps bearer channels (B channels) for data, and one delta channel (D channel) at 16 kbps used for signaling and other link-management tasks. PPP typically is used to carry data over the B channels.

The increasing demand for residential broadband (high-speed) services has increased the popularity for DSL and cable modem connections. DSL service can achieve T1/E1 speeds over the existing telephone line. Cable services, which work over the existing coaxial cable TV line, also offer high-speed connectivity matching or surpassing that of DSL.

 Interactive Media Activity   Drag and Drop: WAN Physical Layer Implementation

After completing this activity, you will be able to identify the components in the WAN physical layer.

WAN Serial Connections

Serial transmission is a method of data transmission in which bits of data are transmitted sequentially over a single channel. This one-bit-at-a-time transmission contrasts with parallel data transmission, which transmits several bits at a time. For long-distance communication, WANs use serial transmission. To carry the energy represented in bits, serial channels use a specific electromagnetic or optical frequency range.

Frequencies, described in terms of their cycles per second (hertz), function as a band or spectrum for communication. For example, the signals transmitted over voice-grade telephone lines use up to 3 kHz (kilohertz, or thousand hertz). The size of this frequency range is called the bandwidth.

Another way to express bandwidth is to specify the amount of data in bits per second that the serial channel can carry.

Table 5-5 compares physical standards for EIA/TIA-232 and EIA/TIA-449, v.35, X.21, and EIA-530 WAN serial connection options.

Table 5-5 Comparison of Physical Standards

Data (bps)	Distance (Meters) EIA/TIA-232	Distance (Meters) EIA/TIA-449, V.35, X.21, EIA-530
2400	60	1250
4800	30	625
9600	15	312

Table 5-5 Comparison of Physical Standards (Continued)

Data (bps)	Distance (Meters) EIA/TIA-232	Distance (Meters) EIA/TIA-449, V.35, X.21, EIA-530
19,200	15	156
38,400	15	78
115,200	3.7	—
T1 (1.544 Mbps)	—	15

Several types of physical connections enable you to connect to serial WAN services. You must select the correct serial cable type to use with the router, depending on the physical implementation that you choose or the physical implementation that your service provider imposes. Figure 5-27 shows all the different serial connector options available. Serial connectors are used to connect end-user devices and service providers. Note that serial ports on Cisco routers use a proprietary 60-pin connector or smaller "smart serial" connector, which enables two serial connections on a WAN interface card. The type of connector on the other end of the cable is dependent on the service provider or end-device requirements, but V.35 is common.

Figure 5-27 WAN Serial Connection Options

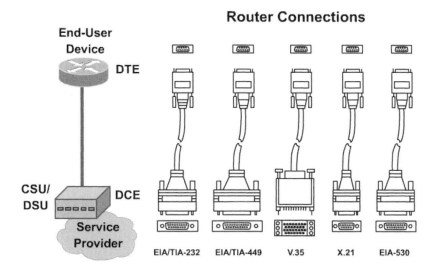

Netwok Connections at the CSU/DSU

If the connection is made directly to a service provider or a device that provides signal clocking, such as a channel/data service unit (CSU/DSU), the router will be a data terminal equipment (DTE) and use a DTE serial cable. Typically, this is the case. However, occasions arise where the local router is required to provide the clocking rate and, therefore, will use a data communications equipment (DCE) cable. In the curriculum router labs, one of the connected routers will need to provide the clocking function. Therefore, the connection will consist of a DCE and a DTE cable.

Routers and Serial Connections

NOTE

Clocking is a method used to synchronize data transmission between devices. In a WAN serial connection, the CSU/DSU handles the clocking of the transmitted data.

Routers are responsible for routing data packets from source to destination within the LAN, and for providing connectivity to the WAN. Within a LAN environment, the router contains broadcasts, provides local-address resolution services, such as ARP and RARP, and can segment the network using a subnetwork structure. To provide these services, the router must be connected to the LAN and WAN.

In addition to determining the cable type, you need to determine whether you need DTE or DCE connectors for your equipment. The DTE is the endpoint of the user's device on the WAN link. The DCE is the device used to convert the user data from the DTE into a form acceptable to the facility providing WAN services.

As shown in Figure 5-28, if connecting directly to a service provider or to a device that performs signal clocking (such as a channel service unit/data service unit [CSU/DSU]), the router is a DTE and needs a DTE serial cable. This situation is typically the case for routers.

Figure 5-28 Serial Implementation of DTE and DCE

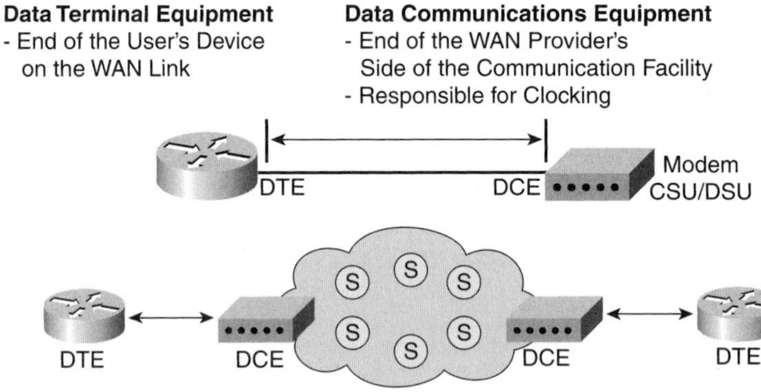

However, in some cases the router must be the DCE, as shown in Figure 5-29. For example, if performing a back-to-back router scenario (meaning that routers are used at both ends of the connection) in a test environment, one of the routers is a DTE, and the other is a DCE and *must* provide the clock.

Figure 5-29 Back-to-Back Serial Connection

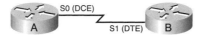

When you are cabling routers for serial connectivity, the routers have either fixed or modular ports. The type of port being used affects the syntax that you use later to configure each interface.

Figure 5-30 shows an example of a router with fixed serial ports (interfaces). Each port is given a label of port type and port number—for example, serial 0. To configure a fixed interface, you specify the interface using the port type and port number convention—for example, serial 0.

Figure 5-30 Fixed Interfaces

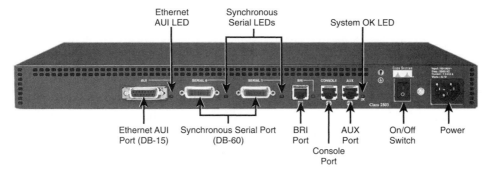

Figure 5-31 shows examples of routers with modular serial ports. Usually, each port is given a label of port type, slot (the location of the module), and port number. To configure a port on a modular card, you are asked to specify the interface using the convention "port type slot number/port number"—for example, serial 1/0, in which the type of interface is a serial interface, the slot number where the serial interface module is installed is slot 1, and the specific port that you are referencing on that serial interface module is port 0.

Figure 5-31 Modular Serial Port Interfaces

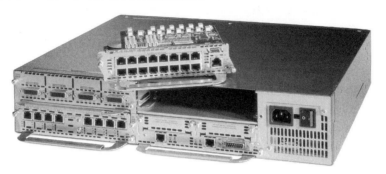

 Lab 5.2.3a Connecting Router LAN Interfaces

In this lab, you identify the Ethernet or Fast Ethernet interfaces on the router. Then, identify and locate the proper cables to connect the routers to hubs or switches. Finally, use the cables to connect the router and computers to the hub or switch.

 Lab 5.2.3b Building a Basic Routed WAN

In this lab, you connect two simple LANs, each consisting of a workstation and a switch (or hub), to form a basic router-to-router WAN.

 Lab 5.2.3c Troubleshooting Interconnected Devices

In this lab, you create a simple routed WAN with two PCs, two switches or hubs, and two routers. You configure workstation IP address information and identify and correct networking problems related to cabling issues and workstation IP addressing issues.

Routers and ISDN BRI Connections

With ISDN BRI, you can use two types of interfaces: BRI S/T and BRI U. In ISDN BRI service, a user (U) interface is the electrical interface for the twisted-pair wire connection from a user to a Network Termination 1 (NT1) device. A terminal (T) interface is the electrical interface between an NT1 device and an NT 2 device, which is usually a private branch exchange (PBX). A system (S) interface is the electrical interface between an NT1 and ISDN devices such as a computer or a telephone. In BRI, the T interface is electrically identical to the S interface. Thus, the two interfaces are typically combined in a single interface, referenced as an S/T interface.

To determine which interface type you need, you must find out whether you or the service provider provides an NT1 device. An NT1 device is an intermediate device between the router and the service-provider ISDN switch (cloud) that is used to connect four-wire subscriber wiring to the conventional two-wire local loop. In the United States, a U interface is typically used because the service provider does not provide the NT1. The rest of the world usually uses an S/T interface because the service provider provides the NT1. The NT1 converts a line from a single-pair, full-duplex wiring on the service provider side to a two-pair line with separate transmit and receive lines on the subscriber side. This allows multiple devices to co-exist on the circuit, like an ISDN telephone and an ISDN router.

CAUTION

It is important to insert a cable running from an ISDN BRI port only to an ISDN jack or an ISDN switch. ISDN BRI uses voltages that can seriously damage non-ISDN devices.

More Information: Cabling Routers for ISDN Connections

If the NT1 device needs to be provided by the customer, an ISDN BRI with a U interface can be used. A U interface has an NT1 built in. If an external NT1 device is used or if the service provider uses an NT1 device, the router needs an ISDN BRI S/T interface. Because routers can have multiple ISDN interface types, the interface needed must be determined when the router is purchased. Some routers have both a U and an S/T interface. The type of ISDN connector that the router has can be determined by looking at the port label. Figure 5-32 shows the different port types for the ISDN interface.

Figure 5-32 Cabling Routers for ISDN Connections

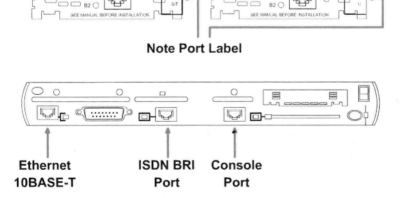

To interconnect the ISDN BRI port on the router to the service-provider device, use a UTP CAT 5 straight-through cable with RJ-45 connectors. Note that the ISDN BRI cable pinouts are different than the pinouts for Ethernet. Table 5-6 shows the ISDN BRI S/T interface connector pinouts.

More Information: Cabling Routers for ISDN Connections (Continued)

Table 5-6 ISDN BRI S/T Interface Connector Pinouts

Pin	Signal
1	Unused
2	Unused
3	Transmit (Tx+)
4	Receive (Rx+)
5	Receive (Rx-)
6	Transmit (Tx-)
7	Unused
8	Unused

Routers and DSL Connections

DSL technology is a modem technology that enables inexpensive, high-speed digital transmission over existing twisted-pair telephone lines. For most small offices or home offices today, DSL technology is a good choice for many business applications, such as file transfer and access to a corporate intranet. Asymmetric digital subscriber line (ADSL) is the most common and is part of a larger family of technologies generically referred to as xDSL.

The Cisco 800 series of fixed-configuration DSL routers provides enhanced security, low cost of ownership, proven reliability, and safe investment through the power of Cisco IOS Software tailored for small offices and telecommuters.

The Cisco 827-4V ADSL router has one ADSL interface, as shown in Figure 5-33, that can connect users to the Internet or to a corporate LAN via DSL.

Figure 5-33 Cisco 827-4V Router

NOTE

If you are connecting non-DSL devices to a phone line with DSL service, you need to install a filter to prevent interference between data and voice services.

Cisco 827-4V Router

Wall Jack

More Information: Connecting a Router for DSL Service
To connect an ADSL line to the ADSL port on a router, perform the following simple steps: **Step 1**   Connect the phone cable to the ADSL port on the router. **Step 2**   Connect the other end of the phone cable to the external wall phone jack. To connect a router for DSL service, you need a phone cable with RJ-11 connectors. DSL works over standard telephone lines. It uses only two pins on the RJ-11 connector, as shown in Table 5-7. **Table 5-7** Telephone Connector Pinouts (RJ-11)

Pin	Signal
1	Unused
2	Unused
3	Transmit (Tx)
4	Receive (Rx)
5	Unused

Routers and Cable Connections

NOTE

RF coaxial cable connects radio frequencies to antennas. The majority of cable TV systems use coaxial cable as their wiring system. The main trunk lines that run from the cable provider to neighborhood distribution boxes might be fiber-optic, but coaxial cables are likely to be used in runs between the distribution boxes and the end user.

Cable modems enable two-way, high-speed data transmissions using the same coaxial lines that transmit cable television. Some cable service providers are promising data speeds up to six and a half times that of T1 leased lines. With the demand for broadband services, cable modem connection is becoming more popular.

The Cisco uBR905 cable access router provides high-speed network access on the cable television system to residential and Small Office, Home Office (SOHO) subscribers. The uBR905 router has a coaxial cable (F-connector) interface that can be connected to a cable system. Coaxial cable and an F connector are used to connect the router and cable system. The coaxial cable can be either radio grade 59 (RG-59) or RG-6, although RG-6 is recommended.

To connect the Cisco uBR905 cable access router to the cable system, follow these steps:

Step 1   Verify that the router is not connected to power.

Step 2   Locate the RF coaxial cable coming from the coaxial cable CATV wall outlet.

Step 3   Install a cable splitter/directional coupler, if needed, to separate signals for TV and computer use. If necessary, also install a high-pass filter to prevent interference between the TV and computer signals.

CAUTION

Do not overtighten the connector; doing so can break off the connector. Use of a torque wrench is not recommended because of the danger of tightening the connector more than the recommended 1/6 turn after it is finger-tight.

Step 4   Connect the coaxial cable to the F connector of the router, as shown in Figure 5-34. Hand-tighten the connector, making sure that it is finger-tight, and then give it a 1/6 turn with a wrench.

Figure 5-34 F Connector

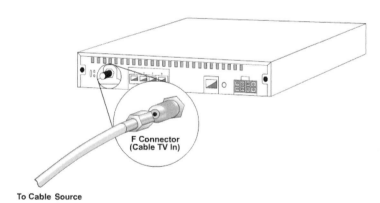

Step 5   Make sure that all other coaxial cable connectors—all intermediate splitters, couplers, or ground blocks—are securely tightened from the distribution tap to the Cisco uBR905 router, following the instructions in Step 4.

Setting Up Console Connections

To initially configure your Cisco device, you need to provide a management connection directly to the device. For Cisco equipment, this management attachment is called a console port. The console port enables you to monitor and configure a Cisco hub, switch, or router.

The cable used between a terminal and a console port is a rollover cable with RJ-45 connectors, as illustrated in Figure 5-35.

Figure 5-35 Setting Up a Console Connection

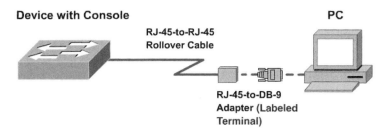

The rollover cable, also known as a console cable, has a different pinout than the straight-through or crossover RJ-45 cables used with Ethernet or the ISDN BRI. The pinout for a rollover is as follows:

1 to 8

2 to 7

3 to 6

4 to 5

5 to 4

6 to 3

7 to 2

8 to 1

To set up a connection between your terminal and the Cisco console port, you must perform the following steps:

Step 1   Cable the devices using a rollover cable. You likely need an RJ-45-to-DB-9 or an RJ-45-to-DB-25 adapter for your PC or terminal.

Step 2   Configure your terminal emulation application with the following common equipment (COM) port settings:

— 9600 bps

— 8 data bits

NOTE

The auxiliary (AUX) port on the router is used to provide remote management through a modem. The AUX port must be configured using the console port before it can be used. The AUX port can use the settings of 9600 bps, 8 data bits, no parity, 1 stop bit, and hardware flow control. The speed can be set up to 115,000 bps, but the speed will typically be no greater than 33,600 bps because of pulse code modulation (PCM).

—No parity

—1 stop bit

—Hardware flow control

Photozoom   Console Cable

In this PhotoZoom, you view a console cable.

Lab 5.2.7   Establishing a Console Connection to a Router or Switch

In this lab, you connect a PC to a router or a switch to establish a console session and observe the user interface.

Summary

In this chapter, you learned the following key points:

- A NIC provides network communication capabilities to and from a PC.

- The three common LAN media types are Ethernet, Token Ring, and FDDI.

- The term Ethernet often refers to all CSMA/CD LANs that conform to the Ethernet specifications.

- The four main categories of the Ethernet family of LAN implementations are Ethernet (10 Mbps), Fast Ethernet (100 Mbps), Gigabit Ethernet (1000 Mbps), and 10-Gb Ethernet (10,000 Mbps).

- Use a straight-through cable to connect dissimilar devices, such as a switch to a router, a switch to a PC, a hub to a router, or a hub to a PC.

- Use a crossover cable to connect similar devices, such as a switch to a switch, a router to a router, a PC to a PC, or a hub to a hub.

- The two major types of LANs are peer-to-peer and client-server.

- WANs use serial data transmission. WAN connection types include ISDN, DSL, and cable modems.

- A router is usually the DTE and needs a serial cable to connect to a DCE device, such as a CSU/DSU.

- The ISDN BRI has two types of interfaces: S/T and U interfaces. To interconnect the ISDN BRI port to the service-provider device, a UTP Category 5 straight-through cable with RJ-45 connectors is used.

- A phone cable and an RJ-11 connector connect a router for DSL service.

- Coaxial cable and a BNC connector connect a router for cable service.

- Rollover cable connects a terminal and the console port of an internetworking device.

To supplement all that you have learned in this chapter, refer to the chapter-specific Interactive Media Activity and PhotoZooms on the CD-ROM that accompanies this book.

Key Terms

active hub   Must be plugged into an electrical outlet because it needs power to amplify the incoming signal before passing it out to the other ports.

AUI (attachment unit interface)   The 15-pin physical connector interface between a computer's NIC and Ethernet cable.

crossover cable   A cable that crosses the critical pair to properly align, transmit, and receive signals on the device with line connections.

GBIC (Gigabit Interface Converter)   A hot-swappable input/output device that plugs into a Gigabit Ethernet port.

intelligent hub   Sometimes called "smart hubs." These devices basically function as active hubs, but also include a microprocessor chip and diagnostic capabilities. They are more expensive than active hubs, but are useful in troubleshooting situations.

peer-to-peer network   Networked computers act as equal partners, or peers, to each other. As peers, each computer can take on the client function or the server function.

repeater   A device that regenerates and retimes network signals at the bit level to allow them to travel a longer distance on the media.

RJ-45   A connector commonly used for finishing a twisted-pair cable.

straight-through cable   A cable that maintains the pin connection all the way through the cable. Thus, the wire connected to pin 1 is the same on both ends of the cable.

switch   Sometimes described as a multiport bridge. While a typical bridge might have just two ports (linking two network segments), the switch can have multiple ports, depending on how many network segments are to be linked.

WEP (wired equivalent privacy)   A security mechanism, defined within the 802.11 standard, that is designed to protect the over-the-air transmission between wireless LAN access points and NICs.

Check Your Understanding

Complete all the review questions to test your understanding of the topics and concepts in this chapter. Answers are listed in Appendix B, "Check Your Understanding Answer Key."

1. Which of the following is an 802.3u specification?

   A. 10BASE-F

   B. 10BASE-T

   C. 100BASE-TX

   D. 1000BASE-CX

2. Which of the following is the most appropriate choice for Ethernet connectivity?

   A. Use 10-Mbps Ethernet as a connection between server and LAN.

   B. Use Gigabit Ethernet as the link at the user level to provide good performance.

   C. Use Fast Ethernet as a link between the user level and network devices to support the aggregate traffic from each Ethernet segment on the access link.

   D. None of the above.

3. Which standards body created the cables and connector specification used to support Ethernet implementation?

   A. ISO

   B. ANSI

   C. EIA/TIA

   D. IETF

4. Which of the following statements does not correctly describe a media connector?

   A. An RJ-45 connector is an 8-pin connector used mainly for terminating coaxial cable.

   B. An AUI is a 15-pin connector used between a NIC and an Ethernet cable.

   C. The GBIC is a transceiver that converts serial electric currents to optical signals, and vice versa.

   D. None of the above.

5. For which of the following would you not need to provide a crossover cable?

   A. Connecting uplinks between switches

   B. Connecting routers to switches

   C. Connecting hubs to switches

   D. None of the above

6. Which technology is not a type of wireless communication?

   A. Cellular

   B. Broadband

   C. Infrared

   D. Spread spectrum

7. Which of the following is not a WAN implementation?

   A. DSL

   B. ISDN

   C. Frame Relay

   D. Ethernet

8. What type of data-transmission method is used by a WAN?

   A. Parallel

   B. Serial

   C. Single

   D. None of above

9. What best describes a DCE?

   A. User device at the end of a network

   B. Equipment that serves as the data source or destination

   C. Physical devices such as protocol translators and multiplexers

   D. Devices that make up the network end of the user-to-network interface

10. Which of the following media is used to interconnect the ISDN BRI port to the service-provider device?

    A. CAT 5 UTP straight-through

    B. CAT 5 UTP crossover

    C. Coaxial

    D. Fiber-optic

11. What type of connector is used for DSL connection?

    A. RJ-45

    B. RJ-11

    C. F

    D. DB-9

12. What type of connector is used to connect a router and a cable system?

    A. RJ-45

    B. RJ-11

    C. F

    D. AUI

13. What type of cable is used to connect a terminal and a console port?

    A. Straight-through

    B. Rollover

    C. Crossover

    D. Coaxial

CHAPTER 6

Ethernet Fundamentals

Objectives

Upon completion of this chapter, you should be able to answer the following questions:

- What are the Ethernet IEEE naming standards?

- Ethernet operates at which layers of the OSI reference model?

- What are the 802.3 frame formats?

- What is the Media Access Control (MAC)?

- What is the CSMA/CD process?

- What is link establishment?

- What is full duplex?

Additional Topics of Interest

In addition to the core objective areas, this chapter introduces you to the following topics of interest to networkers:

- How to identify computers and interfaces

- Layer 2 framing

- Ethernet frame structure

- Ethernet timing

- Interface spacing and backoff

- Error handling

- Three types of collisions

- Sources of Ethernet errors

- Frame Check Sequence (FCS)

- Ethernet auto-negotiation

Key Terms

The following is a list of key terms introduced in this chapter. For your reference, a definition for each term can be found at the end of the chapter.

Ethernet   page 247

carrier sense multiple access collision detect (CSMA/CD)   page 248

Institute of Electrical and Electronic Engineers (IEEE)   page 248

Fast Ethernet   page 249

Gigabit Ethernet   page 249

10-Gb Ethernet   page 249

Media Access Control (MAC)   page 250

Logical Link Control (LLC)   page 250

IEEE 802.2   page 250

encapsulation   page 250

IEEE 802.3   page 251

MAC address   page 253

organizationally unique identifier (OUI)   page 253

header   page 253

trailer   page 253

maximum transmission unit (MTU)   page 259

Token Ring   page 262

FDDI   page 262

backoff   page 263

connectionless   page 265

simplex   page 265

half duplex   page 265

full duplex   page 266

propagation delay   page 266

Simple Network Management Protocol (SNMP)   page 270

jabber   page 276

long frame   page 276

alignment error   page 277

range error   page 277

ghost   page 278

Ethernet, in its various forms, is the most widely used local-area network (LAN) technology. Ethernet was designed to fill the middle ground between long-distance, low-speed networks and specialized, computer-room networks carrying data at high speeds for very limited distance.

Ethernet is well suited to applications in which a local communication medium must carry sporadic, occasionally heavy traffic at high-pack data rates. It was designed to enable sharing resources on a local workgroup level. Design goals include simplicity, low cost, compatibility, fairness, low delay, and high speed.

In this chapter, you learn about the history of Ethernet and IEEE Ethernet standards. This chapter discusses the operation of Ethernet, Ethernet framing, and error handling, as well as the different types of collisions on Ethernet networks. In addition, this chapter introduces collision domains and broadcast domains. Finally, this chapter describes segmentation and the devices used to create network segments.

Please be sure to look at the associated Interactive Media Activity for this chapter that you will find on the CD-ROM accompanying this book.

Ethernet Fundamentals

LANs are high-speed, low-error data networks that cover a relatively small geographic area (up to a few thousand meters). LANs connect workstations, peripherals, terminals, and other devices in a single building or other geographically limited area.

Ethernet is the dominant LAN technology in the world. Most of the traffic on the Internet originates and ends with an Ethernet connection. From its beginning in the 1970s, Ethernet has evolved to meet the increasing demand for high-speed LANs. When a new medium, fiber optics, was produced, Ethernet adapted to take advantage of the great bandwidth of fiber and low error rate. Now the same basic protocol that transported data at 3 megabits per second (Mbps) in 1973 is carrying data at 10 gigabits per second (Gbps).

The success of Ethernet is a result of its simplicity and ease of maintenance, its capability to incorporate new technologies, its reliability, and its low cost of installation and upgrade. With the introduction of Gigabit Ethernet, what started as a LAN technology has now had its reach extended to distances that make Ethernet a metropolitan-area and even a wide-area networking standard. This section provides an overview of the Ethernet, including the history of Ethernet, Ethernet naming conventions, and Ethernet frame formats.

Introduction to Ethernet

The original idea for Ethernet grew out of the problem of allowing two or more users to use the same medium without each user's signals interfering with each other. This problem of multiple-user access to a shared medium was studied in the early 1970s at the University of Hawaii. A system called Alohanet was developed to allow various stations on the Hawaiian

Islands to have structured access to the shared radio frequency band in the atmosphere. The original technology that today's Ethernet is based on was wireless. This work later formed the basis for the Ethernet Media Access Control (MAC) method known as *carrier sense multiple access collision detect (CSMA/CD)*. CSMA/CD is discussed in more detail later in this chapter.

The original version of Ethernet was the first LAN of the world. It was designed more than 30 years ago by Robert Metcalfe and his coworkers at Xerox. The first Ethernet standard was published by a consortium of Digital Equipment Company, Intel, and Xerox (DIX) in 1980. Metcalfe wanted Ethernet to be a shared standard from which everyone could benefit. Therefore, DIX made the new standard an open standard, meaning that it was available to any company. This was not often done in the computer industry. The first products developed using the Ethernet standard were sold during the early 1980s. Ethernet products transmitted at 10 Mbps over thick (about the diameter of your smallest finger) coaxial cable up to a distance of 2 km. Ethernet was an instant success.

The *Institute of Electrical and Electronic Engineers (IEEE)* is a professional organization that defines network standards. In 1985, the IEEE standards committee for local and metropolitan networks published its standards for LANs. The IEEE LAN standards are the predominant and best-known LAN standards in the world today. These standards start with the number 802. The standard that was based on Ethernet is 802.3. The IEEE wanted to make sure that its standards were compatible with and fit into the ISO's OSI reference model. The IEEE divides the OSI data link layer into two separate sublayers: Media Access Control (MAC) and Logical Link Control (LLC). The 802.3 standard addresses the needs of Layer 1 (Physical) and the lower portion of Layer 2 (MAC).

Some small modifications to the original Ethernet standard were made in the 802.3 standard. Some differences exist between the DIX Ethernet and the 802.3 specifications. However, the differences between the two standards are so minor that any Ethernet network interface card (NIC) can transmit and receive Ethernet and 802.3 packets and frames. Essentially, Ethernet and IEEE 802.3 are the same standards. Just remember that 802.3 is now the official IEEE Ethernet standard.

During the mid-1980s, Ethernet's 10-Mbps bandwidth was more than enough for the PCs of that era. By the early 1990s, PCs had become much faster and people were beginning to complain about the bottleneck caused by the small bandwidth of Ethernet LANs. In 1995, the IEEE announced a standard for a 100-Mbps Ethernet. This was followed by standards for Gigabit (1 billion bits per second) Ethernet in 1998 and 1999. IEEE approved the standards for 10-Gb Ethernet in June 2002. These more modern standards are still Ethernet (802.3).

All the new Ethernet standards are essentially compatible with the original Ethernet standard. An Ethernet frame could leave an older 10-Mbps NIC in a PC, eventually be placed by a router onto a 10-Gbps Ethernet fiber link, and then end up at a 100-Mbps Ethernet card. As long as the frame stayed on Ethernet networks, it would not be changed. This illustrates one of the main reasons for Ethernet's great success—it is very scalable. That means that the bandwidth of the network could be increased again and again without changing the underlying Ethernet technology.

The original Ethernet (IEEE 802.3) has been supplemented a number of times to incorporate new transmission media and to enable higher transmission rates. However, it is important to understand that the essential qualities of the original Ethernet have been retained. The Ethernet 802.3 standards all belong to the same family. Differences exist between the standards, but their similarities are greater than their differences. What has been retained from the original in each new standard means that the 802.3 family of Ethernet is all compatible.

IEEE Ethernet Naming Rules

The term *Ethernet* refers to a family of networking technologies that include original Ethernet, *Fast Ethernet*, *Gigabit Ethernet* (or Gig-E), and *10-Gb Ethernet* (or 10-G). Ethernet interfaces can range from US $10 to $100,000. Ethernet speeds can be 10, 100, 1000, or 10,000 Mbps. This section explores more details of original Ethernet (10BASE-T), Fast Ethernet (100BASE-TX and 100BASE-FX), Gigabit Ethernet (1000BASE-T and 1000BASE-X), and 10-Gb Ethernet. Two features of Ethernet remain consistent across all forms of Ethernet: the basic frame format and the IEEE sublayers of OSI Layer 2.

When Ethernet needs to be expanded to add a new medium or capability, the IEEE issues a new supplement to the 802.3 standard. The new supplements are given a one- or two-letter designation—for example, 802.3u is Fast Ethernet. An abbreviated description (called an identifier) also is assigned to the supplement. The following are examples of some of the supplements:

- 10BASE2 (IEEE 802.3a)

- 10BASE5 (IEEE 802.3)

- 100BASE-T (IEEE 802.3i)

- 1000BASE-TX (IEEE 802.3X)

As you can see, the abbreviated description consists of these parts:

- A number indicating the number of megabits per second transmitted

- The word BASE, indicating that baseband signaling is used

- Numbers (the 2 and 5) that refer to the coaxial cable segment length (the 185m length has been rounded up to 2, for 200)

- One or more letters of the alphabet indicating the type of medium used (F = fiber-optic cable, T = copper unshielded twisted-pair)

Baseband signaling is the simplest method of signaling. In baseband signaling, the whole bandwidth of the transmission medium is used for the signal. The data signal (a voltage on UTP or a flash of light on fiber) is transmitted directly over the transmission medium. No other special signal (known as a carrier signal) is required. Ethernet uses baseband signaling.

A second method of signaling, broadband signaling, is not used in Ethernet. In broadband signaling, the data signal is never placed directly on the transmission medium. Instead, an analog signal called the carrier signal is modulated by the data signal. Then this modulated carrier signal is transmitted. Radio broadcasts and cable TV use broadband signaling. Like the International Organization for Standardization (ISO), the IEEE is a standards-making organization. The manufacturers of networking equipment are not required to fully comply with all the specifications of any standard. The goals of IEEE are as follows:

- To supply the engineering information necessary to build devices that comply with an Ethernet standard

- To not stifle innovation by manufacturers

If you are setting up or maintaining a small LAN, you can buy all your equipment from one reputable manufacturer. Then you can be assured of the compatibility of all the devices. However, if you are responsible for a large network made up of many smaller Ethernet LANs with equipment from a mix of vendors, your situation is very different. The capability to use equipment from a variety of vendors to interoperate reliably is a very important issue. It is unfortunate that no industry or governmental agency exists to test and certify that a device fully meets an IEEE standard. However, that is a very good reason for you to educate yourself about the standards and the industry. The fact is, you have only your own knowledge and that of your coworkers on which to base your design and purchasing decisions.

 Interactive Media Activity   Drag and Drop: IEEE 802 Standards

This activity tests familiarity with all the IEEE 802 standards.

Ethernet and the OSI Model

LAN standards define the physical media and the connectors used to connect devices to media at the physical layer of the OSI reference model. In addition, LAN standards define how to encapsulate protocol-specific traffic in such a way that traffic going to different upper-layer protocols can use the same channel that passes through that layer of the OSI model. To provide these functions, the IEEE Ethernet data link layer has two sublayers:

- *Media Access Control (MAC)* **(802.3)**—As the name implies, the MAC sublayer defines how to transmit frames on the physical wire. It handles physical addressing associated with each device, network topology definition, and line discipline.

- *Logical Link Control (LLC)* **(802.2)**—As the name implies, the LLC sublayer is responsible for logically identifying different protocol types and then encapsulating them. A type code or a service access point (SAP) identifier performs the logical identification. The type of LLC frame used by an end station depends on what identifier the upper-layer protocol (such as IP) expects. Although *IEEE 802.2* represents one standard type of frame *encapsulation*, there are others, such as Ethernet II (used primarily with TCP/IP–based Ethernet LANS). These are discussed later in the chapter.

As shown in Figure 6-1, the *IEEE 802.3* standard defines the physical layer (Layer 1) and the MAC portion of the data link layer (Layer 2).

Figure 6-1 802.3 Ethernet and the OSI Model

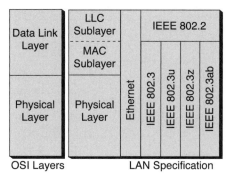

Figure 6-2 maps a variety of technologies to OSI Layer 1 and the lower half of Layer 2. In this book, we focus primarily on Ethernet LAN technology. Layer 1, the physical layer, involves interfacing with media, signals, bit streams that travel on media, components that put signals on media, and various topologies. The physical layer performs a key role in the communication that takes place between computers, but its efforts alone are not enough. Each of its functions has its limitations. Layer 2 addresses these limitations.

Figure 6-2 LAN Specifications and OSI Model

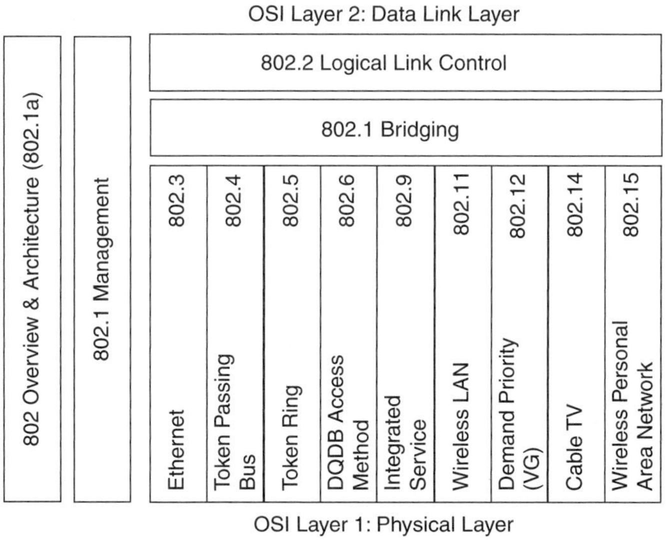

OSI Layer 2: Data Link Layer

802 Overview & Architecture (802.1a)	802.1 Management	802.2 Logical Link Control								
		802.1 Bridging								
		802.3	802.4	802.5	802.6	802.9	802.11	802.12	802.14	802.15
		Ethernet	Token Passing Bus	Token Ring	DQDB Access Method	Integrated Service	Wireless LAN	Demand Priority (VG)	Cable TV	Wireless Personal Area Network

OSI Layer 1: Physical Layer

For each limitation in Layer 1, Layer 2 has a solution, as documented in Table 6-1.

Table 6-1 Layer 1 Limitations Versus Layer 2 Solutions

Layer 1 Limitation	Layer 2 Solution
Layer 1 cannot communicate with the upper-level layers.	Layer 2 communicates with upper-level layers via the LLC sublayer.
Layer 1 cannot identify computers.	Layer 2 identifies computers using the MAC addressing scheme.
Layer 1 can only describe streams of bits.	Layer 2 uses framing to organize or group the bits. (This process ultimately provides a way for the bits to convey meaning.)
Layer 1 cannot decide which computer will transmit binary data from a group that is all trying to transmit at the same time.	Layer 2 uses the MAC sublayer to accomplish this.

The Layer 2 sublayers, LLC and MAC, are active, vital agreements that make technology compatible and computer communication possible. The MAC sublayer is concerned with the physical components that will be used to communicate the information. Like the other layers, the LLC remains relatively independent of the physical equipment that will be used for the communicative process. The LLC allows multiple Layer 3 protocols, such as IP and IPX, to be simultaneously supported along with multiple frame types.

Figure 6-3 maps a variety of Ethernet technologies to the lower half of OSI Layer 2, and all of Layer 1. Although there are other varieties of Ethernet, the ones depicted are the most widely used and are the focus of this course.

Figure 6-3 Ethernet Technologies and OSI Model

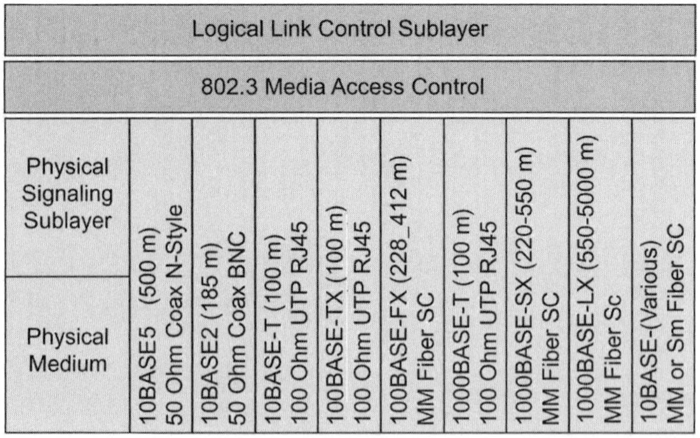

Naming

To allow for local delivery of frames on the Ethernet, there must be an addressing system, a way of naming the computers and interfaces. Every computer has a unique way of identifying itself. Each computer on a network has a physical address. No two physical addresses on a network should ever be alike. Referred to as the ***Media Access Control (MAC) address***, the physical address is located on the NIC. Other terms for the MAC address include the hardware address, the NIC address, the Layer 2 address, and the Ethernet address.

Ethernet uses MAC addresses to uniquely identify individual devices. Every device (PC, router, switch) with an Ethernet interface to the LAN must have a MAC address; otherwise, other devices cannot communicate with it. A MAC address is 48 bits in length and is expressed as 12 hexadecimal digits. The first six hexadecimal digits, which are administered by the IEEE, identify the manufacturer or vendor and thus comprise the ***organizationally unique identifier (OUI)***. The remaining six hexadecimal digits comprise the interface serial number, or another value administered by the specific vendor. MAC addresses sometimes are referred to as burned-in addresses (BIAs) because they are burned into read-only memory (ROM) and are copied into random-access memory (RAM) when the NIC initializes. Figure 6-4 illustrates the MAC address format.

Figure 6-4 MAC Address Format

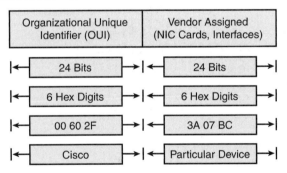

Without MAC addresses, the LAN would be a group of computers without identifiers, and it would be impossible to deliver an Ethernet frame. Therefore, at the data link layer, a ***header*** and a ***trailer*** are added to upper-layer data. The header and trailer contain control information intended for the data link layer entity in the destination system. Data from upper-layer entities is encapsulated in the data link layer header and trailer.

Ethernet and 802.3 LANs are broadcast networks. All stations see all frames. Each station must examine every frame to determine whether that station is the desired destination.

On an Ethernet network, when one device wants to send data to another device, it can open a communication pathway to the other device by using its MAC address. When a source device sends data out on a network, the data carries the MAC address of its intended destination. As this data propagates along the network medium, the NIC in each device on the network checks to see if its MAC address matches the physical destination address carried by the data frame. If there is no match, the NIC discards the data frame.

If there is a match, the NIC verifies the destination address in the frame header to determine whether the packet is properly addressed. When the data passes its destination station, the NIC for that station makes a copy, takes the data out of the envelope, and gives the data to the computer to be processed by upper-layer protocols such as IP and TCP.

Layer 2 Framing

Encoded bit streams on physical media represent a tremendous technological accomplishment, but they alone are not enough to make communication happen. Framing helps obtain essential information that could not otherwise be obtained with coded bit streams alone. Examples of such information are listed here:

- Which computers are communicating with one another
- When communication between individual computers begins and when it terminates
- Recognition of errors that occur during the communication
- Whose turn it is to "talk" in a computer "conversation"
- Where the data is located within the frame

When you have a way to identify computers, you can move on to framing. Framing is the Layer 2 encapsulation process. A frame is the Layer 2 protocol data unit. Figure 6-5 illustrates the ideas of bits and frames.

Figure 6-5 From Bits to Frame

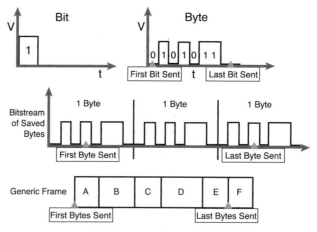

A, B, C, D, E, F Multiple, Often Many, Bytes

When you work with bits, the most accurate diagram you can use to visualize them is a graph showing voltage versus time. However, because you usually deal with larger units of data and addressing and control information, this type of graph could become ridiculously large and confusing. Another type of diagram you could use is the frame format diagram, which is based on voltage versus time graphs. You read them from left to right, just like an oscilloscope graph. The frame format diagram in Figure 6-5 shows different groupings of bits (fields) that perform other functions.

Many different types of frames are described by various standards. A single generic frame has sections called *fields*, and each field is composed of bytes (see Figure 6-6). The names of the fields commonly found in a data link layer frame are as follows:

- Frame Start field

- Address field

- Length/Type/Control field

- Data field

- Frame Check Sequence (FCS) field

Figure 6-6 A Generic Frame Format

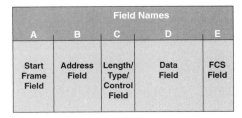

The sections that follow describe the different frame fields in more detail.

More Information: Frame Fields

Frame Start Field

When computers are connected to a physical medium, there must be a way for them to grab the attention of other computers to broadcast the message, as in, "Here comes a frame!" Various technologies have different ways of doing this process, but, regardless of technology, all frames have a beginning signaling sequence of bytes.

Address Field

All frames contain identification information, such as the address of the source computer (MAC address) and the address of the destination computer (MAC address).

Length and Type Fields

Most frames have some specialized fields. In some technologies, a Length field specifies the exact length of a frame. Some have a Type field, which specifies the Layer 3 protocol making the sending request. There is also a set of technologies in which no such fields are used.

More Information: Frame Fields (Continued)
Data Field
The reason for sending frames is to get higher-layer data, ultimately the user application data, from the source computer to the destination computer. The data package that you want to deliver includes the message that you want to send (the data). Padding bytes are added sometimes so that the frames have a minimum length. Logical Link Control (LLC) bytes also are included with the data field in the IEEE standard frames. Remember that the LLC sublayer adds control information to the network protocol data, a Layer 3 packet, to help deliver that packet to its destination. Layer 2 communicates with upper layers through LLC.
Frame Check Sequence Field
All frames (and the bits, bytes, and fields contained within them) are susceptible to errors from a variety of sources. The Frame Check Sequence (FCS) field contains a number based on the data in the frame; this number is calculated by the source computer. When the destination computer receives the frame, it recalculates the FCS number and compares it with the FCS number included in the frame. If the two numbers are different, an error is assumed and the frame is discarded.
The Frame Check Sequence number normally is calculated through the use of a cyclic redundancy check (CRC), which performs polynomial calculations on the data.

Ethernet Frame Structure

At the MAC sublayer, the frame structure is nearly identical for all speeds of Ethernet (10/100/1,000/10,000 Mbps). Half-duplex Gigabit Ethernet 1000BASE-T and the "W" versions of 10-Gb Ethernet have certain timing issues that require minor differences in how the interframe spacing is handled by the MAC sublayer, but these are otherwise the same as the other speeds. However, at the physical layer, almost all versions of Ethernet are substantially different from one another, and each speed has its own set of architecture design rules.

IEEE 802.3 Ethernet Frame

In addition to the 802.2 frame type discussed previously, there is a simpler IEEE 802.3 frame type, which was the first developed by the IEEE. As with 802.2, however, it is not used widely in today's Ethernet LANs. Figure 6-7 shows the basic IEEE 802.3 Ethernet frame format.

Figure 6-7 IEEE 802.3 Ethernet Frame Structure

						FCS Calculation	
Preamble	SFD	Destination	Source	Length/ Type	Data	Pad	FCS
7	1	6	6	2	46 to 1500		4

Table 6-2 lists the octet number and name for each 802.3 Ethernet frame field.

Table 6-2 IEEE 802.3 Ethernet Frame Fields

Octets in Each Frame Field	Frame Field
7	Preamble
1	Start Frame Delimiter (SFD)
6	Destination MAC Address
6	Source MAC Address
2	Length/Type Field (Length if less than 0600 in hexadecimal—otherwise, protocol Type)
46 to 1500	Data and Pad
4	Frame Check Sequence (CRC Checksum)

More Information: Ethernet II Frame

In the DIX version of Ethernet that was developed before the adoption of the IEEE 802.3 version of Ethernet, the Preamble and Start Frame Delimiter (SFD) fields were combined into a single field, although the binary pattern was identical. The field labeled Length/Type was listed only as Length in the early IEEE versions and only as Type in the DIX version. These two uses of the field officially were combined in a later IEEE version because both uses of the field were common throughout the industry. The early DIX Ethernet frame format, also known as Ethernet Version2 or Ethernet II, is the most commonly used frame type with TCP/IP–based Ethernet LANs. Figure 6-8 illustrates the Ethernet II frame format.

Figure 6-8 Ethernet II Frame Format

Preamble	Destination	Source	Type	Data ¦ Pad	FCS
8	6	6	2	46 to 1500	4

Table 6-3 lists the octet number and name for each Ethernet II frame field.

Table 6-3 Ethernet II Frame Fields

Octets in Each Frame Field	Frame Field
8	Preamble (ending in pattern 10101011, the 802.3 SFD)
6	Destination MAC Address
6	Source MAC Address
2	Type Field (46 to 1500 data—if less than 46 octets, a pad must be added to the end)
46 to 1500	Data and Pad
4	Frame Check Sequence (CRC Checksum)

More Information: Ethernet II Frame (Continued)

As indicated in Table 6-3, use of the Ethernet II Type field is incorporated into the current 802.3 frame definition. Upon receipt, a station must determine which higher-layer protocol is present in an incoming frame. This first is attempted by examining the Length/Type field. If the two-octet value is equal to or greater than 600 hex, the frame is interpreted according to the Ethernet II type code indicated. If it is less than 600 hex, the frame is interpreted as an 802.3 frame and the length of the frame is indicated. Further investigation is required to determine how to proceed. To proceed from here, the first four octets of the 802.3 Data field are examined. The value found in those first four octets usually is checked for two unique values; if they are not present, the frame is assumed to be an 802.2 Logical Link Control (LLC) sublayer encapsulation and is decoded according to the 802.2 LLC encapsulation indicated. One of the two values tested for is AAAA in hexadecimal, which indicates an 802.2/ 802 (Subnetwork Access Protocol [SNAP]) encapsulation. The other value tested for is FFFF in hexadecimal, which might indicate an old Novell Internetwork Packet Exchange (IPX) "raw" encapsulation.

Ethernet Frame Fields

The following list shows most of the fields permitted or required in an 802.3 Ethernet frame. Refer back to Figure 6-8 for an illustration of the 802.3 Ethernet frame:

- **Preamble**—This field contains an alternating pattern of 1s and 0s that was used for timing synchronization in the asynchronous 10-Mbps and slower implementations of Ethernet. Faster versions of Ethernet are synchronous, so this timing information is redundant but is retained for compatibility. The preamble is seven octets in length and is represented by the following binary pattern:

  10101010 10101010 10101010 10101010 10101010 10101010 10101010

- **Start Frame Delimiter (SFD)**—This one-octet field marks the end of the timing information. It is represented by the binary pattern 10101011. In the early DIX form of Ethernet, this octet was the last in the eight-octet preamble.

  Although the old DIX Ethernet described the first eight octets differently than the IEEE Ethernet, the pattern and usage is identical. Also, the timing information represented by the preamble and SFD is discarded and is not counted toward the minimum and maximum frame sizes.

- **Destination Address**—This field contains the six-octet MAC destination address. The destination address can be a unicast (single node), multicast (group of nodes), or broadcast address (all nodes).

- **Source Address**—This field contains the six-octet MAC source address. The source address is supposed to be only the unicast address of the transmitting Ethernet station. However, there are an increasing number of virtual protocols in use, which use and sometimes share a specific source MAC address to identify the virtual entity.

In the early Ethernet specifications, MAC addresses were optionally two or six octets, as long as the size was constant throughout the broadcast domain. Two-octet addressing first was excluded explicitly in paragraph 3.2.3 in the 1998 version of 802.3 and no longer is supported in 802.3 Ethernet.

■ **Length/Type**—If the value is less that 1536 decimal (0600 hexadecimal), then the value indicates Length . The Length interpretation is used where the LLC layer provides the protocol identification.

— **Type (Ethernet)**—The Type specifies the upper-layer protocol to receive the data after Ethernet processing is complete.

— **Length (IEEE 802.3)**—The Length indicates the number of bytes of data that follows this field. If the value is equal to or greater than 1536 decimal (0600 hexadecimal), the value indicates Type, and the contents of the Data field are decoded per the protocol indicated. A list of common Ethertype protocols is found on page 168 of RFC 1700.

■ **Data and Pad**—This field can be of any length that does not cause the frame to exceed the maximum frame size. The *maximum transmission unit (MTU)* for Ethernet is 1500 octets, so the data should not exceed that size. The content of this field is unspecified. An unspecified pad is inserted immediately after the user data when there is not enough user data for the frame to meet the minimum frame length.

The frame structure figures depict the Data field as being between 46 and 1500 octets. In fact, Ethernet does not specify this. The frame is required to be not less than 64 octets or more than 1518 octets, without actually specifying the size of the data field. This left the user to calculate the size of the data field by subtracting all the other fields from the frame size. If the currently required six-octet MAC addresses are used, the data field size will be between 46 (padded, if necessary) and 1500 octets.

Data (IEEE 802.3)—After physical layer and data link layer processing is complete, the data is sent to an upper-layer protocol, which must be defined within the data portion of the frame. If data in the frame is insufficient to fill the frame to its minimum 64-byte size, padding bytes are inserted to ensure at least a 64-byte frame.

■ **Frame Check Sequence (FCS)**—This sequence contains a 4-byte CRC value that is created by the sending device and is recalculated by the receiving device to check for damaged frames. The mathematical result of a cyclic redundancy check algorithm is placed in this four-octet field. The sending station calculates the checksum for the transmitted frame, and the resulting four-octet value is appended following the Data/Pad. Receiving station(s) perform the same calculation and compare the new checksum against the checksum found at the end of the transmitted frame. If the two match, the frame is good. The fields used in the calculation include everything from the beginning of the destination address to the end of the Data/Pad, as shown in Figure 6-7.

The preamble, shown in Figure 6-8, illustrates that SFD and Extension fields are not included in the calculation. The FCS is the only Ethernet field transmitted in noncanonical order (Most Significant Bit [MSB] first).

Because the corruption of a single bit anywhere from the beginning of the destination address through the end of the FCS field causes the checksum to be different, the coverage of the FCS includes itself. It is not possible to distinguish between corruption of the FCS itself and corruption of any preceding field used in the calculation.

Ethernet Operation

When multiple stations (nodes) must access physical media and other networking devices, various media access control strategies are used. This section briefly reviews the access-control strategies and focuses on Ethernet access control method—CSMA/CD.

It should be noted that although CSMA/CD has immense historical importance and practical importance in original Ethernet, it is diminishing somewhat in implementation for two reasons:

- When four-pair UTP is used, separate wire pairs for transmission (Tx) and reception (Rx) exist, making copper UTP potentially free from collisions and capable of full-duplex operation, depending on whether it is deployed in a shared (hub) or switched environment.

- Similar logic applies to optical fiber links, where separate optical paths—a transmission fiber and a reception fiber—are used.

One new form of Ethernet, 1000BASE-TX, Gigabit Ethernet over copper, uses all four wire pairs simultaneously in both directions, resulting in a permanent collision. In older forms of Ethernet, such a permanent collision precludes the system from working. Yet in 1000BASE-TX, sophisticated circuitry can accommodate this permanent collision, resulting from an attempt to get as much data as possible over UTP.

Media Access Control (MAC)

Media Access Control (MAC) refers to protocols that determine which computer on a shared-medium environment (collision domain) is allowed to transmit the data. MAC, with LLC, comprises the IEEE version of Layer 2. MAC and LLC are both sublayers of Layer 2. Two broad categories of MAC exist:

- Deterministic (taking turns)

- Nondeterministic (first come, first served)

Token Ring and FDDI are deterministic, and Ethernet/802.3 is nondeterministic (also called probabilistic).

Deterministic MAC Protocols

Deterministic MAC protocols use a form of taking turns. Token passing is an example of the deterministic MAC protocol. Some Native American tribes used the custom of passing a "talking stick" during gatherings. Whoever held the talking stick was allowed to speak. When that person finished, he or she passed it to another person.

In this analogy, the shared medium is the air, the data is the words of the speaker, and the protocol is possession of the talking stick. The stick might even be called a token. This situation is similar to a data link protocol called a Token Ring. In a Token Ring network, individual hosts are arranged in a ring, as shown in Figure 6-9. A special data token circulates around the ring. When a host wants to transmit, it seizes the token, transmits the data for a limited time, and then places the token back in the ring, where it can be passed along, or seized, by another host.

Figure 6-9 A Token Ring Network

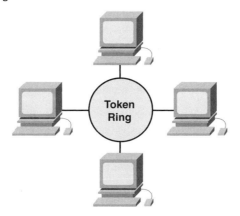

Nondeterministic MAC Protocols

Nondeterministic MAC protocols use a first-come, first-served (FCFS) approach. CSMA/CD is an example of a nondeterministic MAC protocol.

To use this shared-medium technology, Ethernet allows the networking devices to arbitrate for the right to transmit. Stations on a CSMA/CD network listen for quiet, at which time it's okay to transmit. However, if two stations transmit at the same time, a *collision* occurs and neither station's transmission succeeds. All other stations on the network also hear the collision and wait for silence. The transmitting stations, in turn, each wait a random period of time (a backoff period) before retransmitting, thus minimizing the probability of a second collision.

Three Specific Topological Implementations and Their MACs

Three well-known Layer 2 technologies are Token Ring, FDDI, and Ethernet. Of these, Ethernet is by far the most common; however, they all serve to illustrate a different approach to LAN requirements. All three specify Layer 2 elements (for example, LLC, naming, framing, and MAC), as well as Layer 1 signaling components and media issues. The specific technologies for each are as follows:

- **Ethernet**—Logical bus topology (information flow on a linear bus) and physical star or extended star (wired as a star)

- *Token Ring*—Logical ring topology (in other words, information flow controlled in a ring) and a physical star topology (in other words, wired as a star)

- *FDDI*—Logical ring topology (information flow controlled in a ring) and physical dual-ring topology (wired as a dual-ring)

MAC Rules and Collision Detection/Backoff

Ethernet is a shared-media broadcast technology. The access method CSMA/CD used in Ethernet performs three functions:

- Transmitting and receiving data packets

- Decoding data packets and checking them for valid addresses before passing them to the upper layers of the OSI model

- Detecting errors within data packets or on the network

In the CSMA/CD access method, networking devices with data to transmit over the networking media work in a listen-before-transmit mode (CS = carrier sense). With shared Ethernet, this means that when a device wants to send data, it first must check to see whether the networking medium is busy. The device must check whether there are any signals on the networking media. After the device determines that the networking media is not busy, the device begins to transmit its data. While transmitting its data in the form of signals, the device also listens, to ensure that no other stations are transmitting data to the networking medium at the same time. If two stations send data at the same time, a collision occurs, as shown in the upper half of Figure 6-10. When it completes transmitting its data, the device returns to listening mode. With traditional shared Ethernet, only one device can transmit at a time. This is not true with switched Ethernet, which is covered in Chapter 8, "Ethernet Switching."

Figure 6-10 CSMA/CD

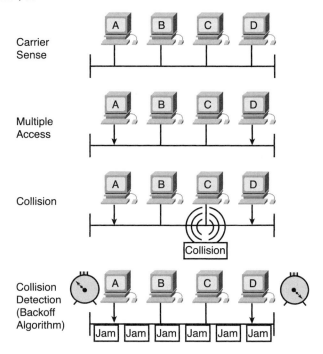

Networking devices are capable of detecting when a collision has occurred because the amplitude of the signal on the networking media increases (CD = collision detect). When a collision occurs, each device that is transmitting continues to transmit data for a short time, to ensure that all devices see the collision. When all devices on the network have seen that a collision has occurred, each transmitting device invokes an algorithm, known as a *backoff* algorithm. When all transmitting devices on the network have backed off for a certain period of time (random and, therefore, different for each device), any device can attempt to gain access to the networking media once again. When data transmission resumes on the network, the devices that were involved in the collision do not have priority to transmit data. Figure 6-11 summarizes the CSMA/CD process.

Figure 6-11 CSMA/CD Process

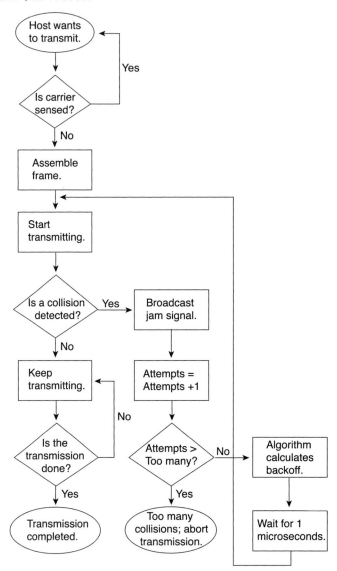

Ethernet is a broadcast transmission technology. This means that all devices on a network can see all frames that pass along the networking medium. However, not all the devices on the network will process the data. Only the device whose MAC address matches the destination MAC address carried by the frame copies the frame into its buffer. Ethernet is not concerned with Layer 3 network addresses such as IP or IPX. If the MAC addresses match, the frame is copied and passed up to Layer 3 to check the destination IP or IPX address for a match.

After a device has verified the destination MAC and IP addresses carried by the data, it checks the data packet for errors. If the device detects errors, the data packet is discarded. The destination device does not notify the source device, regardless of whether the packet arrived successfully. Ethernet is a *connectionless* network architecture and is referred to as a *best-effort delivery system*.

More Information: Simplex, Half-Duplex, and Full-Duplex Operation

The data channels over which a signal is sent can operate in one of three ways: simplex, half duplex, or full duplex. The distinction among these is in the way the signal can travel.

Simplex transmission, as its name implies, is simple. It is also called unidirectional because the signal travels in only one direction, just like traffic flows on a one-way street. Television or radio transmission is an example of simplex communication, as illustrated in Figure 6-12.

Figure 6-12 Simplex Transmission

Half-duplex transmission is an improvement over simplex transmission; the traffic can travel in both directions. Half-duplex transmission enables signals to travel in either direction, but not in both directions simultaneously, as illustrated in Figure 6-13. Half-duplex Ethernet, defined in the original 802.3 Ethernet, uses only one wire, with a digital signal running in both directions on the wire. It allows data transmission in only one direction at a time between a sending station and a receiving station. It also uses the CSMA/CD protocol to help prevent collisions and retransmit if a collision does occur.

Figure 6-13 Half-Duplex Transmission

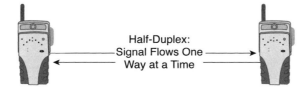

> **More Information: Simplex, Half-Duplex, and Full-Duplex Operation (Continued)**
>
> *Full-duplex transmission*, as illustrated in Figure 6-14, operates like a two-way, two-lane street. Traffic can travel in both directions at the same time. Ethernet full-duplex operation is made possible using switch technology, which is covered in greater depth in Chapter 8, "Ethernet Switching." Full-duplex switched networking technology increases performance because data can be sent and received at the same time. Full-duplex Ethernet uses two pairs of wires, which allow simultaneous data transmission between a sending station and a receiving station. Virtually no collisions occur in full-duplex Ethernet because switching technology creates a two-station, point-to-point virtual circuit, or "microsegments," when two devices need to communicate. Full-duplex Ethernet is supposed to offer 100 percent efficiency in both directions. This means that you can get 20 Mbps with a 10-Mbps Ethernet running in full-duplex operation. A 100-Mbps switch potentially can offer 200 Mbps to a station in full-duplex mode.
>
> **Figure 6-14** Full-Duplex Transmission
>
>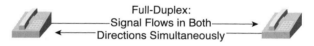
>
> Full-Duplex:
> Signal Flows in Both Directions Simultaneously

Ethernet Timing

Ethernet was designed to operate on a bus structure, which is a technical way to say that every station always hears all messages at almost the exact same time. The official designation is CSMA/CD. CSMA/CD can be interpreted simplistically to mean that when two stations realize that they are talking at the same time, they are supposed to stop and wait a polite amount of time before trying again.

The basic rules and specifications for proper operation of Ethernet are not particularly complicated, although some of the faster physical layer implementations are becoming so. Despite the basic simplicity, when a problem occurs in Ethernet, it is often quite difficult to isolate the source of the problem. Because of the common bus architecture of Ethernet (which can be described as a distributed single point of failure), the scope of the problem is usually all stations within the collision domain that are attached to the segment. When repeaters are used, this can include stations up to four segments away.

According to the rules, any station on an Ethernet network that wants to transmit a message first listens to ensure that no other station currently is transmitting. If the cable is quiet, the station begins transmitting immediately. But because the electrical signal takes a small amount of time to travel down the cable (called *propagation delay*), and each subsequent repeater encountered introduces a small amount of latency in forwarding the frame from one port to the next, it is possible for more than one station to begin transmitting at or near the same time. A collision then results.

If the attached station is operating in full duplex, the station can send and receive simultaneously, and collisions should not be present. Full-duplex operation also changes the timing considerations and eliminates the concept of slot time. Full-duplex operation allows for larger network architecture designs because the timing restriction for collision detection is removed.

In half-duplex operation, assuming that a collision does not occur, the sending station transmits 64 bits of timing synchronization information that often is known collectively as the preamble. The contents are as follows:

- Destination and source MAC addressing information
- Certain other header information
- The actual data payload
- A checksum (FCS) used to ensure that the message was not corrupted along the way

Stations receiving the frame recalculate the FCS to determine whether the incoming message is valid, and hand good messages to the next higher layer in the protocol stack.

For 10-Mbps Ethernet and slower versions, which are asynchronous, each receiving station uses the eight octets of timing information to synchronize its receive circuit to the incoming data but then discard it. The 100 Mbps higher-speed implementations of Ethernet are synchronous, so the timing information is not actually required at all. However, for compatibility reasons, the preamble and SFD are present. All information following the SFD at the end of the timing information is passed to the next higher layer. A new checksum is calculated and compared with the checksum found at the end of the received frame. If the frame is intact, it then must be interpreted according to the rules for whichever protocol is indicated by the Length/Type field or the LLC-layer protocol indicated by the first few octets of the data.

For all speeds of Ethernet transmission at or below 1000 Mbps, the standard describes how a transmission can be no smaller than *slot time*. Slot time for 10- and 100-Mbps Ethernet is 512 bit-times (64 octets). Slot time for 1000-Mbps Ethernet is 4096 bit-times (512 octets, including the extension). Slot time is not defined for 10-Gbps Ethernet because it does not permit half-duplex operation. Slot time is just longer than the longest possible round-trip delay time when maximum cable lengths are used on the largest legal network architecture and all hardware propagation delay times are at the legal maximum; the 32-bit jam signal is used when collisions are detected. In other words, slot time is just longer than the time it theoretically can take to go from one extreme end of the largest legal Ethernet collision domain to the other extreme end, collide with another transmission at the last possible instant, and then have the collision fragments return to the sending station and be detected.

For the system to work, the first station must learn about the collision before it finishes sending the smallest legal frame size. To allow 1000-Mbps Ethernet to operate in half duplex, the Extension field was added when sending small frames, purely to keep the transmitter busy long enough for a collision fragment to make it back. This field is present only on 1000-Mbps half-duplex links, and it allows minimum-size, 64-octet frames to be stretched long enough to meet slot-time requirements. Extension bits are discarded by the receiving station.

To examine the issue briefly, consider the following: On a 10-Mbps Ethernet, 1 bit at the MAC sublayer requires 100 nanoseconds (ns) to transmit. At 100 Mbps, that same bit requires 10 ns to transmit, and at 1000 Mbps, it takes only 1 ns. Table 6-4 summarizes the bit-time of different types of Ethernet.

Table 6-4 Bit-Time

Ethernet Speed	Bit-Time
10 Mbps	100 nanosecond
100 Mbps	10 nanosecond
1000 Mbps = 1 Gbps	1 nanosecond
10,000 Mbps = 10 Gbps	.1 nanosecond

As a rough estimate, 8 inches (2.3 cm) per nanosecond often is used for calculating propagation delay down a UTP cable. For 100m of UTP, this means that it takes just under 5 bit-times for a 10BASE-T signal to travel the length of a 100m cable (about 4.92 bit-times). Simply moving the decimal point over results in 49.2 bit-times at 100 Mbps, and 492 bit-times at 1000 Mbps.

For CSMA/CD Ethernet to operate, the sending station must become aware of a collision before it has completed transmission of a minimum-size frame. At 100 Mbps, the system timing is barely capable of accommodating 100m cables. At 1000 Mbps, special (very inefficient) adjustments were required because nearly an entire minimum-size frame has been transmitted before the first bit reaches the end of the first 100 meters of UTP cable. It is easy to see why half duplex was not permitted in 10-Gb Ethernet.

Interframe Spacing and Backoff

Table 6-5 shows the minimum spacing between two noncolliding packets, also called the interframe spacing, from the last bit of the FCS field of the first frame to the first bit of the preamble of the second frame.

Table 6-5 Interframe Spacing

Speed	Interframe Spacing	Time Required
10 Mbps	96 bit-times	9.6 μsec
100 Mbps	96 bit-times	0.96 μsec
1 Gbps	96 bit-times	0.096 μsec
10 Gbps	96 bit-times	0.0096 μsec

After a frame has been sent, all stations on a 10-Mbps Ethernet are required to wait a minimum of 96 bit-times (9.6 microseconds) before any station legally can transmit the next frame. On faster versions of Ethernet, the spacing remains the same: 96 bit-times. However, the time required for that interval grows correspondingly shorter, as shown in Table 6-6. This interval alternately is referred to as the interframe spacing, the interframe gap, and the interpacket gap, and it is intended to allow slow stations time to process the previous frame and prepare for the next frame.

Table 6-6 Slot Time Parameter

Speed	Slot Time*	Time Interval
10 Mbps	512 bit-times	51.2 μsec
100 Mbps	512 bit-times	5.12 µsec
1 Gbps	4096 bit-times	4.096 µsec
10 Gbps	Not applicable	—

*Slot time applies only to half-duplex Ethernet links.

However, a repeater is expected to regenerate the full 64 bits of timing information (preamble and SFD) at the start of any frame, despite the potential loss of some of the beginning preamble bits to slow synchronization. Thus, because of this forced reintroduction of timing bits, some minor reduction of the interframe gap is not only possible, but expected. Some Ethernet chip sets are sensitive to a shortening of the interframe spacing and begin failing to see frames as the gap is reduced. With the increase in processing power at the desktop, it would be very easy for a personal computer to saturate an Ethernet segment with traffic and to begin transmitting again before the interframe spacing delay time is satisfied. Over the years, some vendors deliberately have violated the interframe gap a little to improve throughput testing results in competitive product comparisons. For the most part, this cheating on the interframe spacing has not caused problems, but it has the potential to do so.

After a collision occurs and all stations allow the cable to become idle (each waits the full interframe spacing), the stations that collided must wait an additional—and potentially progressively longer—period of time before attempting to retransmit the collided frame. The waiting period intentionally is designed to be semi-random so that two stations do not delay for the same amount of time before retransmitting; otherwise, the result would be more collisions. This is accomplished in part by expanding the interval from which the random retransmission time is selected on each retransmission attempt. The waiting period is measured in increments of the parameter slot time.

More Information: Retransmission

Retransmission is controlled by this formula:

$$0 = r < 2k$$

Here, *r* is some random number of slot times and *k* is the number of backoff attempts (up to a maximum of 10 for the backoff value). Backoff time is defined as follows:

$$r * \text{slot time}$$

The total maximum number of retransmission attempts is 16, although the backoff value remains at 10 for the last few attempts. The formula specifies the minimum waiting period for a retransmission attempt. It is quite acceptable, though not necessarily desirable, for a station to introduce extra delays that will degrade its own throughput.

As an example, after the fifth consecutive collision without being able to transmit the current 10BASE-T frame, the waiting time would be a random delay interval between 0 and 32 slot times ($0 = r < 2^5$). Restated, the delay would be a random number of 51.2 microsecond time units, ranging from an immediate retry attempt up to 1638.4 microseconds later.

If the MAC sublayer still cannot send the frame after 16 attempts, it gives up and generates an error to the next layer up. Such an occurrence is fairly rare and happens only under extremely heavy network loads or when a physical problem exists on the network.

In a special situation, the MAC sublayer experiences much more frequent failures to send a frame despite the 16 attempts, usually found on switched links. This is called the capture effect or the packet starvation effect. When two devices (switches, stations, or both) connect in half-duplex operation and each is attempting to send a large block of traffic, a collision will certainly occur. Whichever station "wins" the first retransmission has a progressively greater chance to transmit with each subsequent collision. Assume that a second collision has taken place. The first station, which was capable of transmitting its first frame, again selects its random delay between 0 and 1 time intervals, while the second station now selects from 0, 1, 2, and 3 time intervals. It is highly likely that the first station will again select a shorter delay time and be capable of transmitting. The first station will probably win the retransmission for 16 consecutive attempts by the second station. The second station then will give up and discard that frame. It also will record an excessive collisions error. This type of error usually is revealed using the *Simple Network Management Protocol (SNMP)* to query a switch port, and it often is found even where only a single device is attached to the affected port. Because Ethernet is inherently bursty, this might be reported on ports with relatively low average utilization.

Error Handling

The most common (and usually benign) error condition on Ethernet networks are collisions. Collisions are the mechanism for resolving contention for network access. A few collisions provide a smooth, simple, low-overhead way for network nodes to arbitrate contention for the network resource. When the network cannot operate properly because of various problems, collisions can become a significant impediment to useful network operation. Collisions are possible only on half-duplex segments.

Collisions waste time in two ways:

- Network bandwidth loss is equal to the initial transmission and the collision jam signal. This is called *consumption delay*, and it affects all network nodes. Consumption delay can significantly reduce network throughput. Following each successful or failed transmission attempt is an enforced idle time (backoff period) for all stations, called the interframe spacing (or interframe gap), that further impacts throughput.

- A delay caused by the result of this collision backoff algorithm. Backoff delays are not usually significant.

The considerable majority of collisions occur very early in the frame, often before the SFD. Collisions occurring before the SFD usually are not reported to the higher layers, as if the collision did not occur. As soon as a collision is detected, the sending station(s) transmit a 32-bit jam signal that will enforce the collision. This is done so that any data being transmitted thoroughly is corrupted and all stations have a chance to detect the collision.

In Figure 6-15, two stations are listening to ensure that the cable is idle and then transmit. The 802.3 standard provides worst-case limits on how long each component in the system can delay a signal. The maximum allowed round-trip delay for a 10-Mbps collision domain is 512 bit-times, a value that determines the minimum frame size. Station 1 is the first station transmitting, so that station sends the most data before a collision is detected. Station 2 is capable of sending only a few bits before the collision is detected.

Examine Figure 6-15 closely. Station 1 can transmit a significant percentage of the frame before the signal even reaches the last cable segment. Station 2 does not receive the first bit of the transmission before beginning its own transmission. Station 2 can send only several bits before the NIC senses the collision. Station 2 immediately truncates the current transmission and substitutes the 32-bit jam signal in its place. Then Station 2 ceases all transmissions. During the collision and jam event that Station 2 is experiencing, the collision fragments work their way back through the repeated collision domain toward Station 1. Station 2 completes transmission of the 32-bit jam signal and becomes silent before the collision can propagate back to Station 1. Station 1, still unaware of the collision, continues to transmit. When the collision fragments finally reach Station 1, it also truncates the current transmission and substitutes a 32-bit jam signal in place of the remainder of the frame being transmitted. Upon sending the 32-bit jam signal, Station 1 ceases all transmissions.

Figure 6-15 Routine Error Handling in a 10-Mbps Collision Domain

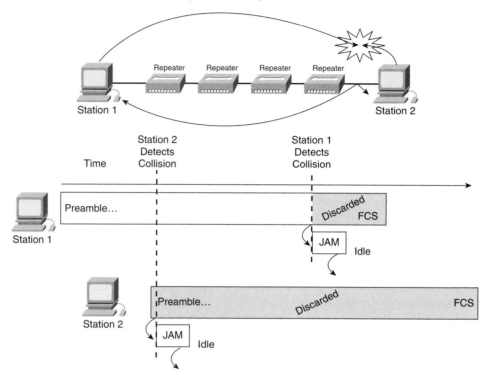

A jam signal can be composed of any binary data, as long as it does not form a proper check-sum for the portion of the frame already transmitted. The most commonly observed data pattern for a jam signal is simply a repeating 1, 0, 1, 0 pattern, the same as the preamble. When viewed by a protocol analyzer, this pattern appears as a repeating hexadecimal 5 or A sequence. The corrupted, partially transmitted messages often are referred to as collision fragments and sometimes by the slang term runts. Compared to late collisions, normal collisions are less than 64 octets in length and, therefore, fail both the minimum length test and the FCS checksum test.

Types of Collisions

Collisions typically take place when two or more Ethernet stations transmit simultaneously within a collision domain. Collisions are reported by event counts by most diagnostic tools, but they might be reported separately as single collisions or multiple collisions when a switch or other station is queried with SNMP. A single collision refers to a collision that was detected while trying to transmit a frame, but, on the next attempt, the frame was transmitted successfully. Multiple collisions indicate that the same frame collided repeatedly before being successfully transmitted. This is different from frames with deferred transmissions because the deferred transmission frame did not collide. The medium was busy when the station or switch sought to transmit, and it was required to wait its turn to transmit. Because of repeated collisions of the same frame, the frame might not be transmitted at all, which would be reported as being aborted as the result of excessive collisions.

The results of collisions—partial and corrupted frames that are less than 64 octets and that have an invalid FCS—often are called collision fragments. Some protocol analyzers and network monitors call these fragments runts, but the term is imprecise.

The main Ethernet frame error types that can be captured through a protocol-analysis session are local collision, remote collision, and late collision. Figure 6-16 illustrates those collision types. The sections that follow briefly describe each frame error type.

Figure 6-16 Summary of Collision Types: Local, Remote, and Late

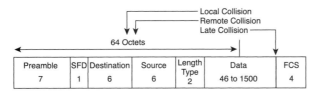

Preamble	SFD	Destination	Source	Length Type	Data	FCS
7	1	6	6	2	46 to 1500	4

More Information: Local, Remote, and Late Collisions

Local Collision

To create a local collision on coax cable (10BASE2 and 10BASE5), the signal travels down the single cable until it encounters a signal from the other station. The waveforms then overlap, canceling out some parts of the signal and reinforcing (doubling) other parts. The doubling of the signal pushes the voltage level of the signal beyond the allowed maximum. This overvoltage condition is sensed by all of the stations on the local cable segment as a collision. A special circuit in the NIC monitors for this overvoltage condition. The overvoltage threshold is around –1.5 volts, as measured on the coax cable. Figure 6-17 shows a midframe in 10BASE2/10BASE5 collision captured by a digital storage oscilloscope.

Figure 6-17 10BASE2/10BASE5 Local Collision

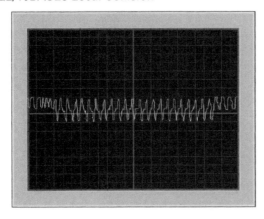

> **More Information: Local, Remote, and Late Collisions (Continued)**
>
> In Figure 6-17, the beginning of the waveform represents normal Manchester-encoded data. A few cycles into the sample, the amplitude of the wave doubles. That is the beginning of the collision, where the two waveforms overlap. Just before the end of the sample, the amplitude returns to normal when the first station to detect the collision quits transmitting, and a jam from the second colliding station still is observed.
>
> On UTP cable (such as 10BASE-T, 100BASE-TX, and 1000BASE-T), a collision is detected on the local segment only when a station detects a signal on the RX (receive) pair at the same time it is sending on the TX (transmit) pair. Because the two signals are on different pairs, there is no characteristic change in the signal, as shown in Figure 6-17. Collisions are recognized on UTP only when the station is operating in half duplex. The only functional difference between half- and full-duplex operation in this regard is whether both transmit and receive pairs are permitted to be used simultaneously. If the station is not engaged in transmitting, it cannot detect a local collision. Conversely, a cable fault, such as excessive crosstalk, can cause a station to perceive its own transmission as a local collision.
>
> **Remote Collision**
>
> The characteristics of a remote collision are a frame that is less than the minimum length has an invalid FCS checksum, but does not exhibit the local collision symptom of overvoltage or simultaneous RX/TX activity. This sort of collision usually results from collisions that occur on the far side of a repeated connection. A repeater will not forward an overvoltage state and cannot cause a station to have both the TX and RX pairs active at the same time. The station would have to be transmitting to have both pairs active, and that would constitute a local collision. On UTP networks, this is the most common sort of collision observed. Nearly all monitoring tools that report collisions, such as software protocol analyzers and Remote Monitoring (RMON) probes, will detect only remote collisions because they are passive listening devices.
>
> **Late Collision**
>
> No possibility exists for a normal or legal collision after the first 64 octets of data have been transmitted by the sending station(s). The theoretical maximums for legal network propagation times are exceeded before then. Collisions that occur after the first 64 octets are called late collisions. The most significant difference between late collisions and collisions that occur before the first 64 octets is that the Ethernet NIC retransmits a normally collided frame automatically but does not automatically retransmit a frame that collided late. As far as the NIC is concerned, everything went out fine, and the upper layers of the protocol stack must deduce that the frame was lost. Other than retransmission, a station that detects a late collision handles it in exactly the same way as a normal collision.
>
> In all but one case, the 802.3 standard permits a station to attempt to retransmit a frame that collided late, but it does not require this. Gigabit Ethernet explicitly denies late-collided frames from being retransmitted.

> **More Information: Local, Remote, and Late Collisions (Continued)**
>
> A late remote collision takes place after slot time has elapsed *and* on the far side of a repeater. However, because the repeater would prevent observation of the local collision symptoms of an overvoltage state or simultaneous receive/transmit event, monitoring hardware would have to be present on the distant segment to detect a late collision and report that information to the monitoring station. You also can infer that a late remote collision took place somewhere on the other side of a repeater by analyzing the last few octets of a bad frame for the presence of the pattern normally associated with a jam signal. Typically, this type of collision would be detected on the local segment simply as an FCS error.

Ethernet Errors

Why learn about Ethernet errors? Because Ethernet is a dominant LAN technology, an intimate knowledge of typical errors is invaluable for understanding both the operation and troubleshooting of Ethernets.

Whereas local and remote collisions are considered to be a normal part of Ethernet operation, the late collision is considered to be an error. The presence of errors on Ethernet always suggests that further investigation is warranted. The severity of the problem indicates the troubleshooting urgency related to the detected error(s). A handful of errors detected over many minutes or over hours would be a low priority. Thousands detected over a few minutes suggest that urgent attention is warranted. Situations that are considered Ethernet errors are as follows:

- Simultaneous transmission occurring before the slot time has elapsed (collision or runt)
- Simultaneous transmission occurring after the slot time has elapsed (late collision)
- Excessively or illegally long transmission (jabber, long frame, and range errors)
- Illegally short transmission (short frame, collision fragment, or runt)
- Corrupted transmission (FCS error)
- Insufficient or excessive number of bits transmitted (alignment error)
- Mismatch of actual and reported number of octets in frame (range error)
- Unusually long preamble or jam event (ghost or jabber)

Each situation is defined separately. Frames associated with error conditions are frequently, but not always, discarded. Normal collisions are included simply to provide a more complete list but are not actually considered errors. The sections that follow briefly describe some of the Ethernet errors.

Jabber

Jabber is defined several places in the 802.3 standard as being a transmission of at least 20,000 to 50,000 bit-times in duration. However, most diagnostic tools report jabber whenever a detected transmission exceeds the maximum legal frame size—which is considerably smaller than 20,000 to 50,000 bit-times. This presents a rather fuzzy definition because the reporting device *might* or *might not* consider a 1518-octet frame with VLAN tagging added to be larger than the legal limit. Also, no indication exists as to whether jabber has a good or bad FCS. Most references to jabber more properly are called long frames.

Long Frame

A *long frame* is one that is longer than the maximum legal size and that takes into consideration whether the frame was tagged. It does not consider whether the frame had a valid FCS checksum. This error usually is meant when someone says that jabber was detected on the network. Figure 6-18 illustrates that a long frame is longer than 1518 octets.

Figure 6-18 Long Frame

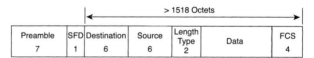

Jabber and long frames are both in excess of the maximum frame size. Jabber is significantly larger, however. If the frame is 802.1q tagged, that usually is not counted toward being illegally large. The IEEE 802.1Q standard defines the operation of virtual LAN (VLAN) bridges that permit the definition, operation, and administration of VLAN topologies within a bridged LAN infrastructure. The IEEE's 802.1Q standard was developed to address the problem of how to break large networks into smaller parts so that broadcast and multicast traffic would not grab more bandwidth than necessary.

Short Frame

A short frame is a frame smaller than the minimum legal size of 64 octets, with a good frame check sequence. Some protocol analyzers and network monitors call these frames runts, but the term is imprecise. In general, you should not see short frames, although their presence is no guarantee that the network is failing.

Short frames are formed properly in all but one aspect and have valid FCS checksums; they are less than the minimum frame size (64 octets), however. Figure 6-19 illustrates that a short frame is shorter than 64 octets.

Figure 6-19 Short Frame

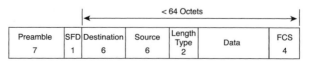

Runt

The term *runt* is generally an imprecise slang term that means something less than a legal frame size. It can refer to short frames with a valid FCS checksum. It usually refers to collision fragments.

FCS and Beyond

A received frame with a bad frame check sequence (also referred to as a checksum or CRC error) is different by at least 1 bit from what was transmitted. In a frame with an FCS error, the header information is probably correct (the addressing and such), but the checksum calculated by the receiving station does not match the checksum appended to the end of the frame by the sending station. Trusting the accuracy of the addressing in a single frame is probably a bad idea, but if many frames have the same source address, there is a pretty good chance that the source address is correct.

A high number of FCS errors from a single station usually indicates a faulty NIC or faulty or corrupted software drivers, or a bad cable connecting that station to the network. If FCS errors are associated with many stations, it generally is traceable to bad cabling, a faulty version of a NIC driver, a faulty hub port, or induced noise in the cable system.

FCS errors are reported when at least 1 bit in the transmission is different. When a new checksum is calculated by the receiving station and compared to the checksum in the FCS field, the two do not match. The frame then is discarded.

Alignment Error

A message that does not end on an octet boundary is known as an ***alignment error***. That is, instead of the correct number of binary bits to form complete octet groupings, some additional bits (less than 8) are left over. Such a frame is truncated to the nearest octet boundary; if the FCS checksum fails, an alignment error is reported. This often is caused by bad software drivers or a collision, and frequently is accompanied by a failure of the FCS checksum. Other causes are characterized by a read and write operation error, which is caused by software bugs. If an alignment error is not corrected, this can cause a crash. Usually, the software corrects itself, but this causes a sudden spike in CPU resources for the router.

Range Error

A frame that has a legal-size value in the Length field but that does not match the actual number of octets counted in the Data field of the received frame is known as a ***range error***. This error also appears when the Length field value is less than the minimum legal unpadded size of the Data field. A similar error, Out of Range, is reported when the value in the Length field indicates a data size that is too large to be legal.

Ghost

Fluke Networks has coined the term *ghost* to mean energy (noise) detected on the cable that appears to be a frame but that lacks a valid SFD. To qualify as a ghost, this "frame" must be at least 72 octets long (including the preamble); otherwise, it is classified as a remote collision. Because of the peculiar nature of ghosts, it is important to note that test results largely are dependent upon where on the segment the measurement is made.

Some types of noise fool nodes on a network segment into thinking they are receiving a frame. However, the sensed frame never comes, so no data is passed up into the NIC to be processed. After a while, the sensed transmission ceases and the NIC resumes sending its own messages. Different network interfaces react differently, and no standards define how or when a NIC should react to a noisy segment. Repeaters usually propagate these noise signals into other segments of the collision domain.

The visible symptom of ghosting is a network that is slow for no apparent reason. The file servers are nearly idle, and network-monitoring equipment shows very low network utilization, yet users complain that the network is excessively slow or completely down. The symptom might be geographically limited, with one end of a large/long segment seeming to operate and the other being slow or completely down.

Ground loops and other wiring problems are usually the cause of ghosting. Ghosts cause some repeaters to respond as though a frame is being received. Because the repeater reacts only to an AC voltage riding on the cable, there is no valid frame to pass on to the other ports. The repeater, however, transmits this energy on to its other port(s). The retransmitted ghost might appear as a jam pattern or a very long preamble.

Most network-monitoring tools do not recognize the existence of ghosts for the same reason that they do not recognize preamble collisions—they rely entirely on what the chip set tells them. Software-only protocol analyzers, many hardware-based protocol analyzers, and handheld diagnostic tools, as well as most remote monitoring (RMON) probes do not report these events.

Ethernet Autonegotiation

As Ethernet grew from 10 to 100 and 1000 Mbps, one goal was to make each technology interoperable, even to the point that 10, 100, and 1000 interfaces could be directly connected. A process called autonegotiation (of speeds and half duplex or full duplex) was developed. Specifically, at the time that Fast Ethernet was introduced, the standard included a method of automatically configuring a given interface to match the speed and capabilities of the link partner. This process defines how two link partners automatically can negotiate a configuration that offers the best common performance level. It has the additional advantage of involving only the lowest part of the physical layer.

10BASE-T required each station to transmit a link pulse about every 16 milliseconds whenever the station was not engaged in transmitting a message. Autonegotiation adopted this signal and renamed it a Normal Link Pulse (NLP). When a series of NLPs are sent in a group for the purpose of autonegotiation, the group is called a Fast Link Pulse (FLP) burst. Each FLP burst is sent at the same timing interval as an NLP and is intended to allow older 10BASE-T devices to operate normally if they receive an FLP burst. Figure 6-20 illustrates the NLP and FLP timing.

Figure 6-20 NLP Versus FLP Timing

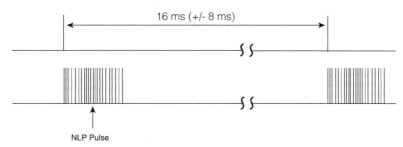

10BASE-T transmits using signaling between +1 and –1 volts, for a 2-volt peak-to-peak differential signal. NLP signaling uses only the range from 0 to +1 volts. The duration of a single NLP pulse is 100 ns. Figure 6-21 illustrates two sample NLP pulses. The left pulse is very sharp and clean, and is from an interface capable of 1000-Mbps operation. The right pulse is from an older device capable of only 10/100-Mbps operation, which does not require as precise of a signal.

Figure 6-21 NLP Pulses

Autonegotiation is accomplished by transmitting a burst of 10BASE-T link pulses from each of the two link partners. The burst communicates the capabilities of the transmitting station to its link partner. After both stations have interpreted what the other partner is offering, both switch to the highest-performance common configuration and establish link at that speed. If anything interrupts communications and the link is lost, the two link partners first attempt to link again at the last negotiated speed. If that fails, or if it has been too long since the link was lost, the autonegotiation process starts over. The link can be lost because of external influences, such as a cable fault, or because one of the partners issues a reset.

Figure 6-22 shows the actual FLP autonegotiation burst. The FLP burst is made up of multiple NLP link pulses.

Figure 6-22 FLP Autonegotiation Burst

An FLP burst consists of 33 pulse positions, which represent a 16-bit link code word that is framed by 17 clocking pulses. Pulses within a burst are separated by 62.5 ms (±7 ms). Data pulse positions are found between each clocking pulse. If a data pulse is present, it is interpreted as a binary 1. The absence of a data pulse in the window between two clocking pulses is interpreted as a binary 0. As shown in Figure 6-23, the 17 clocking pulses are always present. The 16 data pulses are present only if they represent binary 1; they are absent if they represent binary 0 in the encoded 16-bit data word. The pulses interpreted as binary 1s for data are highlighted in gray.

Figure 6-23 Interpretation of Autonegotiation Pulse

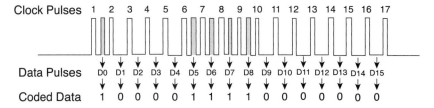

When autonegotiation is implemented, additional information can be added using the concept of pages. Pages are additional bits representing more sophisticated negotiation and link parameters.

After a device has decoded the link code word offered by its link partner, it acknowledges receipt of the current word by sending at least three FLP bursts with the Acknowledge bit set. After both link partners acknowledge the current FLP link code word exchange in that manner, the link partners either move on to the next page or enable the agreed configuration and attempt to link accordingly. Link partners can send any number of next pages following the initial configuration base page and any necessary next pages that are associated with the base page.

Link Establishment and Full and Half Duplex

Link partners are allowed to skip offering configurations that they are capable of offering, but are not allowed to include configurations that they are not capable of offering. This enables the network administrator to force ports to a selected speed and duplex setting, without disabling autonegotiation.

Autonegotiation is optional for most Ethernet implementations. Gigabit Ethernet requires its implementation, although the user can disable it. Autonegotiation originally was defined for UTP implementations of Ethernet.

When an autonegotiating station first attempts to link, it is supposed to enable 10BASET parts of the front-end chip set to attempt to immediately establish a link. If 10BASET signaling is present and the station supports 10BASET, it attempts to establish a link without negotiating. If either signaling produces a link, or if FLP bursts are received, the station proceeds with that technology. If a link partner does not offer an FLP burst, but instead offers NLPs, that device automatically is assumed to be a 10BASET station. During this initial interval of testing for other technologies, the transmit path sends FLP bursts. The standard does not permit parallel detection of any other technologies.

If a link is established through parallel detection, it is required to be half duplex. Only two methods of achieving a full-duplex link exist:

- Through a completed cycle of autonegotiation
- By administratively forcing both link partners to full duplex

If one link partner is forced to full duplex but the other partner parallel-detects while attempting to autonegotiate, there is certain to be a duplex mismatch, resulting in collisions and errors on that link. If you force one end, you *must* force the other. The exception to this is that 10 Gigabit Ethernet does not support half duplex.

Many vendors implement their hardware in such a way that it cycles through the various possible states. It transmits FLP bursts to autonegotiate for a while, then it configures itself for Fast Ethernet and attempts to link for a while, and finally, it simply listens for a while. Some vendors do not offer any transmitted attempt to link until the interface first hears an FLP burst or some other signaling scheme. In the silent listening state, a portable computer is capable of conserving enough battery power to be quite worthwhile, although this mode is not supported by the standard.

Ethernet Duplex Operation

Two duplex modes exist: half and full. For shared media, the half-duplex mode is mandatory. All of the coaxial implementations are inherently half duplex in nature and cannot operate in full duplex. UTP and fiber implementations can be operated in half duplex, but that mode is an administrative imposition. All 10-Gbps implementations are specified for full duplex only.

In half duplex, only one station can transmit at a time. For the coaxial implementations, a second station transmitting causes the signals to overlap and collide, becoming corrupted. Because UTP and fiber generally transmit on separate pairs, the signals have no opportunity to overlap and become corrupted. Ethernet has established arbitration rules for resolving conflicts that arise when more than one station attempts to transmit at the same time. Both stations in a point-to-point full-duplex link are permitted to transmit at any time, regardless of whether the other station is transmitting at the same time.

Autonegotiation avoids most situations in which one station in a point-to-point link is transmitting under half-duplex rules and the other is operating under full-duplex rules.

Only two methods exist of achieving a full-duplex connection at speeds below 10 Gigabit Ethernet:

- By using autonegotiation
- By administratively forcing the interface mode

If one station in a point-to-point link is autonegotiating and the other is not, the auto-negotiating station is required to select half duplex. Thus, if one end of a link is forced, it is incumbent upon the network support staff to force the other end as well. Failure to force both ends results in an artificially elevated error level and poor performance on the link. Duplex mismatches are perhaps the most common problem found on switched networks.

Priority Resolution

In the anticipated event that link partners share more than one common technology capability, the following list is used to determine which technology should be chosen from the offered configurations. In other words, it is desirable for 10-/100-/1000-Mbps versions of copper-based Ethernet to agree automatically on the best way for two interfaces to link. The list is ranked by priority, with the most desirable link configuration at the top:

- Full duplex
- Half duplex
- Full duplex
- Half duplex
- Full duplex
- Half duplex

Fiber-optic Ethernet implementations are not included in this priority resolution list because the interface electronics and optics do not permit easy reconfiguration between implementations. It is assumed that the interface configuration is fixed. If the two interfaces are capable of autonegotiating, they are already using the same Ethernet implementation, although there remain a number of configuration choices, such as the duplex setting or which station will act as the master for clocking purposes.

Summary

In this chapter, you learned the following key points:

- IEEE is a professional organization that defines network standards. IEEE LAN standards are the best-known IEEE communication standards and are the predominant LAN standards in the world.

- The two IEEE sublayers of the OSI data link layer are MAC and LLC.

- Ethernet uses the MAC address, which is the physical address located on a NIC.

- Framing helps obtain essential information that could not be obtained from coded bit streams alone.

- The two broad categories of MAC are deterministic, or taking turns, and nondeterministic, or first come, first served.

- Ethernet uses CSMA/CD.

- Half-duplex transmission enables signals to travel in either direction, but not in both directions simultaneously. Full-duplex transmission enables data to be sent and received at the same time. The most common error condition on an Ethernet is a collision.

To supplement all that you have learned in this chapter, refer to the chapter-specific Interactive Media Activity on the CD-ROM that accompanies this book.

Key Terms

10-Gb Ethernet   Built on the Ethernet technology used in most of today's LANs, 10-Gb Ethernet is described as a technology that offers a more efficient and less expensive approach to moving data on backbone connections between networks, while also providing a consistent technology end to end. Ethernet now can step up to offering data speeds at 10 Gbps.

alignment error   A message that does not end on an octet boundary.

backoff   The retransmission delay enforced when a collision occurs.

connectionless   Data transfer without the existence of a virtual circuit.

CSMA/CD (carrier sense multiple access collision detect)   A media-access mechanism wherein devices ready to transmit data first check the channel for a carrier. If no carrier is sensed for a specific period of time, a device can transmit. If two devices transmit at once, a collision occurs and is detected by all colliding devices. This collision subsequently delays retransmissions from those devices for some random length of time. CSMA/CD access is used by Ethernet and IEEE 802.3.

encapsulation   Wrapping of data in a particular protocol header. For example, upper-layer data is wrapped in a specific Ethernet header before network transit. Also, when bridging dissimilar networks, the entire frame from one network simply can be placed behind the header used by the data link layer protocol of the other network.

Ethernet   A baseband LAN specification invented by Xerox Corporation and developed jointly by Xerox, Intel, and Digital Equipment Corporation. Ethernet networks use CSMA/CD and run over a variety of cable types at 10, 100, and 1000 Mbps. Ethernet is similar to the IEEE 802.3 series of standards.

Fast Ethernet   Any of a number of 100-Mbps Ethernet specifications. Fast Ethernet offers a speed increase 10 times that of the 10BASE-T Ethernet specification, while preserving such qualities as frame format, MAC mechanisms, and MTU. Such similarities allow the use of existing 10BASE-T applications and network-management tools on Fast Ethernet networks. Fast Ethernet is based on an extension to the IEEE 802.3 specification.

FDDI (Fiber Distributed Data Interface)   A LAN standard, defined by American National Standards Institute (ANSI) 3T9.5, specifying a 100-Mbps token-passing network using fiber-optic cable, with transmission distances of up to 2 km. FDDI uses a dual-ring architecture to provide redundancy.

full duplex   The capability for simultaneous data transmission between a sending station and a receiving station.

ghost   Fluke Networks coined this new term to mean energy (noise) detected on the cable that appears to be a frame but that lacks a valid SFD. To qualify as a ghost, this "frame" must be at least 72 octets long (including preamble); otherwise, it is classified as a remote collision.

Gigabit Ethernet   Standard for a high-speed Ethernet, approved by the IEEE 802.3z standards committee in 1996.

half duplex   A capability for data transmission in only one direction at a time between a sending station and a receiving station.

header   Control information placed before data when encapsulating that data for network transmission.

IEEE 802.2   An IEEE LAN protocol that specifies an implementation of the LLC sublayer of the data link layer. IEEE 802.2 handles errors, framing, flow control, and the network layer (Layer 3) service interface.

IEEE (Institute of Electrical and Electronic Engineers)   A professional organization whose activities include the development of communications and network standards. IEEE LAN standards are the predominant LAN standards today.

IEEE 802.3   An IEEE LAN protocol that specifies an implementation of the physical layer and the MAC sublayer of the data link layer. IEEE 802.3 uses CSMA/CD access at a variety of speeds over a variety of physical media. Extensions to the IEEE 802.3 standard specify implementations for Fast Ethernet. Physical variations of the original IEEE 802.3 specification include 10BASE2, 10BASE5, 10BASE-F, 10BASE-T, and 10BROAD36. Physical variations for Fast Ethernet include 100BASE-TX and 100BASE-FX.

jabber   Defined several places in the 802.3 standard as being a transmission of at least 20,000 to 50,000 bit-times in duration. However, most diagnostic tools report jabber whenever a detected transmission exceeds the maximum legal frame size—which is considerably smaller than 20,000 to 50,000 bit-times.

LLC (Logical Link Control)   The higher of the two data link layer sublayers defined by the IEEE. The LLC sublayer handles error control, flow control, framing, and MAC-sublayer addressing. The most prevalent LLC protocol is IEEE 802.2, which includes both connectionless and connection-oriented variants.

long frame   A frame that is longer than the maximum legal size and that takes into consideration whether the frame was tagged.

MAC (Media Access Control)   The lower of the two sublayers of the data link layer defined by the IEEE. The MAC sublayer handles access to shared media, such as whether token passing or contention will be used. See also *LLC*.

MAC address   A standardized data link layer address that is required for every device that connects to a LAN. Other devices in the network use these addresses to locate specific devices in the network and to create and update routing tables and data structures. MAC addresses are 6 bytes long and are controlled by the IEEE. Also known as a hardware address, a MAC-layer address, or a physical address.

MTU (Maximum Transmission Unit)   The maximum packet size, in bytes, that a particular interface can handle.

OUI (organizationally unique identifier)   Three octets assigned by the IEEE in a block of 48-bit LAN addresses.

propagation delay   The time required for data to travel over a network from its source to its ultimate destination.

range error   A frame that had a legal-size value in the Length field but that did not match the actual number of octets counted in the Data field of the received frame.

simplex   The capability for transmission in only one direction between a sending station and a receiving station. Broadcast television is an example of a simplex technology.

SNMP (Simple Network Management Protocol)   A network-management protocol used almost exclusively in TCP/IP networks. SNMP provides a means of monitoring and controlling network devices and managing configurations, statistics collection, performance, and security.

Token Ring   A token-passing LAN developed and supported by IBM. Token Ring runs at 4 or 16 Mbps over a ring topology.

trailer   Controls information appended to data when encapsulating the data for network transmission.

Check Your Understanding

Complete all the review questions to test your understanding of the topics and concepts in this chapter. Answers are listed in Appendix B, "Check Your Understanding Answer Key."

1. Which of the following is *not* one of the recognized IEEE sublayers?

   A. Media Access Control

   B. Data Link Control

   C. Logical Link Control

   D. None of the above

2. The recognized IEEE 802.3 sublayers are concerned with what layers of the OSI reference model?

   A. 2 and 3

   B. 1 and 2

   C. 3 and 4

   D. 1 and 3

3. The LLC, as a sublayer, participates in which process?

   A. Encryption

   B. Encapsulation

   C. Framing

   D. All of the above

4. What do the first six hexadecimal numbers in a MAC address represent?

   A. Interface serial number

   B. Organizationally unique identifier

   C. Interface unique identifier

   D. None of the above

5. MAC addresses are how many bits in length?

   A. 12

   B. 24

   C. 48

   D. 64

6. What is the name of the access method used in Ethernet that explains how Ethernet works?

   A. TCP/IP

   B. CSMA/CD

   C. CMDA/CS

   D. CSMA/CA

7. Where does the MAC address reside?

   A. Transceiver

   B. Computer BIOS

   C. NIC

   D. CMOS

8. Which of the following statements best describes communication between two devices on a LAN?

   A. The source device encapsulates data in a frame with the MAC address of the destination device and then transmits it. Everyone on the LAN sees it, but the devices with nonmatching addresses otherwise ignore the frame.

   B. The source encapsulates the data and places a destination MAC address in the frame. It puts the frame on the LAN, where only the device with the matching address can check the address field.

   C. The destination device encapsulates data in a frame with the MAC address of the source device and puts it on the LAN. The device with the matching address removes the frame.

   D. Each device on the LAN receives the frame and passes it up to the computer, where software decides whether to keep or to discard the frame.

9. Which functions are associated with framing?

   A. Identifies which computers are communicating with one another

   B. Signals when communication between individual computers begins and when it ends

   C. Flags corrupted frames

   D. All of the above

10. Media Access Control refers to what?

    A. The state in which a NIC has captured the networking medium and is ready to transmit

    B. Rules that govern media capture and release

    C. Rules that determine which computer on a shared-medium environment is allowed to transmit the data

    D. A formal byte sequence that has been transmitted

11. Which best describes a CSMA/CD network?

    A. One node's transmission traverses the entire network and is received and examined by every node.

    B. Signals are sent directly to the destination if the source knows both the MAC and IP addresses.

    C. One node's transmission goes to the nearest router, which sends it directly to the destination.

    D. Signals always are sent in broadcast mode.

12. In an Ethernet or IEEE 802.3 LAN, when do collisions occur?

    A. When one node places a packet on a network without informing the other nodes

    B. When two stations listen for traffic, hear none, and transmit simultaneously

    C. When two network nodes send packets to a node that no longer is broadcasting

    D. When jitter is detected and traffic is disrupted during normal transmission

13. Which is an important Layer 2 data link layer function?

    A. Logical link control

    B. Addressing

    C. Media access control

    D. All of the above

14. Which is true of a deterministic MAC protocol?

    A. It defines collisions and specifies what to do about them.

    B. It allows the hub to determine the number of users active at any one time.

    C. It allows hosts to "take turns" sending data.

    D. It allows the use of a "talking stick" by network administrators to control the media access of any users considered "troublemakers."

CHAPTER 7

Ethernet Technologies

Objectives

Upon completion of this chapter, you should be able to answer the following questions:

- What are the different types of 10-Mbps Ethernet?

- What is 10BASE-T?

- How is 10BASE-T wired?

- What are the basic architectural considerations of 10BASE-T?

- What are the different types of 100-Mbps Ethernet?

- What are three characteristics of Fast Ethernet?

- What is 100BASE-TX and which type of UTP cable made 100BASE-TX commercially successful?

- What is 1000-Mbps Ethernet?

- What are the differences between Ethernet, Fast Ethernet, and Gigabit Ethernet?

- What is 100BASE-T and why was it created?

- What is the future of Ethernet technologies?

Additional Topics of Interest

In addition to the core objective areas, this chapter introduces you to the following topics of interest to networkers:

- 10BASE5

- 10BASE2

- 100BASE-FX

- Fast Ethernet architecture and cable distances

- 1000BASE-SX and LX

- Basic architectural considerations of Gigabit Ethernet

- 10 Gigabit Ethernet and the major conceptual changes

- Basic architectural considerations of 10 Gigabit Ethernet

Key Terms

The following is a list of key terms introduced in this chapter. For your reference, a definition for each term can be found at the end of this chapter.

10BASE5   page 293

10BASE2   page 293

10BASE-T   page 293

encoding   page 295

nonreturn to zero (NRZ)   page 295

Manchester encoding   page 295

Thinnet   page 298

100BASE-TX   page 303

100BASE-FX   page 303

signal-to-noise ratio (SNR)   page 304

nonreturn to zero inverted (NRZI)   page 305

1000BASE-T   page 313

1000BASE-SX   page 313

1000BASE-LX   page 313

8B1Q4F   page 314

4D-PAM5   page 314

WDM (wavelength-division multiplexing)   page 323

Ethernet, along with its associated IEEE 802.3 protocols, is one of the world's most important networking standards. Because of the great success of the original Ethernet and the soundness of its design, it has evolved over time. This evolution was in response to the developing needs of modern LANs. Ethernet most likely will continue to evolve in response to future demands for network capability.

The previous chapter introduced both the history of Ethernet and the standards associated with Ethernet. You also learned that the term *Ethernet* refers to a family of the Ethernet technologies. This chapter discusses the Ethernet technologies in more detail.

Please be sure to look at this chapter's associated Interactive Media Activity that you will find on the CD-ROM accompanying this book. This CD element is designed to supplement the material and reinforce the concepts introduced in this chapter.

10-Mbps and 100-Mbps Ethernet

This section introduces the specifics of the most important varieties of Ethernet. The goal is not to memorize all the facts about each type of Ethernet, but rather to develop a sense of what is common to all forms of Ethernet and what are the specific strengths and weaknesses of the commercially important forms of Ethernet.

The popularity of Ethernet began with 10BASE5 coaxial cable (Thicknet). Thinnet 10BASE2, a thinner coaxial cable, was easier to install and terminate. The maximum length for Thinnet decreased from 500 to 180 meters (m). This trend toward easy installation and lower cost took a great step forward with the introduction of UTP-based 10BASE-T. However, the length that an unrepeated signal could travel decreased to 100m, necessitating the introduction of repeaters and then multiport repeaters (hubs). The repeater concept allowed 10BASE-T networks of up to 500m. As workgroups grew in size and applications increased in complexity, the shared bandwidth of the hub became a limiting factor. The introduction of Ethernet 10BASE-T switches addressed both the length and bandwidth limitations. Station-to-switch links were now point-to-point.

The power, versatility, and cost-effectiveness of 10BASE-T coincided with an explosion in the number of LAN users, the number of Internet users (which also increased LAN traffic), and the complexity of applications. Demand for higher bandwidth grew, and Fast Ethernet was introduced. The copper cable version of Fast Ethernet that became commercially successful was 100BASE-TX, and many clever features were developed for interoperability with 10BASE-T systems (the emergence of 10/100 interfaces, for example). To compete with the backbone/LAN technology of FDDI, fiber-based 100BASE-FX was introduced. Throughout all of these Ethernet technologies, the MAC addressing concept, the frame format, and the CSMA/CD media access control method were maintained.

10-Mbps Ethernet

Figure 7-1 shows a subset of physical layer implementations that you can deploy to support Ethernet. The *10BASE5*, *10BASE2*, and *10BASE-T* implementations of Ethernet are considered legacy implementations and are referred to as such in the sections that follow.

Figure 7-1 Types of Ethernet

Logical Link Control Sublayer								
802.3 Media Access Control								
Physical Signaling Sublayer / Physical Medium	10BASE5 (500 m) 50 Ohm Coax N-Style	10BASE2 (185 m) 50 Ohm Coax BNC	10BASE-T (100 m) 100 Ohm UTP RJ45	100BASE-TX (100 m) 100 Ohm UTP RJ45	100BASE-FX (228_412 m) MM Fiber SC	1000BASE-T (100 m) 100 Ohm UTP RJ45	1000BASE-SX (220-550 m) MM Fiber SC	1000BASE-LX (550-5000 m) MM Fiber Sc	10BASE-(Various) MM or Sm Fiber SC

Four things are common among legacy Ethernet:

- Timing parameters
- Frame format
- Transmission process
- A basic design rule

After you learn about what these three historically important versions have in common, you will examine each in more detail.

10BASE5, 10BASE2, and 10BASE-T all share the same timing parameters, as shown in Table 7-1. Note that 1 bit-time at 10 Mbps = 100 nanosecond = 0.1 μ second = 1 ten-millionth of a second.

Table 7-1 Parameters for 10-Mbps Ethernet Operation

Parameter	Value
Bit-time	100 nsec
Slot time	512 bit-times
Interframe spacing	96 bits*
Collision attempt limit	16
Collision backoff limit	10
Collision jam size	32 bits
Maximum untagged frame size	1518 octets
Minimum frame size	512 bits (64 bytes)

*The value listed is the official interframe spacing.

The frame format is common to 10BASE5, 10BASE2, and 10BASE-T. Figure 7-2 shows an Ethernet frame as observed at the MAC sublayer.

Figure 7-2 Ethernet Frame

Preamble	SFD	Destination	Source	Length/ Type	Data ¦ Pad	FCS
7	1	6	6	2	46 to 1500	4

The Legacy Ethernet transmission process is identical until the lower part of the OSI physical layer. As the frame passes from the MAC sublayer to the physical layer, further processes occur before the bits are placed on the medium from the physical layer. One process that is particularly important at this level is the signal quality error (SQE) signal. This signal is typical of what you will see in many networking technologies. At the physical layer, the network is "alive" with communications other than the user data to ensure a properly functioning network. SQE is always used in half duplex. SQE can be used in full-duplex operation but is not required. SQE is active in the following instances:

- Within 4 to 8 microseconds following a normal transmission, to indicate that the outbound frame was successfully transmitted.

- Whenever there is a collision on the medium.

- Whenever there is an *improper* signal on the medium. Improper signals might include detected jabber, or the reflections that result from a cable fault, such as a short. (There are separate conditions depending on which medium is attached.)

- Whenever a transmission has been interrupted as jabber—that is, it has transmitted longer than allowed.

NOTE

In NRZ encoding, signals are maintained at constant voltage llevels, with no signal transitions (no return to a 0V level) during a bit interval.

All 10-Mbps forms of Ethernet take octets received from the MAC sublayer and perform a process called *line encoding*. Line encoding describes how the bits actually are signaled on the wire. The simplest *encodings* (such as *nonreturn to zero* [NRZ] in which a 1 bit is 5 volts [V] and the 0 bits are 0V) typically have undesirable timing and electrical characteristics. Therefore, line codes have been engineered to have desirable transmission properties and tailored to each medium. The form of line encoding used in 10-Mbps systems is called *Manchester encoding*. Figure 7-3 shows a Manchester encoding example. The y-axis is voltage; the x-axis is time.

Figure 7-3 Manchester Encoding Examples

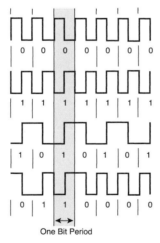

Manchester encoding relies on the direction of the edge transition in the middle of the timing window to determine the binary value for that bit period. In the encoding example shown in Figure 7-3, one timing window is highlighted vertically through all four waveform examples. The top waveform has a falling edge in the center of the timing window, so it is interpreted as a binary 0.

The result is that in the center of the timing window for the second waveform, there is a rising edge, which is interpreted as a binary 1.

Instead of a repeating sequence of the same binary value in the third waveform example, there is an alternating binary sequence. In the first two examples, the signal must transition back between each bit period so that it can make the same-direction transition each time in the center of the timing window. With alternating binary data, there is no need to return to the previous voltage level in preparation for the next edge in the center of the timing window. Thus, any time there is a long separation between one edge and the next, you can be certain that both edges represent the middle of a timing window. The fourth waveform example is random data that enables you to verify that whenever there is a wide separation between two transitions, both edges are in the center of a timing window and represent the binary value for that timing window. Manchester Encoding translates a 1 into a low to high transition [01], and a 0 is translated into a high to low transition (10), which is also called Biphase Code. This uses double the bandwidth and, therefore, Manchester encoding is considered to be self-clocking, which means that accurate synchronization of a data stream is possible. This means that each bit is transmitted over a predefined time period.

Legacy (10-Mbps) Ethernet has some common architectural features. All of these legacy versions are referred to as *shared Ethernet* because they share a common collision domain. It is not only allowed, but it is expected that an Ethernet network could contain multiple types of media (for example, 10BASE5, 10BASE2, 10BASE-T, and so on). The standard goes out of its way to ensure that interoperability is maintained. However, when implementing a mixed-media network, it is important to pay particular attention to the overall architecture design. It becomes easier to violate maximum delay limits as the network grows and becomes more complex. The timing limits are based on parameters such as these:

- Cable length and its propagation delay

- Delay of repeaters

- Delay of transceivers (including NICs, hubs, and switches)

- Interframe gap shrinkage

- Delays within the station

More Information: 5-4-3 Rule

10-Mbps Ethernet operates within the timing limits offered by a series of no more than five segments separated by no more than four repeaters. That is, no more than four repeaters can be connected in series between any two distant stations. The coaxial implementations have a further requirement that there can be no more than three populated segments between any two distant stations. The other two allowed coaxial segments are used to extend the diameter of the collision domain and are called link segments. The primary characteristic of a link segment is that it has exactly two devices attached. All twisted-pair links, such as 10BASE-T, meet the definition of a link segment.

10BASE5

The original (1980) Ethernet product (10BASE5) transmitted 10 Mbps over a single thick coaxial cable bus, thus the name *Thicknet*. 10BASE5 is important for historical reasons. It was the first medium used for Ethernet. 10BASE5 was part of the original 802.3 standard. It can be found today as part of legacy installations. It is not a preferred choice for new networks because its primary benefit, length, can be accomplished in other ways. Although 10BASE5 systems are inexpensive and require no configuration (there is no need for hubs to extend the length of the system), basic components such as NICs are very difficult to find, and the technology is very sensitive to signal reflections on the cable. In addition, 10BASE5 systems are very cable-dependent across the whole collision domain and thus represent a large single point of failure.

The timing, frame format, and transmission process were described previously in Chapter 6, "Ethernet Fundamentals," and are common to all 10-Mbps legacy Ethernet.

10BASE5 uses Manchester-encoded signals on thick coaxial cable. Figure 7-4 is an example of a 10BASE5 signal. It is transmitted from approximately 0V to –1V. 10BASE5 potentially could be idle (0V) for days if no station wanted to transmit. 10BASE5 is asynchronous.

Figure 7-4 10BASE5 Signal Decoded

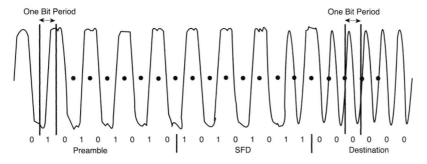

In Figure 7-4, timing marks have been added to aid you in recognizing the timing windows from which the binary data was decoded. The y-axis is voltage; the x-axis is time. Voltage has been measured between the central conductor and the outer sheathing of the coaxial cable.

A 10BASE5 *thick* coax cable, as shown in Figure 7-5, has a solid central conductor, a minimum nominal velocity of propagation (NVP) of 0.77c, and 50 ohms of impedance/termination resistance; it uses N-style screw-on connections.

Each of the maximum five segments of thick coax can be up to 500m (1640 ft.) long, and each station is connected to a transceiver on the coax via an Attachment Unit Interface (AUI) cable that can be up to 50m (164 ft.) long. The cable is large, heavy, and difficult to install, but the distance limitations were favorable; this prolonged its use in certain applications.

NOTE

Nominal velocity of propagation refers to the speed a signal will travel down an electrical cable measured as a percentage of the speed of light in a vacuum, normally 70% to 75%.

Figure 7-5 10BASE5 Thicknet Cable

Other specifications or limitations of 10BASE5 cable include the following:

- Only one station can transmit at a time (or a collision will occur).

- 10BASE5 can run *only* in half-duplex mode, subject to the CSMA/CD rules.

- Up to 100 stations, including repeaters, can exist on any individual 10BASE5 segment.

Lab 7.1.2 Waveform Decoding

The purpose of this lab is to integrate knowledge of networking media; OSI Layers 1, 2, and 3; and Ethernet by decoding a digital waveform of an Ethernet frame.

10BASE2

10BASE2 (originally 802.3a) was introduced in 1985. Because of its smaller size, lighter weight, and greater flexibility, it was easier to install than 10BASE5. Because of its use of thinner cable, 10BASE2 often is referred to as *Thinnet*. 10BASE2 still exists in legacy networks. Although there is little reason to install a 10BASE2 network today, its low cost and lack of need for hubs are attractive. Essentially, 10BASE2 requires no configuration, although obtaining NICs is increasingly difficult. Just like 10BASE5 systems, 10BASE2 systems are very cable-dependent across the whole collision domain and represent a large single point of failure.

The timing, frame format, and transmission are common to all 10-Mbps Legacy Ethernet.

10BASE2 uses Manchester-encoded signals on thin coaxial cable. A 10BASE2 signal is transmitted from approximately 0V to –1V. (The y-axis is voltage; the x-axis is time. Voltage is measured between the center conductor and the outer sheathing conductor.) 10BASE2 potentially could be idle (0V) for days if no station wanted to transmit. 10BASE2 is asynchronous.

The computers on the LAN were linked together like the beads of a necklace by an unbroken series of coaxial cable lengths. These lengths of coaxial cable were attached by British Naval Connectors (BNCs) to a T-shape connector on the NIC, as shown in Figure 7-6. This single coaxial cable was the shared bus for the network. Workstations easily could be moved and reattached, or new workstations could be added to the LAN. Otherwise, 10BASE2 used the same original Ethernet half-duplex protocol.

A 10BASE2 *thin* coax cable has a stranded central conductor. (Be sure that stranded coax is specified when new cable is ordered. Some installers find it hard to work with and use solid-core coax when possible.) It has a minimum nominal velocity of propagation (NVP) of 0.65c, has 50 ohms of impedance/termination resistance, and uses BNC T-style connections. Each of the maximum five segments of thin coax can be up to 185m long (600 ft.), and each station is connected directly to the BNC T connector on the coax.

Figure 7-6 Thinnet and BNC Connector

10BASE-T

10BASE-T (originally 802.3i-1990) substituted the cheaper and easier-to-install UTP copper cable for coaxial cable. This cable plugged into a central connection device, a hub or a switch, that contained the shared bus. The type of cable used in 10BASE-T, the distances that the cable could extend from the hub, and the way in which the UTP was installed, interconnected, and tested were standardized in a "structured cabling system," which increasingly specified a star or extended star topology. 10BASE-T was originally a half-duplex protocol, but full-duplex features were added later. The explosion in Ethernet's popularity in the 1990s—when Ethernet came to dominate LAN technology—was 10BASE-T running on Category (Cat) 5 UTP. To reacquaint yourself with network topologies and networking media, refer back to Chapter 2, "Networking Fundamentals," and Chapter 3, "Networking Media."

The timing, frame format, and transmission were described previously and are common to all 10-Mbps Legacy Ethernet.

10BASE-T uses Manchester encoding signals over Category 3 (now 5, 5e, or better) UTP.

10-Mbps Ethernet is asynchronous, and the cable often is completely idle (0V) for long periods of time between transmissions. 10BASE-T links have a *link pulse* present about every 125 milliseconds (eight times per second), but can otherwise be idle. 10BASE-T networks are "alive" with link pulses.

A 10BASE-T unshielded twisted-pair (UTP) cable has a solid conductor for each wire in the maximum 90m horizontal cable, which should be 0.4 mm to 0.6 mm (26 to 22 American Wire Gauge [AWG]) in diameter. The 10m of allowed patch cables use similar-dimension stranded cable for durability because it is expected to experience repeated flexing. Suitable UTP cable has a minimum NVP of 0.585c, has 100 ohms of impedance, and uses eight-pin RJ-45 modular connectors, as specified in ISO/IEC 8877. Cables between a station and a hub generally are described as between 0m and 100m long (0 ft. to 328 ft.), although the precise maximum length is determined by propagation delay through the link segment (any length that does not exceed 1000 ns of delay is acceptable). Usually, 0.5mm (24 AWG) diameter UTP wire in a multipair cable will meet the requirements at 100m.

Although Category 3 cable is adequate for use on 10BASE-T networks, it is strongly recommended that any new cable installations be made with Category 5e or better materials and wiring practices. Use all four pairs, and use either the T568A or T568B cable pinout arrangement. With this type of cable installation, it should be possible to operate many different media access protocols (including 1000BASE-T) over the same cable plant, without rewiring.

Table 7-2 shows the pinout for a 10BASE-T connection. Notice that two separate transmit/receive paths exists (whereas coaxial cable has only one).

Table 7-2 10BASE-T Cable Pinouts

Pin Number	Signal
1	TD+ (Transmit Data, positive-going differential signal)
2	TD– (Transmit Data, negative-going differential signal)
3	RD+ (Receive Data, positive-going differential signal)
4	Unused
5	Unused
6	RD– (Receive Data, negative-going differential signal)
7	Unused
8	Unused

Figure 7-7 shows conceptual and physical connections between two stations. A crossover cable is required, so Tx on device A sends signals to Rx on device B. Note that two point-to-point connections exist (TxA to RxB, and TxB to RxA).

Figure 7-8 shows the connection between stations and repeaters, multiport repeaters (hubs), or switches. The same connection would be used between a router and a hub or a switch. A straight-through cable is used. Note that inside the hub is a bus topology, which is a collision domain. When a workstation is connected to a switch using a straight-through cable, all individual links are point-to-point. The switch fabric circuitry allows full bandwidth simultaneously between pairs of ports without collisions.

Figure 7-7 10BASE-T Station to Station

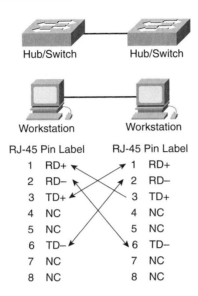

Hub/Switch   Hub/Switch

Workstation   Workstation

RJ-45 Pin Label		RJ-45 Pin Label	
1	RD+	1	RD+
2	RD–	2	RD–
3	TD+	3	TD+
4	NC	4	NC
5	NC	5	NC
6	TD–	6	TD–
7	NC	7	NC
8	NC	8	NC

Figure 7-8 10BASE-T Straight-Through Cable

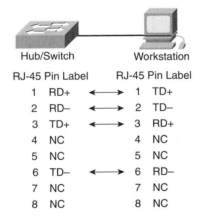

Hub/Switch   Workstation

RJ-45 Pin Label			RJ-45 Pin Label	
1	RD+	⟷	1	TD+
2	RD–	⟷	2	TD–
3	TD+	⟷	3	RD+
4	NC		4	NC
5	NC		5	NC
6	TD–	⟷	6	RD–
7	NC		7	NC
8	NC		8	NC

Because station-to-station, switch-to-switch, and station-to-switch connections all are point-to-point links, they have two physically separate communication pathways, channels on two separate UTP wire pairs. In this case, collisions are not physical events, but rather the result of the decision to not allow simultaneous Tx and Rx. Thus, either half duplex (subject to the administrative imposition of CSMA/CD) or full duplex (no physical collisions occur) is a configuration choice. Most of the time, you run these connections in full duplex, which not only eliminates collisions, but also doubles the throughput of the connection. When first introduced, the relevant IEEE standard was entitled 802.3x-1997 Full-Duplex. However, station-to-hub connections involve the bus topology within the hub, an actual physical collision domain. Hence, this connection can run *only* half duplex and is subject to CSMA/CD because of the physical nature of the structure.

10BASE-T carries 10 Mbps of traffic in half-duplex mode; however, 10BASE-T in full-duplex mode actually can exchange 20 Mbps of traffic (although, again, some of this is overhead, not user data). This concept will become increasingly important with the desire to increase the speed of Ethernet links.

10BASE-T Wiring and Architecture

10BASE-T links generally consist of a connection between the station and a hub or switch. Hubs should be thought of as multiport repeaters and count toward the limit on repeaters between distant stations. Switches can be thought of as multiport bridges and are subject to 100 m length limitations.

Although hubs can be linked in series (sometimes called daisy-chaining, or cascading), it is best to avoid this arrangement when possible, to keep from violating the limit for maximum delay between distant stations. The physical size of a 10BASE-T network is subject to the same rules as 10BASE5 and 10BASE2 concerning the number of repeaters. When multiple hubs are required, it is best to arrange them in hierarchical order, to create a tree structure instead of a chain. Also, performance will be improved if fewer repeaters separate stations. "Stackable" hubs, or concentrators with common backplanes that will support several multiport adapter cards, permit large numbers of stations to be connected to a device that counts as a single hub (repeater).

All distances between stations are acceptable, although in one direction, the architecture is at its limit. The most important aspect to consider is how to keep the delay between distant stations to a minimum—regardless of the architecture and media types involved. A shorter maximum delay provides better overall performance. Consider the following architectures:

In Figure 7-9, there are five segments and four repeaters from Station 1 to any other station in these paths. For 10BASE-T connections, the maximum of three segments with stations does not apply because no other stations are on the same cable. Each connection is described as a link segment.

Figure 7-9 Example 10-Mbps Mixed Architecture 1

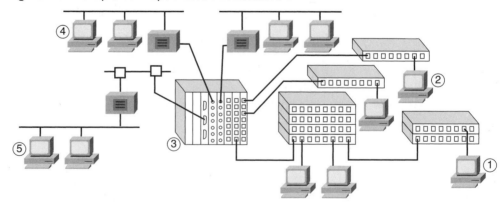

In Figure 7-10, from any station (except Station 1) to any other station, the path is only three repeaters. Because these alternate paths include 10BASE5 and 10BASE2 links, the other requirements still apply there (such as only three segments with stations).

Figure 7-10 Example 10-Mbps Mixed Architecture 2

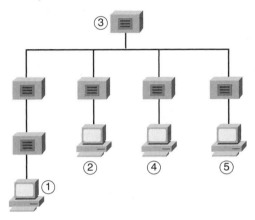

10BASE-T links can have unrepeated distances up to 100m. This might seem like a long distance, but it typically is used up quickly when wiring an actual building. Hubs can solve this distance issue, although a maximum of four repeaters could be chained together because of timing considerations. The widespread introduction of switches has made this distance limitation less important. As long as workstations are located within 100m of a switch, the 100m distance starts over at the switch, which could be connected via another 100m to another switch, and so on. Because most modern 10BASE-T Ethernet is switched, these are the practical limits between devices. Ring, star, and extended star topologies all are allowed. The issue then becomes one of logical topology and data flow, not timing or distance limitations.

Table 7-3 shows a chart of the 10BASE-T link characteristics.

Table 7-3 BASE-T Link Characteristics Chart

Connection	Maximum Segment
Station to station, station to switch, switch to switch	100m, with no limitations on daisy chaining
Station to hub	100m, but subject to four-repeater rule

100-Mbps Ethernet

100-Mbps Ethernet, also known as Fast Ethernet (in comparison to the original 10-Mbps Ethernet), was a series of technologies. The two technologies that became commercially important are ***100BASE-TX*** (copper UTP-based) and ***100BASE-FX*** (multimode optical fiber-based). This section examines the commonalities between these two technologies and then examines their differences individually.

Three things are common to 100BASE-TX and 100BASE-FX:

- The timing parameters
- The frame format
- Parts of the transmission process

Table 7-4 shows the parameters for 100-Mbps Ethernet operation.

Table 7-4 Parameters for 100-Mbps Ethernet Operation

Parameter	Value
Bit-time	10 nsec
Slot time	512 bit-times
Interframe spacing	96 bits
Collision attempt limit	16
Collision backoff limit	10
Collision jam size	32 bits
Maximum untagged frame size	1518 octets
Minimum frame size	512 bits (64 octets)

100BASE-TX and 100BASE-FX both share timing parameters. Note that 1 bit-time in 1000-Mbps Ethernet is 10 nsec = .01 microseconds = 1 100-millionth of a second.

The 100-Mbps frame format is the same as the 10-Mbps frame. This is unlike 10-Mbps Ethernet, in which the process was the same for all technologies until the signal was applied to the medium.

Fast Ethernet represents a tenfold increase in speed. With this increase in speed comes extra requirements. The bits being sent get shorter in duration and occur more frequently. They require more careful timing, and their transmission requires frequencies closer to medium-bandwidth limitations and become more susceptible to noise. In response to these issues of synchronization, bandwidth, and *signal-to-noise ratio (SNR)*, two separate encoding steps are used by 100-Mbps Ethernet. The basic idea is to use codes—which can be engineered to have desirable properties—to represent the user data in a way that is efficient to transmit, including synchronization, efficient usage of bandwidth, and improved SNR characteristics. The first part of the encoding uses a technique called 4-bit/5-bit (4B/5B); the second part of the encoding is the actual line encoding specific to copper or fiber.

The two forms of 100-Mbps Ethernet of consideration in this course, 100BASE-TX and 100BASE-FX, encode nibbles (4-bit groupings) from the upper parts of the MAC sublayer. The 4-bit patterns are converted into 5-bit symbols; symbols sometimes control information (such as start frame, end frame, or medium-is-idle conditions). The entire frame to be transmitted is comprised of control symbols and data symbols (data code groups). Again, all of this extra complexity is necessary to achieve the tenfold increase in network speed.

After the 4B/5B encoding, the bits (in the form of code groups) still need to be placed on the medium (that is, they must be line-encoded). The conversion from 4 bits to 5 bits also means that there are now 125 Mbps to be transmitted instead of 100 Mbps during the same time interval. This puts more strict requirements on the medium, transmitters, and receivers used. For example, the cable must be tested at higher frequencies to ensure proper transmission characteristics. Any time that there is no data to be sent, "idle code" groups still are sent to fill the empty periods and maintain synchronization. At this point, the data path diverges depending on whether you are using copper (100BASE-TX) or fiber (100BASE-FX) media.

100BASE-TX

The need for faster networks led to the announcement of the 100BASE-T Fast Ethernet and autonegotiation standard in 1995 (originally 802.3u-1995). 100BASE-T increased Ethernet's bit rate to 100 Mbps. 100BASE-TX was the Category 5 UTP version of 100BASE-T that became commercially successful. Soon 10/100 hubs and switches enabled Ethernet transmissions at the original rate of 10 Mbps to share the network with frames sent at 100 Mbps.

The original coaxial Ethernet used half-duplex transmission; therefore, only one device could transmit at a time. In 1997, Ethernet was expanded to include a full-duplex capability (originally 802.3x) that allowed more than one PC on a network to transmit at the same time. Devices called Ethernet switches were developed that enabled this full-duplex communication and handled network traffic more efficiently than hubs. These switches increasingly replaced hubs in high-speed networks because of their full-duplex capability and rapid handling of Ethernet frames.

100BASE-TX uses 4B/5B encoded data, which then is scrambled and converted to multilevel transmit—three levels, or MLT-3, line encoding on Category 5 UTP (or better). The MLT-3 encoding converts the binary data stream to an electrical waveform using a continuous signaling system. MLT-3 is different from *nonreturn to zero inverted (NRZI)*, in that the signal level alternates between above and below the zero level instead of using only two levels.

Figure 7-11 shows some MLT-3 encoding examples. The basic rule of MLT-3 is that binary 1s cause the voltage level to cycle to the next level down and then back up again. Binary 0s do not cause a level transition.

NOTE

In NRZI encoding, signals maintain constant voltage levels with no signal transitions (no return to a 0V level) but interpret the presence of data at the beginning of a bit interval as a signal transition. Likewise, they interpret the absence of data as no transition.

Figure 7-11 MLT-3 Encoding Examples

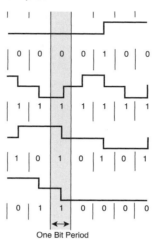

In the encoding example in Figure 7-11, one timing window is highlighted vertically through all four waveform examples. The top waveform has no transition in the center of the timing window. No transition indicates that a binary 0 is present. If the example waveform was all 0s on that line, the signal level represented would be either a constant high, 0, or low across the waveform. A single 1 was introduced to move the remaining 0s to a different voltage level and show that 0s can appear at more than one voltage level. The level depends upon what the previous (high or low) voltage level was and moves in the opposite direction. In this first waveform, it is thus evident that the previous voltage level (not shown) was low level. The second waveform in Figure 7-11 has a transition in the center of the timing window. A binary 1 is represented by a transition. It does not matter whether the transition is rising or falling, or whether the new level reached is high, 0, or low. Instead of a repeating sequence of the same binary value in the third waveform example, there is an alternating binary sequence. Again, this pattern helps demonstrate that the absence of a transition indicates a binary 0, and the presence of a transition indicates a binary 1. Rising or falling edges indicate 1s. The very steep signal changes from one extreme to the other, with a slight decrease in gradient at 0, indicate consecutive 1s. Any noticeable horizontal line in the signal indicates a 0, or consecutive 0s.

Figure 7-12 is an example of a 100BASE-TX signal taken from an oscilloscope. (In Figure 7-12, the y-axis is voltage; the x-axis is time. Voltage is measured as a differential signal between 2.)

Figure 7-12 100BASE-TX Signal Sample

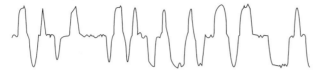

During the initial process of establishing synchronization with the link partner to establish a link, the receiver circuit expects to see only 4B/5B idle code groups.

The cable pinout for a 100BASE-TX connection is identical to the one for 10BASE-T. Two separate transmit/receive paths exist. For the connection between two stations or two switches, a crossover cable is required. As for the connection between stations and repeaters/multiport repeaters (hubs), a straight-through cable is used. Note, that inside an exclusively 100-Mbps hub is a bus topology, which is a collision domain. However, if the hub is a 10/100 autosensing hub, which is vastly more common, the internal topology is more complex, to account for the speed differential between 10BASE-T and 100BASE-TX. It should be noted that, even though a 100-Mbps Ethernet hub is significantly faster than a 10-Mbps hub, collisions are still a problem because both are based on a shared bus architecture. Only through the use of switches and full duplex are collisions avoided.

For the connection between a station and a switch, a straight-through cable is used. The switch fabric circuitry allows full bandwidth simultaneously on multiple ports without collisions.

Station-to-station, switch-to-switch, and station-to-switch connections in Fast Ethernet all are point-to-point links. They have two physically separate communication pathways/channels. In this case, collisions are not physical events, but rather the result of an administrative decision to not allow simultaneous Tx and Rx. Therefore, either half duplex (subject to the administrative imposition of CSMA/CD) or full duplex (no physical collisions occur) is a configuration choice. Most of the time, you run these connections in full duplex.

However, station-to-hub connections must account for the bus topology within the hub, a collision domain. Hence, this connection can *only* run half duplex and is subject to CSMA/CD because of the physical nature of the structure.

Can a 100-Mbps technology allow 200 Mbps of traffic? 100BASE-TX carries 100 Mbps of traffic in half-duplex mode (although some of this is overhead, not user data). But 100BASE-TX in full-duplex mode can exchange 200 Mbps of traffic (although, again, some of this is overhead, not user data). The concept of full duplex will become increasingly important with the desire to increase the speed of Ethernet links. You will learn about the 100BASE-TX architecture rules later in this chapter.

100BASE-FX

Why use 100BASE-FX (introduced as part of the 802.3u-1995 standard)? At the time copper-based Fast Ethernet was introduced, a fiber version was desired for backbone applications, connections between floors and buildings where copper is less desirable, and high-noise environments. 100BASE-FX also was positioned as an alternative to the then-popular FDDI (100-Mbps dual fiber-optic Token Ring). However, the vast majority of Fast Ethernet installations today are 100BASE-TX. One reason for the relative lack of adoption of 100BASE-FX was the rapidity of the introduction of Gigabit Ethernet copper and fiber standards, which are now the dominant technology for backbone installations, high-speed cross-connects, and general infrastructure needs.

100BASE-FX uses 4B/5B encoded data with NRZI line encoding. Signals are LED pulses on multimode optical fiber. NRZI encoding relies on the presence or absence of a transition in the middle of the timing window to determine the binary value for that bit period. 100BASE-FX is synchronous.

Figure 7-13 illustrates the NRZI encoding examples. (The y-axis is optical power; the x-axis is time.)

Figure 7-13 NRZI Encoding Examples

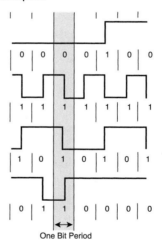

One Bit Period

In the encoding examples in Figure 7-13, one timing window is highlighted vertically through all four waveform examples. The top waveform has no transition in the center of the timing window, so it is interpreted as a binary 0. No transition indicates that a binary 0 is present. If the example waveform was all 0s on that line, the signal level represented would be either low or high across the waveform. A single 1 was introduced to indicate that 0s could be either level.

The second waveform has a transition in the center of the timing window. A binary 1 is represented by a transition. It does not matter whether the transition is rising or falling. Instead of a repeating sequence of the same binary value in the third waveform, there is an alternating binary sequence. In this example, it is more obvious that no transition indicates a binary 0, and the presence of a transition indicates a binary 1.

The NRZI-encoded, serialized bit stream is ready for transmission using pulsed light. Because of cycle time problems related to turning the transmitter completely on and off each time, the light is pulsed using low and high power. A logic 0 is represented by low power, and a logic 1 is represented by high power.

Table 7-5 summarizes a 100BASE-FX link and the pinouts. A fiber pair with either (ST) or (SC) connectors most commonly is used.

Table 7-5 100BASE-FX Pinout

Fiber	Signal
1	Tx (LED and laser transmitters)
2	Rx (high-speed photodiode detectors)

Figure 7-14 shows an interface-to-interface fiber link. The two separate strands of multimode fiber are often in the same cable structure, with dual connectors on each end.

Figure 7-14 Fiber Interface-to-Interface Connection

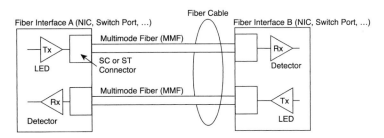

The MAC method treats the link as point-to-point, and fiber is intrinsically full duplex because of separate Tx and Rx fibers. 100BASE-TX could run in half duplex, but this would have length implications (the timing is actually a codeterminant, along with attenuation/dispersion/fiber properties of length limitations and restrictions on numbers of segments). Again, physical collisions between voltages are not an issue—these are serial streams of light pulses on an optical fiber—but administratively can impose CSMA/CD based on not allowing simultaneous Tx and Rx.

Can 100-Mbps fiber technology allow 200 Mbps of traffic? Somewhat analogous to the separate transmit and receive paths in UTP, there are two such paths in 100BASE- FX optical fiber, and 200 Mbps is possible.

Fast Ethernet Architecture

Fast Ethernet links generally consist of a connection between the station and a hub or switch. Hubs should be thought of as multiport repeaters and count toward the limit on repeaters between distant stations. Switches can be thought of as multiport bridges. They are subject to the 100m UTP media distance limitation.

Repeaters must be labeled with the word *Class* followed by a Roman numeral I or II inside a circle, indicating Class I or Class II. A Class I repeater can introduce up to 140 bit-times of latency (delay). Any repeater that changes between one Ethernet implementation and another (for example, 100BASE-TX and 100BASE-FX) is a Class I repeater. Also assume that any unlabeled repeater is a Class I device. Figure 7-15 illustrates the maximum collision domain diameter for a Class I repeater for 100BASE-TX. Using switches removes these restrictions, and the limiting factor becomes the media-determined maximum length between interfaces.

Figure 7-15 Maximum Collision Domain Diameter for a Class I Repeater

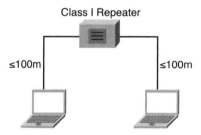

A Class II repeater can introduce only a maximum of 92 bit-times of latency. Because of the reduced latency, it is possible to have two Class II repeaters in a series, but only if the cable between them is very short. Figure 7-16 illustrates the maximum collision domain diameter for a Class II repeater for 100BASE-TX. Using switches removes these restrictions, and the limiting factor becomes the media-determined maximum length between interfaces.

Figure 7-16 Collision Domain Diameter for a Class II Repeater

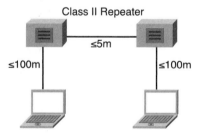

If your network is implemented using new high-performance hardware, it is possible that some of these limits can be exceeded. For example, if a longer cable is used between repeaters, shorter cables would have to be used to each station. Modification of the architecture rules is *strongly* discouraged for 100BASE-TX. Refer to the technical timing descriptions detailed in Clause 29 of the current 802.3 standard and the technical information about your hardware performance before attempting it. Any device that adapts between different Ethernet speeds, such as between 10 Mbps and 100 Mbps, is an OSI Layer 2 bridge. It is not possible to adapt between speeds and still be a repeater. However, the same device can repeat between ports linked at the same speed.

A 100BASE-TX UTP cable is about the same as a 10BASE-T cable, except that link performance must meet the higher-quality Category 5 or ISO Class D requirements. The 100BASE-TX cable between Class II repeaters cannot exceed 5m.

Links operating in full duplex can be substantially longer than what is shown in Table 7-6 because they are limited only by the capability of the medium to deliver a robust enough signal for proper decoding, not the round-trip delay. It is not uncommon to find Fast Ethernet operating in half duplex. However, half duplex is undesirable because the signaling scheme is inherently full duplex, and forcing half-duplex communications rules onto a full-duplex signaling system is not a wise use of resources.

It is recommended that all links between a station and a hub or switch be configured for autonegotiation, to permit the highest common performance configuration to be established without risking misconfiguration of the link. Disable autonegotiation and force connection configurations only if autonegotiation fails or on certain selected connections. The average station connection should be established by autonegotiation.

Table 7-6 summarizes the architectural rules for Fast Ethernet.

Table 7-6 Architecture Configuration Cable Distances

Architecture	100BASE-TX	100BASE-FX	100BASE-FX and 100BASE-TX
Station to station, station to switch, switch to switch (half or full duplex)	100m	412m	—
One Class I repeater (half duplex)	200m	272m	100m TX 160.8m FX
One Class II repeater (half duplex)	200m	320m	100m TX 208m FX
Two Class II repeaters (half duplex)	205m	228m	105m TX 211.2m FX

100BASE-TX links can have unrepeated distances up to 100m. This might seem like a long distance, but it typically is used up quickly when wiring an actual building. Hubs can solve this distance issue, subject to the restrictions in Table 7-6, because of timing considerations. The widespread introduction of switches has made this distance limitation less important. As long as workstations are located within 100m of a switch, the 100m distance starts over at the switch, which could be connected via another 100m to another switch, and so on. Because most Fast Ethernet is switched, these are the practical limits between devices. Ring, star, and extended star topologies all are allowed. The issue then becomes one of logical topology and data flow, not timing or distance limitations.

Lab 7.1.9a   Introduction to Fluke Network Inspector

This lab demonstrates how to use the Fluke Network Inspector (NI) to discover and analyze network devices within a broadcast domain.

Lab 7.1.9b   Introduction to Fluke Protocol Inspector

This lab demonstrates how to use the Fluke Network Protocol Inspector to analyze network traffic and data frames.

Interactive Media Activity   Drag and Drop: Fast Ethernet Architecture

After completing this activity, you understand the architecture of Fast Ethernet.

Gigabit and 10-Gigabit Ethernet

Fast Ethernet (100 Mbps) represented a major improvement over legacy Ethernet (10 Mbps). Yet the even more rapid progression from Fast Ethernet to Gigabit Ethernet is testimony to the power of IEEE standards, engineering advances, and market forces. Gigabit Ethernet, 1000 Mbps, is a hundredfold increase in network speed over the wildly popular 10BASE-T. Although MAC addressing, CSMA/CD, and, most important, the frame format from earlier versions of Ethernet are preserved, many other aspects of the MAC sublayer, the physical layer, and the medium have been changed.

Copper interfaces capable of 10/100/1000 operation are now common. Gigabit switch and router ports and blades are becoming routine in wiring closets. More multimode and single-mode optical fiber is being installed. One major emphasis of Gigabit Ethernet is optical fiber technology, but the need for a copper version—to use existing cable plants and to use the ruggedness of copper in user environments—led to a very clever scheme to get 1000 Mbps down the same Category 5 UTP used so successfully in 10-Mbps and 100-Mbps Ethernet. All of the Gigabit technologies are intrinsically full duplex. The inexorable forward march of technology continues as standards and technologies for 40 Gbps, 100 Gbps, and 160 Gbps currently are being implemented. Most dramatic is the evolution of Ethernet from LAN applications only to an end-to- end LAN, MAN, and WAN technology.

1000-Mbps Ethernet

In 1998, the IEEE 802.3z committee adopted the 1000BASE-X standard. This standard raised the data transmission rate to 1 Gbps full duplex over optical fiber, a hundredfold increase in speed over 10BASE-T. The 1000BASE-T standard, specifying 1 Gbps full duplex over Category 5 or higher UTP, was adopted in 1999.

Table 7-7 shows the parameters for 1000-Mbps Ethernet operation.

Table 7-7 Parameters for Gigabit Ethernet Operation

Parameter	Value
Bit-time	1 nsec
Slot time	4096 bit-times
Interframe spacing	96 bits
Collision attempt limit	16
Collision backoff limit	10
Collision jam size	32 bits
Maximum untagged frame size	1518 octets
Minimum frame size	512 bits (64 octets)
Burst limit	65,536 bits

1000BASE-T, *1000BASE-SX*, and *1000BASE-LX* all share the same timing parameters. Note that bit-time at 1000 Mbps = 1 nsec = .001 microseconds = 1 billionth of a second. You also need to note that some differences in timing relative to legacy and Fast Ethernet now are appearing because of the special issues that arise with such short bit and slot times.

The 1000-Mbps (Gigabit) Ethernet frame has the same format as is used for 10- and 100-Mbps Ethernet. 1000-Mbps Ethernet has different paths for the process of converting frames to bits on the cable, depending on which implementation is used.

Gigabit Ethernet is a tenfold increase in speed over Fast Ethernet. Just as with Fast Ethernet, with this increase in speed comes extra requirements—the bits being sent get shorter in duration (1 nanosecond), occur more frequently, and require more careful timing. Their transmission also requires frequencies closer to medium bandwidth limitations, and they become more susceptible to noise. In response to these issues of synchronization, bandwidth, and signal-to-noise ratio, Gigabit Ethernet uses two separate encoding steps. The basic idea is to use codes—which can be engineered to have desirable properties—to represent the user data in a way that is efficient to transmit, including synchronization, efficient usage of bandwidth, and improved SNR characteristics. Bit patterns from the MAC sublayer are converted into symbols, with symbols sometimes controlling information (such as start frame, end frame, and medium idle conditions). The entire frame is broken up into control symbols and data symbols (data code groups). All of this extra complexity is necessary to achieve the tenfold increase in network speed over Fast Ethernet. For 1000BASE-T, the first part of the encoding uses a technique called *8Bit-1Quinary quarter (8B1Q4)*; the second part of the encoding is the actual line encoding specific to copper, called *4-dimensional 5 level pulse amplitude modulation (4D-PAM5)*. The 8B1Q4 encoding followed by the 4D-PAM5 line encoding provide the synchronization, bandwidth, and SNR characteristics needed to make possible the four wire pairs (working in parallel) running full duplex on each wire pair simultaneously. For 1000BASE-X, 8-bit/10-bit (8B/10B) encoding (similar to the 4B/5B concept) is used, followed by the simple NRZ line encoding of light on optical fiber.

1000BASE-T

Goals for 1000BASE-T (introduced as 802.3ab-1999 1000BASE-T Gigabit Ethernet over twisted-pair) included these:

- Capability to function over existing Category 5 copper cable plants

- Assurance that this cable would work by passing a Category 5e test, which most cable can pass after a careful retermination

- Interoperability with 10BASE-T and 100BASE-TX

- Applications such as building backbones, interswitch links, wiring closet applications, server farms, and high-end desktop workstations

- Provision of 10x bandwidth of Fast Ethernet, which became very widely installed by end users, helping to necessitate more speed upstream in the network

To achieve this speed running over Category 5e copper cable, 1000BASE-T needed to use all four pairs of wires. Category 5e cable reliably can carry up to 125 Mbps of traffic. Using sophisticated circuitry, full-duplex transmissions on the same wire pair allows 250 Mbps per pair; multiplied by four wire pairs, this gives a total of 1000 Mbps (1 Gbps). For some purposes, it is helpful to think of these four wire pairs as "lanes" over which the data travels simultaneously (to be reassembled carefully at the receiver).

1000BASE-T uses 8B1Q4 encoding with 4D-PAM5 line encoding on Cat 5e or better UTP. Achieving the 1-Gbps rate required use of all four pairs in full-duplex simultaneously. This results in a permanent collision on the wire pairs, which is very different from the first coaxial Ethernet systems. The "permanent" collisions—transmission and receipt of data happens in both directions on the same wire at the same time—results in very complex voltage patterns.

But using sophisticated integrated circuits, which, among other things, use a technique called *echo cancellation*, works well.

Despite the constant collision of the signals, the system is capable of operating through a careful selection of voltage levels and use of Layer 1 forward error correction (FEC).

Figure 7-17 shows the outbound (transmitting [Tx]) 1000BASE-T signal (the y-axis is voltage; the x-axis is the time taken from an oscilloscope—voltage is a "differential signal" measured between two paired wires in one of the four pairs present in UTP cable).

Figure 7-17 Outbound (Tx) 1000BASE-T Signal

Figure 7-18 actually shows a 1000BASE-T signal captured with a digital storage oscilloscope after several meters of cable. (the y-axis is voltage; the x-axis is time—voltage is a "differential signal" measured between two paired wires in one of the four pairs present in UTP cable).

Figure 7-18 Actual 1000BASE-T Signal

It is quite remarkable that the signal can be recovered at all when it is revealed that during idle periods, there are nine voltage levels found on the cable, and during data transmission periods, there are 17 voltage levels on the cable. Note the complex line encoding to begin with. Then, in Figure 7-18, look at the actual signal on the wire with constant collisions, as well as attenuation effects and noise. The signal looks analog. The key here is that sophisticated circuitry is decoding all of this. However, the system is susceptible to cable problems, termination problems, and noise unless standards are followed. Gigabit Ethernet works very well if the cabling, termination, and noise guidelines are followed.

Table 7-8 summarizes the use of all four pairs in the UTP cable. A, B, C, and D could be considered "lanes" of data. The data from the sending station is carefully divided into four parallel streams, encoded, transmitted and detected in parallel, and then reassembled into one received bit stream.

Table 7-8 1000BASE-T Pinout

Pin Number	Signal
1	BI_DA+ (bidirectional data, positive going)
2	BI_DA- (bidirectional data, negative going)
3	BI_DB+ (bidirectional data, positive going)
4	BI_DC+ (bidirectional data, positive going)
5	BI_DC- (bidirectional data, negative going)
6	BI_DB- (bidirectional data, negative going)
7	BI_DD+ (bidirectional data, positive going)
8	BI_DD- (bidirectional data, negative going)

Figure 7-19 is a schematic representation of simultaneous full duplex on four wire pairs. Station-to-station, switch-to-switch, and station-to-switch cabling connections are the same as in Fast Ethernet.

Figure 7-19 1000BASE-T Signal Transmission

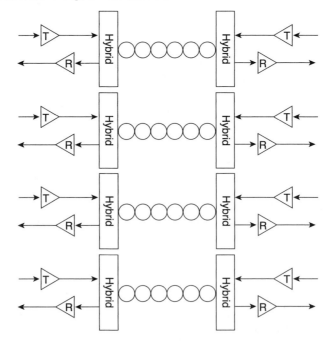

It is especially important to desktop, office, and wiring closet applications that there be interoperability among Gigabit, Fast, and 10BASE-T Ethernet. This might seem to be a hopeless affair. But upon close inspection, note that if the cabling installed in the walls tests out (as it often does or easily can be made to by retermination) at Category 5e and if all eight wires in the RJ-45 connectors and jacks are connected, the signal paths exists for Gigabit, Fast, and 10BASE-T Ethernet to interoperate. Just as 10/100 devices emerged in Fast Ethernet, 10/100/1000 interfaces have been developed for interoperability. By using the same frame format, compatible wiring paths, and clever interface engineering, it all works well.

For historical reasons, CSMA/CD and half duplex are options on 1000BASE-T. But the overwhelming use of 1000BASE-T is full duplex. This is accomplished with sophisticated hybrid circuits that can act as Tx and Rx at the same time for the same wires.

Before communications can begin, the two link partners must determine which will source the master clock and which will use the data stream to recover the slave clock. The master clock and slave clock are used as time markers for signal transmission. This process usually is determined during autonegotiation, although it can be configured manually. A number of other parameters also are determined in the same manner, including duplex type. Autonegotiation usually determines that a multiport device (a switch or hub) should become the master clock. The overall message here is that with the 1 nanosecond bit-times, 1 billion bps data transfer rate, and four wire pairs simultaneously transmitting and receiving, synchronization is extremely important.

When the topic of 1000BASE-X (1000BASE-SX and 1000BASE-LX) is presented, comparisons with 1000BASE-T architecture are included.

1000BASE-SX and LX

Gigabit Ethernet over fiber is one of the most recommended backbone technologies. Its benefits are tremendous:

- 1000-Mbps data transfer, which can aggregate groupings of widely deployed Fast Ethernet devices

- Noise immunity

- Lack of any ground potential problems between floors or buildings

- An explosion in 1000BASE-X device options

- Excellent distance characteristics

Gigabit Ethernet over fiber originally was introduced in the IEEE 802.3 supplement entitled "802.3z-1998 1000BASE-X Gigabit Ethernet." The only application for which 1000BASE-SX and 1000BASE-LX have not caught on as rapidly is the office desktop—1000BASE-TX is considered more "user-proof" in terms of day-to-day wear, and 10-/100-/1000-Mbps copper interfaces are common.

1000BASE-X uses 8B/10B encoding converted to NRZ line encoding, with either lower-cost short-wavelength 850 nm laser (or sometimes LED) sources and multimode optical fiber (1000BASE-SX, S for short), or long-wavelength 1310 nm laser sources and single-mode optical fiber (1000BASE-LX, L for long).

NRZ encoding relies on the signal level found in the timing window to determine the binary value for that bit period. Unlike most of the other encoding schemes described, this encoding system is *level*-driven instead of *edge*-driven.

In the encoding example in Figure 7-20, one timing window is highlighted vertically through all four waveform examples. The top waveform is low across the timing window. A low signal level represents a binary 0. A single 1 was introduced at the end of the waveform to show the other signal level.

Figure 7-20 NRZ Encoding Example

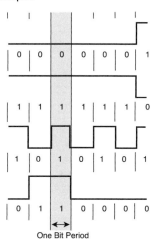

One Bit Period

The second waveform is high across the timing window. A high signal level represents a binary 1. Again, a single 0 was introduced at the end of the waveform to show the other signal level. Instead of a repeating sequence of the same binary value in the third waveform, there is an alternating binary sequence. In this example, it is more obvious that a low signal level indicates a binary 0 and a high signal indicates a binary 1.

The fourth waveform example is random data. Three of these examples are good examples of why this encoding scheme has the potential to cause dc voltage drift on copper media. The second example is changing levels each bit period and would not suffer from dc voltage drift. It is very easy for a string of the same binary signal to cause a dc voltage bias on the cable, which has the potential of causing clocking errors. On fiber media, this is not an issue.

The NRZ-encoded serialized bit stream is ready for transmission using pulsed light, as specified for 1000BASE-SX or 1000BASE-LX. Because of cycle time problems related to turning the transmitter completely on and off each time, the light is pulsed using low and high power. A logical 0 is represented by low power, and a logical 1 is represented by high power.

Table 7-9 shows the amazingly simple interface-to-interface interconnection for Gigabit Ethernet over fiber. SC fiber-optic connectors most commonly are used.

Table 7-9 Interface-to-Interface Interconnection for Gigabit Ethernet

Fiber	Signal
1	Tx (laser transmitters)
2	Rx (high-speed photodiode detectors)

Figure 7-21 shows the interface-to-interface connection for 1000BASE-SX. Short-wave-length laser (or sometimes LED) sources typically are used with multimode optical fiber.

Figure 7-21 1000BASE-SX Fiber Interface-to-Interface Connection

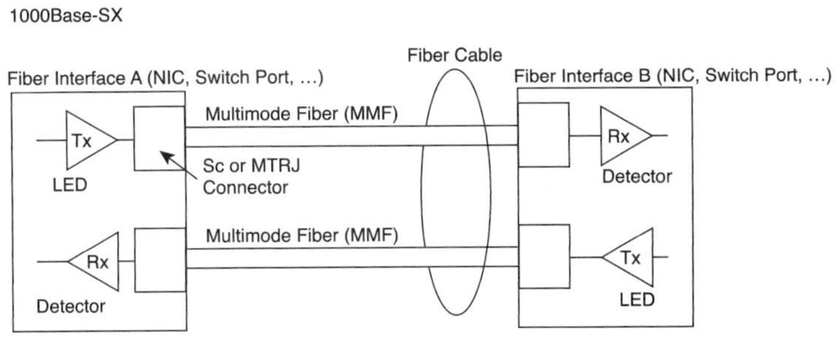

Figure 7-22 shows the interface-to-interface connection for 1000BASE-LX. Laser sources typically are used with single-mode fiber to achieve distances of up to 5000m.

Figure 7-22 1000BASE-LX Interface-to-Interface Connection

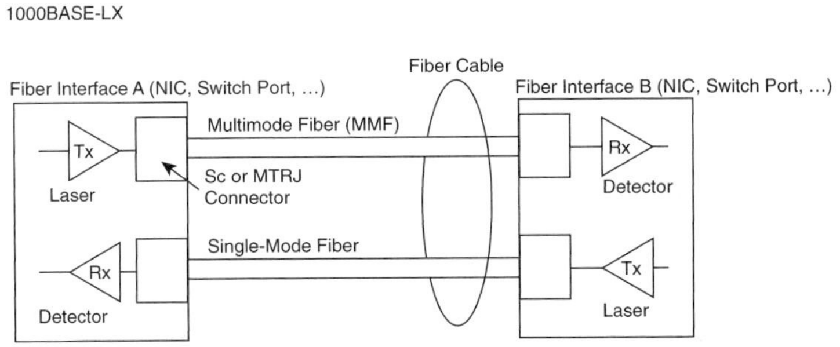

The MAC method used treats the link as point-to-point, and fiber is intrinsically full duplex because of separate Tx and Rx fibers. Gigabit Ethernet permits a single repeater between two stations.

Gigabit Ethernet Architecture

Any device that adapts between different Ethernet speeds, such as between 100 Mbps and 1000 Mbps, is an OSI Layer 2 bridge. It is not possible to adapt between speeds and still be a repeater.

Full-duplex links can be substantially longer that what is shown in Tables 7-9 and 7-10 because they are limited only by the medium, not by the round-trip delay. Gigabit Ethernet architecture is overwhelmingly station-to-station, station-to-switch, switch-to-switch, and switch-to-router connections running at full duplex. 1000BASE-SX is specified for multi-mode fiber. 1000BASE-LX is specified for multimode and single-mode fiber.

Tables 7-10 and 7-11 show distance limitations for 1000BASE-SX and 1000BASE-LX. Because most Gigabit Ethernet is switched, these are the practical limits between devices. Daisy-chaining, star, and extended star topologies all are allowed. The issue then becomes one of logical topology and data flow, not timing or distance limitations.

Table 7-10 Maximum 1000BASE-SX Cable Distances

Medium	Modal Bandwidth	Maximum Distance
62.5 μm MMF	160	220m
62.5 μm MMF	200	275m
50 μm MMF	400	500m
50 μm MMF	500	550m

The maximum 1000BASE-SX cable distances at 805 nm (minimum overfilled launch).

Table 7-11 Maximum 1000BASE-LX Cable Distances

Medium	Modal Bandwidth	Maximum Distance
62.5 μm MMF	500	550m
50 μm MMF	400	550m
50 μm MMF	500	550m
10 μm SMF	—	5000m

The maximum 1000BASE-LX cable distances at 805 nm (minimum overfilled launch).

A 1000BASE-T UTP cable is about the same as a 10BASE-T and 100BASE-TX cable, except that link performance must meet the higher-quality Category 5e or ISO Class D (2000) requirements.

As with 10-Mbps and 100-Mbps versions, it is possible to modify some of the architecture rules slightly; however, there is virtually no allowance for additional delay in half duplex. Modification of the architecture rules is strongly discouraged for 1000BASE-T. At 100m, 1000BASE-T is operating close to the edge of the hardware's capability to recover the transmitted signal. Any cabling problems or environmental noise could render an otherwise-compliant cable inoperable even at distances that are within the specification. Refer to the technical timing descriptions in the current 802.3 standard and the technical information about your hardware performance before attempting any adjustments to the architecture rules.

Links operating in full-duplex links might be longer than what is indicated in Table 7-12 because they are limited only by the capability of the medium to deliver a robust enough signal to decode the signaling; they are not limited by the round-trip delay. It is extremely rare to find Gigabit Ethernet operating in half duplex. Half duplex is undesirable because the signaling scheme is inherently full duplex, and forcing half-duplex communications rules onto a full-duplex signaling system is not a wise use of resources. Operating under half-duplex rules requires adherence to slot time round-trip delay limitations that reduce the effective cable lengths, and there is also a substantial increase in overhead introduced by the carrier extension. Furthermore, very few Gigabit repeaters are in service, which means that the link is probably between a station and an OSI Layer 2 bridge, or between two bridges, so the collision domain would end at the bridge anyway.

It is recommended that all links between a station and a switch be configured for autonegotiation, to permit the highest common performance configuration to be established without risking misconfiguration of the link, and to avoid accidental misconfiguration of the other required parameters for proper Gigabit Ethernet operation.

Table 7-12 shows the speed case for half-duplex operation. But because most Gigabit Ethernet is switched, it is subject to link-by-link rules shown previously in Tables 7-10 and 7-11.

Table 7-12 Architecture Configuration Cable Distances for Half-Duplex Operation

Architecture	1000BASE-T	1000BASE-SX/LX	1000BASE-SX/LX and 1000BASE-T
Station to station	100m	316m	—
One repeater	200m	220m	100m 1000BASE-T (plus) 110m 1000BASE-SX/LX

10-Gigabit Ethernet

Most recently, in 2002, IEEE 802.3ae was adapted. This standard specifies 10-Gbps full-duplex transmission over fiber-optic cable. Taken as a whole, the similarities between 802.3ae and 802.3 (the original Ethernet) and all of the other varieties of Ethernet are remarkable. Metcalfe's original design has evolved, but it is still very apparent in the modern Ethernet. Recently, 10-Gb Ethernet (10GbE) has emerged as the latest example of the extensibility of the Ethernet system. Usable for LANs, storage-area networks (SANs), metropolitan-area networks (MANs), and WANs, 10GbE offers exciting new networking possibilities. What is 10GbE, and why should it be used?

Legacy Ethernet, Fast Ethernet, and Gigabit Ethernet now dominate the LAN market. The next step in the evolution of Ethernet is to move to 10-Gb Ethernet (10GbE, operating at 10,000,000,000 bps). By maintaining the frame format and other Ethernet Layer 2 specifications, increasing bandwidth needs can be accommodated with the low-cost, easily implementable, and easily interoperable 10GbE. 10GbE runs only over optical fiber media. End-to-end Ethernet networks become possible.

Because of massive growth in Internet- and intranet-based traffic, and the rapidly increasing use of Gigabit Ethernet, even higher bandwidth interconnections are needed. Internet service providers (ISPs) and network service providers (NSPs) can use 10GbE to create high-speed, low-cost, easily interoperable connections between colocated carrier switches and routers. Points of presence (POPs), intranet server farms comprised of Gigabit Ethernet servers, digital video studios, SANs, and backbones already are envisaged applications.

Perhaps most significantly, a major conceptual change comes with 10GbE. Ethernet traditionally is thought of as a LAN technology. But 10GbE physical layer standards allow both an extension in distance (to 40 km over single-mode fiber) and compatibility with Synchronous Optical Network (SONET)/Synchronous Digital Hierarchy (SDH) networks. Operation at a 40 km distance makes 10GbE a viable MAN technology. Compatibility with SONET/SDH networks operating up to OC-192 speeds (9.584640 Gps) makes 10GbE a viable WAN technology. 10GbE also might compete with Asynchronous Transfer Mode (ATM) for certain applications.

The following summarizes how 10GbE compares to other varieties of Ethernet:

- Frame format is the same, allowing interoperability among all varieties of Legacy, Fast, Gigabit, and 10-Gb Ethernet, with no reframing or protocol conversions.

- Bit-time now at 0.1 nanoseconds. All other time variables scale accordingly.

- No need for CSMA/CD because only full-duplex fiber connections are used.

- IEEE 802.3 sublayers within OSI Layers 1 and 2 that are mostly preserved, with a few additions to accommodate 40-km fiber links and interoperability with SONET/SDH technologies.

- Possibility of flexible, efficient, reliable, relatively low-cost, end-to-end Ethernet networks.

- Capability to run TCP/IP over LANs, MANs, and WANs with one Layer 2 transport method.

The basic standard governing CSMA/CD is IEEE 802.3. An IEEE 802.3 supplement, entitled 802.3ae, governs the 10GBASE family. As is typical for new technologies, a variety of implementations are being considered, including these:

- **10GBASE-SR**—Intended for short distances over already-installed multimode fiber, supports a range between 26 m and 82 m.

- **10GBASE-LX4**—Uses *wavelength-division multiplexing (WDM)*. Supports 240 m to 300 m over already-installed multimode fiber, and 10 km over single-mode fiber.

- **10GBASE-LR and 10GBASE-ER**—Supports 10 km and 40 km over single-mode fiber.

- **10GBASE-SW, 10GBASE-LW, and 10GBASE-EW**—Intended to work with OC-192/STM SONET/SDH WAN equipment.

The IEEE 802.3ae task force and the 10-Gb Ethernet Alliance (10 GEA) are working to standardize these emerging technologies.

10-Gb Ethernet (IEEE 802.3ae) was standardized in June 2002. It is a full-duplex protocol that uses only fiber-optic fiber as a transmission medium. The maximum transmission distances depend on the type of fiber being used. When using single-mode fiber as the transmission medium, the maximum transmission distance is 40 km (25 miles). Some discussions between IEEE members suggest the possibility of standards for 40-Gbps, 80-Gbps, and even 100-Gbps Ethernet.

Given the history of Ethernet, there is no reason to expect that its evolution will cease. The higher speeds and greater transmission distances that are making Ethernet both a LAN and a MAN protocol are not the only additions to the Ethernet standard that we are likely to see. Because fiber is being used as the transmission medium, the likelihood that an error in the data might occur during the passage of the Ethernet packet across the network is very low, much lower than in the original Ethernet. On a network with a very low error rate, it makes sense to transmit larger packets of data.

The upper limit on the amount of data that can be carried in an Ethernet packet (a frame) is 1500 bytes. Sending more data than that in a frame would make it an invalid Ethernet frame and cause the network to discard it. This has been the standard since Ethernet was created. Given a low likelihood of errors on a network, large files could be moved over the network more efficiently if a larger amount of data could be carried in each frame. The reason for this is that it takes time for computers to generate and to process Ethernet headers and trailers. Each Ethernet frame must have a header and a trailer. For example, if six times as much data could be sent per frame, there would be fewer frames (only one sixth as many) needed to carry all the data in a file. This means that fewer headers and trailers would have to be generated by the transmitter and processed by the receiver. The result is a shorter amount of time needed to move a large file over a network between two computers. WANs that use fiber as their transmission medium routinely transmit large data packets.

For this reason, especially when multigigabit LANs are connected to WANs, it is likely that we will see the use of Jumbo Ethernet frames. A Jumbo frame is any Ethernet frame that is carrying more than 1500 bytes of data. The proposed upper limit for the amount of data carried in a Jumbo frame is about 9,000 bytes. Jumbo frames are not currently a part of the new IEEE 802.3ae standard. However, it is very likely that some vendors of Ethernet networking equipment will allow Jumbo frames to be carried on Ethernet networks built using only their equipment. This might force the IEEE 802.3 committee to make support for larger frame sizes an option in new multigigabit standards.

Table 7-13 shows the parameters for 10-Gb Ethernet operation.

Table 7-13 Parameters for 10-Gbps Ethernet Operation

Parameter	Value
Bit-time	0.1 nsec
Slot time	N/A*
Interframe spacing	96 bits**
Collision attempt limit	N/A*
Collision backoff limit	N/A*
Collision jam size	N/A*
Maximum untagged frame size	1518 octets
Minimum frame size	512 bits (64 bytes)
Burst limit	N/A*
Interframe spacing stretch ratio	104 bits***

*10-Gbps Ethernet does not permit half-duplex operation, so parameters related to slot timing and collision handling do not apply.

**The value listed is the official interframe spacing.

***The interframe spacing stretch ratio applies exclusively to 10GBASE-W definitions.

Amazingly, 10GbE uses the same frame format (with a few special case exceptions) as 10-, 100-, and 1000-Mbps Ethernet.

10-Gigibit Ethernet Architectures

10-Gb Ethernet is a tenfold increase in speed over Gigabit Ethernet. Just as with Gigabit Ethernet, with this increase in speed comes extra requirements—the bits being sent get shorter in duration (1 ns), occur more frequently, and require more careful timing. In addition, their transmission requires frequencies closer to medium bandwidth limitations and they become more susceptible to noise. In response to these issues of synchronization, bandwidth, and SNR, two separate encoding steps are used by 10-Gb Ethernet. The basic idea is to use codes—which can be engineered to have desirable properties— to represent the user data in a way that is efficient to transmit, including synchronization, efficient usage of bandwidth, and improved SNR characteristics.

Bit patterns from the MAC sublayer are converted into symbols, with symbols sometimes controlling information (such as start frame, end frame, and medium idle conditions). The entire frame is broken up into control symbols and data symbols (data code groups). All of this extra complexity is necessary to achieve the tenfold increase in network speed over Gigabit Ethernet. 8B/10B encoding (similar to the 4B/5B concept) is used, followed by several different types of line encoding on the optical fiber.

Figure 7-23 represents what happens to the 8B-10B before it is line-encoded. 10-Gb Ethernet uses a variety of complex encodings before line encoding, including 8B/10B and 64B/66B. Bits from these codes then are converted to line signals: low power light for binary 0 and higher power light for binary 1. Complex serial bit streams are used for all versions of 10GbE except for 10GBASE-LX4, which uses wide wavelength-division multiplexing (WWDM) to multiplex 4-bit simultaneous bit streams as four wavelengths of light launched into the fiber at one time.

Figure 7-23 How 10GbE Converts MAC Frames to Four Lanes of Bits

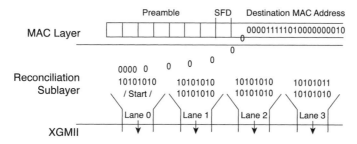

Figure 7-23 shows how 10GbE converts MAC frames to four lanes of bits for parallel transmission on four wire pairs of UTP or as a bit stream that is then serialized for laser transmission on single-mode fiber.

Figure 7-24 represents the particular case of using four slightly different-colored laser sources. Upon receipt from the medium, the optical signal stream is demultiplexed into four separate optical signal streams. The four optical signal streams then are converted back into four electronic bit streams as they travel in approximately the reverse process back up through the sublayers to the MAC sublayer.

Currently, most 10GbE products are in the form of modules (line cards) for addition to high-end switches and routers. As the 10GbE technologies evolve, an increasing diversity of signaling components can be expected. As optical technologies evolve, improved transmitters and receivers will be incorporated into these products, further taking advantage of modularity. All 10GbE varieties use optical-fiber media. Fiber types include 10μm single-mode fiber, and 50μm and 62.5 μm multimode fibers. A range of fiber attenuation and dispersion characteristics are supported, but they limit operating distances.

Figure 7-24 10GBASE-LX4 Signal Multiplexing

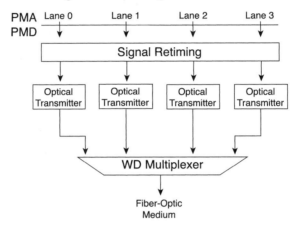

SC fiber-optic connectors most commonly are used. Because optical fiber is the medium used by 10GbE, typically a fiber pair connects Tx for device 1 to Rx for device 2, and vice versa. The primary devices connecting currently via 10GbE are high-end modular switches and routers. Table 7-14 lists the pinout options for 10GbE.

Table 7-14 10GbE Pinout

Fiber	Signal
1	Tx (laser transmitters)
2	Rx (high-speed photodiode detectors)

10-Gb Ethernet is available in full-duplex mode only and runs only over optical fiber. Hence, collisions are nonexistent and CSMA/CD is unnecessary.

As 10GbE standards and products evolve, a wide range of architectures and application guidelines is becoming possible. Most important to consider is that the addition of 10GbE, with its LAN, SAN, MAN, and WAN capabilities, enables network engineers to consider very sophisticated end-to-end Ethernet networks. LAN, SAN, MAN, and WAN topologies using Gigabit Ethernet are all being implemented.

10-Gb Ethernet is supported only over fiber-optic media. Support is available for 62.5 µm and 50 µm multimode fiber, as well as 10 µm single-mode fiber. Even though support is limited to fiber-optic media, some of the maximum cable lengths are surprisingly short. No repeater is defined for 10-Gb Ethernet because half duplex explicitly is not supported.

As with 10-Mbps, 100-Mbps, and 1000-Mbps versions, it is possible to modify some of the architecture rules slightly. Possible architecture adjustments are related to signal loss and distortion along the medium. Because of dispersion of the signal and other issues, the light pulse becomes undecipherable beyond certain distances. Refer to the technical timing and spectral requirements in the current 802.3 standard, as well as the technical information about your hardware performance, before attempting any adjustments to the architecture rules.

Table 7-15 shows the 10-Gb Ethernet implementations. Both R and W specifications are covered by each appropriate entry (for example, 10GBASE-E covers both 10GBASE-ER and 10GBASE-EW).

Table 7-15 10-Gb Ethernet Implementations

Implementation	Wavelength	Medium	Minimum Modal Bandwidth	Operating Distance
10GBASE-LX4	1310 nm	62.5 µm MMF	500 MHz/km	2m to 300m
10GBASE-LX4	1310 nm	50 µm MMF	400 MHz/km	2m to 240m
10GBASE-LX4	1310 nm	50 µm MMF	500 MHz/km	2m to 300m
10GBASE-LX4	1310 nm	10 µm SMF	—	2 km to 10 km
10GBASE-S	850 nm	62.5 µm MMF	160 MHz/km	2m to 26m
10GBASE-S	850 nm	62.5 µm MMF	200 MHz/km	2m to 33m
10GBASE-S	850 nm	50 µm MMF	400 MHz/km	2m to 66m
10GBASE-S	850 nm	50 µm MMF	500 MHz/km	2m to 82 m
10GBASE-S	850 nm	50 µm MMF	2000 MHz/km	2m to 300 m
10GBASE-L	1310 nm	10 µm SMF	—	2 km to 10 km
10GBASE-E	1550 nm	10 µm SMF	—	2 km to 30 km*

*The standard permits 40-km lengths if link attenuation is low enough.

Note the versatility of 10GbE. A diverse set of fiber types and laser sources can be used to achieve not only LAN, but also MAN and WAN distances.

Future of Ethernet

As the last several sections have documented, Ethernet has gone through an evolution from Legacy to Fast to Gigabit to multigigabit technologies. Although other LAN technologies are still in place (legacy installations), Ethernet dominates new LAN installations—so much so that some have referred to Ethernet as the LAN "dial tone." Ethernet is now the standard for horizontal, vertical, and interbuilding connections. In fact, recently developing versions of Ethernet are blurring the distinction between LANs, MANs, and WANs in terms of geographic distance covered as part of one network.

Figure 7-25 illustrates the expanding scope of Ethernet.

Figure 7-25 Ethernet's Expanding Scope

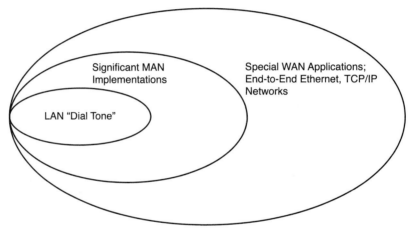

Although Gigabit Ethernet is now widely available and 10-Gb products are becoming more available, the IEEE and the 10-Gb Ethernet Alliance currently have released 40-Gbps, 100-Gbps, and even 160-Gbps standards. Which technologies actually are adopted will depend on a number of factors, including the rate of maturation of the technologies and standards, the rate of adoption in the market, and cost.

Proposals for Ethernet arbitration schemes other than CSMA/CD have been made. But the problem of collisions, so fundamental to physical bus topologies of 10BASE5, 10BASE2, 10BASE-T, and 100BASE-TX hubs, is no longer so common. Use of UTP and optical fiber, both of which have separate Tx and Rx paths, and the decreasing costs of switched instead of hubbed connections, make single shared-media, half-duplex media connections much less important.

The future of networking media is threefold:

- Copper (up to 1000 Mbps, perhaps more)

- Wireless (approaching 100 Mbps, perhaps more)

- Optical fiber (currently at 10,000 Mbps and soon to be more)

Unlike copper and wireless media, in which certain physical and practical limitations on the highest-frequency signals that can be transmitted are being approached, the bandwidth limitation on optical fiber is extremely large and is not a limiting factor for the foreseeable future. In fiber systems, the electronics technology (such as emitters and detectors) and the fiber-manufacturing processes most limit the speed. Therefore, upcoming developments in Ethernet likely will be heavily weighted toward laser light sources and single-mode optical fiber.

When Ethernet was slower, half duplex (subject to collisions and a "democratic" process for prioritization) was not considered to have the quality of service (QoS) capabilities required to handle certain types of traffic. This included such things as IP telephony and video multicast.

However, the full-duplex, high-speed Ethernet technologies that now dominate the market are proving to be sufficient at supporting even QoS-intensive applications. This makes the potential applications of Ethernet even wider. Ironically, end-to-end QoS capability helped drive a push for ATM to the desktop and to the WAN in the mid-1990s, but now Ethernet, not ATM, is approaching this goal.

At 30 years old, Ethernet technologies continue to grow and have a very bright future.

Summary

In this chapter, you learned the following key points:

- Several types of Ethernet exist, such as Ethernet, Fast Ethernet, Gigabit Ethernet, and 10-Gb Ethernet. Each type is associated with a different transfer rate:
    — 10-Mbps Ethernet operates within the timing limits of up to five segments separated up to four repeaters.
    — 10BASE-T uses cheaper and easier-to-install Category 3 or Category 5 UTP copper cable instead of coaxial cable.
    — 10BASE-T wiring parameters consist of a connection between a station and a hub or switch.
- The three connection types in the future of networking media are
    — Copper, which offers up to 1000 Mbps or more
    — Wireless, which offers up to 100 Mbps or more
    — Optical fiber, which is currently at 10,000 Mbps and soon to be more

To supplement all that you have learned in this chapter, refer to the chapter-specific Interactive Media Activity on the CD-ROM that accompanies this book.

Key Terms

10BASE2   10-Mbps baseband Ethernet specification using 50-ohm thin coaxial cable. 10BASE2, which is part of the IEEE 802.3 specification, has a distance limit of 185m (606 ft.) per segment.

10BASE5   10-Mbps baseband Ethernet specification using standard (thick) 50-ohm baseband coaxial cable. 10BASE5, which is part of the IEEE 802.3 baseband physical layer specification, has a distance limit of 500m (1640 ft.) per segment.

10BASE-T   10-Mbps baseband Ethernet specification using two pairs of twisted-pair cabling (Category 3, 4, or 5): one pair for transmitting data and the other for receiving data. 10BASE-T, which is part of the IEEE 802.3 specification, has a distance limit of approximately 100m (328 ft.) per segment.

100BASE-FX   100-Mbps baseband Fast Ethernet specification using two strands of multimode fiber-optic cable per link. To guarantee proper signal timing, a 100BASE-FX link cannot exceed 400m (1312 ft.) in length. It is based on the IEEE 802.3 standard.

100BASE-TX   100-Mbps baseband Fast Ethernet specification using two pairs of either UTP or STP wiring. The first pair of wires is used to receive data; the second is used to transmit. To guarantee proper signal timing, a 100BASE-TX segment cannot exceed 100m (328 ft.) in length. It is based on the IEEE 802.3 standard.

1000BASE-T   1000-Mbps baseband Gigabit Ethernet specification using four pairs of Category 5 UTP cable for a maximum length of 100m (328 ft.).

1000BASE-SX   1000-Mbps baseband Gigabit Ethernet specification using a short laser wavelength on multimode fiber-optic cable for a maximum length of 550m (1804.5 ft.).

1000BASE-LX   1000-Mbps baseband Gigabit Ethernet specification using a long wavelength for a long-haul fiber-optic cable for a maximum length of 10,000 (32808.4 ft.).

4D-PAM5   The symbol-encoding method used in 1000BASE-T. The four-dimensional quinary symbols (4D) received from the 8B1Q4 data encoding are transmitted using five voltage levels (PAM5). Four symbols are transmitted in parallel each symbol period.

8B1Q4   For IEEE 802.3, the data-encoding technique used by 1000BASE-T when converting GMII data (8B-8 bits) to four quinary symbols (Q4) that are transmitted during one clock (1Q4).

encoding   Process by which bits are represented by voltages.

Manchester encoding   Digital encoding scheme, used by IEEE 802.3 and Ethernet, in which a mid–bit-time transition is used for clocking; a 1 is denoted by a high level during the first half of the bit time.

NRZ (nonreturn to zero)   Signals that maintain constant voltage levels with no signal transitions (no return to a 0V level) during a bit interval.

NRZI (nonreturn to zero inverted)   Signal that maintains constant voltage levels with no signal transitions (no return to a 0V level). It interprets the presence of data at the beginning of a bit interval as a signal transition and interprets the absence of data as no transition.

SNR (signal-to-noise ratio)   The ratio of useable signal being transmitted to the undesired signal (noise). It is a measure of transmission quality. The ratio of good data (signal) to bad (noise) on a line, expressed in decibels (dB).

Thinnet   Term used to define a thinner, less-expensive version of the cable specified in the IEEE 802.3 10BASE2 standard.

WDM (wavelength-division multiplexing)   Multiple optical wavelengths can share the same transmission fiber. The spectrum occupied by each channel must be separated adequately from the other.

Check Your Understanding

Complete all the review questions to test your understanding of the topics and concepts in this chapter. Answers are listed in Appendix B, "Check Your Understanding Answer Key."

1. What is the name of the method used in Ethernet that explains how Ethernet works?

   A. TCP/IP

   B. CSMA/CD

   C. CMDA/CS

   D. CSMA/CA

2. What is the maximum distance for thick Ethernet without using a repeater?

   A. 185m (606.95 ft.)

   B. 250m (820.2 ft.)

   C. 500m (1640.4 ft.)

   D. 800m (2624.64 ft.)

3. 10-Mbps Ethernet operates within the timing limits offered by a series of no more than _____ segments separated by no more than _____ repeaters.

   A. Three, two

   B. Four, three

   C. Five, four

   D. Six, five

4. Fast Ethernet supports up to what transfer rate?

   A. 5 Mbps

   B. 10 Mbps

   C. 100 Mbps

   D. 1000 Mbps

5. Identify two Gigabit Ethernet over fiber cable specifications

   A. 1000BASE-TX

   B. 1000BASE-FX

   C. 1000BASE-SX

   D. 1000BASE-LX

   E. 1000BASE-X

6. What is the transmission medium for 1000BASE-SX?

    A. Long-wave laser over single-mode and multimode fiber

    B. Category 5 UTP copper wiring

    C. Balanced, shielded, 150-ohm, two-pair STP copper cable

    D. Short-wave laser over multimode fiber

7. 4D-PAM5 encoding method is used in which of the following Gigabit Ethernet?

    A. 1000BASE-LX

    B. 1000BASE-SX

    C. 1000BASE-T

    D. 1000BASE-CX

8. What is the IEEE standard for 10-Gb Ethernet?

    A. 802.3z

    B. 802.3u

    C. 802.3ae

    D. 803.3

9. What happens when 1000BASE-T sends and receives data in a full-duplex mode on the same conductor?

    A. A permanent collision on the wire

    B. Increased symbol decoding

    C. The addition of two hops to any transmission

    D. Increased signal-to-noise ratio

10. What is the maximum transmission distance supported by 10 Gigabit Ethernet?

    A. 82m

    B. 240m

    C. 10km

    D. 40km

    E. 82km

    F. Unlimited

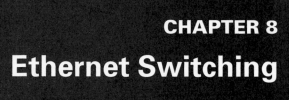

CHAPTER 8

Ethernet Switching

Objectives

Upon completion of this chapter, you should be able to answer the following questions:

- What is Layer 2 bridging?

- How does a LAN switch operate?

- What is latency?

- What are the differences among common switching methods such as cut-through switching, store-and-forward switching, and fragment-free switching?

- What are the functions and features of the Spanning Tree Protocol (STP)?

- How does STP work?

- What is the difference between a collision domain and a broadcast domain?

- Which Layer 1, 2, and 3 devices create collision domains and broadcast domains?

- What is segmentation?

- What is a broadcast?

- How does data flow through a network?

- What is network segmentation? Which devices create segments?

Key Terms

The following is a list of key terms introduced in this chapter. For your reference, a definition for each term can be found at the end of this chapter.

collision   page 336

broadcasts   page 336

Spanning Tree Protocol (STP)   page 336

microsegmentation   page 338

latency   page 341

store-and-forward switching   page 342

cut-through switching   page 342

fragment-free switching   page 343

bridge protocol data units (BPDUs)   page 345

collision domain   page 350

broadcast domain   page 356

segment   page 359

Shared Ethernet works extremely well under ideal conditions. When the number of devices trying to access the network is low, the number of collisions stays well within acceptable limits. However, when the number of users on the network increases, the increased number of collisions can cause intolerably bad performance. Bridging was developed to help ease the performance problems that arose from increased collisions. Switching evolved from bridging to become the key technology in modern Ethernet LANs.

Collisions and *broadcasts* are expected events in modern networking. In fact, they are engineered into the design of Ethernet and higher-layer technologies. However, when collisions and broadcasts occur in numbers that are above the optimum, network performance suffers. The concept of collision domains and broadcast domains is concerned with the ways that networks can be designed to limit the negative effects of collisions and broadcasts. This chapter explores the effects of collisions and broadcasts on network traffic, and then describes how bridges and routers segment networks to improve performance.

As more nodes are added to an Ethernet physical segment, the contention for the medium increases. The addition of more nodes increases the demands on the available bandwidth and places additional loads on the medium. With additional traffic, collisions increase, which results in more retransmissions. A solution to this problem is to break the large segment into parts and separate it using Catalyst switches. This isolates the newly segmented sections into isolated collision domains, which reduces the number of collisions and increases the network's reliability.

Bridging and switching are technologies that decrease congestion in LANs by reducing traffic and increasing bandwidth. LAN switches and bridges, operating at Layer 2 of the OSI reference model, forward frames based on the MAC addresses to perform the switching function. If the Layer 2 MAC address is unknown, the device floods the frame in an attempt to reach the desired destination. LAN switches and bridges also forward all broadcast frames. The result could be storms of traffic being looped endlessly through the network. The *Spanning Tree Protocol (STP)* is a loop-prevention protocol; it enables switches to communicate with each other to discover physical loops in the network.

Be sure to look at this chapter's associated Interactive Media Activities and Videos, which you can find on the CD-ROM accompanying this book. These CD elements are designed to supplement the material and reinforce the concepts introduced in this chapter.

Ethernet Switching

The following sections discuss some of the features of Ethernet Switching. Some of the topics that will be discussed include the following:

- Layer 2 bridging
- Layer 2 switching
- Switch operation

- Latency

- Switch modes

- Spanning-Tree Protocol

Layer 2 Bridging

A *bridge* is a Layer 2 device designed to create two or more LAN segments, each of which is a separate collision domain. In other words, bridges were designed to create more usable bandwidth. The purpose of a bridge is to filter traffic on a LAN to keep local traffic local, yet allow connectivity to other parts (segments) of the LAN for traffic that is directed there. To filter or selectively deliver network traffic, bridges build tables of all MAC addresses located on a network segment and other networks, and map them to associated ports. The process is as follows:

- If data comes along the network medium, a bridge compares the destination MAC address carried by the data to MAC addresses contained in its tables.

- If the source MAC address is not already known, the bridge creates a new entry in the MAC address table with the source port. This mapping determines future switching of frames to the new source device.

- If the bridge determines that the destination MAC address of the data is from the same network segment as the source, it does not forward the data to other segments of the network. This process is known as *filtering*. By performing this process, bridges can significantly reduce the amount of traffic between network segments by eliminating unnecessary traffic.

- If the bridge determines that the destination MAC address of the data is not from the same network segment as the source, it forwards the data to the appropriate segment.

- If the destination MAC address is unknown to the bridge, the bridge broadcasts the data to all devices on a network except the one on which it was received. The process is known as *flooding*.

Video and Animation   Bridging Overview

In this video, you learn how a bridge forwards and learns where stations are located.

Layer 2 Switching

Generally, a bridge has only two ports and divides a collision domain into two parts. All decisions made by a bridge are based on MAC addresses or Layer 2 addressing, and do not affect the logical or Layer 3 addressing. Thus, a bridge divides a collision domain but not a logical or broadcast domain. No matter how many bridges are in a network, unless a device such as a router works on Layer 3 addressing, the network all shares the same logical (broadcast) address space. A bridge creates more (and smaller) collision domains, but won't add broadcast domains. Because every device on the network must pay attention to broadcasts, bridges always forward them. Therefore, all segments in a bridged environment are considered to be in the same broadcast domain.

LAN switches are essentially multiport bridges that use *microsegmentation* to reduce the number of collisions in a LAN and increase the available bandwidth. LAN switches also support features such as full-duplex communication and multiple simultaneous conversations. Figure 8-1 shows a LAN with three workstations, a LAN switch, and the LAN switch's address table. The LAN switch has four *interfaces* (or network connections). Stations A and C are connected to the switch's Interface 3, and Station B is on Interface 4. As indicated in Figure 8-2, Station A needs to transmit data to Station B.

Figure 8-1 Transmitting Data to a Known Station

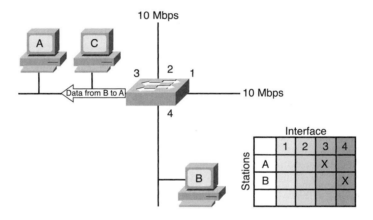

Figure 8-2 LAN Switch Operation

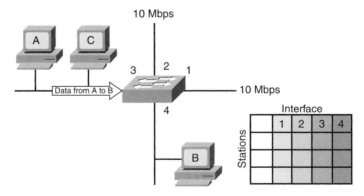

Remember that as this traffic goes through the network, the switch operates at Layer 2, meaning that the switch can look at the MAC layer address. When Station A transmits and the switch receives the frames, the switch assesses the traffic as it goes through to discover the source MAC address and store it in the address table, as shown in Figure 8-3.

Figure 8-3 Building an Address Table

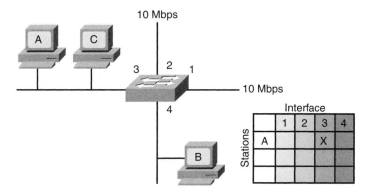

As the traffic goes through the switch, an entry is made in the address table identifying the source station and the interface that it is connected to on the switch. The switch now knows where Station A is connected. When that frame of data is in the switch, it floods to all ports because the destination station is unknown, as shown in Figure 8-4.

Figure 8-4 Flooding Data to All Switch Ports

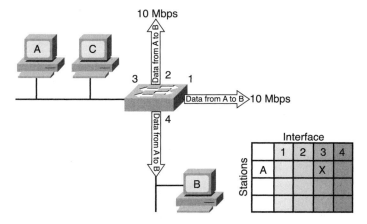

After the address entry is made in the table, however, a response comes back from Station B to Station A. The switch now knows that Station B is connected to Interface 4, as shown in Figure 8-5.

Figure 8-5 Responding to the Flooding Message

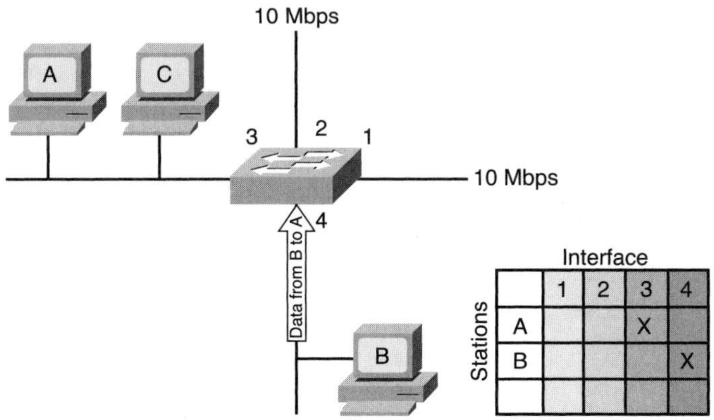

The data is transmitted into the switch, but notice that the switch does not flood the traffic this time. The switch sends the data out of only Interface 3 because it knows where Station A is on the network, as shown in Figure 8-1.

The original transmission indicated where that MAC address came from, enabling the switch to deliver traffic in the network more efficiently.

Switch Operation

As technology improved, it became possible to build bridges with more capability. Naturally, the ultimate goal is to have only one node on each port of a bridge. This would reduce the collision domains so that collisions would be nearly nonexistent. A switch does exactly that and is simply a bridge with many ports. These small physical segments are called microsegments.

In addition to faster microprocessors and memory, two other technological advances made switches possible. Content Addressable Memory (CAM) is memory that essentially works backward compared to conventional memory. Entering data into the memory returns the associated address. Using CAM allows a switch to directly find the port that is associated with a MAC address without using search algorithms. An application-specific integrated circuit (ASIC) is a device consisting of undedicated logic gates that can be programmed to perform functions at logic speeds. Operations that might have been done in software now can be done in hardware using an ASIC. The use of these technologies greatly reduced the delays caused by software processing and enabled a switch to keep pace with the data demands of many microsegments and high bit rates.

Full-Duplex Transmission

Another function of LAN switching that dramatically improves bandwidth is full-duplex transmission, which effectively doubles the amount of bandwidth between nodes. Full-duplex transmission between stations is achieved by using point-to-point Ethernet connections. This feature can be important, for example, between high-bandwidth consumers, such as a connection between a switch and a server. Full-duplex transmission provides a collision-free transmission environment. Because both nodes can transmit and receive at the same time, there are no negotiations for bandwidth.

In 10-Mbps connections, for example, full-duplex transmission provides 10 Mb of transmit capacity and 10 Mb of receive capacity, for effectively 20 Mb of capacity on a single connection. Likewise, a 100-Mbps connection offers effectively 200 Mbps of throughput, as illustrated in Figure 8-6. Full-duplex communication also supports two data transmission paths, with speeds up to 1 Gbps.

Figure 8-6 Switching Technology: Full Duplex

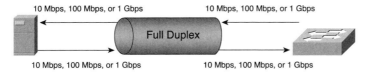

Microsegmentation

Microsegmentation facilitates the creation of a dedicated segment and provides dedicated bandwidth to each user on the network. Each user receives instant access to the full bandwidth and does not have to contend for available bandwidth with other users. This means that pairs of devices on the same switch can communicate in parallel with a minimum number of collisions. Microsegmentation reduces collisions in a network and effectively increases the capacity for each station connected to the network.

Latency

Latency, sometimes called *propagation delay*, is the time that a frame, or packet, of data takes to travel from the source station or node to its final destination on the network. A wide variety of conditions can cause delays as a frame travels from source to destination:

- Media delays caused by the finite speed that signals can travel through the physical media.

- Circuit delays caused by the electronics that process the signal along the path.

- Software delays caused by the decisions that software must make to implement switching and protocols.

- Delays caused by the content of the frame and where in the frame switching decisions can be made. For example, a device cannot route a frame to a destination until the destination MAC address has been read.

Latency is the time delay between when a frame first starts to leave the source device and when the first part of the frame reaches its destination.

Switch Modes

How the content of a frame is switched to the destination port is a trade-off of latency and reliability. The three modes of switching, store-and-forward, cut-through, and fragment-free switching, offer different performance and latency.

Store-and-Forward Switching

In *store-and-forward switching*, the switch reads the entire frame of data, checks the frame for errors, decides where it needs to go, and then sends it on its way. Figure 8-7 illustrates the operation of store-and-forward switching. The obvious trade-off here is that it takes the switch longer to read the entire frame. As it reads the entire frame, however, it detects any errors on that frame. If the frame is in error, the frame is not forwarded and is discarded. Although cut-through switching is faster, it offers no error detection. The latency introduced by store-and-forward switching is usually not a significant issue.

Figure 8-7 Store-and-Forward Switching

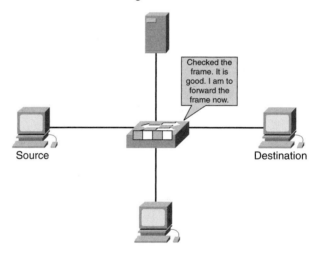

Cut-Through Switching

In *cut-through switching*, the switch reads the beginning of the frame up to the destination MAC address as the traffic flows through the switch and "cuts through" to its destination without continuing to read the rest of the frame, as illustrated in Figure 8-8.

Cut-through switching decreases the latency of the transmission. However, cut-through switching has no error detection.

Figure 8-8 Cut-Through Switching

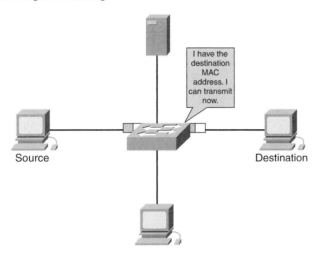

Fragment-Free Switching

Fragment-free switching is a modified form of cut-through switching. Fragment-free switching filters out collision fragments, which are the majority of packet errors, before forwarding begins. Fragment-free switching waits until the received packet has been determined not to be a collision fragment before forwarding the packet.

When to Use Each Switching Mode

When using cut-through and fragment-free modes, both the source port and the destination port must be operating at the same bit rate to keep the frame intact. This is called symmetric switching. If the bit rates are not the same, the frame must be stored at one bit rate before it is sent out at the other bit rate. This is known as asymmetric switching. Store-and-forward mode must be used for asymmetric switching. Asymmetric switching provides switched connections between ports of unlike bandwidths, such as a combination of 100 Mbps and 1000 Mbps. Asymmetric switching is optimized for client/server traffic flows in which multiple clients simultaneously communicate with a server, requiring more bandwidth dedicated to the server port to prevent a bottleneck at that port.

Spanning-Tree Protocol

When multiple switches are connected, there is a possibility of creating a loop where there is no clear path from source to destination. If switches are arranged in a simple hierarchical tree, no loops will occur, as shown in Figure 8-9.

Figure 8-9 STP Reducing Routing Loops

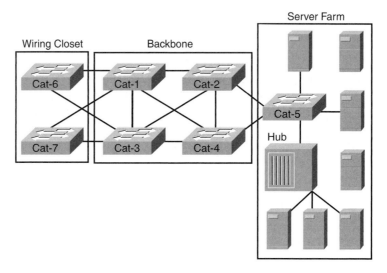

However, when extra switches and bridges are added to provide redundant paths for reliability and fault tolerance, loops can occur, as shown in Figure 8-10.

Figure 8-10 Broadcast Storms

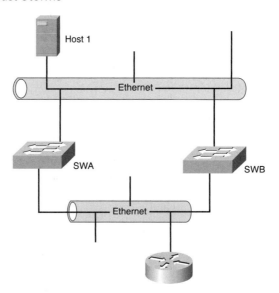

In Figure 8-10, the following steps are occurring:

1. Host 1 broadcasts.

2. SWA and SWB receive the frame.

3. SWA forwards to SWB.

4. SWB forwards to SWA.

5. Each switch now begins to see multiple frames of the same broadcast, thus resulting in bridging loops.

To counteract the possibility of loops, switches are provided with a protocol for them to talk with each other to resolve the condition. A switch sends special messages called ***bridge protocol data units (BPDUs)*** out all its ports to let other switches know of its existence, as shown in Figures 8-11 and 8-12. The switches use a spanning tree algorithm (STA) to resolve and shut down the redundant paths. The process of shutting down a port is called *blocking*. The result of resolving and eliminating the loops is a logical hierarchical tree created with no loops. However, the alternate paths are still available, in case they are needed. The protocol used to resolve and eliminate loops is known as the Spanning Tree Protocol (STP).

Figure 8-11 BPDU Communication

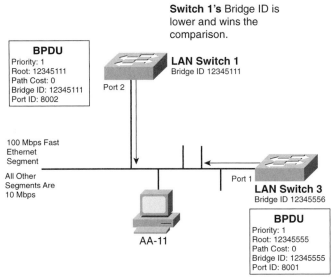

Consequently, switches have five operating modes:

- **Blocking**—A port in blocking state sends and listens to BPDUs but does not forward frames. By default, all ports are in blocking state when the switch is turned on.

- **Listening**—In listening state, a port listens to the BPDUs to make sure there are no loops on the network. No frames are forwarded in this state.

- **Learning**—In this state, a port learns MAC addresses and builds an address table, but it does not forward frames.

- **Forwarding**—A port in the forwarding state forwards frames. BPDUs are sent and listened to.

- **Disabled**—A port in the disabled state does not participate in the operation of STP. Therefore, it does not listen to BPDUs or forward frames. This port is in a "shutdown" state.

Figure 8-12 BPDU Protocol Layout

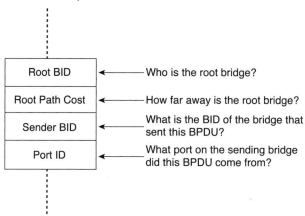

Figure 8-13 illustrates some of the port states and operating modes in a switched network using STP.

Figure 8-13 Port States

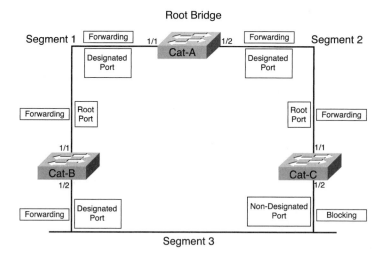

Collision Domains and Broadcast Domains

This section presents topics that relate to collision and broadcast domains. Excessive broadcasts and collisions can affect the network performance. This section discusses how to reduce the impact of broadcasts and collisions on the performance of the network. The term segment is defined, and different types of segmentation are discussed.

Shared Media Environments

To understand collision domains, it is first necessary to examine the issues of what a collision is and how it is caused. To help explain collisions, it is useful to review Layer 1 media and topologies.

As illustrated in Figure 8-14, some of the various types of directly connected networks include the following:

- **Shared-media environment**—A shared-media environment occurs when multiple hosts have access to the same medium. For example, if several PCs are attached to the same physical wire or optical fiber, or share the same airspace, they all share the same media environment. In this case, they are said to share the same collision domain. Traditional bus-based (coaxial cable) Ethernet and hub-based Ethernet (UTP cable) are shared-media environments.

- **Extended shared-media environment**—This is a special type of shared-media environment in which networking devices can extend the environment so that it can accommodate multiple access or longer cable distances. Using Ethernet repeaters or multiple hubs can create an extended shared-media environment. This creates an extended collision domain.

- **Point-to-point network environment**—This is widely used in dialup network connections and is the most familiar to the home user. It is a shared networking environment in which one device is connected to only one other device, such as connecting a computer to an Internet service provider by modem and a phone line. Because this is a point-to-point dedicated connection, there is no potential for collisions. No other devices share the link.

Figure 8-14 Directly Connected Networks

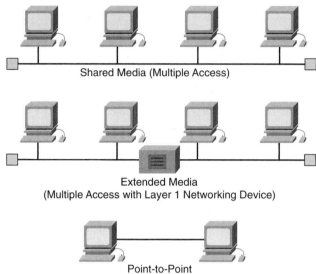

Shared Media (Multiple Access)

Extended Media
(Multiple Access with Layer 1 Networking Device)

Point-to-Point

More Information: Indirectly Connected Networks
Some networks are indirectly connected, meaning that some higher-layer networking devices or some geographical distance is between the two communicating hosts. Figure 8-15 also shows the two types of indirectly connected networks, which are described as follows:

- **Circuit-switched**—An indirectly connected network in which actual electrical circuits are maintained for the duration of the communication. Circuit switching sets up a physical, end-to-end connection between the endpoints. The bandwidth is dedicated to this point-to-point connection. The current telephone system is still, in part, circuit-switched, although the telephone systems in many countries now are concentrating less on circuit-switched technologies. Because this is not a shared environment, there are no collisions.

- **Packet-switched**—Instead of dedicating a link as an exclusive circuit connection between two communicating hosts, the source sends messages in packets. Each packet contains enough information for it to be routed to the proper destination host. Packet-switched networks frequently share physical media, but because logical point-to-point connections are created, there are no collisions.

More Information: Indirectly Connected Networks (Continued)

Figure 8-15 Indirectly Connected Networks

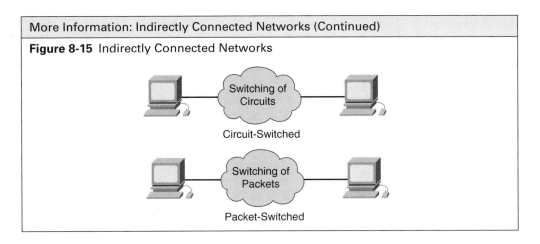

Collision Domains

It is important to identify the medium as a shared environment because this shared environment causes collisions. A similar situation can occur with an automobile on a highway. If there is only one car, there is nothing to collide with. However, if more than one automobile is trying to use the same section of road at the same time, as shown in Figure 8-16, a collision occurs. The same is true for networks: If more than one computer tries to transmit data on the same network segment at the same time, a collision occurs.

A collision is a situation that can occur when 2 bits propagate at the same time on the same network. A small, slow network could work out a system that allows only two computers to send messages, with both agreeing to take turns. The problem is that many computers are connected to large networks, with each one wanting to communicate millions of bits every section.

Figure 8-16 Collision

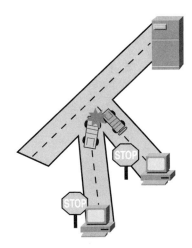

Collision domains are the connected physical network segments where collisions can occur. Collisions cause the network to be inefficient. Every time there is a collision on a network, all transmission stops for a period of time. This time is variable, as determined by a backoff algorithm for each network device, which is necessary to allow broadcast transmission to resume.

Except for a single isolated Ethernet LAN environment, the types of devices that interconnect the media segments define collision domains. These devices have been classified as OSI Layer 1, 2, or 3 devices. Layer 1 devices do not break up collision domains; Layers 2 and 3 devices do break up collision domains, as described in Figure 8-17. Breaking up or increasing the number of collision domains with Layer 2 and 3 devices is known as segmentation.

Figure 8-17 Collision Domain Segmentation

Application	
Presentation	
Session	
Transport	
Network	Breaks Up Collision Domain
Data Link	Breaks Up Collision Domain
Physical	One Collision Domain

Layer 1 devices, such as repeaters and hubs, serve the primary function of extending the Ethernet cable segments. By extending the network, more hosts can be added. However, every host that is added increases the amount of potential traffic on the network. Because Layer 1 devices pass on everything that is sent on the medium, the more traffic that is transmitted within a collision domain, the greater the chances of collisions are. The final result is diminished network performance, which is even more pronounced if all the computers on that network demand large amounts of bandwidth. Simply put, Layer 1 devices extend collision domains, as shown in Figure 8-18, but the length of a LAN also can be overextended and can cause other collision issues.

Figure 8-18 A Repeater Increases the Collision Domain

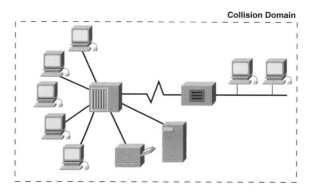

The four-repeater rule in Ethernet states that no more than four repeaters or repeating hubs can be between any two computers on the network, as shown in Figure 8-19. To ensure that a repeated 10BASET network will function properly, the round-trip delay calculation must be within certain limits; otherwise, all the workstations will not be capable of hearing all the collisions on the network.

Figure 8-19 A Repeater Increases the Collision Domain

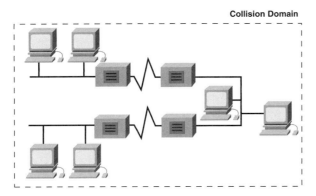

Repeater latency, propagation delay, and NIC latency all contribute to the four-repeater rule. Exceeding the four-repeater rule can lead to violating the maximum delay limit. When this delay limit is exceeded, the numbers of late collisions dramatically increase. A late collision occurs when a collision happens after the first 64 bytes of the frame are transmitted. The chip sets in NICs are not required to retransmit automatically when a late collision occurs. These late-collision frames add delay that is referred to as consumption delay. As consumption delay and latency increase, network performance decreases. This Ethernet rule of thumb also is known as the 5-4-3-2-1 rule. This means that the following guidelines should not be exceeded:

- Host sections consist of
  - 5 sections of network media
  - 4 repeaters or hubs
  - 3 sections of the network
- **2** sections are link sections (no hosts)
- **1** large collision domain

Video and Animation   Collisions

In this video, you learn how collisions occur in CSMA/CD networks.

Segmentation

For a networking professional, one important skill is the ability to recognize collision domains. Connecting several computers to a single shared-access medium that has no other networking devices attached creates a collision domain. This situation limits the number of computers that can use the medium, also called a segment. As illustrated in Figure 8-20, Layer 1 devices extend but do not control collision domains.

Layer 2 devices segment or divide collision domains. Controlling frame propagation using the MAC address assigned to every Ethernet device performs this function. Layer 2 devices, bridges and switches, keep track of the MAC addresses and which segment they are on. By doing this, these devices can control the flow of traffic at the Layer 2 level. This function makes networks more efficient by allowing data to be transmitted on different segments of the LAN at the same time, without the frames colliding. By using bridges and switches, the collision domain effectively is broken up into smaller parts, each being its own collision domain.

These smaller collision domains will have fewer hosts and less traffic than the original domain, and thereby increase the amount of bandwidth available to each host in that domain. The lower the amount of traffic is in a collision domain, the greater the chance there is that when a host wants to transmit data, the media will be available. This works well as long as the traffic between segments is not too heavy. Otherwise, the Layer 2 device actually can slow communication and become a bottleneck itself.

Layer 3 devices, like Layer 2 devices, do not forward collisions. Because of this, the use of Layer 3 devices in a network has the effect of breaking up collision domains into smaller domains. Layer 3 devices perform more functions than just breaking up a collision domain. These devices and their functions are covered in more depth in the section, "Broadcast Domains." Figure 8-21 illustrates that Layer 2 and Layer 3 devices can break up the collision domain.

 Interactive Media Activity   Fill In the Blank: Segmentation

After completing this activity, you will learn about segmentation of a network.

Figure 8-20 Layer 1 Devices Extend the Collision Domains

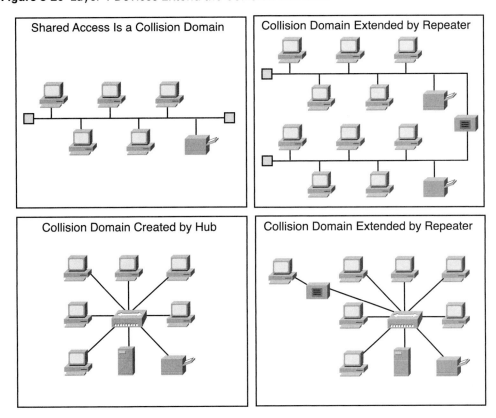

Figure 8-21 Limiting the Collision Domain

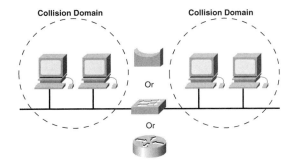

Layer 2 Broadcasts

To communicate with all collision domains, protocols use broadcast and multicast frames at Layer 2 of the OSI model. When a node needs to communicate with all hosts on the network, it sends a frame with a destination MAC address 0xFFFFFFFFFFFF (a broadcast). This is an address to which the NIC of every host must recognize.

Layer 2 devices must flood all broadcast and multicast traffic because they cannot learn the broadcast or multicast MAC address. The accumulation of broadcast and multicast traffic from each device in the network is referred to as broadcast radiation. Figure 8-22 illustrates a bridge forwarding the broadcast to all hosts on the network.

Because the NIC must interrupt the CPU to process each broadcast or multicast group that it belongs to, broadcast radiation affects the performance of hosts in the network. Most often, the host does not benefit from processing the broadcast because it is not the destination being sought. Either the host does not care about the service that is being advertised or it already knows about the service. High levels of broadcast radiation can noticeably degrade host performance, as shown in Figure 8-23. The three sources of broadcasts and multicasts in IP networks are workstations, routers, and multicast applications.

Workstations broadcast an Address Resolution Protocol (ARP) request every time they need to locate a MAC address that is not in the ARP table. For example, the command telnet mumble.com translates into an IP address through a Domain Name System (DNS) search, and then an ARP request is broadcast to find the actual station. Generally, IP workstations cache 10 to 100 addresses in about 2 hours. The ARP rate for a typical workstation might be about 50 addresses every 2 hours, or 0.007 ARPs per second. Thus, 2000 IP end stations produce about 14 ARPs per second.

Table 8-1 lists the average number of broadcast and multicasts for IP networks.

Table 8-1 Average Number of Broadcast and Multicasts for IP Networks

Number of Hosts	Average Percentage of CPU Loss Per Host
100	0.14
1000	0.96
10,000	9.15

Figure 8-22 Layer 2 Broadcast

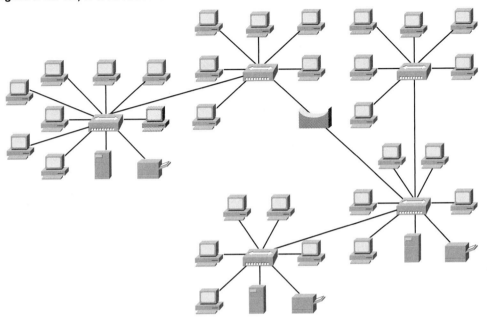

Figure 8-23 Effect of Broadcast Radiation on Hosts in IP Network

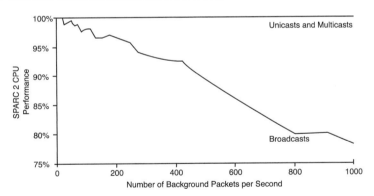

Although the numbers in Table 8-1 might appear low, they represent an average, well-designed IP network that is not running the Routing Information Protocol (RIP). When broadcast and multicast traffic peak because of storm behavior, peak CPU loss can be orders of magnitude greater than average. Broadcast storms can be caused by a device requesting information from a network that has grown too large. So many responses are sent to the original request that the device cannot process them, or the first request triggers similar requests from other devices that effectively block normal traffic flow on the network.

An IP router is a router or workstation that runs any distance vector routing protocol. Some administrators configure all workstations to run RIP (a routing protocol) as a redundancy and reachability policy. Every 30 seconds, RIP uses broadcasts to retransmit the entire RIP routing table to other RIP routers. If a large number of routers were configured to run RIP and, on average, 50 packets were required to transmit the routing table, the routers would generate 3333 broadcasts per second. Most network administrators configure only a small number of routers—usually five to ten—to run RIP. For a routing table that has a size of 50 packets, 10 RIP routers would generate about 16 broadcasts per second. (Routing protocols and routing table are discussed in Chapter 10, "Routing Fundamentals and Subnets.")

IP multicast applications can adversely affect the performance of large, scaled, switched networks. Although multicasting is an efficient way to send a stream of multimedia data to many users on a shared-media hub, it affects every user on a flat-switched network. A flat-switched network is a network of interconnected switches that does not utilize Layer 3 routing or something similar. A particular packet video application can generate a 7-megabyte (MB) stream of multicast data that, in a switched network, would be sent to every segment, resulting in severe congestion.

Broadcast Domains

A *broadcast domain* is a grouping of collision domains that are connected by Layer 2 devices. Breaking up a LAN into multiple collision domains improves network efficiency by allowing multiple transmissions of data simultaneously on separate collision domains. But broadcasts travel across the Layer 2 devices and, if excessive, can reduce the efficiency of the overall LAN. Broadcasts must be controlled at Layer 3 because Layer 1 and 2 devices have no way of controlling them. The total size of a broadcast domain can be identified by looking at all of the collision domains that the same broadcast frame is processed by. In other words, all the nodes are a part of that network segment bounded by a Layer 3 device. Broadcast domains are controlled at Layer 3 because routers do not forward broadcasts. In Figure 8-24, the router will not forward the broadcast from the blue-highlighted workstation in the left side to the hosts on the right.

Routers actually work at Layers 1, 2, and 3. Like all Layer 1 devices, they have a physical connection to and transmit data onto the medium. They have a Layer 2 encapsulation on all interfaces and perform just like any other Layer 2 device. Layer 3 allows the router to segment broadcast domains.

For a packet to be forwarded through a router, it must have been processed already by Layer 2, and the frame information must have been stripped off. Layer 3 forwarding is based on the destination IP address, not the MAC address. For a packet to be forwarded, it must contain an IP address that is outside the range of addresses assigned to the LAN segment, and the router must have a destination to send the specific packet to in its routing table.

Figure 8-24 Broadcast Domain Segmentation

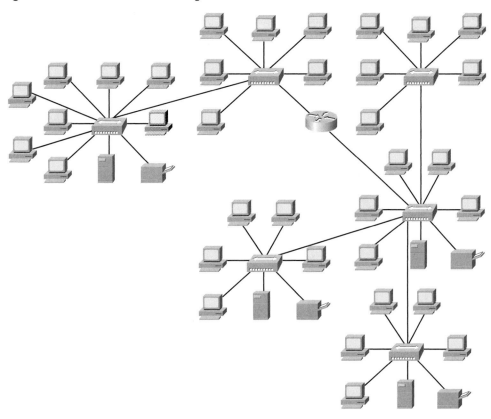

Introduction to Data Flow

Data flow in the context of collision and broadcast domains focuses on how data frames propagate through a network. It refers to the movement of data through Layer 1, 2, and 3 devices, as well as how data must be encapsulated to effectively make that journey. Remember that data is encapsulated at the network layer with an IP source and destination address, and at the data link layer with a MAC source and destination address.

The basic rule to follow here is that a Layer 1 device always forwards the frame, a Layer 2 device wants to forward the frame (in other words, it forwards unless something prevents it), and a Layer 3 device does not forward unless it has to. Using this rule helps identify how data flows through a network.

Layer 1 devices (repeaters and hubs) do no filtering, so everything that is received is passed on to the next segment. The frame simply is regenerated and retimed, thus returned to its original transmission quality. Any segments connected by Layer 1 devices are part of the same domain, both collision and broadcast.

Layer 2 devices (bridges and switches) filter data frames based on the destination MAC address. A frame is forwarded if it is going to an unknown destination (outside the collision domain). The frame also is forwarded if it is a broadcast, multicast, or unicast going outside the local collision domain. The only time that a frame is not forwarded is when the Layer 2 device finds that the sending host and the receiving host are in the same collision domain. A bridging device (Layer 2) creates multiple collision domains but maintains only one broadcast domain.

Layer 3 devices (routers and some high-end switches) filter data packets based on IP destination address. The only way that a packet is forwarded is if its destination IP address is outside the broadcast domain and the router has an identified location to send the packet. A Layer 3 device creates multiple collision and broadcast domains.

Data flow through a routed IP-based network involves data moving across traffic-management devices at Layers 1, 2, and 3 of the OSI model. Layer 1 is used for transmission across the physical medium, Layer 2 is used for collision domain management, and Layer 3 is used for broadcast domain management. Figure 8-25 shows data flowing from Workstation X through Routers A, B, and C to Workstation Y.

Figure 8-25 Data Flow Through a Network

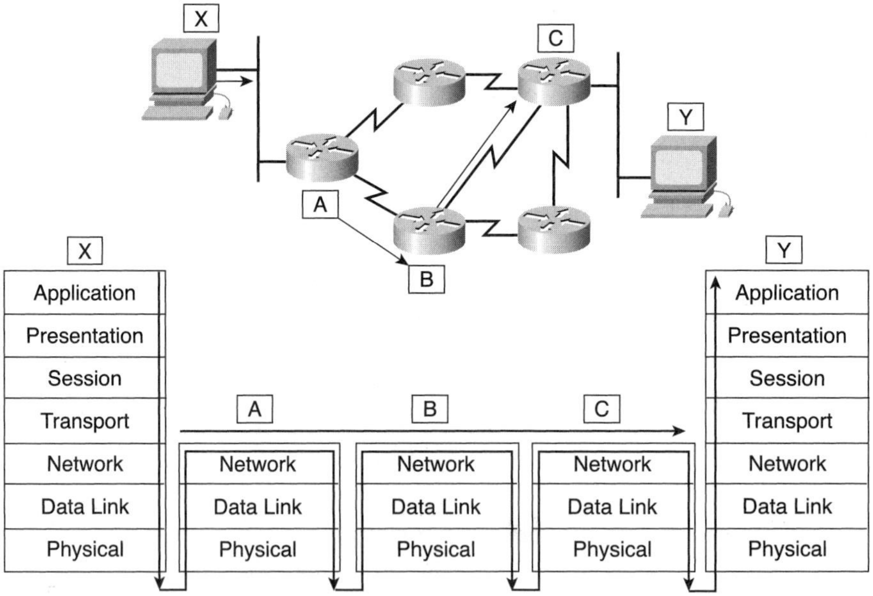

What Is a Network Segment?

As with many terms and acronyms, *segment* has multiple meanings. The dictionary definition of the term is as follows:

- A separate piece of something
- One of the parts into which an entity or quantity is divided or marked off by, or as if by natural boundaries

In the context of data communication, the following definitions are used:

- Section of a network that is bounded by bridges, routers, or switches.
- In a LAN using a bus topology, a continuous electrical circuit that is often connected to other such segments with repeaters.
- Term used in the TCP specification to describe a single transport layer unit of information. The terms datagram, frame, message, and packet also are used to describe logical information groupings at various layers of the OSI reference model and in various technology circles.

Figure 8-26 illustrates the three definitions of the term segment within the content of the data communication.

Figure 8-26 Segments

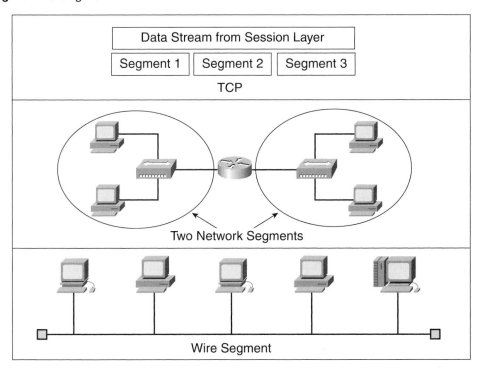

To define the term segment properly, the context of the usage must be presented with the word. If segment is used in the context of TCP, it is defined as a separate piece of the data. If segment is being used in the context of physical networking media in a routed network, it is seen as one of the parts or sections of the total network.

Interactive Media Activity   Point and Click: Types of Segments

After completing this activity, you will understand the various meanings of the term segment.

Summary

In this chapter, you learned the following key points:

- Switches can provide dedicated access to improve the performance of shared LAN technologies.

- A switch segments a LAN into microsegments. Microsegmentation reduces the number of collisions to a minimum and increases the effective bandwidth.

- Switches read the destination Layer 2 MAC addresses of frame packets to achieve transfers.

- Full-duplex communication allows two devices to communicate with each other simultaneously and doubles the throughput that a LAN switch can translate.

- Switches can support multiple conversations at the same time in a network.

- The three switching modes that can be used to forward frames through a switch are store-and-forward, cut-through, and fragment-free switching.

- The main task of STP is to prevent the occurrence of network loops.

- The five possible states of a port on an STP bridge or switch are blocking, listening, learning, forwarding, or disabled.

- The fundamental grouping of devices in a shared-media environment is a collision domain.

- Collision domains can be segmented to reduce congestion and improve network efficiency.

- Collision domains are segmented by both Layer 2 and Layer 3 devices.

- Broadcasts are designed to travel throughout collision domains and can cause network inefficiency.

- Layer 3 devices can be used to segment broadcast domains.

To supplement all that you have learned in this chapter, refer to the chapter-specific Videos and Interactive Media Activities on the CD-ROM that accompanies this book.

Key Terms

bridge protocol data unit (BPDU)   Spanning Tree Protocol hello packet that is sent out at configurable intervals to exchange information among bridges in the network.

broadcasts   Data packets that are sent to all nodes on a network. Broadcasts are identified by a broadcast address.

broadcast domain   A set of all devices that will receive broadcast frames originating from any device within the set. Broadcast domains typically are bounded by routers (or, in a switched network, by VLANs) because routers do not forward broadcast frames.

collision   In Ethernet, the result of two nodes transmitting simultaneously. The frames from each device impact and are damaged when they meet on the physical media.

collision domain   In Ethernet, the network area within which frames that have collided are propagated. Repeaters and hubs propagate collisions; LAN switches, bridges, and routers do not.

contention   Occurs when there is competition for resources, such as when two or more nodes try to send frames simultaneously.

cut-through switching   A packet-switching approach that streams data through a switch so that the leading edge of a packet exits the switch at the output port before the packet finishes entering the input port. A device using cut-through packet switching reads, processes, and forwards packets as soon as the destination address is looked up and the outgoing port is determined. *See also* store-and-forward switching.

fragment-free switching   Switching that filters out collision fragments, which are the majority of packet errors, before forwarding begins.

latency   Delay between the time when a device receives a frame and the time when that frame is forwarded out the destination port.

microsegmentation   The division of a network into smaller segments, usually with the intention of increasing aggregate bandwidth to network devices.

segment   A section of a network that is bounded by bridges, routers, or switches.

store-and-forward switching   A packet-switching technique in which frames are processed completely before being forwarded out the appropriate port. This processing includes calculating the CRC and checking the destination address. In addition, frames must be stored temporarily until network resources (such as an unused link) are available to forward the message.

STP (Spanning Tree Protocol)   Bridge protocol that uses the spanning tree algorithm, enabling a learning bridge to dynamically work around loops in a network topology by creating a spanning tree. Bridges exchange BPDU messages with other bridges to detect loops and then remove the loops by shutting down selected bridge interfaces.

Check Your Understanding

Complete all the review questions to test your understanding of the topics and concepts in this chapter. Answers are listed in Appendix B, "Check Your Understanding Answer Key."

1. Which of the following is *not* a feature of microsegmentation?

   A. It enables dedicated access.

   B. It supports multiple conversations at any given time.

   C. It increases the capacity for each workstation connected to the network.

   D. It increases collisions.

2. Which of the following is used by LAN switches for making the forwarding decision?

   A. IP address

   B. MAC address

   C. Network address

   D. Host address

3. Which of the following is a feature of full-duplex transmission?

   A. It offers two 10- to 1-Gbps data-transmission paths.

   B. It doubles bandwidth between nodes.

   C. It provides collision-free transmission.

   D. All of the above.

4. What are the three common types of switching methods?

5. The Spanning Tree Protocol allows which of the following?

   A. Bridges to communicate Layer 3 information

   B. A redundant Layer 2 network path without suffering the effects of loops in the network

   C. Static network paths for loop prevention

   D. None of the above

6. Which of the following is *not* one of the STP port states?

   A. Blocking

   B. Learning

   C. Listening

   D. Transmitting

7. Which of the following is true concerning a bridge and its forwarding decisions?

    A. Bridges operate at OSI Layer 2 and use IP addresses to make decisions.

    B. Bridges operate at OSI Layer 3 and use IP addresses to make decisions.

    C. Bridges operate at OSI Layer 2 and use MAC addresses to make decisions.

    D. Bridges operate at OSI Layer 3 and use MAC addresses to make decisions.

8. Which of the following is a feature of bridges?

    A. They operate at Layer 2 of the OSI model.

    B. They are more intelligent than hubs.

    C. They do not make any forwarding decisions.

    D. They build and maintain address tables.

9. Which of the following statements is true of microsegmentation?

    A. Each workstation gets its own dedicated segment through the network.

    B. All the workstations are grouped as one segment.

    C. Microsegmentation increases the number of collisions on a network.

    D. None of the above.

10. Which of the following is true for LAN switches?

    A. They repair network fragments known as microsegments.

    B. They are very high-speed multiport bridges.

    C. Lower bandwidth makes up for higher latency.

    D. They require new network interface cards on attached hosts.

11. What is a network area called where two or more Ethernet stations are separated by a bridge or Layer 2 switch, in which data frames originate and collide?

    A. Collision domain

    B. Network domain

    C. Broadcast domain

    D. Network segment

12. Using repeaters does which of the following to the collision domain?

    A. Reduces

    B. Has no effect on

    C. Extends

    D. None of the above

13. The process of using the complex networking devices, such as bridges, switches, and routers, to break up the collision domains is known as which of the following?

A. Sectioning

B. Segmentation

C. Collision domain reduction

D. None of the above

CHAPTER 9

TCP/IP Protocol Suite and IP Addressing

Objectives

Upon completion of this chapter, you will be able to answer the following questions:

- What are the TCP/IP model components?

- What is the order of the four TCP/IP layers, and how are they related to each other?

- What is the application layer responsible for, and what are some common applications?

- What is the transport layer responsible for, and what are some common services?

- What is the Internet layer responsible for, and what are some common protocols?

- What is the network access layer responsible for, and what are some common functions?

- How does TCP/IP compare to the OSI model?

- What is the format and significance of each component of an IP network such as IP

address, IP address classes, reserved IP address space, private IP address space, and IP subnetting?

- How do you calculate valid IP subnetwork addresses and mask values so that all requirements are met for an IP address scheme?

- What is the basis for the evolution of IP addressing and the need for an increase in the size of IP address space?

- What is the difference between IPv4 and IPv6 addressing?

- Which IP address format will be used in the future?

- What is a static assignment of an IP address?

- What is ARP and how does it work?

Key Terms

The following is a list of key terms introduced in this chapter. For your reference, a definition for each term can be found at the end of this chapter.

This chapter presents an overview of the *Transmission Control Protocol/Internet Protocol (TCP/IP)* protocol suite. It starts with the history and future of TCP/IP. Then it compares the TCP/IP protocol model to the OSI model, identifying and describing each layer of the TCP/IP protocol suite and how it relates to the Internet architecture.

This chapter also discusses IP addressing in depth. This includes how to convert decimal and binary numbers and how to identify the different classes of IP addresses—Class A, B, C, D, and E. IPv4 has been the standard by which IP addresses have been assigned for years. Today, IPv4 is beginning to be replaced by a more advanced IP addressing scheme called IPv6. This chapter describes and compares IPv4 and IPv6.

Be sure to look at this chapter's associated Videos and Interactive Media Activities, which you will find on the CD-ROM accompanying this book. These CD elements are designed to supplement the material and reinforce the concepts introduced in this chapter.

Introduction to TCP/IP

The Internet was developed to provide a communication network that could continue to function in wartime. Although the Internet has evolved in ways very different from those imagined by its architects, it is still based on the TCP/IP protocol suite. The design of TCP/IP is ideal for the decentralized and robust network that is the Internet. Many protocols used today were designed using the four-layer TCP/IP model.

It is useful to know both the TCP/IP and OSI networking models. Each model offers its own structure for explaining how a network works, but there is overlap between the two. Without an understanding of both, a system administrator might not have sufficient insight into why a network functions the way it does.

History and Future of TCP/IP

The U.S. Department of Defense (DoD) created the TCP/IP reference model, shown in Figure 9-1, because it wanted a network that could survive any conditions. To illustrate further, imagine a world criss-crossed by different kinds of connections—wires, microwaves, optical fibers, and satellite links. Then imagine a need for data to be transmitted, regardless of the condition of any particular node or network on the internetwork. The DoD wants its packets to get through every time, under any conditions, from any one point to any other point. It was this very difficult design problem that brought about the creation of the TCP/IP model, which has since become the standard on which the Internet has grown.

Figure 9-1 TCP/IP Protocol Suite Layers

Application
Transport
Internet
Network Access

When reading about the TCP/IP model layers, keep in mind the original intent of the Internet because it will help explain why certain things are as they are. The TCP/IP model has four layers: the application layer, the transport layer, the Internet layer, and the network access layer. It is important to note that some of the layers in the TCP/IP model have the same names as layers in the OSI model. Do not confuse the layer functions of the two models. The layer numbers are different, so the functions Layer 2 performs in the OSI model might not be the same as Layer 2 in the TCP/IP model. For example, in the OSI model, Layer 3 is IP, just as Layer 2 in the TCP/IP model is IP. Another case is the TCP/UDP functions at Layer 4 (the transport layer) in the OSI model and Layer 3 (the transport layer) in the TCP/IP model.

The present version of TCP/IP is old. Internet Protocol Version 4 (IPv4) was standardized in September 1981. In 1992 the standardization of a new generation of Internet Protocol (IP), often called IPng, was supported by the Internet Engineering Task Force (IETF). IPng is now called ***Internet Protocol Version 6 (IPv6)***. IPv6, shown in Figure 9-2, has not yet gained wide implementation, but it has already been released by most vendors of networking equipment and will become the dominant standard in the future.

Figure 9-2 IPv4 Versus IPv6

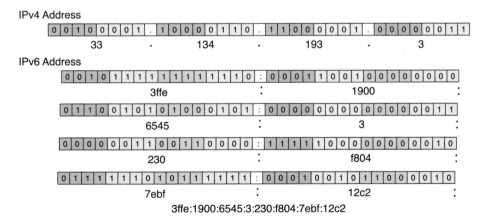

Application Layer

TCP/IP was designed with a high-level protocol layer that includes OSI session, presentation, and application layer details. The *application layer*, shown in Figure 9-3, handles high-level protocols and issues of representation, encoding, and dialog control.

Figure 9-3 TCP/IP Application Layer Protocols

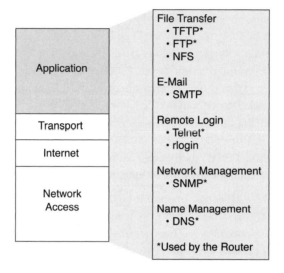

The TCP/IP protocol suite combines all application-related issues into one layer and ensures that this data is properly packaged for the next layer. TCP/IP includes not only Internet and transport layer specifications (such as IP and TCP), but also specifications for common applications. TCP/IP has protocols to support file transfer, e-mail, and remote login, including the following protocols:

- **Hypertext Transfer Protocol (HTTP)**—The underlying protocol used by the World Wide Web. HTTP defines how messages are formatted and transmitted and what actions web servers and browsers should take in response to various commands.

- **Trivial File Transfer Protocol (TFTP)**—A connectionless service that uses User Datagram Protocol (UDP). TFTP is used on the router to transfer configuration files and Cisco IOS images and to transfer files between systems that support TFTP. It is useful in some LANs because it operates faster than FTP in a stable environment.

- **File Transfer Protocol (FTP)**—A reliable, connection-oriented service that uses TCP to transfer files between systems that support FTP. It supports bidirectional binary files and ASCII file transfers.

- **Network File System (NFS)**—A distributed file system protocol suite developed by Sun Microsystems that allows remote file access across a network.

- **Simple Mail Transfer Protocol (SMTP)**—Governs the transmission of e-mail over computer networks. It does not provide support for transmission of data other than plain text.

- **Terminal emulation (Telnet)**—Provides the capability to remotely access another computer. It lets a user log into an Internet host and execute commands. A Telnet client is called a local host; a Telnet server is called a remote host.

- **Simple Network Management Protocol (SNMP)**—A protocol that provides a means to monitor and control network devices and to manage configurations, statistics collection, performance, and security.

- **Domain Name System (DNS)**—A system used on the Internet to translate names of domains and their publicly advertised network nodes into IP addresses.

Transport Layer

The *transport layer* provides transport services from the source host to the destination host. It constitutes a logical connection between the network's endpoints: the sending host and the receiving host. Transport protocols, shown in Figure 9-4, segment and reassemble upper-layer applications into the same data stream between endpoints. The transport layer data stream provides end-to-end transport services, sometimes called end-to-end services.

Figure 9-4 TCP/IP Transport Layer Protocols

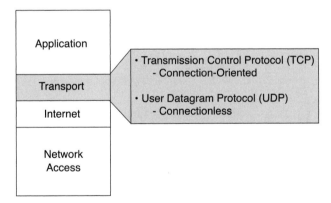

The transport layer data stream is a logical connection between a network's endpoints. Using UDP, the transport layer's primary duty is to transport data from source to destination. End-to-end control, provided by sliding windows and reliability in sequencing numbers and acknowledgments, is the primary duty of the transport layer when using TCP. The transport layer defines end-to-end connectivity between host applications. Transport services using TCP include all of the following services, whereas using UDP provides only the first two:

- Segmenting upper-layer application data

- Sending segments from one end device to another end device

- Establishing end-to-end operations

- Flow control provided by sliding windows

- Reliability provided by sequence numbers and acknowledgments

The transport layer assumes that it can use the network as a "cloud" to send data packets from the sender source to the receiver destination, as shown in Figure 9-5. The cloud deals with issues such as which of several paths is best for a given route, as shown in Figure 9-6.

Figure 9-5 Internet Cloud

Figure 9-6 Internet Paths

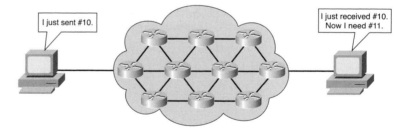

Internet Layer

In the OSI reference model, the network layer isolates the upper-layer protocols from the details of the underlying network and manages the connections across the network. IP is normally described as the TCP/IP network layer. Because of TCP/IP's internetworking emphasis, this is commonly called the Internet layer in the TCP/IP model (see Figure 9-7). All upper- and lower-layer communications travel through IP as they are passed through the TCP/IP protocol stack. The purpose of the Internet layer is to send packets from a device using the correct protocol that functions at this layer. Best path determination and packet switching occur at this layer. Think of it in terms of the postal system. When a letter is mailed, it doesn't matter how it gets there (there are various possible routes), but it is important that it arrives.

Figure 9-7 TCP/IP Internet Layer Protocols

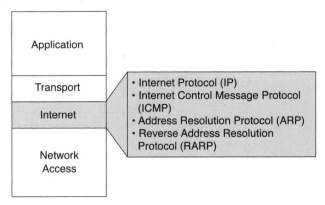

Several protocols operate at the TCP/IP Internet layer:

- **IP**—Provides connectionless, best-effort delivery routing of packets. IP is not concerned with the content of the packet. Instead, it looks for a way to move the packets to their destination.

- **Internet Control Message Protocol (ICMP)**—Provides control and messaging capabilities.

- **Address Resolution Protocol (ARP)**—Determines the data link layer addresses (Media Access Control [MAC] addresses) for known IP addresses.

- **Reverse Address Resolution Protocol (RARP)**—Determines IP addresses when data link layer addresses (MAC addresses) are known.

IP performs the following operations:

- Defining a packet and an addressing scheme

- Transferring data between the Internet layer and the network access layer

- Routing packets to remote hosts

Finally, to clarify terminology, IP is sometimes referred to as an unreliable protocol. This does not mean that IP does not accurately deliver data across a network; it simply means that IP does not perform error checking and correction. That function is handled by upper-layer protocols from the transport or application layer.

Network Access Layer

The *network access layer*, shown in Figure 9-8, is also called the host-to-network layer. It is the layer that is concerned with all the issues that an IP packet requires to make a physical link to the network medium. It includes the LAN and WAN technology details and all the details contained in the OSI physical and data link layers.

Figure 9-8 TCP/IP Network Access Layer Protocols

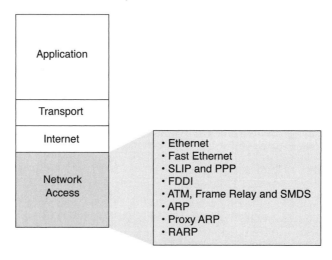

Software applications and drivers that are designed for individual pieces of hardware, such as Ethernet or Token Ring network interface cards (NICs), ISDN, or modem cards, often handle the network access layer. This causes confusion for users because a wide variety of protocols are defined by other standards that reside at the network access layer. The Internet and transport layer protocols (IP, TCP, and UDP) are more quickly recognized, as are the application protocols (SMTP, HTTP, and FTP), as being part of TCP/IP.

Network access layer functions include mapping IP addresses to physical hardware addresses and encapsulating IP packets into frames. Based on the hardware type of the network interface, the network access layer defines the connection with the physical network medium.

A good example of network access layer configuration is setting up a Windows system using a third-party NIC. Depending on the version of Windows, the operating system automatically detects the NIC, and the proper drivers are installed. If an older version of Windows is being used, the user must specify the network card driver. The card manufacturer supplies these drivers on disks or CD-ROMs.

The OSI Model and the TCP/IP Model

Figure 9-9 compares the OSI model and the TCP/IP model.

Figure 9-9 Comparing the TCP/IP Model to the OSI Model

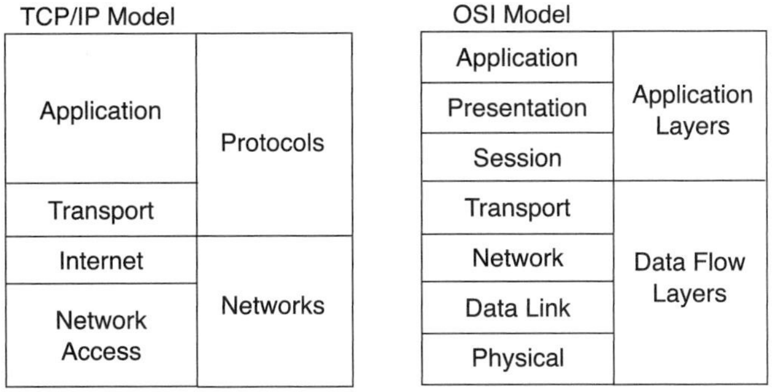

TCP/IP Model

Application	Protocols
Transport	
Internet	Networks
Network Access	

OSI Model

Application	Application Layers
Presentation	
Session	
Transport	Data Flow Layers
Network	
Data Link	
Physical	

Notice that the models have similarities and differences:

■ Similarities

  – Both have layers.

  – Both have application layers, although they include very different services.

  – Both have comparable transport and network layers.

  – Packet-switched (not circuit-switched) technology is assumed.

  – Networking professionals need to know both.

■ Differences

  – TCP/IP combines the presentation and session layers into its application layer.

  – TCP/IP combines the OSI data link and physical layers into its network access layer.

  – TCP/IP appears simpler because it has fewer layers.

  – The TCP/IP transport layer using UDP does not always guarantee reliable delivery of packets, as the transport layer in the OSI model does.

■ TCP/IP protocols are the standards around which the Internet developed, so the TCP/IP model gains credibility just because of its protocols. In contrast, networks typically aren't built on the OSI protocol. The OSI reference model is used as a guide for understanding the communication process.

 Interactive Media Activity   Drag and Drop: Comparing the TCP/IP and OSI Model

After completing this activity, you will be able to identify the differences between the TCP/IP model and OSI model.

Internet Architecture

Although the Internet is complex, some basic ideas underlie its operation. This section examines the basic architecture of the Internet. The Internet is a deceptively simple idea that, when repeated on a large scale, enables nearly instantaneous worldwide data communications between anyone, anywhere, at any time. In Figure 9-10, X and Y represent computers that are connected and that can communicate with each other from across the world.

Figure 9-10 Routers Connecting Two Networks

One limitation of LANs is that they do not scale

- Beyond a certain number of stations

- Beyond a certain geographic separation

Astonishing progress is being made in the number of stations that can be efficiently attached to a hierarchical LAN, and there have been advances in technologies such as Metro Optical and Gigabit Ethernet and 10 Gigabit Ethernet. However, ultimately, stations must make recourse to a long-distance, WAN-like, packet-switching network.

One assumption of the Internet's architecture is that the details of host computers, and the LANs on which they reside, are separate from the details of getting messages from one network to another.

One approach to the big-picture architecture for the Internet was to focus on the application layer interactions between the source and destination computers and any intermediate computers. Identical instances of an application, put on all the computers in the network, could facilitate delivery of messages across the large network. However, this does not scale well. New software functionality would require new applications to be installed on every computer in the network. New hardware functionality would require modifying the software. Failure of an intermediate computer or its application would break the chain on which the messages are passed.

Instead, the Internet uses the principle of network layer interconnection. Using the OSI model as an example, the goal is to build the network's functionality in independent modules. The desire is to allow a diversity of LAN technologies at Layers 1 and 2. You want to allow a diversity of applications functioning at Layers 5, 6, and 7. However, you want a system that hides the details of the lower and upper layers, allowing intermediate networking devices to relay traffic without having to bother with the details of the LAN (best administered locally, and the network envisioned will be global) or the applications generating network traffic.

This leads to the concept of *internetworking*—building networks of networks. A network of networks is called an internet (with a lowercase i). (An uppercase I is used to refer to the networks that grew out of the DoD on which the WWW runs, and to refer to *the* Internet.) Internetworking must have the following characteristics:

- It must be scalable in the number of networks and computers attached.

- It must be able to handle the transport of data across vast distances, including entire-earth and near-earth space.

- It must be flexible to account for constant technological innovations.

- It must adjust to dynamic conditions on the network.

- It must be cost-effective.

- It must be a system that permits anytime, anywhere data communications to anyone.

Figure 9-10 illustrated the connection of one physical network to another through a special-purpose computer called a router. This diagram is not unlike the problem that led to the beginning of Cisco Systems at Stanford University in 1984 and the invention of the router. These networks are described as "directly connected" to the router. The router here is useful for handling any "translations" required for the two networks to communicate. However, because users seek an anytime/anywhere connection to anyone, this scheme for connecting just two networks quickly becomes inadequate.

Figure 9-11 shows two routers connecting three physical networks. Now the routers must make more complex decisions. Because all users on all networks want to communicate with each other, even without being directly connected to one another, the router must have some way of dealing with this.

Figure 9-11 Local and Remote Networks

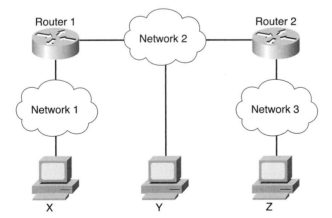

One way would be for the router to keep a list of all user computers and the paths to them. The router would decide whether and where to forward data packets based on this table of all users, forwarding based on the destination computer. However, this would quickly become problematic as the number of users grows—it is not scalable. What if the router could instead keep a list of all networks, leaving the local delivery details to the local physical networks? This solution is better and more scalable—forwarding based on the destination network. In this case, the routers relay messages. In principle, if the routers can share some information about which networks they are connected to, doing so can scale this idea to many routers.

Figure 9-12 shows the results of this extension, showing the user's desired view: universal interconnections, with a minimum of details required by the end users to get their packets across the "cloud." Yet the physical/logical structure to accomplish this can be extremely complex. Indeed, the Internet cloud has grown exponentially, with devices and protocols constantly being improved to allow more users. The fact that the Internet has grown so large, with more than 90,000 core routes and more than 300,000,000 end users, is testimony to the soundness of the basic Internet architecture.

Thus, two computers, anywhere in the world, following certain hardware, software, and protocol specifications, can communicate reliably ("anyplace/anytime/anyone"). Even when they are not directly connected (or even not close to being directly connected), cooperation and procedures for moving data across this network of networks have made the Internet possible.

Figure 9-12 Physical Details Hidden from the User

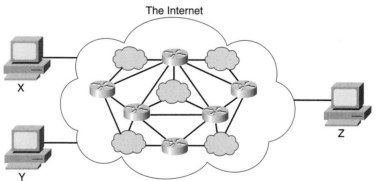

Internet Addresses

The network layer is responsible for navigating data through a network. The function of the network layer is to find the best path through a network. Devices use the network layer addressing scheme to determine the destination of data as it moves through the network. This section examines IP addressing and the five classes of IP addresses, along with subnetworks and subnet masks and their roles in IP addressing schemes. In addition, this portion of the chapter discusses the differences between public and private addresses, IPv4 and IPv6 addressing, and unicast and broadcast messages.

IP Addressing

For any two systems to communicate, they must be able to identify and locate each other, as shown in Figure 9-13. Although these addresses are not actual network addresses, they represent the concept of address grouping. The A and B identify the network, and the number sequence identifies the individual host. The combination of letter (network address) and number (host address) creates a unique address for each device on the network. In everyday life, names or numbers (such as telephone numbers) are often used as unique identifiers. Similarly, each computer in a TCP/IP network must be given at least one unique identifier, or address. This address allows one computer to locate another on a network.

Figure 9-13 Host Addresses

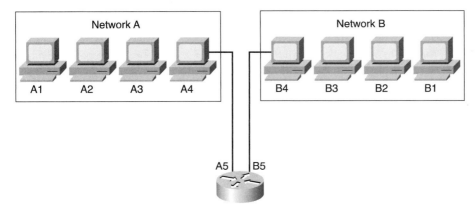

A computer might be connected to more than one network, as shown in Figure 9-14. This is an example of a computer that is connected to two different networks. This is done by having two network interface cards in the computer. This is called a dual-homed device. The important thing to notice here is that the computer's two interfaces are in completely different networks and, consequently, have different network identifiers in the addresses. One other important note is that this computer doesn't pass data through it unless it is specifically configured to do so. The computer merely has access to both networks. If this is the case, the system must be given more than one address, each address identifying its connection to a different network. Strictly speaking, a device cannot be said to have an address, but each of its connection points (or interfaces) to a network has an address that allows other computers to locate it on that particular network.

Figure 9-14 Dual-Homed Computers

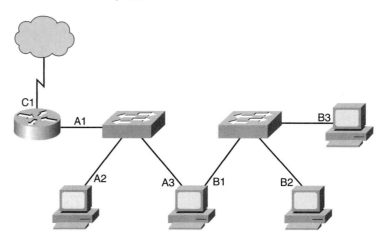

Inside a computer, an IP address is stored as a 32-bit sequence of 1s and 0s, as shown in Figure 9-15. To make the IP address easier to use, it is usually written as four decimal numbers separated by periods. For instance, an IP address of one computer is 192.168.1.2. Another computer might have the address 128.10.2.1. This way of writing the address is called *dotted-decimal format*. In this notation, each IP address is written as four parts separated by periods, or dots. Each part of the address is called an *octet* because it is made up of 8 binary digits. For example, the IP address 192.168.1.8 is 11000000.10101000.00000001.00001000 in binary notation. The dotted-decimal notation is an easier method for humans to understand than the binary 1s and 0s methods. The dotted-decimal notation also prevents a large number of transposition errors that would result if only the binary numbers were used.

Figure 9-15 IP Addressing Format

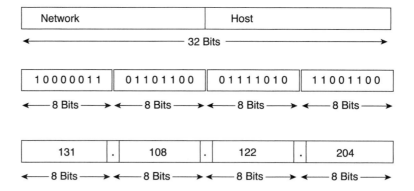

Using dotted-decimal also allows number patterns to be more quickly understood, as shown in Figure 9-15. Both the binary and decimal numbers in the figure represent the same values, but it is much easier to see with the dotted-decimal values. This is one of the common problems with working directly with binary numbers. The long strings of repeated 1s and 0s make these numbers prone to transposition and omission errors. In other words, it is easier to see the relationship between these two numbers:

> 192.168.1.8

> 192.168.1.9

than it is to recognize the relationship between their dotted-decimal binary equivalents:

> 11000000.10101000.00000001.00001000

> 11000000.10101000.00000001.00001001

Looking at the binaries, it is almost impossible to see that they are consecutive numbers.

Video   IP Numbering Basics

In this video, you learn about the structure of an IP address and its globally unique nature. In addition, you learn about the different classes of IP addresses and how to identify them.

Decimal and Binary Conversion

There is usually more than one way to solve a math problem, and decimal-to-binary conversion is no exception. This section explores one method, but feel free to use another method if it is easier.

To convert a decimal number to binary, the idea is to first find the biggest power of 2 that "fits" into the decimal number, as shown in Table 9-1. If this process is designed to work with computers, the most logical place to start is with the largest values that fit into 1 or 2 bytes.

Table 9-1 Calculating Available Host Addresses

2^{15}	2^{14}	2^{13}	2^{12}	2^{11}	2^{10}	2^9	2^8	2^7	2^6	2^5	2^4	2^3	2^2	2^1	2^0
32678	16384	8192	4096	2048	1024	512	256	128	64	32	16	8	4	2	1

As mentioned, the most common grouping of bits is 8, which make up one byte. But sometimes the largest value that can be held in 1 byte (255) is not large enough for the values needed. In this situation you must combine bytes, so instead of having two 8-bit numbers you have one 16-bit number, or instead of three 8-bit numbers you have one 24-bit number. The same rules apply as for 8-bit numbers: You multiply the previous position value by 2 to get the present column value. Table 9-1 documents these values (starting with a 2-byte/16-bit number), which are very important when you're learning the mechanics of subnetting.

Because working with computers often is referenced by bytes, it is easiest to start with byte boundaries and calculate from there, as shown in Table 9-2. To better demonstrate, look at the next couple of calculation examples, the first being 6783. Because this number is greater than 255, the largest value possible in a single byte, you use 2 bytes. Start calculating from 2^{15}. The result is that 6783 equals 00011010 01111111.

Table 9-2 Decimal-to-Binary Conversion Chart

Position Power	Decimal Value	Position Value	Binary Count	Remainder
2^{15}	6783	32678	0	6783
2^{14}	6783	16384	0	6783
2^{13}	6783	8192	0	6783
2^{12}	6783	4096	1	2687
2^{11}	2687	2048	1	639
2^{10}	639	1024	0	639
2^9	639	512	1	127
2^8	127	256	0	127
2^7	127	128	0	127
2^6	127	64	1	63
2^5	63	32	1	31
2^4	31	16	1	15
2^3	15	8	1	7
2^2	7	4	1	3
2^1	3	2	1	1
2^0	1	1	1	0

The second example is 104. Because this number is less than 255, the conversion can be done in 1 byte, as shown in Table 9-3.

Table 9-3 Converting an 8-Bit Number

Position Power	Decimal Value	Position Value	Binary Count	Remainder
2^7	104	128	0	104
2^6	104	64	1	40
2^5	40	32	1	8
2^4	8	16	0	8
2^3	8	8	1	0
2^2	0	4	0	0
2^1	0	2	0	0
2^0	0	1	0	0

So 104 is 01101000.

This method works for any decimal number. Consider the decimal number 1,000,000. Because 1,000,000 is greater than the largest value that can be held in 2 bytes (65,535), you need at least 3 bytes. By multiplying by two until 24 bits (3 bytes) is reached, the value will be 2^{23} or 8,388,608. This means that the largest value that 24 bits can hold is 16,777,215 (2^{24} − 1). So starting at the 24 bit, follow the process until you get to 0. Continuing with the procedure, you'll determine that the decimal number 1,000,000 equals the binary number 00001111 01000010 01000000.

Binary-to-decimal conversion is just the opposite. Simply place the binary number in the table. If there is a 1 in a column position, add that value to the total. Table 9-4 demonstrates an example of this It shows converting 00000100 00011101 to decimal, resulting in 1053.

Table 9-4 Decimal-to-Binary Conversion of a 16-Bit Number

Position Power	Position Value	Binary Count	Decimal Value
2^{15}	32678	0	0
2^{14}	16384	0	0
2^{13}	8192	0	0

continues

Table 9-4 Decimal-to-Binary Conversion of a 16-Bit Number (Continued)

Position Power	Position Value	Binary Count	Decimal Value
2^{12}	4096	0	0
2^{11}	2048	0	0
2^{10}	1024	1	1024
2^9	512	0	1024
2^8	256	0	1024
2^7	128	0	1024
2^6	64	0	1024
2^5	32	0	1024
2^4	16	1	1040
2^3	8	1	1048
2^2	4	1	1052
2^1	2	0	1052
2^0	1	1	1053

IPv4 Addressing

IP forwards packets from the network on which they originate to the destination network, as shown in Figure 9-16. This addressing scheme, therefore, must include an identifier for both the source and destination networks. By using the destination network identifier, IP can deliver a packet to the destination network. When the packet arrives at a router connected to the destination network, IP must then locate the particular computer connected to that network. This works in much the same way as the postal system. When the mail is routed, it must first be delivered to the post office at the destination city using the zip code, and then that post office must locate the final destination in that city using the street address. This is a two-step process.

Figure 9-16 Communication Path

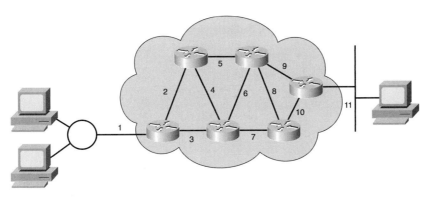

Accordingly, every IP address has two parts, as shown in Figure 9-17. One part identifies the network to which the system is connected, and a second part identifies that particular system on the network. This kind of address is called a hierarchical address, because it contains different levels, as shown in Figure 9-18. As Figure 9-18 illustrates, each octet ranges from 0 to 255. Each octet breaks down into 256 subgroups, and they break down into another 256 subgroups with 256 addresses in each. By referring to the group address directly above a group in the hierarchy, all the groups that branch from that address can be referenced as a single unit. An IP address combines these two identifiers into one number. This number must be unique, because duplicate addresses are not allowed. The first part identifies the system's network address. The second part, the host part, tells which particular machine it is on that network.

Figure 9-17 Network and Host Portions of the IP Address

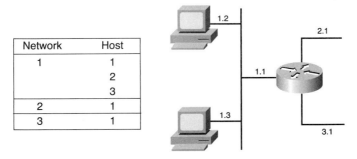

Network	Host
1	1
	2
	3
2	1
3	1

Figure 9-18 Hierarchical IP Addresses

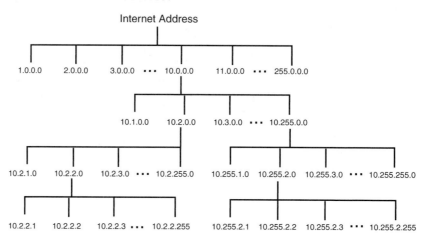

How does a user determine which portion of the address identifies the network and which portion identifies the host? The answer begins with the designers of the Internet, who thought networks would be built in different sizes, depending on the number of computers (hosts) they contained, as shown in Table 9-5.

Table 9-5 IP Address Classes

Address Class	Number of Networks	Number of Hosts Per Network
A	126*	16,777,216
B	16,384	65,535
C	2,097,152	254
D (multicast)	—	—

*The 127.x.x.x address range is reserved as a loopback address, used for testing and diagnostic purposes

The assumption was that there would be a relatively small number of large networks, possibly with millions of computers. The designers envisioned a larger number of medium-sized networks, with perhaps thousands of computers each. Finally, they saw a great number of networks having several hundred or fewer machines. Thus, the designers divided the available IP addresses into classes to define the large (Class A), medium (Class B), and small (Class C) networks, as shown in Table 9-6. Knowing the class of an IP address is the first step in deter-mining which part of the address identifies the network and which part identifies the host.

Table 9-6 Identifying Address Classes

Address Class	High-Order Bits	First Octet Address Range	Number of Bits in the Network Address
A	0	0 to 127*	8
B	10	128 to 191	16
C	110	192 to 223	24
D (Multicast	1110	224 to 239	28

*127 (01111111) is a Class A address reserved for loopback testing and cannot be assigned to a network.

Class A, B, C, D, and E IP Addresses

To accommodate different-sized networks and to aid in classifying them, IP addresses are divided into groupings called classes, as shown in Figure 9-19. This is called classful address-ing. Each complete 32-bit IP address is broken into a network part and a host part. A bit or bit sequence at the start of each address determines the class of the address, as shown in Figure 9-20. There are five *IP address classes*.

Figure 9-19 Network and Host Division

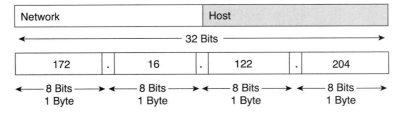

Figure 9-20 Address Class Prefixes

No. of Prefix Bits	1	7	24
Class A: Prefix Value	0	Network Bits	Host Bits

No. of Prefix Bits	2	14	16
Class B: Prefix Value	10	Network Bits	Host Bits

No. of Prefix Bits	3	21	8
Class C: Prefix Value	110	Network Bits	Host Bits

No. of Prefix Bits	4	28
Class D: Prefix Value	1110	Address

No. of Prefix Bits	4	28
Class E: Prefix Value	1111	Address

Class D addresses are used for multicast groups. There is no need to allocate octets or bits to separate network and host addresses.

Class E addresses are reserved for research use only.

Class A Addresses

The 127.0.0.0 network is reserved for loopback testing (routers or local machines can use this address to send packets to themselves). Therefore, it cannot be assigned to a network.

The *Class A address*, shown in Figure 9-21, was designed to support extremely large networks. A Class A IP address uses only the first octet to indicate the network address. The remaining three octets are used for host addresses.

Figure 9-21 Class A Addresses

The first bit of a Class A address is always 0. With that first bit a 0, the lowest number that can be represented is 00000000 (decimal 0), and the highest number that can be represented is 01111111 (decimal 127). However, these two numbers, 0 and 127, are reserved and cannot be used as a network address. Any address that has a value between 1 and 126 in the first octet is a Class A address.

Class B Addresses

The *Class B address*, shown in Figure 9-22, was designed to support the needs of moderate-to large-sized networks. A Class B IP address uses two of the four octets to indicate the network address. The other two octets specify host addresses.

Figure 9-22 Class B Addresses

The first 2 bits of the first octet of a Class B address are always 10. The remaining 6 bits may be populated with either 1s or 0s. Therefore, the lowest number that can be represented with a Class B address is 10000000 (decimal 128), and the highest number that can be represented is 10111111 (decimal 191). Any address that starts with a value in the range of 128 to 191 in the first octet is a Class B address.

Class C Addresses

The *Class C address*, shown in Figure 9-23, is the most commonly used of the original address classes. This address space was intended to support a lot of small networks.

Figure 9-23 Class C Addresses

A Class C address begins with binary 110. Therefore, the lowest number that can be represented is 11000000 (decimal 192), and the highest number that can be represented is 11011111 (decimal 223). If an address contains a number in the range of 192 to 223 in the first octet, it is a Class C address.

Class D Addresses

The *Class D address*, shown in Figure 9-24, was created to enable multicasting in an IP address. A *multicast address* is a unique network address that directs packets that have that destination address to predefined groups of IP addresses. Therefore, a single station can simultaneously transmit a single stream of data to multiple recipients.

Figure 9-24 Class D Addresses

The Class D address space, much like the other address spaces, is mathematically constrained. The first 4 bits of a Class D address must be 1110. Therefore, the first octet range for Class D addresses is 11100000 to 11101111, or 224 to 239. An IP address that starts with a value in the range of 224 to 239 in the first octet is a Class D address.

Class E Addresses

A *Class E address*, shown in Figure 9-25, has been defined. However, the Internet Engineering Task Force (IETF) reserves these addresses for its own research. Therefore, no Class E addresses have been released for use in the Internet. The first 4 bits of a Class E address are always set to 1. Therefore, the first octet range for Class E addresses is 11110000 to 11111111, or 240 to 255.

Figure 9-25 Class E Addresses

Table 9-7 shows the IP address range of the first octet (in decimal and binary) for each IP address class.

Table 9-7 IP Address Classes: Range of the First Octet

IP Address Class	IP Address Range (First Octet Decimal Value)
Class A	1 to 126 (00000001 to 01111110)[*]
Class B	128 to 191 (10000000 to 10111111)
Class C	192 to 223 (11000000 to 11011111)
Class D	224 to 239 (11100000 to 11101111)
Class E	240 to 255 (11110000 to 11111111)

Determine the class based on the decimal value of the first octet.

 Lab 9.2.7   IP Addressing Basics

This lab helps you develop an understanding of IP addresses and how TCP/IP networks operate.

Reserved IP Addresses

Certain addresses are reserved and cannot be assigned to devices on a network. These reserved host addresses include the following:

- Network addresses are used to identify the network itself (see Figure 9-26). The upper box represents the 198.150.11.0 network. Data that is sent to any host on that network (198.150.11.1 to 198.150.11.254) is seen outside the LAN as 198.159.11.0. The only time the host numbers matter is when the data is on the LAN. The LAN in the lower box is treated the same as the upper LAN, except that its network number is 198.150.12.0.

■ The *broadcast address* is used to broadcast packets to all the devices on a network (see Figure 9-27). The upper box represents the 198.150.11.255 broadcast address. Data that is sent to the broadcast address is read by any host on that network (198.150.11.1 to 198.150.11.254). The LAN in the lower box is treated the same as the upper LAN, except that its broadcast address is 198.150.12.255.

Figure 9-26 Network Address

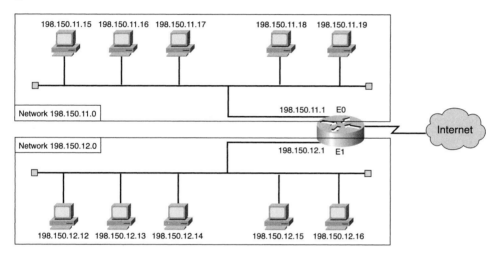

Figure 9-27 Broadcast Address

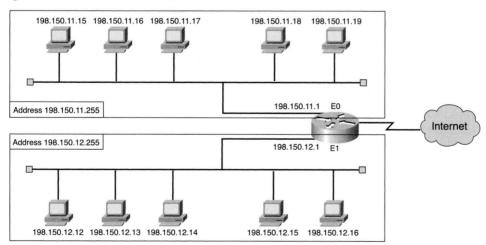

An IP address that has binary 0s in all host bit positions is reserved for the *network address,* as shown in Figure 9-28. This Class B address has all its host bits set to 0. That is why it is identified as the network address. Therefore, as a Class A network example, 113.0.0.0 is the IP address of the network containing the host 113.1.2.3. A router uses the network IP address when it forwards data on the Internet. As a Class B network example, the IP address 176.10.0.0 is a network address, as shown in Figure 9-28.

Figure 9-28 Network Address

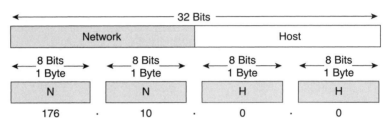

Network Address (Host Bits = All Zeros)

In a Class B network address, the first two octets, written as dotted-decimal numbers, are assigned by default. The last two octets contain 0s because those 16 bits are for host numbers and identify devices that are attached to the network. This is called a *unicast address* (*uni* means *one*). A unicast address points to just one host on the network. The IP address in the example (176.10.0.0) is reserved for the network address and is never used as an address for any device that is attached to it. An example of an IP address for a device on the 176.10.0.0 network is 176.10.16.1. In this example, 176.10 is the network address portion, and 16.1 is the host address portion.

To send data to all the devices on a network, a broadcast address is needed. A broadcast occurs when a source sends data to all devices on a network, as shown in Figure 9-29. This Class B address is the broadcast address for this network. When packets are received with this destination address, the data is processed by every computer. To ensure that all the other devices on the network process the broadcast, the sender must use a destination IP address that they can recognize and process. Broadcast IP addresses end with binary 1s in the entire host part of the address (the Host field).

For the network 176.10.0.0, where the last 16 bits make up the Host field (or the host part of the address), the broadcast that is sent to all devices on that network includes a destination address of 176.10.255.255 (because 255 is the decimal value of an octet containing 11111111).

Figure 9-29 Broadcast Address

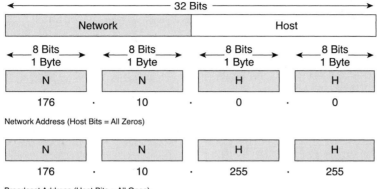

Network Address (Host Bits = All Zeros)

Broadcast Address (Host Bits = All Ones)

Public and Private IP Addresses

Internet stability depends directly on the uniqueness of publicly used network addresses. As shown in Figure 9-30, there is an issue with the networking addressing scheme. Both networks have a network address of 198.150.11.0. When data transmissions reach the router, which network would it forward to? A scheme such as this one would greatly increase the amount of network traffic and would defeat a router's basic function. Therefore, some mechanism was needed to ensure that addresses were, in fact, unique. This responsibility originally rested with the InterNIC (Internet Network Information Center). This organization is now defunct and has been succeeded by the Internet Assigned Numbers Authority (IANA). IANA carefully manages the remaining supply of IP addresses to ensure that duplication of publicly used addresses does not occur. Such duplication would cause instability in the Internet and compromise its capability to deliver datagrams to networks using the duplicated addresses.

Figure 9-30 Required Unique Addresses

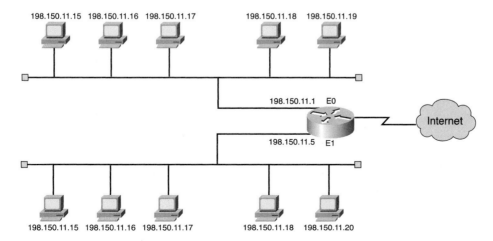

Public IP addresses are unique. No two machines that connect to a public network can have the same IP address, because public IP addresses are global and standardized. All machines connected to the Internet agree to adhere to the system. Public IP addresses must be obtained from an Internet service provider (ISP) or a registry at some expense.

With the rapid growth of the Internet, public IP addresses were beginning to run out, so new addressing schemes, such as classless interdomain routing (CIDR) and IPv6, were developed to help solve the problem. CIDR and IPv6 are discussed later.

Another solution that was developed is the use of private IP addresses, as shown in Table 9-8. As stated previously, Internet hosts require a globally unique IP address. However, private networks that are not connected to the Internet can use any valid address, as long as it is unique within the private network. Many private networks exist alongside public networks. Grabbing "just any address" is strongly discouraged because that network might eventually be connected to the Internet.

RFC 1918 sets aside three blocks of IP addresses (a single Class A address, a range of Class B addresses, and a range of Class C addresses) for private, internal use. Addresses in this range are not routed on the Internet backbone. Internet routers immediately discard private addresses.

Table 9-8 Private IP Addresses

IP Address Class	RFC 1918 Internal Address Range
Class A	10.0.0.0 to 10.255.255.255
Class B	172.16.0.0 to 172.31.255.255
Class C	192.168.0.0 to 192.168.255.255

If you are addressing a nonpublic intranet, a test lab, or a home network, these private addresses can be used instead of globally unique addresses. Private IP addresses can be inter-mixed with public IP addresses, as shown in Figure 9-31, to conserve the number of addresses used for internal connections.

Connecting a network to the Internet using private addresses requires translating the private addresses to public addresses. This translation process is called Network Address Translation (NAT). A router usually is the device that performs NAT.

Figure 9-31 Using Private IP Addresses Within the WAN

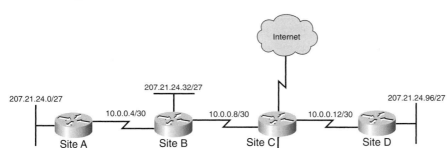

Introduction to Subnetting

Another way to conserve IP addresses, like CIDR, IPv6, and private addresses, is the use of *subnetting*. This method of dividing full network address classes into smaller pieces has helped prevent complete IP address exhaustion. Figure 9-32 shows a Class B network (131.108.0.0) divided into three subnetworks. It is impossible to cover TCP/IP without mentioning subnetting. As a system administrator, you must understand subnetting as a means of dividing and identifying separate networks throughout the LAN. It is not always necessary to subnet a small network, but for large or extremely large networks, subnetting is required. Simply stated, subnetting a network means using the subnet mask to divide the network and break a large network into smaller, more efficient, more manageable segments, or subnets, as shown in Figure 9-33. This is like the American telephone system, which breaks the system into area codes, and then exchange codes, and finally local numbers. These elements of the phone system are comparable to network numbers, subnets, and individual host addresses, respectively, in an IP internetwork.

Figure 9-32 Addressing with Subnets

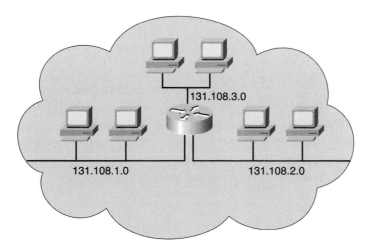

Figure 9-33 Subnet Addresses

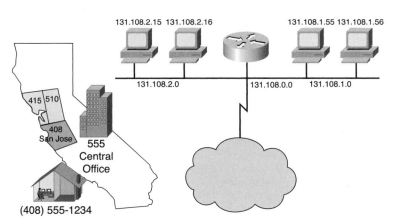

The system administrator must resolve these issues when adding and expanding the network. It is important to know how many subnet/networks are needed and how many hosts are allowed to be on each network. With subnetting, the network is not limited to the standard Class A, B, or C network masks, and there is more flexibility in the network design.

Subnet addresses include the Class A, Class B, or Class C network portion, plus a Subnet field and a Host field. These fields are created from the original host portion for the entire network. The ability to decide how to divide the original host portion into the new Subnet and Host fields provides addressing flexibility for the network administrator.

To create a subnet address, a network administrator borrows bits from the Host field and designates them as the Subnet field, as shown in Table 9-9. The minimum number of bits that can be borrowed is 2. If you were to borrow only 1 bit, to create a subnet, you would have only a network number (the .0 network) and a broadcast number (the .255 network). The maximum number of bits that can be borrowed can be any number that leaves at least 2 bits for the host number. In Table 7-9's example of a Class C IP address, bits from the Host field have been borrowed for the Subnet field.

Table 9-9 Subnet Addresses

Decimal Notation for First Host Octet	Number of Subnets	Number of Class A Hosts Per Subnet	Number of Class B Hosts Per Subnet	Number of Class C Hosts Per Subnet
.192	2	4,194,302	16,382	62
.224	6	2,097,150	8,190	30
.240	14	1,048,574	4,094	14

Table 9-9 Subnet Addresses (Continued)

Decimal Notation for First Host Octet	Number of Subnets	Number of Class A Hosts Per Subnet	Number of Class B Hosts Per Subnet	Number of Class C Hosts Per Subnet
.248	30	524,286	2,046	6
.252	62	262,142	1,022	2
.254	126	131,070	510	—
.255	254	65,534	254	—

IPv4 Versus IPv6

When TCP/IP was adopted in the 1980s, it relied on a two-level addressing scheme, which at the time offered adequate scalability. Unfortunately, the architects of TCP/IP could not have predicted that their protocol would eventually sustain a global network of information, commerce, and entertainment. More than 20 years ago, IPv4 offered an addressing strategy that, although scalable for a time, resulted in an inefficient allocation of addresses.

Class A and B addresses make up 75 percent of the IPv4 address space, as shown in Figure 9-34, but a relative handful of organizations (fewer than 17,000) can be assigned a Class A or B network number. Class C network addresses are far more numerous than Class A and Class B addresses, but they account for only 12.5 percent of the possible 4 billion IP addresses.

Figure 9-34 IPv4 Address Allocation

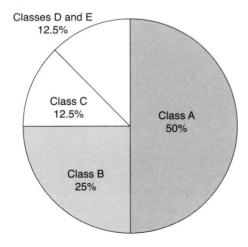

Unfortunately, Class C addresses are limited to 254 hosts, not meeting the needs of larger organizations that cannot acquire a Class A or B address. Even if there were more Class A, B, and C addresses, too many network addresses would cause Internet routers to grind to a halt under the weight of the enormous routing tables required to store the routes to reach the networks.

As early as 1992, the IETF identified two specific concerns:

- **Exhaustion of the remaining, unassigned IPv4 network addresses**—At the time, the Class B space was about to be used up.

- **The rapid and substantial increase in the size of Internet routing tables because of the Internet's growth**—As more Class C networks came online, the resulting flood of new network information threatened the capability of Internet routers to cope effectively.

Over the past two decades, numerous extensions to IPv4 have been developed that are specifically designed to improve the efficiency with which the 32-bit address space can be used. Two of the more important are subnet masks and classless interdomain routing (CIDR).

Meanwhile, an even more extensible and scalable version of IP, IPv6, has been defined and developed. IPv6 uses 128 bits rather than the 32 bits currently used in IPv4, as shown in Figure 9-35. IPv6 uses hexadecimal numbers to represent the 128 bits. It provides 16 billion IP addresses ($3.4 * 10^{38}$ addresses). This version of IP should provide sufficient addresses for future communication needs.

Figure 9-35 IPv4 and IPv6

Internet Protocol Version 4 (IPv4)   4 Octets
11010001.11011100.11001001.01110001
209.156.201.113
4,294,467,295 IP Addresses

Internet Protocol Version 6 (IPv6)   16 Octets
11010001.11011100.11001001.01110001.11010001.11011100. 110011001.01110001.11010001.11011100.11001001. 01110001.11010001.11011100.11001001.01110001
A524:72D3:2C80:DD02:0029:EC7A:002B:EA73
3.4 x 10^{38} IP Addresses

The IPv6 shorthand representation of the 128 bits uses eight 16-bit numbers, shown as four hexadecimal digits, as shown in Figure 9-36. The groups of four hex digits are separated by colons. If there are leading 0s in the hex digits, they may be omitted.

Figure 9-36 Pv4 and IPv6

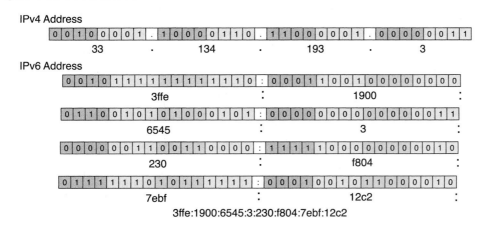

After years of planning and development, IPv6 is slowly being implemented in select networks. Eventually, IPv6 might replace IPv4 as the dominant IP.

Obtaining an IP Address

This section discusses how network devices obtain IP addresses. For a network to keep functioning, the IP addresses must be assigned according to a specific hierarchy. How and why this is done are discussed in the following section. IP addresses can be assigned either statically or dynamically. Both methods are covered here.

Obtaining an Internet Address

For a host on a network to function on the Internet, it needs to obtain a globally unique address. A host's physical or MAC address is only locally significant. Being locally significant means that the address can only identify the host in its own LAN. It has no meaning to any device that is not in that LAN.

IP is the most widely used global addressing scheme. It is a hierarchical addressing scheme that allows individual addresses to be associated and treated as groups, as shown in Figure 9-37. These groups of addresses allow efficient transfer of data across the Internet.

Figure 9-37 Internet Address Hierarchy

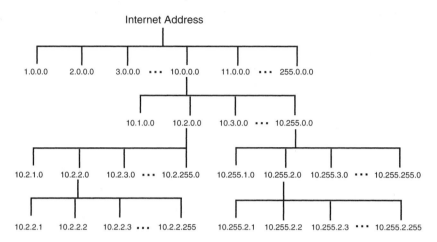

There are essentially two methods for assigning IP addresses—*static addressing* and *dynamic addressing*. The next few sections cover static and dynamic addressing. Regardless of which addressing scheme is chosen, no two interfaces can have the same IP address. This would cause a conflict that might cause both the hosts involved not to operate properly.

Static Assignment of an IP Address

When IP addresses are assigned statically, each device must be configured with an IP address. Each operating system has its own way of configuring TCP/IP. This method requires records of the address assignments to be kept, because problems can occur in a network if duplicate IP addresses are used. Some operating systems, such as Windows 95 and Windows NT, send an ARP request to check for a duplicate IP address when they attempt to initialize TCP/IP. If a duplicate is discovered, the operating system does not initialize TCP/IP and generates an error message. Not all operating systems identify duplicate IP addresses. This again emphasizes the need for good record-keeping.

The main reason that a device would be assigned a static IP address is if the device needs to be referenced by other devices. A good example is a web server. If a web server got a new IP address each time it started up, it would be difficult to find the web server. As an example of this address changing, if a city were to constantly change street names and building addresses, maps would no longer help you locate a particular building. If an address changes, it is no longer easy to return to the location. If a building is difficult to get to, people will stop trying to locate it.

Certain types of devices need to maintain a static IP address. Web servers, network printers, application servers, and routers are good examples of devices that require permanent IP addresses.

RARP IP Address Assignment

Reverse Address Resolution Protocol (RARP) binds MAC addresses to IP addresses. This binding allows some network devices to encapsulate data before sending it out on the network. A network device or workstation might know its MAC address but not its IP address. Devices using RARP require that a RARP server be present on the network to answer RARP requests, as shown in Figure 9-38.

Figure 9-38 RARP IP Address Assignment

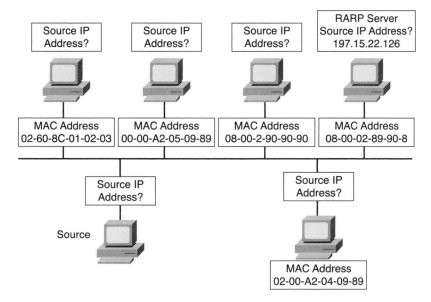

Consider an example in which a source device wants to send data to another device. The source knows the destination's MAC address but is unable to locate its IP address in the ARP table. For the destination device to retrieve the data, pass it to higher layers of the OSI model, and respond to the originating device, the source must include both its MAC address and IP address. Therefore, the source initiates a process called a RARP request, which helps it detect its own IP address. The device builds a RARP request packet, as shown in Figure 9-39, and sends it out on the network. To ensure that all devices see the RARP request on the network, the device uses a broadcast MAC address.

Figure 9-39 ARP/RARP Message Structure

0-15 Bits		16-31 Bits
Hardware Type		Protocol Type
HLen (1 Byte)	Plen (1 Byte)	Operation
Sender HA (Bytes 1-4)		
Sender HA (Bytes 5-6)		Sender PA (Byte 1-2)
Sender PA (Byte 3-4)		Target HA (Byte 1-2)
Target HA (Bytes 3-6)		
Target PA (Bytes 1-4)		
RARP Header Structure		

The various parts of the RARP header structure are as follows:

- **Hardware type**—Specifies a hardware interface type for which the sender requires a response.

- **Protocol type**—Specifies the type of high-level protocol address the sender has supplied.

- **HLen**—Hardware address length

- **PLen**—Protocol address length

- **Operation**—Values are as follows:
  - 1: ARP request
  - 2: ARP response
  - 3: RARP request
  - 4: RARP request
  - 5: Dynamic RARP request
  - 6: Dynamic RARP reply
  - 7: Dynamic RARP error
  - 8: InARP request
  - 9: InARP reply

- **Sender (HA) hardware address**—HLen bytes in length

- **Sender (PA) protocol address**—PLen bytes in length

- **Target (HA) hardware address**—HLen bytes in length

- **Target (PA) protocol address**—PLen bytes in length

RARP uses the same packet format as ARP. But in a RARP request, the MAC headers and operation code are different from an ARP request. The RARP packet format contains places for MAC addresses of both destination and source. The source IP address field is empty. The broadcast goes to all devices on the network; therefore, the destination MAC address is set to all binary 1s. Workstations running RARP have codes in ROM that direct them to start the RARP process. Figure 9-40 shows the RARP process.

Figure 9-40 RARP Process

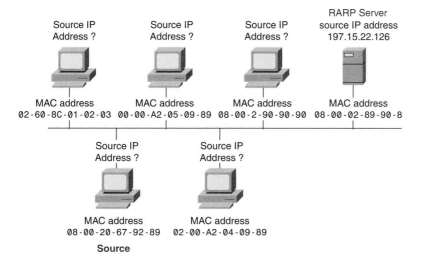

BOOTP IP Address Assignment

Like RARP, BOOTP operates in a client/server environment and requires only a single packet exchange to obtain IP information. However, unlike RARP, which sends back only a four-octet IP address, BOOTP packets can include the IP address as well as the address of a router (default gateway), the address of a server, and vendor-specific information, as shown in Figure 9-41.

One of the problems with BOOTP is that it was not designed to provide dynamic address assignment. With BOOTP, a network administrator creates a configuration file that specifies the parameters for each device. The administrator must add hosts and maintain the BOOTP database. Also, even though the addresses are dynamically assigned, there is still a one-to-one relationship between the number of IP addresses and the number of hosts. This means that for every host on the network, there must be a BOOTP profile with an IP address assignment. No two profiles can have the same IP address, because those profiles might be used at the same time, and that would mean that two hosts have the same IP address.

Figure 9-41 BOOTP Message Structure

0-7 Bits	8-15 Bits	16-24 Bits	25-31 Bits
Op (1)	Htype (1)	Hlen (1)	Hops (1)
Xid (4 Bytes)			
Seconds (2 Bytes)		Unused	
Ciaddr (4 Bytes)			
Yiaddr (4 Bytes)			
Siaddr (4 Bytes)			
Giaddr (4 Bytes)			
Chaddr (16 Bytes)			
Server Host Name (32 Bytes)			
Boot File Name (64 Bytes)			
Vendor Specific Area (32 Bytes)			
BOOTP Message Structure			

A device uses BOOTP when it starts up to obtain an IP address. BOOTP uses UDP to carry messages; the UDP message is encapsulated in an IP packet. A computer uses BOOTP to send a broadcast IP packet (using a destination IP address of all 1s—255.255.255.255—in dotted-decimal notation). A BOOTP server receives the broadcast and then sends back a broadcast. The client receives a frame and checks the MAC address. If it finds its own MAC address in the destination address field and a broadcast in the IP destination field, it takes and stores the IP address and other information supplied in the BOOTP reply message.

DHCP IP Address Management

Dynamic Host Configuration Protocol (DHCP) is the successor to BOOTP. Unlike BOOTP, DHCP allows a host to obtain an IP address dynamically without the network administrator's having to set up an individual profile for that machine. All that is required for using DHCP is a defined range of IP addresses on a DHCP server. As hosts come online, they contact the DHCP server and request an address. The DHCP server chooses an address and leases it to that host. With DHCP, the entire computer's TCP/IP configuration can be obtained in one message. This includes all the data supplied by the BOOTP message, plus a leased IP address and subnet mask.

The major advance that DHCP makes over BOOTP is that it allows users to be mobile. This allows them to freely change network connections from location to location. There is no longer a requirement for a fixed profile for every device attached to the network as there is with the BOOTP system. The key to this DHCP advancement is its capability to lease an IP address to a device and then reclaim that IP address for another user after the first user releases it. This means that there is now a one-to-many ratio of IP addresses and that an address is available to anyone who connects to the network.

More Information: DHCP Message and States

DHCP uses the same message format as BOOTP, as shown in Figure 9-42, with the following exceptions. The unused field in the BOOTP format now represents a Flags field. The most significant bit is the only flag defined currently. It represents a broadcast message. DHCP and BOOTP also define the vendor-specific area, as follows:

- 1-byte Option field
- 1-byte Length field
- Variable-length (specified by the Length field) Option Data field

Figure 9-42 DHCP Message Structure

0-7 Bits	8-15 Bits	16-24 Bits	25-31 Bits
Op (1)	Htype (1)	Hlen (1)	Hops (1)
Xid (4 Bytes)			
Seconds (2 Bytes)		Flags (2 Bytes)	
Ciaddr (4 Bytes)			
Yiaddr (4 Bytes)			
Siaddr (4 Bytes)			
Giaddr (4 Bytes)			
Chaddr (16 Bytes)			
Server Host Name (32 Bytes)			
Boot File Name (64 Bytes)			
Vendor Specific Area (32 Bytes)			
DHCP Message Structure			

For DHCP message types, the values for the fields are as follows:

- 53 for the Option field, indicating a DHCP message
- 1 for the Length field, indicating that the Data field is 1 byte long

> ### More Information: DHCP Message and States (Continued)
>
> When a DHCP client boots, it enters an initialize state. It sends DHCPDISCOVER broadcast messages, which are UDP packets with the port number set to the BOOTP port. After sending the DHCPDISCOVER packets, the client moves into the select state and collects DHCPOFFER responses from DHCP servers. The client then selects the first response it receives and negotiates the lease time (how long it can keep the address without renewing it) with the DHCP server by sending a DHCPREQUEST packet. Next, the DHCP server acknowledges a client request with a DHCPACK packet. The client can now enter the bound state and begin using the address. Figure 9-43 summarizes the DHCP state.
>
> **Figure 9-43** DHCP Startup States
>
>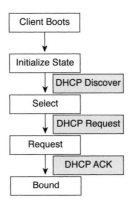

Lab 9.3.5 DHCP Client Setup

In this lab, you set up a networked computer as a DHCP client to use DHCP services.

Problems in Address Resolution

One of the major problems in networking is how to communicate with other network devices. In TCP/IP communications, a datagram on a LAN must contain both a destination MAC address and a destination IP address. In Figure 9-44, computer 176.10.16.1 wants to send data to 176.10.16.4. It has its IP address, but data transmission requires both the IP and MAC address of 176.10.16.4. How does it get that MAC address to perform the data transmission?

These addresses must be correct and match the destination host's MAC and IP addresses, or the destination host discards them. So, on LANs, there must be a way to automatically resolve (or translate) IP addresses to MAC addresses. Doing the resolution manually would be much too rigid and time-consuming for the user. This solution covers only LAN issues; a different set of issues are raised when data is sent outside the LAN.

Figure 9-44 Address Resolution Issues

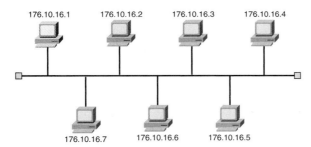

There are two parts to the problem in communicating with devices that are not on the same physical network segment:

- Obtaining the MAC address of the intermediate devices
- Transferring the data packets from one network segment to another to get to the destination host

Figure 9-45 illustrates this problem with an example. Computer 192.168.10.34 needs to communicate with computer 192.168.1.1. How does it get the MAC address for 192.168.1.1, and would it do any good if it *could* get the MAC address? Remember that MAC addresses are useful only in LANs. They won't be any help outside the 192.168.10.0 network. So you need the router's MAC address to get the data out of the LAN and onto the WAN system.

Figure 9-45 Remote Address Resolution Issues

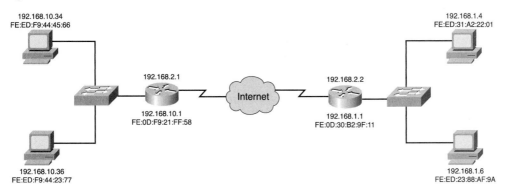

More Information
Routers running proxy ARP capture ARP packets. They respond with their MAC addresses for those requests in which the IP address is not in the range of addresses of the local subnet. For example, in Figure 9-46, if Machine A sends an ARP request to Machine F, the router processes the request and replies to A with its own MAC address to be mapped to the IP address of Machine F. In the previous description of how data is sent to a host on a different subnet, the default gateway is configured. If the source host does not have a default gateway configured, it sends an ARP request. All hosts on the segment, including the router, receive the ARP request. The router compares the IP destination address with the IP subnet address to determine whether the destination IP address is on the same subnet as the source host. If the subnet address is the same, the router discards the packet. The packet is discarded because the destination IP address is on the same segment as the source's IP address. This means that the destination device on the segment should respond to the ARP request. The exception to this is that the destination IP address is not currently assigned, which generates an error response on the source host.

Figure 9-46 Proxy ARP Network Example

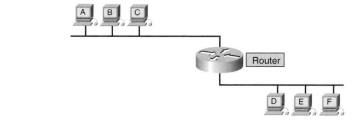

Address Resolution Protocol

For devices to communicate, the sending device needs the destination device's IP address and MAC address. When a device tries to communicate with a device whose IP addresses it knows, it must determine the MAC addresses. The TCP/IP suite has a protocol called Address Resolution Protocol (ARP) that can automatically obtain the MAC address. ARP lets a computer find the MAC address of the computer that is associated with an IP address, as shown in Figure 9-47.

Some devices keep ARP tables, which contain the MAC addresses and IP addresses of other devices that are connected to the same LAN. ARP tables map IP addresses to the corresponding MAC addresses. ARP tables are sections of RAM memory that are maintained automatically on each device, as shown in Tables 9-10 and 9-11. It is rare that you must manually make an ARP table entry. Each computer on a network maintains its own ARP table.

Figure 9-47 ARP Obtains the IP Address Via the MAC Address

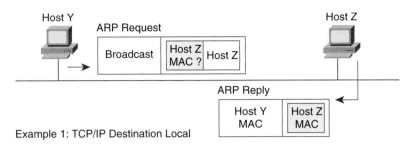

Example 1: TCP/IP Destination Local

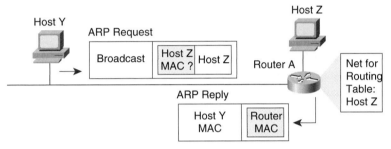

Example 2: TCP/IP Destination not Local

Table 9-10 ARP Table Entry

Internet Address	Physical Address	Type
68.2.168.1	00-50-57-00-76-84	Dynamic

Table 9-11 ARP Table for 198.150.11.36

MAC Address	IP Address
FE:ED:F9:44:45:66	198.150.11.34
DD:EC:BC:AB:04:AC	198.150.11.33
DD:EC:BC:00:94:D4	198.150.11.35
FE:ED:F9:23:44:EF	198.150.11.36

Whenever a network device wants to send data across a network, it uses information provided by its ARP table. In Figure 9-48, a source device wants to send data to another device.

Figure 9-48 ARP Tables

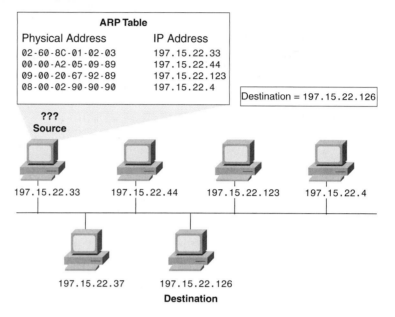

ARP Operation Within a Subnet

If a host wants to send data to another host, it must know the destination IP and MAC addresses. If it cannot locate a MAC address for the destination IP address in its ARP table, the host initiates a process called an ARP request, as shown in Figure 9-48.

An ARP request lets a host discover the destination MAC address. A host builds an ARP request packet and sends it to all devices on the network. This ARP request packet is divided into two parts:

- The frame header

- The ARP message

To ensure that all devices see the ARP request, the source uses a broadcast MAC address. The broadcast address in a MAC addressing scheme has all places set to hexadecimal F. Thus, a MAC broadcast address has the form FF-FF-FF-FF-FF-FF. Because ARP request frames travel in a broadcast mode, all devices on the local network receive the frames and pass them up to the network layer for further examination. If a device's IP address matches the destination IP address in the ARP request, that device responds by sending the source its MAC address and possibly other information. This is called the ARP reply.

When the originating device receives the ARP reply, it extracts the MAC address from the sender hardware address field and updates its ARP table. The originating device can then properly address its data with both a destination MAC address and a destination IP address.

It uses this new information to perform Layer 2 and Layer 3 encapsulations of the data before it sends them out over the network. When the data arrives at the destination, the data link layer makes a match, strips the MAC header, and transfers the data up to the network layer. The network layer examines the data and finds that its IP address matches the destination IP address carried in the IP header. The network layer strips the IP header and transfers the encapsulated data to the next-highest layer in the OSI model, the transport layer (Layer 4). This process is repeated until the rest of the packet's partially de-encapsulated data reaches the application, where the user data can be read.

Default Gateway

A default gateway is the IP address of the interface on the router that connects to the network segment on which the source host is located. The default gateway's IP address must be in the same network segment as the source host, as shown in Figure 9-49.

Figure 9-49 Default Gateway

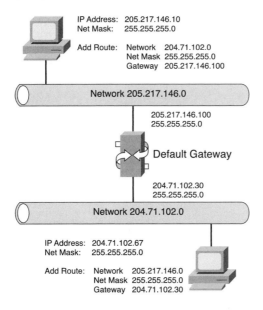

Lab 9.3.7   Workstation ARP

In this lab, you use the workstation ARP table and the **arp -a** command to confirm that a computer is successfully resolving network (Layer 3) addresses to MAC (Layer 2) addresses.

Video   ARP

In this video, you learn how ARP works to discover the MAC address of the destination.

Summary

In this chapter, you learned the following key points:

- The U.S. DoD created the TCP/IP reference model because it wanted a network that could survive any conditions.

- The application layer of the TCP/IP model handles high-level protocols, issues of representation, encoding, and dialog control.

- The transport layer provides transport services from the source host to the destination host.

- The purpose of the Internet layer is to select the best path through the network for packets to travel.

- The network access layer handles all the requirements for an IP packet to make a physical link to the network media.

- Large networks are often divided into smaller networks called subnetworks or subnets. This allows a network administrator to get around the limitations of IPv4. Administrators can divide a single network address into many subnets that are only visible within that network.

- A subnet mask tells devices which part of an address contains the network number and the subnet, and which part is the host.

- Communication functions of the network layer include network addressing and best-path selection for data.

- The evolution of IP addressing includes the need for an increase in the size of the IP address space.

- A computer needs an IP address, which is a hierarchical address, to communicate on the Internet.

- IP addresses can either be configured statically or dynamically.

- There are multiple ways to assign an IP address dynamically.

- DHCP allows computers to be mobile and connected to different networks, as needed.

To supplement all that you have learned in this chapter, refer to the chapter-specific Videos and Interactive Media Activities on the CD-ROM that accompanies this book.

Key Terms

application layer   Handles high-level protocols and issues of representation, encoding, and dialog control. The TCP/IP protocol suite combines all application-related issues into one layer and ensures that this data is properly packaged for the next layer.

broadcast address   Used to broadcast packets to all the devices on a network.

Class A address   Designed to support extremely large networks. A Class A IP address uses only the first octet to indicate the network address. The remaining three octets enumerate host addresses.

Class B address   Designed to support the needs of moderate- to large-sized networks. A Class B IP address uses two of the four octets to indicate the network address. The other two octets specify host addresses.

Class C address   The most commonly used of the original address classes. This address space was intended to support a lot of small networks.

Class D address   Created to enable multicasting in an IP address.

Class E address   The IETF reserves these addresses for its own research. Therefore, no Class E addresses have been released for use on the Internet.

dotted-decimal format   In this notation, each IP address is written as four parts separated by periods, or dots.

IP address class   A 32-bit IP address is broken into a network part and a host part. A bit or bit sequence at the start of each address determines the address's class.

IP Version 6 (IPv6)   The replacement for the current version of IP (Version 4). IPv6 includes support for flow ID in the packet header, which can be used to identify flows. Formerly called IPng (IP next generation).

multicast address   A unique network address that directs packets that have that destination address to predefined groups of IP addresses.

network access layer   The layer that is concerned with all the issues that an IP packet requires to make a physical link to the network medium.

subnetting   The method of dividing full network address classes into smaller pieces. This has prevented complete IP address exhaustion.

Transmission Control Protocol/Internet Protocol (TCP/IP)   The common name for the suite of protocols developed by the U.S. DoD in the 1970s to support the construction of worldwide internetworks. TCP and IP are the two best-known protocols in the suite.

transport layer   Provides transport services from the source host to the destination host. It constitutes a logical connection between the network's endpoints: the sending host and the receiving host.

Check Your Understanding

Complete all the review questions to test your understanding of the topics and concepts in this chapter. Answers are listed in Appendix B, "Check Your Understanding Answer Key."

1. What transport layer protocol does TFTP use?

   A. TCP

   B. IP

   C. UDP

   D. CFTP

2. Which of the following is a basic service of the transport layer?

   A. Provides reliability by using sequence numbers and acknowledgments

   B. Segments upper-layer application data

   C. Establishes end-to-end operations

   D. All of the above

3. Which of the following protocols operate at the TCP/IP Internet layer?

   A. IP

   B. ICMP

   C. ARP

   D. All of the above

4. What is the first thing that happens when a DHCP client boots?

   A. DHCPREQUEST

   B. DHCPBOOT

   C. DHCPDISCOVER

   D. None of the above

5. How does the network layer forward packets from the source to the destination?

   A. By using a routing table

   B. By using ARP responses

   C. By referring to a name server

   D. By referring to the bridge

6. If a device doesn't know the MAC address of a device on an adjacent network, it sends an ARP request to what?

   A. The default gateway

   B. The closest router

   C. The router interface

   D. All of the above

7. What are the two parts of an IP address?

   A. Network address and host address

   B. Network address and MAC address

   C. Host address and MAC address

   D. MAC address and subnet mask

8. What Internet protocol is used to map a known IP address to an unknown MAC address?

   A. UDP

   B. ICMP

   C. ARP

   D. RARP

9. Which of the following initiates an ARP request?

   A. A device that can locate the destination IP address in its ARP table

   B. The RARP server in response to a malfunctioning device

   C. A diskless workstation with an empty cache

   D. A device that cannot locate the destination MAC address in its ARP table

10. Which of the following best describes an ARP table?

    A. A way to reduce network traffic by providing lists of shortcuts and routes to common destinations

    B. A way to route data within networks that are divided into subnetworks

    C. A protocol that performs an application layer conversion of information from one stack to another

    D. A section of RAM on each device that maps IP addresses to MAC addresses

11. Which of the following best describes the ARP reply?

    A. A device sends its MAC address to a source in response to an ARP request

    B. The shortest path between the source and the destination

    C. The updating of ARP tables through intercepting and reading messages traveling on the network

    D. The method of finding IP addresses based on the MAC address, used primarily by RARP servers

12. Why are current, updated ARP tables important?

    A. For testing links in the network

    B. For limiting the number of broadcasts

    C. For reducing network administrator maintenance time

    D. For resolving addressing conflicts

13. Which of the following best describes TCP/IP?

    A. It is a suite of protocols that can be used to communicate across any set of inter connected networks.

    B. It is a suite of protocols that allows LANs to connect to WANs.

    C. It is a suite of protocols that allows for data transmission across a multitude of networks.

    D. It is a suite of protocols that allows different devices to be shared by interconnected networks.

14. Which of the following does not describe the TCP/IP protocol stack?

    A. It maps closely to the OSI reference model's upper layers.

    B. It supports all standard physical and data link protocols.

    C. It transfers information in a sequence of datagrams.

    D. It reassembles datagrams into complete messages at the receiving location.

15. The TCP/IP protocol suite has specifications for which layers of the OSI model?

    A. 1 through 3

    B. 1 through 4 and 7

    C. 3, 4, and 5 through 7

    D. 1, 3, and 4

16. Which of the following is not a function of the network layer?

    A. RARP determines network addresses when data link layer addresses are known.

    B. ICMP provides control and messaging capabilities.

    C. ARP determines the data link layer address for known IP addresses.

    D. UDP provides connectionless exchange of datagrams without acknowledgments.

17. Which of the following is one of the protocols found at the transport layer?

    A. UCP

    B. UDP

    C. TDP

    D. TDC

CHAPTER 10

Routing Fundamentals and Subnets

Objectives

Upon completion of this chapter, you should be able to answer the following questions:

- What is the purpose of routable and routed protocols, such as IP?

- What is the function of IP as a connectionless versus connection-oriented networking service?

- How do routers operate at the network layer?

- How do routed protocols define the format and use of the fields in a packet?

- In the OSI model, how does Layer 2 LAN switching compare to Layer 3 routing?

- Why are routing protocols used between routers to determine paths and maintain routing tables?

- What process do routers use to accomplish path selection and switching functions to transport packets through an internetwork?

- What is the differences between static and dynamic routing?

- What is the difference between distance vector and link-state routing protocols, including convergence?

- What are the differences between interior and exterior routing protocols? What are some examples of each?

- What are some of the purposes and benefits of subnetting?

- How is a resident network calculated through the ANDing process?

Key Terms

The following is a list of key terms introduced in this chapter. For your reference, a definition for each term can be found at the end of this chapter.

routed protocol   page 419

packet   page 419

routing protocol   page 420

IP address   page 420

connectionless   page 421

datagrams   page 422

collision domain   page 423

connection-oriented   page 425

router   page 427

routing metrics   page 428

NetBIOS Extended User Interface (NetBEUI)   page 429

broadcast domain   page 430

subnetwork   page 430

routing table   page 431

hop   page 435

MAC address   page 437

broadcasts   page 437

hop count   page 438

algorithm   page 439

Interior Gateway Protocol (IGP)   page 440

Exterior Gateway Protocol (EGP)   page 440

autonomous system   page 441

distance vector routing   page 442

Routing Information Protocol (RIP)   page 442

Interior Gateway Routing Protocol (IGRP)   page 442

Enhanced Interior Gateway Routing Protocol (EIGRP)   page 442

link-state routing protocol   page 442

protocol stack   page 445

classless interdomain routing (CIDR)   page 445

octet   page 447

subnet address   page 447

subnet mask   page 450

This chapter covers topics related to the Internet Protocol (IP). IP is the fundamental protocol used in the Internet. Topics discussed include how IP is delivered, how the header is modified at Layer 3 devices, and the actual layout of the IP packet. This chapter also covers the relationship between connectionless and connection-oriented networking services. You learn the difference between routing and routed protocols and how routers track distance between locations. This chapter introduces the distance vector, link-state, and hybrid routing approaches and how each resolves common routing problems.

Be sure to look at this chapter's associated Videos and Interactive Media Activities, which you will find on the CD-ROM accompanying this book. These CD elements are designed to supplement the material and reinforce the concepts introduced in this chapter.

Routed Protocol

Internet Protocol (IP) is the routed protocol of the Internet. IP addressing enables packets to be routed from source to destination using the best available path. The propagation of packets, encapsulation changes, and connection-oriented and connectionless protocols are also critical to ensure that data is properly transmitted to its destination. This section provides an overview for each.

Routable and Routed Protocols

A protocol is a standards-based set of rules that determines how computers communicate with each other across networks. A protocol also serves as the common denominator or medium by which different applications, hosts, or systems communicate. When computers communicate with one another, they exchange data messages. To accept and act on these messages, computers must have definitions of how a message is defined and what it means. Examples of messages include establishing a connection to a remote machine, sending or receiving e-mail, and transferring files and data.

A protocol describes

- The format that a message must take

- The way in which computers must exchange a message within the context of a particular activity, such as sending messages across networks

Because of the similarity of a routed/routable protocol versus a routing protocol, confusion over these terms often exists. The following provides some clarification:

- *Routed protocol* — Any network protocol that provides enough information in its network layer address to allow a packet to be forwarded from one host to another host based on the addressing scheme. Routed protocols define the field formats within a *packet*. Packets are generally conveyed from end system to end system. A routed protocol uses the routing table to forward packets. Examples of routed or routable protocols are shown in the routing table in Figure 10-1. They include the following:

    — Internet Protocol (IP)

    — Internetwork Packet Exchange (IPX)

    — AppleTalk

Figure 10-1 Routed/Routable Protocols

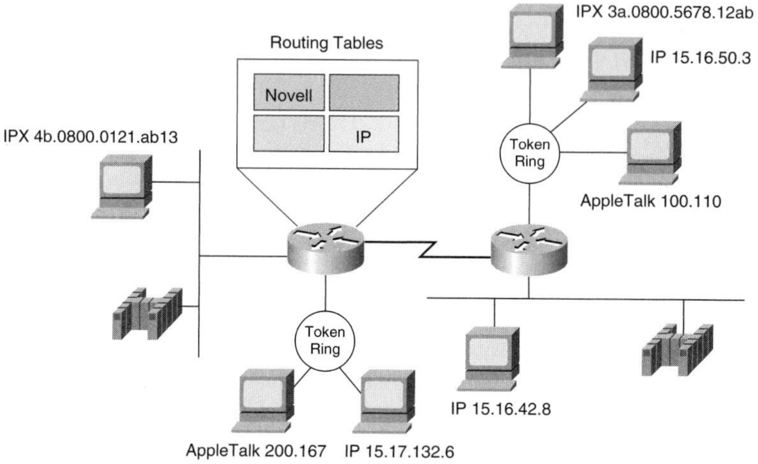

- *Routing protocol*—Supports a routed protocol by providing mechanisms for sharing routing information. Routing protocol messages move between the routers. A routing protocol allows the routers to communicate with other routers to update and maintain tables. Here are some TCP/IP examples of routing protocols:

    — Routing Information Protocol (RIP)

    — Interior Gateway Routing Protocol (IGRP)

    — Enhanced Interior Gateway Routing Protocol (EIGRP)

    — Open Shortest Path First (OSPF)

For a protocol to be routable, it must provide the capability to assign a network number, as well as a host number, to each individual device. Some protocols, such as Internetwork Packet Exchange (IPX), only require that an administrator assign a network number, because they use a host's Media Access Control (MAC) address for the physical number. Other protocols, such as IP, require that a complete address be provided, as well as a network mask.

Both the *IP address* and network mask are required to have a routed network. A network mask separates the network and host portions of a 32-bit IP address. IPX uses the MAC address with an administrator-assigned network address to create the complete address and does not use a network mask. With IP addresses, the network address is obtained by comparing the address with the network mask.

A network mask allows groups of sequential IP addresses to be treated as a single unit. If this grouping were not allowed, each host would have to be mapped individually for routing. That would not be possible with the millions of hosts on the Internet. As shown in Figure 10-2, all 254 addresses in the sequence of 192.168.10.1 to 192.168.10.254 can be represented by the network address 192.168.10.0. This allows data to be sent to any one of these hosts just by locating the network address. This means that routing tables need to contain only one entry of 192.168.10.0 instead of all 254 individual entries. This is according to the Internet Software Consortium (http://www.isc.org). For routing to function, this process of grouping must be used.

The following sections describe the router's use and operations in performing the key inter-networking function of the Open System Interconnection (OSI) reference model's network layer, Layer 3. In addition, you'll learn about the difference between routing and routed pro-tocols and how routers track distance between locations. Finally, you'll learn more about dis-tance vector, link-state, and hybrid routing approaches and how each resolves common routing problems.

Figure 10-2 Network and Host Addresses

Host Addresses	Network Address
192.168.10.1	
192.168.10.2	
192.168.10.3	
192.168.10.4	
192.168.10.5	
192.168.10.6	
192.168.10.7	
.	
.	192.168.10.0
.	
192.168.10.250	
192.168.10.251	
192.168.10.252	
192.168.10.253	
192.168.10.254	

Video   Routed Versus Routing Protocols

In this video, you learn about some of the differences between routed and routing protocols. You also learn about some of the uses for these protocols.

IP as a Routed Protocol

IP is the most widely used implementation of a hierarchical network addressing scheme. IP is a connectionless, unreliable, best-effort delivery system protocol used on the Internet. The term *connectionless* means that no dedicated circuit connection is required, as there would be for a telephone call. There is no call setup before data is transferred between hosts. The IP protocol takes whichever route is the most efficient based on the routing protocol decision. Unreliable and best-effort do not mean that the system is unreliable and doesn't work well, but that the IP protocol does not make any effort to see if the packet was delivered. This func-tion is handled by the upper-layer protocols.

As information flows down the layers of the OSI model, the data is processed at each layer. At the network layer, the data is encapsulated within packets called *datagrams*, as shown in Figure 10-3.

Figure 10-3 Encapsulation

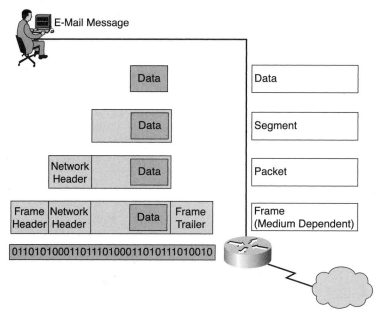

IP determines the form of the IP packet header (which includes addressing and other control information) but does not concern itself with the actual data. It accepts whatever is passed down from the higher layers, as shown in Figure 10-4.

Figure 10-4 IP Header

IP Header Information	Data (From Upper Layers)

Packet Propagation and Switching Within a Router

As a packet travels through an internetwork to get to its final destination, the frame's headers and trailers are stripped and replaced at every router (Layer 3) device, as shown in Figure 10-5. The reason for this is that Layer 2 units (frames) are for local addressing and Layer 3 units (packets) are for end-to-end addressing.

Layer 2 Ethernet frames are meant to work within a broadcast domain and to work with the MAC addresses that are assigned to the physical devices. Other Layer 2 frame types include point-to-point serial links and Frame Relay WAN connections that use their own Layer 2 addressing scheme. The main point is that no matter what type of Layer 2 addressing is used, it is designed to stay within a Layer 2 broadcast domain. As the data crosses a Layer 3 device, the Layer 2 information changes.

Figure 10-5 Network Layer Device Data Flow

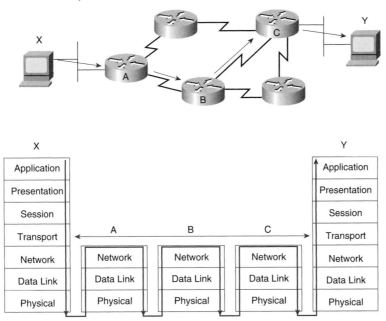

The exact process that is performed at a Layer 3 device is detailed in Figure 10-6 and the following paragraph.

As a frame is accepted at a router interface, the destination MAC address is extracted and checked, as is done by all devices in a *collision domain*, to see if the frame is directly addressed to the interface or is a broadcast. In either of these cases, the packet is accepted; otherwise, it is discarded, because it was destined for another device on the collision domain. The accepted frame has the cyclic redundancy check (CRC) extracted from the frame trailer and is calculated to verify that the frame arrived without error at the interface. If the check fails, the frame is discarded. If the check is valid, the frame header and trailer are stripped, and the packet is passed up to Layer 3. The packet is then checked to see if it is destined for the router or is to be routed to another device in the internetwork. The types of packets that are destined for the router have an IP address of one of the router interfaces as the destination IP address. This packet has the Layer 3 header stripped and passed up to Layer 4. If the packet is to be routed, the destination IP address is compared to the routing table. If a match is found or there is a default route, the packet is sent to the interface specified in the matching routing table statement.

Figure 10-6 Encapsulation Changes in a Router

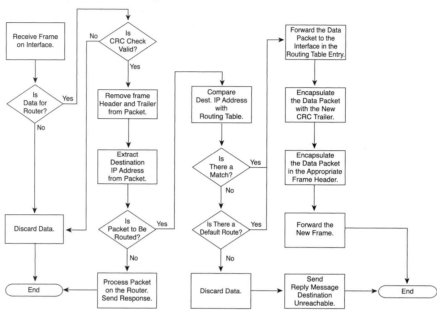

When the packet is switched to the outgoing interface, a new CRC value is added as a frame trailer, and, depending on the type of interface (Ethernet, serial, or Frame Relay), the proper frame header is added to the packet. The frame is then transmitted to the next broadcast domain for the next part of the trip to the final destination.

Connectionless and Connection-Oriented Delivery

Most OSI model network services use a connectionless delivery system (TCP), as shown in Figure 10-7. They treat each packet separately and send it on its way through the network. The packets might take different paths to get through the network, but they are reassembled when they arrive at the destination. In a connectionless system, the destination is not contacted before a packet is sent. A good analogy for a connectionless system is the postal system. The recipient is not contacted before a letter is sent from one destination to another. The letter is sent on its way, and the recipient learns of the letter when it arrives.

Connectionless network processes are often referred to as being *packet-switched*. In these processes, as the packets pass from source to destination, they can switch to different paths, as well as (possibly) arrive out of order. Devices make the path determination for each packet based on a variety of criteria. Some of the criteria (such as available bandwidth) might differ from packet to packet.

The Internet is a huge connectionless internetwork in which all packet deliveries are handled by IP. TCP (Layer 4) adds connection-oriented and reliable services on top of IP (Layer 3). TCP segments are encapsulated into IP packets for transport across the Internet.

Figure 10-7 Connectionless Delivery System for Network Services

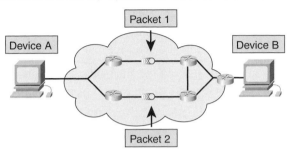

IP is a connectionless system; it treats each packet independently. For example, if you use an FTP program to download a file, IP does not send the file in one long stream of data; it treats each packet independently. Each packet can travel different paths; some can even get lost. IP relies on the transport layer protocol to determine whether packets have been lost and to request retransmission. The transport layer is also responsible for reordering the packets.

In *connection-oriented* systems, a connection is established between the sender and the recipient before any data is transferred, as shown in Figure 10-8. An example of a connection-oriented network is the telephone system. You place a call, a connection is established, and then communication occurs. Connection-oriented network processes first establish a connection with the recipient and then begin the data transfer. All packets travel sequentially across the same physical circuit—or, more commonly, across the same virtual circuit.

Figure 10-8 Connection-Oriented Delivery System for Network Services

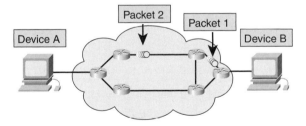

Anatomy of an IP Packet

The Layer 3 packet/datagram becomes Layer 2 data, which is then encapsulated into frames as previously discussed.

Similarly, the IP packet, shown in Figure 10-9, consists of the data from upper layers plus an IP header:

- **Version**—A 4-bit field that indicates the version of IP currently used. All devices must be running the same version of IP, or the device that is different rejects the packets.

- **IP Header Length (HLEN)**—A 4-bit field that indicates the datagram header length in 32-bit words. This is the total length of all header information, accounting for the two variable-length header fields.

- **Type of Service (TOS)**—An 8-bit field that specifies the level of importance that has been assigned by a particular upper-layer protocol.

- **Total Length**—A 16-bit field that specifies the length of the entire packet in bytes, including data and header. To get the length of the data payload, subtract the HLEN from the total length.

- **Identification**—A 16-bit field that contains an integer that identifies the current datagram. This is the sequence number.

- **Flags**—A 3-bit field in which the 2 low-order bits control fragmentation. The first bit specifies whether the packet can be fragmented, and the second bit specifies whether the packet is the last fragment in a series of fragmented packets.

- **Fragment Offset**—A 13-bit field that helps piece together datagram fragments. This field allows the Flags field to end at a 16-bit boundary.

- **Time-to-Live (TTL)**—An 8-bit field that maintains a counter that gradually decreases, in increments, to 0. At this point, the datagram is discarded, keeping the packets from looping endlessly. An example is hop count.

- **Protocol**—An 8-bit field that indicates which upper-layer protocol receives incoming packets after IP processing has been completed. Examples are TCP and UDP.

- **Header Checksum**—A 16-bit field that helps ensure IP header integrity.

- **Source IP Address**—A 32-bit field that specifies the sending node IP address.

- **Destination IP Address**—A 32-bit field that specifies the receiving node IP address.

- **Options**—A variable-length field that allows IP to support various options, such as security.

- **Padding**—Extra 0s are added to this field to ensure that the IP header is always a multiple of 32 bits.

- **Data**—A variable-length (maximum 64 Kb) field that contains upper-layer information.

Figure 10-9 IP Packet Contents

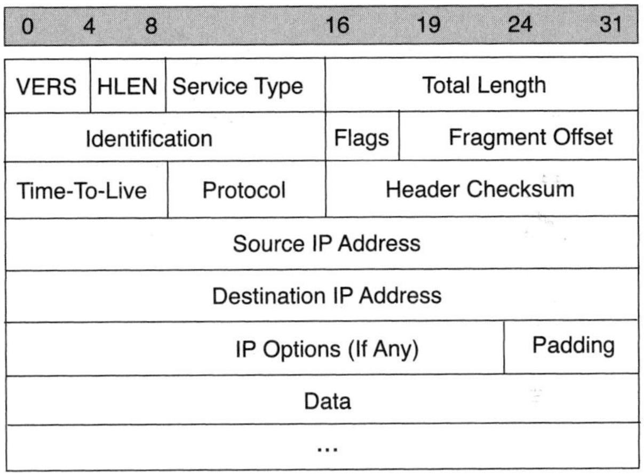

0	4	8		16	19	24	31

VERS	HLEN	Service Type	Total Length		
Identification			Flags	Fragment Offset	
Time-To-Live		Protocol	Header Checksum		
Source IP Address					
Destination IP Address					
IP Options (If Any)				Padding	
Data					
...					

The IP packet consists of upper-layer data and the header information just described. Although the focus of this book so far has been the IP source and destination addresses, the other header fields are what make IP so flexible and resilient. The header fields are the information that is provided to the upper-layer protocols that defines the data in the packet. Several earlier chapters discussed the idea of layer independence; the header information in the preceding list is what allows that independence to happen.

IP Routing Protocols

The difference between routing and routed protocols is a common source of confusion for individuals who are just learning about networking. The two words sound similar, but they are different. This section introduces routing protocols, which allow routers to build tables from which to determine the best path to a host on the Internet.

Routing Overview

Routing is an OSI Layer 3 function. It functions as a hierarchical organizational scheme that allows individual addresses to be grouped and treated as a single unit until the individual address is needed for final delivery of the data. Routing is the process of finding the most efficient path from one device to another, as shown in Figure 10-10. The main device that performs this process is the *router*.

Figure 10-10 Network Layer Protocol Operation

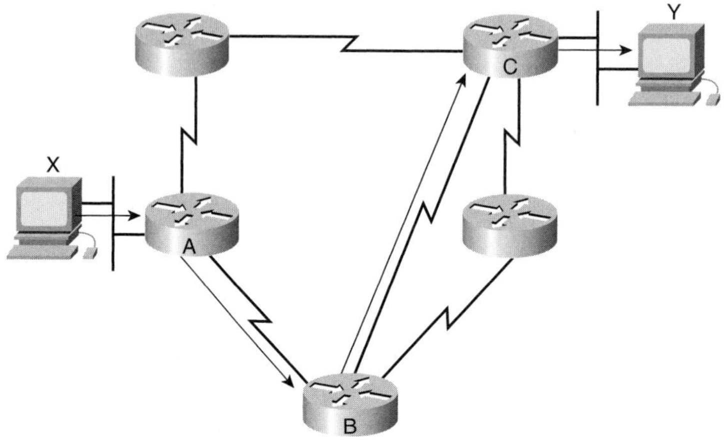

A router has two key functions:

- To maintain routing tables and make sure other routers know of changes in the network topology. This function is performed using a routing protocol to communicate network information to other routers.

- When packets arrive at an interface, the router must use the routing table to determine where to send the packets. It switches them to the appropriate interface, adds the necessary framing for the interface, and then transmits the frame.

A router is a network layer device that uses one or more ***routing metrics*** to determine the optimal path along which network traffic should be forwarded. The routing metric is a value used to determine the route's desirability. Routing protocols use various combinations of criteria for determining the routing metric, as shown in Figure 10-11.

Figure 10-11 Routing Protocol Metrics

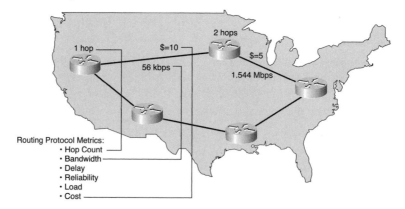

The metrics of hop count, bandwidth, delay, reliability, load, and cost are calculated in various combinations to determine the best path through an internetwork. Routers interconnect network segments or entire networks. They pass data frames between networks based on Layer 3 information. Routers make logical decisions regarding the best path for the delivery of data on an internetwork and then direct packets to the appropriate output port to be encapsulated for transmission. The encapsulation/de-encapsulation process occurs each time a packet passes through a router and data is sent from one device to another, as shown in Figure 10-12. Encapsulation breaks the data stream into segments, adds the appropriate headers and trailers, and transmits the data. The de-encapsulation process is the opposite, removing the headers and trailers and then recombining the data into a seamless stream. Routers take frames from LAN devices (for example, workstations) and, based on Layer 3 information, forward them through the network.

Figure 10-12 Data Encapsulation

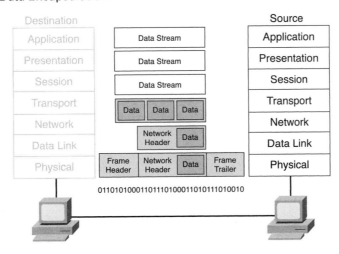

It is important to know that there are other routable protocols, such as IPX/SPX and Apple-Talk, for example. Protocols such as IP, IPX/SPX, and AppleTalk provide Layer 3 support and therefore are routable. Protocols that do not support Layer 3 are called nonroutable protocols. The most common of these is *NetBIOS Extended User Interface (NetBEUI)*—a small, fast, efficient protocol that is limited to running on one segment.

Routing Versus Switching

Routing is often contrasted with Layer 2 switching, which might seem to perform the same function to the casual observer. The primary difference between the two is that switching occurs at Layer 2 (the data link layer) of the OSI model, and routing occurs at Layer 3. This distinction means that routing and switching use different information in the process of moving data from source to destination.

The relationship between switching and routing parallels that of local and long distance telephone calls. When a telephone call is made to another local number (a number with the same area code), a local switch handles the call. However, the local switch cannot keep track of all the telephone numbers in the world—only its own local numbers. When the switch receives a request for a call outside its area, it switches the call to a higher-level switch that recognizes area codes. The higher-level switch switches the call so that it eventually gets to the local switch for the area code dialed.

The router performs a function similar to that of the higher-level switch in the telephone network, as shown in Figure 10-13. Layer 2 switching takes place within the LAN, also called a *broadcast domain*. Layer 3 routing moves traffic between broadcast domains. This requires the hierarchical addressing scheme that a Layer 3 addressing scheme like IP provides. The Layer 2 switch cannot recognize the Layer 3 IP address—only local MAC addresses. When a host has data for a nonlocal IP address, it sends the frame to its default gateway, the router, by using the router's MAC address.

Figure 10-13 Layer 2 Switching and Layer 3 Routing

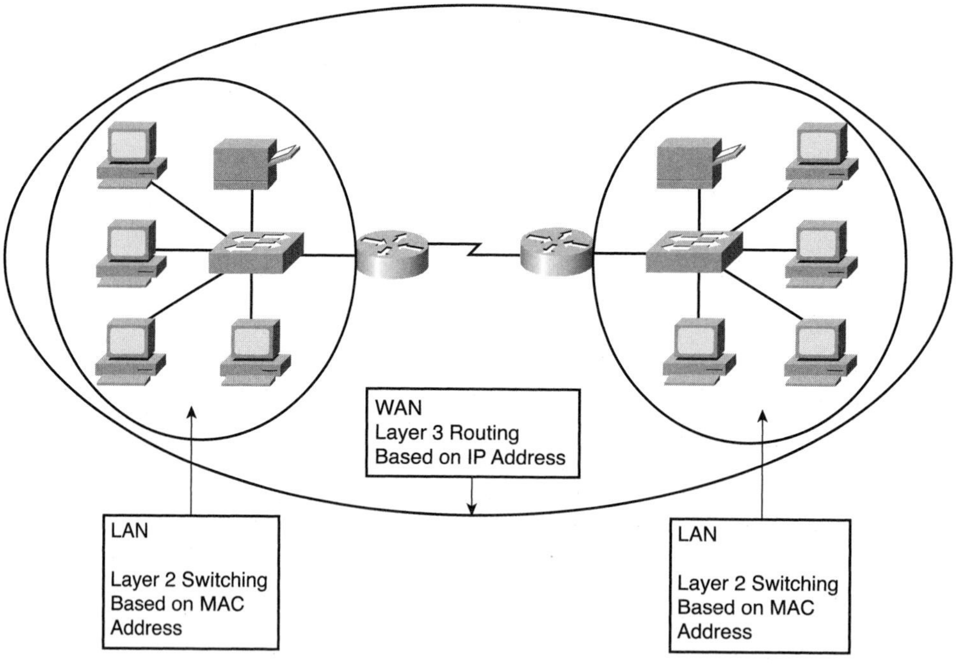

A Layer 2 switch interconnects segments belonging to the same logical network or *subnetwork*. If Host X needs to send a frame to another host on a different network or subnetwork, Host X sends the frame to the router that is also connected to the switch. Host X knows the router IP address because the Host IP configuration includes the IP address of the default gateway, but it does not know its MAC address. Host X learns the router's MAC address by using an Address Resolution Protocol (ARP) request, which translates IP addresses to MAC addresses. The switch forwards the frame to the router based on the router's destination MAC address. The router examines the packet's Layer 3 destination address to make the forwarding decision. The default gateway is the router that is on the same network or subnetwork as Host X.

Much like the way a Layer 2 switch keeps a table of known MAC addresses, the router keeps a table of IP network addresses called a *routing table*, as shown in Figure 10-14. Each computer and router Ethernet interface maintains an ARP table for Layer 2 communication. The ARP table is effective only for the broadcast domain that it is connected to. The router also maintains a routing table that allows it to route data outside the broadcast domains. Each ARP table contains the IP-MAC address pair. (The MAC address in Figure 10-14 is represented by the acronym MAC because the actual addresses are too long to fit in the figure.) The routing tables show how the route was learned—in this case, directly connected (C) and RIP (R)— the network IP address for reachable networks, the hop count to get those networks, and the interface the data must be sent out to get to the destination network.

The difference between these two types of addresses is that the MAC address is not organized in any particular way. This is OK, though, because any individual network segment does not have a large number of hosts, so it is manageable. If the IP network addresses were treated the same way, the Internet simply would not work. There would be no way to organize all the addresses and the directions on how to get to them (hierarchically or otherwise).

Organizing IP addresses hierarchically enables you to group addresses to be treated as a single unit until you need to locate an individual host. A way to understand this is to think of a library that contains only millions of individual pages in a large pile. This material is useless, because it is impossible to locate an individual document. If the pages were organized into books, and each page were individually identified, and if the books were listed in an index, it would be much easier to find and use the data.

Another difference between switched and routed networks is that Layer 2 switched networks do not block Layer 3 broadcasts. As a result, they can be swamped by broadcast storms. Routers normally block broadcasts so that a broadcast storm affects only the broadcast domain it originated on. Routers also provide higher security and bandwidth control than Layer 2 switches because they block broadcasts.

Figure 10-14 Router ARP Tables

Table 10-1 compares routers and switches.

Table 10-1 Router and Switch Feature Comparison

Feature	Router	Switch
Speed	Slower	Faster
OSI layer	Layer 3	Layer 2
Addressing used	IP	MAC
Broadcasts	Blocks	Forwards
Security	Higher	Lower
Segment networks	Segment broadcast domains	Segment collision domains

Interactive Media Activity   Drag and Drop: Routing Versus Switching

After completing this activity, you will be able to identify the differences between routing and switching.

Routed Versus Routing

Two categories of protocols exist at the network layer: routed and routing (see Figure 10-15). Routed protocols transport data across a network, and routing protocols allow routers to properly direct the data from one location to another.

Protocols that transfer data from one host to another across a router are routed or routable protocols.

A routed protocol operates as shown in Figure 10-16:

- It includes any network protocol suite that provides enough information in its network layer address to allow a router to forward it to the next device and ultimately to its destination.

- It defines the format and use of the fields within a packet. Packets generally are conveyed from end system to end system.

IP and IPX are examples of routed protocols. Other examples include DECnet, AppleTalk, Banyan VINES, and Xerox Network Systems (XNS).

Routers use routing protocols to exchange routing tables and share routing information. In other words, *routing* protocols let routers route *routed* protocols after a path has been determined.

Figure 10-15 Routed and Routing Protocols

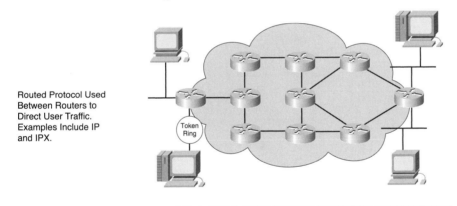

Routed Protocol Used
Between Routers to
Direct User Traffic.
Examples Include IP
and IPX.

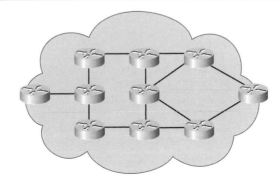

Routing Protocol Used
Between Routers to
Maintain Tables.
Examples Include RIP,
IGRP, and OSPF.

Figure 10-16 Routed Protocol

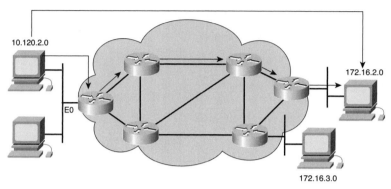

A routing protocol operates as shown in Figure 10-17:

- It provides processes for sharing routing information.

- It allows routers to communicate with other routers to update and maintain the routing tables.

Examples of routing protocols that support IP routed protocols include RIP, IGRP, OSPF, Border Gateway Protocol (BGP), and EIGRP.

Figure 10-17 Routing Protocol

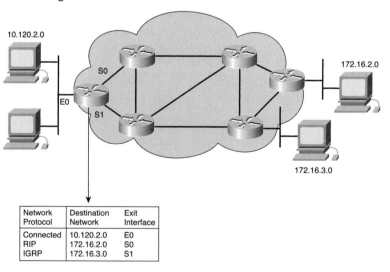

Network Protocol	Destination Network	Exit Interface
Connected	10.120.2.0	E0
RIP	172.16.2.0	S0
IGRP	172.16.3.0	S1

Path Determination

Path determination occurs at Layer 3 (the network layer). It lets a router evaluate the available paths to a destination and establish the preferred handling of a packet. Routing services use network topology information when evaluating network paths, as shown in Figure 10-18. Path determination is the process that a router uses to choose the next hop in a path toward a packet's ultimate destination. This process is also called *routing* the packet.

Figure 10-18 Choosing a Path

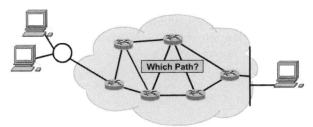

Path determination for a packet can be compared to a person driving a car from one side of a city to another. The driver has a map that shows the streets to take to get to the destination. The drive from one intersection to another is a *hop*. Similarly, a router uses a map that shows the available paths to a destination. Routers can also make their decisions based on the traffic density and the link's speed (bandwidth), just as a driver might choose a faster path (a highway) or use less-crowded back streets.

The decisions of a driver are influenced by factors such as traffic, the speed limit, the number of lanes, tolls, and whether a road is frequently closed. Sometimes, it's faster to take a longer route on a smaller, less-crowded back road instead of a highway with serious traffic. Similarly, routers can make decisions based on the load, bandwidth, delay, cost, and reliability of a network link. The following process determines the path for every packet that is routed:

- The destination address is obtained from the packet.

- The mask of the first entry in the routing table is applied to the destination address.

- The masked destination and the routing table entry are compared.

- If a match occurs, the packet is forwarded to the port that is associated with that table entry.

- If no match occurs, the next entry in the table is checked.

- If the packet does not match any entries in the table, the router checks to see if a default route has been set.

- If a default route has been set, the packet is forwarded to the associated port. A *default route* is a route that is configured by the network administrator as the route to use if no matches exist in the routing table.

- If there is no default route, the packet is discarded. A message is often sent back to the device that sent the data to indicate that the destination was unreachable.

More Information: Voice Gateway

Network Layer Addressing

A network address helps the router identify a path within the network cloud and also provides hierarchical or subnet information. The router uses the network address to identify the destination network of a packet within an internetwork. In addition to the network address, network protocols use some form of host, or node, address. For some network layer protocols, a network administrator assigns host addresses according to some predetermined network addressing plan. For other network layer protocols, assigning host addresses is partially or completely dynamic or automatic. Figure 10-19 shows three devices in Network 1 (two workstations and a router), each with its own unique host address. (The figure also shows that the router is connected to two other networks—networks 2 and 3.)

Figure 10-19 Network Addresses

Network	Host
1	1 2 3
2	1
3	1

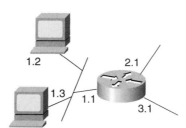

Logical addressing occurs at the network layer. Recall the analogy that compares network addresses to telephone numbers. The first portions of a phone number are the area code and the first three digits. The last four digits of a phone number tell the phone company equipment which specific phone to ring. This is similar to the function of the host portion of an address. The host portion tells the router the specific device to which it should deliver a packet.

Without network layer addressing, routing cannot take place. Routers require network addresses to ensure proper delivery of packets. Without some hierarchical addressing structure, packets could not travel across an internetwork. Similarly, without some hierarchical structure to telephone numbers, postal addresses, or transportation systems, there would be no smooth delivery of goods and services.

More Information: Voice Gateway (Continued)

A *MAC address* can be compared to your name, and a network layer address can be compared to your mailing address (network and host address). For example, if you were to move to another town, your name would remain unchanged, but your mailing address would indicate your new location. Network devices (routers as well as individual computers) have both a MAC address and a protocol (network layer) address. When you move a computer to a different network, the computer maintains the same MAC address, but you must assign it a new network layer address.

The Communication Path

The function of the network layer is to find the best path through the network. To be truly practical, a network must consistently represent the paths available between routers. As Figure 10-20 shows, each line between the routers has a number that the routers use as a network address. These addresses must convey information that can be used by a routing process. This means that an address must have information about the path of media connections that the routing process uses to pass packets from a source toward a destination.

Figure 10-20 Network Media Connections

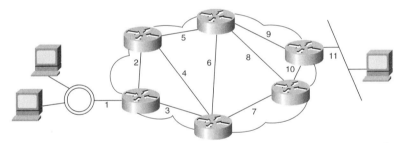

Using these addresses, the network layer can provide a relay connection that interconnects independent networks. The consistency of Layer 3 addresses across the entire internetwork also improves the use of bandwidth by preventing unnecessary broadcasts. *Broadcasts* invoke unnecessary process overhead and waste capacity on any devices or links that do not need to receive the broadcast. By using consistent end-to-end addressing to represent the path of media connections, the network layer can find a path to the destination without unnecessarily burdening the devices or links on the internetwork with broadcasts.

Routing Tables

To aid in the process of path determination, routing protocols build and maintain routing tables, which contain route information, as shown in Figure 10-21. Route information varies, depending on the routing protocol used. Routing protocols fill routing tables with a variety of information.

Figure 10-21 Routing Tables

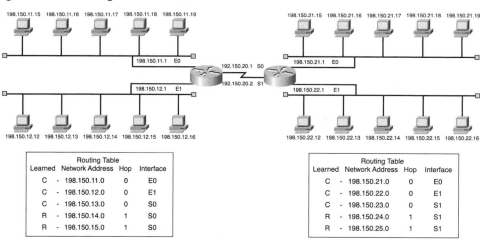

Routers keep track of important information in their routing tables:

- **Protocol type**—The type of routing protocol that created the routing table entry.

- **Destination/next-hop associations**—Tells a router that a particular destination is either directly connected to the router or that it can be reached via another router called the *next hop* on the way to the final destination. When a router receives an incoming packet, it checks the destination address and attempts to match it with a routing table entry.

- **Routing metrics**—Different routing protocols use different routing metrics. Routing metrics are used to determine a route's desirability. For example, RIP uses **hop count** as its routing metric. IGRP uses bandwidth, load, delay, and reliability to create a composite metric value. This is covered in more depth in CCNA2.

- **Outbound interface**—The interface that the data must be sent out to reach the final destination.

Routers communicate with one another to maintain their routing tables through the transmission of routing update messages. Depending on the particular routing protocol, routing update messages can be sent periodically or only when there is a change in the network topology. The routing protocol also determines whether just the changed routes or the entire routing table is sent in the routing update. By analyzing the routing updates from the neighboring routers, a router can build and maintain its routing table.

Routing Algorithms and Metrics

Routing protocols often have one or more of the following design goals:

- **Optimization**—Optimization describes the capability of the routing protocol/algorithm to select the best route, depending on metrics and metric weightings used in the calculation. For example, one algorithm might use hop count and delay for its metric but might weigh delay more heavily in the calculation.

- **Simplicity and low overhead**—Ideally, efficient routing algorithm functionality is achieved if the routers have minimum CPU and memory overhead. This is important so that the network can scale to large proportions, such as the Internet.

- **Robustness and stability**—A routing algorithm should perform correctly in the face of unusual or unforeseen circumstances, such as hardware failures, high load conditions, and implementation errors.

- **Rapid convergence**—Convergence is the process of all routers agreeing on routes. When a network event causes changes in router availability, recalculations are needed to reestablish network connectivity. Routing algorithms that converge slowly can cause data to not be delivered.

- **Flexibility**—A routing algorithm should quickly adapt to a variety of network changes. These changes include router availability, changes in bandwidth, queue size, and network delay.

- **Scalability**—Some routing protocols are better designed for scalability than others. It is important to keep in mind that if the network is intended to grow (or even if this option is to be left open), a routing protocol such as EIGRP rather than RIP should be used.

When a routing *algorithm* updates a routing table, its primary objective is to determine the best information to include in the table. Routing algorithms use different metrics to determine the best route. Each routing algorithm interprets what is best in its own way. The routing algorithm generates a number, called the metric value, for each path through the network. Sophisticated routing algorithms can base route selection on multiple metrics, combining them in a single composite metric, as shown in Figure 10-22. Typically, the smaller the metric, the better the path.

Figure 10-22 Routing Metrics

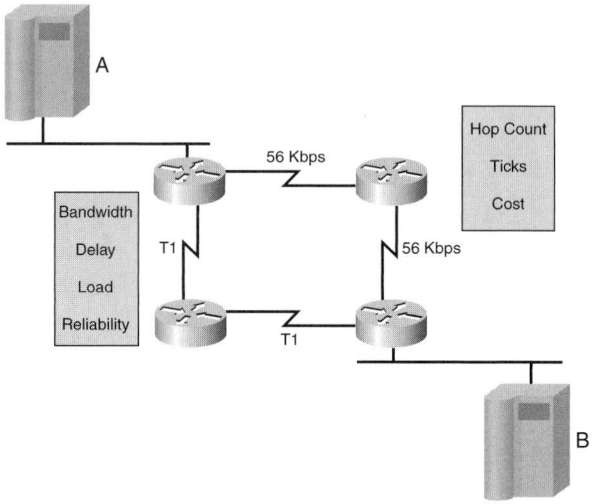

Metrics can be based on a single characteristic of a path or can be calculated based on several characteristics. The metrics that are most commonly used by routing protocols are as follows:

- **Bandwidth**—A link's data capacity. (Normally, a 10-Mbps Ethernet link is preferable to a 64-kbps leased line.)

- **Delay**—The length of time required to move a packet along each link from source to destination. Delay depends on the bandwidth of intermediate links, port queues at each router, network congestion, and physical distance.

- **Load**—The amount of activity on a network resource such as a router or link.

- **Reliability**—Usually refers to the error rate of each network link.

- **Hop count**—The number of routers that a packet must travel through before reaching its destination. Whenever data goes through a router, this is one hop. A path that has a hop count of 4 indicates that data traveling along that path passes through four routers before reaching its final destination. If there are multiple paths to a destination, the router chooses the path with the fewest hops.

- **Cost**—An arbitrary value, usually based on bandwidth, monetary expense, or another measurement, that is assigned by a network administrator.

IGP and EGP

Routers use routing protocols to exchange routing information. In other words, routing protocols determine how routed protocols are routed. Two families of routing protocols are the *Interior Gateway Protocols (IGPs)* and the *Exterior Gateway Protocols (EGPs)*, as shown in

Figure 10-23. These families are classified based on how they operate with regard to autonomous systems.

Figure 10-23 IGPs and EGPs

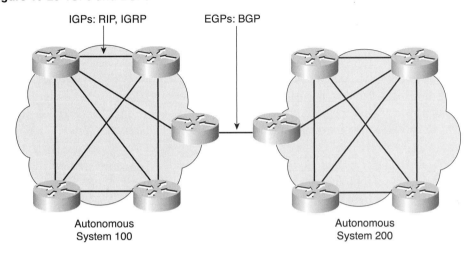

An *autonomous system* is a network or set of networks that are under the administrative control of a single entity, such as the cisco.com domain. An autonomous system consists of routers that present a consistent view of routing to the external world. The Internet Assigned Numbers Authority (IANA) allocates autonomous system numbers to the regional registries. These registries are ARIN (hostmaster@arin.net) for the Americas, the Caribbean, and Africa; RIPE-NCC (ncc@ripe.net) for Europe; and AP-NIC (admin@apnic.net) for the Asia Pacific region. This autonomous system is a 16-bit number. A routing protocol such as BGP requires that you specify this unique, assigned autonomous system number in your configuration.

IGPs route data within an autonomous system. Here are some examples of IGPs:

- Routing Information Protocol (RIP) and RIP V2
- Interior Gateway Routing Protocol (IGRP)
- Enhanced IGRP (EIGRP)
- Open Shortest Path First (OSPF)
- Intermediate System-to-Intermediate System (IS-IS) protocol

EGPs route data between autonomous systems. BGP is the most pervasive example of an EGP.

Link-State and Distance Vector

Routing protocols can be classified in many different ways, such as IGPs or EGPs. Another classification that describes routing protocols is distance vector or link-state. Whereas IGP and EGP describe the physical relationships of routers, the distance vector and link-state categories describe how routers interact with each other in terms of routing updates.

Distance Vector Protocols

The *distance vector routing* approach determines the direction (vector) and distance (hop count) to any link in the internetwork. Distance vector algorithms periodically (such as every 30 seconds) send all or some portion of their routing table to their adjacent neighbors. Routers running a distance vector routing protocol send periodic updates even if there are no changes in the network. By receiving a neighbor's routing table, a router can verify all the known routes and make changes to the local routing table based on updated information received from the neighboring router. This process is called "routing by rumor" because the understanding that a router has of the network is based on the neighbor's perspective of the network topology. Distance vector protocols use the Bellman-Ford Algorithm to calculate the best paths.

Examples of distance vector protocols include the following:

- *Routing Information Protocol (RIP)*—The most common IGP in the Internet, RIP uses hop count as its routing metric.

- *Interior Gateway Routing Protocol (IGRP)*—Cisco developed this IGP to address the issues associated with routing in large, heterogeneous networks.

- *Enhanced Interior Gateway Routing Protocol (EIGRP)*—Advanced version of IGRP developed by Cisco. Provides superior convergence properties and operating efficiency, and combines the advantages of link-state protocols with those of distance vector protocols.

Link-State Protocols

Link-state routing protocols were designed to overcome the limitations of distance vector routing protocols. Link-state routing protocols respond quickly to network changes, send trigger updates only when a network change has occurred, and send periodic updates (called link-state refreshes) at long time intervals, such as every 30 minutes.

When a link changes state, the device that detected the change creates a link-state advertisement (LSA) concerning that link (route), and that LSA is propagated to all neighboring devices. Each routing device takes a copy of the LSA, updates its link-state (topological) database, and forwards the LSA to all neighboring devices. This flooding of the LSA is required to ensure that all routing devices update their databases before creating an updated routing table that reflects the new topology, as shown in Figure 10-24.

Figure 10-24 Link-State Routing Protocols

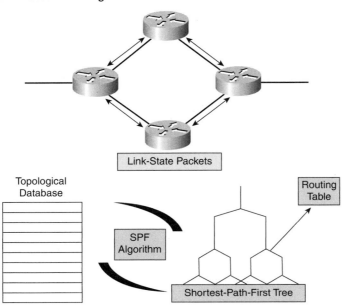

The link-state database is used to calculate the best paths through the network. Link-state routers find the best paths to destinations by applying the Dijkstra Shortest Path First (SPF) algorithm against the link-state database to build the SPF tree. The best (shortest) paths are then selected from the shortest-path-first tree and are placed in the routing table.

Examples of link-state protocols are OSPF and IS-IS, the characteristics for which are illustrated by Figure 10-25.

Figure 10-25 Comparing Distance Vector and Link-State Routing Protocols: RIP, IS-IS, and OSPF

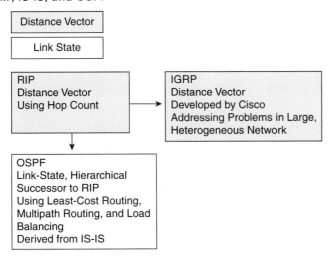

Interactive Media Activity Checkbox: Link-State and Distance Vector Routing Protocols

After completing this activity, you will be able to identify the difference between link-state and distance vector routing protocols.

Routing Protocols

The following sections describe the metrics, network usability, and other significant characteristics of the most commonly used routing protocols.

RIP

RIP uses hop count to determine the direction and distance to any link in the internetwork, as shown in Figure 10-26. If there are multiple paths to a destination, RIP selects the path with the fewest hops. However, because hop count is the only routing metric RIP uses, it does not necessarily select the fastest path to a destination. RIP-1 uses only classful routing. This means that all devices in the network must use the same subnet mask, because RIP-1 does not include the subnet information with the routing update.

RIP-2 provides what is called *prefix routing* and sends subnet mask information with the route updates. This supports the use of classless routing. With classless routing protocols, different subnets within the same network can have different subnet masks. The use of different subnet masks within the same network is called variable-length subnet masking (VLSM).

Figure 10-26 RIP Uses Hop Count as Its Metric

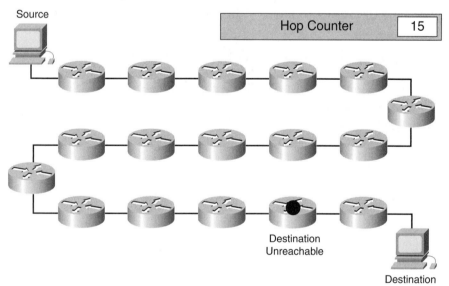

IGRP

IGRP is a distance vector routing protocol developed by Cisco specifically to address problems associated with routing in large networks that are beyond the scope of protocols such as RIP. IGRP can select the fastest path based on the delay, bandwidth, load, and reliability. By default, IGRP uses bandwidth and delay metrics only and uses a 24-bit metric. IGRP also has a much higher maximum hop-count limit than RIP to allow the network to scale. IGRP uses only classful routing.

EIGRP

Like IGRP, EIGRP is a proprietary Cisco protocol. EIGRP is an advanced version of IGRP and uses a 32-bit metric. Specifically, EIGRP provides superior operating efficiency such as faster convergence and lower-overhead bandwidth. It is an advanced distance vector protocol. EIGRP also uses some of the link-state protocol functions. Hence, the term *hybrid* is also used to describe EIGRP.

OSPF

OSPF is a link-state routing protocol. The Internet Engineering Task Force (IETF) developed OSPF in 1988. The most recent version, OSPF Version 2, is described in RFC 2328. OSPF is an IGP, which means that it distributes routing information between routers belonging to the same autonomous system. OSPF was written to address the needs of large, scalable internetworks that RIP could not.

IS-IS

Intermediate System-to-Intermediate System (IS-IS) is the dynamic link-state routing protocol for the OSI *protocol stack*. As such, it distributes routing information for routing Connectionless Network Protocol (CLNP) data for the ISO Connectionless Network Service (CLNS) environment. Integrated IS-IS is an implementation of the IS-IS protocol for routing multiple network protocols. Integrated IS-IS tags CLNP routes with information about IP networks and subnets. It provides an alternative to OSPF in the IP world, mixing ISO CLNS and IP routing in one protocol. It can be used purely for IP routing, purely for ISO routing, or for a combination of the two.

> **NOTE**
>
> CLNP refers to the OSI network layer protocol that does not require a circuit to be established before data is transmitted.

BGP

Border Gateway Protocol (BGP) is an example of an EGP. BGP exchanges routing information between autonomous systems while guaranteeing loop-free path selection. It is the principal route advertising protocol used by major companies and ISPs on the Internet. BGP-4 is the first version of BGP that supports *classless interdomain routing (CIDR)* and route aggregation. Unlike common IGPs such as RIP, OSPF, and EIGRP, BGP does not use metrics such as hop count or bandwidth or delay. Instead, BGP makes routing decisions based on network policies or rules using various BGP path attributes.

Lab 10.2.9   Small Router Purchase

The purpose of this lab is to introduce the variety and prices of network components in the market. This lab looks specifically at small routers used by telecommuters when working from home.

The Mechanics of Subnetting

The Internet's original two-level hierarchy assumed that each site would have only a single network. Therefore, each site would need only a single connection to the Internet. Initially, these were safe assumptions. Over time, however, network computing matured and expanded. By 1985, it was no longer safe to assume that an organization would have only a single network or that it would be satisfied with a single connection to the Internet.

As sites began to develop multiple networks, it became obvious to the IETF that a mechanism was needed to differentiate among the multiple logical networks that were emerging as subsets of the Internet's second tier. Otherwise, there could be no efficient way to route data to specific end systems in sites with multiple networks.

Classes of Network IP Addresses

Classes of IP addresses offer a range from 256 to 16.8 million hosts, as discussed previously. To efficiently manage a limited supply of IP addresses, all classes can be subdivided into smaller subnetworks. Figure 10-27 provides an overview of the division between networks and hosts.

Figure 10-27 Class A–D IP Addresses: Network and Host Portions

Class A	Network	Host		
Octet	1	2	3	4

Class B	Network		Host	
Octet	1	2	3	4

Class C	Network			Host
Octet	1	2	3	4

Class D	Host			
Octet	1	2	3	4

Introduction to and Reasons for Subnetting

To create the subnetwork structure, host bits must be reassigned as subnetwork bits by dividing the host *octet*(s). This is often called *borrowing* bits, but a more accurate term would be *lending* bits. The starting point for this process is always the leftmost host bit, dependent on the IP class.

In addition to the need for manageability, subnetworking lets the network administrator provide broadcast containment and low-level security on the LAN. Security, through subnetting on the LAN, is provided because access to other subnets is provided by a router. As you learn in Chapter 11, "Access Control Lists," of the CCNA 2 portion of this book, the router can be configured to permit or deny access to a subnet based on varied criteria, thereby providing security. Some owners of Class A and Class B networks have also discovered that subnetting creates a revenue source for the organization through the leasing or sale of previously unused IP addresses.

In such multiple-network environments, each subnetwork is connected to the Internet via a common point—a router, as shown in Figure 10-28. The details of the internal network environment are inconsequential to the Internet. They comprise a private network that is (or should be) capable of delivering its own datagrams. Therefore, the Internet must concern itself only with how to reach that network's gateway router to the Internet. Inside the private network, the host portion of the IP address can be subdivided to create subnetworks.

Because the ***subnet address*** is taken from the host number portion of Class A, Class B, and Class C addresses, it is assigned locally, usually by the network administrator. Also, like the other portions of IP addresses, each subnet address must be unique within its scope, as shown in Figure 10-29.

Figure 10-28 Subnetworks

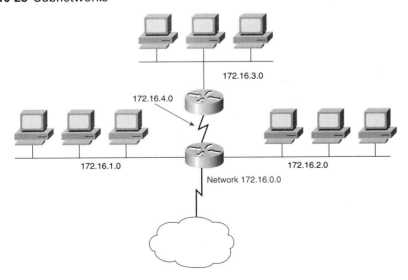

Figure 10-29 Subnet Address

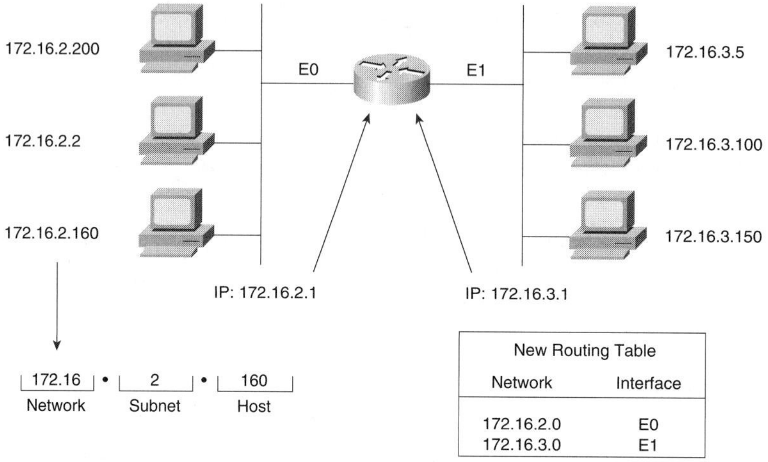

Subnetting is frequently necessary when LANs are to be interconnected to form a WAN. For example, if you want to connect two LANs in geographically separate locations, you can assign a unique subnet to each of the LANs and to the WAN link between them. Two routers can then be used (one on each LAN) to route packets between the LANs (subnets).

Another primary reason for using subnets is to reduce the size of a broadcast domain. Broadcasts are sent to all hosts on a network or subnetwork. When broadcast traffic begins to consume too much of the available bandwidth, network administrators might choose to reduce the size of the broadcast domain.

The outside world sees a LAN as a single network with no knowledge of the internal network structure. This view of the network keeps the routing tables small and efficient. Given a local node address of 192.168.10.14, the world outside the LAN sees only the advertised major network number of 192.168.10.0. The reason for this is that the local address of 192.168.10.14 is valid only within the LAN 192.168.10.0. It cannot function anywhere else.

Subnet addresses include the Class A, Class B, and Class C network portion, plus a subnet field and a host field. These fields are created from the original host portion of the major IP address by assigning bits from the host portion to the original network portion of the address. The ability to divide the original host portion of the address into the new subnet and host fields provides addressing flexibility for the network administrator, as shown in Figures 10-30, 10-31, and 10-32. This simply means that the administrator has more options available when it comes to assigning an IP addressing scheme both initially and when it is time to expand the network.

Figure 10-30 Subdividing the Host Octet of a Class C Address

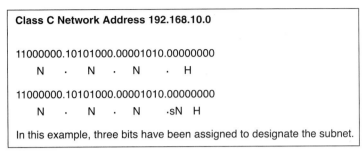

Figure 10-31 Subdividing the Host Octets of a Class B Address

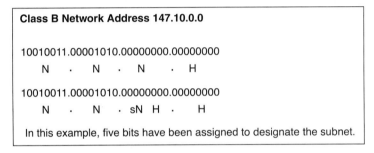

Figure 10-32 Subdividing the Host Octets of a Class A Address

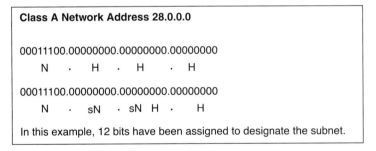

Establishing the Subnet Mask Address

Selecting the number of bits to use in the subnet process depends on the required maximum number of hosts per subnet. To calculate the result of using host bits to create subnetworks, you must understand some basic binary math and the position value of the bits in each octet, as shown in Table 10-2.

Table 10-2 Subnetting Chart: Bit Position and Value

Bit	1	2	3	4	5	6	7	8
Value	128	64	32	16	8	4	2	1

Regardless of the IP address class, the last 2 bits in the last octet can never be assigned to the subnetwork. These are called the *last two significant bits*. Using all the available bits except these two results in subnets with only two usable hosts. This is a practical address conservation method for addressing serial router links. However, for a working LAN, this would result in prohibitive equipment costs.

To create the **subnet mask** that gives the router the information required to compute which subnet a particular host resides on, select the column with the number of bits and refer to the mask number above it, as shown later in Figure 10-36. This number is calculated by adding the position value of the bits used. If 3 bits were used, the mask for a Class C address would be 255.255.255.224, as shown in Table 10-3. This mask can also be illustrated in the slash format as /27. The number following the slash is the total number of bits in the network portion and subnet mask.

Table 10-3 Subnetting Chart: Subnet Mask Identifier (Two Formats)

Slash Format	/25	/26	/27	/28	/29	/30	—	—
Mask	128	192	224	240	248	252	254	255
Bit	1	2	3	4	5	6	7	8
Value	128	64	32	16	8	4	2	1

To determine the number of bits to be used, the network designer needs to calculate how many hosts the largest subnetwork requires and the number of subnetworks. For example, assume that this requirement is 30 hosts and five subnetworks. To calculate how many bits to reassign, consult the Usable Hosts row in Table 10-4. For example, for 30 usable hosts, 3 bits are required. This also creates six usable subnetworks, which satisfies the requirements of this scheme. Again, the difference between usable and total hosts is a result of using the first available address as the ID and the last available address as the broadcast for each subnetwork. Classful routing does not provide the capability to use these subnetworks, whereas classless routing recovers many of these "lost" addresses, as shown in Table 10-4. This table illustrates the loss of subnets and hosts when you don't use a classless routing protocol.

Table 10-4 Subnetting Chart: Subnets and Hosts

Slash Format	/25	/26	/27	/28	/29	/30	—	—
Mask	128	192	224	240	248	252	254	255
Bit	1	2	3	4	5	6	7	8
Value	128	64	32	16	8	4	2	1
Total Subnets		4	8	16	32	64		
Usable Subnets		2	6	14	30	62		
Total Hosts		64	32	16	8	4		
Usable Hosts		62	30	14	6	2		

An alternative way to compute the subnet mask and the number of networks is to use the following formulae:

The number of usable subnets equals 2 to the power of the assigned subnet bits minus 2:

$(2^{\text{power of bits assigned}}) - 2 = \text{usable subnets}$

For example, $2^3 - 2 = 6$

The number of usable hosts equals 2 to the power of the bits remaining minus 2:

$(2^{\text{power of bits remaining}}) - 2 = \text{usable hosts}$

For example, $2^5 - 2 = 30$

Applying the Subnet Mask

To create subnets, you must extend the routing portion of the address. The Internet "knows" your network as a whole, identified by the Class A, B, or C address, which defines 8, 16, or 24 routing bits (the network number). The subnet field represents additional routing bits so that the routers within your organization can recognize different locations, or subnets, within the whole network.

Subnet masks use the same format as IP addresses. In other words, each subnet mask is 32 bits long and is divided into four octets. Subnet masks have all 1s in the network and subnetwork portion and all 0s in the host portion. By default, if no bits are borrowed, the subnet mask for a Class B network is 255.255.0.0. However, if 8 bits were borrowed, the subnet mask for the same Class B network would be 255.255.255.0, as shown in Figures 10-33 and 10-34. However, because there are two octets in the host field of a Class B network, up to 14 bits can be borrowed to create subnetworks. A Class C network has only one octet in the host field. Therefore, only up to 6 bits can be borrowed in Class C networks to create subnetworks.

Figure 10-33 Network and Host Addresses

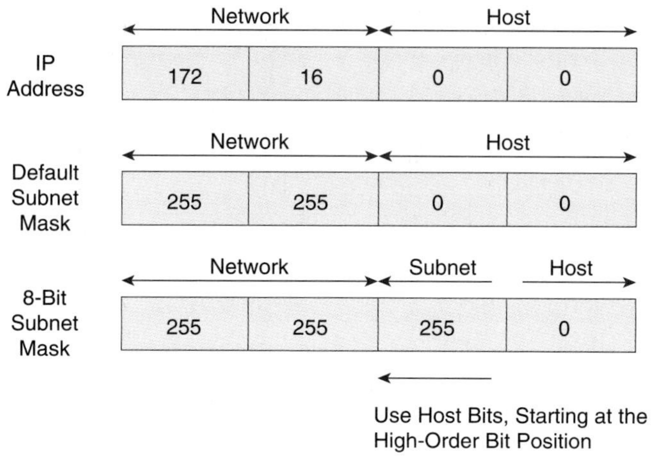

	Network		Host	
IP Address	172	16	0	0

	Network		Host	
Default Subnet Mask	255	255	0	0

	Network		Subnet	Host
8-Bit Subnet Mask	255	255	255	0

Use Host Bits, Starting at the High-Order Bit Position

Figure 10-34 Binary Conversion Chart

128	64	32	16	8	4	2	1		
1	0	0	0	0	0	0	0	=	128
1	1	0	0	0	0	0	0	=	192
1	1	1	0	0	0	0	0	=	224
1	1	1	1	0	0	0	0	=	240
1	1	1	1	1	0	0	0	=	248
1	1	1	1	1	1	0	0	=	252
1	1	1	1	1	1	1	0	=	254
1	1	1	1	1	1	1	1	=	255

The subnet field always immediately follows the network number. That is, the borrowed bits must be the first *n* bits of the default host field, where *n* is the desired size of the new subnet field, as shown in Figure 10-35. The subnet mask is the tool used by the router to determine which bits are routing bits and which bits are host bits.

Figure 10-35 Subnetting a Class B Address

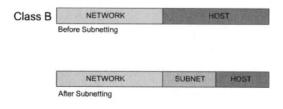

More Information: Determining Subnet Mask Size

Again, subnet masks contain all 1s in the network bit positions (determined by the address class) as well as the subnet bit positions, and they contain all 0s in the remaining bit positions, designating them as the host portion of an address.

By default, if you borrow no bits, the subnet mask for a Class B network would be 255.255.0.0, which is the dotted-decimal equivalent of 1s in the 16 bits corresponding to the Class B network number and 0s in the other 16 bits.

If 8 bits were borrowed for the subnet field, the subnet mask would include 8 additional 1 bits and would become 255.255.255.0. For example, if the subnet mask 255.255.255.0 were associated with the Class B address 130.5.2.144 (8 bits borrowed for subnetting), the router would know to route this packet to subnet 130.5.2.0 rather than just to network 130.5.0.0, as shown in Figure 10-36.

Figure 10-36 Subnet Masking: Class B Address

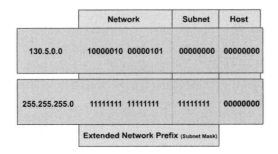

Another example is the Class C address 197.15.22.131 with a subnet mask of 255.255.255.224. With a value of 224 in the final octet (11100000 in binary), the 24-bit Class C network portion has been extended by 3 bits to make the total 27 bits. The 131 in the last octet presents the third usable host address in the subnet 197.15.22.128, as shown in Figure 10-37. The routers in the Internet (that don't know the subnet mask) only worry about routing to the Class C network 197.15.22.0. The routers inside that network, knowing the subnet mask, look at 27 bits to make a routing decision.

Figure 10-37 Subnet Masking: Class C Address

11000101	00001111	00010110	10000011
Network Field		Subnetwork Field	Host Field

> **More Information: Determining Subnet Mask Size (Continued)**
>
> **Computing the Subnet Mask and IP Address**
>
> Whenever you borrow bits from the host field, it is important to note the number of additional subnets that are being created each time you borrow one more bit. You have already learned that you cannot borrow only 1 bit; the fewest you can borrow is 2. Borrowing 2 bits creates four possible subnets (2 * 2) (but you must remember that there are two reserved/unusable subnets). Each time you borrow another bit from the host field, the number of subnets created increases by a power of 2. Eight possible subnets are created by borrowing 3 bits (2 * 2 * 2). Sixteen possible subnets are created by borrowing 4 bits (2 * 2 * 2 * 2). From these examples and from the binary conversion chart that was shown in Figure 10-34, it is easy to see that each time you borrow another bit from the host field, the number of possible subnets doubles.
>
> **Computing Hosts Per Subnetwork**
>
> Each time you borrow 1 bit from a host field, there is 1 less bit remaining that can be used for host numbers. Specifically, each time you borrow another bit from the host field, the number of host addresses that you can assign decreases by a power of 2 (gets cut in half).
>
> To understand how this works, consider a Class C network address. If there is no subnet mask, all 8 bits in the last octet are used for the host field. Therefore, 256 (2^8) possible addresses are available to assign to hosts (254 usable addresses after you subtract the two you know you can't use). Now, imagine that this Class C network is divided into subnets. If you borrow 2 bits from the default 8-bit host field, the host field decreases in size to 6 bits. If you wrote out all the possible combinations of 0s and 1s that could occur in the remaining 6 bits, you would discover that the total number of possible hosts that could be assigned in each subnet would be reduced to 64 (2^6). The number of usable host numbers would be reduced to 62.
>
> In the same Class C network, if you borrow 3 bits, the size of the host field decreases to 5 bits, and the total number of hosts you can assign to each subnet is reduced to 32 (2^5). The number of usable host numbers decreases to 30.
>
> The number of possible host addresses that can be assigned to a subnet is related to the number of subnets that have been created. In a Class C network, for example, if a subnet mask of 255.255.255.224 has been applied, 3 bits (224 in decimal equals 11100000 in binary) are borrowed from the host field. Six usable subnets are created (8 – 2), each having 30 (32 – 2) usable host addresses.

Subnetting Class A and B Networks

The Class A and B subnetting procedure is identical to the process for Class C, except there might be significantly more bits involved. The available bits for assignment to the subnet field in a Class A address are 22 bits, while a Class B address has 14 bits, as shown in Figure 10-38 and Figure 10-39.

Assigning 12 bits of a Class B address to the subnet field creates a subnet mask of 255.255.255.240 or /28. All 8 bits were assigned in the third octet, resulting in 255, which is the total value of all 8 bits. Four bits were assigned in the fourth octet, resulting in 240. Recall that the slash mask is the sum total of all the bits assigned to the subnet field plus the fixed network bits.

Assigning 20 bits of a Class A address to the subnet field creates a subnet mask of 255.255.255.240 (or /28). All 8 bits of the second and third octets were assigned to the subnet field and 4 bits from the fourth octet.

In this situation, it is apparent that the subnet mask for the Class A and Class B addresses appear identical. Unless the mask is related to a network address, it is not possible to decipher how many bits were assigned to the subnet field.

Whichever class of address needs to be subnetted, the following rules are the same:

Total subnets = 2 to the power of the bits borrowed

Total hosts= 2 to the power of the bits remaining

Usable subnets = 2 to the power of the bits borrowed **minus 2**

Usable hosts= 2 to the power of the bits remaining **minus 2**

Figure 10-38 Subdividing the Host Octets of a Class B Network

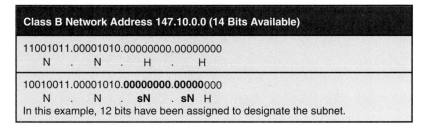

Class B Network Address 147.10.0.0 (14 Bits Available)

11001011.00001010.00000000.00000000
   N   .   N   .   H   .   H

10010011.00001010.**00000000.00000**000
   N   .   N   . **sN**   . **sN** H
In this example, 12 bits have been assigned to designate the subnet.

Figure 10-39 Subdividing the Host Octets of a Class A Network

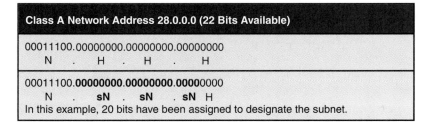

Class A Network Address 28.0.0.0 (22 Bits Available)

00011100.00000000.00000000.00000000
   N   .   H   .   H   .   H

00011100.**00000000.00000000.00000**000
   N   . **sN** . **sN** . **sN** H
In this example, 20 bits have been assigned to designate the subnet.

Lab 10.3.5a Basic Subnetting

This exercise provides a basic overview of the subnetting and the ANDing processes. Given a network address and requirements, you determine the subnet mask, the number of subnets and hosts per subnet, and the number of usable subnets and hosts. You also use the ANDing process to determine if a destination IP address is local or remote. Finally, you identify valid and invalid IP host addresses based on a given a network number and subnet mask.

Lab 10.3.5b Subnetting a Class A Network

In this lab, you analyze a Class A network address with the number of network bits specified to determine the subnet mask, number of subnets, hosts per subnet, and information about specific subnets.

Lab 10.3.5c Subnetting a Class B Network

In this lab, you analyze a Class B network address with the number of network bits specified to determine the subnet mask, number of subnets, hosts per subnet, and information about specific subnets.

Lab 10.3.5d Subnetting a Class C Network

In this lab, you analyze a Class C network address with the number of network bits specified to determine the subnet mask, number of subnets, hosts per subnet, and information about specific subnets.

Calculating the Resident Subnetwork Through ANDing

As previously mentioned, the network or subnet address has all 0s in the host portion. To route a data packet, the router must first determine the destination network/subnet address. To accomplish this, the router performs a logical AND using the destination host's IP address and the subnet mask for that network.

Imagine that you have a Class B network with the network number 172.16.0.0. After assessing your network's needs, you decide to borrow 8 bits to create subnets. As you learned earlier, when you borrow 8 bits with a Class B network, the subnet mask is 255.255.255.0, as shown in Figure 10-40.

Figure 10-40 8 Bits of Subnetting

	Network	Subnet	Host
IP Host Address 172.16.2.120	10101100 00010000	00000010	01111000
Subnet Mask 255.255.255.0 or /24	11111111 11111111	11111111	00000000
Subnet	10101100 00010000 172 16	00000010 2	00000000 0

Someone outside the network sends data to the IP address 172.16.2.120. To determine where to deliver the data, the router ANDs this address with the subnet mask.

When the two numbers are ANDed, the host portion of the result is always 0. What is left is the network number, including the subnet. Thus, the data is sent to subnet 172.16.2.0, and only the final router notices that the packet should be delivered to host 120 in that subnet.

Now, imagine that you have the same network, 172.16.0.0. This time, however, you decide to borrow only 7 bits for the subnet field. The binary subnet mask for this is 11111111.11111111.11111110.00000000. What is this in dotted-decimal notation?

Again, someone outside the network sends data to host 172.16.2.120. To determine where to send the data, the router again ANDs this address with the subnet mask. As before, when the two numbers are ANDed, the host portion of the result is 0. So what is different in this second example? Everything looks the same — at least, in decimal. The difference is in the number of subnets available and the number of hosts available per subnet. You can see this only by comparing the two different subnet masks, as shown in Figure 10-41.

Figure 10-41 Network Number Extended by 7 Bits

	Network	Subnet	Host
IP Host Address 172.16.2.120	10101100 00010000	00000010	01111000
Subnet Mask 255.255.254.0 or /23	11111111 11111111	11111110	00000000
Subnet	10101100 00010000 172 16	00000010 2	00000000 0

With 7 bits in the subnet field, there can be only 126 subnets. How many hosts can there be in each subnet? How long is the host field? With 9 bits for host numbers, there can be 510 hosts in each of those 126 subnets.

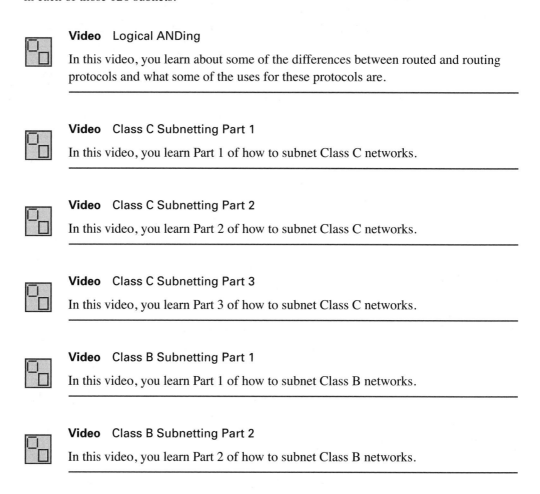

Video   Logical ANDing

In this video, you learn about some of the differences between routed and routing protocols and what some of the uses for these protocols are.

Video   Class C Subnetting Part 1

In this video, you learn Part 1 of how to subnet Class C networks.

Video   Class C Subnetting Part 2

In this video, you learn Part 2 of how to subnet Class C networks.

Video   Class C Subnetting Part 3

In this video, you learn Part 3 of how to subnet Class C networks.

Video   Class B Subnetting Part 1

In this video, you learn Part 1 of how to subnet Class B networks.

Video   Class B Subnetting Part 2

In this video, you learn Part 2 of how to subnet Class B networks.

Summary

In this chapter, you learned the following key points:

IP is referred to as a connectionless protocol because no dedicated circuit connection is established between source and destination prior to transmission. IP is referred to as unreliable because it does not verify that the data reached its destination. If delivery verification is required, a combination of IP and a connection-oriented transport protocol, such as TCP, is required. If verification of error-free delivery is not required, IP can be used in combination with a connectionless transport protocol, such as UDP. Connectionless network processes are often referred to as packet-switched processes. Connection-oriented network processes are often referred to as circuit-switched processes.

Protocols at each layer of the OSI model add control information to the data as it moves through the network. Because this information is added at the beginning and end of the data, this process is referred to as encapsulating the data. Layer 3 adds network, or logical, address information to the data and Layer 2 adds local, or physical, address information.

Layer 3 routing and Layer 2 switching direct and deliver data throughout the network. Initially, the router receives a Layer 2 frame with a Layer 3 packet encapsulated within it. The router must strip off the Layer 2 frame and examine the Layer 3 packet. If the packet is destined for local delivery, the router must encapsulate it in a new frame with the correct local MAC address as the destination. If the data must be forwarded to another broadcast domain, the router must encapsulate the Layer 3 packet in a new Layer 2 frame that contains the MAC address of the next internetworking device. In this way, a frame is transmitted through networks from broadcast domain to broadcast domain and is eventually delivered to the correct host.

Routed protocols, such as IP, transport data across a network. Routing protocols allow routers to choose the best path for data from source to destination. These routes can be either static routes, which are entered manually, or dynamic routes, which are learned through routing protocols. When dynamic routing protocols are used, routers use routing update messages to communicate with one another and maintain their routing tables. Routing algorithms use metrics to process routing updates and populate the routing table with the best routes. Convergence describes the speed at which all routers agree on a change in the network.

Interior gateway protocols (IGPs) are routing protocols that route data within autonomous systems, while exterior gateway protocols (EGPs) route data between autonomous systems. IGPs can be further categorized as either distance vector or link-state protocols. Routers using distance vector routing protocols periodically send routing updates consisting of all or part of their routing tables. Routers using link-state routing protocols use link-state advertisements (LSAs) to send updates only when topological changes occur in the network, and send complete routing tables much less frequently.

As a packet travels through the network, devices need a method of determining what portion of the IP address identifies the network and what portion identifies the host. A 32-bit address mask, called a subnet mask, indicates the bits of an IP address that are being used for the network address. The default subnet mask for a Class A address is 255.0.0.0. For a Class B address, the subnet mask always starts out as 255.255.0.0, and a Class C subnet mask begins as 255.255.255.0. The subnet mask can be used to split up an existing network into subnetworks, or subnets.

Subnetting reduces the size of broadcast domains, allows LAN segments in different geographical locations to communicate through routers, and provides improved security by separating one LAN segment from another.

Custom subnet masks use more bits than the default subnet masks by borrowing these bits from the host portion of the IP address. This creates a three-part address:

- Original network address

- Subnet address made up of the bits borrowed

- Host address made up of the bits left after borrowing some for subnets

Routers use subnet masks to determine the subnetwork portion of an address for an incoming packet. This process is referred to as logical ANDing.

To supplement all that you have learned in this chapter, refer to the chapter-specific Videos and Interactive Media Activities on the CD-ROM that accompanies this book.

Key Terms

algorithm   A well-defined rule or process for arriving at a solution to a problem. In networking, algorithms are commonly used to determine the best route for traffic from a particular source to a particular destination.

autonomous system   A network or set of networks that are under the administrative control of a single entity, such as the Cisco.com domain.

broadcast   A data packet that is sent to all nodes on a network. Broadcasts are identified by a broadcast address.

broadcast domain   A set of all devices that receive broadcast frames originating from any device within the set. Broadcast domains are typically bounded by routers (or, in a switched network, by VLANs) because routers do not forward broadcast frames.

classless interdomain routing (CIDR)   A technique supported by BGP and based on route aggregation. CIDR allows routers to group routes to cut down on the quantity of routing information carried by the core routers. With CIDR, several IP networks appear to networks outside the group as a single, larger entity.

collision domain   In Ethernet, the network area within which frames that have collided are propagated. Repeaters and hubs propagate collisions; LAN switches, bridges, and routers do not.

connectionless   Data transfer without the existence of a virtual circuit.

connection-oriented   Data transfer that requires the establishment of a virtual circuit.

datagram   A logical grouping of information sent as a network layer unit over a transmission medium without prior establishment of a virtual circuit. IP datagrams are the primary information units in the Internet. The terms *cell, frame, message, packet,* and *segment* also describe logical information groupings at various layers of the OSI reference model and in various technology circles.

distance vector routing   A class of routing algorithms that iterate on the number of hops in a route to find a shortest-path spanning tree. Distance vector routing algorithms call for each router to send its entire routing table in each update, but only to its neighbors. Distance vector routing algorithms can be prone to routing loops but are computationally simpler than link-state routing algorithms. Also called the Bellman- Ford routing algorithm.

Exterior Gateway Protocol (EGP)   An Internet protocol used to exchange routing information between autonomous systems. Border Gateway Protocol (BGP) is the most common EGP.

hop   The passage of a data packet from one network node, typically a router, to another.

hop count   A routing metric used to measure the distance between a source and a destination. RIP uses hop count as its sole metric.

Interior Gateway Protocol (IGP)   An Internet protocol used to exchange routing information within an autonomous system. Examples of common Internet IGPs are IGRP, OSPF, and RIP.

Interior Gateway Routing Protocol (IGRP)   An IGP developed by Cisco to address the problems associated with routing in large, heterogeneous networks.

Enhanced Interior Gateway Routing Protocol (EIGRP) — Advanced version of IGRP developed by Cisco. Provides superior convergence properties and operating efficiency, and combines the advantages of link state protocols with those of distance vector protocols.

IP address   A 32-bit address assigned to hosts using TCP/IP. An IP address belongs to one of five classes (A, B, C, D, or E) and is written as four octets separated by periods (that is, dotted-decimal format). Each address consists of a network number, an optional subnetwork number, and a host number. The network and subnetwork numbers together are used for routing, and the host number is used to address an individual host within the network or subnetwork. A subnet mask is used to extract network and subnetwork information from the IP address. CIDR provides a new way to represent IP addresses and subnet masks. Also called an *Internet address*.

link-state routing protocol   A routing algorithm in which each router broadcasts or multicasts information regarding the cost of reaching each of its neighbors to all nodes in the internetwork. Link-state algorithms create a consistent view of the network and are therefore not prone to routing loops. However, they achieve this at the cost of relatively greater computational difficultly and more widespread traffic than do distance vector routing algorithms.

MAC address   A standardized data link layer address that is required for every device that connects to a LAN. Other devices in the network use these addresses to locate specific devices in the network and to create and update routing tables and data structures. MAC addresses are 6 bytes long and are controlled by the IEEE. Also called a *hardware address, MAC-layer address,* or *physical address*.

NetBIOS Extended User Interface (NetBEUI)   An enhanced version of the NetBIOS protocol used by network operating systems such as LAN Manager, LAN Server, Windows for Workgroups, and Windows NT. NetBEUI formalizes the transport frame and adds functions. NetBEUI implements the OSI LLC2 protocol.

octet   8 bits. In networking, the term *octet* is often used (rather than *byte*) because some machine architectures employ bytes that are not 8 bits long.

packet   A logical grouping of information that includes a header containing control information and (usually) user data. Packets most often refer to network-layer units of data. The terms *datagram, frame, message,* and *segment* also describe logical information groupings at various layers of the OSI reference model and in various technology circles.

protocol stack   A set of related communications protocols that operate together and, as a group, address communication at some or all of the seven layers of the OSI reference model. Not every protocol stack covers each layer of the model, and often a single protocol in the stack addresses a number of layers at once. TCP/IP is a typical protocol stack.

routed protocol   Any network protocol that provides enough information in its network layer address to allow a packet to be forwarded from one host to another host based on the addressing scheme.

router   A network-layer device that uses one or more metrics to determine the optimal path along which network traffic should be forwarded. Routers forward packets from one network to another based on network-layer information contained in routing updates. Occasionally called a *gateway* (although this definition of *gateway* is becoming increasingly outdated).

Routing Information Protocol (RIP)   An IGP supplied with UNIX BSD systems. The most common IGP in the Internet. RIP uses hop count as a routing metric.

routing metric   A method by which a routing algorithm determines that one route is better than another. This information is stored in routing tables and is sent in routing updates. Metrics include bandwidth, communication cost, delay, hop count, load, MTU, path cost, and reliability. Sometimes simply called a *metric*.

routing protocol   A protocol that accomplishes routing through the implementation of a specific routing algorithm. Examples of routing protocols are IGRP, OSPF, and RIP.

routing table   A table stored in a router or some other internetworking device that keeps track of routes to particular network destinations and, in some cases, metrics associated with those routes.

subnet address   A portion of an IP address that is specified as the subnetwork by the subnet mask.

subnet mask   A 32-bit address mask used in IP to indicate the bits of an IP address that are used for the subnet address. Sometimes simply called a *mask*.

subnetwork   1. In IP networks, a network sharing a particular subnet address. Subnetworks are networks arbitrarily segmented by a network administrator to provide a multilevel, hierarchical routing structure while shielding the subnetwork from the addressing complexity of attached networks. Sometimes called a *subnet*. 2. In OSI networks, a collection of ESs and ISs under the control of a single administrative domain and using a single network access protocol.

Check Your Understanding

Complete all the review questions to test your understanding of the topics and concepts in this chapter. Answers are listed in Appendix B, "Check Your Understanding Answer Key."

1. How many bits are in an IP address?

   A. 16

   B. 32

   C. 64

   D. None of the above

2. What is the maximum value of each octet in an IP address?

   A. 28

   B. 255

   C. 256

   D. None of the above

3. The network number plays what part in an IP address?

   A. It specifies the network to which the host belongs.

   B. It specifies the identity of the computer on the network.

   C. It specifies which node on the subnetwork is being addressed.

   D. It specifies which networks the device can communicate with.

4. The host number plays what part in an IP address?

   A. It designates the identity of the computer on the network.

   B. It designates which node on the subnetwork is being addressed.

   C. It designates the network to which the host belongs.

   D. It designates which hosts the device can communicate with.

5. What is the decimal equivalent of the binary number 101101?

   A. 32

   B. 35

   C. 45

   D. 44

6. Convert the decimal number 192.5.34.11 to its binary form.

   A. 11000000.00000101.00100010.00001011

   B. 11000101.01010111.00011000.10111000

   C. 01001011.10010011.00111001.00110111

   D. 11000000.00001010.01000010.00001011

7. Convert the binary IP address 11000000.00000101.00100010.00001011 to its decimal form.

   A. 190.4.34.11

   B. 192.4.34.10

   C. 192.4.32.11

   D. None of the above

8. What portion of the Class B address 154.19.2.7 is the network address?

   A. 154

   B. 154.19

   C. 154.19.2

   D. 154.19.2.7

9. What portion of the IP address 129.219.51.18 represents the network?

   A. 129.219

   B. 129

   C. 14.1

   D. 1

10. Which of the following addresses is an example of a broadcast address on the network 123.10.0.0 with a subnet mask of 255.255.0.0?

   A. 123.255.255.255

   B. 123.10.255.255

   C. 123.13.0.0

   D. 123.1.1.1

11. How many host addresses can be used in a Class C network?

   A. 253

   B. 254

   C. 255

   D. 256

12. What is the minimum number of bits that can be borrowed to form a subnet?

    A. 1

    B. 2

    C. 4

    D. None of the above

13. What is the primary reason for using subnets?

    A. To reduce the size of the collision domain

    B. To increase the number of host addresses

    C. To reduce the size of the broadcast domain

    D. None of the above

14. How many bits are in a subnet mask?

    A. 16

    B. 32

    C. 64

    D. None of the above

15. Performing the Boolean function as a router would on the IP addresses 121.8.2.5 *and* 255.0.0.0, what is the network/subnetwork address?

    A. 121.8.1.0

    B. 121.8.0.0

    C. 121.8.2.0

    D. None of the above

16. With a Class C address of 197.15.22.31 and a subnet mask of 255.255.255.224, how many bits have been borrowed to create a subnet?

    A. 1

    B. 2

    C. 3

    D. None of the above

17. Performing the Boolean function as a router would on the IP addresses 172.16.2.120 *and* 255.255.255.0, what is the subnet address?

    A. 172.0.0.0

    B. 172.16.0.0

    C. 172.16.2.0

    D. None of the above

18. Which of the following best describes one function of Layer 3, the network layer, in the OSI model?

    A. It is responsible for reliable network communication between nodes.

    B. It is concerned with physical addressing and network topology.

    C. It determines which is the best path for traffic to take through the network.

    D. It manages data exchange between presentation layer entities.

19. What function allows routers to evaluate available routes to a destination and to establish the preferred handling of a packet?

    A. Data linkage

    B. Path determination

    C. SDLC interface protocol

    D. Frame Relay

20. How does the network layer forward packets from the source to the destination?

    A. By using an IP routing table

    B. By using ARP responses

    C. By referring to a name server

    D. By referring to the bridge

21. What are the two parts of a network layer address that routers use to forward traffic through a network?

    A. Network address and host address

    B. Network address and MAC address

    C. Host address and MAC address

    D. MAC address and subnet mask

CHAPTER 11

TCP/IP Transport and Application Layers

Objectives

Upon completion of this chapter, you should be able to answer the following questions:

- What are some functions of the TCP/IP transport layer?

- How does flow control affect data transmission?

- What are some of the processes of establishing a connection between peer systems?

- How does windowing affect data transmission?

- How does acknowledgment affect data transmission?

- What are the transport layer protocols, and what purpose do they serve?

- What are the major protocols of the TCP/IP application layer?

- What are some well-known TCP/IP applications?

Key Terms

The following is a list of key terms introduced in this chapter. For your reference, a definition for each term can be found at the end of this chapter.

The transport layer uses the services provided by the network layer, such as best-path selection and logical addressing, to provide end-to-end communication between source and destination. This chapter describes how the transport layer regulates the flow of information from source to destination reliably and accurately. The primary characteristics of the transport layer are discussed, including the following:

- The transport layer data stream is a logical connection between the endpoints of a network.

- End-to-end control and reliability are provided by sliding windows, sequencing numbers, and acknowledgments.

- Layer 4 protocols TCP and UDP use *port* numbers to keep track of different conversations that cross the network at the same time, and to pass information to the upper layers.

The primary characteristics of the TCP/IP application layer include the following:

- End-user applications reside at this layer.

- Commonly used applications include NFS, DNS, ARP, rlogin, talk, FTP, NTP, and traceroute.

Please be sure to look at this chapter's associated Videos that you will find on the CD-ROM accompanying this book. These CD elements are designed to supplement the material and reinforce the concepts introduced in this chapter.

TCP/IP Transport Layer

As its name implies, the TCP/IP transport layer transports data between applications on source and destination devices. A thorough understanding of the operation of the transport layer is essential to understanding modern data networking. This section describes the functions and services of this critical layer of the TCP/IP network model.

Introduction to the TCP/IP Transport Layer

The phrase *quality of service* often is used to describe the purpose of Layer 4, the transport layer. UDP, which is covered later, also operates at Layer 4 and provides connectionless transport services. However, the primary protocol operating at this layer is connection-oriented TCP. Its main function is to transport and regulate the flow of information from source to destination reliably and accurately. The primary duties of the transport layer are to provide end-to-end control, to provide flow control via sliding windows, and to ensure reliability via sequencing numbers and acknowledgments.

To understand reliability and flow control, think of a person who speaks really fast. In conversation, the listener might need to ask this person to repeat some words if they are not understood (for reliability) and to speak slowly, so the listener can catch the words (flow control), as shown in Figure 11-1.

Figure 11-1 Transport Layer Analogies

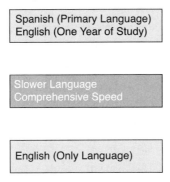

The transport layer provides transport services from the source host to the destination host. It constitutes a logical connection between the endpoints of the network. Transport services segment and reassemble data that is sent by several upper-layer *applications* onto the same transport layer data stream. This transport layer data stream provides end-to-end transport services.

The transport layer data stream is a logical connection between the endpoints of a network. The transport layer defines end-to-end connectivity between host applications. Figure 11-2 illustrates the transport layer.

Figure 11-2 Transport Layer Role in Communication Between Network Devices

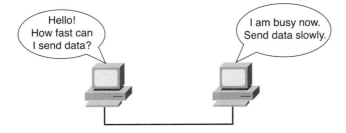

The transport layer provides the following basic services:

- Segmenting upper-layer application data

- Establishing end-to-end operations

- Sending segments from one end host to another end host

- Ensuring flow control provided by sliding windows

- Ensuring reliability provided by sequence numbers and acknowledgments

The transport layer assumes that it can use the network as a "cloud," to send data packets from source to destination. The cloud deals with issues of which one of the several paths are best for a given route. This starts to illustrate the role that routers perform in this process.

TCP/IP is a combination of two individual protocols, TCP and IP. IP is a Layer 3 protocol, a connectionless service that provides best-effort delivery across a network. TCP is a Layer 4 protocol, a connection-oriented service that provides flow control as well as reliability. Pairing the protocols enables them to provide a wider range of services. The TCP/IP protocol suite is made up of many protocols, but TCP and IP are the key ones. TCP/IP is the protocol suite on which the Internet is based.

Flow Control

As the TCP transport layer protocol sends data segments, it can ensure the integrity of the data. One method of doing this is called *flow control*. Flow control avoids the problem of a transmitting host overflowing the buffers in the receiving host. Overflows can present serious problems because they can result in the loss of data.

Transport layer services enable reliable data transport between hosts and destinations. To obtain such reliable transport of data, a connection-oriented relationship is used between the communicating end systems. Reliable transport can accomplish the following:

- Ensure that segments delivered will be acknowledged to the sender

- Provide for retransmission of any segments that are not acknowledged

- Put segments back into their correct sequence at the destination

- Provide congestion avoidance and control

Session Establishment, Maintenance, and Termination

In the OSI and TCP/IP reference models, multiple applications can share the same transport connection. Transport functionality is accomplished segment by segment. This means that different applications can send data segments on a first-come, first-served basis. Such segments can be intended for the same destination or for different destinations. This setup sometimes is referred to as the multiplexing of upper-layer conversations, as shown in Figure 11-3.

Figure 11-3 Multiple Types of Application Layer Data Share the Transport Layer

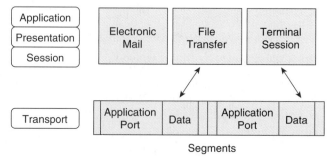

One function of the transport layer is to establish a connection-oriented session with its peer system. For data transfer to begin, both the sending and the receiving applications inform their respective operating systems that a connection will be initiated. One machine initiates a connection that must be accepted by the other. Protocol software modules in the two operating systems communicate by sending messages across the network to verify that the transfer is authorized and that both sides are ready.

After all synchronization has occurred, a connection is said to be established and the transfer of data begins. During transfer, the two machines continue to communicate with their protocol software to verify that data is received correctly.

Figure 11-4 shows a typical connection between sending and receiving systems. The first handshake requests synchronization. The second and third handshakes acknowledge the initial synchronization request, as well as synchronize connection parameters in the opposite direction. The final handshake segment is an *acknowledgment* used to inform the destination that both sides agree that a connection has been established. After the connection is established, data transfer begins.

Figure 11-4 Establishing a Connection with a Peer System

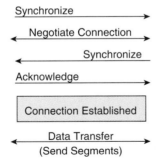

When data transfer is in progress, congestion can occur for two reasons. First, a high-speed computer might be capable of generating traffic faster than a network can transfer it. Second, if many computers simultaneously need to send datagrams to a single destination, that destination can experience congestion, although no single source caused the problem.

When datagrams arrive too quickly for a host or gateway to process, they temporarily are stored in memory. If the traffic continues, the host or gateway eventually exhausts its memory and must discard additional datagrams that arrive.

Instead of allowing data to be lost, the receiving host can issue a "not ready" indicator to the sender. Acting like a stop sign, this indicator signals the sender to stop sending data. When the receiver can handle additional data, the receiver sends a "ready" transport indicator, which is like a go signal. When it receives this indicator, the sender can resume segment transmission.

At the end of data transfer, the sending host sends a signal that indicates the end of the transmission. The receiving host at the end of the data sequence acknowledges the end of transmission, and the connection is terminated.

Three-Way Handshake

TCP is connection-oriented, so it requires connection establishment before data transfer begins. For a connection to be established or initialized, the two hosts must synchronize their Initial Sequence Numbers (ISNs). Synchronization is done in an exchange of connection-establishing segments that carry a control bit called SYN (for synchronize) and the ISNs. Segments that carry the SYN bit also are called SYNs. Hence, the solution requires a suitable mechanism for picking an initial sequence number and a slightly involved handshake to exchange the ISNs.

The synchronization requires each side to send its own initial sequence number and to receive a confirmation of it in an acknowledgment (ACK) from the other side. Each side also must receive the other side's ISN and send a confirming ACK. This exchange, shown in Figure 11-5, is called the ***three-way handshake***.

Figure 11-5 Three-Way Handshake

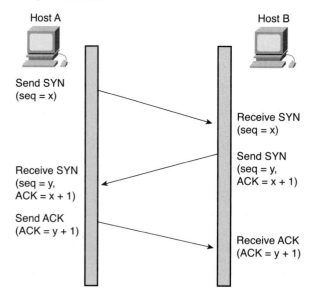

1. **A->B SYN**—Host A initial sequence number is X, the ACK number is 0, and the SYN bit is set, but the ACK bit is not set.

2. **B->A ACK**—Host B sequence number is X+1, Host A initial sequence number is Y, and the SYN and ACK bits are set.

3. **A->B ACK**—Host B sequence number is Y+1, Host A sequence number is X+1, and the ACK bit is set, but the SYN bit is not set.

A three-way handshake is an asynchronous connection mechanism, which is necessary because sequence numbers are not tied to a global clock in the network. Therefore, TCP protocols can have different mechanisms for picking the ISN. The three-way handshake addresses a lot more issues than just the sequence numbers. Other issues that are addressed include window size and any network latency to expect. The receiver of the first SYN has no way of knowing whether the segment was an old delayed one, unless it remembers the last sequence number used on the connection (which is not always possible), so it must ask the sender to verify this SYN.

Video   Three-Way Handshakes

In this video, you learn how TCP hosts establish a connection with a three-way handshake verification.

Windowing

In the most basic form of reliable, connection-oriented data transfer, data packets must be delivered to the recipient in the same order in which they were transmitted. The protocol fails if any data packets are lost, damaged, duplicated, or received in a different order. The basic solution is to have a recipient acknowledge the receipt of each data segment.

If the sender must wait for an acknowledgment after sending each segment, as shown in Figure 11-6, throughput is low. Therefore, most connection-oriented, reliable protocols allow more than one frame or segment to be outstanding at a time. Because time is available after the sender finishes transmitting the data packet and before the sender finishes processing any received acknowledgment, the interval is used for transmitting more data. The number of data packets that the sender is allowed to have outstanding without having received an acknowledgment is known as the window.

TCP uses expectational acknowledgments, meaning that the acknowledgment number refers to the octet that is expected next. Windowing refers to the fact that the window size is negotiated dynamically during the TCP session. *Windowing* is a flow-control mechanism requiring that the source device receive an acknowledgment from the destination after transmitting a certain amount of data.

Figure 11-6 Window Size of 1

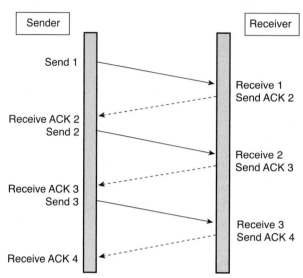

To govern the flow of data between devices, TCP uses a flow-control mechanism. The receiving TCP device reports a "window" to the sending TCP device. This window specifies the number of octets, starting with the acknowledgment number, that the receiving TCP device currently is capable of receiving.

For example, with a window size of 3, the source device can send three octets to the destination. It then must wait for an acknowledgment. If the destination receives the three octets, it sends an acknowledgment to the source device, which now can transmit three more octets. If the destination does not receive the three octets—for example, because of overflowing buffers—it does not send an acknowledgment. Because the source does not receive an acknowledgment, it knows that the octets should be retransmitted and that the transmission rate should be slowed.

TCP window sizes are variable during the lifetime of a connection. Each acknowledgment contains a window advertisement that indicates the number of bytes that the receiver can accept. TCP also maintains a congestion-control window, which is normally the same size as the receiver's window but is cut in half when a segment is lost (for example, there is congestion). This approach permits the window to be expanded or contracted, as necessary, to manage buffer space and processing. A larger window size controls the permissible number of octets that can be transmitted.

If the sender sends three octets, it is expecting an ACK of 4. If the receiver can handle a window size of only two octets, it drops packet 3, specifies 3 as the next octet, and specifies a new window size of 2. The sender sends the next two octets but still specifies its own window size of 3 (for example, it still can accept three octets from the receiver). The receiver replies by requesting octet 5 and specifying a window size of 2.

Video   Sliding Window

In this video, you learn how routers manage flow control with sliding windows.

Acknowledgment

Reliable delivery guarantees that a stream of data sent from one machine is delivered through a data link to another machine without duplication or data loss. Positive acknowledgment with retransmission is one technique that guarantees reliable delivery of data. Positive acknowledgment requires a recipient to communicate with the source, sending back an acknowledgment message when it receives data. The sender keeps a record of each data packet (TCP segment) that it sends and expects an acknowledgment. The sender also starts a timer when it sends a segment, and it retransmits a segment if the timer expires before an acknowledgment arrives.

Figure 11-7 shows the sender transmitting data packets 1, 2, and 3. The receiver acknowledges receipt of the packets by requesting packet 4. Upon receiving the acknowledgment, the sender sends packets 4, 5, and 6. If packet 5 does not arrive at the destination, the receiver acknowledges with a request to resend packet 5. The sender resends packet 5 and then receives an acknowledgment to continue with the transmission of packet 7.

Figure 11-7 Window Size of 3

Sender			Receiver
Send 1			
Send 2			
Send 3			Receive 1
			Receive 2
			Receive 3
			Send ACK 4
Receive ACK 4			
Send 4			
Send 5			
Send 6			
			Receive 4
			Receive 5
			Receive 6
			Send ACK 7
Receive ACK 7			

Window Size = 3

TCP provides sequencing of segments with a forward reference acknowledgment. Each datagram is numbered before transmission, as shown in Figure 11-8. At the receiving station, TCP reassembles the segments into a complete message. TCP must recover from data that is damaged, lost, duplicated, or delivered out of order by the Internet communication system. This is achieved by assigning a sequence number to each octet transmitted and requiring a positive acknowledgment (ACK) from the receiving TCP. If the ACK is not received within a timeout interval, the data is retransmitted. At the receiver, the sequence numbers are used to correctly order segments that might be received out of order and to eliminate duplicates. Damage is handled by adding a checksum to each segment transmitted, checking it at the receiver, and discarding damaged segments.

Figure 11-8 TCP Sequence and Acknowledgment

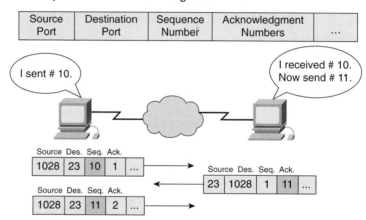

Transmission Control Protocol (TCP)

Transmission Control Protocol (TCP) is a connection-oriented transport layer protocol that provides reliable full-duplex data transmission. TCP is part of the TCP/IP protocol stack. In a connection-oriented environment, a connection is established between both ends before transfer of information can begin. TCP is responsible for breaking messages into segments, reassembling them at the destination station, resending anything that is not received, and reassembling messages from the segments. TCP supplies a virtual circuit between end-user applications.

The following protocols use TCP:

- File Transfer Protocol (FTP)

- Hypertext Transfer Protocol (HTTP)

- Simple Mail Transfer Protocol (SMTP)

- Domain Name System (DNS)

Figure 11-9 shows the TCP segment format.

Figure 11-9 TCP Segment Format

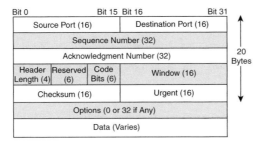

The following list defines the fields in the TCP segment shown in Figure 11-9:

- **Source Port**—Number of the calling port

- **Destination Port**—Number of the called port

- **Sequence Number**—Number used to ensure correct sequencing of the arriving data

- **Acknowledgment Number**—Next expected TCP octet

- **HLEN**—Number of 32-bit words in the header

- **Reserved**—Set to 0

- **Code Bits**—Control functions (such as setup and termination of a session)

- **Window**—Number of octets that the sender is willing to accept

- **Checksum**—Calculated checksum of the header and data fields

- **Urgent Pointer**—Indication of the end of the urgent data

- **Options**—One option currently defined—maximum TCP segment size

- **Data**—Upper-layer protocol data

User Datagram Protocol (UDP)

User Datagram Protocol (UDP), the segment format for which is shown in Figure 11-10, is the connectionless transport protocol in the TCP/IP protocol stack. UDP is a simple protocol that exchanges datagrams without acknowledgments or guaranteed delivery. This simplicity is evident when comparing the UDP segment format with that of TCP. Error processing and retransmission must be handled by upper-layer protocols. For example, if a TFTP download gets interrupted for some reason, the human operator can just retry until it is successfully done.

Figure 11-10 UDP Segment Format

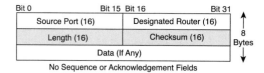

No Sequence or Acknowledgement Fields

The following list defines the fields in the UDP segment shown in Figure 11-10:

- **Source Port**—Number of the calling port

- **Destination Port**—Number of the called port

- **Length**—Number of bytes, including header and data

- **Checksum**—Calculated checksum of the header and data fields

- **Data**—Upper-layer protocol data

UDP does not use windowing or acknowledgments. Therefore, *application layer* protocols are used to provide reliability. UDP is designed for applications that do not need to put sequences of segments together.

The following protocols use UDP:

- Trivial File Transfer Protocol (TFTP)

- Simple Network Management Protocol (SNMP)

- Dynamic Host Configuration Protocol (DHCP)

- Domain Name System (DNS)

TCP and UDP Port Numbers

Both TCP and UDP use port numbers to pass information to the upper layers. The combination of an IP address and a port number is referred to as a socket. Port numbers are used to keep track of different conversations crossing the network at the same time.

Application software developers agree to use well-known port numbers that are controlled by the Internet Assigned Numbers Authority (IANA). For example, any conversation bound for the FTP application uses the standard port numbers 20 (for the data) and 21 (for control), as shown in Figure 11-11. Conversations that do not involve an application with a well-known port number are assigned port numbers randomly from within a specific range above 1023. Some ports are reserved in both TCP and UDP, but applications might not be written to support them, as shown in Table 11-1. Port numbers have the assigned ranges shown in this table.

Figure 11-11 Port Numbers

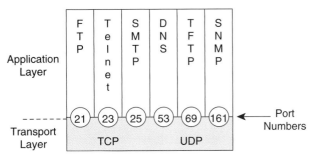

Table 11-1 Reserved TCP and UDP Port Numbers

Decimal Port Number	Keyword	Description
0	—	Reserved
1 to 4	—	Unassigned
5	RJE	Remote job entry
7	Echo	Echo
9	Discard	Discard
11	Users	Active users
13	Daytime	Daytime
15	Netstat	Who is up, or netstat
17	Quote	Quote of the day
19	Chargen	Character generator
20	FTP-data	File Transfer Protocol (data)
21	FTP	File Transfer Protocol
23	Telnet	Terminal connection
25	SMTP	Simple Mail Transfer Protocol
37	Time	Time of day
39	RLP	Resource Location Protocol
42	Nameserver	Host name server
43	nickname	Who is

continues

Table 11-1 Reserved TCP and UDP Port Numbers (Continued)

Decimal Port Number	Keyword	Description
53	Domain	Domain Name Server
67	Bootps	Bootstrap protocol server
68	Bootpc	Bootstrap protocol client
69	TFTP	Trivial File Transfer Protocol
75	—	Any private dial-out service
77	—	Any private RJE service
79	Finger	Finger
80	HTTP	Hypertext Transfer Protocol
95	SUPDUP	SUPDUP Protocol
101	HOSTNAME	NIC Host Name Server
102	ISO-TSAP	ISO-TSAP
113	AUTH	Authentication Service
117	UUCP-PATH	UUCP Path Service
123	NTP	Network Time Protocol
133 to 159		Unassigned
160 to 223		Reserved
224 to 241		Unassigned
242 to 255		Unassigned

As shown in Figure 11-12, end systems use port numbers to select the proper application. Originating source port numbers are assigned dynamically by the source host, with some number greater than 1023. As an example, a host attempting to connect to another using FTP sends a packet with a destination TCP port number of 21 (FTP) and a dynamically generated source port number such as 1028. This pair of port numbers (destination and source) defines the unique "conversation" between these hosts. If the same host initiates another FTP session to a second host, the destination port still is 21, but the source port generated is different (for example, 1030), to keep the two sessions separate.

Figure 11-12 Port Numbers Dictate Application Used

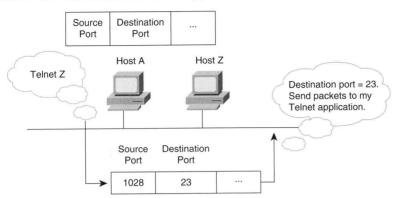

The Application Layer

The last layer of both the OSI and the TCP/IP model is referred to as the application layer. The application layer is the closest to the end user when interacting with software applications, such as sending and receiving e-mail over a network. You see how the application layer deals with data packets from client/server applications, domain name services, and network applications by examining the following elements:

- Client/server
- Redirectors
- Domain Name System
- E-mail
- Telnet
- FTP
- HTTP

Introduction to the TCP/IP Application Layer

In the context of the OSI reference model, the application layer (Layer 7) supports the communicating component of an application, as shown in Figure 11-13. The application layer is responsible for the following:

- Identifying and establishing the availability of intended communication partners
- Synchronizing cooperating applications
- Establishing agreement on procedures for error recovery
- Controlling data integrity

Figure 11-13 Application Layer

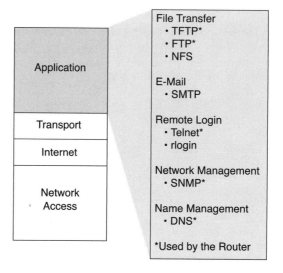

The application layer is the layer closest to the end user. This determines whether sufficient resources exist for communication between systems. Without the application layer, there would be no network communication support. The application layer does not provide services to any other layer, but it does provide services to application processes lying outside the scope of the TCP/IP model, such as spreadsheet programs, word-processing programs, and banking terminal programs. Additionally, the application layer provides a direct interface to the rest of the model for network applications (such as browser or e-mail program) or an indirect interface for standalone applications (such as word processors, spreadsheets, and presentation managers) with a network redirector.

Direct Network Applications

Most applications that work in a networked environment are classified as client/server applications. These applications, such as FTP clients (not protocols), web browsers, and e-mail programs, all have two components that allow them to function—the client side and the server side. The client side is located on the local computer and is the requestor of the services. The server side is located on a remote computer and provides services in response to the client's requests.

A client/server application works by constantly repeating the following looped routine: client request, server response; client request, server response. For example, a web browser accesses a web page by requesting a uniform resource locator (URL), which is resolved to an IP address on a remote web server. After it locates the URL, the web server that is identified by that URL responds to the request. Then, based on the information received from the web server, the client can request more information from the same web server or can access another web page from a different web server.

Netscape Navigator and Internet Explorer are probably the most commonly used network applications. An easy way to understand a web browser is to compare it to a television remote control. A remote control gives you the capability to directly control a TV's functions: volume, channels, brightness, and so on. For the remote control to function properly, you do not need to understand how the remote control functions electronically. The same is true of a web browser. The browser gives you the capability to navigate through the web by clicking hyperlinks. For the web browser to function properly, it is not necessary for you to understand how the lower-layer OSI protocols work and interact.

Indirect Network Support

Within a LAN environment, indirect-application network support is also a client/server function. If a client wants to save a file from a word processor to a network server, the redirector enables the word-processing application to do so transparently. Remember that this transparency is supplied by the session layer Remote Procedure Call (RPC) functionality.

A redirector is an OSI model session layer function that works with computer operating systems and network clients instead of specific application programs.

Examples of protocols that use redirectors are as follows:

- AppleTalk Filing Protocol

- NetBIOS Extended User Interface (NetBEUI)

- Novell IPX/SPX protocols

- Network File System (NFS) of the TCP/IP protocol suite

A redirector enables a network administrator to assign remote resources to logical names on the local client. When you select one of these logical names to perform an operation such as saving a file or printing a file, the network redirector sends the selected file to the proper remote resource on the network for processing. If the resource is on a local computer, the redirector ignores the request and allows the local operating system to process the request.

The advantage of using a network redirector on a local client is that the applications on the client never have to recognize the network. In addition, the application that requests service is located on the local computer, and the redirector reroutes the request to the proper network resource, while the application treats it as a local request.

Redirectors expand the capabilities of non-network software. They also enable users to share documents, templates, databases, printers, and many other resource types without having to use special application software.

Networking has had a great influence on the development of programs such as word processors, spreadsheets, presentation managers, database programs, graphics, and productivity software. Many of these software packages are now network-integrated or network-aware; they have the capabilities of launching integrated web browsers or Internet tools and publishing their output to the *Hypertext Markup Language (HTML)* for easy web integration.

Making and Breaking a Connection

It is important to note that in each of the examples mentioned in the preceding sections, the connection to the server was maintained only long enough to complete a single task. In the web example, the connection was maintained just long enough to download the current web page. In the printer example, the connection was maintained just long enough to send the document to the print server. After the processing was completed, the connection was broken and had to be re-established for the next processing request to take place. This is one of the two ways that communication sessions take place.

Later in this chapter, you learn about the second method in which communication sessions take place. This is illustrated by the Telnet and FTP examples, in which a connection to the server is established and maintained until all processing has been performed. The client computer terminates the connection when the user determines that he or she has finished. All communication activity falls into one of these two categories. In the next section, you learn about the *Domain Name System (DNS)*, which is supported by the application layer processes.

NOTE

For more information on domain names, visit the IANA website (www.iana.org/domain-names.htm).

DNS

The Internet is built on a hierarchical addressing scheme. This allows for routing that is based on classes of addresses, as opposed to individual addresses. The problem that this creates for the user is associating the correct address with the Internet site. The only difference between the addresses 198.151.11.12 and 198.151.11.21 is one transposed digit. It is very easy to forget an address to a particular site because there is nothing to associate the contents of the site with its address.

To associate the contents of the site with its address, a domain-naming system was developed. DNS is a system used on the Internet for translating names of domains and their publicly advertised network nodes into IP addresses. A domain is a group of computers that are associated by their geographical location or their business type. A domain name is a string of characters and/or numbers, usually a name or abbreviation that represents the numeric address of an Internet site. More than 200 top-level domains exist on the Internet. Some examples include the following:

- **.us**—United States
- **.uk**—United Kingdom

There are also generic names, examples of which include the following:

- **.edu**—Educational sites
- **.com**—Commercial sites
- **.gov**—Government sites
- **.org**—Nonprofit sites
- **.net**—Network service

- **.mil**—U.S. military sites

- **.int**—International database/treaty organization sites

The Domain Name System (DNS) server is a device on a network that responds to requests from clients to translate a domain name into the associated IP address. The DNS system is set up in a hierarchy that creates different levels of DNS servers.

If a local DNS server is capable of translating a domain name into its associated IP address, it does so and returns the result to the client. If it cannot translate the address, it passes the request up to the next higher-level DNS server on the system, which then tries to translate the address. If the DNS server at this level is capable of translating the domain name into an associated IP address, it does so and returns the result to the client. If not, it sends the request to the next higher level. This process repeats itself until the domain name has been translated or until the top-level DNS server has been reached. If the domain name cannot be found on the top-level DNS server, it is considered to be an error and the corresponding error message is returned. Any type of application that uses domain names to represent IP addresses uses the DNS server to translate that name into its corresponding IP address.

FTP and TFTP

The *File Transfer Protocol (FTP)* is designed to download files (received or gotten from the Internet) and upload files (sent or put to the Internet). The capability to upload and download files is one of the most valuable features of the Internet. This is especially helpful for people who rely on computers for many purposes and who might need software drivers and upgrades immediately. Network administrators rarely can wait even a few days to get the necessary drivers that enable their network servers to function again. The Internet can provide these files immediately by using FTP. Like e-mail and Telnet, FTP is a client/server application. It requires server software running on a host that can be accessed by client software.

An FTP session is established the same way in which a Telnet session is established. Just like Telnet, the FTP session is maintained until the client terminates it or until there is some sort of communication error. When you establish a connection to an FTP process or daemon, you must supply a login ID and a password. Normally, you use Anonymous as the login ID and your e-mail address as the password. This type of connection is known as *anonymous FTP*. After your identity is established, a command link opens between your client machine and the FTP server. This is similar to a Telnet session, in which commands are sent and executed on the server and the results are returned to the client. This feature enables you to create and change folders, erase and rename files, and execute many other functions associated with file management.

The main purpose of FTP is to transfer files from one computer to another by copying and moving files from servers to clients and from clients to servers. When you copy files from a server, FTP establishes a second connection, a data link between the computers, across which the data is transferred. Data transfer can occur in *American Standard Code for Information*

Interchange (ASCII) mode or binary mode. These two modes determine how the data file is to be transferred between the stations. ASCII format returns a human-readable representation of the number in seven ASCII characters. The first character is a space or a negation sign, followed by three digits, a decimal point, and two more digits. If a number has less than three digits to the left of the decimal point, then the optional sign and digits are right-justified in the seven-character field, and spaces are filled in on the left. Because binary-mode numbers take only 4 bytes each, compared to the 7 of an ASCII representation, the binary representation takes less time to send over the serial link to the computer. However, there are marked advantages to using the ASCII representation. After the file transfer has ended, the data connection terminates automatically. After you complete the entire session of copying and moving files, you might log off, thus closing the command link and ending the session.

The *Trivial File Transport Protocol (TFTP)* is a connectionless service that uses UDP. TFTP is used on routers and switches to transfer configuration files and Cisco IOS Software images, and to transfer files between systems that support TFTP. It is designed to be small and easy to implement. Therefore, it lacks most of the features of regular FTP. The only thing it can do is read or write files from or to a remote server. It cannot list directories, and currently it has no provisions for user authentication. It is useful in some LANs because it operates faster than FTP in a stable environment.

Another protocol that has the capability to download files is Hypertext Transfer Protocol (HTTP), as discussed in the next section. One limitation of HTTP is that you can use it only to download files, not upload them.

HTTP

The *Hypertext Transfer Protocol (HTTP)* works with the World Wide Web, which is the fastest-growing and most used part of the Internet. One of the main reasons for the extraordinary growth of the web is the ease with which it allows access to information. A web browser is a client/server application, which means that it requires both a client and a server component to function. A web browser presents data in multimedia formats on web pages that use text, graphics, sound, and video. The web pages are created with a format language called the Hypertext Markup Language (HTML). HTML directs a web browser on a particular web page to produce the appearance of the page in a specific manner. In addition, HTML specifies locations for the placement of text, files, and objects that are to be transferred from the web server to the web browser.

Hyperlinks make the World Wide Web easy to navigate. A hyperlink is an object (word, phrase, or picture) on a web page that, when clicked, transfers you to a new web page. The web page contains (often hidden within its HTML description) an address location known as a uniform resource locator (URL).

Table 11-2 shows the components of a standard URL address (http://www.cisco.com/edu/ in this case).

Table 11-2 URL Components

http://	www.	Cisco.com	/cgi/
Identifies to the browser what protocol should be used.	Identifies what type of site is being contacted by the browser.	Represents the domain entry of the website.	Identifies the folder where the web page is located on the server. Also, because no name is specified, the browser loads the default page identified by the server.

When you open a web browser, the first thing you usually see is a starting (or "home") page. The URL of the home page already has been stored in the configuration area of your web browser and can be changed at any time. From the starting page, you can click one of the web page hyperlinks or type a URL in the browser's address bar. The web browser then examines the protocol to determine whether it needs to open another program, and it determines the IP address of the web server. After that, the transport layer, network layer, data link layer, and physical layer initiate a session with the web server. The data that is transferred to the HTTP server contains the folder name of the web page location (the data also can contain a specific filename for an HTML page). If no name is given, the server uses a default name (as specified in the server's configuration).

The server responds to the request by sending all of the text, audio, video, and graphic files, as specified in the HTML instructions, to the web client. The client browser reassembles all the files to create a view of the web page and then terminates the session. If you click another page that is located on the same server or a different server, the whole process begins again.

Lab 11.2.4   Protocol Inspector, TCP and HTTP

This exercise provides a basic overview of how to use Protocol Inspector, or equivalent software, to view dynamic Transmission Control Protocol (TCP) operations. The operation that will be specifically looked at is HTTP during web page access.

SMTP

E-mail servers communicate with each other using the Simple Mail Transfer Protocol (SMTP) to send and receive mail. The SMTP protocol transports e-mail messages in ASCII format using TCP. You can connect to an SMTP server by performing a ping test to the SMTP port (25) or to the POP3 port (110). This is a good way to test if a mail server is reachable.

When a mail server receives a message destined for a local client, it stores that message and waits for the client to collect the mail. Mail clients can collect their mail in several ways: They can use programs that access the mail server files directly or can use one of many network protocols. The most popular mail client protocols are Post Office Protocol Version 3 (POP3) and Internet Messaging Access Protocol Version 4 (IMAP4), which both use TCP to transport data. Even though mail clients use these special protocols to collect mail, they almost always use SMTP to send mail. Because two different protocols, and possibly two different servers, are used to send and receive mail, it is possible that mail clients can perform one task and not the other. Therefore, you should troubleshoot the sending of mail and the receiving of mail separately.

When verifying the configuration of a mail client, both the mail relay server (SMTP) and mail servers (POP or IMAP) should be verified. SMTP does not offer much in the way of security and does not require any authentication. To prevent unauthorized users from bouncing mail messages off their servers, administrators often don't allow hosts that are not part of their network to use their SMTP server to send (or relay) mail.

SNMP

The *Simple Network Management Protocol (SNMP)* is an application layer protocol that facilitates the exchange of management information between network devices. SNMP enables network administrators to manage network performance, find and solve network problems, and plan for network growth.

An SNMP-managed network consists of the following three key components:

- **Managed device**—A network node that contains an SNMP agent and that resides on a managed network. Managed devices collect and store management information and make this information available to NMSs using SNMP. Managed devices, sometimes called network elements, can be routers and access servers, switches and bridges, hubs, computer hosts, or printers.

- **Agent**—A network-management software module that resides in a managed device. An agent has local knowledge of management information and translates that information into a form compatible with SNMP.

- **Network-management system (NMS)**—Executes applications that monitor and control managed devices. NMSs provide the bulk of the processing and memory resources required for network management. One or more NMSs must exist on any managed network.

Telnet

Terminal emulation (*Telnet*) software provides the capability to remotely access another computer. It enables you to log in to an Internet host and execute commands. Telnet commonly is used for remote administration of servers and network equipment such as routers and switches. A Telnet client is referred to as a *local host*, and a Telnet server, which uses special software called a daemon, is referred to as a *remote host*, as shown in Figure 11-14.

Figure 11-14 Telnet

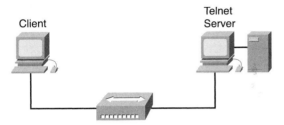

To make a connection from a Telnet client, you must select a connection option. The host name and terminal type will need to be entered on the command-line prompt. The host name is the IP address (DNS) of the remote computer to which you connect. The terminal type describes the type of terminal emulation that you want the computer to perform. The Telnet operation uses none of the transmitting computer's processing power. Instead, it transmits the keystrokes to the remote host and sends the resulting screen output back to the local monitor. All processing and storage takes place on the remote computer.

When a DNS name for a Telnet location is entered, the name must be translated into its associated IP address before a connection can be established. The Telnet application works mainly at the top three layers of the OSI model—the application layer (commands), the presentation layer (formats, usually ASCII), and the session layer (transmits). The data then passes to the transport layer, where it is segmented, and the port address and error checking are added. The data then passes to the network layer, where the IP header (containing the source and destination IP addresses) is added. Next, the packet travels to the data link layer, which encapsulates the packet in a data frame, adds the source and destination MAC address, and adds a frame trailer. If the source computer doesn't have the MAC address of the destination computer, it performs an ARP request. When the MAC address has been determined, the frame travels across the physical medium (in binary form) to the next device. Telnet is a good network troubleshooting tool because it tests all seven layers of the OSI model and allows remote diagnostics to be performed.

When the data reaches the remote host computer, the data link layer, the network layer, and the transport layer reassemble the original data commands. The remote host computer executes the commands and transmits the results back to the local client computer by using the same process of encapsulation that delivered the original commands. This whole process repeats itself, sending commands and receiving results until the local client has completed the work that needs to be done. When the work is done, the client terminates the session.

Summary

In this chapter, you learned about the functions of the TCP/IP application layer and transport layer. You also learned about the different processes that occur as data packets travel through this layer. More specifically, you learned that the application layer is responsible for these actions:

- Identifies and establishes the availability of intended communication partners
- Synchronizes cooperating applications
- Establishes agreement on procedures for error recovery
- Controls data integrity

In addition, you learned that the application layer supports the following:

- Direct and indirect network applications
- The Domain Name System
- Telnet, FTP, and HTTP
- TCP, UDP, SMTP, and SNMP

To supplement all that you've learned in this chapter, refer to the chapter-specific Videos on the CD-ROM accompanying this book.

Key Terms

acknowledgment   Notification sent from one network device to another to acknowledge that some event (for example, receipt of a message) occurred. Sometimes abbreviated ACK.

application   A program that performs a function directly for a user. FTP and Telnet clients are examples of network applications.

application layer   Layer 7 of the OSI reference model. This layer provides services to application processes (such as e-mail, file transfer, and terminal emulation) that are outside the OSI reference model. The application layer identifies and establishes the availability of intended communication partners (and the resources required to connect with them), synchronizes cooperating applications, and establishes agreement on procedures for error recovery and control of data integrity.

ASCII (American Standard Code for Information Interchange)   An 8-bit code (7 bits plus parity) for character representation.

DNS (Domain Name System)   The system used in the Internet for translating names of network nodes into addresses.

flow control   A technique for ensuring that a transmitting entity does not overwhelm a receiving entity with data. When the buffers on the receiving device are full, a message is sent to the sending device to suspend the transmission until the data in the buffers has been processed. In IBM networks, this technique is called pacing.

FTP (File Transfer Protocol)   An application protocol, part of the TCP/IP protocol stack, used for transferring files between network nodes. FTP is defined in RFC 959.

HTML (Hypertext Markup Language)   A simple hypertext document formatting language that uses tags to indicate how a given part of a document should be interpreted by a viewing application, such as a web browser.

HTTP (Hypertext Transfer Protocol)   The protocol used by web browsers and web servers to transfer files, such as text and graphics files.

port   In IP terminology, an upper-layer process that receives information from lower layers. Ports are numbered, and many are associated with a specific process. For example, SMTP is associated with port 25. A port number of this type is called a well-known port or address.

TCP (Transmission Control Protocol)   A connection-oriented transport-layer protocol that provides reliable full-duplex data transmission. TCP is part of the TCP/IP protocol stack.

Telnet   A standard terminal emulation protocol in the TCP/IP protocol stack. Telnet is used for remote terminal connection, enabling users to log in to remote systems and use resources as if they were connected to a local system. Telnet is defined in RFC 854.

TFTP (Trivial File Transfer Protocol)   A simplified version of FTP that allows files to be transferred from one computer to another over a network.

three-way handshake   A sequence of messages exchanged between two or more network devices to ensure transmission synchronization before sending user data.

UDP (User Datagram Protocol)   A connectionless transport layer protocol in the TCP/IP protocol stack. UDP is a simple protocol that exchanges datagrams without acknowledgments or guaranteed delivery, requiring that error processing and retransmission be handled by other protocols. UDP is defined in RFC 768.

windowing   A flow-control mechanism requiring that the source device receive an acknowledgment from the destination after transmitting a certain amount of data.

Check Your Understanding

Complete all the review questions to test your understanding of the topics and concepts in this chapter. Answers are listed in Appendix B, "Check Your Understanding Answer Key."

1. When conversing with an individual whose primary language is different than yours, you might need to repeat your words and speak more slowly. Repeating your words can be compared to _____, and the need to speak slowly can be compared to the _____ functions of the transport layer.

   A. Reliability; flow control

   B. Flow control; reliability

   C. Transport; acknowledgment

   D. Flow control; transport

2. The following characteristics describe what TCP/IP protocol: connection-oriented; resends anything not received; divides outgoing messages into segments?

   A. IPX

   B. TCP

   C. UDP

   D. SPS

3. What does the window field in a TCP segment indicate?

   A. Number of 32-bit words in the header

   B. Number of the called port

   C. Number used to ensure correct sequencing of the arriving data

   D. Number of octets that the device is willing to accept

4. What transport protocol exchanges datagrams without acknowledgments or guaranteed delivery?

   A. UDP

   B. TCP

   C. IRQ

   D. LLC

5. What do TCP and UDP use to keep track of different conversations crossing a network at the same time?

   A. Port numbers

   B. IP addresses

   C. MAC addresses

   D. Route numbers

6. How does TCP synchronize a connection between the source and the destination before data transmission?

   A. Two-way handshake

   B. Three-way handshake

   C. Four-way handshake

   D. Holton functions

7. Which range of port numbers is unregulated?

   A. Below 255

   B. Between 256 and 512

   C. Between 256 and 1023

   D. Above 1023

8. With TCP transmission, what occurs if a segment is not acknowledged in a certain time period?

   A. UDP takes over the transmission.

   B. The virtual circuit is terminated.

   C. Nothing happens.

   D. Retransmission occurs.

9. Which best describes flow control?

   A. A method of managing limited bandwidth

   B. A method of connecting two hosts synchronously

   C. A method of preventing buffer overrun

   D. A method of checking data for viruses before transmission

10. Which of the following best describes the purpose of the TCP/IP protocol stack?

    A. Maps closely to the OSI reference model's upper layers

    B. Supports all standard physical and data link protocols

    C. Transfers information from one host to another in a sequence of datagrams

    D. Reassembles datagrams into complete messages at the receiving location

11. Which of the following is one of the protocols found in the transport layer?

    A. UCP

    B. UDP

    C. TDP

    D. TDC

12. What is the purpose of port numbers?

    A. They keep track of different upper-layer conversations crossing the network at the same time.

    B. Source systems use them to keep a session organized.

    C. End systems use them to assign end users dynamically to a particular session, depending on their application use.

    D. Source systems generate them to predict destination addresses.

13. Why are TCP three-way handshake/open connections used? Select all that apply.

    A. To ensure that lost data can be recovered if problems occur later

    B. To determine how much data the receiving station can accept at one time

    C. To provide efficient use of bandwidth by users

    D. To change binary ping responses into information in the upper layers

14. What does a dynamic TCP window field do?

    A. It makes the window larger so that more data can come through at once, which results in more efficient use of bandwidth.

    B. The window size slides to each section of the datagram to receive data, which results in more efficient use of bandwidth.

    C. It allows the window size to be negotiated dynamically during the TCP session, which results in more efficient use of bandwidth.

    D. It limits the incoming data so that each segment must be sent one by one, which is an inefficient use of bandwidth.

15. UDP segments use what protocols to provide reliability?

    A. Network layer protocols

    B. Application layer protocols

    C. Internet protocols

    D. Transmission control protocols

16. A network redirector enables data to travel _____.

    A. Only to a network print server

    B. Only to a network file server

    C. In a single direction

    D. None of the above

17. Which of the following is an example of a client/server application?

   A. E-mail

   B. A spreadsheet

   C. A NIC

   D. Hard-drive utilities

18. The client side of the client/server relationship is which of the following?

   A. Located on the remote computer

   B. The requestor of services

   C. The most important

   D. Always located on the server

19. Which of the following best describes a domain name?

   A. It translates the name of a network node into a numeric address.

   B. It is the same as the name you give your primary server.

   C. It represents the specific location where your LAN is located.

   D. It is an IP address used to represent a print server.

20. .com is the domain typically assigned to which of the following?

   A. Client machines

   B. Customers

   C. Network provider companies

   D. Corporations

21. During a Telnet connection, the remote computer is responsible for which of the following?

   A. Nothing

   B. Processing

   C. Client-side Telnet application

   D. Client-side printing

22. At which three layers of the OSI model does Telnet primarily work?

   A. Application layer, session layer, transport layer

   B. Presentation layer, session layer, transport layer

   C. Data link layer, transport layer, presentation layer

   D. Application layer, presentation layer, session layer

23. The typical default settings for anonymous FTP sessions use _____ as the login ID and _____ as the password.

   A. Anonymous; the user e-mail address

   B. The user e-mail address; FTP

   C. FTP; FTP

   D. Guest; anonymous

24. Instead of working with specific application programs, redirectors work with which of the following?

   A. Computer operating systems

   B. Spreadsheets

   C. E-mail

   D. Web browsers

Objectives

Upon completion of this chapter, you should be able to answer the following questions:

- What are the different types of WAN connections, encapsulations, and protocols?

- What are the differences between a WAN and LAN? Which type of standards and protocols does each use?

- What is the role of a router in a WAN?

- What are the physical characteristics of a router?

- What are the common ports on a router?

- What organizations are responsible for WAN standards?

- What is the role of a router in a WAN?

- What are the internal components of the router? What are their functions?

- How are Ethernet, serial WAN, and console ports properly connected?

Key Terms

The following is a list of key terms introduced in this chapter. For your reference, a definition for each term can be found at the end of this chapter.

In this chapter, you learn about WAN devices, technologies, and standards. In addition, you learn about the function of a router in a WAN.

Please be sure to look at this chapter's PhotoZooms and Interactive Media Activity that you will find on the CD-ROM accompanying this book. These CD elements are designed to supplement the material and reinforce the concepts introduced in this chapter.

WANs

WANs have several important characteristics that distinguish them from LANs. This first section provides an overview of WAN technologies and protocols. It will also explain how WANs and LANs are different, and ways in which they are similar.

Introduction to WANs

A *wide-area network (WAN)* is a data communications network that extends across a large geographic area. WANs often use transmission facilities provided by common carriers, for example, telephone companies.

A WAN differs from a local-area network (LAN) in several ways. For example, unlike a LAN, which connects workstations, peripherals, terminals, and other devices in a single building or other small geographic area, a WAN makes data connections across a broad geographic area. Companies use a WAN to connect various company sites so that information can be exchanged between distant offices.

A WAN operates at the physical layer (Layer 1) and the data link layer (Layer 2) of the OSI reference model. It interconnects LANs that are usually separated by large geographic areas. WANs provide for the exchange of data packets/frames between *routers/switches* and the LANs they support.

Table 1-1 lists some information indicative of specific examples of data networks.

Table 1-1 Data Networks

Name	Location of Hosts	Distances Between Devices
LAN Classroom	Room	10 m
LAN School	Building	100 m
LAN University	Campus	1000 m = 1 km
WAN Cisco Systems, Inc.	Country	100,000 m = 100 km

Table 1-1 Data Networks (Continued)

Name	Location of Hosts	Distances Between Devices
WAN Africa	Continent	1,000,000 m = 1000 km
WAN Internet	Planet	10,000,000 m = 10,000 km
WAN Earth and Artificial Satellites	Earth-Moon Systems	100,000,000 m = 100,000 km

As shown in Figure 1-1, the major characteristics of WANs are as follows:

- They connect devices that are separated by wide geographical areas.

- They use the services of carriers such as the regional Bell operating companies (RBOCs), Sprint, and MCI in the U.S. Examples of carriers in other countries include British telecom, German Telekom, Telstra, and Data Access Pvt Ltd.

- They use serial connections of various types to access bandwidth over large geographic areas.

Figure 1-1 WAN Connection

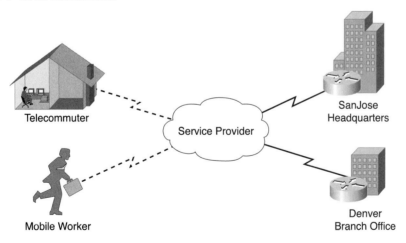

> **More Information: WAN Performance Criteria**
>
> **Component Uptime**
>
> Each physical component of the WAN can be monitored and measured for its availability using uptime. *Uptime* is the opposite of downtime: It is the amount of time that the device is functional and in service relative to the users' requirements for its availability. It is common for uptime to be statistically overstated by measuring it on a 7-day-24-hour basis, even though the users' requirements might be for only 5 days a week 12 hours a day. Remember to tailor this metric and every other metric as closely as possible to your users' stated requirements for network performance.
>
> Although electronic devices are highly reliable, they eventually fail. Most manufacturers provide a *mean time between failure (MTBF)* rating for their equipment as a reassurance of how reliable their products really are. Typically, MTBF ratings are in the tens of thousands of hours. These hours could conceivably translate into years of trouble-free service. Unfortunately, these ratings are statistically derived. The actual time between failures of any given device depends greatly on a number of factors, including the following:
>
> - Ambient temperature ranges of the operating environment
> - Cleanliness of the commercial electric power
> - Quality of the handling of the devices before and during operation
>
> Monitoring and tracking uptime of individual components enables you to demonstrate to your user community how well you are satisfying their requirements for the network's availability. Component uptime data can also be charted over time to identify potentially problematic components in your network infrastructure. Such trends can provide information about the general reliability of a given type or brand of hardware, which then can be used to identify individual components that might be at risk of failure.
>
> Note that the term *availability* is sometimes used to generically describe aggregate network uptime. Unfortunately, it is not a good metric. In theory, network availability provides a quantified synopsis of the network's readiness. In practice, availability is so nebulous that it is virtually meaningless.
>
> To illustrate this point, if a router at a remote location fails, the entire network is unavailable to the users at that location. The network, however, is available to users at every other location. They will not be able to access hosts at the affected location, but they will also not be impeded from accessing every other host in the network. The extent to which the network is available varies greatly by location and by usage requirements. Therefore, quantifying network availability can be more difficult than it is valuable.
>
> **Traffic Volumes**
>
> One of the more important metrics for any WAN is the volume of traffic that it is expected to support. Volume is almost always volatile; it varies with time, business cycles, seasons, and so on. In other words, you can count on traffic volumes being anything but constant. Given this volatility, it is important to measure volumes in two different ways, maximum volumes and average volumes:

More Information: WAN Performance Criteria (Continued)

- The maximum volume that you expect the network to support is known as the *peak volume*. As its name implies, this peak volume is the greatest amount of traffic that you expect the network to have to support.

- *Average volumes* are the traffic loads that you can reasonably expect during the course of a business day from any given work location.

Establishing these two traffic volumes is critical to sizing the WAN's transmission facilities, as well as the facilities of its routers. If you expect any given location to generate a traffic load of 100 kbps during the course of a business day, for example, a 56-kbps transmission facility is clearly inadequate.

Delay

Delay is one of the more common metrics that can be used to measure network performance. *Delay* is the time that elapses between two events. In data communications, these two events are typically the transmission and reception of data. Therefore, delay is the total amount of time that is required by the network to transport a packet from its point of origin to its destination. Given this definition, delay is a combined phenomenon with many potential causes. Three of the more common types of delay are the following:

- *Propagation delay*—The cumulative amount of time required to transmit, or propagate, the data across an end-to-end transmission path. The network infrastructure within each transmission facility in the network path directly contributes to the aggregate forwarding delay of any given transmission. An additional factor in propagation delay is traffic volume. The more traffic that is flowing across a given facility, the less bandwidth that is available for new transmissions. Propagation delay is inherent in terrestrial circuits, regardless of whether they traverse glass or copper media or are transmitted through the air using microwave radio frequencies. Terrestrial circuits refer to network infrastructure that is bound to a geographical area. For example, satellites extend the reach of the Internet and IP-based private networks to places poorly served by the terrestrial infrastructure.

- **Satellite uplink/downlink delays**—Some transmission facilities are satellite-based, requiring the signal to be transmitted up to the satellite and then transmitted back down from the satellite. Because of the great distances between the terrestrial transmission facilities and the satellite, these delays can be quite noticeable.

- **Forwarding delay**—Forwarding delay, or latency, in a network is the amount of time that a physical device needs to receive, buffer, process, and forward data. The actual forwarding delay or latency of any given device can vary over time. Individual devices operating at or near capacity will likely experience a greater forwarding delay than comparable devices that are less utilized. Additionally, forwarding delay can be made worse by heavy traffic or error conditions in the network. Forwarding delay can be described as latency within individual components.

The following devices are used in WANs, as represented in Figure 1-2:

- **Routers**—Offer many services, including internetworking and WAN interface ports. Their main function is to interconnect two or more networks.

- **Switches**—Connect to WAN bandwidth for voice, data, and video communication. Some examples of WAN switches include Frame Relay switches, ATM switches, and telephone switches located at the telephone company's central office (CO).

- *Modems*—Include interfaces to voice-grade services (analog dialup modems); channel service units/digital service units (CSU/DSUs) that interface T1/E1 services; and terminal adapters/Network Termination 1s (TAs/NT1s) that interface Integrated Services Digital Network (ISDN) services.

- **Communication servers**—Concentrate dial-in and dial-out user communication.

Figure 1-2 Common WAN Devices

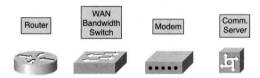

WAN data link protocols describe how frames are carried between systems on a single data link. They include protocols designed to operate over dedicated point-to-point, multipoint, and multiaccess switched services, such as Frame Relay. WAN standards are defined and managed by a number of recognized authorities, including the following agencies:

- **International Telecommunication Union-Telecommunication Standardization Sector (ITU-T)**, formerly the Consultative Committee for International Telegraph and Telephone (CCITT)

- International Organization for Standardization (ISO)

- Internet Engineering Task Force (IETF)

- Electronic Industries Association (EIA)

- Institute of Electrical and Electronics Engineers (IEEE)

Synchronous serial lines have several data link encapsulations associated with them, the characteristics for which are listed in Table 1-2.

Table 1-2 Synchronous Serial Line Data Link Encapsulations

Encapsulation	Characteristics
High-Level Data Link Control (HDLC)	An IEEE standard. It is the default encapsulation on point-to-point dedicated links and circuit-switch connections. Cisco HDLC is a proprietary version, bit-oriented, synchronous data link layer protocol typically used when communicating between two Cisco devices. Cisco HDLC might be incompatible with other vendors' versions due to the method of implementation those vendors have chosen. Supports both point-to-point and multipoint configurations with minimal overhead.
Frame Relay	Uses high-quality digital facilities. Uses simplified framing with no error correction mechanisms, which means it can send Layer 2 information much more rapidly than other WAN protocols. Industry-standard switched data link layer protocol that handles multiple virtual circuits. Next generation to X.25, Frame Relay is streamlined to eliminate some of the time-consuming processes that were employed in X.25, such as error correction and flow control.
Point-to-Point Protocol (PPP)	Described by RFC 1661. Two standards developed by the IETF. Contains a Protocol field to identify the network layer protocol. Provides router-to-router and host-to-network connections over synchronous and asynchronous circuits. Designed to work with several network layer protocols, such as Internet Protocol (IP) and Internetwork Packet Exchange (IPX). Built-in security mechanisms, such as Password Authentication Protocol (PAP) and Challenge Hand shake Authentication Protocol (CHAP).
Synchronous Data Link Control (SDLC) Protocol	IBM-designed WAN data link protocol for System Net work Architecture (SNA) environments. Largely being replaced by the more versatile HDLC.
Serial Line Internet Protocol (SLIP)	A WAN data link protocol for carrying IP packets. Replaced in many applications by the more versatile PPP. A protocol used for point-to-point serial connections using Transmission Control Protocol/Internet Protocol (TCP/IP).

continues

Table 1-2 Synchronous Serial Line Data Link Encapsulations (Continued)

Encapsulation	Characteristics
Link Access Procedure Balanced (LAPB)	Used by X.25. Has extensive error-checking capabilities.
Link Access Procedure on the D channel (LAPD)	Protocol used for signaling and call setup on an Integrated Services Digital Network (ISDN) D channel.
Link Access Procedure Frame (LAPF)	Used for Frame-Mode Bearer Services. Similar to LAPD, used with Frame Relay technologies.
X.25/Link Access Procedure Balanced (LAPB)	An ITU-T standard that defines how connections between DTE and DCE are maintained for remote terminal access and computer communications in public data networks. Specifies LAPB, a data link layer protocol. Predecessor to Frame Relay.

Figure 1-3 illustrates some of the common data link encapsulations associated with synchronous serial lines. HDCL, PPP, ISDN, and Frame Relay will be discussed in more detail in subsequent chapters.

Figure 1-3 Data Link Encapsulations

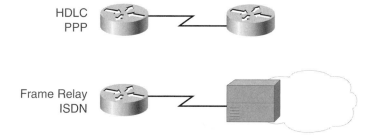

Figure 1-4 illustrates the synchronous serial communications model where services offered to the router are made available through a modem or a CSU/DSU.

Figure 1-4 CSU/DSU

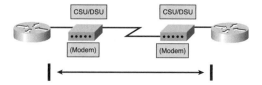

Introduction to Routers in a WAN

Just as computers need operating systems to run software applications, routers also need an operating-system software to run configuration files. On Cisco routers, this is called the Internetwork Operating System (IOS). These configuration files contain the instructions and parameters that control the flow of traffic in and out of the routers. Specifically, by using routing protocols to direct routed protocols and routing tables, routers make decisions regarding the best path for packets. The configuration file specifies all the information the router needs to make these decisions. On Cisco routers, these configuration files are known as the running-config and startup-config files. These files are discussed in later chapters.

A router is a special type of computer. It has the same basic components as a standard desktop PC. It has a CPU, memory, a system bus, and various input/output interfaces. However, routers perform some specific functions that are not typically performed by desktop computers. For example, routers connect and allow communication between two networks and determine the best path for data to travel through the connected networks.

This book demonstrates how to build configuration files from the IOS commands to get the router to perform many essential network functions. The router configuration file might appear complex at first glance, but it will seem less so by the end of this book.

The main internal components of the router, as shown in Figure 1-5, are random-access memory (RAM), nonvolatile random-access memory (NVRAM), Flash memory, read-only memory (ROM), and interfaces.

Figure 1-5 Router Internal Components

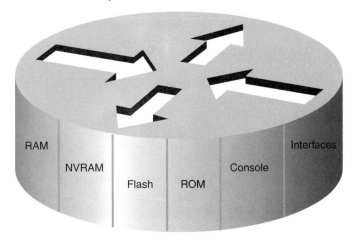

Router LANs and WANs

Routers have both LAN and WAN interfaces. WAN technologies are frequently used to connect routers. These routers communicate with each other through WAN connections, such as

Frame Relay or a dedicated T1 line. Routers are the backbone devices of intranets and the Internet. They operate at Layer 3 of the OSI model, making decisions based on network addresses (or by using IP on the Internet). The major role of a router is not as a WAN device, except on a small network where you only have a router to connect to an Internet service provider (ISP). Routers are used in any medium-sized and larger network for broadcast segmentation, and other reasons.

The two main functions of a router are as follows:

- Selection of best paths for incoming data packets
- Switching of packets to the proper outgoing interface

Routers accomplish these functions by building routing tables and exchanging the network information with other routers.

An administrator can maintain routing tables by configuring static routes. However, routing tables are generally maintained dynamically through the use of a routing protocol that exchanges network topology, or path, information with other routers.

For example, if a company has a Main office located in Arizona, and employees need to send/receive data to users located in their branch offices located in Mexico City and London, a routing feature for information flow as well as redundant paths for reliability must be configured on the routers interconnecting these remote locations. Many network design decisions and technologies can be traced to this desire for computers on the Arizona, Mexico City, and London LANs to be able to communicate, send, and receive data.

A correctly configured internetwork provides the following:

- Consistent end-to-end addressing
- Addresses that represent network topologies
- Best path selection
- Dynamic routing and/or static routing
- Switching

More Information: WAN Services and Router Roles

More often than not, internetworks are extensive in terms of the number of routers, transmission facilities, and attached end systems. In an extensive internetwork, such as the Internet or even large private networks, it is virtually impossible for any given machine to know about every other machine. Therefore, some semblance of hierarchy is needed. Hierarchical organization of internetworked machines creates the need for specialized routing functions.

Routers can specialize in learning about and distributing routing information within their domain. These routers are called *interior gateways*. Alternatively, routers can specialize in collecting routing information about networks that lie beyond their domain. These routers are known as *exterior gateways*.

More Information: WAN Services and Router Roles (Continued)

Networking is often used as a generic or universal term. However, networked machines communicate in tremendously different ways. Routers can function in different capacities in an internetwork, for example, as interior, exterior, or border routers.

As you might have noticed in the previous paragraphs, finding interior routers, exterior routers, and border routers described as *interior gateways, exterior gateways,* and *border gateways*, respectively, is not uncommon. The term *gateway* is as old as routing itself. Over time, this term has lost some of its descriptive value. Consequently, both sets of terms are technically correct, except in the presence of technological purists. Then, you must determine which terminology they consider correct!

These functional specializations are more than merely academic. Understanding the differences among them requires examining them in the context of a WAN. Therefore, a logical starting point is an examination of the context. The terms *WAN, network, internetwork,* and *autonomous system* are all used interchangeably, yet each term has a slightly different meaning:

- **WAN**—A collection of related LANs linked via routers and serial transmission facilities, such as leased lines or Frame Relay circuits. Implicit in this definition is that the LANs in the WAN might be geographically dispersed, but they still fall under the control of a single organization, such as a company or school.

- **Network**—A network can sometimes be a difficult term to describe. Everything from LANs to WANs can be classified as a network. A single subnet can be a network or a collection of subnets. Consequently, for the purposes of this book, a network identifies a generic collection of related networking mechanisms. Therefore, a network can be a LAN or a WAN, but it must belong to a single organization and feature a consistent addressing architecture. This term is sometimes used to indicate an internetwork or even the Internet.

- **Internetwork**—A collection of loosely related networks that are interconnected. The interconnected networks can belong to different organizations. For example, two companies can use the Internet to interconnect their private WANs. The resulting internetwork consists of one public network and two private networks linked together. The most common definition of internetwork is a set of networks linked by routers. This internetwork is not necessarily a loosely related set of networks, although the term is applied to both a single domain or autonomous system (AS) internetwork or an internetwork comprised of separate autonomous systems.

More Information: WAN Services and Router Roles (Continued)

■ **Autnomous system**—A collection of networks under a common administration that share a common routing strategy. This routing strategy can include multiple routing protocols within the AS and even different, independent organizations or companies. To the outside world, an AS is viewed as a single entity. The AS can be run by one or more operators while presenting a consistent view of routing to the external world. The American Registry of Internet Numbers (ARIN) or a service provider assigns an identifying number to each AS. An autonomous system connects to other autonomous systems by using the exterior routing protocol Border Gateway Protocol (BGP) or using static routes (which is explained later). Autonomous systems are usually ISPs or large enterprise networks.

Given these definitions, it is possible to better define the functional classes of routers. An internal router interconnects networks within a LAN or autonomous system. Interior routers use Interior Gateway Routing Protocols such as OSPF and/or static routes. Figure 1-6 illustrates a small network and identifies those devices that function as interior routers.

Figure 1-6 Interior Routers in a Network

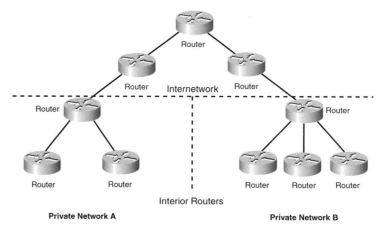

An exterior router lies beyond the boundaries of any given network. Figure 1-7, although not pretending to depict the Internet's actual topology, presents a highly simplified Internet topology that is solely intended to demonstrate what an exterior router is.

More Information: WAN Services and Router Roles (Continued)

Figure 1-7 Exterior Routers

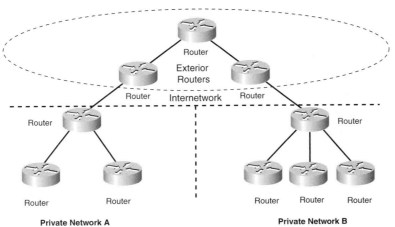

The last functional class of router is the border router. A border router connects to another router in a different AS. Both routers are usually running BGP. Border routers are sometimes known as exterior routers because they run BGP, which is an exterior routing protocol. It is important to note that a single entity might own and operate multiple autonomous systems. Therefore, a border router might denote the boundary between two autonomous systems rather than the border between a private network and some other network. Figure 1-8 identifies the border routers in the sample network that was used in Figure 1-6 and Figure 1-7.

Figure 1-8 Border Routers

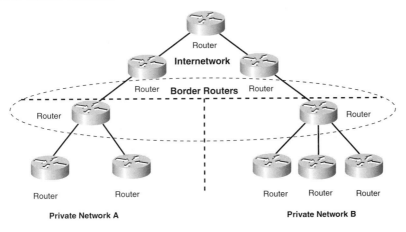

More Information: WAN Services and Router Roles (Continued)

You can use different WAN connection options to interconnect LANs. The following subsections give a brief description of the most common WAN connection services:

- Circuit-switched services

- Packet-switched services

- Cell-switched services

- Dedicated digital services

- Dialup, cable, and wireless services

Figure 1-9 depicts the different WAN connection services.

Figure 1-9 WAN Connection Services

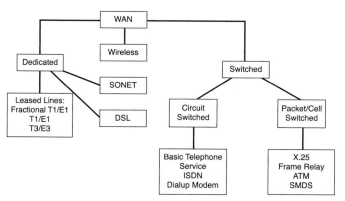

Circuit-Switched Services

Circuit switching is a WAN switching method in which a dedicated physical circuit through a carrier network is established, maintained, and terminated for each communication session. ISDN is an example of a circuit-switched WAN technology. Figure 1-10 illustrates a network topology that supports circuit switching.

Figure 1-10 Circuit Switching

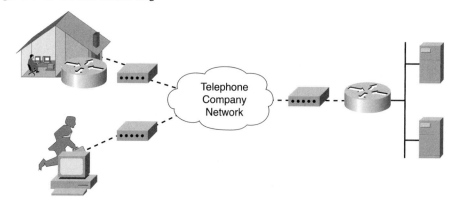

More Information: WAN Services and Router Roles (Continued)

Table 1-3 describes the characteristics of two most common circuit-switched services—plain old telephone service (POTS) and narrowband Integrated Services Digital Network (ISDN).

Table 1-3 Circuit-Switched Services

Circuit-Switched Service	Characteristics
POTS	Not a computer data service, but included because many of its technologies are part of the growing data infrastructure, and it is an incredibly reliable, easy-to-use, wide-area communications network. Typical medium is twisted-pair copper wire.
ISDN	A versatile, widespread, historically important technology. Was the first all-digital dialup service. Cost is moderate. Maximum bandwidth is 128 kbps for the lower-cost Basic Rate Interface (BRI) and about 3 Mbps for the Primary Rate Interface (PRI). Usage is fairly widespread, though it varies considerably from country to country. Typical medium is twisted-pair copper wire.

POTS and ISDN are dialup services, which means that when the call is made, an end- to-end physical path is set up and the bandwidth is reserved end to end. ISDN and POTS use synchronous time-division multiplexing (TDM), which is sometimes referred to as synchronous transfer mode.

Packet-Switched Services

Packet-switched services route small units of data called *packets* through a network based on the destination address contained within each packet. Figure 1-11 shows an example network topology that supports packet-switched services.

Figure 1-11 Packet Switching

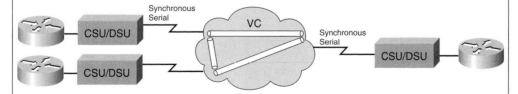

Table 1-4 describes the characteristics of two most common packet-switched services—X.25 and Frame Relay.

More Information: WAN Services and Router Roles (Continued)

Table 1-4 Packet-Switched Services

Packet-Switched Service	Characteristics
X.25	An older technology, but still widely used. Has extensive error-checking capabilities from the days when WAN links were more prone to errors. This makes it reliable but limits its bandwidth. Bandwidth can be as high as 2 Mbps. Usage is fairly extensive. Cost is moderate. Typical medium is twisted-pair copper wire.
Frame Relay	A packet-switched version of narrowband ISDN. Has become an extremely popular WAN technology in its own right. More efficient than X.25, but with similar services. Maximum bandwidth is 44.736 Mbps. 56 kbps and 384 kbps are extremely popular in the U.S. Usage is widespread. Cost is moderate to low. Typical media include twisted-pair copper wire and optical fiber.

X.25 is both connection-oriented and reliable at both Layers 2 and 3, which is a big part of why it is so much slower than Frame Relay.

Frame Relay is typically regarded as a much faster, sleeker version of X.25; it has no defined Layer 3 protocol, nor is it reliable. However, it is connection-oriented. Frame Relay has since replaced X.25 as the packet-switched service of choice because the error-checking reliability of TCP and physical reliability of the WAN infrastructure has made the reliability features of X.25 obsolete.

Circuit-switched services use time-division multiplexing (TDM) and are said to be synchronous, whereas packet-switched services use statistical TDM and are sometimes said to be asynchronous (similar to ATM).

Cell-Switched Services

Cell-switched services provide a dedicated-connection switching technology that organizes digital data into cell units and transmits them over a physical medium using digital signal technology.

More Information: WAN Services and Router Roles (Continued)

Table 1-5 describes the characteristics of two most common cell-switched services—Asynchronous Transfer Mode (ATM) and Switched Multimegabit Data Service (SMDS). ATM and SMDS are not part of CCNA.

Table 1-5 Cell-Switched Services

Cell-Switched Service	Characteristics
ATM	Is becoming an increasingly important WAN technology. Uses small, fixed 53-byte length cells to carry data. Maximum bandwidth is currently 622 Mbps, though higher speeds are being developed. Typical media are twisted-pair copper wire and optical fiber. Usage is widespread and increasing. Cost is high.
SMDS	Closely related to ATM, and typically used in metropolitan-area networks (MANs). Maximum bandwidth is 44.736 Mbps. Typical media are twisted-pair copper wire and optical fiber. Usage is not very widespread. Cost is relatively high.

Dedicated Digital Services

Dedicated digital services also provide circuit-switched services but the connection is "always-up."

Table 1-6 describes the characteristics of the most common dedicated digital services—T1, T3, E1, E3; digital subscriber line (xDSL); and Synchronous Optical Network (SONET).

Dialup, Cable, and Wireless Services

Table 1-7 describes the characteristics of other WAN services that do not fall into any of the previously covered categories of WAN technologies. Among these miscellaneous technologies are dialup modems, cable modems, and terrestrial and satellite wireless.

More Information: WAN Services and Router Roles (Continued)

Table 1-6 Dedicated Digital Services

Dedicated Digital Service	Characteristics
T1, T3, E1, E3	The T series of services in the U.S. and the E series of services in Europe are extremely important WAN technologies. They use TDM to slice up and assign time slots for data transmission. Bandwidths for the T and E series lines are 1.544 Mbps for T1, 44.736 Mbps for T3, 2.048 Mbps for E1, and 34.368 Mbps for E3. Other bandwidths are also available. The media used are typically twisted-pair copper wire and optical fiber. Usage is extremely widespread. Cost is moderate.
xDSL	A new and developing family of WAN technologies intended primarily for home use. xDSL indicates the entire family of DSL technologies, including high-bit-rate DSL (HDSL), single-line DSL (SDSL), asymmetric DSL (ADSL), and very-high-data-rate DSL (VDSL). Bandwidth decreases with increasing distance from the phone company's equipment. Top speeds of 51.84 Mbps are possible near a phone company office; however, most bandwidths are much lower from hundreds of kbps to several Mbps. Cost is moderate and decreasing.
SONET	A family of very high-speed physical layer technologies. Designed for optical fiber, but can also run on copper cables. Has a series of data rates available with special designations. Implemented at different Optical Carrier (OC) levels, ranging from 51.84 Mbps (OC-1) to 9,952 Mbps (OC-192). Can achieve high data rates by using wavelength division multiplexing (WDM). WDM is when lasers are tuned to slightly different colors, or wavelengths, to send huge amounts of data optically. Usage is widespread among Internet backbone entities. The cost is expensive. This is not a technology that connects to homes.

More Information: WAN Services and Router Roles (Continued)	

Table 1-7 Dialup, Cable, and Wireless Services

WAN Service	Characteristics
Dialup modem (switched analog)	Limited in speed, but quite versatile. Works with existing phone network. Maximum theoretical bandwidth is 56 kbps, but actual maximum bandwidth is 53 kbps. Cost is low. Usage is still very widespread. Typical medium is the twisted-pair phone line.
Cable modem (shared analog)	Puts data signals on the same cable as television signals. Increasing in popularity in regions that have large amounts of existing cable TV coaxial cable. Ninety percent of homes in United States have existing cable TV coaxial cable. Maximum bandwidth can be 10 Mbps, though this decreases as more users attach to a given network segment. Behaves like an unswitched (shared) LAN. Cost is relatively low. The medium is coaxial cable.
Wireless	Wireless requires no medium since the signals are electromagnetic waves that are transmitted through the air. A variety of wireless WAN links exist, including the following: Terrestrial has bandwidths typically in the 11-Mbps range (for example, microwave). Cost is relatively low, line of sight (LOS) is usually required, and usage is moderate. Satellite can serve mobile users such as those in a cellular telephone network and remote users that are too far from any wires or cables. Usage is widespread, and the cost is high.

Figure 1-12 illustrates different WAN technologies connected by routers.

Figure 1-12 WAN Technologies Connected by Routers

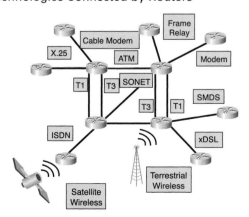

More Information: WAN Services and Router Roles (Continued)			

Comparison of WAN Technologies

Table 1-8 shows an overview of the previously discussed WAN technologies.

Table 1-8 WAN Technologies

WAN Term	WAN Name	Maximum Bandwidth	Comments
POTS	plain old telephone service	4 kHz analog	Standard for reliability
ISDN	Integrated Services Digital Network	128 kbps	Data and voice together
X.25	X.25	2 Mbps	Old reliable workhorse
Frame Relay	Frame Relay	Up to 44.736 Mbps	New workhorse
ATM	Asynchronous Transfer Mode	622 Mbps	High-powered networks
SMDS	Switched Multimegabit Data Service	1.544 Mbps and 44.736 Mbps	MAN variant of ATM
T1, T3	T1, T3	1.544 Mbps and 44.736 Mbps	Widely used telecommunications
xDSL	digital subscriber line	384 kbps	Technology over phone lines
SONET	Synchronous Optical Network	9,992 Mbps	Fast optical fiber transmission
Dialup modem	Modem	56 kbps	Mature technology using phone lines
Cable modem	Cable modem	10 Mbps	Technology using cable TV
Terrestrial wireless	Wireless	11 Mbps	Microwave and laser links
Satellite wireless	Wireless	2 Mbps	Microwave and laser links

| More Information: WAN Services and Router Roles (Continued) |

Costs of the WAN

Tempering the various performance criteria of the WAN is cost. The costs of owning and operating a WAN include the initial startup costs, as well as the monthly recurring expenses. Not surprisingly, the larger and more powerful network components are much more expensive than smaller, less-robust components. Therefore, designing a WAN becomes an economic exercise in which a careful balance of performance and cost is achieved.

Achieving this balance can be painful. No one wants to design a WAN that disappoints the users with its performance, but no one wants to design a WAN that blows the budget, either! Fortunately, the following suggestions can help guide the design of a WAN that satisfies existing requirements, provides flexibility for future growth, and doesn't exceed the budget:

- The capital investments in routers and other network hardware become a fixed part of the network. After the hardware components are placed in operation, the logistics of replacing hardware become quite complicated. And, depending on your depreciation schedule for capital equipment, you might find yourself obligated to use the hardware for five or more years! It might be better if you to purchase a larger router that is relatively low in port density. You can add hardware (memory, CPUs, and interfaces) in the future as the need for them arises. This method allows future expansion at modest incremental costs and little (if any) operational downtime.

- The transmission facilities are relatively easy to replace with other transmission facilities. They are an expense item, not a capital investment, so there is no depreciation expense to retire. These can be replaced with other facilities as often as your lease agreement with the carrier permits. Therefore, you might want to explore your options for meeting performance requirements with the various available transmission facilities and technologies.

Resource Utilization Rates

The degree to which the various physical resources of the WAN are being utilized is also a good indicator of how well, or how poorly, the WAN is performing relative to the performance requirements. Two main categories of resource utilization rates should be monitored carefully:

- Router CPU and memory utilization rates
- Transmission facility utilization rates

Router Physical Resource Rates

Routers are one of the most vital components of any WAN. And, unlike the transmission facilities, they are outside the view of the telecommunications carrier. Therefore, they are distinctly the responsibility of the customer. Fortunately, routers are intelligent devices that contain their own CPU and memory. These physical resources are indispensable in the calculation of WAN routes and the forwarding of packets. They can also be used to monitor the performance of the router.

More Information: WAN Services and Router Roles (Continued)

If either CPU or memory utilization rates approach 100 percent, performance suffers. Numerous conditions can result in either utilization rate temporarily spiking upward with subsequent performance degradation. One example is a sudden increase in transmissions from the LAN to the WAN. LANs can operate at speeds of up to 1 Gbps, and more, but they usually operate only at 10, Mbps, or 100 Mbps. Any of these speeds is a gross mismatch against the typical WAN transmission facility, which offers a paltry 1.544 Mbps of bandwidth. This mismatch in bandwidth must be buffered by the router's memory. It won't take long for a router to become resource constricted given a sustained period of heavy LAN transmissions.

If such situations are rarely experienced, they should be considered irregularity. Irregularity should be monitored, but shouldn't drive physical upgrades. If these resource constrictions recur or constitute a trend, however, something needs to be done. Usually this requires an upgrade, either to the next larger router or via an expansion of memory. If a router is chronically at or near 100 percent of capacity with its memory, it may be time to purchase additional memory.

However, responding to chronically high CPU utilization rates might not be as simple as a memory upgrade. Really, only three options exist for improving high CPU utilization rates:

- If possible, add another CPU to the router.
- Upgrade to a more powerful router.
- Investigate the WAN's traffic patterns to see if the load on the problematic router can be reduced.

Manipulating traffic patterns is really only a viable option in larger WANs with complex topologies that can afford route redundancy.

Transmission Facility Rates

Transmission facilities can also be monitored for utilization. Typically, this utilization rate is expressed in terms of the percentage of consumed bandwidth. If you are using a T1, for example, a given sample might indicate that 30 percent of its 1.544 Mbps of available bandwidth is currently being utilized.

These rates can be tricky to analyze and might even be misleading. It is not uncommon, for example, for network-management software packages to capture utilization data in time intervals. These intervals can be 1 hour, 5 minutes, or just about any other interval. If set too coarsely, the sampling frequency can miss short-duration fluctuations in bandwidth consumption. If the sampling is too frequent, you can find yourself mired in a meaningless morass of data points. The trick is finding the right frequency that provides meaningful data about how the network is performing relative to the users' expectations.

More Information: WAN Services and Router Roles (Continued)

Beyond merely selecting the sampling rate is the issue of sampling window. The sampling window should be determined by the users' requirements for WAN availability. If the utilization samples are spread over a 24-hour day and a 7-day week, whereas the users work only 10 hours per day, 5 days per week, the statistical data is not indicative of how well the users' requirements are being met.

Utilization rates are a wonderful statistical tool for monitoring and measuring the status of transmission facilities. However, they are not the only metric for assessing a network's performance. The network is successful only if it satisfies the users' requirements. Therefore, a combination of performance metrics that provides a multifaceted, composite perspective is likely to provide a better assessment of the network's success than any single metric can offer.

Role of Routers in a WAN

A WAN is said to operate at the physical layer and at the data link layer. This does not mean that the other five layers of the OSI model are not found in a WAN. It simply means that the characteristics that separate a WAN from a LAN are typically found at the physical layer and the data link layer. In other words, the standards and protocols used in WANs at Layer 1 and Layer 2 are different from those used in LANs at the same layers.

The WAN physical layer describes the interface between the *data terminal equipment (DTE)* and the *data circuit-terminating equipment (DCE)*. Typically, a DCE device provides a physical connection to the network, forwards traffic, and provides a clocking signal used to synchronize data transmission between DCE and DTE devices. Examples include modems and CSU/DSUs. A DTE device is the user end of a user-network interface that serves as a data source, destination, or both. A router is an example of a DTE device. (See Figure 1-13.)

Figure 1-13 WAN Services

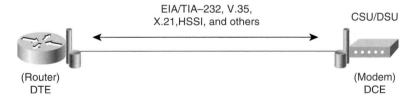

To ensure that the correct protocol is used, you must configure the appropriate Layer 2 encapsulation on the router. The choice of the protocol depends on the WAN technology and communicating equipment being utilized.

WAN physical layer protocols describe how to provide electrical, mechanical, operational, and functional connections for WAN services. These services are usually obtained from WAN service providers, such as RBOCs; alternate carriers; and Post, Telephone, and Telegraph (PTT) agencies.

The following physical layer standards are specified:

- **EIA/TIA-232**—Common physical layer interface standard that supports unbalanced circuits at signal speeds of up to 64 kbps. Closely resembles the V.24 specification.

- **EIA/TIA-449**—A faster (up to 2 Mbps) version of EIA/TIA-232 capable of longer cable runs.

- **V.24**—Physical layer interface between DTE and DCE. V.24 is essentially the same as the EIA/TIA-232.

- **V.35**—A synchronous, physical layer protocol for communications between a network access device and a packet network. V.35 is most commonly used in the United States and in Europe. V.35 cabling and interfaces are capable of much higher throughput (over 2 Mbps). They are used when connecting a Cisco router to a T1/E1 or fractional T1/E1 via a CSU/DSU.

- **X.21**—Protocol for serial communications over synchronous digital lines. The X.21 protocol is used primarily in Europe and Japan.

- **G.703**—ITU-T electrical and mechanical specifications for connections between telephone company equipment and DTE using BNC connectors and operating at E1 data rates.

- **EIA-530**—Refers to two electrical implementations of EIA/TIA-449: RS-422 (for balanced transmission) and RS-423 (for unbalanced transmission).

Academy Approach to Hands-On Labs

A viable WAN connection can connect routers from around the world. In an academy lab, all the networks are connected with a serial or Ethernet cable, and the students can see and physically touch the equipment. In a real-world situation, one router could be in New York, while another router could be in Sydney, Australia. An administrator located in Sydney would have to connect to the router in New York through the WAN cloud to troubleshoot the New York router.

In the academy lab, the entire dedicated circuit cloud has been made extremely small and put in the "crack" between the back-to-back DTE-DCE cables. The connection from one router's interface s0/0 to another's router interface s0/1 simulates the entire circuit cloud.

Note that because a CSU/DSU is not normally used in a lab situation, clocking must be configured on the DCE side of a connection between two routers that are directly attached to each other.

More Information: Internetworking Scenarios

Having examined the concepts underlying routing and internetworking, as well as some of the terminology inherent with these topics, you can see how they are used by examining three internetworking scenarios. Each scenario demonstrates some of the issues that need to be addressed in any network or internetwork:

- Routing within a network
- Routing between adjacent networks
- Routing between nonadjacent networks

These three generic aspects encompass virtually every form of internetworking that you are likely to encounter. Each one holds different implications for the network administrator, including such routing aspects as route calculation and distribution, convergence, and security. The following sections provide an overview of each internetworking scenario and highlight the areas of concern for a network administrator. The various potential resolutions to these routing concerns are presented throughout this book.

Routers

It is important to have an understanding of the physical layer components of a router. This understanding builds a foundation for other knowledge and skills needed to configure routers and manage routed networks. This section closely examines the internal and external physical components of the router. This chapter also describes techniques for physically connecting the various router interfaces.

Router Internal Components

Table 1-9 outlines the main internal configuration components of the router.

Table 1-9 Main Internal Configuration Components of a Router

Internal Component	Characteristics
Random-access memory (RAM/ DRAM)	Stores routing tables. Address Resolution Protocol (ARP) cache. Fast-switching cache. Packet buffering (shared RAM). Packet-hold queues. Provides temporary and running memory for the configuration file of the router while the router is powered on. RAM content is lost when powered down or restarted.

continues

Table 1-9 Main Internal Configuration Components of a Router (Continued)

Internal Component	Characteristics
Nonvolatile random-access memory (NVRAM)	Stores the backup/startup configuration file for the router. Retains content when the router is powered down or restarted.
Flash memory	Erasable, programmable read-only memory (EPROM). Holds the operating system image and microcode. Allows software to be updated without removing and replacing chips on the processor. Content remains when powered down or restarted. Multiple versions of Cisco IOS Software can be stored in Flash memory.
Read-only memory (ROM)	Maintains instructions for power-on self test (POST) diagnostics. Stores a bootstrap program and basic operating system software. Software upgrades in ROM require replacing pluggable chips on the CPU.
Interface	Network connection through which packets enter and exit a router. Located on the motherboard or on a separate interface module.

Interactive Media Activity   Drag and Drop: Router Internal Components

When you complete this activity, you will be able to define the internal components of a router.

More Information: A Closer Look at Routers

Routers are designed to interconnect multiple networks. This interconnection enables machines on different networks to communicate with each other. Interconnected networks can be co-located or geographically dispersed. Networks that are geographically dispersed are usually interconnected via a WAN. WANs are constructed of numerous different technologies, including routers and transmission facilities. It is the router's capability to interconnect networks in a WAN that has made it indispensable.

More Information: A Closer Look at Routers (Continued)

A router is an intelligent network device that operates predominantly at the first three layers of the OSI reference model. Routers, like any host, are actually capable of operating at all seven layers of the OSI reference model, but this does not usually include the routing function of the router. For example, upper-layer protocols allow the network administrator to telnet into the router. However, the need for the first three layers is virtually universal. Communication across the first two layers allows routers to communicate directly with LANs and WANs as part of the router's switching function (data link layer constructs). More importantly, routers can identify routes through networks based on Layer 3 addresses. This enables routers to inter-network multiple networks by using network layer addressing, regardless of how near or far they might be relative to each other.

Understanding routers and routing requires examining a router from two different perspectives: physical and logical. From a physical perspective, routers contain myriad parts, each of which has a specific function. From a logical perspective, routers perform many functions, including finding other routers in the network, learning about potential destination networks and hosts, discovering and tracking potential routes, and forwarding datagrams, or packets, toward their specified destination. Together, these physical components and logical functions enable you to build and use internetworks, including WANs.

Physical Components of a Router

A router is a remarkably complex device. Its complexity lies in its routing engine logic that enables the physical device to perform the various routing functions. The complexity of routing logic is hidden by the relative simplicity of the router's physical form. The most common type of router is actually a highly specialized type of computer; it contains the same basic components as any other computer. These components include the following:

- A central processing unit (CPU)

- Random-access memory (RAM)

- A basic input/output system (BIOS)

- An operating system (OS)

- A motherboard

- Physical input/output (I/O) ports

- A power supply, chassis, and sheet-metal skin

The vast majority of a router's components will remain forever shielded from the eyes of network administrators by the chassis' sheet-metal skin. These components are extremely reliable and, under normal operating conditions, shouldn't see the light of day. The obvious exceptions to this general statement are born of expansion. Any time you need to add more resources to the router, you might have to take off its cover. Such resources usually include either memory or I/O ports.

More Information: A Closer Look at Routers (Continued)

The components that a network administrator will encounter most often are the OS and the I/O ports. A router's OS (in Cisco Systems case, the Internetwork Operating System or IOS) is the software that controls the various hardware components and makes them usable. Network administrators mostly use a command-line interface to develop a logical configuration. The configuration is a profile of the system: the numbers, the locations, the types of each I/O port, and details such as addressing and bandwidth information. A router's configuration can also include security information such as which users are permitted access to specific I/O ports and configuration modes.

The I/O ports are the one physical router component that network administrators see on a routine basis. These ports bear out the router's unique capability to interconnect seemingly endless combinations of LAN and WAN transmission technologies. Each one of these ports, whether LAN or WAN, must have its own I/O port on the router. These ports function like a network interface card (NIC) in a LAN-attached computer; they are related to the medium and framing mechanisms expected and provide the appropriate physical interfaces. Many of these physical interfaces appear quite similar to each other. This physical similarity belies the differences between the higher-layer functions of those technologies. Therefore, you will find it more useful to examine transmission technologies than to examine specific physical interfaces.

Functions of a Router

The logical functions that a router performs are just as important as providing physical interconnectivity for multiple networks. These functions make the physical interconnections usable. For example, internetworked communications require that at least one physical path interconnect the source and destination machines. However, having and using a physical path are two very different things. Specifically, the source and destination machines must speak a common language (a *routed protocol*). It also helps if the routers that lie between them also speak a common language (a *routing protocol*) and agree on which specific physical path is the best one to use.

Therefore, some of the more salient functions that a router provides are

- Physical interconnectivity
- Logical interconnectivity
- Route calculation and maintenance
- Security

Physical Interconnectivity

A router has a minimum of two (and frequently many more) physical I/O ports. I/O ports, or *interfaces* as they are better known, are used to physically connect multiple networks or subnets. Each port is connected to a circuit board that is attached to the router's mother board. Thus, the motherboard actually provides the interconnectivity among these multiple networks.

More Information: A Closer Look at Routers (Continued)

The network administrator must initially configure each interface via the router's console. Configuration includes defining the interface's port number in the router, the specific transmission technology and bandwidth available on the network connected to that interface, and the type of Layer 2 protocols that will be used through that interface. The actual parameters that must be defined vary based on the type of network interface.

Logical Interconnectivity

As soon as a router interface is configured, it can be activated. The interface's configuration identifies the interface's IP address, and the address of the network that it connects to. Upon activation of a port and when routing is enabled, the router will immediately begin monitoring all the packets that are being transmitted on the network attached to the newly activated port. With dynamic routing, this is only done after convergence. This monitoring allows it to "learn" about network and host IP addresses that reside on the networks that can be reached via that port.

A router can also be configured with a *default route*. A default route associates a specific router interface with all unknown destination addresses, addresses that do not match more specific routes in the routing table. This association allows a router to forward a datagram to destinations that are not in its routing table. Default routes can be useful in other ways, too. Default routes can be used to minimize the size of routing tables, for example, or can be used to reduce the amount of traffic generated between routers as they exchange routing information.

Route Calculation and Maintenance

Routers communicate with each other using a predetermined protocol, a routing protocol. Routing protocols enable routers to do the following:

- Identify potential routes to specific destination networks

- Perform a mathematical calculation, based on the routing protocol's algorithm, to determine the best path to each destination

- Continuously monitor the network to detect any topology changes that might render known routes invalid

Many different types of routing protocols exist. Some, such as the Routing Information Protocol (RIP), are simple. Others, such as Open Shortest Path First (OSPF), are remarkably powerful and feature-rich but more complicated. In general, routing protocols use two different approaches to make routing decisions: distance vectors and link states. A distance-vector routing protocol makes its decision based on information from neighboring routers. This process is also known as "routing-by-rumor."

A link-state protocol bases its decisions upon a topology map it creates of the entire routing domain. However, the routing decisions result in different levels of performance, including convergence times.

More Information: A Closer Look at Routers (Continued)

You can evaluate routing protocols using numerous, more-specific criteria than just which approaches they use. Some of the more meaningful criteria include the following:

- **Optimality**—Optimality describes a routing protocol's capability to select the best available route. Unfortunately, the word *best* is ambiguous. Many different ways exist to evaluate different routes to any given destination. Each way could result in the selection of a different "best" route depending on the criteria used. The criteria used by routing protocols to calculate and evaluate routes are known as *routing metrics*. A wide variety of metrics are used, and they vary widely by routing protocol. One simple metric is *hop count*, the number of hops, or routers, that lie between the source and destination machines.

- **Efficiency**—Another criterion to consider when evaluating routing protocols is their operational efficiency. Operational efficiency can be measured by examining the physical resources, including router RAM and CPU time, and network bandwidth required by a given routing protocol. You might need to consult your router manufacturer or vendor to determine the relative efficiencies of any protocols you are considering.

- **Robustness**—A routing protocol should perform reliably at all times, not just when the network is stable. Error conditions, including hardware or transmission-facility failures, router configuration errors, and even heavy traffic loads, adversely affect a network. Therefore, that a routing protocol functions properly during periods of network failure or instability is critical.

- **Convergence**—Because they are intelligent devices, routers can automatically detect changes in the internetwork. When a change is detected, all the routers involved must converge on a new agreement of the network's topology and recalculate the routes to known destinations accordingly. This process of reaching mutual agreement is called *convergence*. Each routing protocol uses different mechanisms for detecting and communicating network changes. Therefore, each one converges at a different rate. In general, the slower a routing protocol converges, the greater the potential for disrupting service across the internetwork.

- **Scalability**—A network's scalability is its capability to grow. Although growth isn't a requirement in every organization, the routing protocol that you select should be capable of scaling upward to meet your network's projected growth.

Router Physical Characteristics

It is not critical to know the location of the physical components inside the router to understand how to use the router. However, in some situations, such as adding memory, it can be helpful.

The exact components used and their location varies between router models. Figure 1-14 identifies the internal components of a 2600 router.

Figure 1-14 Internal Components of a 2600 Router

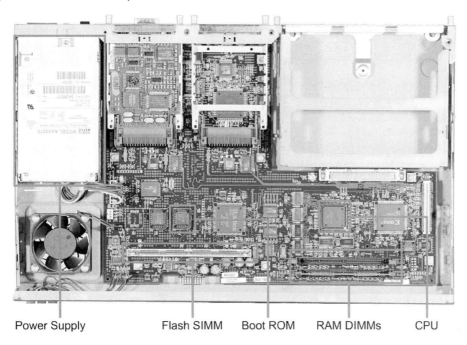

Power Supply   Flash SIMM   Boot ROM   RAM DIMMs   CPU

Figure 1-15 shows some of the external connectors on a 2600 router.

Figure 1-15 External Connection on a 2600 Router

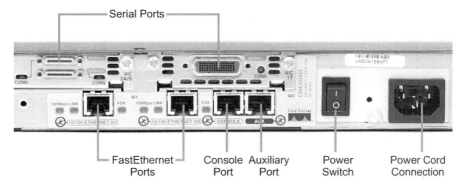

Serial Ports

FastEthernet   Console Auxiliary   Power   Power Cord
Ports   Port   Port   Switch   Connection

PhotoZoom   Cisco 1721 Router

In this PhotoZoom, you view a Cisco 1721 router.

PhotoZoom   Cisco 2621 Router

In this PhotoZoom, you view a Cisco 2621 router.

Router External Connections

The three basic types of connections on a router are LAN interfaces, WAN interfaces, and management ports, as illustrated by Figure 1-16. LAN interfaces allow the router to connect to the LAN media, which is usually some form of Ethernet. However, it could be some other LAN technology such as Token Ring or FDDI.

Figure 1-16 Router External Connections

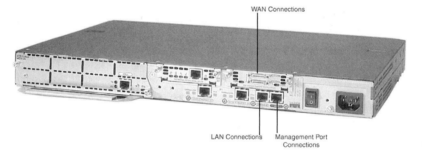

WAN connections provide connections through a service provider to a distant site or to the Internet. These connections can be serial connections or any number of other WAN interfaces. With some types of WAN interfaces, an external device such as a CSU/DSU is required to connect the router to the service provider's local connection. With other types of WAN connections, the router might be directly connected to the service provider.

The function of management ports is different from that of the other connections. The LAN and WAN connections provide network connections through which packets are passed. The management port provides a text-based connection for the configuration and troubleshooting of the router. The common management interfaces are the console and auxiliary ports. These are EIA-232 asynchronous serial ports. They are connected to a communications port on a computer. The computer will run a terminal emulation program to provide a text-based session with the router. Through this session the network administrator can manage the device.

Management Port Connections

The console port and (on some routers) the auxiliary (AUX) port are management ports. These asynchronous serial ports are not designed as networking ports. The console port is required for the configuration of the router. Not all routers have an auxiliary port.

When the router is first put into service, no networking parameters are configured. Therefore, the router cannot communicate with any network. To prepare for initial startup and configuration, attach an RS-232 ASCII terminal, or attach the rollover cable to a personal computer running terminal emulating software, such as HyperTerminal, to the system console port. Then you can enter configuration commands to set up the router.

Once you enter this initial configuration into the router through the console or auxiliary port, you can then connect the router to the network for troubleshooting or monitoring.

You can remotely configure the router through the configuration port across an IP network using Telnet, or by dialing to a modem connected to the console or auxiliary port on the router.

The console port is also preferred over the auxiliary port for troubleshooting. This preference for the console port is because it displays router startup, debugging, and error messages by default. You can use the console port when the networking services have not been started or have failed. Therefore, you can use the console port for disaster and password recovery procedures. The auxiliary port can be used to set up a modem to a dialup line so the network administrator can dial in to fix a problem.

Console Port Connections

The console port, as shown in Figure 1-17, is a management port used to provide out-of-band access to the router. Out-of-band access is reserved for network administration. It enables an administrator to have access to the router regardless of the state of the other interfaces or networks attached to the router. It is used for the initial configuration of the router, monitoring, and disaster-recovery procedures.

Figure 1-17 A Console Port

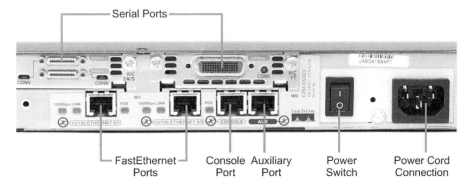

To connect to the console port, a rollover cable and an RJ-45 to DB-9 adapter are used to connect a PC, as shown in Figure 1-18. Cisco supplies the necessary adapter to connect to the console port.

Figure 1-18 Connecting to the Console Port

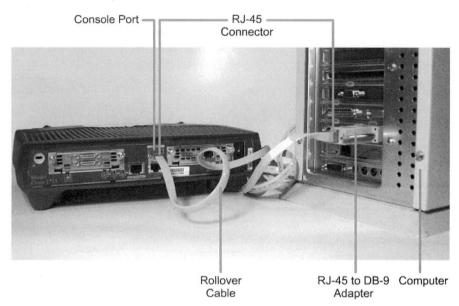

The PC or terminal must support VT100 terminal emulation. Terminal emulation software, such as HyperTerminal, as shown in Figure 1-19, is usually used.

Figure 1-19 HyperTerminal

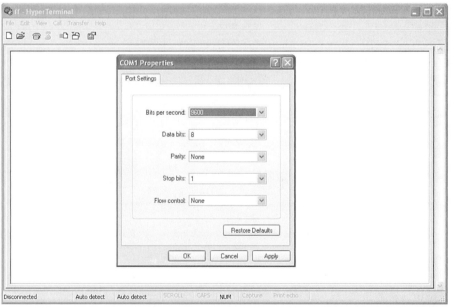

To connect the PC to a router, complete the following steps:

Step 1   Configure terminal emulation software on the PC for the following:

- The appropriate com port

- 9600 baud

- 8 data bits

- No parity

- 1 stop bit

- No flow control

Step 2   Connect the RJ-45 connector of the rollover cable to the router console port.

Step 3   Connect the other RJ-45 end of the rollover cable to the DB-9 adapter.

Step 4   Attach the female DB-9 adapter to a PC.

Lab 1.2.5   Connecting Console Interfaces

In this activity, you identify the console interfaces on the router. You then identify and locate the proper cable to connect a PC to the router to serve as its management console.

Connecting Router LAN Interfaces

In most LAN environments, the router is connected to the LAN using an Ethernet or Fast Ethernet interface. The router is a host that communicates with the LAN via a hub or a switch. A straight-through cable makes this connection. A 10/100BASE-TX router interface requires Category 5 or better unshielded twisted-pair (UTP), regardless of the router type, as shown in Figure 1-20.

Figure 1-20 UTP Cable Connection

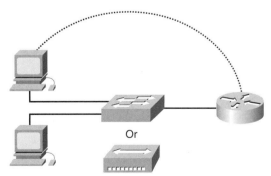

In some cases, the Ethernet connection of the router is connected directly to the computer or to another router. For this type of connection, a crossover cable is required.

The correct interface must be used. If the wrong interface is connected, damage can result to the router or other networking devices. Many different types of connections use the same style of connector. For example, Ethernet, ISDN BRI, console, AUX, integrated CSU/DSU, and Token Ring interfaces use the same 8-pin connector, RJ-45, RJ-48, or RJ-49. To help distinguish the connections on the router, Cisco uses a color-code scheme to identify connector use.

Lab 1.2.6   Connecting Router LAN Interfaces

In this activity, you identify the Fast Ethernet interfaces on the router. You then identify and locate the proper cables to connect the router. Finally, you use the cables to connect the router and computer to the hub.

Connecting WAN Interfaces

WAN connections can take any number of forms. A WAN makes data connections across a broad geographic area using many different types of technology. These WAN services are usually leased from service providers. Among these WAN connection types are leased line, circuit-switched, and packet-switched, as shown in Figure 1-21.

Figure 1-21 WAN Types

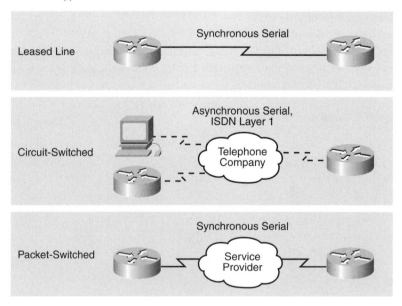

For each type of WAN service, the customer premises equipment (CPE), which is often a router, is the data terminal equipment (DTE). This is connected to the service provider using a data circuit-terminating equipment (DCE) device, which is commonly a modem or channel service unit/data service unit (CSU/DSU). This device converts the data from the DTE into a form that's acceptable to the WAN service provider.

Perhaps the most commonly used router interfaces for WAN services are serial interfaces. Selecting the proper serial cable is as easy as knowing the answers to four questions:

- What is the type of connection to the Cisco device? Cisco routers might use different connectors for the serial interfaces, as shown in Figure 1-22. The interface on the left is a smart serial interface. The interface on the right is a DB-60 connection. This makes the selection of the serial cable connecting the network system to the serial devices a critical part in setting up a WAN.

Figure 1-22 Router Serial Ports

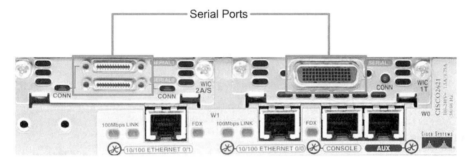

- Is the network system being connected to a DTE or DCE device? DTE and DCE are the two types of serial interfaces that devices use to communicate. The key difference between these two is that the DCE device provides the clock signal for the communications on the bus. The device documentation should specify whether it is DTE or DCE.

- What signaling standard does the device require? For each different device, a different serial standard could be used, as shown in Figure 1-23. Each standard defines the signals on the cable and specifies the connector at the end of the cable. Device documentation should always be consulted for the signaling standard.

- Is a male or female connector required on the cable? If the connector has visible projecting pins, it is male. If the connector has sockets for projecting pins, it is female, as shown in Figure 1-24.

Figure 1-23 Router Serial WAN Connectors

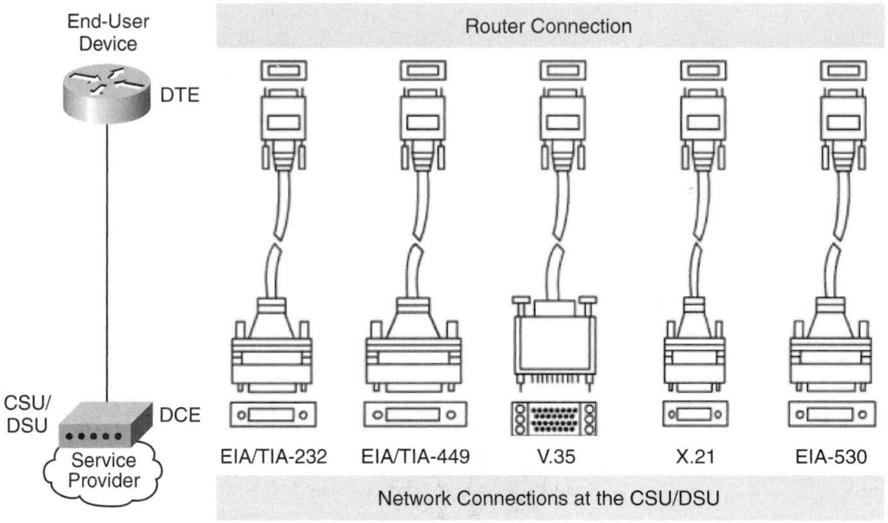

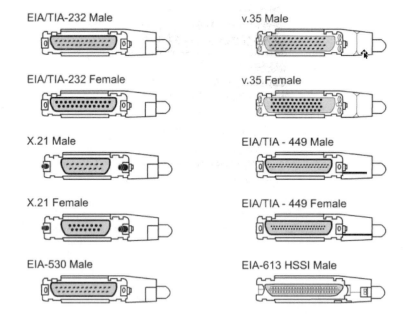

Figure 1-24 DCE Serial Connections

Lab 1.2.7   Connecting WAN Interfaces

In this activity, you identify the serial interfaces on the router. You then identify and locate the proper cables to interconnect the routers. Finally, you use the cables to connect the routers.

Summary

In this chapter, you learned the following the key points:

- The Internet is the interconnection of thousands of large and small networks all over the world.

- A WAN is used to interconnect LANs that are separated by a large geographic distance.

- Dedicated line, circuit-switching, packet-switching, and cell-switching are some of the common WAN connection types.

- Many types of WAN services are available to the WAN subscriber, who must know how to interface to the WAN provider's service.

- WAN devices include routers, WAN switches, modems, CSUs/DSUs, and access servers.

- WAN physical layer protocols describe how to provide electrical, mechanical, operational, and functional connection for WAN services.

- WAN data link layer protocols describe how frames are carried between systems on a single data link.

To supplement all that you've learned in this chapter, refer to the chapter-specific PhotoZooms and Interactive Media Activity on the CD-ROM accompanying this book.

Key Terms

cell-switched services   Provide a dedicated-connection switching technology that organizes digital data into cell units and transmits them over a physical medium using digital signal technology.

circuit switching   A WAN switching method in which a dedicated physical circuit through a carrier network is established, maintained, and terminated for each communication session. ISDN is an example of a circuit-switched WAN technology.

DCE (data circuit-terminating equipment)   Devices and connections of a communications network that comprise the network end of the user-to-network interface. The DCE provides a physical connection to the network, forwards traffic, and provides a clocking signal used to synchronize data transmission between DCE and DTE devices. Modems and interface cards are examples of DCE.

DTE (data terminal equipment)   Device at the user end of a user-network interface that serves as a data source, destination, or both. DTE connects to a data network through a DCE device (for example, a modem) and typically uses clocking signals generated by the DCE. DTE includes such devices as computers, protocol translators, and multiplexers.

modem   Device that converts digital and analog signals. At the source, a modem converts digital signals to a form suitable for transmission over analog communication facilities. At the destination, the analog signals are returned to their digital form. Modems allow data to be transmitted over voice-grade telephone lines. The term *modem* is also used to describe various digital devices such as CSU/DSUs and ISDN terminal adapters.

packet-switched services   Routes small units of data called packets through a network based on the destination address contained within each packet.

propagation delay   Time required for data to travel over a network from its source to its ultimate destination.

router   Network layer device that uses one or more metrics to determine the optimal path along which network traffic should be forwarded. Routers forward packets from one network to another based on network layer information.

switch   Network device that filters, forwards, and floods frames based on the destination address of each frame. The switch operates at the data link layer of the OSI model.

uptime   The amount of time that the device is functional and in service relative to the users' requirements for its availability.

WAN (wide-area network)   A data communications network spanning a large geographic area, such as a state, province or country. WANs often use transmission facilities provided by common carriers, for example, telephone companies.

Check Your Understanding

Complete all the review questions to test your understanding of the topics and concepts in this chapter. Answers are listed in Appendix B, "Check Your Understanding Answer Key."

1. Which of the following best describes a WAN?

    A. Connects LANs that are separated by a large geographic area

    B. Connects workstations, terminals, and other devices in a metropolitan area

    C. Connects LANs within a large building

    D. Connects workstations, terminals, and other devices within a building

2. How do WANs differ from LANs?

    A. WANs provide access over serial interfaces operating at lower speeds than LAN interfaces.

    B. WANs provide high-speed multiple access services.

    C. WANs typically exist in small geographic areas.

    D. WANs use tokens to regulate network traffic.

3. Which of the following are examples of WAN technologies?

    A. Token Ring, ARCNet

    B. Frame Relay, ISDN

    C. Star, Banyan VINES

    D. CSU/DSU, ARCView

4. Which layers of the OSI model do WAN standards describe?

    A. Data link and network

    B. Data link and presentation

    C. Physical and application

    D. Physical and data link

5. Which best describes data circuit-terminating equipment (DCE)?

    A. Consists of the user device at the end of a network

    B. Serves as the data source or destination

    C. Consists of physical devices such as protocol translators and multiplexers

    D. Consists of physical devices at the end of a WAN connection that provide a clocking signal used to synchronize data transmission between DCE and DTE devices.

6. Which of the following components provides an interface for voice-grade services and channel service units/digital service units (CSUs/DSUs) that interface T1/E1 services?

    A. Switches

    B. Routers

    C. Modems

    D. Communication servers

7. Which of the following concentrates the dial-in and dial-out user connections?

    A. Switches

    B. Routers

    C. Modems

    D. Communication servers

8. Some WAN physical and data link layer standards are:

    A. EIA/TIA-232

    B. PPP

    C. Frame Relay

    D. All of the above

9. Match the functions with the components.

    1) RAM/DRAM   A. RAM that retains its contents when a unit is powered off

    2) NVRAM   B. Volatile memory that can be read and written by the microprocessor

    3) ROM   C. Nonvolatile memory that can be read but not written by a microprocessor

    4) Flash memory D. Nonvolatile storage that can be electrically erased and reprogrammed so that software images can be stored, booted, and rewritten as necessary

    5) Interface   E. Connection between two systems or devices

    Select your answer:

    A. 1-B, 2-A, 3-C, 4-E, 5-D

    B. 1-A, 2-B, 3-C, 4-E, 5-D

    C. 1-B, 2-A, 3-E, 4-C, 5-D

    D. 1-B, 2-A, 3-C, 4-D, 5-E

10. Any internetwork will probably include the following:

    A. Consistent end-to-end addressing

    B. Addresses that represent network topologies

    C. Best path selection static and/or dynamic routing

    D. All of the above

11. Which of the following are data link encapsulations for WAN?

    A. High-Level Data Link Control (HDLC)

    B. Frame Relay

    C. Point-to-Point Protocol (PPP)

    D. All of the above

12. What are the main functions of routers?

    A. The determination of best paths for incoming data packets and the switching of packets to the proper outgoing interface

    B. Replying to ARP requests when two nodes are on different LANs

    C. Building routing tables and exchanging the network information contained within them with other routers

    D. Both A and C

13. Which is an IBM-designed WAN data link for Systems Network Architecture (SNA) environments, largely being replaced by the more versatile HDLC?

    A. Serial Line Interface Protocol

    B. Point-to-Point Protocol

    C. Synchronous Data Link Control Protocol

    D. Simple Data Level Control Protocol

14. Which WAN data link protocol is used for signaling and call setup on an ISDN D channel?

    A. LAPD

    B. LAPF

    C. LAPB

    D. LAPR

15. Identify the WAN circuit-switched service(s):

    A. Plain old telephone services (POTS)

    B. Narrowband ISDN with a maximum bandwidth of 1.544 Mbps

    C. Narrowband ISDN with a maximum bandwidth of 128 kbps

    D. Both A and C

16. Which service has become an extremely popular WAN technology in its own right, is more efficient than X.25 but with similar services, has a maximum bandwidth of 44.736 Mbps, and offers extremely popular 56-Kbps and 384-Kbps implementations in the United States?

    A. Frame Relay

    B. X.25

    C. POTS

    D. ATM

17. Identify the common type(s) of DSL technology/technologies:

    A. High-bit-rate DSL (HDSL)

    B. Single-line DSL (SDSL)

    C. Asymmetric DSL (ADSL)

    D. All of the above

18. Which is a family of very high-speed physical layer technologies with a series of data rates available with special designations, implemented at different Optical Carrier (OC) levels ranging from 51.84 Mbps (OC-1) to 9952 Mbps (OC-192), that can achieve these amazing data rates by using wavelength division multiplexing (WDM)?

    A. SONET

    B. HDSL

    C. ATM

    D. SMDS

Objectives

Upon completion of this chapter, you should be able to answer the following questions:

- What steps are required to establish a HyperTerminal session?

- What steps are required to log in to a router?

- How do you use the Help feature in the command-line interface?

- What are some ways to troubleshoot command errors?

- What are some of the basic operation and features of Cisco IOS Software?

- What are the methods of troubleshooting Cisco IOS Software?

- What are some uses of the **show version** command?

- What are the various router user interfaces and modes used for?

- What is the purpose of Cisco IOS Software?

- What are some of the methods used to establish a command-line interface (CLI) session with the router?

- What commands and steps are used to alternate between the user command executive (EXEC) and privileged EXEC modes?

Key Terms

The following is a list of key terms introduced in this chapter. For your reference, a definition for each term can be found at the end of this chapter.

Cisco Internetwork Operating System (IOS) Software　page 548

command-line interface (CLI)　page 548

bootstrap　page 553

nonvolatile RAM (NVRAM)　page 554

power-on self-test (POST)　page 555

Flash memory　page 555

light-emitting diode (LED)　page 560

daughter card　page 560

In this chapter, you learn how to start a router for the first time by using the correct commands and startup sequence to do an initial configuration of the router. This chapter also explains the startup sequence of a router and the setup dialog that the router uses to create an initial configuration file using current versions of Cisco Internetwork Operating System (IOS) Software.

Please be sure to look at this chapter's associated Interactive Media Activity that you will find on the CD-ROM accompanying this book. This CD element is designed to supplement the material and reinforce the concepts introduced in this chapter.

Operating Cisco IOS Software

Cisco technology is built around the *Cisco Internetwork Operating System (IOS)*, which is the software that controls the routing and switching functions of internetworking devices. A solid understanding of the IOS is essential for a network administrator. This section presents an introduction to the fundamentals of the IOS and provides practice in examining the features of the IOS.

The Purpose of Cisco IOS Software

Like any computer, a router or switch cannot function without an operating system (OS). Cisco calls its operating system the Cisco Internetwork Operating System, or Cisco IOS Software. It is the embedded software architecture in almost all the Cisco routers and Catalyst switches. Some Catalyst switches use a Cisco command-line interface (CLI). A router does not become functional until it loads Cisco IOS Software. Without an operating system, the hardware has no capability. Cisco IOS Software provides the following network services:

- Basic routing and switching functions
- Reliable and secure access to networked resources
- Network scalability

Router User Interface

Recall that the Cisco IOS Software uses a *command-line interface (CLI)* as its traditional console environment. Cisco IOS Software is a core technology that extends across most of the Cisco product line. Its operation details vary, depending upon the internetworking device using it.

This CLI environment is accessible through several methods:

- Through a console session. A console uses a low-speed serial connection directly from a computer or terminal to the console connection on the router. This method does not require the configuration of network services on the router or the computer.

- Through a dialup connection by using a modem connected to the router AUX port. This method does not require the configuration of IP services on the router, either.

- Through a Telnet connection to the router as a virtual terminal. To establish a Telnet session to the router, at least one interface must be configured for IP. Virtual terminal sessions also must be configured for login and passwords.

Router User Interface Modes

The Cisco CLI uses a hierarchical structure. This structure requires entry into different modes to accomplish particular tasks. For example, interface configuration mode must be entered to configure a router interface. From interface configuration mode, all configurations entered apply only to that particular interface, such as the IP address and subnet mask. Each command mode is indicated with a distinctive prompt and allows only commands that are appropriate for that mode.

Cisco IOS Software provides a command interpreter service known as the command executive (EXEC). After each command is entered, the EXEC validates and executes the command.

As a security feature, Cisco IOS Software separates the EXEC sessions into two access levels. These levels are user EXEC mode and privileged EXEC mode, which is also known as enable mode.

User EXEC mode allows only a limited number of basic monitoring commands. This often is referred to as a view-only mode. The user EXEC level does not allow any commands that could change the configuration of the router. The user EXEC level does not mean this is for the typical "user" on the network. The user EXEC mode is for network technicians and others in the Information Technology (IT) department who need access to basic monitoring commands, but do not have the authorization to make modifications to the networking device. The user EXEC mode can be identified by the > prompt.

Privileged EXEC mode provides access to all router commands. Privileged EXEC mode can be protected by requiring a user ID and a password. This mode allows only authorized users to access the router. Configuration and management commands require that the network administrator be at the privileged EXEC level. Global configuration mode and all other more specific configuration modes can be reached only from privileged EXEC mode. Privileged EXEC mode can be identified on the CLI session by the # prompt.

To access the privileged EXEC level from the user EXEC level, enter the **enable** command at the > prompt. If a password is configured, the router asks for a password at this point. For security reasons, a Cisco network device will not show the password that is entered. When the correct password is entered, the router prompt changes to #, indicating that the user is now at the privileged EXEC level. Entering a question mark (?) at the privileged EXEC level reveals many more command options than those available at the user EXEC level.

Cisco IOS Software Features

Cisco provides Cisco IOS Software images for devices spanning a wide range of network product platforms. To optimize the Cisco IOS Software required by various product platforms, Cisco is working to develop many different Cisco IOS Software files, known as images. Each image represents a different feature set that serves the various device platforms, available memory resources, and customers' needs.

Numerous Cisco IOS Software images exist for different Cisco device models and feature sets. However, the basic configuration command structure is the same. The configuration and troubleshooting skills acquired on any one device apply across a wide range of products.

The naming convention for the different Cisco IOS Software releases contains three parts:

- The platform on which the image runs
- The special capabilities supported in the image
- Where the image runs and whether it has been zipped or compressed

This material is covered in more detail in Chapter 5, "Managing Cisco IOS Software."

The Cisco IOS Software naming conventions, image content, and other details are subject to change.

One of the main considerations when selecting a new IOS image is that it is compatible with the router Flash and RAM memory. In general, the newer the release is and the more features it provides, the more Flash memory and RAM it requires. Use the **show version** command, as shown in Example 2-1, from the Cisco device to check the current image and available Flash memory.

The Cisco support site has tools available to help determine the amount of Flash memory and RAM required for each image. For example, after choosing the options that meet the network requirements, select a Cisco IOS Software release that is supported by the hardware. The software requirements of each device are listed in the "Cisco Product Documentation" section of the Documentation CD. The Cisco Software Advisor, which is an interactive tool, provides the most current information.

Before installing a new Cisco IOS Software image on the router, check to see if the router meets the Flash memory and RAM requirements for that image. To see the amount of RAM, issue the **show version** command and look for the following output in Example 2-1.

Example 2-1 **show version** Command Output

```
Cisco> show version
Cisco Internetwork Operating System Software
--- output omitted ---
 image file is "flash:/c2500-i-l.121-16.bin"


cisco 2600 (68030) processor (revision N) with 6144K/2048K bytes of memory.
```

The highlighted line shows how much main and shared memory is installed in the router. Some platforms use a fraction of dynamic RAM (DRAM) as shared memory. The memory requirements take this into account, so both numbers must be added to determine the amount of DRAM installed on the router.

To determine the amount of Flash memory, issue the **show flash** command, as shown in Example 2-2.

Example 2-2 **show flash** *Command Output*

```
Cisco> show flash

System flash directory:
File  Length    Name/status
   1  8022152   /c2500-i-l.121-16.bin
[8022216 bytes used, 366392 available, 8388608 total]
8192K bytes of processor board System flash (Read ONLY)
```

Troubleshooting Cisco IOS Software

Several things could prevent the router from booting properly:

- Configuration file with a missing or incorrect **boot system** statement
- Incorrect configuration register value
- Corrupted Flash image
- Hardware failure

When the router boots, it looks in the configuration file for a **boot system** statement. By default, the router selects the first IOS image in Flash. This statement can force the router to boot from a specific IOS image in Flash or from an image in another location, such as a TFTP server. This command is discussed in more detail in Chapter 5, "Managing Cisco IOS Software." To identify the boot image source, type the **show version** command and look for the line that identifies the image boot source, as shown in Example 2-3.

Example 2-3 *Image Boot Source*

```
Cisco> show version
--- output omitted ---

ROM: System Bootstrap, Version 11.0(10c), SOFTWARE
BOOTLDR: 3000 Bootstrap Software (IGS-BOOT-R), Version 11.0(10c), RELEASE
  SOFTWARE (fc1)
```

An incorrect configuration register setting prevents the Cisco IOS Software from loading from Flash memory. The value in the configuration register tells the router where to get the Cisco IOS Software image. This can be confirmed by using the **show version** command and looking at the last line for the configuration register, as shown in Example 2-4.

Example 2-4 *Configuration Register*

```
Cisco> show version
---- output omitted ----


Configuration register is 0x2102
```

The correct value varies in different hardware platforms. The Cisco IOS Software documentation should include a printed copy of the **show version** output. If that documentation is not available, there are resources on the Cisco Documentation CD or at Cisco.com to identify the correct configuration register value. Correct this by changing the configuration register in the configuration and saving this as the startup configuration.

If there is still a problem, the router might have a corrupted Flash image file. If this is the case, an error message should be displayed during boot. The error message might display as follows:

```
open: read error...requested 0x4 bytes, got 0x0
trouble reading device magic number
boot: cannot open "flash:"
boot: cannot determine first file name on device "flash:"ú
```

If the Flash image is corrupt, a new Cisco IOS Software image should be uploaded into the router. If the problem has not been identified in this section, the router could have a hardware failure. If this is the case, you should contact the Cisco Technical Assistance Center (TAC). Although hardware failures are rare, they do occur.

Table 2-1 lists and describes other helpful router status commands. You can obtain a list of all **show** commands by entering the **show** command followed by a space and a question mark.

Table 2-1 Router Status Commands

Command	Description
show version	Displays the configuration of the system hardware, the software version, names and sources of the system images, and the boot images, and displays the reason for the last system reboot. Also shows the directory structure of Flash memory, including image names and how much memory is used and how much is available.

Table 2-1 Router Status Commands (Continued)

Command	Description
show processes	Displays information about the active processes.
show protocols	Displays the configured protocols. This command shows the status of any configured Layer 3 (network layer) protocol.
show memory	Shows statistics about the router's memory, including memory-free pool statistics.
show stacks	Monitors the stack use of processes and interrupt routines.
show buffers	Provides statistics for the buffer pools on the router.
show flash	Shows information about the Flash memory device.
show running-config (**write term** on Cisco IOS Software Release 10.3 or earlier)	Displays the active configuration file.
show startup-config (**show config** on Cisco IOS Software Release 10.3 or earlier)	Displays the backup configuration file.
show interface	Displays statistics for all interfaces configured.

Operation of Cisco IOS Software

Cisco IOS Software devices have three distinct operating environments or modes:

- ROM monitor
- Boot ROM
- Cisco IOS

The startup process of the router normally loads into RAM and performs in one of these operating environments. The configuration register setting can be used by system administrators to control which of these modes is used by the router to load.

The ROM monitor performs the *bootstrap* process and provides low-level functionality and diagnostics. The ROM monitor is used to recover from system failures and to recover a lost password. The ROM monitor cannot be accessed through any of the network interfaces, but only through a console port session.

When the router is running in ROM monitor mode, only a limited subset of the Cisco IOS Software feature set is available. ROM monitor mode allows write operations to Flash memory and is used primarily to replace the Cisco IOS Software image that is stored in Flash memory. The Cisco IOS Software image can be modified in boot ROM mode by using the **copy tftp flash** command, which copies an IOS image stored on a TFTP server into the Flash memory of the router. This is covered in more detail in Chapter 5, "Managing Cisco IOS Software."

The normal operation of a router requires the full Cisco IOS Software image from Flash memory. In some devices, such as the 2500 series routers, IOS operates out of Flash and is not loaded into RAM. However, most Cisco routers require a copy of the Cisco IOS Software image to be loaded into RAM and also executed from RAM. Some Cisco IOS Software images are stored in Flash in a compressed format and must be expanded when copied to RAM.

To see the Cisco IOS Software image and version that is running, use the **show version** command, which also indicates the configuration register setting. The **show flash** command in Example 2-5 verifies that the system has sufficient memory to load a new Cisco IOS Software image.

Example 2-5 *Verifying the Cisco IOS Software Image*

```
Cisco> show flash

System flash directory:
File  Length   Name/status
  1   8022152  /c2500-i-l.121-16.bin
[8022216 bytes used, 366392 available, 8388608 total]
8192K bytes of processor board System flash (Read ONLY)
```

Starting a Router

All network configuration tasks, from the most basic to the most complex, require a strong foundation in the basics of router configuration. This section provides the tools and techniques for basic router startup and configuration that will be used throughout this book.

Initial Startup of Cisco Routers

A router initializes by loading the bootstrap, the operating system, and a configuration file. If the router cannot find a configuration file, it prompts the user to enter setup mode. If the setup mode is selected, the user is prompted to help create an initial router configuration. The router stores a backup copy of the new configuration created from setup mode in *nonvolatile random- access memory (NVRAM)*. If the setup mode is not selected, the user needs to use the IOS CLI to configure the router. Setup mode is not commonly used because of the limits in what the user can actually configure.

When a Cisco router powers up, it performs a *power-on self-test (POST)*. During this self-test, the router performs diagnostics from ROM on all hardware modules. These diagnostics verify the basic operation of the CPU, memory, and network interface ports. After verifying the hardware functions, the router proceeds with software initialization, characterized by the following two processes:

- System startup routines initiate router software.
- Fallback routines provide startup alternatives as needed.

These routines and processes are discussed in more detail in Chapter 5, "Managing Cisco IOS Software," and included here only as an introduction.

The goal of the startup routines for Cisco IOS Software is to start the router operations. The router must deliver reliable performance in its job of connecting the user networks that it was configured to serve. To do this, the startup routines must do the following:

1. Make sure that the router hardware is tested and functional.

2. Find and load the Cisco IOS Software that the router uses for its operating system.

3. Find and apply the startup configuration file or enter the setup mode.

Router Startup Sequence

After the POST, the following events occur as the router initializes:

1. The generic bootstrap loader in ROM is carried out. A bootstrap is a simple, preset operation that loads instructions. These instructions then cause other instructions to be loaded into memory or cause entry into other configuration modes.

2. The Cisco IOS Software image can be found in several places. The boot field of the configuration register determines the location to be used in loading Cisco IOS Software images. If the boot field indicates a *Flash memory* or network load (from a TFTP server), the **boot system** commands in the configuration file indicate the exact name and location of the image. The configuration file, known as the startup-configuration, is stored in NVRAM and would contain the commands that were previously configured and saved on the router. If no boot system commands are present in the startup-configuration, the router has a default process of looking for the IOS image, starting with looking at Flash memory.

3. The Cisco IOS Software image is loaded. After the Cisco IOS Software is loaded and operational, the operating system locates the hardware and software components and lists the results on the console terminal.

4. The configuration file (startup-configuration) saved in NVRAM is loaded into main memory and the commands are executed one line at a time. The configuration commands start routing processes, supply addresses for interfaces, set media characteristics, and so on.

5. If no valid configuration file exists in NVRAM, or if NVRAM is erased, the operating system executes a question-driven initial configuration routine referred to as the system configuration dialog, also called the setup dialog when the router is rebooted.

Figure 2-1 shows the startup sequence.

Figure 2-1 Startup Sequence

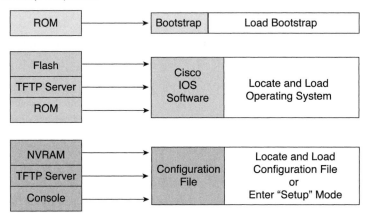

More Information: System Configuration Dialog

Setup is not intended as the mode for entering complex protocol features in the router. Although the main purpose of setup mode is to quickly install a minimal configuration for any router that cannot find its configuration from another source, it is usually not a recommended way of configuring the router. Most administrators find it easier to skip this mode and completely configure the router from the IOS CLI commands.

For many of the prompts in the system configuration dialog of the setup command facility, default answers appear in square brackets ([ ]) following the question. Press the Enter key to use these defaults.

If the system has been previously configured, the defaults that appear will be the currently configured values. To get a fresh start, the command **erase startup-config** can be used to remove the current configuration file from NVRAM. The **reload** command reboots the router and initiates setup again. If the system is being configured for the first time, the factory defaults are provided. If there is no factory default, as in the case of passwords, nothing is displayed after the question mark (?). During the setup process, you can press Ctrl-C at any time to terminate the process and start over. When setup is terminated, all interfaces are administratively shut down. Example 2-6 shows the **setup** command.

More Information: System Configuration Dialog (Continued)

Example 2-6 setup *Command*

```
# setup

-- System Configuration Dialog --
At any point you may enter a question mark '?' for help.
Use ctrl-c to abort configuration dialog at any prompt.
Default settings are in square brackets '[]'.

Basic management setup configures only enough connectivity
for management of the system, extended setup will ask you
to configure each interface on the system

Would you like to enter basic management setup? [yes/no]: no

First, would you like to see the current interface summary? [yes]: yes

Interface       IP-Address      OK? Method Status                 Protocol
Ethernet0       198.133.219.1   YES NVRAM  up                     down
Serial0         unassigned      YES NVRAM  administratively down   down
Serial1         unassigned      YES NVRAM  administratively down   down
```

When the configuration process is completed in setup mode, the screen displays the configuration that was created. When you are asked whether to use this configuration, enter **yes**; the configuration executes and is saved to NVRAM. If you enter **no**, the configuration is not saved and the process begins again. If a --More-- prompt appears, press the spacebar to continue to another screen of information.

Setting Up Global Parameters

After you view the current interface summary, a prompt appears on your monitor, as shown in Example 2-7, indicating that you must enter the global parameters for your router. These parameters are the configuration values that you select.

The first statement indicates that you are configuring the global parameters in the router. The first global parameter enables you to set the router host name. This host name will be part of the Cisco IOS Software prompts for all EXEC modes. At initial configuration, the router name default is displayed between square brackets as [Router]. After you set the router name default, you need to set the various passwords used on the router.

You must enter an enable password. When you enter a string of password characters for the prompt Enter enable secret, the characters are processed by Cisco-proprietary encryption. This enhances the security of the password string. Whenever anyone lists the contents of the router configuration file, this enable password appears as a meaningless string of characters.

More Information: System Configuration Dialog (Continued)

Example 2-7 *Global Parameters*

```
Configuring global parameters:

  Enter host name [Router]: Cisco

  The enable secret is a password used to protect access to
  privileged EXEC and configuration modes. This password, after
  entered, becomes encrypted in the configuration.
  Enter enable secret: cougars

  The enable password is used when you do not specify an
  enable secret password, with some older software versions, and
  some boot images.
  Enter enable password: lumberjacks

  The virtual terminal password is used to protect
  access to the router over a network interface.
  Enter virtual terminal password: matadors
  Configure SNMP Network Management? [yes]: no
```

Setup recommends, but does not require, that the *enable password* be different than the *enable secret word*. The enable secret word is a one-way cryptographic secret word that is used instead of the enable password, when it exists. The enable password is used when no enable secret word exists. Because of this one-way encryption, the enable secret password cannot be recovered if forgotten, whereas the enable password is clear text and can be read from the config file.

The enable password also is used with other versions of Cisco IOS Software. All passwords are case sensitive and can be alphanumeric.

It is possible to secure the router by using passwords to restrict access to individual lines as well. Example 2-8 uses the **line console 0** command followed by the **login** and **password** subcommands to establish a login password for the console terminal. The purpose here is to establish the need for a user to log into the console before gaining access to the router through the console port. **console 0** designates the router's console connection, and **login** prompts the user for a password before allowing console connectivity.

Example 2-8 *Configuring the Router's Console Password*

```
Router(config)# line console 0
Router(config-line)# password cisco
Router(config-line)# login
```

As demonstrated in Example 2-9, the **line vty 0 4** command followed by the **password** subcommand establishes a login password on incoming Telnet sessions.

More Information: System Configuration Dialog (Continued)

Example 2-9 *Configuring the Router's Virtual Terminal Password*

```
Router(config)# line vty 0 4
Router(config-line)# password sanjose
Router(config-line)# login
```

After you enter the passwords for the various ports, the router asks you to enter the routing protocols that are to be used, as shown in Example 2-10. When you are prompted for parameters for each protocol, use the configuration values that you have selected for your router. Whenever you answer **yes** to a prompt, additional questions might appear regarding the protocol.

Example 2-10 *Prompts for Global Parameters at the Console*

```
Configure IP? [yes]:
        Configure IGRP routing? [yes]: yes
      Your IGRP autonomous system number [1]: 200
Configuring interface parameters:

Do you want to configure Ethernet0 interface? [yes]: yes
  Configure IP on this interface? [yes]: yes
    IP address for this interface: 10.10.10.1
    Subnet mask for this interface [255.0.0.0] :
    Class A network is 10.0.0.0, 8 subnet bits; mask is /8

Do you want to configure Serial0  interface? [yes]: n

Do you want to configure Serial1  interface? [yes]: n

The following configuration command script was created:

hostname Cisco
enable secret 5 $1$37Kq$vA6UckClKEBzOIWGIF54U/
enable password lumberjacks
line vty 0 4
password wildcats
no snmp-server
!
no bridge 1
ip routing
!
interface Ethernet0
ip address 10.10.10.1 255.0.0.0
!
--- output omitted ---
```

Lab 2.2.1   Router Configuration Using Setup

In this lab, you use the System Configuration Dialogue (setup) to establish some of the basic router configuration parameters

Router LED Indicators

Cisco routers use *light-emitting diode (LED)* indicators to provide status information. Depending on the Cisco router model, the LED indicators vary.

The upper LED on the *daughter card* indicates the activity on serial 1 port on the daughter card. The lower LED on the daughter card indicates the activity of the WAN, or BRI port. Figures 2-2 and 2-3 illustrate the router LED indicators.

The LEDs on the interface indicate the activity of the corresponding interface. If the LED is not on when the interface is active, *and* the interface is correctly connected, this might indicate a problem. If an interface is extremely busy, its LED is always on. The green OK LED on the bottom of both WAN interface cards comes on after the system initializes correctly.

Figure 2-2 2500 Series Router LED Indicators

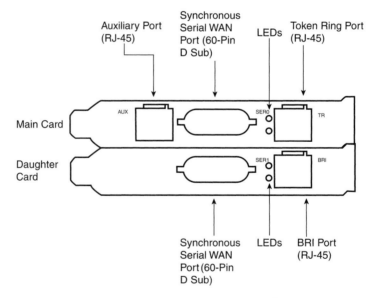

Figure 2-3 1721 Series Router LED Indicators

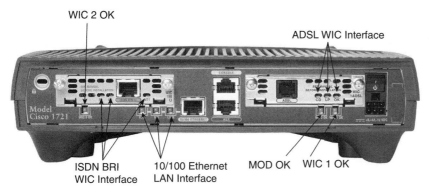

The Initial Router Boot Up

Each time a router is powered on, it goes through the following boot sequence:

1. The router goes through POST diagnostics to verify basic operation of the CPU, memory, and interfaces.

2. To verify that the system bootstrap software is loaded correctly, the boot image executes and searches for a valid Cisco IOS Software image (router operating system software). The source of the Cisco IOS Software image, whether a Flash memory or a Trivial File Transfer Protocol (TFTP) server, is determined by the configuration register setting. The factory-default setting for the configuration register is 0x2102. This indicates that the router should look to the configuration file saved in NVRAM for any **boot system** commands. These commands specify the order in which the router is supposed to look for the IOS. If no **boot system** commands are stored in NVRAM, the router resorts to the default fallback sequence. This means that the router first looks in Flash for its IOS image.

3. If after five attempts a valid Cisco IOS Software image is not found in Flash memory, the router reverts to boot ROM mode. This mode is used to install or upgrade a Cisco IOS Software image.

4. If a valid Cisco IOS Software image is found, the router searches for a valid configuration file.

5. If a valid configuration file is not found in NVRAM, the router searches for a TFTP server over all interfaces. If a configuration file is not found, the router runs the system configuration dialog so a configuration can be manually configured.

In Examples 2-11 and 2-12, the messages displayed vary, depending on the interfaces in the router and the Cisco IOS release. The screen displays in this graphic are for reference only and might not exactly reflect the screen displays on the console.

Example 2-11 *NVRAM Invalid*

```
System Bootstrap, Version X.X(XXXX) [XXXXX XX], RELEASE SOFTWARE

Copyright (c)  1986-199X by Cisco Systems

1721 processor with 4096 Kbytes of main memory


Notice:     NVRAM invalid, possibly due to write erase.


--- output omitted ---
```

Example 2-12 *Bootstrap and Cisco IOS Software Version*

```
--- output omitted ---

IOS (tm) 1721 Software (XXX-X-X), Version  [XXXXX XXX]

Copyright (c)  1986-199X by Cisco Systems, Inc.
```

NOTE

The **write erase** command is the old command for **erase start,** and NVRAM is invalid possibly due to a user issuing the **erase start.**

Notice in Example 2-11 that the NVRAM is invalid; this is possibly because of write erase. This tells the user that the router has not been previously configured or that the configuration file, startup-config, in NVRAM has been erased. A router cannot be used until it is configured.

In Example 2-12, the user can determine the bootstrap version and the Cisco IOS Software version that the router is using. The user also can determine the router model, the processor, and the amount of memory that the router contains. Other information listed in this output includes the following information and is shown in Example 2-13:

- How many interfaces the router has

- What types of interfaces the router has

- The amount of NVRAM

- The amount of Flash memory

Example 2-13 *Bootstrap and Cisco IOS Software Version*

```
Processor board ID 10226279

R4700 CPU at 100Mhz, Implementation 33, Rev 1.0

MICA-6DM Firmware: CP ver 2730 - 5/23/2001, SP ver 2730 - 5/23/2001.
```

Example 2-13 *Bootstrap and Cisco IOS Software Version (Continued)*

```
Bridging software.

X.25 software, Version 3.0.0.

SuperLAT software (copyright 1990 by Meridian Technology Corp).

TN3270 Emulation software.

Primary Rate ISDN software, Version 1.1.

2 Ethernet/IEEE 802.3 interface(s)

24 Serial network interface(s)

4 Low-speed serial(sync/async) network interface(s)

6 terminal line(s)

1 Channelized T1/PRI port(s)

DRAM configuration is 64 bits wide with parity disabled.

125K bytes of non-volatile configuration memory.

32768K bytes of processor board System flash (Read/Write)


Configuration register is 0x2102
```

Establish a Console Connection

All Cisco routers include an EIA/TIA-232 asynchronous serial console port (RJ-45). Cables and adapters are needed to connect a console terminal (an ASCII terminal or PC running terminal emulation software) to the console port. To connect a PC running terminal emulation software to the console port, use the RJ-45–to–RJ-45 rollover cable with a female RJ-45–to–DB-9 or RJ-45–to–DB-25 adapter.

The default parameters for the console port are 9600 baud, 8 data bits, no parity, 1 stop bit, and no flow control. The console port does not support hardware flow control.

Take the following steps to connect a terminal to the console port on the router:

Step 1   Connect the terminal or PC using the RJ-45–to–RJ-45 rollover cable and an RJ-45–to–DB-9 adapter.

Step 2   Configure the terminal or PC terminal emulation software for 9600 baud, 8 data bits, no parity, 1 stop bit, and no flow control.

Figure 2-4 shows an example of the console connection to a PC, to establish a HyperTerminal connection with a PC.

Figure 2-4 Terminal Console Cable

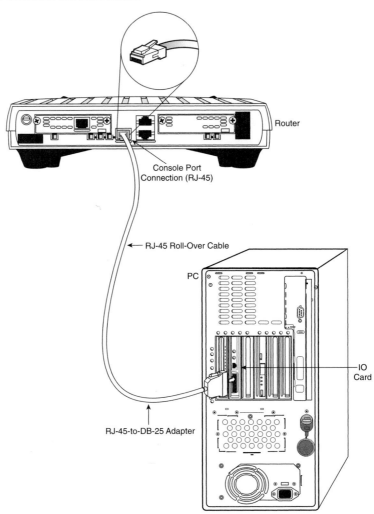

Table 2-2 shows a list of operating systems and the terminal emulation software that can be used with each operating system.

Table 2-2 Available Terminal Emulation Software

PC Operating System	Software
Windows 9x, NT, 2000, and XP	HyperTerminal (included with Windows software), ProComm Plus, and TeraTerm
Windows 3.1	Terminal (included with Windows software)
Macintosh	ProComm, VersaTerm, ZTerm (supplied separately)

 Lab 2.2.4 Establishing a Console Connection with HyperTerminal

In this lab, a workstation will be connected to the router using a console cable and HyperTerminal will be configured to establish a console session with router.

Router Login

To configure Cisco routers, the user interface must be accessed on the router using a terminal or remotely if the router has been configured for network access. When accessing a router, if the console or Telnet (vty) passwords have been configured, a user must log into the router before any other commands are entered.

For security purposes, the router has two levels of access to commands, as demonstrated by Example 2-14:

- **User EXEC mode**—Typical tasks include those that check the router status. In this mode, router configuration changes are not allowed.

- **Privileged EXEC mode**—Typical tasks include those that change the router configuration. The main concept to understand about privileged EXEC mode is that it allows the administrator full control over the router.

The user EXEC mode prompt is displayed upon login to a router. Commands available at this user level are a subset of the commands available at the privileged EXEC level. For the most part, these commands enable a user to display information without changing router configuration settings.

Example 2-14 *Router Modes*

```
Router>     -------------- User Mode
Router>enable
Password:
Router#    -------------- Privileged-Mode
Router>disable
Router>
```

To access the full set of commands, privileged EXEC mode must be entered. At the > prompt, type **enable**. At the password prompt, enter the password that has been set with the **enable secret** command. When the login steps have been completed, the prompt changes to a #, to indicate that you are now in privileged EXEC mode. If **enable secret** was not configured, the enable password will work. If neither were configured, no password is required to enter privileged EXEC mode. From privileged EXEC mode, global configuration mode and other specific modes, including the following, can be accessed:

- Interface: router(config-if)#
- Subinterface: router(config-subif)#
- Line: router(config-line)#
- Router: router(config-router)#

To return to user EXEC mode, type **disable**. To log out of the router, type **exit**. Screen output varies with the specific Cisco IOS Software level and router configuration.

More Information: Basic Operation of Cisco IOS Software

The Cisco Internetwork Operating System (IOS) Software platform is implemented on the various hardware used in this course. It is the embedded software architecture in all the Cisco routers. Cisco IOS Software enables the following network services in these products:

- Features to carry the chosen network protocols and functions
- Connectivity for high-speed traffic between devices
- Security to control access and discourage unauthorized network use
- Scalability to add interfaces and capability, as needed, for network growth
- Reliability to ensure dependable access to networked resources

The Cisco IOS Software command-line interface (CLI) can be accessed through a console connection, a modem connection, or a Telnet session. Regardless of which connection method is used, access to the IOS command-line interface generally is referred to as an EXEC session.

Keyboard Help In the Router CLI

Typing a question mark (**?**) at the user EXEC mode prompt or the privileged EXEC mode prompt displays a list of available commands, as demonstrated in Example 2-15.

Notice the --More-- at the bottom of the sample display. The screen displays 22 lines at one time. The --More-- prompt at the bottom of the display indicates that multiple screens are available as output. Whenever a --More-- prompt appears, you can view the next available screen by pressing the spacebar. To display just the next line, press the Enter key. Press any other key to return to the prompt.

Example 2-15 *Keyboard Help*

```
?
Exec commands:
access-enable    Create a temporary Access-List entry
access-profile   Apply user-profile to interface
access-template  Create a temporary Access-List entry
archive          manage archive files
bfe              For manual emergency modes setting
cd               Change current directory
clear            Reset functions
clock            Manage the system clock
configure        Enter configuration mode
connect          Open a terminal connection
copy             Copy from one file to another
debug            Debugging functions (see also 'undebug')
delete           Delete a file
dir              List files on a filesystem
disable          Turn off privileged commands
disconnect       Disconnect an existing network connection
elog             Event-logging control commands
enable           Turn on privileged commands
erase            Erase a filesystem
exit             Exit from the EXEC
help             Description of the interactive help system

--More--
isdn             Make/disconnect an isdn data call on a BRI interface
lock             Lock the terminal
login            Log in as a particular user
logout           Exit from the EXEC
more             Display the contents of a file
mrinfo           Request neighbor and version information from a multicast router
mrm              IP Multicast Routing Monitor Test
mstat            Show statistics after multiple multicast traceroutes
```

continues

NOTE

At this point, the list of
commands displayed is
context sensitive. You
see a different list when
you are in user mode
versus enable mode,
and when in global con-
figuration versus con-
figure interface modes.

Example 2-15 *Keyboard Help (Continued)*

```
 mtrace            Trace reverse multicast path from destination to source
 name-connection  Name an existing network connection
 no               Disable debugging functions
 pad              Open a X.29 PAD connection
 ping             Send echo messages
 ppp              Start IETF Point-to-Point Protocol (PPP)
 pwd              Display current working directory
 reload           Halt and perform a cold restart
 resume           Resume an active network connection
 rlogin           Open an rlogin connection
 rsh              Execute a remote command
 send             Send a message to other tty lines
 setup            Run the SETUP command facility
 show             Show running system information


 --More--
 slip             Start Serial-line IP (SLIP)
 start-chat       Start a chat-script on a line
 systat           Display information about terminal lines
 telnet           Open a telnet connection
 terminal         Set terminal line parameters
 test             Test subsystems, memory, and interfaces
 traceroute       Trace route to destination
 tunnel           Open a tunnel connection
 udptn            Open an udptn connection
 undebug          Disable debugging functions (see also 'debug')
 verify           Verify a file
 where            List active connections
 write            Write running configuration to memory, network, or terminal
 x28              Become an X.28 PAD
 x3               Set X.3 parameters on PAD
```

To access privileged EXEC mode, type **enable** or the abbreviation **ena**. Typing **enable** causes
the router to prompt the user for a password. Typing a question mark at the privileged EXEC
mode prompt (see Example 2-16) displays a longer list of commands than would be displayed at the user EXEC mode prompt.

Example 2-16 *Privileged EXEC Mode Commands*

```
Cisco# ?
Exec commands:
  access-enable   Create a temporary Access-List entry
  access-profile  Apply user-profile to interface
  access-template Create a temporary Access-List entry
  archive         manage archive files
  bfe             For manual emergency modes setting
  cd              Change current directory
  clear           Reset functions
  clock           Manage the system clock
  configure       Enter configuration mode
  connect         Open a terminal connection
  copy            Copy from one file to another
  debug           Debugging functions (see also 'undebug')
  delete          Delete a file
  dir             List files on a filesystem
  disable         Turn off privileged commands
  disconnect      Disconnect an existing network connection
  elog            Event-logging control commands
  enable          Turn on privileged commands
  erase           Erase a filesystem
  exit            Exit from the EXEC
  help            Description of the interactive help system
--More--
```

Screen output varies, depending on Cisco IOS Software level and router configuration.

Router Help Functions

Suppose that a user wants to set the router clock. If the necessary command is not known, that user can use the help function to check the syntax for setting the clock. The following exercise illustrates one of the many uses of the help function. The task is to set the router clock. Assuming that the command is not known, proceed using the following steps:

Step 1   Use **?** to find the command for setting the clock. The help output shows that the **clock** command is required.

Step 2   Check the syntax for changing the time.

Step 3   Enter the current time by using hours, minutes, and seconds, as shown. The system indicates that additional information needs to be provided to complete the command. The help output in Example 2-17 shows that the **set** keyword is required.

Example 2-17 *Clock* **set** *Keyword*

```
Cisco# cl?
clear   clock


Cisco# clock
% Incomplete command.


Cisco# clock ?
  set  Set the time and date


Cisco# clock set
% Incomplete command.


Cisco# clock set ?
  hh:mm:ss  Current Time
```

Step 4 Check the syntax for entering the time, and enter the current time using hours, minutes, and seconds. As shown in Example 2-18, the system again indicates that additional information is required to complete the command.

Example 2-18 *Clock Time and Date Set Format*

```
Cisco# clock set 19:50:00
% Incomplete command.


Cisco# clock set 19:50:00 ?
  <1-31>  Day of the month
  MONTH   Month of the year


Cisco# clock set 19:50:00 14 7
                            ^
% Invalid input detected at '^' marker.


Cisco# clock set 19:50:00 14 July
% Incomplete command.


Cisco# clock set 19:50:00 14 July ?
  <1993-2035>  Year
```

Example 2-18 *Clock Time and Date Set Format (Continued)*

```
Cisco# clock set 19:50:00 14 July 2003

Cisco#
```

Step 5   Press **Ctrl + P** or the up arrow to repeat the previous command entry automatically. Then add a space and a question mark (?) to reveal the additional arguments. Now the command entry can be completed.

Step 6   The caret symbol (^) and help response indicate that there is an error. The placement of the caret symbol shows where the possible problem is located. To input the correct syntax, re-enter the command up to the point where the caret symbol is located, and then enter a question mark (**?**).

Step 7   Enter the year, using the correct syntax, and press Enter to execute the command.

The user interface provides syntax checking by placing a ^ where the error occurred. The ^ appears at the point in the command string where an incorrect command, keyword, or argument was entered. The error location indicator and interactive help system enable syntax errors to be found and easily corrected.

Enhanced Editing Commands

The user interface includes an enhanced editing mode that provides a set of editing key functions with which the user can edit a command line as it is being typed. Use the key sequences indicated in Table 2-3 to move the cursor at the command line for corrections or changes. Although enhanced editing mode automatically is enabled with the current software release, it can be disabled if written scripts do not interact well while enhanced editing is enabled. To disable enhanced editing mode, type **terminal no editing** at the privileged EXEC mode prompt.

Table 2-3 Editing Commands

Command	Description
Ctrl + a	Moves to the beginning of the command line
Ctrl + e	Moves to the end of the command line
Esc + b	Moves back one word
Ctrl + f (or right arrow)	Moves forward one character
Ctrl + b (or left arrow)	Moves back one character
Esc + f	Moves forward one word

The editing command set provides a horizontal scrolling feature for commands that extend beyond a single line on the screen. When the cursor reaches the right margin, the command line shifts ten spaces to the left. The first ten characters of the line cannot be seen, but a user can scroll back and check the syntax at the beginning of the command. To scroll back, press Ctrl+ b or the left arrow key repeatedly until the beginning of the command entry is reached. Ctrl + a returns a user directly to the beginning of the line.

In the following command line, the command entry extends beyond one line:

```
Cisco>$ value for our customers, employees, investors, and partners
```

When the cursor first reaches the end of the line, the line is shifted ten spaces to the left and is redisplayed. The dollar sign ($) indicates that the line has been scrolled to the left. Each time the cursor reaches the end of the line, the line again is shifted ten spaces to the left.

Screen output varies, depending on the Cisco IOS Software level and router configuration.

The **Ctrl + z** command backs out of configuration mode. This commands will return the user to the privileged EXEC mode prompt.

Router Command History

The user interface provides a history, or record, of commands that have been entered. This feature is particularly useful for recalling long or complex commands or entries. With the command history feature, the following tasks can be completed:

- Set the command history buffer size
- Recall commands
- Disable the command history feature

By default, the command history is enabled and the system records ten command lines in its history buffer. To change the number of command lines that the system records during a terminal session, use the **terminal history size** or the **history size** commands. The maximum number of commands is 256. Table 2-4 shows command history commands.

Table 2-4 Router Command History

Command	Description
Ctrl + p	This key sequence or the up arrow key recalls the last (previous) command in the history buffer
Ctrl + n	This key sequence or the down arrow key recalls the most recent command in the history buffer
show history	Displays the command buffer

NOTE

Students tend to not learn these commands and rely on the arrow keys. It is important that you practice using these commands for two reasons: (1) Some terminal emulators do not support the arrow keys, including telneting through a workstation's DOS window; (2) The CCNA exam tests your knowledge of these commands. The best practice is to use these commands exclusively until they become a habit.

Table 2-4 Router Command History (Continued)

Command	Description
terminal history [**size** *number-of-lines*]	Sets the command buffer size
terminal no editing	Disables advanced editing features
Router> terminal editing	Re-enables advanced editing features
Tab	Completes the entry

To recall commands in the history buffer, beginning with the most recent command, press **Ctrl + p.** Continue to press **Ctrl + p** or the up arrow key to recall successively older commands. To return to more recent commands in the history buffer, after using the **Ctrl + p** or the up arrow, press **Ctrl + n** or the down arrow key repeatedly to recall successively more recent commands.

When typing commands, as a shortcut, you can enter the unique characters for a command. Press the **Tab** key, and the interface finishes the entry. When the typed letters uniquely identify the command, the Tab key simply acknowledges visually that the router has understood the specific command that was intended.

On most computers, additional select and copy functions are available. A previous command string can be copied and then pasted or inserted as the current command entry.

Lab 2.2.9   Command Line Fundamentals

In this lab, you log into a router in both user and privilege modes. You use several basic router commands to determine how the router is configured. You also become familiar with the router help facility and use the command history and editing features.

Interactive Media Activity   Drag and Drop: Router Command History

When you complete this activity, you will be able to identify the correct usage for keystrokes relating to router command history.

Troubleshooting Command-Line Errors

Command-line errors primarily occur from typing mistakes. If a command keyword is incorrectly typed, the user interface provides error isolation in the form of an error indicator (^). The ^ symbol appears at the point in the command string where an incorrect command, keyword, or argument was entered. The error-location indicator and interactive help system allow the user to easily find and correct syntax errors:

```
Router#clock set 13:32:00 23 February 04
                                         ^
% Invalid input detected at "^" marker.
```

The caret symbol (^) and help response indicate an error at 04. To list the correct syntax, enter the command up to the point where the error occurred, and then enter a question mark (**?**):

```
Router#clock set 13:32:00 23 February ?
<1993-2035> Year
Router#clock set 13:32:00 23 February
```

Enter the year using the correct syntax and press **Return** to execute the command:

```
Router#clock set 13:32:00 23 February 2004
```

If a command line is entered incorrectly, and the **Enter** key is pressed, the up arrow can be pressed to repeat the last command. Use the right and left arrow keys to move the cursor to the location where the mistake was made. Then, type the correction that needs to be made. If something needs to be deleted, use the **Backspace** key.

The show version Command

The **show version** command displays information about the Cisco IOS Software version that currently is running on the router as well as the following information:

- Cisco IOS Software version and descriptive information
- Bootstrap ROM version
- Boot ROM version
- Router up time
- Last restart method
- System image file and location
- Router platform
- Configuration register setting

Summary

The keys points discussed in this chapter were the following:

- Establishing a HyperTerminal session
- Logging into the router
- Using the help feature in the command-line interface
- Using enhanced editing commands
- Using command history
- Troubleshooting command errors
- The router can boot into either ROM monitor, boot ROM, or Cisco IOS mode.
- The **show version** and **show flash** commands provide information on Cisco IOS Software and configuration register settings currently on the router.
- Router commands are entered at the command-line interface (CLI) in either user EXEC, privileged EXEC, global configuration, or specific configuration mode.

To supplement all that you've learned in this chapter, refer to the chapter-specific Interactive Media Activity on the CD-ROM accompanying this book.

Key Terms

bootsrap   The protocol used by a network node to determine the IP address of its Ethernet interfaces to affect network booting.

Cisco Internetwork Operating System (IOS) Software   Software stored as an image file in Flash memory on the router that, when loaded into RAM, provides the operating system that runs the router.

command-line interface (CLI)   An interface that enables the user to interact with the operating system by entering commands and optional arguments.

daughter card   Similar to an expansion board, but it accesses the motherboard components (memory and CPU) directly instead of sending data through the slower expansion bus.

Flash memory   A special type of EEPROM that can be erased and reprogrammed in blocks instead of 1 byte at a time. Many modern PCs have their BIOS stored on a Flash memory chip so that it can be updated easily, if necessary. Flash memory is also popular in modems because it enables the modem manufacturer to support new protocols as they become standardized.

light-emitting diode (LED)   Semiconductor device that emits light produced by converting electrical energy. Status lights on hardware devices are typically LEDs.

nonvolatile RAM (NVRAM)   RAM that retains its contents when a unit is powered off.

power-on self-test (POST)   Set of hardware diagnostics that runs on a hardware device when that device is powered up.

Check Your Understanding

Complete all the review questions to test your understanding of the topics and concepts in this chapter. Answers are listed in Appendix B, "Check Your Understanding Answer Key."

1. A router initializes by doing which of the following?

   A. Loading the NVRAM, the setup procedure, and the operating system

   B. Loading the bootstrap, the operating system, and a configuration file

   C. Loading the bootstrap, the setup procedure, and the operating system

2. During the setup process in a router, what keys can be used to escape the sequence?

   A. Ctrl-A

   B. Ctrl-E

   C. Ctrl-C

3. Match the configuration settings on the right with the items on the left that are needed to establish a HyperTerminal session.

BAUD	None
DATA BITS	1
PARITY	8
STOP BITS	None
FLOW CONTROL	9600

4. Which of the following is true at initial boot-up output?

   A. The Cisco IOS Software version that the router uses can be seen.

   B. The Cisco IOS Software version that the router uses cannot be seen.

5. Which of the following is true at initial boot-up output?

   A. The amount of Flash memory can be seen.

   B. The amount of Flash memory cannot be seen.

6. Match the commands on the left with the correct descriptions on the right.

Ctrl + a	Moves out of configuration mode
Ctrl + b	Moves to the end of the command line
Ctrl + e	Moves back one word
Ctrl + f	Moves to the beginning of the command line
Esc + b	Moves forward one character
Esc + f	Moves forward one word
Ctrl + z	Moves back one character

7. Match the commands on the left with the correct descriptions on the right.

Tab	Enables advanced editing
Ctrl + p	Sets the command buffer size
Ctrl + n	Recalls the most recent command
show history	Shows the command buffer
terminal history size #	Recalls the last command
terminal editing	Completes the entry
no Terminal editing	Disables advanced editing features

8. Which of the following correctly describes a method for specifying how a router loads the Cisco IOS Software?

   A. Designate fallback sources for the router to use in sequence from NVRAM.

   B. Configure the Cisco IOS Software image for the location where it will bootstrap.

   C. Manually boot a default system image at a virtual terminal.

   D. Manually boot a default system image at the network server.

9. Which of the following is not a boot option that can be set with the configuration register boot field?

   A. Cisco IOS Software boots in ROM monitor mode.

   B. Cisco IOS Software automatically boots from ROM.

   C. Cisco IOS Software automatically boots from a TFTP server.

   D. NVRAM is examined for **boot system** commands.

10. Which of the following is information displayed by the Cisco IOS Software
show version command?

  A. Detailed statistics about each page of the router's memory

  B. The name of the system image

  C. The names and sizes of all files in Flash memory

  D. The status of configured network protocols

11. Which of the following has a limited version of router Cisco IOS Software?

  A. ROM

  B. Flash memory

  C. TFTP server

  D. Bootstrap

12. If you want to completely back out of configuration mode, which of the following must
you enter?

  A. **exit**

  B. **no config-mode**

  C. **Ctrl + e**

  D. **Ctrl + z**

13. If you are planning to configure an interface, what prompt should be on the router?

  A. router(config)#

  B. router(config-in)#

  C. router(config-intf)#

  D. router(config-if)#

14. What is the acronym used to describe the Cisco text-based user interface?

  A. IOS

  B. TCP/IP

  C. OSPF

  D. OSI

15. What two modes of access to router commands exist for Cisco routers?

  A. User and privileged

  B. User and guest

  C. Privileged and guest

  D. Guest and anonymous

16. Which mode do you use to make router configuration changes on Cisco routers?

A. User

B. Privileged

C. Administrator

D. Root

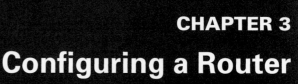

Objectives

Upon completion of this chapter, you should be able to answer the following questions:

- What are the commands to name a router?

- How does an administrator set passwords on a router?

- What are the **show** commands used for?

- What are the command and steps required to configure a serial interface?

- What are the command and steps required to configure an Ethernet interface?

- How does an administrator execute changes to a router?

- How does and administrator save changes to a router?

- What are the command and steps required to configure an interface description?

- What are the command and steps required to configure a message-of-the-day banner?

- What are the command and steps required to configure host tables?

- What purposes does backup documentation serve?

- How does and administrator recover passwords on a router?

Key Terms

The following is a list of key terms introduced in this chapter. For your reference, a definition for each term can be found at the end of this chapter.

global configuration mode   page 584

interface   page 584

privileged mode   page 584

nonvolatile RAM (NVRAM)   page 588

Trivial File Transfer Protocol (TFTP)   page 601

This chapter covers the router modes and configuration methods to update a router's configuration file. It is important to have a firm understanding of Cisco IOS Software and know the procedures for starting a router. In addition, this chapter describes the tasks necessary for password recovery.

Be sure to look at this chapter's associated Interactive Media Activities, which you will find on the CD-ROM accompanying this book. These CD elements are designed to supplement the material and reinforce the concepts introduced in this chapter.

Configuring a Router

To gain access to a router, a login is required. After login, there is a choice of modes. The modes interpret the commands that are typed and carry out the operations. Two EXEC modes exist:

- User mode
- Privileged EXEC mode

The following sections define the two command modes and their associated commands.

CLI Command Modes

More Information: Command Modes

A user is automatically in user EXEC mode upon first login to the router. *User mode* is a limited examination of the router. Table 3-1 provides the user mode commands and their descriptions.

Table 3-1 User Mode Commands

Command	Description
access-enable	Creates a temporary access list entry
atmsig	Executes ATM signaling commands
cd	Changes current device
clear	Resets functions
connect	Opens a terminal connection
dir	Lists files on a given device
disable	Turns off privileged commands
disconnect	Disconnects an existing network
enable	Turns on privileged commands
exit	Exits EXEC

More Information: Command Modes (Continued)

Table 3-1 User Mode Commands *(Continued)*

Command	Description
help	Gets a description of the interactive help system
lat	Opens a LAT connection
lock	Locks the terminal
login	Logs in as a particular user
logout	Exits EXEC mode
mrinfo	Requests neighbor and version information from a multicast router
mstat	Shows statistics after multiple multicast traceroutes
mtrace	Traces the reverse multicast path from destination to source
name-connection	Names an existing network connection
pad	Opens an X.29 PAD connection
ping	Sends echo messages
ppp	Starts IETF Point-to-Point Protocol (PPP)
pwd	Displays current device
resume	Resumes an active network connection
rlogin	Opens an rlogin connection
show	Shows running system information
slip	Starts Serial Line IP (SLIP)
systat	Displays information about terminal lines
telnet	Opens a Telnet connection
terminal	Sets terminal line parameters
tn3270	Opens a TN3270 connection
traceroute	Sets a traceroute to the destination
tunnel	Opens a tunnel connection
where	Lists active connections
x3	Sets X.3 parameters on PAD
xremote	Enters Xremote mode

NOTE

At this point, the list of commands displayed is context sensitive. You see a different list when you are in user mode versus enable mode, and when in *global configuration mode* versus configure *interface* modes.

More Information: Command Modes (Continued)

Privileged Mode Command List

Privileged EXEC mode provides a detailed examination of the router and allows configuration changes to be made to the router. A specific mode is entered depending upon the configuration change that is required. From privileged EXEC mode, other modes can be entered; privileged EXEC mode must be entered before entering these other modes (see the next section, "Router Configuration Modes").

To access *privileged mode* from user EXEC mode, type **enable** (or the abbreviation **en**):

```
Router>enable
Password:


Router>en
Password:
```

You are prompted for a password. If you type a question mark (?) at the privileged mode prompt Router#?, the screen displays a longer list of commands than it would at the user mode prompt. Table 3-2 provides a complete list with descriptions of privileged mode commands.

Note that the list of commands varies depending on the IOS version and the type of router platform being configured.

Table 3-2 Privileged Mode Commands

Command	Description
access-enable	Creates a temporary access list entry
access-template	Creates a temporary access list entry
appn	ends a command to the APPN subsystem
atmsig	Executes ATM signaling commands
bfe	Sets manual emergency modes
calendar	Manages the hardware calendar
cd	Changes the current device
clear	Resets functions
clock	Manages the system clock
cmt	Starts or stops FDDI connection-management functions
configure	Enters configuration mode
connect	Opens a terminal connection
copy	Copies configuration or image data
debug	Uses debugging functions (see also undebug)

More Information: Command Modes *(Continued)*

Table 3-2 Privileged Mode Commands *(Continued)*

Command	Description
delete	Deletes a file
dir	Lists files on a given device
disable	Turns off privileged commands
disconnect	Disconnects an existing network connection
enable	Turns on privileged commands
erase	Erases Flash or configuration memory
exit	Exits EXEC mode
format	Formats a device
help	Gets a description of the interactive help system
lat	Opens a LAT connection
lock	Locks the terminal
login	Logs in as a particular user
logout	Exits EXEC mode
mbranch	Traces the multicast route down the tree branch
mrbranch	Traces the reverse multicast up the tree branch
mrinfo	Requests neighbor and version information from a multicast router
mstat	Shows statistics after multiple multicast traceroutes
mtrace	Traces reverse multicast path from destination source
name-connection	Names an existing network connection
ncia	Starts or stops an NCIA server
pad	Opens an X.29 PAD connection
ping	Sends echo messages
ppp	Starts the IETF Point-to-Point Protocol (PPP)
pwd	Displays current device
reload	Halts and performs a cold return
resume	Resumes an active network connection
rlogin	Opens an rlogin connection
rsh	Executes a remote command
sdlc	Sends SDLC test frames

More Information: Command Modes (Continued)	

Table 3-2 Privileged Mode Commands *(Continued)*

Command	Description
send	Sends a message over tty lines
setup	Runs the setup command facility
show	Shows running system information
slip	Starts Serial Line IP (SLIP)
squeeze	Squeezes a device
start-chat	Starts a chat script on a line
systat	Displays information about terminal lines
tarp	Targets ID Resolution Process (TARP) commands
telnet	Opens a Telnet connection
terminal	Sets terminal-line parameters
test	Tests subsystems, memory, and interfaces
tn3270	Opens a TN3270 connection
traceroute	Sets a traceroute to the destination
tunnel	Opens a tunnel connection
undebug	Disables debugging functions (see also debug)
undelete	Undeletes a file
verify	Verifies the checksum of a Flash file
where	Lists active connections
which-route	Does an OSI route table lookup and displays results
write	Writes running configuration to memory, network, or terminal
x3	Sets X.3 parameters on PAD
xremote	Enters Xremote mode

Router Configuration Modes

Global configuration commands are used in a router to apply configuration statements that affect the system as a whole, such as the hostname. Use the privileged EXEC command **configure** to enter global configuration mode. After this command is entered, a prompt asking for the source of the configuration commands appears, at which you can specify **terminal**, **nvram**, or **network**. The default selection is to type in commands from the terminal console. Pressing the **Enter** key begins this configuration method.

The first configuration mode is referred to as global configuration mode, or global config, for short. Table 3-3 describes some of the configuration modes that you access from global configuration mode.

Table 3-3 Router Configuration Modes

Configuration Mode	Prompt
Interface	Router(config-if)#
Subinterface	Router(config-subif)#
Controller	Router(config-controller)#
Map-list	Router(config-map-list)#
Map-class	Router(config-map-class)#
Line	Router(config-line)#
Router	Router(config-router)#
IPX-router	Router(config-ipx-router)#
Route-map	Router(config-route-map)#

Typing **exit** at one of these specific configuration modes returns the router to global configuration mode. Pressing **Ctrl-Z** or typing **end** leaves the configuration modes completely and returns the router to privileged EXEC mode.

Example 3-1 demonstrates this sequence of transitioning between configuration modes.

Example 3-1 *Navigating Privileged EXEC, Global Config, and Specific Configuration Modes*

```
Router# configure terminal
Router(config)#(commands)
Router(config)# exit
Router#

Router#configure terminal
Router(config)# router protocol
Router(config-router)#(commands)
Router(config-router)# exit
Router(config)#interface type port
Router(config-if)#(commands)
Router(config-if)# end
Router#
```

More Information: Router Startup Modes

Whether it is accessed from the console or through the auxiliary port, a router can be placed in several modes. Each mode provides different functions:

- **ROM monitor** mode is generally a recovery mode. It allows certain configuration tasks, such as recovering a lost password or downloading software (IOS). The router boots into ROM monitor mode if the router does not find a valid system image or if the boot sequence is interrupted during startup. In many routers, Rommon> is the default prompt for ROM monitor mode.

- **Setup** mode is a prompted dialog that helps users create a first-time basic configuration. Setup mode consists of a series of questions with default answers in brackets. Setup mode does not have a defining default prompt. The router prompts the user to enter setup mode if a valid startup configuration file is not found. Setup can also be entered by typing **setup** from privileged mode. Note that setup mode also can be invoked manually if the user erased the *nonvolatile random-access memory (NVRAM)* and rebooted the router.

- **RXBoot** mode is a special mode that the router can enter by changing the settings of the configuration register and rebooting the router. RXBoot mode provides the router with a subset of Cisco IOS Software and enters a streamlined setup mode. The streamlined setup mode differs from the standard setup mode because streamlined setup does not configure global router parameters. There are prompts only to configure interface parameters, which permit the router to boot. This allows the router to boot when it cannot find a valid Cisco IOS Software image in Flash memory. The default prompt is the host name followed by <boot>.

Table 3-4 briefly describes some of the commonly used configuration commands. These commands will be discussed later in this chapter.

Table 3-4 Selection of Router Configuration Commands

Command	Description
configure terminal	Configures manually from the console terminal
copy tftp running-config	Loads configuration information from a network TFTP server into RAM
show running-config	Displays the current configuration in RAM
copy running-config startup-config	Stores the current configuration from RAM into NVRAM
copy running-config tftp	Stores the current configuration from RAM on a network TFTP server
show startup-config	Displays the saved configuration, which is the contents of NVRAM
erase startup-config	Erases the contents of NVRAM

More Information: Router Startup Modes (Continued)

Use the commands shown in Figure 3-1 for routers running Cisco IOS Software Release 11.0 or later.

Figure 3-1 Configuration File Commands

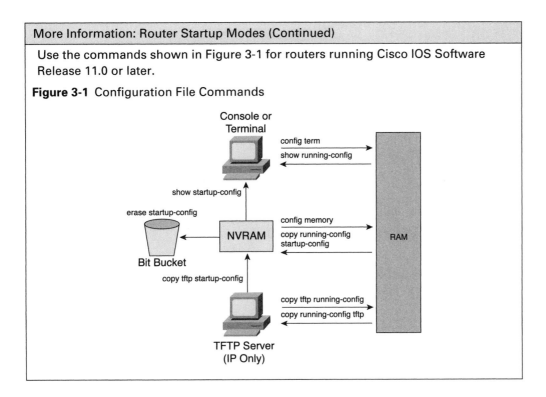

Configuring a Router Name

One of the first basic configuration tasks is to name the router, as shown in the following command line:

```
Router(config)#hostname SunDevils
SunDevils(config)#
```

Naming a router helps to better manage the network by uniquely naming each router within the network. The router is named in global configuration mode. The name of the router is called the host name and is displayed as the system prompt. If a router is not named, the system default is Router.

Lab 3.1.2   Command Modes and Router Identification

In this lab, you identify the basic router modes of user and privileged. You also use several commands that will enter specific modes to become familiar with the router prompt for each mode. In addition, you name the router.

Configuring Router Passwords

A router can be secured to restrict access by using passwords. Passwords can be established for virtual terminal lines and the console line. Privileged EXEC mode also can have a password.

From global configuration mode, use the **enable password** command to restrict access to privileged mode. This password, however, will be visible from the router's configuration files. To enter an encrypted password in privileged mode, use the command **enable secret**. If an enable secret password and an enable password is configured, the **enable secret** command is used instead of the **enable password**. From the configuration files, a person can view only the encryption, not the actual password.

Enable secret passwords cannot be read; another user might be able to break into the configuration, but the only thing that can be done is to overwrite the password because it is one-way encrypted and cannot be converted back to clear text.

The line console 0 configuration mode can be used to establish a login password on the console terminal. This is useful on a network on which multiple people have access to the router. This prevents anyone not authorized from accessing the router.

Telnet requires a password check. Different hardware platforms have different numbers of vty lines defined. The range 0 through 4 is used to specify five vty lines. These five incoming Telnet sessions can be simultaneous. The same password can be used for all lines, or one line can be set uniquely. This often is used in large networks with many network administrators. If a catastrophic problem occurs on a network and all common vty lines are used, the one unique line can be reserved for recovery.

Use the command **line vty 0 4** to establish a login password on incoming Telnet sessions. Example 3-2 demonstrates the different ways to configure and protect passwords.

By default, the console and vty passwords are displayed in clear text in the configuration file. They can be protected from display through the use of the **service password-encryption** command. This command is entered from global configuration mode. the **service password-encryption** command will encrypt all the other passwords, not the "enable secret" password, because the enable secret password is already encrypted. The global command **service password-encryption** will encrypt the "enable password" password and the passwords configured on the vty, aux, and console lines.

Example 3-2 *Configuring/Protecting Passwords*

```
! Console Password
Router(config)# line console 0
Router(config-line)# login
Router(config-line)# password cisco
! Virtual Terminal Password
Router(config)# line vty 0 4
```

Example 3-2 *Configuring/Protecting Passwords (Continued)*

```
Router(config-line)# login
Router(config-line)# password cisco
! Enable Password
Router(config)# enable password san-fran
!Perform Password Encryption
Router(config)# enable secret <password>
```

 Lab 3.1.3 Configuring Router Passwords

In this lab, you configure passwords for the console, virtual terminals, and a secret password.

Examining the show Commands

Many **show** commands exist, which help examine the contents of files in the router and are useful in troubleshooting. From each mode in the router, the **show ?** command can be used to see all the available options. Table 3-5 lists some of the **show** command options.

Table 3-5 show Commands

Command	Description
show interfaces	Displays all the statistics for all the interfaces on the router. If a user wants to view the statistics for a specific interface, he can enter the **show interfaces** command followed by the specific interface slot/port number. This is shown in the following example: Router#**show interfaces serial 1**
show controllers serial	Displays information specific to the interface hardware. This command must also include the port or slot/port number of the serial interface. For example: Router#**show controllers serial 0/1**
show clock	Displays the time set in the router.
show hosts	Displays a cached list of host names and addresses.
show users	Displays all users who are connected to the router.
show history	Displays a history of commands that have been entered.
show flash	Displays information about Flash memory and what Cisco IOS Software files are stored there.

continues

Table 3-5 **show** Commands (Continued)

Command	Description
show version	Displays information about the currently loaded software version along with hardware and device information.
show arp	Displays the router's address resolution (ARP) table.
show protocols	Displays the global and interface-specific status of any configured Layer 3 protocols.
show startup-config	Displays the saved configuration located in NVRAM.
show running-config	Displays the contents of the currently running configuration file or the configuration for a specific interface, or map class information.

Examples 3-3, 3-4, and 3-5 display sample output from the **show protocols**, **show version**, and **show interfaces** commands, respectively.

Example 3-3 **show protocols** *Command Output*

```
Router# show protocols
Global values:
Internet Protocol routing is enabled
DECnet routing is enabled
XNS routing is enabled
Vines routing is enabled
AppleTalk routing is enabled
Novell routing is enabled
--More--
Ethernet0 is up, line protocol is up
Internet address is 183.8.126.2, subnet mask is 255.255.255.128
DECnet cost is 5
XNS address is 3010.aa00.0400.0284
CLNS enabled
Vines metric is 32
AppleTalk address is 3012.93, zone ld-e0
Novell address is 3010.aa00.0400.0284
--More--
```

Example 3-4 show version *Command Output*

```
Router# show version
Cisco Internetwork Operating System Software
IOS (tm) 4500 Software (C4500-J-M). Version 12.1.5
Copyright (c) 1986-1996 by Cisco Systems, Inc.
Compiled Fri 28-Jun-96 16:32 by rbeach
Image text-base: 0x600088A0, data-base: 0x6076E000
ROM: System Bootstrap, Version 5.1(1) RELEASE SOFTWARE (fc1)
ROM: 4500-XBOOT Bootstrap Software, Version 10.1(1) RELEASE SOFTWARE (fc1)
router uptime is 1 week, 3 days, 32 minutes
System restarted by reload
System image file is c4500-j-mz, booted via tftp from 171.69.1.129
--More--
```

Example 3-5 show interfaces *Command Output*

```
Router# show interfaces
Serial0 is up, line protocol is up
Hardware is MK5025
Internet address is 183.8.64.129, subnet mask is 255.255.255.128
MTU 1500 bytes, BW 56 kbit, DLY 20000 usec, rely 255/255. load 9/255
Encapsulation HDLC, loopback not set, keepalive set (10 sec)
Last input 0:00:00, output 0:00:01, output hang never
Last clearing of show interfaces counters never
Output queue 0/40, 0 drops, input queue 0/75, 0 drops
Five minute input rate 1000 bits/sec, 0 packets/sec
331885 packets input, 62400237 bytes, no buffer
Received 230457 broadcasts, 0 runts, 0 giants
3 input errors, 3 CRC, 0 frame, 0 overrun, 0ignored, 0 abort
403591 packets output, 66717279 bytes, 0 underruns
0 output errors, 0 collisions, 8 interface resets, 0 restarts
45 carrier transitions
--More--
```

Lab 3.1.4 Using Router **show** Commands

This lab helps you become familiar with the router **show** commands. The **show** commands are the most important information-gathering commands available for the router.

Configuring a Serial Interface

A serial interface can be configured from the console or through a virtual terminal line. Serial interfaces require a clock signal to control the timing of the communications. In most environments, a data communications equipment (DCE) device such as a channel service unit/data service unit (CSU/DSU) provides the clock. By default, Cisco routers are data terminal equipment (DTE) devices, but they can be configured as DCE devices.

When routers are directly connected to each other through their serial links in a lab environment, one side must be considered as a DCE and provide a clocking signal. The clock is enabled and its speed is specified with the **clockrate** command. The available clock rates in bits per second are 1200, 2400, 9600, 19,200, 38,400, 56,000, 64,000, 72,000, 125,000, 148,000, 500,000, 800,000, 1,000,000, 1,300,000, 2,000,000, and 4,000,000. However, some bit rates might not be available on certain serial interfaces depending on their capacity. Keep in mind that in production networks, routers are almost always the DTE, and the CSU/DSU or modem sets the clock rate.

To configure a serial interface, perform the following steps and see Example 3-6:

Step 1 Enter global configuration mode. Enter interface mode.

Step 2 Configure the IP address and subnet mask.

Step 3 Set the DCE clock rate (skip this step on DTE).

Step 4 Turn on the interface.

Example 3-6 *Configuring a Serial Interface*

```
Router(config)# interface serial 1/0
Router(config-if)# bandwidth 56
Router(config-if)# clockrate 56000
Router(config-if)# no shutdown
```

By default, interfaces are turned off. To turn on an interface, you must enter the command **no shutdown**. The interface might need to be administratively turned off to perform hardware maintenance, change the interface configuration, perform troubleshooting, or perform other maintenance. The command **shutdown** turns off an interface.

The following command administratively turns off the interface:

```
Router(config-if)# shutdown
```

The following command turns on an interface that has been shut down:

```
Router(config-if)# no shutdown
```

The following command quits the current interface configuration mode:

```
Router(config-if)# exit
```

 Lab 3.1.5   Configuring a Serial Interface

In this lab, you configure a serial interface on two routers so that they can communicate with each other.

Making Configuration Changes

If a change is needed to a configuration, enter the appropriate mode and make the change. For example, if an interface was not turned on, enter global configuration mode and then enter interface mode, and issue the command **no shutdown**.

To verify changes, use the **show running-config** command. This command displays the current configuration. If the variables displayed are not what was intended, the environment can be corrected by doing one of the following:

- Issuing the **no** form of a configuration command

- Restarting the system and reloading the original configuration file from NVRAM

- Removing the startup configuration file with the **erase startup-configuration** command, restarting the router, and entering setup mode

To save the configuration variables to the startup configuration file in NVRAM, enter the following command at the privileged EXEC prompt:

```
Router# copy running-configuration startup-configuration
```

Table 3-6 shows commands used to manage the contents of NVRAM in Cisco IOS Software Release 11.*x* and later.

Table 3-6 Commands Used to Manage the Contents of NVRAM in Cisco IOS Software Release 11.x and Later

Command	Description
copy startup-config running-config	Loads configuration information from NVRAM
erase startup-config	Erases the contents of NVRAM
copy running-config startup-config	Stores the current configuration in RAM (that is, the running configuration) into NVRAM (as the startup configuration)
show startup-config	Displays the saved configuration, which is the contents of NVRAM

Lab 3.1.6 Making Configuration Changes

In this lab, you prepare to make changes to the existing configuration in a router. You bring an interface down and then back up and view its status.

Configuring an Ethernet Interface

An Ethernet interface can be configured from the console or a virtual terminal line. Each Ethernet interface must have an IP address and subnet mask.

To configure an Ethernet interface, perform the following steps and see Example 3-7:

Step 1 Enter global configuration mode.

Step 2 Enter interface configuration mode.

Step 3 Specify the interface address and subnet mask.

Step 4 Turn on the interface.

Example 3-7 *Configuring an Ethernet Interface*

```
Router(config)# interface ethernet0
Router(config-if)#ip address 192.168.1.150 255.255.255.128
Router(config-if)# no shutdown
```

By default, interfaces are turned off. To turn on an interface, enter the command **no shutdown**. The interface might need to be administratively turned off to perform hardware maintenance, change the interface configuration, perform troubleshooting, or perform other maintenance. The command **shutdown** turns off an interface.

 Lab 3.1.7 Configuring an Ethernet Interface

In this lab, you configure an Ethernet or FastEthernet interface on the router for a LAN.

Finishing the Configuration

The following lists recommended tasks for finishing the configuration. (Some organizations do not have some of the recommended configuration tasks, such as a message-of-the-day.)

■ Establishing configuration standards

■ Providing and configuring interface descriptions

- Configuring login banners
- Configuring a message-of-the-day (MOTD) banner
- Performing host name resolution
- Performing configuration backup and documentation

Importance of Configuration Standards

It is important to develop standards for configuring files within an organization. This facilitates control of the number of configuration files that must be maintained, how the files are stored, and where the files are stored.

A standard is a set of rules or procedures that are either widely used or officially specified. Without standards in an organization, a network could be in chaos if an interruption in service occurs.

To manage a network, there must be a centralized support standard. Configuration, security, performance, and other issues must be adequately addressed for the network to function smoothly. Creating standards for network consistency helps reduce network complexity, the amount of unplanned downtime, and exposure to events that might have an impact on network performance.

Interface Descriptions

An interface description should be used to identify important information such as a distant router, a circuit number, or a specific network segment. A description of an interface can help a network user remember specific information about the interface, such as what network the interface services. The next section, "Configuring Interface Description," provides a specific example.

The description is meant solely as a comment about the interface. Although the description appears in the configuration files that exist in router memory, a description does not affect the operation of the router. Descriptions are created by following a standard format that applies to each interface. The description can include the purpose and location of the interface, other devices or locations connected to the interface, and circuit identifiers. Descriptions enable support personnel to better understand the scope of problems related to an interface and allow for faster resolution of problems.

Configuring Interface Description

Enter global configuration mode to configure an interface description. Perform the following steps and see Example 3-8:

Step 1   Enter global configuration mode by entering the command **configure terminal**.

Step 2   Enter specific interface mode (for example, interface Ethernet 0) by entering the command **interface ethernet 0**.

Step 3   Enter the command **description**, followed by the information that is to be displayed (for example, XYZ Network, Building 10).

Step 4   Exit interface mode back to privileged EXEC mode by pressing **Ctrl-z**.

Step 5   Save the configuration changes to NVRAM by using the command **copy running-config startup-config**.

Example 3-8 Configuring an Interface Description

```
Router(config)# interface ethernet 0
Router(config-if)# description SkyDome LAN Communication Building
Router(config-if)# exit
! Results of issuing the show running-config command
interface Ethernet0
 description SkyDome LAN Communication Building
 ip address 198.133.215.1 255.255.255.0
```

Lab 3.2.3   Configuring Interface Descriptions

In this lab, you choose a description for an interface and use interface configuration mode to enter that description.

Login Banners

A login banner is a message that is displayed at login. The login banner is useful for conveying messages that affect all network users, such as notices of impending system shutdowns.

Anyone can see login banners. Therefore, careful attention should be used in the wording of a banner message. "Welcome" is an invitation for anyone to enter a router and is probably not an appropriate message.

A login banner should be a warning not to attempt login unless authorized. A message such as, "This is a secure system, authorized access only!" instructs unwanted visitors that any further intrusion or attempt is unwanted and illegal. Example 3-9 shows an example of a login banner.

Example 3-9 *Login Banner*

```
Tokyo con0 is now available
Press RETURN to get started.
```

Example 3-9 *Login Banner (Continued)*

```
This is a secure system.  Authorized Access ONLY!!!
User Access Verification
Password:
Tokyo>enable
Password:
Tokyo#
```

Configuring Message-of-the-Day (MOTD)

A message-of-the-day (MOTD) or login banner can be displayed on all connected terminals.

Enter global configuration mode to configure a MOTD banner. Use the **banner motd** command, followed by a space and a delimiting character, such as the pound sign (#). Add a message of the day followed by a space and a delimiting character, such as the pound sign (#). The delimiting character tells IOS when the message text begins and when the message text ends. Use the delimiting character once before typing the message text and again after finishing the message text. Any keyboard character can serve as the delimiting character, as long as it is not used in the banner. Just make sure that the character does not occur in the message text. Otherwise, the router assumes that you have finished entering the message text.

Perform the following steps to create and display a message of the day. See Example 3-10:

Step 1   Enter global configuration mode by using the command **configure terminal.**

Step 2   Enter the command **banner motd # The message of the day goes here #**.

Step 3   Save changes by issuing the command **copy running-configuration startup-configuration**, or **copy run start** for a shortcut.

Example 3-10 *MOTD Display*

```
Tokyo(config)# banner motd #
You have entered a secure system, authorized access ONLY!#
```

 Lab 3.2.5   Configuring Message-of-the-Day (MOTD)

In this lab, you use global configuration mode to enter a message-of-the-day into the router. This procedure enables all users to view the message upon entering the router.

Host Name Resolution

Host name resolution is the process that a computer system uses to associate a host name with a network address.

Protocols such as Telnet use host names to identify network devices. To use host names to communicate with other IP devices, network devices, such as routers, must be capable of associating the host names with IP addresses. A list of host names and their associated IP addresses is called a *host table*. Table 3-7 shows a sample host table.

Table 3-7 Host Table

Router Name	Router Type	E0	E1	S0
Tokyo	2601	10.10.1.1	192.168.1.150	172.16.150.1
Paris	2621	10.10.1.2		172.16.151.1

A host table might include all devices in a network organization. Each unique IP address can have a host name associated with it. Cisco IOS Software maintains a cache of host name-to-address mappings for use by EXEC commands. This cache speeds up the process of converting names to addresses.

Host names, unlike Domain Name System (DNS) names, are significant only on the router on which they are configured and used only by the router IOS commands. Host names on the router do not make the router a DNS server for host computers. Example 3-11 shows the configuration of a host table on a router.

Example 3-11 *Host Table Configuration*

```
Router(config)# ip host Auckland 172.16.32.1
Router(config)# ip host Beirut 192.168.53.1
Router(config)# ip host Capetown 192.168.89.1
Router(config)# ip host Denver 10.202.8.1
```

This host table enables the network administrator to type either the host name or the IP address to obtain access to a remote host. An example to use as the host name would be Auckland or 172.16.32.1 for the IP address. To display a list of hosts and their associated IP addresses that are defined for a particular router, use the command **show hosts**.

Configuring Host Tables

To assign host names to addresses, first enter global configuration mode. Issue the command **ip host** followed by the name of the destination and all IP addresses by which the device can be reached. This maps the host name to each of its interface IP addresses. To reach the host, use a **telnet** or **ping** command with the name of the router or an IP address that is associated with the router's name.

The procedure to configure the host table is as follows:

Step 1   Enter global configuration mode in the router.

Step 2   Enter the command **ip host** followed by the name of the router and the IP addresses associated with the interfaces on each router.

Step 3   Continue entering IP addresses until all routers in the network are entered.

Step 4   Save the configuration to NVRAM.

 Lab 3.2.7   Configuring Host Tables

In this lab, you use global configuration mode to create IP host tables to allow a router to translate router names with all the attached interfaces on that router.

Configuration Backup and Documentation

The configuration of network devices determines the way the network behaves or acts. Management of device configuration includes the following tasks:

- Listing and comparing configuration files on running devices
- Storing configuration files on network servers
- Performing software installations and upgrades

Configuration files should be stored as backup files in case a problem arises. Configuration files can be stored on a network server, on a *Trivial File Transfer Protocol (TFTP)* server, or on a disk stored in a safe place. Documentation should be included with this offline information.

The configuration on the router also can be saved to a disk by capturing text in the router and saving it to the disk or hard drive. If the file needs to be copied back to the router, it can be pasted into the router. These methods of saving and restoring the router configuration are covered in greater detail in Chapter 5, "Managing Cisco IOS Software."

Figure 3-2 shows an overview of the router configuration process.

Figure 3-2 Router Configuration Process Flowchart

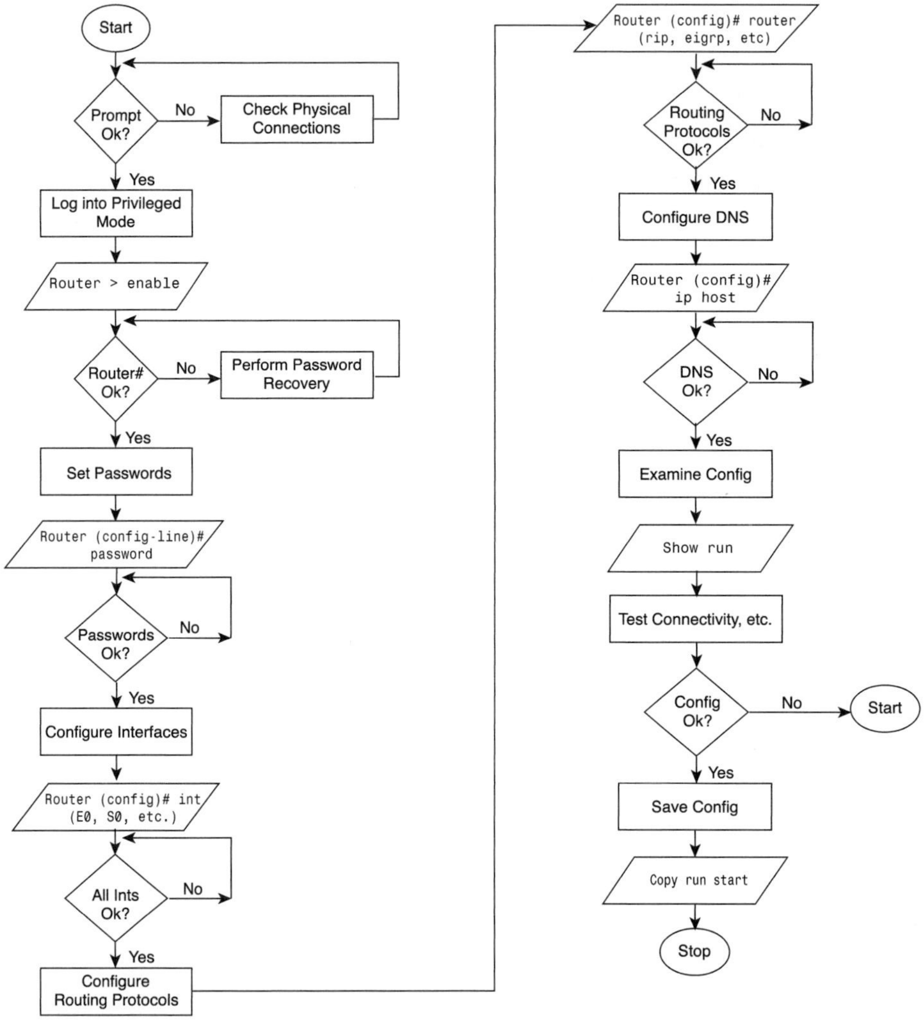

Backing Up Configuration Files

A current copy of the configuration can be stored on a TFTP server. The **copy running-config tftp** command can be used to store the current configuration on a network TFTP server. To do so, complete the following tasks:

Step 1   Enter the **copy running-config tftp** command.

Step 2   Enter the IP address of the host where the configuration file will be stored.

Step 3   Enter the name to assign to the configuration file.

Step 4   Confirm the choices by answering yes each time.

A configuration file stored on one of the network servers can be used to configure a router. To do so, complete the following tasks:

Step 1   Enter configuration mode by entering the **copy tftp running-config** command.

Step 2   At the system prompt, select a host or network configuration file. The network configuration file contains commands that apply to all routers and terminal servers on the network. The host configuration file contains commands that apply to one router in particular. At the system prompt, enter the IP address of the remote host where the TFTP server is located. In this example, the router is configured from the TFTP server at IP address 10.10.1.2.

Step 3   At the system prompt, enter the name of the configuration file or accept the default name. The filename convention is UNIX-based. The default filename is **hostname-config** for the host file and **network-config** for the network configuration file. In the DOS environment, filenames are limited to eight characters plus a three-character extension (for example, **router.cfg**). Confirm the configuration filename and the TFTP server address that the system supplies.

The router configuration can also be saved to a disk by capturing text in the router and saving it to the disk or hard drive. If the file needs to be copied back to the router, use the standard edit features of a terminal emulator program to paste the command file into the router.

Lab 3.2.9   Backing Up Configuration Files

In this lab, you learn how to capture the running configuration of a router to an ASCII text file with HyperTerminal.

More Information: Password Recovery
This section explains several password-recovery techniques for Cisco routers and Catalyst switches. You can perform password recovery on most of the platforms without changing hardware jumpers, but all platforms require that the router be rebooted. Password recovery can be done only from the console port (physically attached to the router).

Overview of Password Recovery

Three ways exist for restoring access to a router when the password is lost. You can view the password, change the password, or erase the configuration and start over as if the box was new.

Each procedure follows these basic steps:

Step 1   Configure the router to start up without reading the configuration memory (NVRAM). This is done from what sometimes is called test system mode, ROM mode, or boot mode.

More Information: Password Recovery (Continued)	
Step 2	Reboot the system.
Step 3	Access enable mode (which can be done without a password if you set the configuration register correctly in Step 1).
Step 4	View or change the password, or erase the configuration.
Step 5	Reconfigure the router to boot up and read the NVRAM as it normally does.
Step 6	Reboot the system.

Some password recovery requires a terminal to issue a BREAK signal; you must be familiar with how your terminal or PC terminal emulator issues this signal. In Pro-Comm, for example, the keys Alt-B generate the BREAK signal by default; in Windows HyperTerminal, you press Break or Ctrl-Break. Windows HyperTerminal also enables you to define a function key as BREAK. From the terminal window, select Function Keys and define one as Break by filling in the characters ^$B (Shift-6, Shift-4, and uppercase B). Several free terminal-emulation packages also are available for download on the Internet, which you might find preferable.

The following sections contain detailed instructions for specific Cisco routers. Locate your product at the beginning of each section to determine which technique to use.

Password Recovery Technique 1

The following are the relevant devices for this technique:

- Cisco 2500 series
- Cisco 3000 series
- Cisco 7000 series running Cisco IOS Software Release 10.0 or later in ROMs

This technique can be used on the Cisco 7000 and Cisco 7010 series only if the router has Cisco IOS Software Release 10.0 ROMs installed on the Route Processor (RP) card. It might be booting Flash Cisco IOS Software Release 10.0, but it needs the actual ROMs on the processor card as well. The following steps outline password recovery technique 1:

Step 1	Attach a terminal or PC with terminal emulation to the console port of the router. To connect a PC to the console port, attach a null modem adapter (Tandy Null Modem Adapter No. 26-1496 has been tested) to the console port, and then attach a straight-through modem cable to the null modem adapter.
Step 2	Type **show version** and record the setting of the configuration register. It is usually 0x2102 or 0x102. If you do not get the router prompt to do a **show version**, look on a similar router to obtain the configuration register number, or try using 0x2102.
Step 3	Power-cycle the router.
Step 4	Press the **Break** key on the terminal within 60 seconds of the power-up. You should see the > prompt with no router name. If you don't see this, the terminal is not sending the correct BREAK signal. In that case, check the terminal or terminal emulation setup.

More Information: Password Recovery (Continued)

Step 5   Type **o/r 0x42** at the > prompt to boot from Flash memory, or type **o/r 0x41** to boot from the boot ROMs. (Note that this is the letter *o*, not the numeral zero.) If you have Flash memory and it is intact, 0x42 is the best setting because it is the default. Use 0x41 only if the Flash memory is erased or is not installed. If you use 0x41, you can either view or erase the configuration. You cannot change the password.

Step 6   Type **i** at the > prompt. The router reboots but ignores its saved configuration.

Step 7   Answer **no** to all the setup questions, or press **Ctrl-C**.

Step 8   Type **enable** at the Router> prompt. You're then in enable mode and can see the Router# prompt.

Step 9   Choose one of the following three options:

 ■ To view the password, type **show start**.

 ■ To change the password (in case it is encrypted, for example), do the following:

   a   Type **copy start run** to copy the NVRAM into memory.

   b   Type **show run**.

   c   If you have the enable secret password set, perform the following:

   Type **config term** and make the changes.

   Type **enable secret** *new_password*.

   Press **Ctrl-Z**.

   d   If you do not have **enable secret xxxx**, type **enable password** *new_password* and press **Ctrl-Z**.

   e   Type **copy run start** to commit the changes.

Step 10   Type **config term** at the prompt.

Step 11   Type **config-register 0x2102**, or whatever value you recorded in Step 2.

Step 12   Press **Ctrl-Z** to return to privileged EXEC mode.

Step 13   Type **reload** at the prompt. You do not need to write memory.

Password Recovery Technique 2

Use this procedure to recover lost passwords on the following routers:

 ■ Cisco 1003

 ■ Cisco 1600 series

 ■ Cisco 2600 series

 ■ Cisco 3600 series

 ■ Cisco 4500 series

 ■ Cisco 7100 series

NOTE

To erase the config, type **erase start**.

More Information: Password Recovery (Continued)

- Cisco 7200 series

- Cisco 7500 series

- IDT Orion-based routers

- AS5200 and AS5300 platforms

To recover a password using procedure 2, perform the following steps:

Step 1   Attach a terminal or PC with terminal-emulation software to the console port of the router.

Step 2   Enter **show version** and record the setting of the configuration register. It is usually 0x2102 or 0x102.

The configuration register value is on the last line of the display. Note whether the configuration register is set to enable Break or disable Break.

The factory-default configuration register value is 0x2102. Notice that the third digit from the left in this value is 1, which disables Break. If the third digit is *not* 1, Break is enabled.

Step 3   Turn off the router and then turn it on again.

Step 4   Press the Break key on the terminal within 60 seconds of turning on the router. The rommon> prompt appears. If it does not appear, the terminal is not sending the correct Break signal.

If the prompt does not appear, check the terminal or terminal emulation setup.

Step 5   Enter **confreg** at the rommon> prompt.

The following prompt appears:

```
Do you wish to change configuration [y/n]?
```

Step 6   Enter **yes** and press Return.

Step 7   Enter **no** to subsequent questions until the following prompt appears:

```
ignore system config info [y/n]?
```

Step 8   Enter **yes**.

Step 9   Enter **no** to subsequent questions until the following prompt appears:

```
change boot characteristics [y/n]?
```

Step 10   Enter **yes**.

The following prompt appears:

```
enter to boot:
```

Step 11   At this prompt, either enter **2** and press **Enter** if booting from Flash memory, or, if Flash memory is erased, enter **1**.

More Information: Password Recovery (Continued)

If Flash memory is erased, the Cisco 4500 must be returned to Cisco for service. If you enter **1**, you can only view or erase the configuration; you cannot change the password.

A configuration summary is displayed and the following prompt appears:

```
Do you wish to change configuration [y/n]?
```

Step 12 Enter **no** and press Return.

The following prompt appears:

```
rommon>
```

Step 13 Enter **reset** at the privileged EXEC prompt or, for Cisco 4500 series and Cisco 7500 series routers, power-cycle the router.

Step 14 As the router boots, enter **no** to all the setup questions until the following prompt appears:

```
Router>
```

Step 15 Enter **enable** to enter enable mode.

The Router# prompt appears.

Step 16 Choose one of the following options:

- To view the password, if it is not encrypted, enter **more nvram:startup-config**.

- To change the password (if it is encrypted, for example), enter the following commands:

```
Router# configure memory
Router# configure terminal
Router(config)# enable secret 1234abcd
Router(config)# ctrl-z
Router# write memory
```

The **enable secret** command provides increased security by storing the enable secret password using a nonreversible cryptographic function; however, you cannot recover a lost password that has been encrypted.

Step 17 Enter **configure terminal** at the prompt.

Step 18 Type **config-register** and whatever value you recorded in Step 2.

Step 19 Press **Ctrl-Z** to quit the configuration editor.

Step 20 Enter **reload** at the prompt and enter **write memory** to save the configuration.

Summary

This chapter summarized the key points in configuring a router:

- The router has several modes:
  - User mode
  - Privileged mode
  - Global configuration mode
  - Other configuration modes

- The command-line interface (CLI) is used to change configurations, including doing the following:
  - Setting the host name
  - Setting passwords
  - Configuring interfaces
  - Modifying configurations
  - Showing configurations

- Interface descriptions include important information to help network administrators understand and troubleshoot their networks.

- Login banners and messages-of-the-day provide users with information upon login to the router.

- Host name resolutions translate names to IP addresses to allow the router to quickly convert names to addresses.

- Three ways exist for restoring access to a router when the password is lost:
  - You can view the password.
  - You can change the password.
  - You can erase the configuration and start over as if the box was new.

- Configuration standards are key elements in the success of any organization in maintaining an efficient network. Configuration backup and documentation is extremely important to keep a network operating smoothly.

To supplement all that you have learned in this chapter, refer to the chapter-specific Interactive Media Activities on the CD-ROM that accompanies this book.

Key Terms

global configuration mode   Used for one-line commands and commands that make global changes to the router configuration.

interface   Connection between two systems or devices. In routing terminology, a network connection.

nonvolatile RAM (NVRAM)   RAM that retains its contents when a unit is powered off.

privileged mode   Used for copying and managing entire configuration files.

Trivial File Transfer Protocol (TFTP)   Simplified version of FTP that allows files to be transferred from one computer to another over a network, usually without the use of client authentication (for example, username and password).

Check Your Understanding

Complete all the review questions to test your understanding of the topics and concepts in this chapter. Answers are listed in Appendix B, "Check Your Understanding Answer Key."

1. What is a standard?

    A. A formal description of a set of rules and conventions that govern how devices on a network exchange information

    B. A set of rules or procedures that is either widely used or officially specified

    C. A way in which network devices access the network medium

2. Using the **description** command on an interface does what?

    A. Welcomes users to the router

    B. Warns users not to enter the router

    C. Displays a comment about the interface

3. A good example of a login banner is what?

    A. Welcome everyone

    B. Everyone please log in

    C. Authorized access only

4. What is host name resolution?

    A. The process of associating a name with a network address

    B. The process of displaying a login message

    C. The process of displaying a description on a router

5. Configuration backup and documentation is necessary to an organization to maintain an efficient network. True or false?

    A. True

    B. False

6. Backup of configuration files is not necessary. True or false?

    A. True

    B. False

7. A TFTP server is the only location where backup files can be stored. True or false?

    A. True

    B. False

8. If you are planning to configure an interface, what prompt should be on the router?

   A. router(config)#

   B. router(config-in)#

   C. router(config-intf)#

   D. router(config-if)#

9. Which of the following is the correct order for the process of configuring a router? (Assume that you have already made router changes in configuration mode.)

   A. Save changes to backup, decide whether the changes are your intended results, examine the results, and examine the backup file.

   B. Examine the results, decide whether the changes are your intended results, save the changes to backup, and examine the backup file.

   C. Decide whether the changes are your intended results, examine the backup file, save the changes to backup, and examine the results.

   D. Examine the results, save the changes to backup, decide whether the changes are your intended results, and examine the backup file.

10. Which of the following is a command that can be used to save router configuration changes to a backup?

   A. Router# **copy running-config tftp**

   B. Router# **show running-config**

   C. Router# **config mem**

   D. Router# **copy tftp running-config**

11. Which of the following does not describe password configuration on routers?

   A. Passwords can be established in every configuration mode.

   B. A password can be established on the console port.

   C. The enable secret password uses an encryption process to alter the password character string.

   D. All password establishment begins in global configuration mode.

12. What is used for one-line commands that change the entire router?

   A. Global configuration mode

   B. Privileged mode

   C. User EXEC mode

   D. Interface mode

13. What does the **exit** command do in a configuration mode with the prompt Router (config-if)#?

   A. It quits the current configuration interface mode.

   B. It reaches the privileged EXEC prompt.

   C. It exits the router.

   D. It switches to the user EXEC prompt.

14. What are the major elements of a typical router configuration?

   A. Passwords, interfaces, routing protocols, DNS

   B. Boot sequence, interfaces, TFTP server, NVRAM

   C. NVRAM, ROM, DRAM, interfaces

   D. Interfaces, routing protocols, configuration register, Flash memory

15. In a password-recovery procedure, immediately after issuing a Ctrl-Break upon router startup, what value should the config register be set to?

   A. 0x2102

   B. 0x2142

   C. 0x0000

   D. 0x10F

CHAPTER 4

Learning About Other Devices

Objectives

Upon completion of this chapter, you should be able to answer the following questions:

- What are some of the methods to implement, monitor, and maintain CDP?

- How does CDP create a network map of the environment?

- What are the commands to disable and trouble-shoot CDP?

- What are some of the reasons to Telnet remotely to other routers?

- What are the commands to verify, disconnect, and suspend a Telnet connection?

- What are some forms of alternative connectivity tests?

- What are some of the uses of the **show cdp neighbors** command?

- How do you determine which neighboring devices are connected to which local interfaces?

- How does CDP gather the neighboring devices' network address information?

- What are some methods to troubleshoot remote terminal connections?

Key Terms

The following is a list of key terms introduced in this chapter. For your reference, a definition for each term can be found at the end of this chapter.

In this chapter, you learn how to implement, monitor, and maintain Cisco Discovery Protocol (CDP) by using the correct router commands. In addition, this chapter explains the commands most often used to perform address-related troubleshooting.

Be sure to look at this chapter's associated Interactive Media Activities, which you will find on the CD-ROM accompanying this book. These CD elements are designed to supplement the material and reinforce the concepts introduced in this chapter.

Discovering and Connecting to Neighbors

Sometimes, network administrators are faced with situations in which network documentation is incomplete or inaccurate. Cisco Discovery Protocol (CDP) is a useful tool in these situations because it can help to build a basic picture of the network. CDP shows only information about directly connected neighbors; nevertheless, it is a powerful tool.

Introduction to CDP

Cisco Discovery Protocol (CDP) is a Layer 2 protocol that connects lower physical media and upper network layer protocols, as shown in Figure 4-1. CDP is used to obtain information about neighboring Cisco devices. This information shows the types of devices connected, the router interfaces they are connected to, the interfaces used to make the connections, and the model numbers of the devices. CDP is media and protocol independent, and runs on all Cisco equipment over the *Subnetwork Access Protocol (SNAP)*. CDP is a proprietary protocol native to Cisco networking devices and will run only on Cisco networking devices.

CDP Version 2 (CDPv2) is the most recent release of the protocol. Cisco IOS Software Release 12.0(3)T version or later supports CDPv2. CDP Version 1 (CDPv1) is enabled globally by default with Cisco IOS Software Release 10.3 or later.

Figure 4-1 Where CDP Fits In

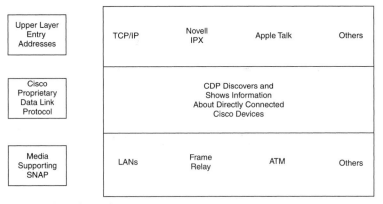

• Media and Protocol Interactions

When a Cisco device boots up, CDP starts up automatically and allows the device to detect neighboring devices that are also running CDP. CDP runs over the data link layer and allows two systems to learn about each other, even if they are using different network layer protocols.

Each device configured for CDP sends periodic messages, known as advertisements, to multiple Cisco routers. Each Cisco device advertises at least one address at which it can receive *Simple Network Management Protocol (SNMP)* messages. The advertisements also contain Time-To-Live (TTL) or holdtime information. This holdtime information indicates the length of time that receiving devices hold CDP information before discarding it. Additionally, each device listens to periodic CDP messages sent by others to learn about neighboring devices.

Information Obtained with CDP

The primary use of CDP is to discover all Cisco devices that are directly connected to a local device. A CDP frame can be small, yet can retrieve useful information about neighboring routers and switches.

More Information: Displaying a CDP Entry

Use the command **show cdp entry** [*device name*], as demonstrated in Example 4-1, to display a single cached CDP entry.

Example 4-1 **show cdp entry** *Command Output*

```
routerA# show cdp entry routerB
-----------------------------
Device ID: routerB
Entry address(es):
IP address: 198.92.68.18
Platform: 2501. Capabilities: Router
Interface: Ethernet), Port ID (outgoing port): Ethernet0
Holdtime: 155 sec

--- output omitted ---
```

Notice that the output from this command includes the Layer 3 addresses configured on the interface that the neighbor is using to send CDP updates to the local router. An administrator can view the IP addresses of the targeted CDP neighbor (Router B) with the single command entry on Router A. The holdtime value indicates the amount of elapsed time since the CDP frame arrived with this information. The **show cdp entry** [*device name*] command includes abbreviated information about Router B. Knowing this information about neighboring devices provides you with an idea of the exact physical topology of the network to properly configure the devices.

Showing CDP Neighbors

Figure 4-2 displays an example of how CDP delivers its collection of information to a network administrator. Each router that is running CDP exchanges protocol information with its neighbors. The network administrator displays the results of this CDP information exchange on a console that is connected to a local router.

Figure 4-2 CDP Neighbors

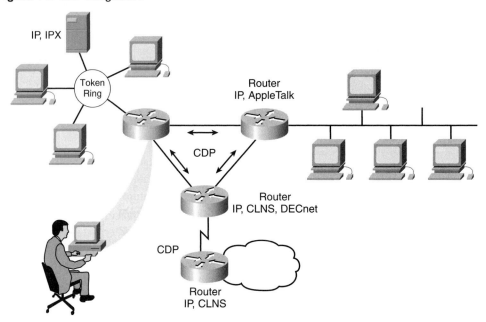

You use the **show cdp neighbors** command to display information about the networks directly connected to the router. CDP provides information about each CDP neighbor device by transmitting *Type Length Values (TLVs)*. TLVs are blocks of information embedded in CDP advertisements.

Device TLVs displayed by the **show cdp neighbors** command, and as shown in Example 4-2, include the following:

- Device ID
- Local Interface
- Holdtime
- Capability
- Platform
- Port ID

- VTP Management Domain Name (CDPv2 only)

- Native VLAN (CDPv2 only)

- Full/Half-Duplex (CDPv2 only)

Example 4-2 **show cdp neighbors** *Command Output*

```
routerA# show cdp neighbors
Capability Codes:
R - Router, T - Trans Bridge,
B - Source Route Bridge,
S - Switch, H - Host, I - IGMP


Device ID     Local Interface    Holdtime    Capability    Platform Port    ID
routerB       Eth 0              151         R             2501     Eth     0
routerB       Ser 0              165         R             2501     Ser     0
```

To display all the information output generated by **show cdp neighbors**, as well as information like that from **show cdp entry**, you use the optional **show cdp neighbors detail** command, as demonstrated in Example 4-3.

Example 4-3 **show cdp neighbors detail** *Command Output*

```
routerA# show cdp neighbors detail
Device ID: routerB
Entry address(es):
  IP address: 198.92.68.18
Platform: 2501, Capabilities: Router
Interface: Ethernet0, Port ID (outgoing port): Ethernet0
Holdtime: 143 sec
```

Notice that the lowest router in Figure 4-2 is not directly connected to the administrator's console router. To obtain CDP information about this device, the administrator needs to *Telnet* to a router that is directly connected to this device. As previously stated, you will find this information helps you gain full knowledge about the devices that are on the network, which provides you a better understanding of the physical topology.

Implementation, Monitoring, and Maintenance of CDP

The commands shown in Table 4-1 are used to implement, monitor, and maintain CDP information.

Table 4-1 CDP Commands

Command	Mode	Description
cdp run	Global configuration mode	Enables CDP globally on the router.
cdp enable	Interface configuration mode	Enables CDP on an interface.
clear cdp counters	Privileged EXEC mode	Resets the traffic counters to zero.
show cdp	User or Privileged EXEC mode	Displays the interval between transmissions of CDP advertisements, the number of seconds the CDP advertisement is valid for a given port, and the version of the advertisement.
show cdp entry {*entry-name* [**protocol** | **version**]}	User or Privileged EXEC mode	Displays information about a specific neighbor. Display can be limited to protocol or version information.
show cdp interface [*type number*]	User or Privileged EXEC mode	Displays information about interfaces on which CDP is enabled.
show cdp neighbors [*type number*] [**detail**]	User or Privileged EXEC mode	Displays the type of device that has been discovered, the name of the device, the number and type of the local interface (port), the number of seconds the CDP advertisement is valid for the port, the device type, the device product number, and the port ID. Issuing the **detail** keyword displays information on the native VLAN ID, the duplex mode, and the VLAN Trunking Protocol (VTP) domain name associated with neighbor devices.

Use the **cdp run** command to enable CDP globally on the router. By default, CDP is globally enabled. Use the **cdp enable** command to enable CDP on a particular interface. On Cisco IOS Software Release 10.3 and later, CDP could be enabled on each interface of the device by using the **cdp enable** command. Even though CDP is enabled by default on most Cisco devices, you might encounter instances in which you need to manually enable CDP on a per interface basis. Examples of when this manual enabling might need to be done occur on 1900 series switches that do not support using the **cdp run** command. On 1900 series switches, you need to enable or disable CDP on a per interface basis. Other examples include particular interfaces that might not have CDP enabled for security purposes.

More Information: The show cdp interface Command

Use the **show cdp interface** command to gather information that CDP uses for its advertisement and discovery frame transmission. Example 4-4 demonstrates some sample output from this command. This information helps provide detailed information about such things as the holdtime, the frequency at which CDP packets are sent, the encapsulation time for the interface, and the administrative and protocol conditions of the interface.

Example 4-4 show cdp interface *Command Output*

```
routerA# show cdp interface
Serial 0 is up, line protocol is up, encapsulation is Frame Relay
  Sending CDP packets every 60 seconds
  Holdtime is 180 seconds
Ethernet0 is up, line protocol is up, encapsulation is ARPA
  Sending CDP packets every 60 seconds
  Holdtime is 180 seconds
```

Creating a Network Map of the Environment

CDP was designed and implemented as a simple, low-overhead protocol. Though a CDP frame can be very small, CDP can retrieve a great deal of useful information about connected neighboring routers.

The **show cdp neighbors** command can be used to obtain the following information:

- Device ID
- Address
- Port ID
- Capabilities
- Version
- Platform
- IP Network Prefix
- VTP Management Domain Name (CDPv2 only)

- Native VLAN (CDPv2 only)

- Full/Half-Duplex (CDPv2 only)

This information can be used to create a network map of the connected devices. Devices connected to neighboring devices can be discovered by using Telnet to connect to the neighbors. Use the **show cdp neighbors detail** command to discover what devices are connected to those neighbors.

Lab 4.1.4   Creating a Network Map Using CDP

In this Lab, you use the CDP commands to get information about neighboring networks and routers.

Disabling CDP

As previously mentioned, CDP is globally enabled on the router by default. To disable CDP at the global level, use the **no cdp run** command in global config mode. If CDP is disabled globally, the interface cannot be enabled for CDP. For example, you might disable CDP for security purposes when you do not want information made available about a particular device.

On Cisco IOS Software Release 10.3 and later, CDP is disabled by default on each of interface of the device. You must use the **cdp enable** command before CDP is enabled and CDP messages can be sent and received. To disable CDP on a specific interface after it has been enabled, use the **no cdp enable** command in interface config mode.

Troubleshooting CDP

Table 4-2 lists and describes troubleshooting commands that you can use to show the version, update information, tables, and traffic.

Table 4-2 CDP Troubleshooting Commands

Command	Description
clear cdp table	Deletes the CDP table of information about neighbors.
show cdp traffic	Displays CDP counters, including the number of packets sent and received and checksum errors.
show debugging	Displays information about the types of debugging that are enabled for your router.
debug cdp adjacency	Displays information about CDP neighbors.
debug cdp events	Displays information about CDP events.
debug cdp ip	Displays information about CDP IP information.

Table 4-2 CDP Troubleshooting Commands (Continued)

Command	Description
debug cdp packets	Displays information about CDP packet-related information.
cdp timers	Specifies how often Cisco IOS Software sends CDP updates.
cdp holdtime	Specifies the holdtime the receiving device should hold a CDP packet from your router before discarding.
show cdp	Displays information about CDP update packets.

Lab 4.1.6   Using CDP Commands

In this activity, you use the CDP commands to get information about neighboring networks and routers. You display information on how CDP is configured for its advertisement and discovery frame transmission.

Getting Information About Remote Devices

This section describes Telnet, *ping*, and *traceroute*, which can be used to obtain information about remote devices, as shown in Figure 4-3.

Figure 4-3 Testing Process Overview

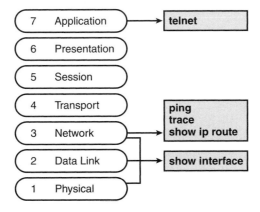

Telnet

Telnet is a virtual terminal protocol that is part of the TCP/IP protocol suite. Telnet enables you to make connections to remote hosts and makes it possible for a network terminal to remotely log in. **telnet** is a Cisco IOS Software EXEC command used to verify the application layer software between source and destination. This command is the most complete test mechanism available.

Telnet performs at the application layer of the OSI model, and it depends on TCP to guarantee the correct and orderly delivery of data between the client and server.

A router can have simultaneous incoming Telnet sessions. The range 0 through 4 specifies five vty or Telnet lines. These five incoming Telnet sessions can take place at one time.

Verifying the application layer connectivity is a byproduct of Telnet. Telnet is mainly used to connect to remote network devices, such as routers, switches, and servers, to gather information or perform maintenance. It is a simple and universal application program.

Establishing and Verifying a Telnet Connection

The **telnet** Cisco IOS Software EXEC command allows a user to Telnet from one Cisco device to another. With the Cisco implementation of TCP/IP, you do not have to enter the command **connect** or **telnet** to establish a Telnet connection. Just enter the host name or the IP address of the remote router. To end a Telnet session, use the EXEC commands **exit** or **logout**. Figure 4-4 demonstrates initiating and exiting a Telnet connection.

Figure 4-4 Telnet Operation

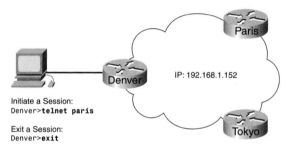

A host name table or access to DNS for Telnet must be present for a name to work in a Telnet session; otherwise, the IP address of the host must be entered. To initiate a Telnet session, use any of the following alternatives:

```
Denver>connect paris
Denver>paris
Denver>192.168.1.152
Denver>telnet paris
```

You can use Telnet to perform a test to determine whether access can or cannot be obtained from a remote router. As shown in Figure 4-5, if Telnet is successful in connecting the York router to the Paris router, a basic test of the network connection is successful. This operation can be performed at either the user or privileged EXEC levels.

If remote access can be obtained through another router, at least one TCP/IP application can reach the remote router. A successful Telnet connection indicates that the upper-layer application functions properly.

Figure 4-5 Testing the Application Layer

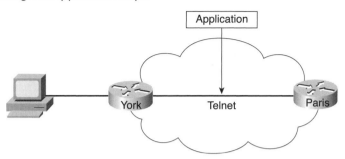

A successful Telnet can occur to one router, but fail to another router. Specific addressing, naming, or access permission problems are likely culprits for Telnet failure. Further, it is possible that the problem exists on the source router or on the router that failed as a Telnet target. In this case, the next step is to try **ping**, which is covered later in this chapter. **ping** allows testing of end-to-end connections at the network layer.

Once the Telnet is completed, log off the host. The EXEC terminates any connection after ten minutes of inactivity by default or when you enter the **exit** command at the EXEC prompt.

Lab 4.2.2   Establishing and Verifying a Telnet Connection

In this lab, you establish a Telnet connection to a remote router and gather information from it.

Disconnecting and Suspending Telnet Sessions

One important feature of the **telnet** command is the suspend feature. However, one potential problem exists, which occurs when a Telnet session is suspended and the **Enter** key is pressed. Cisco IOS software resumes the connection to the most recently suspended Telnet connection. The **Enter** key is used frequently. With a suspended Telnet session, it is possible to reconnect to another router. This is dangerous when changes are made to the configuration or when EXEC commands are used. Always pay particular attention to what router is being used when utilizing the suspended Telnet feature.

A session is suspended for a limited time. To resume a suspended Telnet session, press **Enter**. The command **show sessions** will show what Telnet sessions occur.

The procedure for disconnecting a Telnet session is as follows:

Step 1   Enter the command **disconnect**.

Step 2   Follow the command with the name or IP address of the router. For example:

```
Denver>disconnect paris
```

To suspend a Telnet session, simultaneously press the **Ctrl-Shift-6** keys**,** and then type **x**.

Lab 4.2.3   Suspending and Disconnecting Telnet Sessions

In this lab, you establish a Telnet session to a remote router. You temporarily suspend and then resume the session.

Advanced Telnet Operation

You might have several concurrent Telnet sessions open, and you can switch back and forth between these sessions. The number of open sessions that are allowed at one time is defined by the **session limit** command.

To switch between sessions by escaping from one session and resuming a previous opened session, use the following commands:

- **Ctrl + Shift + 6** followed by hitting the letter **x**—Suspends the current connection and returns to the EXEC prompt.

- **resume**—Resumes a specific Telnet session that was previously created. The **resume** command requires a connection ID to specify which session to resume.

It is possible to make a new connection while at the EXEC prompt.

You can use and suspend multiple Telnet sessions with the **Ctrl + Shift + 6** followed by hitting the letter **x** sequence. The session can be resumed by using the **Enter** key. If the **Enter** key is used, Cisco IOS Software resumes the connection to the most recently suspended Telnet connection. Using the **resume** command requires a connection ID, and you can display the connection IDs for all open sessions by using the **show sessions** command.

Lab 4.2.4   Advanced Telnet Operations

In this lab, you use the **telnet** command to remotely access other routers, verifying that the application layer between source and destination is working properly. You suspend a Telnet session and engage in multiple Telnet sessions. You return to the suspended session and disconnect from the Telnet session.

Alternative Connectivity Tests

The following sections cover many of the commands that can be used to test and examine connectivity between devices. The tools and commands described in this section are as follows:

- **ping**
- **traceroute**
- **show ip route**

- **show interfaces serial**
- **show interfaces/clear counter**
- **debug**

ping Command

Many network protocols support an echo protocol as an aid to diagnosing basic network connectivity. Echo protocols test whether or not protocol packets are being routed.

The **ping** command sends a packet to the destination host and then waits for a reply packet from that host. Results from this echo protocol can help evaluate the path-to-host reliability, delays over the path, and if the host can be reached or is functioning. This command is a basic testing mechanism, and its operation can be performed in either the user or privileged EXEC modes.

The **ping** user EXEC command can be used to diagnose basic network connectivity. Use the **ping** command as follows:

Step 1   **ping** IP address or name of destination.

Step 2   Press the **Enter** key.

More Information: ping Return Codes

Table 4-3 shows the Cisco **ping** return codes. **ping** uses Internet Control Message Protocol (ICMP).

Table 4-3 Cisco **ping** Return Codes

Code	Meaning	Possible Cause(s)
!	Each exclamation point indicates receipt of an ICMP echo reply.	The **ping** completed successfully.
.	Each period indicates that the network server timed out while waiting for a reply.	This message can indicate many problems: **ping** was blocked by an access list or firewall. A router along the path did not have a route to the destination and did not send an ICMP destination unreachable message. A physical connectivity problem occurred somewhere along the path.
U	An ICMP unreachable message was received.	A router along the path did not have a route to the destination address.
C	An ICMP source quench message was received.	A device along the path—possibly the destination—might be receiving too much traffic; check input queues.
&	An ICMP time exceeded message was received.	A routing loop might have occurred.

Figure 4-6 offers a sample diagram to demonstrate how **ping** works.

Figure 4-6 Testing with the **ping** Command

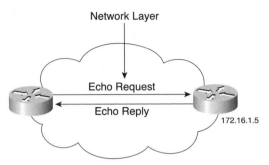

The **ping** target 172.16.1.5 in Figure 4-6 responded successfully to all five datagrams sent as indicated by the following:

```
Router>ping 172.16.1.5
Type escape sequence to abort.
Sending 5, 100 byte ICMP Echos to 172.16.1.5,
timeout is 2 seconds:
!!!!!
Success rate is 100 percent,
round-trip min/avg/max - 1/3/4 ms
Router>
```

The exclamation points (!) indicate each successful echo. If one or more periods (.) are received instead of exclamations on the display, the application on the router timed out waiting for a given packet echo from the **ping** target.

Lab 4.2.5a Connectivity Tests—**ping**

In this lab, you use the **ping** command to send ICMP datagrams to a target host and verify that the network layer between source and destination is working properly. You retrieve information to evaluate the path-to-host reliability, determine delays over the path, and determine if the host can be reached or is functioning.

traceroute Command

The **traceroute** command, which is often referred to as the **trace** command in reference materials, can be used to find the path that data is sent in a network. The **traceroute** command is similar to the **ping** command, except that instead of testing end-to-end connectivity, **traceroute** tests each step along the way. This operation can be performed at either the user or privileged EXEC levels.

Use the **traceroute** command as follows:

Step 1   **traceroute** IP address or name of destination.

Step 2   Press the **Enter** key.

More Information: **traceroute** Return Codes

Table 4-4 shows the Cisco **traceroute** return codes.

Table 4-4 Cisco **traceroute** Return Codes

Code	Meaning	Possible Cause(s)
nn msec	This gives, for each node, the round-trip time (in milliseconds) for the specified number of probes.	This is normal.
*	The probe timed out.	A device along the path either did not receive the probe or did not reply with an ICMP "packet life exceeded" message.
A	Administratively prohibited.	A device along the path, such as a firewall or router, might be blocking the probe and possibly other or all traffic; check access lists.
Q	Source quench.	A device along the path might be receiving too much traffic; check input queues.
H	An ICMP unreachable message has been received.	A routing loop might have occurred.

To demonstrate how **traceroute** works, look at the sample diagram in Figure 4-7.

Figure 4-7 traceroute Command

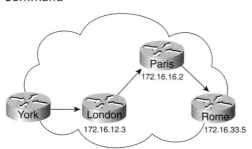

In this example, the path from York to Rome is being traced with the following results:

```
York# trace Rome
Type escape to abort.
Tracing the route to Rome (172.16.33.5)
   1 LONDON (172.16.12.3) 1000 msec 8 msec 4 msec
   2 PARIS (172.16.16.2) 8 msec 8 msec 8 msec
   3 ROME (172.16.35.5) 8 msec 8 msec 4 msec

York#
```

Along the way, the path must go through London and Paris. If one of these routers is unreachable, three asterisks (*) are returned instead of the name of the router. The **traceroute** command will continue attempting to reach the next step until the **Ctrl-Shift-6** escape sequence is used.

The **traceroute** command takes advantage of the error messages generated by routers when a packet exceeds its TTL or hop count value. The **traceroute** command sends several **ping** packets with an incrementing TTL value and displays the round-trip time for each. Because the TTL value is incremented each time a **ping** is sent, each successive **ping** gets closer to the destination. The benefit of the **traceroute** command is that it also tells which router in the path was the last one to be reached, which allows for fault isolation.

 Lab 4.2.5b   Connectivity Tests—**traceroute**

In this lab, you use the **traceroute** Cisco IOS Software command to verify that the network layer between source, destination, and each router along the way is working properly. The **tracert** Windows OS command is used from source workstation to destination router. You also use the **show ip route** command to display the router's routing table.

More Information: Testing the Network Layer with the **show ip route** Command
The router offers some powerful tools at this point in the search. You can actually look at the routing table, which contains directions that the router uses to determine how it will direct traffic across the network, and use another basic test that focuses on the network layer. Use the **show ip route** command, as demonstrated in Example 4-5, to determine whether a routing table entry exists for the target network. The output in Example 4-5 shows that the 172.16.33.5 Rome network is reachable by the Paris network 172.16.16.2 via the Ethernet1 interface in Figure 4-7.

More Information: Testing the Network Layer with the
show ip route Command (Continued)

Example 4-5 show ip route *Command Output*

```
Paris# show ip route
I - IGRP derived, R - RIP derived, O - OSPF derived C - connected,
  S - static, E - EGP derived, B - BGP derived i - IS-IS derived, D - EIGRP derived
  * - candidate default route, IA - OSPF inter area route E1 - OSPF external type 1
  route, E2 - OSPF external type 2 route L1 - IS-IS level-1 route, L2 - IS-IS level-
  2 route EX - EIGRP external route
Gateway of last resort is not set
I     10.10.0.1 [100/1300] via 172.16.12.3 0:00:22 Ethernet1
172.16.0.0 is subnetted (mask is 255.255.0.0), 3 subnets
I     172.16.33.5 [100/180771] via 172.16.16.2, 0:01:29, Ethernet1
C     172.16.12.3 is directly connected, Ethernet1
C     101.108.16.0 is directly connected, Ethernet0
I     219.100.103.0 [100/1200] via 172.16.32.2, 0:00:22, Ethernet1
```

Testing the Physical and Data Link Layers with the show interfaces serial Command

When you test the physical and data link layers, ask these questions:

- Is there a carrier detect signal?
- Is the physical link between devices good?
- Are the keepalive messages being received?
- Can data packets be sent across the physical link?

One of the most important elements of the **show interfaces serial** command output is the display of the line and data link protocol status. Figure 4-8 indicates the key summary line used to check the status of the line and the data link protocol.

Figure 4-8 Identifying Line and Protocol Problems

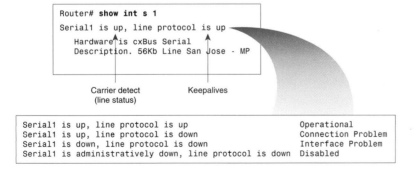

The line status in this example is triggered by a carrier detect signal and refers to the physical layer status. However, the line protocol, triggered by keepalive frames, refers to data link framing (a Layer 2 function).

continues

More Information: Testing the Network Layer with the
show ip route Command (Continued)

Using the show interfaces and clear counters Commands

The router tracks statistics that provide information about the interfaces. Use the
show interfaces command to display the statistics, as demonstrated in Example 4-6.

Example 4-6 show interfaces *Command Output*

```
Router# show interfaces serial 1
Serial1 is up, line protocol is up
Hardware is cxBus Serial
Description: 56Kb Line San Jose - MP
Internet address is 150.136.190.203, subnet mask is 255.255.255.0
MTU 1500 bytes, BW 56 Kbit, DLY 20000 usec, rely 255/255, load 1/255
Encapsulation HDLC, loopback not set, keepalive set (10 sec)
Last input 0:00:07, output 0:00:)), output hang never
Last clearing of show interfaces counters 2w4d
Output queue 0/40, 0 drops; input queue 0/75, 0 drops
Five minute input rate 0 bits/sec, 0 packets/sec
Five minute output rate 0 bits/sec, 0 packets/sec
     16263 packets input, 1347238 bytes, no buffer
     Received 13983 broadcasts, 0 runts, 0 giants
     2 input errors, 0 CRC, 0 frame, 0 overrun, 0 ignored, 2 abort
     0 input packets with dribble condition detected
     22146 packets output, 2383680 bytes, 0 underruns
     0 output errors, 0 collisions, 2 interface resets, 0 restarts
     1 carrier transitions
     DCD=up DSR=up DTR=up RTS=up CTS=up
```

CAUTION

Be careful with the
debug command on a
live network. Substan-
tial debugging on a
busy network slows the
network significantly.
Do not leave debug-
ging turned on; use it to
diagnose a problem,
and then turn it off.
Excessive debugging
on routers with minimal
RAM can cause the
router to force a reload.

The statistics reflect router operation since the last time the counters were cleared.
Use the **clear counters** command to reset the counters to 0. By starting from 0, you
get a better picture of the current status of the network. The **show interfaces** command can also be used to check the status of other interface types, such as Ethernet
(E0), Fast Ethernet (Fa0), and Integrated Services Digital Network (ISDN) (BRI0).

Checking Real-Time Traffic with the debug Command

The router includes hardware and software to aid it in tracking down problems on it or
on other hosts in the network. The *debug* privileged EXEC command starts the console
display of the network events specified in the command parameter. Use the **terminal
monitor** command to forward **debug** output to your Telnet session terminal. In fact,
during *all* Telnet sessions, use the **terminal monitor** command. With this command, *all*
normal console output is forwarded across the Telnet session. For example, this occurs
when an interface is activated or deactivated or when a neighbor adjacency moves to
the full state in OSPF. It is important to understand how helpful the **terminal monitor**
command is at *all* times and when debugging across a Telnet session.

Use the **undebug all** (or **no debug all**) command to turn off debugging when you no
longer need it. Debugging is really intended for solving problems.

By default, the router sends system error messages and output from the **debug** EXEC
command to the console terminal. However, you can redirect messages to a UNIX
host or to an internal buffer. The **terminal monitor** command enables you to redirect
these messages to a terminal, which can be useful in cases where you use a UNIX or
Linux host instead of the console terminal as a means of administering the devices.

Troubleshooting IP Addressing Issues

Addressing problems occur on IP networks. The following three commands are used to perform address-related troubleshooting:

- **ping** uses the ICMP protocol to verify the hardware connection and the IP address of the network layer. This is a basic testing mechanism.

- **telnet** verifies the application layer software between the source and destination. This is the most complete test mechanism available.

- **traceroute** verifies the location of failures in the path from the source to the destination. **trace** uses Time-To-Live values to generate messages from each router along the path.

Lab 4.2.6   Troubleshooting IP Address Issues

In this lab, you configure IP addresses for workstations and the test end-to-end network connectivity.

Summary

In this chapter, you learned the following key points:

- CDP is a media- and protocol-independent, Cisco-proprietary protocol used for neighbor discovery.

- CDP shows information only about directly connected neighbors.

- You use CDP to show Layer 2 and 3 information about neighbors.

- You should test network connectivity layer by layer.

- **ping** uses the ICMP protocol to verify the hardware connection and the IP address of the network layer. This command is a very basic testing mechanism.

- **telnet** verifies the application layer software between source and destination. This command is the most complete test mechanism available.

- **traceroute** allows the location of failures in the path from the source to destination.

- **traceroute**, or **trace**, uses TTL values to generate messages from each router along the path.

To supplement all that you have learned in this chapter, refer to the chapter-specific Interactive Media Activities on the CD-ROM that accompanies this book.

Key Terms

Cisco Discovery Protocol (CDP)   Used to obtain information about neighboring devices, such as the types of devices connected, the router interfaces they are connected to, the interfaces used to make the connections, and the model numbers of the devices.

debug   A command used to find and remove errors (bugs) from a program or design.

ping   Packet internet groper. ICMP echo message and its reply. Often used in IP networks to test the reachability of a network device.

Simple Network Management Protocol (SNMP)   Network management protocol used almost exclusively in TCP/IP networks. SNMP provides a means to monitor and control network devices, and to manage configurations, statistics collection, performance, and security.

Subnetwork Access Protocol (SNAP)   Internet protocol that operates between a network entity in the subnetwork and a network entity in the end system. SNAP specifies a standard method of encapsulating IP datagrams and ARP messages on IEEE networks. The SNAP entity in the end system makes use of the services of the subnetwork and performs three key functions: data transfer, connection management, and QoS selection.

Telnet   Standard terminal emulation protocol in the TCP/IP protocol stack. Telnet is used for remote terminal connection, enabling users to log in to remote systems and use resources as if they were connected to a local system.

Type Length Values (TLVs)   Blocks of information embedded in CDP advertisements.

traceroute   Program available on many systems that traces the path a packet takes to a destination. It is used mostly to debug routing problems between hosts.

Check Your Understanding

Complete all the review questions to test your understanding of the topics and concepts in this chapter. Answers are listed in Appendix B, "Check Your Understanding Answer Key."

1. What is a definition for **telnet**?

   A. A command to determine whether a specific IP address is accessible. It works by sending a packet to the specified address and waiting for a reply.

   B. A command that uses Time-To-Live (TTL) values to generate messages from each router used along the path.

   C. The virtual terminal protocol in the Internet suite of protocols. Allows users of one host to log into a remote host and act as normal terminal users of that host.

2. What information does testing a network by using the **show interfaces** command provide?

   A. It displays line and data link protocol status.

   B. It displays how the router directs traffic across the network.

   C. It displays the path that packets follow across the network.

   D. It displays the names of routers on the network.

3. What information does the **show cdp neighbors** command provide for each CDP neighbor?

   A. Device identifiers

   B. Address list

   C. Port identifier

   D. All of the above

4. The **show cdp interface** command is used to display which of the following?

   A. The values of the CDP timers and the interface status

   B. The encapsulation used by CDP for its advertisement and discovery frame transmission

   C. The interface configuration of the neighboring routers

   D. Both A and B

5. Which of these is true for the output of the command **show cdp entry** [*device name*]?

    A. It displays the Layer 3 addresses configured on the interface that the neighbor uses to send CDP updates to the local router.

    B. It displays the value of neighbors that the router has.

    C. It displays the list of the device numbers of all the neighboring routers.

    D. It displays all the Layer 2 addresses on the interfaces of the neighbor router.

6. To display the information that is obtained both from the **show cdp neighbors** and **show cdp entry** [*device name*] commands, which of the following commands is used?

    A. **show cdp neighbors detail**

    B. **show cdp interface entry**

    C. **show cdp neighbors entry**

    D. **show cdp details**

7. What information is displayed by the **show cdp neighbors** command?

    A. Neighbor device ID

    B. Local port type and number

    C. Decremental holdtime value, in seconds

    D. All of the above

8. What four important pieces of information do you receive after issuing a **ping** command?

    A. The size and quantity of ICMP packets; the timeout duration; the success rate; and the minimum, average, and maximum round-trip times

    B. The size and quantity of ICMP packets; the MAC address; the success rate; and the minimum, average, and maximum round-trip times

    C. All of the above

    D. None of the above

9. What information does testing a network by using the **traceroute** command provide?

    A. It determines if the line protocol is operational.

    B. It determines if a routing table entry exists for the target network.

    C. It maps every router that a packet goes through to reach its destination.

    D. It determines if upper-layer applications are functioning properly.

10. In reply to the **ping** command, exclamation points (!) indicate which of these?

   A. The number of successful echo requests

   B. The number of unsuccessful echo requests

   C. The number of hops before reaching the destination

   D. All of the above

11. What is true of the router **debug** commands?

   A. The **debug** privileged EXEC command starts the console display of the network events specified in the command parameter.

   B. The **undebug all** command (or **no debug all**) turns off debugging.

   C. The **buffer debug** command is used to buffer the login.

   D. Both A and B.

Objectives

Upon completion of this chapter, you should be able to answer the following questions:

- What are the stages of the router boot sequence?

- How do Cisco devices locate and load Cisco IOS Software?

- What is the **boot system** command used for?

- What are the configuration register values?

- What are the methods or processes used to locate Cisco IOS Software?

- What are the processes and commands used to create and load a software image and configuration file backup?

- What are some of the Cisco IOS Software naming conventions?

- What files are used by the Cisco IOS and what are their functions?

- What are the locations on the router of the different file types?

- What does each part of the IOS name represent?

- What are the steps and processes to save and restore configuration files using TFTP and copy-and-paste?

- What are the steps and commands to load an IOS image using TFTP?

- What are the steps and commands to load an IOS image using XModem?

- How do the **show** commands verify the file system?

Key Terms

The following is a list of key terms introduced in this chapter. For your reference, a definition for each term can be found at the end of this chapter.

bootstrap   page 638

nonvolatile random-access memory (NVRAM)   page 638

Flash memory   page 640

Trivial File Transfer Protocol (TFTP)   page 640

random-access memory (RAM)   page 645

remote copy protocol (RCP)   page 646

This chapter examines the stages of the router boot sequence, including how the Cisco router locates and loads Cisco IOS Software. This chapter also introduces the **boot system** command and explains how the **boot system** command tells the router to boot up. Also, you learn how to use a variety of Cisco IOS Software source options and execute commands to load Cisco IOS Software onto the router, maintain backup files, and upgrade Cisco IOS Software. In addition, you learn about the functions of the configuration register and how to determine which version of the Cisco IOS Software image file you have. Finally, this chapter describes how to use a TFTP server as a software source for the Cisco IOS Software image and configuration files.

Please be sure to look at this chapter's associated Interactive Media Activities that you will find on the CD-ROM accompanying this book. These CD elements are designed to supplement the material and reinforce the concepts introduced in this chapter.

Router Boot Sequence and Verification

A Cisco router cannot operate without the Cisco Internetworking Operating System (IOS). Each Cisco router has a predetermined boot-up sequence for locating and loading the IOS. This chapter describes the stages and importance of this boot-up procedure.

Stages of the Router Power-On Boot Sequence

A router initializes by loading the *bootstrap*, the operating system, and a configuration file. If the router cannot find a configuration file, then it enters setup mode. The router stores a backup copy of the new configuration from setup mode in *nonvolatile random-access memory (NVRAM)*. Figure 5-1 shows the events that occur as the router initializes.

Figure 5-1 Router Startup Sequence

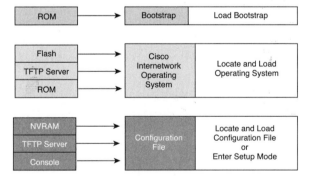

The goal of the startup routines for Cisco IOS Software is to start the router operations. The router must deliver reliable performance in connecting to the user networks it was configured to serve. To do this, the startup routines must do the following:

1. Make sure that the router loads ROM.

2. Find and load the Cisco IOS Software image that the router uses for its operating system.

3. Find and apply configuration statements, including protocol functions and interface addresses.

More Information: POST

When a Cisco router powers up, it performs a power-on self test (POST). During this self test, the router executes diagnostics from ROM on all hardware modules. These diagnostics verify the basic operation of the CPU, memory, and network interface ports. After verifying the hardware functions, the router proceeds with software initialization.

How a Cisco Device Locates and Loads IOS

The default source for Cisco IOS Software startup depends on the hardware platform. However, the router usually looks to the **boot system** commands saved in NVRAM. Cisco IOS Software does, however, allow you to use several alternatives. You can specify that the router look at other sources for software. Also, the router can use its own fallback sequence, as necessary, to load the software. Figure 5-2 illustrates some of the methods that can be used to locate and load the Cisco IOS Software image.

Figure 5-2 Locating Cisco IOS Software

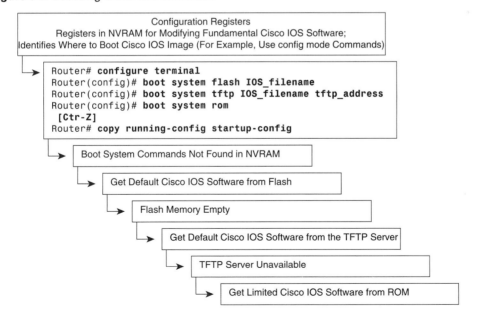

The settings in the configuration register enable the following alternatives:

- You can specify global configuration mode **boot system** commands to enter fallback sources for the router to use in sequence. When the router restarts, it uses these commands in sequence as needed.

- If NVRAM does not have **boot system** commands that the router can use, the system uses the Cisco IOS Software in *Flash memory* by default.

- If Flash memory is empty, the router next attempts to use *Trivial File Transfer Protocol (TFTP)* to load a Cisco IOS Software image from the network. The router uses the configuration register value to form a filename from which to boot a default system image stored on a network server.

- If a TFTP server is unavailable, the router will load the limited version Cisco IOS Software image stored in ROM.

 Interactive Media Activity   Drag and Drop: How a Cisco Device Locates and Loads IOS

After you complete this activity, you can identify the process a Cisco device goes through to find IOS during boot up.

Using the boot system Command

You can enter multiple boot system commands to specify the fallback sequence for booting Cisco IOS Software. Examples 5-1, 5-2, and 5-3 show **boot system** entries that specify that a Cisco IOS Software image will load first from Flash memory, then from a network server, and finally from ROM.

The command **copy running-config startup-config** saves the commands in NVRAM. The router executes the **boot system** commands as needed and in the order in which they were originally entered into configuration mode. To see if any **boot system** commands have been entered, issue the **show startup-config** command.

Booting from Flash Memory

Booting from Flash memory involves loading a system image from electrically erasable programmable read-only memory (EEPROM). The advantage here is that information stored in Flash memory is not vulnerable to network failures that can occur when loading system images from TFTP servers. Example 5-1 specifies that the *c2691-a3js-mz.123-3.bin* Cisco IOS Software file be loaded from Flash.

Example 5-1 *Booting from Flash Memory*

```
Router#config t
Router(config)#boot system flash c2691-a3js-mz.123-3.bin
Router(config)#boot system tftp IOS-image 10.1.1.1
Router(config)#boot system rom
Router(config)#end
Router#copy running-config startup-config
```

Booting from a Network Server

In case Flash memory becomes corrupted, a system image can provide a backup by specifying that it should be loaded from a TFTP server. Example 5-1 specifies that the image file be loaded from the TFTP server at IP address 172.16.13.111.

Booting from ROM

If Flash memory is corrupted and the network server fails to load the image, booting from ROM is the final bootstrap option in software. However, the system image in ROM will likely be a subset of Cisco IOS Software. This subset lacks the protocols, features, and configurations of full Cisco IOS Software. Also, if the software has been updated since the router was purchased, the router might have an older version of Cisco IOS Software. Example 5-1 demonstrates this last bootstrap option.

Lab 5.1.3   Using the **boot system** Command

In this lab, you gather information about the Cisco IOS Image and determine its boot source. You also check the config register settings and document a fallback boot sequence.

Configuration Register

The order in which the router looks for Cisco IOS Software images to load depends on the boot field setting in the configuration register. You can change the default configuration register setting with the global configuration command **config-register**. Use a hexadecimal number as the argument for this command, as shown in Example 5-2.

Example 5-2 *Changing the Boot Field Setting in the Configuration Register*

```
Router# configure terminal
Router(config)# config-register 0x210F
[Ctrl - Z]
```

The configuration register is set so that the router examines the startup file in NVRAM for boot system options. The configuration register is a 16-bit register in NVRAM that is represented as 4 hexadecimal digits. The lowest 4 bits of the configuration register (bits 3, 2, 1, and 0) form the boot field. To change the boot field and leave all other bits set at their original values, follow these guidelines:

- To enter the ROM monitor mode, set the configuration register value to 0xnnn0, where nnn represents the previous value of the non-boot field digits. This value sets the boot field bits to 0000 binary. After a reload or power cycle, the device boots to ROM monitor prompt. Use the **b** command to manually boot the operating system.

- To boot from the first image in Flash or to boot to the IOS in ROM (platform-dependent), set the configuration register to 0xnnn1, where nnn represents the previous value of the non-boot field digits. This value sets the boot field bits to 0001 binary. Older platforms, such as Cisco 1600 and 2500 routers, boot to a limited IOS in ROM. Newer platforms, such as Cisco 1700, 2600, and high end routers, boot from the first image in Flash.

- To configure the system to use the **boot system** commands in NVRAM, set the configuration register to any value from 0xnnn2 to 0xnnnF, where nnn represents the previous value of the non-boot field digits. These values set the boot field bits to a value between 0010 and 1111 binary. The router sequentially processes each **boot system** command in NVRAM until the process is successful or the end of the list is reached. If there are no **boot system** commands in the startup configuration file, the router attempts to boot the first file in Flash memory.

If there are no **boot system** commands in NVRAM, the system will typically look to Flash memory for the Cisco IOS Software image.

Table 5-1 shows the boot field values in the configuration register for the 1600 series router.

Table 5-1 Boot Field Values in the Configuration Register for the 1600 Series Router

Value	Description
0x2100	Use ROM monitor mode (System enters ROM monitor mode and waits for user intervention. Use the **b** or **boot** command to boot the system).
0x2101	Automatically boot from ROM. (Boots the first image in Flash. However, on older platforms, it would boot to a limited IOS located in ROM.)
0x2102 to 0x210F	Examines NVRAM for **boot system** commands. If there are none, it attempts to boot the first file in Flash memory.

To check the boot field setting and to verify the **config-register** command, use the **show version** command.

Troubleshooting IOS Boot Failure

If the router does not boot properly, there are several things that might be wrong:

- The configuration file has a missing or incorrect **boot system** statement
- Incorrect configuration register value
- Corrupted Flash image
- Hardware failure

When the router boots, it looks for a **boot system** statement in the startup configuration file. This **boot system** statement can force the router to boot from another image instead of the IOS in Flash. To identify the boot image source, type the **show version** command and look for the line that identifies the image boot source, as shown in Example 5-3.

Example 5-3 *Configuration Register*

```
Router# show version
Cisco Internetwork Operating System Software IOS (tm)    2500 Software
  (C2500-JS-L),
  Version 12.1(5), RELEASE SOFTWARE (fc1) Copyright (c)  1986-2000 by
  Cisco Systems, Inc. Compiled Wed 25-Oct-00 05:18 by cmong Image text-base:
  0x03071DB0, data-base: 0x00001000
ROM: System Bootstrap, Version 5.2(8a), RELEASE SOFTWARE BOOTFLASH:
  3000 Bootstrap Software (IGS-RXBOOT), Version 10.2(8a), RELEASE SOFTWARE (fc1)
Router uptime is 7 minutes System returned to ROM by reload System image file
  is   "flash:c2500-js-l_121-5.bin"
Cisco 2500 (68030) processor (revision D) with 16384K/2048K bytes of memory.
  Processor board ID 03867477, with hardware revision 00000000 Bridging software.
  X.25 software, Version 3.0.0. SuperLAT software (copyright 1990 by
  Meridian Technology Corp). TN3270 Emulation software. 1 Token Ring/IEEE 802.5
  interface(s) 2 Serial network interface(s) 32K bytes of non-volatile
  configuration memory. 16384K bytes of processor board System flash (Read ONLY)
Configuration register is 0x2142
```

Use the **show running-config** command and look for a **boot system** statement near the top of the configuration. If the **boot system** statement points to an incorrect IOS image, delete the statement using the no version of the command.

An incorrect configuration register setting prevents the IOS from loading from Flash. The value in the configuration register tells the router where to get the IOS. This can be confirmed by using the **show version** command and looking at the last line for the configuration register. The correct value varies from hardware platform to hardware platform. A part of the documentation of the internetwork is a printed copy of the **show version** output. If that documentation is not available, there are resources on the Cisco documentation CD or the Cisco website to identify the correct configuration register value. Correct this by changing the configuration register in the configuration and saving this as the start-up configuration.

If there is still a problem, the router might have a corrupted Flash image file. If this is the case, an error message should be displayed during boot. That message can take one of several forms. Some examples are:

```
open: read error...requested 0x4 bytes, got 0x0
trouble reading device magic number
boot: cannot open "flash:"
boot: cannot determine first file name on device "flash:"ú
```

If the Flash image is corrupt, a new IOS should be uploaded into the router.

If none of the previous messages appear to be the problem, the router might have a hardware failure. If this is the case, contact the Cisco Technical Assistance (TAC) center. Although hardware failures are rare, they do occur.

 Lab 5.1.5 Troubleshooting Configuration Register Boot Problems

In this lab, check and document the configuration register settings related to the boot method and configure the router to boot from Flash.

NOTE

There is no evidence of any config-register setting in output from either the **show running-config** or **show startup-config** command.

More Information: Displaying the Currently Running Cisco IOS Software Version

The **show version** command, as shown in Example 5-3, displays information about the Cisco IOS Software version that is currently running on the router. This version information includes the configuration register and the boot field setting.

In the example, the Cisco IOS Software version and descriptive information are highlighted on the second line of output. The screen captured shows Software Release 12.1(5).

The next highlighted portion of the output shows the system image file is c2500-js-l, booted using Flash. Notice the portion of the filename that indicates that this image is for a Cisco 2500 platform.

As the output of the **show version** command continues, information is displayed about the type of platform on which the version of Cisco IOS Software is currently running. The final highlighted output provides the targeted results of the command **config- register 0x2102**. This information is used to enter configuration register values.

Managing the Cisco File System

Cisco internetworking devices operate using several different files including Cisco Internetwork Operating System (IOS) images and configuration files. A network administrator who wishes to keep the network running smoothly and reliably must carefully manage these files to ensure that the proper versions are used and that necessary backups are performed. This section also describes the Cisco file system and the tools to manage it effectively.

IOS File System Overview

Routers and switches depend on software for their operation. The two types of software required are operating systems and configuration.

The operating system used in almost all Cisco devices is the Cisco Internetwork Operating System (IOS). Cisco IOS Software allows the hardware to function as a router or switch. The Cisco IOS Software file is several megabytes in size. Cisco IOS Software is the platform that ensures that the network provides the connectivity, reliability, security, quality of service, scalability, and management capabilities required for applications.

The software a router or switch uses is referred to as the *configuration file* or the *config*. The configuration file contains the instructions that define how the device is to route or switch. A network administrator creates a configuration file that defines the desired functions of the Cisco device. Examples of the functions that can be specified by the config are the IP addresses of the interfaces, routing protocols, and networks to be advertised. The configuration file typically is a few hundred to a few thousand bytes in size.

Each of the software components is stored in memory as a separate file. These files are also stored in different types of memory.

The Cisco IOS Software image is stored in a memory area called Flash. Flash memory provides nonvolatile storage of a Cisco IOS Software image that can be used as an operating system at startup. Flash allows you to upgrade Cisco IOS Software or to store multiple Cisco IOS Software files. In many router architectures, the Cisco IOS Software image is copied from Flash and run from *random-access memory (RAM)*.

A copy of the configuration file is stored in NVRAM to be used as a configuration during startup. This NVRAM configuration is referred to as the *startup config*. The startup config is copied into RAM at boot time. This configuration in RAM is the configuration used to operate the router. The RAM configuration is referred to as the *running config*.

A single interface to all the file systems that a router uses is provided in Software Release 12 of Cisco IOS Software. This version is referred to as the Cisco IOS File System (IFS). The IFS provides a single method to perform all the file system management that a router uses. This IFS includes the Flash memory file systems, the network file systems, and reading or writing data. The network file systems include TFTP, *remote copy protocol (RCP)*, and File Transfer Protocol (FTP). The reading or writing data includes NVRAM, the running configuration, and ROM. The IFS uses a common set of prefixes to specify file system devices. Table 5-2 provides an overview of the IFS.

Table 5-2 IOS File System

Prefix	Description
bootflash:	Boot Flash memory.
flash:	Flash memory. This prefix is available on all platforms. For platforms that do not have a device named Flash, the prefix flash: is aliased to slot0:. Therefore, the prefix flash: can be used to refer to the main Flash memory storage area on all platforms.
flh:	Flash load helper log files.
nvram:	NVRAM.
rcp:	Remote copy protocol (RCP) network server.
Slot0:	First Personal Computer Memory Card Industry Association (PCMCIA) Flash memory card.
Slot1:	Second PCMCIA Flash memory card.
system:	Contains the system memory, including the running configuration.
Tftp:	TFTP network server.

The IFS uses the Universal Resource Locator (URL) convention to specify files on network devices and the network. The URL convention identifies the location of the configuration files following the colon as **[[[///*location*]/*directory*]/*filename*]**. The IFS also supports FTP file transfer. Table 5-3 lists the commands used to manage Cisco IOS Software for Software Release 12.0 and compares them against counterpart commands used in Cisco IOS Software releases prior to 12.0.

Table 5-3 Commands for Managing Cisco IOS Software Release 12.0 and Earlier

Pre-Cisco IOS Software Release 12.0 Commands	Cisco IOS Software Release 12.x Commands
configure network (pre-Cisco IOS Software Release 10.3) **copy rcp running-config** **copy tftp running-config**	**copy ftp: system:running-config** **copy rcp: system:running-config** **copy tftp: system:running-config**
configure overwrite-network (pre-Cisco IOS Software Release 10.3) **copy rcp startup-config** **copy tftp startup-config**	**copy ftp: nvram:startup-config** **copy rcp: nvram:startup-config** **copy tftp: nvram:startup-config**
show configuration (pre-Cisco IOS Software Release 10.3) **show startup-config**	**more nvram:startup-config**
write erase (pre-Cisco IOS Software Release 10.3) **erase startup-config**	**Erase nvram:**
write memory (pre-Cisco IOS Software Release 10.3) **copy running-config startup-config**	**copy system:running-config nvram:startup-config**
write network (pre-Cisco IOS Software Release 10.3) **copy running-config rcp** **copy running-config tftp**	**copy system:running-config: ftp** **copy system:running-config: rcp** **copy system:running-config: tftp**
write terminal (pre-Cisco IOS Software Release 10.3) **show running-config**	**more system:running-config**

 Interactive Media Activity   Drag and Drop: IOS File System Overview

After you finish this activity, you can list the configuration files and their locations.

IOS Naming Conventions

Cisco develops many different versions of Cisco IOS Software. Cisco IOS Software supports varied hardware platforms and features. Cisco continuously develops and releases new versions of Cisco IOS Software.

Cisco has a naming convention for Cisco IOS Software files to identify the different versions of these Cisco IOS Software files, as illustrated by Figure 5-3.

Figure 5-3 Cisco IOS Software Naming Conventions

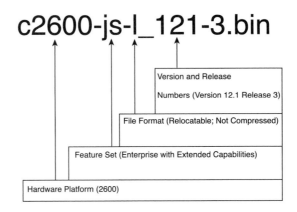

As Figure 5-3 shows, this Cisco IOS Software naming convention uses different fields in the name:

- **Hardware Platform**—The first part of the filename identifies the hardware platform. This image is designed for the hardware platform.

- **Feature Set**—The second part of the filename identifies the various features that the Cisco IOS Software file contains. You can choose from many different features, and these features are packaged in "software images." Each feature set contains a specific subset of Cisco IOS Software features. Examples of the feature set categories are as follows:

  - **Basic**—Basic is a basic feature set for the hardware platform. Examples of Basic are IP and IP/FW.

  - **Plus**—Plus is a basic feature set plus additional features such as IP Plus, IP/FW Plus, and Enterprise Plus.

  - **Encryption**—Encryption has the 56-bit data encryption feature sets added to either a Basic or Plus feature set. Examples include IP/ATM PLUS IPSEC 56 or Enterprise Plus 56. The encryption designators are k8/k9 starting with the Cisco IOS Software Release 12.2. k8 is less than or equal to 64-bit encryption on Release 12.2 and up. k9 is greater than 64-bit encryption on Release 12.2 and up.

- **File Format**—The third part of the IOS filename indicates the file format. The third part specifies if Cisco IOS Software is stored in Flash memory in a compressed format and if the Cisco IOS Software image is relocatable. If the Flash image is compressed, Cisco IOS Software must be expanded during boot as the image is copied to RAM. A relocatable image is copied from Flash memory into RAM to run. A non-relocatable image is run directly from Flash memory.

- **Version and Release**—The fourth part of the IOS filename identifies the version number and release of Cisco IOS Software. As Cisco develops newer versions of Cisco IOS Software, the numerical version number increases.

 Interactive Media Activity   Drag and Drop: IOS Naming Conventions

After you complete this activity, you can identify the different fields in an IOS image name.

Managing Configuration Files Using TFTP

In a Cisco router or switch, the active configuration is in RAM. The default location for the startup configuration in a Cisco router or switch is NVRAM. In the event the configuration is lost, you should back up this startup configuration. You can store one of these backup copies of the configuration on a TFTP server. You can use the **copy running-config tftp** command to back up the configuration. The steps to perform this backup process are as follows:

Step 1   Enter **copy running-config tftp**.

Step 2   Enter the IP address of the TFTP server that is to store the configuration file at the prompt.

Step 3   Enter the name to assign to the configuration file or accept the default name.

Step 4   Confirm the choices by typing **yes** each time.

Example 5-4 demonstrates the actual process.

Example 5-4 *Backing Up the Startup Configuration on a TFTP Server*

```
Cougar# copy running-config tftp
Address or name of remote host [] 192.168.119.20
Destination file name [Cougar-config]?
!!!!!!!!!!!!!!!!!!!!!!!!!
624 bytes copied in 7.05 secs
Cougar#
```

> **NOTE**
>
> If the router config file is missing or if the **erase startup-config** and **reload** commands have been used, the router will not have any interfaces configured. TFTP requires IP to make a connection, so you will need to connect to the router using the console port and configure an IP address for the interface that will provide access to the TFTP server.

You can restore the router configuration by loading the backup configuration file from a TFTP server. The steps you can take to restore the configuration are as follows:

Step 1   Enter **copy tftp running-config**.

Step 2   Select a host or network configuration file at the prompt.

Step 3   At the system prompt, enter the IP address of the TFTP server where the configuration file is located.

Step 4   At the system prompt, enter the name of the configuration file or accept the default name.

Step 5   Confirm the configuration filename and the server address that the system supplies.

Example 5-5 demonstrates the process of restoring the configuration from a TFTP server.

Example 5-5 *Restoring the Startup Configuration from a TFTP Server*

```
Cougar# copy tftp running-config
Address or name of remote host [] 192.168.119.20
Source filename []?  Cougar-confg
Destination filename [running-config]?


Accessing tftp://192.168.119.20/GAD-confg…
Loading GAD-confg from 192.168.119.20
   (via FastEthernet 0/0): !!!!!!!!!!!!!!!!!!!!!!!!!!!!!!!!!!!!!
[OK-624 bytes]
624 bytes copied in 9.45 secs Cougar#
```

More Information: Copying the Configuration File from the TFTP Server Back to the Router

To copy the configuration file from the TFTP server back to the router, perform the following steps:

Step 1   Enter configuration mode by entering the **copy tftp running-config** command.

Step 2   At the system prompt, select a host or network configuration file. The network configuration file contains commands that apply to all routers and terminal servers on the network. The host configuration file contains commands that apply to one router in particular. At the system prompt, enter the optional IP address of the remote host where the configuration file is located. In Example 5-6, the router is configured from the TFTP server at IP address 172.16.2.2.

Step 3   At the system prompt, enter the name of the configuration file or accept the default name. The filename convention is UNIX-based. The default filename is **hostname-config** for the host file and **network-config** for the network configuration file. In the DOS environment, the server filenames are limited to eight characters plus a three-character extension. An example is **router.cfg**. Confirm the configuration filename and the server address that the system supplies. Notice in Example 5-6 that the router prompt changes to **tokyo** immediately. This change is evidence that the reconfiguration happens as soon as the new file is downloaded.

> **More Information: Copying the Configuration File from the TFTP Server Back to the Router (Continued)**
>
> Example 5-6 demonstrates the process of copying the configuration file from a TFTP server.
>
> **Example 5-6** *Copying the Configuration File from a TFTP Server*
>
> ```
> tokyo# copy tftp running-config
> Host or network configuration file [host]?
> IP address of remote host [255.255.255.255]? 131.108.2.155
> Name of configuration file [Router-config]? tokyo.2
> Configure using tokyo.2 from 131.108.2.155? [confirm] y
> Booting tokyo.2 from 131.108.2.155:!! [OK-874/16000 bytes]
> tokyo#setup
> ```

Lab 5.2.3   Managing Configuration Files with TFTP

In this activity, you copy a router configuration file to a TFTP server and then configure the router by copying the file back from the TFTP server.

Managing Configuration Files Using Copy and Paste

Capturing the output of the **show running-config** command is another way to create a backup copy of the configuration. You can perform this backup from the terminal session by copying the output, pasting to a text file, and saving the text file. However, this file needs some editing done before you can use it to restore configuration to the router. Figure 5-4 shows an example of cutting and pasting configurations.

To capture the configuration in HyperTerminal text that is displayed on the screen to a text file, use the following steps:

Step 1   Select **Transfer**.

Step 2   Select **Capture Text**.

Step 3   Specify the name for the text file to the capture configuration.

Step 4   Select **Start** to start capturing text.

Step 5   Display the configuration to the screen by entering **show running-config**.

Step 6   Press the space bar when each "-More -" prompt appears, which continues with the configuration until the end is reached.

Step 7   When the complete configuration has been displayed, stop the capture using the following steps:

a. Select **Transfer**.

b. Select **Capture Text**.

c. Select **Stop**.

Figure 5-4 Capturing the Config File

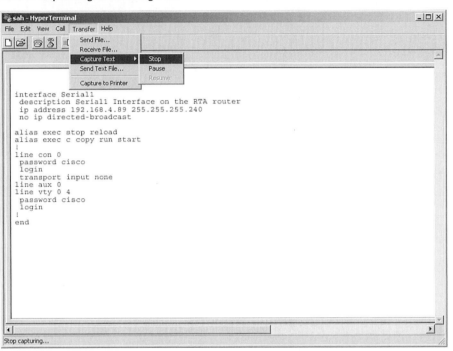

After the capture is complete, you need to edit the configuration file to remove extra text. To create this file in a form to be copied and pasted back into the router, remove any unnecessary information from the captured configuration. You can add comments to the text to explain the various parts of the configuration. Add a comment by beginning a line with an exclamation mark (!).

You can edit the configuration file from a text editor such as Notepad. To edit the file from Notepad, complete the following steps:

Step 1   Click **File > Open**.

Step 2   Find the captured file and select it.

Step 3   Click **Open**.

The lines you need to delete contain the following:

- show running-config

- Building configuration...

- Current configuration:

- - More -

- Any lines that appear after the word *End*

At the end of each of the interface sections, add the **no shutdown** command. Clicking **File > Save** saves the clean version of the configuration.

You can then restore the backup configuration from a HyperTerminal session. However, before you restore the configuration, remove any remaining configuration from the router, which you can do by entering the command **erase startup-config** at the enable router prompt and then restarting the router by entering **reload**.

After you remove any remaining configuration, you can use HyperTerminal to restore a configuration. You can copy the clean backup of the configuration into the router as follows:

Step 1 Go into the router global configuration mode.

Step 2 From the HyperTerminal, choose **Transfer > Send > Text File**.

Step 3 Select the name of the file for the saved backup configuration.

Step 4 The lines of the file are entered into the router as if the lines are being typed.

Step 5 Look for any errors.

Step 6 After the configuration is entered, press **Ctrl + z** to exit the global configuration mode.

Step 7 Restore the startup configuration with **copy running-config startup-config**.

Managing IOS Images Using TFTP

Occasionally, the router will need to have the Cisco IOS Software image upgraded or restored. The first time a router is used, the Cisco IOS Software should be backed up to a TFTP server using the **copy flash tftp** command. This Cisco IOS Software image can be stored in a central server with other Cisco IOS Software images to restore or upgrade the Cisco IOS Software image on routers and switches in the internetwork.

A TFTP service should run on this server. The IOS backup can be initiated from the privileged EXEC mode with the **copy flash tftp** command. The router prompts the user to enter the IP address of the TFTP server and to specify a destination filename.

IOS can be restored or upgraded from the server with the **copy tftp flash** command. The router prompts the user to enter the IP address of the TFTP server, as shown in Example 5-7. Next, the router prompts the user for the filename of the IOS image on the server. The router can then prompt the user to erase Flash. This often happens if there is not sufficient Flash available for the new image. As the image is erased from Flash, a series of Es (lowercased) appear to show the erase process.

Example 5-7 *Backing Up Cisco IOS Software to a TFTP Server*

```
Cougar# copy tftp flash
Address or name of remote host []? 192.168.119.20
Destination filename [C2600-js-l_121-3.bin]?
```

continues

Example 5-7 *Backing Up Cisco IOS Software to a TFTP Server (Continued)*

```
Accessing tftp://192.168.119.20/C2600-js-l_121-3.bin

Erase flash: before copying? [confirm]

Erasing the flash file system will remove all files

Continue? [confirm]

Erasing device   eeeeee…eeeeeeeeeeeee…erased

Loading C2600-js-l_121-3.bin from 192.168.119.20 (via FastEthernet 0/
0):!!!!!!!!!!!!!!!!!!!!!!!!!!!!!!!!!!!

Verifying Check sum……………..OK

[OK-8906589 bytes]

8906589 bytes copied in 277.45 secs

Cougar#
```

NOTE

The symbol "!" means
that the Flash file is
loading successfully.
The symbol "." means
that the Flash file can-
not be found. If the
symbol "." appears,
make sure you typed
the correct command
syntax.

As each datagram of the Cisco IOS Software image file is downloaded, an "!" will be displayed. This Cisco IOS Software image is several megabytes in size and might take some time to download.

The new Flash image is verified after it is downloaded. The router is now ready to be reloaded to use the new Cisco IOS Software image.

More Information: Copying an IOS Image from the TFTP Server to the Router

Example 5-8 uses a different router and TFTP server and provides additional information on the steps used to copy the Cisco IOS Software image from the TFTP server back to the router.

After you enter the **copy tftp flash** command, as shown in Example 5-8, the system prompts you for the IP address (or name) of the TFTP server. This address or name can be another router serving ROM or Flash software images. The system then prompts you for the filename of the software image. Example 5-8 shows sample output from copying a system image, named C4500-I, into Flash memory.

Example 5-8 *Copying the Cisco IOS Software Image from the TFTP Server to the Router*

```
Router# copy tftp flash
IP address or name of remote host [255.255.255.255]? 172.16.13.111
Name of tftp filename to copy into flash []? c4500-I
copy C4500-I already exists; it will be invalidated!
Copy C4500-I from 172.16.13.111 into flash memory? [confirm]
xxxxxxxx bytes available for writing without erasure.
erase flash before writing? [confirm]
Clearing and initializing flash memory [please wait] ####...##
Loading from 172.16.13.111: !!!!!!!!!!!!!!!!!!!!!!!!!!!!!
!!!!!!! (text omitted) [OK - 324572/524212 bytes]
Verifying checksum...
VVVVVVVVVVVVVVVVVVVVVVVVVVVVVVVVVVVVVVVVVVVVVVVVVVVVV
VVVVVVVVV (text omitted)
Flash verification successful. Length = 1204637, checksum = 0x95D9
```

> **More Information: Copying an IOS Image from the TFTP Server to the Router (Continued)**
>
> If you attempt to copy into Flash memory a file that is already there, a prompt tells you that a file with the same name already exists. This file is deleted when you copy the new file into Flash memory. If there is room for both copies in Flash memory, the first copy of the file still resides within Flash memory, but is rendered unusable in favor of the newest version; it will be listed with the [deleted] tag when you use the **show flash** command.
>
> If you abort the copy process, the newer file will be marked (deleted) because the entire file was not copied and is, therefore, not valid. In this case, the original file still resides within Flash memory and is available to the system.

Lab 5.2.5   Managing IOS Images with TFTP

In this activity, you back up a copy of a router's Cisco IOS image to a TFTP server. You then reload the backup copy from the TFTP server into Flash memory on the router.

Managing IOS Images with Xmodem

If the Cisco IOS Software image in Flash has been erased or corrupted, you might need to restore the Cisco IOS Software image from the ROM monitor mode (ROMmon). In many of the Cisco hardware architectures, the ROMmon mode is identified by the **rommon# >** prompt.

The first step in this process is to identify why the Cisco IOS Software image did not load from Flash. This problem could be due to a corrupt or missing image or damaged Flash memory. Examine the Flash memory with the **dir flash:** command.

If you locate an image that appears to be valid, attempt to boot from that image. You perform this boot attempt by using the **boot flash:** command. For example, if the image name is c2600-is-mz.121-5, the command is as follows:

```
rommon > boot flash:c2600-is-mz.121-5
```

You need to check a couple of items if the router boots properly because you need to determine why the router booted to the ROMmon instead of using Cisco IOS Software from Flash. First, use the **show version** command to check the configuration register to ensure that it is configured for the default boot sequence. If the configuration register value is correct, use the **show startup config** command. This command shows if there is a **boot system** command instructing the router to use the Cisco IOS Software for ROMmon.

If the router will not properly boot from the image or there is no Cisco IOS Software image, you need to download a new Cisco IOS Software image. You can recover the Cisco IOS Software file either through using Xmodem to restore the image through the console or by downloading the image using TFTP from the ROMmon mode.

Downloading Cisco IOS Software Using Xmodem from ROMmon

To restore the Cisco IOS Software image through the console, the local PC needs to have a copy of the Cisco IOS Software file to restore and a terminal emulation program such as HyperTerminal. You can restore the Cisco IOS Software image using the default console speed of 9600 bps. You can change the baud rate to 115,200 bps to speed up the download. You can change the console speed from ROMmon mode using the **confreg** command. After you enter the **confreg** command, the router will prompt for the various parameters that can be changed, as shown in Example 5-9.

Example 5-9 *Changing the Console Speed*

```
rommon 1 >confreg

Configuration Summary

…<output omitted>…

 console baud: 9600

boot: the ROM Monitor

do you wish to change the configuration? y/n [n]: y

enable "diagnostic mode"? y/n [n]:

…<output omitted>…

enable "ignore system config info"? y/n [n]:

change console baud rate? y/n [n]: y

enter rate: 0 = 9600, 1 = 4800, 2 = 1200, 3 = 2400

4 = 19200, 5 = 38400, 6 = 57600, 7 = 115200 [0]: 7

change the boot characteristics? y/n [n]:


Configuration Summary

enabled are:

break/abort has effect

console baud: 115200

boot: the ROM Monitor


do you wish to change the configuration? y/n [n]:
```

You must reset or power cycle for the new config to take effect.

When prompted: **change console baud rate? y/n [n]:** selecting **y** provides you with a prompt to select the new speed. After changing the console speed, restart the router into the ROMmon mode. The terminal session at 9600 bps is terminated, and a new session is started at 115,200 bps to match the console speed.

You can use the **xmodem** command from the ROMmon mode to restore a Cisco IOS Software image from the PC. The format for the **xmodem** command is as follows:

xmodem -c image_file_name

For example, to restore a Cisco IOS Software image file with the name *c2600-is- mz.122-10a.bin*, type the command as shown in Example 5-10.

Example 5-10 *Restoring a Cisco IOS Software Image File with the* **xmodem** *Command*

```
rommon 1 >

          rommon 1 >xmodem -?

          xmodem: illegal option -- ?

          usage: xmodem [-cyrx] <destination filename>

          -c  CRC-16

                     -y  ymodem-batch protocol

                     -r  copy image to dram for launch

                     -x  do not launch on download completion

   rommon 2 > xmodem -c c2600-is-mz.122-10a.bin


 Do not start the sending program yet...


          Warning:  All existing data in bootflash will be lost!


 Invoke this application only for disaster recovery.

 Do you wish to continue? y/n [n]: y

 Ready to receive file c2600-is-mz.122-10a.bin ...
```

The **-c** in the command format instructs the Xmodem process to use cyclic redundancy check (CRC) for error checking during the download.

You will receive a prompt from the router to not begin the transfer and a warning message will be shown. The warning message indicates that the bootflash will be erased, and the router asks to confirm whether or not to continue with the process. When you continue the process, the router then prompts to start the transfer.

You now need to start the Xmodem transfer from the terminal emulator. In HyperTerminal, select **Transfer > Send.** Then, in the Send File popup, specify the image name/location, select Xmodem as the protocol, and start the transfer. During the transfer, the Sending File popup displays the status of the transfer.

After the transfer is complete, a message appears indicating that Flash is being erased. This message is followed by the "Download Complete!" message. Before restarting the router, you need to set the console speed back to 9600 bps and the configuration register back to 0x2102. Use the **confreg 0x2102** command at the privileged EXEC prompt to set back the configuration register.

While the router is rebooting, you need to end the 115,200-bps terminal session and begin a 9600-bps session.

 Lab 5.2.6a   Password Recovery Procedures

In this lab, you gain access to a router with an unknown privileged mode (enable) password.

 Lab 5.2.6b   Managing IOS Images with ROMmon and Xmodem

In this lab, you recover a Cisco 1700 series router from ROM monitor mode due to missing or corrupt IOS / bootflash image.

NOTE

All environmental variable names are case sensitive.

Environmental Variables

You can also restore the Cisco IOS Software from a TFTP session. Downloading the image using TFTP from ROMmon is the fastest way to restore a Cisco IOS Software image to the router. You perform this process by setting the environmental variables and then using the **tftpdnld** command.

Because ROMmon has limited functions, no configuration file is loaded during boot. The router, therefore, has no IP or interface configuration. The environmental variables provide a minimal configuration to allow for the TFTP of the Cisco IOS Software image. The ROMmon TFTP transfer works only on the first LAN port, so a simple set of IP parameters are set for this interface. To set a ROMmon environment variable, you type the variable name, then the equal sign (=), and the value for the variable (*VARIABLE_NAME=value*). For example, to set the IP address to 10.0.0.1, type **IP_ADDRESS=10.0.0.1** at the ROMmon prompt.

The minimum variables required to use **tftpdnld** are as follows:

- **IP_ADDRESS**—The IP address on the LAN interface
- **IP_SUBNET_MASK**—The subnet mask for the LAN interface
- **DEFAULT_GATEWAY**—The default gateway for the LAN interface
- **TFTP_SERVER**—The IP address of the TFTP server
- **TFTP_FILE**—The Cisco IOS Software filename on the server

To check the ROMmon environment variables, you can use the **set** command, as shown in Example 5-11.

Example 5-11 *Checking ROMmon Environmental Variables*

```
rommon 10> set
        IP_ADDRESS=10.0.0.1
        IP_SUBNET_MASK=255.255.255.0
        DEFAULT_GATEWAY=10.0.0.254
        TFTP_SERVER=192.168.1.1
        TFTP_FILE=GAD/original_2003_Jan_22/c2600-i-mz.121-5
```

Once you set the variables for the Cisco IOS Software download, you enter the **tftpdnld**
command, as shown in Example 5-12, with no arguments. The ROMmon echoes the variables, and then a confirmation prompt appears with a warning that this process will erase the
Flash memory.

Example 5-12 **tftpdnld**

```
rommon 12 > tftpdnld
IP_ADDRESS: 10.0.0.1
IP_SUBNET_MASK: 255.255.255.0
DEFAULT_GATEWAY: 10.0.0.254
TFTP_SERVER: 192.168.1.1
TFTP_FILE: GAD/original_2003_Jan_22/c2600-i-mz.121-5
Invoke this command for disaster recovery only.
WARNING: all existing data in all partitions on flash will be lost!
Do you wish to continue? y/n:  [n]:  y
Receiving GAD/original_2003_Jan_22/c2600-i-mz.121-5 from
192.168.1.1!!!!.!!!!!!!!!!!!!!!!!!!!.!!
File reception completed.
Copying file GAD/original_2003_Jan_22/c2600-i-mz.121-5 to flash.
Erasing flash at 0x607c0000
program flash location 0x60440000
rommon 13>
```

As each datagram of the Cisco IOS Software file is received, a "!" is displayed. When the
complete Cisco IOS Software file has been received, the Flash is erased and the new IOS
image file is written. Appropriate messages are displayed as the process is completed.

When the new image is written into Flash and the ROMmon prompt is displayed, type the
reset command or **i** to restart the router. The router now boots from the new Cisco IOS Software image in Flash memory.

File System Verification

You can use several commands to verify the router file system. One of those commands is the **show version** command, which you can use to check the current image and the total amount of Flash memory. This command also verifies two other items concerning loading the Cisco IOS Software image. The **show version** command identifies the source of the Cisco IOS Software image that the router used to boot and displays the configuration register. You can examine the boot field setting of the configuration register to determine where the router is to load the Cisco IOS Software image. If the current image and the boot field setting of the configuration register do not agree, there might be a corrupt or missing Cisco IOS Software image in Flash or there might be **boot system** commands in the startup config.

Example 5-13 demonstrates use of the **show version** command.

Example 5-13 *Verifying the Router File System*

```
HMH# show version
Cisco Internetwork Operating System Software
IOS (tm) 1700 Software (C1700-BNSY-L), Version 12.2(11)P, RELEASE SOFTWARE (fc1)
… <output omitted>…
System image file is "flash:c1700-bnsy-l.122-11.p", booted via flash
cisco 171 (68360) processor (revision C) with 3584K/512K bytes of memory.
Processor board ID 12014633, with hardware revision 00000000
Bridging software.
X.25 software, Version 2.0, NET2, BFE and GOSIP compliant.
1 Ethernet/IEEE 802.3 interface(s)
2  serial(sync/async) network interface(s)
System/IO memory with parity disabled
2048K bytes of DRAM onboard 2048K bytes of DRAM on SIMM
System running from FLASH
8K bytes of non-volatile configuration memory.
6144K bytes of processor board PCMCIA flash (Read ONLY)
Configuration register is 0x2102
HMH#
```

You can also use the **show flash** command to verify the file system and to identify the Cisco IOS Software image or images in Flash and the amount of Flash memory that is available. The **show flash** command is often used to confirm that there is enough space to store a new Cisco IOS Software image. Example 5-14 demonstrates sample output from the **show flash** command.

Example 5-14 show flash *Command Output*

```
Router# show flash
4096 bytes of flash memory on embedded flash (in XX).
file offset length name
0 0x40 1204637 xk09140z
[903848/2097152 bytes free]
```

As mentioned, the configuration file might contain **boot system** commands. You can use these commands to identify the source of the desired Cisco IOS Software boot image. You can use multiple **boot system** commands to create a fallback sequence to discover and load a Cisco IOS Software image. These **boot system** commands are processed in the order of their appearance in the configuration file.

Summary

In this chapter, you learned the following key points:

- The default source for Cisco IOS Software depends on the hardware platform, but, most commonly, the router looks to the configuration commands saved in NVRAM.

- You can use the **show version** command to display information about the Cisco IOS Software version that is currently running on the router.

- You can enter multiple **boot system** commands to specify the fallback sequence for booting Cisco IOS Software. Routers can boot Cisco IOS Software from Flash memory, from a TFTP server, and from ROM.

- You use the **show flash** command to verify that you have sufficient memory on your system for the Cisco IOS Software that you want to load.

- With Cisco IOS Software Release 11.2 and later, the naming convention for Cisco IOS contains the following three parts:

  - The platform on which the image runs

  - The special capabilities of the image

  - Where the image runs and whether it has been zipped or compressed

- You can copy a system image back to a network server. This copy of the system image can serve as a backup copy and can be used to verify that the copy in Flash memory is the same as the original file.

- If you need to load the backup Cisco IOS Software version, you can use a variation of the **copy** command, **copy tftp flash**, to download the image that you previously uploaded to the TFTP server.

To supplement all that you've learned in this chapter, refer to the chapter-specific Interactive Media Activities on the CD-ROM accompanying this book.

Key Terms

bootstrap   The protocol used by a network node to determine the IP address of its Ethernet interfaces to affect network booting.

Flash memory   A special type of EEPROM that can be erased and reprogrammed in blocks instead of one byte at a time. Many modern PCs have their BIOS stored on a Flash memory chip so that it can be updated easily if necessary. Such a BIOS is sometimes called a Flash BIOS. Flash memory is also popular in modems because it enables the modem manufacturer to support new protocols as they become standardized.

nonvolatile random-access memory (NVRAM)   RAM that retains its contents when a unit is powered off.

random-access memory (RAM)   Volatile memory that can be read and written by a microprocessor.

remote copy protocol (RCP)   Protocol that allows users to copy files to and from a file system residing on a remote host or server on the network.

Trivial File Transfer Protocol (TFTP)   Simplified version of FTP that allows files to be transferred from one computer to another over a network, usually without the use of client authentication (for example, username and password).

Check Your Understanding

Complete all the review questions to test your understanding of the topics and concepts in this chapter. Answers are listed in Appendix B, "Check Your Understanding Answer Key."

1. Which of the following correctly describes a method for specifying how a router loads the Cisco IOS Software?

   A. Designate fallback sources for the router to use in sequence from NVRAM.

   B. Configure the Cisco IOS Software image for the location where it will bootstrap.

   C. Manually boot a default system image at a virtual terminal.

   D. Manually boot a default system image at the network server.

2. Which of the following is not a boot option that can be set with the configuration register boot field?

   A. Cisco IOS Software boots in ROM monitor mode.

   B. Cisco IOS Software automatically boots from ROM.

   C. Cisco IOS Software automatically boots from a TFTP server.

   D. NVRAM is examined for **boot system** commands.

3. Which of the following is information displayed by the **show version** command?

   A. Detailed statistics about each page of the router's memory

   B. The name of the system image

   C. The names and sizes of all files in Flash memory

   D. The status of configured network protocols

4. Which command is used to discover the configuration register setting?

   A. show register

   B. show running-config

   C. show version

   D. show startup-config

5. What information is not provided in the Cisco image filename system?

   A. The capabilities of the image

   B. The platform on which the image runs

   C. Where the image runs

   D. The size of the image

6. Which of the following is not part of the recommended procedure for loading a new Cisco IOS Software image to Flash memory from a TFTP server? (The procedures are listed in correct order.)

   A. Back up a copy of the current software image to the TFTP server.

   B. Enter the **copy flash tftp** command to start downloading the new image from the server.

   C. The procedure asks if you are willing to erase Flash memory.

   D. A series of Vs on the display indicates successful checksum verification.

7. What is the initial boot attempt if the router configuration register is set to 0x2101?

   A. Setup mode

   B. TFTP server

   C. ROM

   D. Flash memory

8. Which of the following has a limited version of router Cisco IOS Software?

   A. ROM

   B. Flash memory

   C. TFTP server

   D. Bootstrap

9. What is the initial boot attempt if the router configuration register is set to 0x2102?

   A. Flash memory

   B. TFTP server

   C. ROM

   D. Check for **boot system** commands

10. Which of the following is the sequence used by the router for automatic fallback to locate the Cisco IOS Software?

    A. Flash memory, (2) NVRAM, (3) TFTP server

    B. NVRAM, (2) TFTP server, (3) Flash memory

    C. NVRAM, (2) Flash memory, (3) TFTP server

    D. Flash memory, (2) TFTP server, (3) ROM

11. Which of the following is not displayed by the Cisco IOS **show version** command?

   A. Statistics for configured interfaces

   B. The type of platform running the Cisco IOS Software

   C. The configuration register setting

   D. The Cisco IOS Software version

12. Which of the following correctly describes preparing to use a TFTP server to copy software to Flash memory?

   A. The TFTP server must be a connected router or a host system, such as a UNIX workstation or a laptop computer.

   B. The TFTP server must be a system connected to an Ethernet network.

   C. The name of the router containing the Flash memory must be identified.

   D. The Flash memory must be enabled.

13. Why do you create a Cisco IOS Software image backup?

   A. To verify that the copy in Flash memory is the same as the copy in ROM

   B. To provide a fallback copy of the current image before copying the image to a new router

   C. To create a fallback copy of the current image as part of the procedures during recovery from system failure

   D. To create a fallback copy of the current image before updating with a new version

14. What is the command you need to issue if you want to upgrade an old version of the Cisco IOS Software by downloading a new image from the TFTP server?

   A. boot system tftp 131.21.11.3

   B. copy tftp flash

   C. show flash

   D. tftp ios.exe

Routing and Routing Protocols

Objectives

Upon completion of this chapter, you should be able to answer the following questions:

- What are some of the basic principles of routing?

- What is the difference between routed and routing protocols?

- What are interior and exterior protocols used for in routing?

- What is the difference between static versus dynamic routes?

- How are static routes configured?

- How are default routes configured?

- What are some methods for troubleshooting static route configurations?

- Why are dynamic routing protocols necessary?

- What is distance vector routing?

- What is link-state routing?

- How are different routing protocols used in context?

Key Terms

The following is a list of key terms introduced in this chapter. For your reference, a definition for each term can be found at the end of the chapter.

In this chapter, you learn more about the router's use and operations in performing the key internetworking function of the Open System Interconnection (OSI) reference model's network layer, Layer 3. In addition, you review the difference between routing and routed protocols and how routers track distance between locations. Finally, you learn more about distance vector, link-state, and hybrid routing approaches and how each resolves common routing problems.

Please be sure to look at the Videos and Interactive Media Activities associated with this chapter that you will find on the CD-ROM accompanying this book. These CD elements are designed to supplement the material and reinforce the concepts introduced in this chapter.

Introduction to Static Routing

Routing is a set of directions used to get from one network to another. These directions, also known as routes, can be dynamically given to the router by another router, or they can be statically assigned to the router by an administrator. This section concentrates on routes that are statically assigned by an administrator.

Introducing Routing

Routing is the process that a router uses to forward packets toward the destination network. A router makes decisions based upon the destination IP address of a packet. Devices along the way use the destination IP address to point the packet in the correct direction so that the packet eventually arrives at its destination. To make the correct decisions, routers must learn the direction to remote networks. When routers use dynamic routing, this information is learned from other routers. When static routing is used, a network administrator manually configures information about remote networks.

Because static routes must be configured manually, network topology changes require the network administrator to add and delete static routes to account for the changes. In a large network, this manual maintenance of routing tables can require a tremendous amount of administrative time. In small networks with few possible changes, static routes require little maintenance. Because of the extra administrative requirements, static routing does not have the scalability of dynamic routing. Even in large networks, static routes that are intended to accomplish a specific purpose are often configured in conjunction with a dynamic routing protocol.

More Information: Static Versus Dynamic Routes

Static route knowledge is administered manually by a network administrator who enters it into a router's configuration. The administrator must update this static route entry manually whenever an internetwork topology change requires an update.

More Information: Static Versus Dynamic Routes (Continued)

Dynamic route knowledge works differently. After a network administrator enters configuration commands to start dynamic routing, the route knowledge automatically is updated by a routing process whenever new information is received from the internetwork. Changes in dynamic knowledge are exchanged between routers as part of the update process.

The Purpose of a Static Route

Static routing has several useful applications. Dynamic routing tends to reveal everything known about an internetwork; for security reasons, however, you might want to hide parts of an internetwork. *Static routing* enables you to specify the information that you want to reveal about restricted networks.

When a network is accessible by only one path, a static route to the network can be sufficient. This type of network is called a *stub network.* A stub network is a network that has only a single route to the outside world. Configuring static routing to a stub network avoids the overhead of dynamic routing, as shown in Figure 6-1 in the next section.

Static Route Operation

Static route operations can be summarized into a three-part sequence:

1. The network administrator configures the route.

2. The router installs the route in the routing table if the network for the outbound interface is up and up.

3. Packets are routed using the static route.

Figure 6-1 Static Route Operation

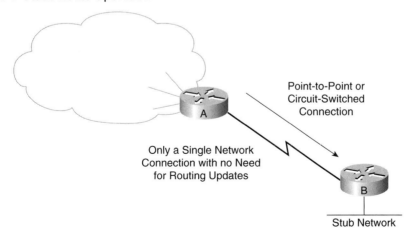

Because a static route is configured manually, the administrator must configure the static route on the router using the **ip route** command, where the *ip-address* argument is the next-hop address, *interface-type interface-number* refers to the outbound interface, and *distance* refers to the administrative distance. The correct syntax for the **ip route** command is as follows:

```
Router(config)#ip route prefix mask {ip-address | interface-type interface-number}
[distance]
```

In Figure 6-2, the network administrator of the Hoboken router needs to configure a static route pointing to the 172.16.1.0/24 and 172.16.5.0/24 networks on the other routers.

Figure 6-2 Static Routes

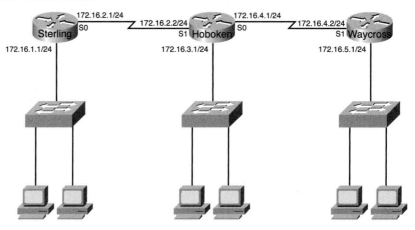

The administrator could enter one of two commands to accomplish this objective. The method in Example 6-1 specifies the outgoing interface (Serial 0). The method in Example 6-2 specifies the next-hop IP address of the adjacent router (172.16.2.2). Either of the commands installs a static route in the routing table of Hoboken.

Example 6-1 *IP Route Using Interface*

```
Sterling(config)# ip route  172.16.3.0  255.255.255.0  s0
```

Example 6-2 *IP Route Using Next-Hop Router IP*

```
Sterling(config)# ip route  172.16.3.0  255.255.255.0  172.16.2.2
```

The static route in Example 6-1 that uses the exit interface instead of the intermediate address is actually a more efficient static route. This is because the routes in the routing table must ultimately be resolved to an exit interface. Using an exit interface (Example 6-1) instead of an intermediate IP address (Example 6-2) requires only one lookup of the routing table instead of two, as in the case of using the intermediate IP address. The intermediate IP address 172.16.2.2 has to be looked up in the routing table before the router knows which exit interface it can use.

The *administrative distance* is an optional parameter that provides a measure of the reliability of the route. A lower value for the administrative distance indicates a more reliable route. This means that a route with a lower administrative distance will be installed before an identical route with a higher administrative distance. When using a static route, the default administrative distance is 1. In the routing table, it shows that the static route with the outgoing interface option is directly connected. This is sometimes confusing because a true directly connected route has an administrative distance of 0. To verify the administrative distance of a particular route, use the **show ip route** *address* command, where the IP address of the particular route is inserted for the *address* option. Table 6-1 show Cisco's administrative distance values for each supported protocol. Routes with lower administrative distances are trusted over identical routes with higher administrative distances. Only directly connected networks can have an administrative distance of 0. This cannot be modified. No other types of routes—static or dynamic—can have an administrative distance of 0. If an administrative distance other than the default is desired, a value between 1 and 255 is entered after the next-hop or outgoing interface, as follows:

```
ip route 172.16.3.0 255.255.255.0 192.168.2.1 255 10
```

Table 6-1 Cisco Administrative Distances

Route Source	Default Distance Values
Connected interface	0
Static route	1
Enhanced Interior Gateway Routing Protocol (EIGRP) summary route	5
External Border Gateway Protocol (BGP)	20
Internal EIGRP	90
IGRP	100
OSPF	110
Intermediate System-to-Intermediate System (IS-IS)	115
Routing Information Protocol (RIP)	120
Exterior Gateway Protocol (EGP)	140
External EIGRP	170
Internal BGP	200
Unknown	255

If the router cannot reach the outgoing or exit interface that is being used in the route, the route will not be installed in the routing table. This means that if the interface is down, the route will not be placed in the routing table. In addition, if the intermediate IP address is not reachable, the static route is installed in the routing table.

Sometimes static routes are used for backup purposes. A static route can be configured on a router that will be used only when the dynamically learned route has failed. To use a static route in this manner, set the administrative distance higher than that of the dynamic routing protocol being used.

Most environments use both a static and a dynamic routing protocol. It is uncommon to find networks that overlap or that use more than one dynamic routing protocol. The exception to this is when the network is physically divided and part of the network uses one dynamic routing protocol while another part of the network uses a different dynamic routing protocol.

Configuring Static Routes

This section lists the steps for configuring static routes and gives an example of a simple network for which static routes might be configured.

Use the following steps to configure static routes:

Step 1   Determine all desired prefixes, masks, and addresses. The address can be either a local interface or a next-hop address that leads to the desired destination.

The term prefix is another name for network address. More specifically, it is the name used to describe a address that has the host bits set to zero (0). A prefix address, therefore, can also refer to a summary address. For example, you can summarize the following addresses into one summary address with the prefix 192.168.0.0/22. The /22 tells us that the first 22 bits are the prefix.

192.168.0.0/24

196.168.1.0/24

196.168.2.0/24

196.168.3.0/24

Step 2   Enter global configuration mode.

Step 3   Type the **ip route** command with a prefix and mask followed by the corresponding address from Step 1. The administrative distance is optional.

Step 4   Repeat Step 3 for as many destination networks as were defined in Step 1.

Step 5   Exit global configuration mode.

Step 6   Save the active configuration to NVRAM by using the **copy running-config startup-config** or **write memory** commands.

The example network in Figure 6-3 is a simple three-router configuration. Hoboken must be configured so that it can reach the 172.16.1.0 network and the 172.16.5.0 network. Both of these networks have a subnet mask of 255.255.255.0.

Figure 6-3 Static Route Operation

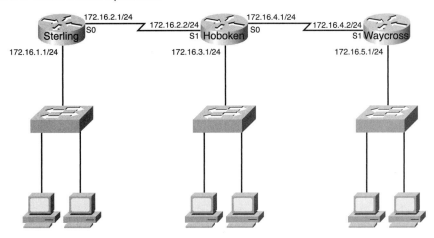

Packets that have a destination network of 172.16.1.0 need to be routed to Sterling. Packets that have a destination address of 172.16.5.0 need to be routed to Waycross. Static routes can be configured to accomplish this using the outgoing router interfaces (S0 and S1), as shown in Example 6-3.

Example 6-3 *IP Route with Outgoing Interfaces*

```
Hoboken(config)#ip route 172.16.1.0 255.255.255.0 s1
Hoboken(config)#ip route 172.16.5.0 255.255.255.0 s0
```

Both static routes first are configured to use a local interface as the gateway to the destination networks, as in Figure 6-4. Because the administrative distance was not specified, it will default to 0 when the route is installed in the routing table. The same two static routes can also be configured using an intermediate address as the gateway. The intermediate address is usually the next-hop IP address, but it does not have to be. Using the next-hop IP address means the network between the routers is directly connected. The intermediate address gets resolved by locating the route as a directly connected network and using that network as the exit interface. If the intermediate address is not a next-hop address, the routing table must contain a route for the network address of that intermediate address; otherwise, the static route is not entered into the routing table.

Figure 6-4 Static Routes Configured by Administrator

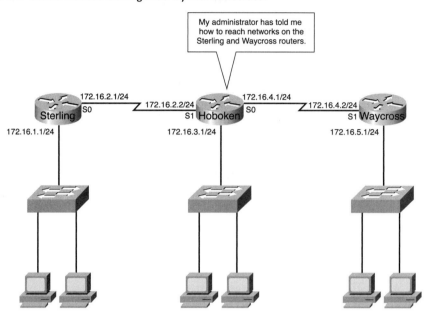

The first route to the 172.16.1.0 network has a gateway of 172.16.2.1. The second route to the 172.16.5.0 network has a gateway of 172.16.4.2. Example 6-4 shows configuring static routes using the intermediate or next-hop interface address and includes comments (preceded by !) that will show up in the configuration file. Because the administrative distance was not specified, it defaults to 1.

Example 6-4 *IP Route with Next Hop and Comment*

```
Hoboken(config)# ip route 172.16.1.0 255.255.255.0 172.16.2.1
!This command points to Sterling's LAN


Hoboken(config)# ip route 172.16.1.0 255.255.255.0 172.16.4.2
!This command points to Waycross LAN
```

More Information: How a Default Route Is Used

Figure 6-5 shows a use for a default route, a routing table entry that directs packets to the next hop when that hop is not explicitly listed in the routing table. You can set default routes as part of the static configuration.

In this example, the Company X routers possess specific knowledge of the topology of the Company X network, but not of other networks. Maintaining knowledge of every other network accessible by way of the Internet cloud is unnecessary and unreasonable, if not impossible.

More Information: How a Default Route Is Used (Continued)

Instead of maintaining specific network knowledge, each router in Company X is informed of the default route that it can use to reach any unknown destination by directing the packet to the Internet.

Figure 6-5 Static Default Route Using Next Hop

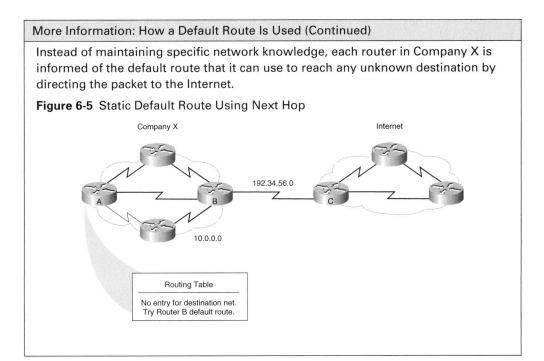

Configuring Default Route Forwarding

Default routes route packets with destinations that do not match any of the other routes in the routing table. Routers typically are configured with a default route for Internet-bound traffic because it is often impractical and unnecessary to maintain routes to all networks in the Internet. A default route is actually a special static route that uses the following format:

```
ip route 0.0.0.0 0.0.0.0 {next-hop-address | outgoing interface}
```

Use the following steps to configure default routes:

Step 1   Enter global configuration mode.

Step 2   Type the **ip route** command with *0.0.0.0* for the prefix and *0.0.0.0* for the mask. The *address* argument for the default route can be either the local router interface that connects to the outside networks or the IP address of the next-hop router.

Step 3   Exit global configuration mode.

Step 4   Save the active configuration to NVRAM by using the **copy running-config startup-config** command.

Figure 6-2, earlier in this chapter, demonstrated static route configuration on router Hoboken to make networks 172.16.1.0 on Sterling and 172.16.5.0 on Waycross accessible. It should now be possible to route packets to both of these networks from Hoboken. However, as configured, neither Sterling nor Waycross will know how to return packets to any network that is

NOTE

The 0.0.0.0 mask, when logically ANDed to the destination IP address of the packet to be routed, always yields the network 0.0.0.0. If the packet does not match a more specific route in the routing table, it is routed to the 0.0.0.0 network.

not directly connected. A static route could be configured on Sterling and Waycross for each of the destination networks that are not directly connected, but on a larger network this would not be a scalable solution.

Sterling connects to all non-directly connected networks via interface s0. Waycross has only one connection to all non-directly connected networks. This is through interface Serial 1. A default route on both Sterling and Waycross provides routing for all packets that are destined for networks that are not directly connected, as demonstrated in Figure 6-6. Examples 6-5 and 6-6 show the commands necessary to define a default static route on Waycross and Sterling, respectively.

Figure 6-6 Static Route for Waycross

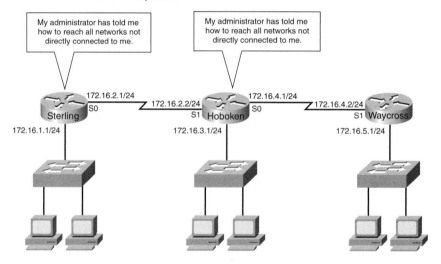

Example 6-5 *Default Route for Waycross*

```
Waycross(config)# ip route 0.0.0.0 0.0.0.0 s1
```

Example 6-6 *Default Route for Sterling*

```
Sterling(config)# ip route 0.0.0.0 0.0.0.0 s0
```

Verifying Static Route Configuration

It is important to verify that the static routes are present in the routing table and that routing is working as expected after the static routes are configured. The command **show running-config** is used to view the active configuration in NVRAM to verify that the static route was entered correctly. The **show ip route** command is used to make sure that the static route is present in the routing table.

Use the following steps to verify static route configuration:

Step 1   In privileged mode, enter the command **show running-config** to view the active configuration.

Step 2   Verify that the static route has been entered correctly. If the route is not correct, it will be necessary to go back into global configuration mode to remove the incorrect static route and enter the correct one.

Step 3   Enter the command **show ip route**.

Step 4   Verify that the route that was configured is in the routing table.

Troubleshooting Static Route Configuration

Having knowledge of troubleshooting tools and procedures is just as important in static routing as in any other aspect of networking. You can use the **show interfaces** command to check the state and configuration of the interface that is to be used for the route gateway. Using the **ping** command helps you to determine whether end-to-end connectivity exists. If an echo reply is not received after a **ping**, you can use the **traceroute** command to determine which router in the route path is dropping the packets. The routing process must happen on each router the packet travels through, or the packet will be dropped. In many cases, packets actually reach their destination, but the remote network router has no knowledge of a route to reply to the sender.

Every router makes its own routing decisions, based only on information in its own routing table. Just because one router might have certain routes in its routing table does not mean that other routers have that same information. In addition, routing information about a path from one router to another router does not provide routing information about the return path.

Use the following steps to troubleshoot a static route configuration:

Step 1   Make sure that the link that is to be used as the gateway by the route is available.

Step 2   Enter the command **show interfaces**, and verify that the interface is up and that the line protocol is up.

Step 3   Verify that the IP address being used on the interface is correct.

Step 4   **ping** the IP address on the remote router interface that is connected directly to the route gateway. If the **ping** is not successful, the problem is not related to routing. The interfaces of one or both of the directly connected routers might be configured incorrectly, or a physical problem might exist with the link. Return to Step 1 to troubleshoot.

Step 5   If the **ping** of the far-end router fails, use the **traceroute** command to determine which router in the route path is dropping the packet.

Step 6   Log into the router with the failed **traceroute.** Return to Step 1 and start again.

Step 7   If the **ping** is successful, attempt to **ping** the far-end router. If this **ping** is successful, complete end-to-end connectivity has been achieved. The test of the static route is complete.

Lab 6.1.6 Configuring Static Routes

In this lab, you configure static routes between routers to allow data transfers between them without the use of dynamic routing protocols.

Dynamic Routing Overview

A network administrator chooses a dynamic routing protocol based upon many considerations. These include the size of the network, the bandwidth of available links, the processing power of the routers, the brands and models of the routers, and the protocols that are used in the network. This section provides more details about the differences between routing protocols that help network administrators make a choice.

More Information: Dynamic Routing

Dynamic routing is necessary to allow networks to update and adapt quickly to changes. The network shown in Figure 6-7 adapts differently to topology changes depending on whether it uses statically or dynamically configured routing information.

Figure 6-7 Dynamic Route

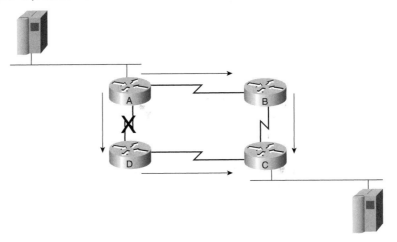

Static routing allows routers to properly route a packet from network to network based on manually configured information. In the example, Router A always sends traffic destined for Router C to Router D. The router refers to its routing table and follows the static knowledge residing there to relay the packet to Router D. Router D does the same and relays the packet to Router C. Router C delivers the packet to the destination host.

More Information: Dynamic Routing (Continued)

If the path between Router A and Router D fails, Router A is not capable of relaying the packet to Router D using that static route. Until Router A is manually reconfigured to relay packets by way of Router B, communication with the destination network is impossible. Dynamic routing offers more flexibility. According to the routing table generated by Router A, a packet can reach its destination over the preferred route through Router D.

However, a second path to the destination is available by way of Router B. When Router A recognizes that the link to Router D is down, it adjusts its routing table, making the path through Router B the preferred path to the destination. The routers continue sending packets over this link.

When the path between Routers A and D is restored to service, Router A again can change its routing table to indicate a preference for the counterclockwise path through Routers D and C to the destination network. Dynamic routing protocols also can direct traffic from the same session over different paths in a network for better performance. This is known as *load sharing* or load balancing.

Dynamic Routing Operations

The success of dynamic routing depends on two basic router functions:

- Maintenance of a routing table
- Timely distribution of knowledge, in the form of routing updates, to other routers (see Figure 6-8)

Figure 6-8 Routing Protocols Maintain Routing Information

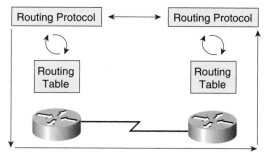

Dynamic routing relies on a routing protocol to share knowledge among routers. A routing protocol defines the set of rules used by a router when it communicates with neighboring routers. For example, a routing protocol describes the following:

- How to send updates
- What knowledge is contained in these updates
- When to send this knowledge
- How to locate recipients of the updates

continues

More Information: Dynamic Routing (Continued)

How Distances on Network Paths Are Determined by Various Metrics

When a routing algorithm updates a routing table, its primary objective is to determine the best information to include in the table. Each routing algorithm interprets what is best in its own way. The algorithm generates a number called the *metric* value for each path through the network. Typically, the smaller the metric number is, the better the path is, as shown in Figure 6-9.

Figure 6-9 Metrics Used to Define Best Path

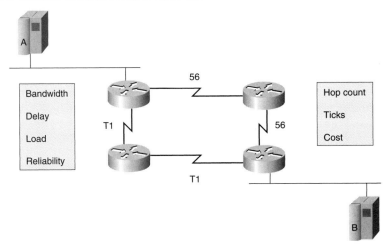

You can calculate simple metrics based on a single characteristic such as path, or you can calculate more complex metrics by combining several characteristics. The metric characteristics that most commonly are used by routers are as follows:

- **Bandwidth**—The data capacity of a link. (Normally, a 10-Mbps Ethernet link is preferable to a 64-kbps leased line.)

- **Delay**—The length of time required to move a packet along each link from source to destination.

- **Load**—The amount of activity on a network resource such as a router or a link.

- **Reliability**—Usually a reference to the error rate of each network link.

- **Hop count**—The number of routers that a packet must travel through before reaching its destination.

- **Cost**—An arbitrary value, usually based on bandwidth, monetary expense, or other measurement, that is assigned by a network administrator.

Introduction to Routing Protocols

This section provides a brief overview of some of the most common routing protocols and their key characteristics.

Routing protocols are different from routed protocols in terms of both function and task. A routing protocol is the communication used between routers. A routing protocol allows one router to share information with other routers regarding the networks it knows about and its proximity to other routers. The information a router gets from another router (using a routing protocol) is used to build and maintain a routing table.

Examples of routing protocols are as follows:

- Routing Information Protocol (RIP)
- Interior Gateway Routing Protocol (IGRP)
- Enhanced Interior Gateway Routing Protocol (EIGRP)
- Open Shortest Path First (OSPF)

A routed protocol is used to direct user traffic. A routed protocol provides enough information in its network layer address to allow a packet to be forwarded from one host to another based on the addressing scheme.

Examples of routed protocols are as follows:

- Internet Protocol (IP)
- Internetwork Packet Exchange (IPX)

Because of the similarity of the two terms, confusion often exists regarding the routed protocol and the routing protocol (see Figure 6-10). The following provides some clarification:

- *Routed protocol*—Any network protocol that provides enough information in its network layer address to allow a packet to be forwarded from one host to another host based on the addressing scheme. Routed protocols define the field formats within a packet. Packets generally are conveyed from end system to end system. A routed protocol uses the routing table to forward packets. The Internet Protocol (IP) is an example of a routed protocol.

- *Routing protocol*—Protocol that supports a routed protocol by providing mechanisms for sharing routing information. Routing protocol messages move between the routers. A routing protocol allows the routers to communicate with other routers to update and maintain tables. TCP/IP examples of routing protocols are listed here:

  - Routing Information Protocol (RIP)
  - Interior Gateway Routing Protocol (IGRP)
  - Enhanced Interior Gateway Routing Protocol (EIGRP)
  - Open Shortest Path First (OSPF)

Figure 6-10 Router and Routing Protocols

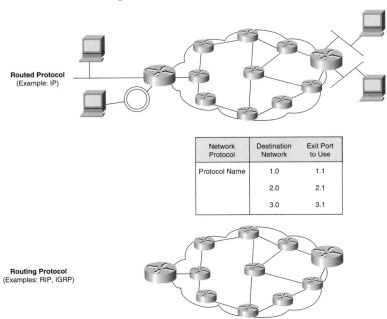

Autonomous Systems

An *autonomous system (AS)* is a collection of networks under a common administration that share a common routing strategy. To the outside world, an AS is viewed as a single entity. The AS might be run by one or more operators while presenting a consistent view of routing to the external world.

The American Registry of Internet Numbers (ARIN), a service provider, or an administrator assigns an identifying number to each AS. This autonomous system number is a 16-bit number. Routing protocols, such as Cisco's IGRP and EIGRP, use the term AS number in their configuration, but this is really used as a process ID. It does not require an actual AS number from ARIN or the use of a private AS number.

Autonomous systems divide the global internetwork into smaller and more manageable networks. Each AS has its own set of rules and policies and an AS number that distinguishes it from all other autonomous systems in the world.

Purpose of a Routing Protocol and Autonomous Systems

The goal of a routing protocol is to build and maintain the routing table. This table contains the learned networks and associated ports for those networks. Routers use routing protocols to manage information received from other routers and information generated from the configuration of its own interfaces.

The routing protocol identifies all available routes, places the best routes into the routing table, and removes routes when they are no longer valid. The router uses the information in the routing table to forward routed protocol packets.

The routing algorithm is fundamental to dynamic routing. Whenever the topology of a network changes because of growth, reconfiguration, or failure, the network knowledge base also must change. The network knowledge needs to reflect an accurate and consistent view of the new topology.

When all routers in an internetwork are operating with the same knowledge, the internetwork is said to have converged. Fast convergence is desirable because it reduces the time period of incorrect routing decisions.

It is common to find individual networks, such as schools and universities, under the control of a single, autonomous system. Each of the schools' networks might be configured to use a dynamic routing protocol and/or static routes. The individual school networks are interconnected either dynamically or statically, and are within the same AS.

Identifying the Classes of Routing Protocols

Most routing algorithms can be classified under one of the following categories:

- Distance vector
- Link-state

The *distance vector routing protocol* approach determines the direction, or the vector, and the distance to any link in the internetwork. The *link-state routing protocol* approach, also called shortest path first (SPF), recreates the exact topology of the entire internetwork. The *balanced hybrid routing protocol* approach, such as EIGRP, is a distance vector routing protocol that includes some of the features found in link-state routing protocols.

Distance Vector Routing Protocol Features

Distance vector routing algorithms pass periodic copies of a routing table from router to router. These regular updates between routers communicate topology changes. Distance vector-based routing algorithms also are known as Bellman-Ford algorithms.

In Figure 6-11, each router receives a routing table from its neighboring routers. Router B receives information from Router A. Router A adds a distance vector number, such as a number of hops, which increases the distance vector before sending the update to Router B. Then Router B passes this new routing table to its other neighbor, Router C, increasing the metric again. This step-by-step process occurs in all directions between all neighbor routers.

Figure 6-11 Distance Vector Concepts

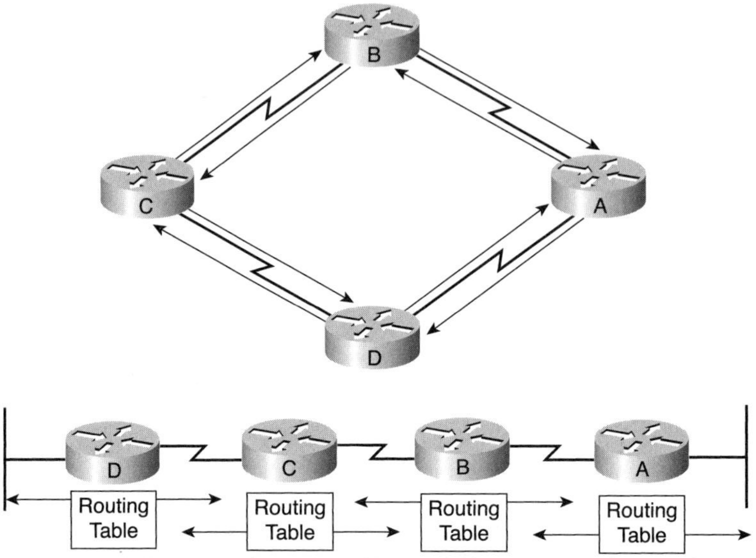

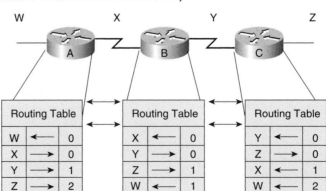

Pass periodic copies of a routing table to neighbor routers and accumulate distance vectors.

The algorithm accumulates network distances so that it can maintain a database of network topology information. However, distance vector algorithms do not provide routers with the exact topology of an internetwork because each router is aware of only its neighbor routers.

Each router that uses distance vector routing begins by identifying its neighbors. Figure 6-12 shows distance vector discovery. The interface that leads to each directly connected network is shown as having a distance of 0. As the distance vector network discovery process proceeds, routers discover the best path to destination networks based on the information they receive from each neighbor. For example, Router A learns about other networks based on the information that it receives from Router B. Each of the other network entries in the routing table has an accumulated distance vector to show how far away that network is in a given direction.

Figure 6-12 Distance Vector Network Discovery

Routing table updates occur when the topology changes. As with the network discovery process, topology change updates proceed step by step from router to router, as shown in Figure 6-13. Distance vector algorithms call for each router to send its entire routing table to each of its adjacent neighbors. The routing tables include information about the total path cost as defined by its metric and the logical address of the first router on the path to each network contained in the table. The metric is made up of several components, as shown in Figure 6-14.

Figure 6-13 Distance Vector Topology Changes

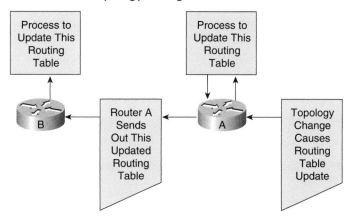

Figure 6-14 Distance Vector Routing Metric Components

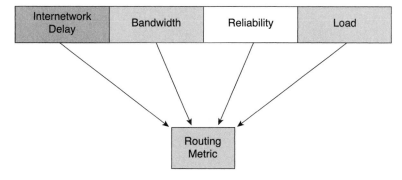

Routing Updates Explained

Each router receives a routing table from its directly connected neighboring routers. For example, in Figure 6-13, Router B receives information from Router A, which increased the metric (number of hops) by 1 before sending it to Router B. This same step-by-step process occurs in all directions between direct-neighbor routers.

A distance vector is comparable to the signs along a highway. Highway signs direct drivers toward a destination and indicate the distance to that destination. Farther down the highway, additional signs point toward the same destination, but now the distance is shorter. As long as the distance continues to become shorter, the traffic is on the right path.

Link-State Routing Protocol Features

The second basic algorithm used for routing is the link-state algorithm. Link-state algorithms are also known as Dijkstra's algorithm or as shortest path first (SPF) algorithms. They maintain a complex database of topology information. Whereas the distance vector algorithm has nonspecific information about distant networks and no knowledge of distant routers, a link-state routing algorithm maintains full knowledge of distant routers and how they interconnect. Link-state routing uses the following:

- *Link-state advertisements (LSAs)*—Small packets of routing information that are sent between routers

- *Topological database*—A collection of information gathered from LSAs

- *Shortest path first (SPF) algorithm*—A calculation performed on the database resulting in the SPF tree

- *Routing table*—A list of the known paths and interfaces

The Internet Engineering Task Force (IETF) implemented this link-state concept in Open Shortest Path First (OSPF) routing. RFC 1583 contains a description of OSPF link-state concepts and operations.

Figure 6-15 illustrates these link-state concepts.

Network Discovery Processes for Link-State Routing

LSAs are exchanged between routers, starting with directly connected networks. Each router, in parallel with others, constructs a topological database consisting of all the exchanged LSAs.

The SPF algorithm computes network accessibility. The router constructs this logical topology as a tree, with itself as the root, consisting of all possible paths to each network in the link-state protocol internetwork. It then sorts these paths using SPF. The router lists the best paths and the interfaces to these destination networks in the routing table. The router also maintains other databases of topology elements and status details.

Figure 6-15 Link-State Concepts

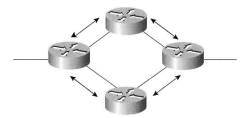

Link-State Advertisement Packets

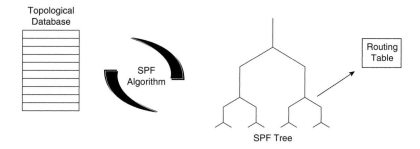

How Link-State Protocols Exchange Routing Information

Link-state network-discovery mechanisms are used to create a common picture of the entire network. All link-state routers share this view of the network. This is similar to having several identical maps of a town. In Figure 6-16, four networks (W, X, Y, and Z) are connected by three link-state routers. Network discovery for link-state routing uses the following processes:

1. Routers exchange LSAs with each other. Each router begins with directly connected networks for which it has direct, firsthand information.

2. Each router, in parallel with the others, constructs a topological database consisting of all the LSAs from the internetwork.

3. The SPF algorithm computes network reachability. The router constructs this logical topology as a tree, with itself as root, consisting of all possible paths to each network in the link-state protocol internetwork. It then sorts these paths by shortest path first (SPF).

4. The router lists its best paths and the ports to these destination networks in the routing table. It also maintains other databases of topology elements and status details.

Figure 6-16 Link-State Algorithm Shortest Path Calculations

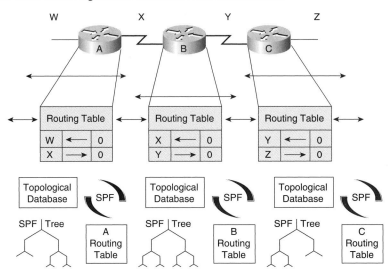

When a router becomes aware of a link-state topology change, it forwards the information so that all other routers can use it for updates. This involves sending common routing information to all routers in the internetwork. To achieve convergence, each router keeps track of its neighbor routers, the router name, interface status, and the cost of the link to the neighbor. The router constructs an LSA packet that lists this information along with new neighbors, changes in link costs, and links that are no longer valid. The LSA packet then is sent out so that all other routers receive it. Figure 6-17 shows an example of link-state topology changes.

Figure 6-17 Link-State Topology Changes

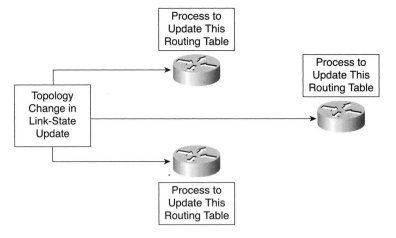

When the router receives an LSA packet, the database is updated with the most recent information. The accumulated data is used to compute a map of the internetwork, and the SPF algorithm calculates the shortest path to other networks. Each time an LSA packet changes the link-state database, SPF recalculates the best paths and updates the routing table. Every router takes the topology change into account to determine the shortest path to use for packet routing.

Three Link-State Concerns

Running link-state protocols brings up three primary concerns:

- Processor overhead
- Memory requirements
- Bandwidth consumption

Routers running link-state protocols require more memory and perform more processing than distance vector routing protocols. Routers must have enough memory to hold all the information from the various databases, the topology tree, and the routing table, as shown in Figure 6-18. Initial link-state packet flooding consumes bandwidth. During the initial discovery process, all routers using link-state routing protocols send LSA packets to all other routers. This action floods the internetwork and temporarily reduces the bandwidth available for routed traffic carrying user data. After this initial flooding, link-state routing protocols generally require only minimal bandwidth to send infrequent or event-triggered LSA packets reflecting topology changes.

Figure 6-18 Link-State Concerns

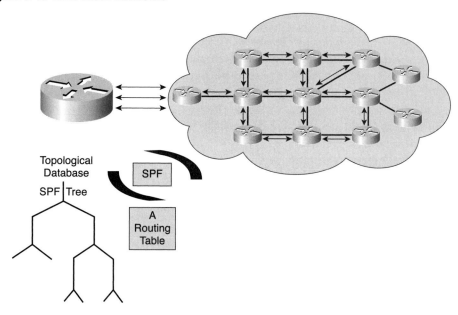

More Information: Hybrid Routing Protocol Features

A third type of routing protocol, balanced hybrid routing, contains features of both distance vector and link-state routing protocols. Balanced hybrid routing protocols use distance vectors to determine the best paths to destination networks. However, they differ from most distance vector protocols by using topology changes to trigger routing database updates instead of periodic updates.

Like link-state protocols, the balanced hybrid routing protocol converges rapidly. However, it differs from distance vector and link-state protocols by using less bandwidth, memory, and processor overhead. Enhanced Interior Gateway Routing Protocol (EIGRP) is an example of a hybrid protocol.

Routing Protocols Overview

The following sections describe and provide an overview of the features of routing protocols. Some of the topics covered include:

- Path determination
- Routing configuration
- Routing protocols
- IGP versus EGP

More Information: Path Determination

Path determination for traffic going through a network cloud occurs at the network layer (Layer 3). The path-determination function enables a router to evaluate the available paths to a destination and to establish the preferred handling of a packet. Routing services use network topology information when evaluating network paths. This information can be configured by the network administrator or can be collected through dynamic processes running in the network.

The network layer provides best-effort end-to-end packet delivery across interconnected networks. The network layer uses the IP routing table to send packets from the source network to the destination network. After the router determines which path to use, it proceeds with forwarding the packet. The router forwards the packet that it accepted on one interface to another interface or port that reflects the best path to the packet's destination.

Routing is the process that a router uses to forward packets toward the destination network. A router makes decisions based upon the destination IP address of a packet. All devices along the way use the destination IP address to point the packet in the correct direction. The destination IP address enables the packet to eventually arrive at its destination. To make the correct decisions, routers must learn the direction to remote networks. When routers use dynamic routing, the direction to remote networks is learned from other routers. When static routing is used, a network administrator configures information about remote networks manually.

More Information: Path Determination (Continued)

Because static routes must be configured manually, any network topology changes require the network administrator to add and delete static routes to account for the changes. In a large network, this manual maintenance of routing tables could require a tremendous amount of administrative time. On small networks with very few possible changes, static routes require very little maintenance. Static routing does not have the scalability of dynamic routing because of the extra administrative requirements. However, even in large networks, static routes that are intended to accomplish a very specific purpose often are configured in combination with a dynamic routing protocol. Although dynamic routing protocols can automatically determine routes, they still must be activated initially and configured by a network administrator to accomplish this.

The sections that follow cover various routing concepts:

- The process of routing packets from source to destination
- Addressing
- Path selection and packet switching
- Routed and routing protocols

How Routers Route Packets from Source to Destination

To be truly practical, a network must consistently represent the paths available between routers. As Figure 6-19 shows, each line between the routers has a number that the routers use as a network address. These addresses must convey information that can be used by a routing process to pass packets from a source toward a destination. Using these addresses, the network layer can provide a relay connection that interconnects independent networks.

The consistency of Layer 3 addresses across the entire internetwork also improves the use of bandwidth by preventing unnecessary broadcasts. Broadcasts invoke unnecessary process overhead and waste capacity on any devices or links that do not need to receive the broadcasts. By using consistent end-to-end addressing to represent the path of media connections, the network layer can find a path to the destination without unnecessarily burdening the devices or links on the internetwork with broadcasts.

Figure 6-19 Network Addresses

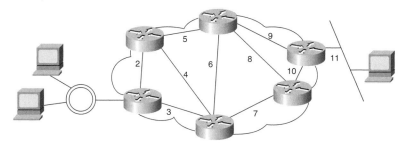

continues

More Information: Path Determination (Continued)

Network and Host Addressing

The router uses the network address to identify the destination network of a packet within an internetwork. Figure 6-20 shows three network numbers identifying segments connected to the router.

Figure 6-20 Network Addresses with Host Portions

Network	Host
1	1 2 3
2	1
3	1

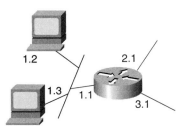

Most network protocol-addressing schemes use some form of host or node address. For some network layer protocols, a network administrator assigns network host addresses according to a predetermined internetwork addressing plan. For other network layer protocols, assignment of host addresses is partially or completely dynamic. In Figure 6-20, three hosts share the network number 1.

Network Layer Protocol Operations

Suppose that a host application needs to send a packet to a destination on a different network. The host addresses the data link frame to the router, using the address of one of the router's interfaces. The router's network layer process examines the incoming packet's Layer 3 header to determine the destination network and then references the routing table, which associates networks to outgoing interfaces (see Figure 6-21). The destination IP address of the packet must match the minimum leftmost bits of the network in the routing table, as specified by the subnet mask. The packet is encapsulated again in the data link frame that is appropriate for the selected interface and is queued for delivery to the next hop in the path.

More Information: Path Determination (Continued)

Figure 6-21 Router Services

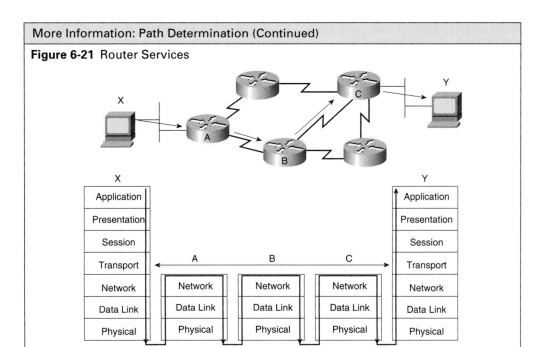

This process occurs each time that the packet is forwarded through another router. When the packet reaches the router that is connected to the destination host's network, it is encapsulated in the destination LAN's data link frame type and is delivered to the destination host.

Multiprotocol Routing

Routers are capable of supporting multiple independent routing protocols and maintaining routing tables for several routed protocols. This capability allows a router to deliver packets from several routed protocols over the same data links (see Figure 6-22).

Figure 6-22 Router Traffic

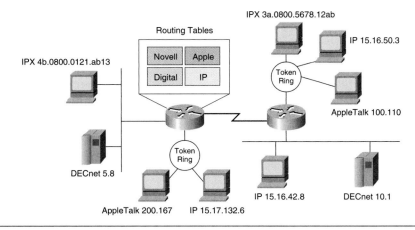

Path Determination

A router generally relays a packet from one data link to another using two basic functions:

- A path-determination function

- A switching function

Figure 6-23 illustrates how routers use addressing for these routing and switching functions. The router uses the network portion of the address to make path selections to pass the packet to the next router along the path.

The switching function allows a router to accept a packet on one interface and forward it through a second interface. The path-determination function enables the router to select the most appropriate interface for forwarding a packet. The node portion of the address is used by the final router (the router connected to the destination network) to deliver the packet to the correct host.

Figure 6-23 How Routers Use Addressing for Routing and Switching Functions

Destination Network	Direction and Router Port
1.0	← 1.1
2.0	→ 2.1
3.0	→ 3.1

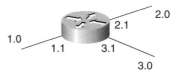

 Video Path Determination

In this video, you learn about how a router uses path determination to relay a packet from one data link to another.

Routing Configuration

To enable an IP routing protocol on a router, both global and interface parameters must be set. Global tasks include selecting a routing protocol, such as RIP, IGRP, EIGRP, or OSPF. The major task in the routing configuration mode is to indicate IP network numbers. Dynamic routing uses broadcasts and multicasts to communicate with other routers. The routing metric helps routers find the best path to each network or subnet.

The **router** command starts a routing process. The syntax for the router command is as follows:

```
Router(config)#router protocol {process-id | autonomous system}
```

where:

- *protocol* is either RIP, IGRP, or EIGRP.
- *process-id | autonomous system* refers to a number such as those used by IGRP and EIGRP.

The **network** command is necessary because it enables the routing process to identify the directly connected interfaces that participate in the sending and receiving of routing updates. The syntax for the **network** command is as follows:

```
Router(config-router)#network network number
```

where *network number* is the IP network number of a directly connected network.

For RIP and IGRP, the network numbers must be based on the network class addresses, not subnet addresses or individual host addresses, of the directly connected networks. Major network addresses are limited to Class A, B, and C network numbers.

At the Internet layer of the TCP/IP suite of protocols, a router can use an IP routing protocol to accomplish routing through the implementation of a specific routing algorithm. Examples of IP routing protocols include the following, as shown in Figure 6-24:

- **Routing Information Protocol (RIP)**—A distance vector interior routing protocol
- **Interior Gateway Routing Protocol (IGRP)**—A distance vector interior routing protocol developed by Cisco
- **Open Shortest Path First (OSPF)**—A link-state interior routing protocol
- **Enhanced Interior Gateway Routing Protocol (EIGRP)**—An interior distance vector routing protocol, described as a balanced hybrid routing protocol, developed by Cisco
- **Border Gateway Protocol (BGP)**—An exterior routing protocol

Figure 6-24 Routing Protocols

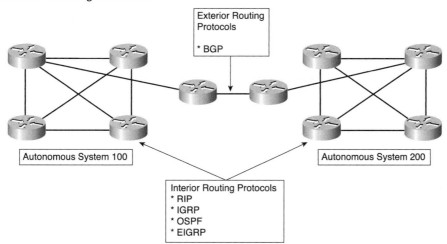

Routing Protocols

At the Internet layer of the TCP/IP suite of protocols, a router can use an IP routing protocol to accomplish routing through the implementation of a specific routing algorithm.

RIP originally was specified in RFC 1058. Its key characteristics include the following:

- It is a distance vector routing protocol.

- It uses hop count as the metric for path selection. If the hop count is greater than 15, the packet is discarded.

- By default, routing updates are broadcast every 30 seconds.

IGRP is a distance vector routing protocol developed by Cisco. IGRP sends routing updates at 90-second intervals, advertising networks for a particular autonomous system. IGRP offers the following design characteristics and features:

- Versatility for automatically handling indefinite or complex topologies

- Flexibility for handling segments with different bandwidth and delay characteristics

- Scalability for functioning in large networks

NOTE

These are the only four metrics used with IGRP and EIGRP. Some documentation incorrectly states that MTU is a metric used by IGRP and EIGRP. The documentation is not accurate, as MTU is not used and has never been used as a routing metric for IGRP or EIGRP.

By default, IGRP uses two metrics, bandwidth and delay. IGRP can be configured to use a combination of variables to determine a composite metric. Possible configurations include the following variables:

- Bandwidth

- Delay

- Load

- Reliability

OSPF is a link-state routing protocol used for IP. Link-state protocols keep a detailed topology, which allows the protocol to use calculations that prevent loops. With OSPF, the subnet mask also is transmitted, enabling features such as variable-length subnet masking (VLSM) and route summarization.

EIGRP is a distance vector routing protocol developed by Cisco. EIGRP has characteristics in common with both distance vector protocols and link-state protocols and is sometimes referred to as a balanced hybrid routing protocol. EIGRP calculates the best route to each network or subnet and provides alternative routes that can be used if the current route fails. EIGRP also transmits the subnet mask for each routing entry. Therefore, features such as VLSM and route summarization easily are supported.

BGP is an exterior routing protocol. BGP is designed to operate between autonomous systems. BGPs can be used between two ISPs or between a company and an ISP.

IGP Versus EGP

An *interior gateway protocol (IGP)* is designed for use in a network controlled or administered by a single organization. An IGP is designed to find the best path through the network. In other words, the metric and how that metric is used is the most important element in an IGP.

An *exterior gateway protocol (EGP)* is designed for use between networks that are controlled by two different organizations. EGPs typically are used between Internet service providers (ISPs) or between a company and an ISP. For example, a company would run BGP, an EGP, between one of its routers and a router inside an ISP. IP EGPs require the following three sets of information before routing can begin:

- A list of neighbor routers to exchange routing information with
- A list of networks to advertise as directly reachable
- The autonomous system number of the local router

An EGP must isolate autonomous systems. Because autonomous systems are managed by different administrations, networks must have a protocol to communicate between different systems. Figure 6-25 shows an autonomous system.

Figure 6-25 Autonomous System

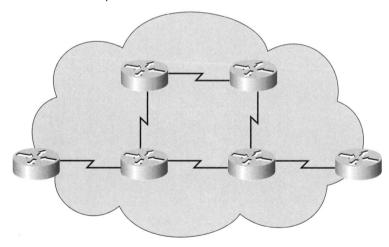

Every autonomous system is assigned a 16-bit identifying number by the American Registry of Internet Numbers (ARIN) or an ARIN provider.

 Interactive Media Activity   Checkbox: IGP Versus EGP

After completing this activity, you will understand IGP and EGP.

Summary

In this chapter, you learned the following points:

- A router will not forward a packet without a route to a destination network.

- Network administrators manually configure static routes.

- Default routes are special static routes that provide routers with gateways of last resort.

- Static and default routes are configured using the **ip route** command.

- Static and default route configuration can be verified using the **show ip route**, **ping**, and **traceroute** commands.

- Three types of routing protocols exist:

  - Distance vector

  - Link-state

  - Balanced hybrid

- An autonomous system (AS) is a collection of networks under a common administration and sharing a common routing strategy.

To supplement all that you've learned in this chapter, refer to the chapter-specific Videos and Interactive Media Activities on the CD-ROM accompanying this book.

Key Terms

administrative distance   A rating that shows trustworthiness of a routing information source. This value is shown as a numeric value between 0 and 255. The higher the value is, the lower the trustworthiness rating is.

autonomous system   A collection of networks under a single administrative domain.

balanced hybrid routing protocol   Routing protocols that utilize elements of distance vector and link-state routing protocols.

distance vector routing protocol   A class of routing algorithms that iterate on the number of hops in a route to find a shortest-path spanning tree. Distance vector routing algorithms call for each router to send its entire routing table in each update, but only to its neighbors. Distance vector routing algorithms can be prone to routing loops but are computationally simpler than link-state routing algorithms. Also called a Bellman-Ford routing algorithm.

dynamic routing   Routing that adjusts automatically to network topology or traffic changes. Also called adaptive routing. Requires that a routing protocol be run between routers.

exterior gateway protocol (EGP)   A routing protocol designed for use between networks that are controlled by two different organizations.

interior gateway protocol (IGP)   A routing protocol that is designed for use in a network controlled or administered by a single organization.

link-state advertisements (LSAs)   Small packets of routing information that are sent between routers.

link-state routing protocol   A routing algorithm in which each router broadcasts or multicasts information regarding the cost of reaching each of its neighbors to all nodes in the internetwork. Link-state algorithms create a consistent view of the network and are therefore not prone to routing loops. However, they achieve this at the cost of relatively greater computational difficulty and more widespread traffic than do distance vector routing algorithms.

load sharing   When dynamic routing protocols direct traffic from the same session over different paths in a network for better performance.

metric   An algorithm that generates a number for each path through the network. Typically, the smaller the metric number is, the better the path is.

routed protocol   A protocol that can be routed by a router. A router must be capable of interpreting the logical internetwork as specified by that routed protocol. Examples of routed protocols are AppleTalk, IPX, and IP.

routing   The process of finding a path to a destination host. Routing is very complex in large networks because of the many potential intermediate destinations that a packet might traverse before reaching its destination host.

routing protocol   A protocol that accomplishes routing through the implementation of a specific routing algorithm. Examples of routing protocols are IGRP, OSPF, and RIP.

routing table   A list of the known paths and interfaces.

shortest path first (SPF) algorithm   A calculation performed on the database resulting in the SPF tree.

static routing   The process of manually defining and configuring the routes.

stub network   An OSPF area that carries a default route, intra-area routes, and inter-area routes, but that does not carry external routes.

topological database   A collection of information gathered from LSAs.

Check Your Understanding

Complete all the review questions to test your understanding of the topics and concepts in this chapter. Answers are listed in Appendix B, "Check Your Understanding Answer Key."

1. Which of the following best describes one function of Layer 3, the network layer, in the OSI model?

    A. It is responsible for reliable network communication between nodes.

    B. It is concerned with physical addressing and network topology.

    C. It determines the best path for traffic to take through the network.

    D. It manages data exchange between presentation layer entities.

2. What function allows routers to evaluate available routes to a destination and to establish the preferred handling of a packet?

    A. Data linkage

    B. Path determination

    C. SDLC interface protocol

    D. Frame Relay

3. How does the network layer forward packets from the source to the destination?

    A. By using an IP routing table

    B. By using ARP responses

    C. By referring to a name server

    D. By referring to the bridge

4. What two parts of a network layer address do routers use to forward traffic through a network?

    A. Network address and destination IP address

    B. Network address and MAC address

    C. Host address and MAC address

    D. MAC address and subnet mask

5. Which of the following best describes a routed protocol?

    A. Its address provides enough information to allow a packet to be forwarded from host to host.

    B. It provides information necessary to pass data packets up to the next-highest network layer.

    C. It allows routers to communicate with other routers to maintain and update address tables.

    D. It allows routers to bind MAC and IP addresses together.

6. Which of the following best describes a routing protocol?

   A. A protocol that accomplishes routing through the implementation of an algorithm

   B. A protocol that specifies how and when MAC and IP addresses are bound together

   C. A protocol that defines the format and use of fields within a data packet

   D. A protocol that allows a packet to be forwarded from host to host

7. What is one advantage of distance vector algorithms?

   A. They are not likely to count to infinity.

   B. You can implement them easily on very large networks.

   C. They are not prone to routing loops.

   D. They are computationally simple.

8. Which of the following best describes a link-state algorithm?

   A. It recreates the exact topology of the entire internetwork.

   B. It requires numerous computations.

   C. It determines distance and direction to any link on the internetwork.

   D. It uses little network overhead and reduces overall traffic.

9. Why do routing loops occur?

   A. Slow convergence occurs after a modification to the internetwork.

   B. Split horizons are artificially created.

   C. Network segments fail catastrophically and take down other network segments in a cascade effect.

   D. Default routes never were established and initiated by the network administrator.

10. Which of the following best describes the concept of describing EIGRP as a balanced hybrid routing protocol?

   A. Being that EIGRP is a distance vector routing protocol, it determines best paths, but topology changes trigger routing table updates.

   B. It uses distance vector routing to determine best paths between topology during high-traffic periods.

   C. It uses topology to determine best paths but does frequent routing table updates.

   D. It uses topology to determine best paths but uses distance vectors to circumvent inactive network links.

11. What is a network with only one path to a router called?

  A. Static network

  B. Dynamic network

  C. Entity network

  D. Stub network

12. Which best describes a default route?

  A. Urgent-data route manually entered by a network administrator

  B. Route used when part of the network fails

  C. Route used when the destination network is not listed explicitly in the routing table

  D. Preset shortest path

CHAPTER 7

Distance Vector Routing Protocols

Objectives

Upon completion of this chapter, you should be able to answer the following questions:

- What are the steps of the initial router configuration?

- What are some of the defining characteristics of RIP?

- What are the steps and commands to configure a RIP routing scenario?

- What are some of the defining characteristics of IGRP?

- What are the steps and commands to configure an IGRP routing scenario?

- What is load balancing over multiple paths and how can it be tested?

- How do routing loops occur in distance vector routing?

- What are the several methods used by distance vector routing protocols to ensure that routing information is accurate?

- What is the **ip classless** command used for?

- What are some methods and techniques to troubleshoot RIP

Key Terms

The following is a list of key terms introduced in this chapter. For your reference, a definition for each term can be found at the end of the chapter.

Now that you have learned about routing protocols, you are ready to configure IP routing protocols. As you know, routers can be configured to use one or more IP routing protocols. In this chapter, you learn the initial configuration of the router to enable the Routing Information Protocol (RIP) and the Interior Gateway Routing Protocol (IGRP). In addition, you learn how to monitor IP routing protocols.

Please be sure to look at this chapter's associated Videos and Interactive Media Activities that you will find on the CD-ROM accompanying this book. These CD elements are designed to supplement the material and reinforce the concepts introduced in this chapter.

More Information: Initial Router Configuration

After testing the hardware and loading the Cisco IOS Software image, the router finds and applies the configuration statements. These entries provide the router with details about router-specific attributes, protocol functions, and interface addresses. Remember that if the router cannot locate a valid startup-config file, it enters an initial router configuration mode called setup mode or system configuration dialog.

With the setup mode command facility, you can answer questions in the system configuration dialog. This facility prompts you for basic configuration information. The answers that you enter enable the router to build a sufficient but minimal router configuration. The setup facility provides the following:

- An inventory of interfaces
- An opportunity to enter global parameters
- An opportunity to enter interface parameters
- A setup script review
- An opportunity to indicate whether or not you want the router to use this configuration

After you confirm setup mode entries, the router uses the entries as a running configuration. The router also stores the configuration in nonvolatile random-access memory (NVRAM) as a new startup-config, and you can start using the router. For additional protocol and interface changes, you can then use the enable mode and enter the command **configure**.

Distance Vector Routing

This section discusses distance vector routing protocols and their shortcomings, as well as identifies solutions to the problems presented by distance vector routing. Distance vector–based routing algorithms pass periodic copies of a routing table from router to router. These regular updates between routers communicate topology changes.

Distance Vector Routing Updates

Routing table updates occur periodically or whenever the topology in a distance vector proto-col network changes. It is important for a routing protocol to be efficient in updating the rout-ing tables. As with the network discovery process, topology change updates proceed systematically from router to router. Figure 7-1 illustrates how distance vector protocols han-dle topology changes.

Figure 7-1 Distance Vector Topology Changes

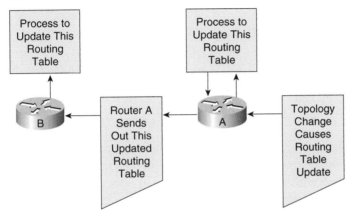

Distance vector algorithms instruct each router to send its entire routing table to each of its *adjacent neighbors*, except in the case where a split horizon is implemented. A split horizon is discussed later in this chapter. The routing tables include information about the total path cost, as defined by the metrics, and the logical address of the advertising router on the path to each network.

Distance Vector Routing Loop Issues

Routing loops can occur if a network experiences slow *convergence* as the result of changes in the network or routing topology causing inconsistent routing entries. Figure 7-2 demon-strates routing loops.

Figure 7-2 Routing Loops

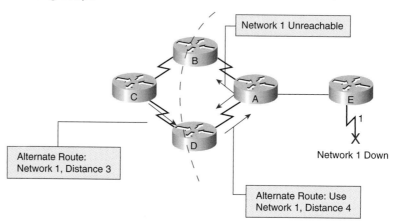

The process of how a routing loop occurs (based on Figure 7-2) is as follows:

1. Just before the failure of Network 1, all routers have consistent knowledge and correct routing tables. The network is said to have converged. Assume for the remainder of this example that for Router C, the preferred path to Network 1 is by way of Router B, and the distance from Router C to Network 1 is three.

2. When Network 1 fails, Router E sends an update to Router A. Router A stops routing packets to Network 1, but Routers B, C, and D continue to do so because they have not yet been informed of the failure. When Router A sends out its update, Routers B and D stop routing to Network 1. However, Router C has not received an update. To Router C, Network 1 is still reachable through Router B.

3. Now Router C sends a periodic update to Router D, indicating a path to Network 1 by way of Router B. Router D changes its routing table to reflect this incorrect information, and sends the information to Router A. Router A sends the information to Routers B and E, and so on. Any packet destined for Network 1 now loops from Router C to B to A to D and back again to C.

Video and Animation   Distance Vector

In this video, you learn how distance vector protocols send routing updates.

Defining a Maximum Count

The invalid updates of Network 1 continue to loop until some other process stops the looping. This condition, called *count to infinity*, loops packets continuously around the network in spite of the fundamental fact that the destination network, Network 1, is down. While the routers are counting to infinity, the invalid information allows a routing loop to exist, as illustrated in Figure 7-3.

Figure 7-3 Counting to Infinity

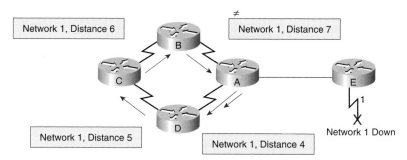

Without countermeasures to stop the process, the distance vector or the metric increases each time the packet passes through another router. Metrics are covered in Chapter 6, "Routing and Routing Protocols." These packets loop through the network because of incorrect information in the routing tables.

Distance vector routing algorithms are self-correcting, but a routing loop problem can require a count to infinity to resolve. To avoid this prolonged problem, distance vector protocols define infinity as a specific maximum number. This number refers to a *routing metric*, which might simply be the hop count. Figure 7-4 demonstrates this concept.

Figure 7-4 Defining a Maximum Metric

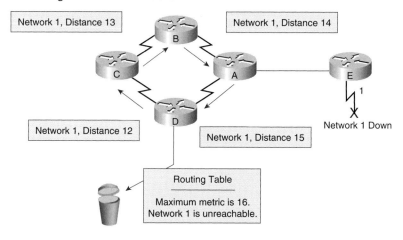

By assigning a maximum number to infinity, the routing protocol permits the routing loop to continue until the metric exceeds its maximum allowed value. Figure 7-4 shows the metric value as 16 hops, which exceeds the distance vector default maximum of 15 hops, and the router discards the packet. In any case, when the metric value exceeds the maximum value, Network 1 is considered unreachable.

If you want to know what happens to the other IP packets (non-routing protocol packets) when a routing loop has occurred, you should know that the packets continue to get passed from router to router. IP has its own built-in mechanism to keep packets from traveling a network continually; this is called the TTL (Time to Live) field. Before an IP packet is transmitted by a host, the TTL field is set to a value between 1 and 255. This value is operating system-independent and common values are between 32 and 128. As a packet is received by a router, the router decrements the TTL by 1. If the TTL becomes 0, the routers discard the IP packet and send an ICMP message back to the sender to inform the host. Chapter 8, "TCP/IP Suite Error and Control Messages," discusses ICMP in greater detail. For several reasons, this keeps IP packets from indefinitely traveling a network and includes routing loops.

Eliminating Routing Loops Through Split Horizon

Another possible source for a routing loop occurs when incorrect information that has been sent back to a router contradicts the correct information that the router originally distributed. The following process explains how this problem occurs:

1. Router A, shown in Figure 7-5, passes a routing update to Router B and Router D indicates that Network 1 is down. However, Router C has not yet converged and transmits an update to Router B, indicating incorrectly that Network 1 is available at a distance of four by way of Router D.

2. Because Router C has not converged and sends out updates about its route to Network 1, Router B will incorrectly conclude that Router C has a valid path to Network 1, although at a much less favorable metric. Router B sends an update to Router A to advise Router A of the new route to Network 1.

3. Router A now determines that it can send information to Network 1 by way of Router B. Router B determines that it can send information to Network 1 by way of Router C, and Router C determines that it can send information to Network 1 by way of Router D. Any packet introduced into this environment loops between the routers.

4. Split horizon attempts to avoid this situation by eliminating these routing loops. Using the split horizon rule, if a routing update for Network 1 arrives from Router A indicating that Network 1 is down, then Router B and Router D cannot send information about Network 1 back to Router A, as in Figure 7-5. Using the split horizon rule, Router C eventually receives the update about Network 1 being down, and Router C correctly converges, and the routing loop is eliminated. *Split horizon* thus reduces incorrect routing information and reduces routing overhead.

Figure 7-5 Split Horizon

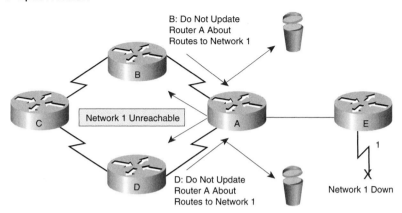

Video and Animation Split Horizon

In this video, you learn how routers use split horizon to prevent routing loops.

Route Poisoning

Route poisoning or split horizon with poison reverse is used by various distance vector protocols to overcome large routing loops and offer explicit information when a subnet or network is not accessible. Route poisoning is usually accomplished by setting the hop count to one more than the maximum.

Poison reverse is another way of avoiding routing loops. Its rule states:

> Once you learn of a route through an interface, advertise it as unreachable back through that same interface. The idea is that it is better to explicitly tell a router to ignore a route than to not tell the router about the route in the first place.

Assume that the routers in Figure 7-6 have poison reverse enabled. When Router One learns about Network A from Router Two, it advertises Network A as unreachable through its link to Routers Two and Three. Router Three, if it shows any path to Network A through Router One, removes that path because of the unreachable advertisement. EIGRP combines these two rules to help prevent routing loops.

Figure 7-6 Route Poisoning

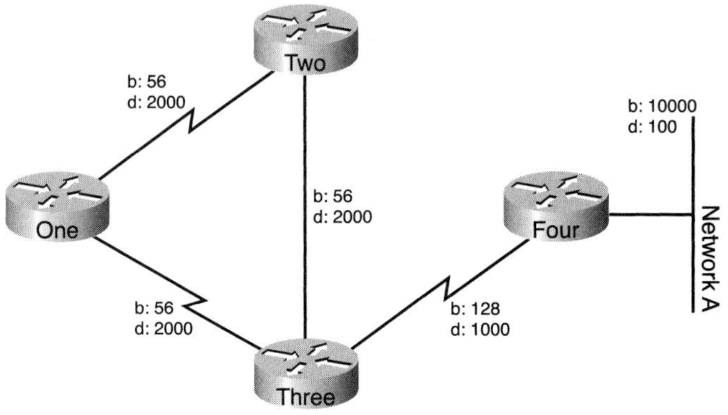

EIGRP uses split horizon or advertises a route as unreachable when

■ Two routers are in startup mode (exchanging topology tables for the first time)

■ Advertising a topology table change

■ Sending a query

When route poisoning is used with triggered updates, it will speed up convergence time because neighboring routers do not have to wait 30 seconds (when using RIP) before advertising the poisoned route. Route poisoning causes a routing protocol to advertise infinite-metric routes for a failed route. Route poisoning does not break split-horizon rules. Split horizon with poison reverse is essentially route poisoning, but specifically placed on links that split horizon would not normally allow routing information to flow across. In either case, the result is that failed routes are advertised with infinite metrics.

Avoiding Routing Loops with Triggered Updates

New routing tables are usually sent to neighboring routers on a regular basis. RIP updates occur every 30 seconds. However, a *triggered update* is sent immediately in response to some change in the routing table. The router that detects a topology change immediately sends an update message to adjacent routers. Those routers then generate triggered updates, notifying their adjacent neighbors of the change. When a route fails, an update is sent, rather than waiting on the update timer to expire. The use of triggered updates, in conjunction with route poisoning, ensures that all routers know of failed routes before any holddown timers can expire.

A triggered update is an update that is sent without waiting for the update timer to expire. The router immediately sends another routing update on its other interfaces, rather than waiting for the routing update timer to expire. This action causes the updated information about the status of the route to be forwarded and starts the holddown timers more rapidly on the neighboring routers. This wave of updates is transmitted throughout the network. Figure 7-7 demonstrates this principle.

Figure 7-7 Triggered Updates

Router C issues a triggered update, announcing that network 10.4.0.0 is unreachable. Upon receipt of this information, Router B announces that network 10.4.0.0 is down through interface S0/1. In turn, Router A sends out an update through interface Fa0/0.

Preventing Routing Loops with Holddown Timers

A count to infinity problem can be avoided by using holddown timers. The correct sequence for this procedure is as follows:

1. When a router receives an update from a neighbor indicating that a previously accessible network is now inaccessible, the router marks the route as inaccessible and starts a holddown timer. If an update is received from the same neighbor before the holddown timer expires indicating that the network is again accessible, the router marks the network as accessible and removes the holddown timer.

2. If an update arrives from a different neighboring router with a better metric than that originally recorded for the network, the router marks the network as accessible and removes the holddown timer.

3. If at any time before the holddown timer expires, an update is received from a different neighboring router with a poorer metric, the update is ignored. Ignoring updates under these conditions allows more time for the knowledge of a disruptive change to travel through the entire network, as Figure 7-8 shows.

Figure 7-8 Holddown Timers

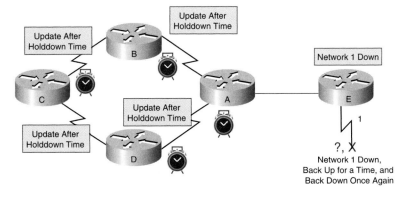

Video and Animation   Holddown Timers

In this video, you learn how holddown timers are used when routing updates are sent.

RIP

Routing Information Protocol (RIP) was originally specified in RFC 1058 in 1988. Its key characteristics include the following:

- It is a distance vector routing protocol.

- Hop count is used as the metric for path selection (see Figure 7-9).

- If the hop count is greater than 15, the packet is discarded.

- By default, *routing updates* are broadcast every 30 seconds.

Note in Figure 7-9 that the 19.2-kbps path between the two hosts using the top routers is 2 hops. The lower alternate path using the three T-1 links is 4 hops. Because RIP path selection is based solely on the number of hops, in this case, RIP path selection chooses the 19.2-kbps link instead of the much faster T1 links.

Figure 7-9 RIP Uses Hop Count as Its Metric

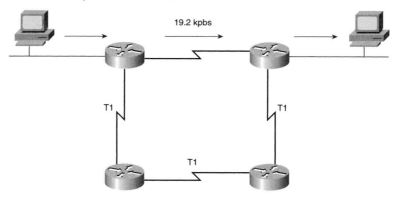

RIP Routing Process

RIP has evolved over the years from a classful routing protocol, RIP Version 1 (RIPv1), to a classless routing Protocol, RIP Version 2 (RIPv2). RIPv2 enhancements include the following:

- Capability to carry additional packet routing information

- Authentication mechanism to secure table updates

- Capability to support subnet masks

RIP prevents routing loops from continuing indefinitely by implementing a limit on the number of hops allowed in a path from the source to a destination. The maximum number of hops allowed in a path is 15. When a router receives a routing update that contains a new or changed entry, the metric value is increased by one. If this causes the metric to be incremented beyond 15, it is considered to be infinity, and the network destination is considered unreachable. RIP includes a number of features that are common in other routing protocols. For example, RIP implements split horizon with poison reverse and holddown mechanisms to prevent incorrect routing information from being propagated.

Configuring RIP

The **router rip** command enables RIP as the routing protocol. The network command is then used to tell RIP which directly connected networks the router will advertise using RIP. The routing process then associates these interfaces with the network addresses and begins sending RIP updates and listening for RIP updates on these interfaces.

Most routing protocols use a combination of time-driven and event-driven updates. RIP is time-driven, but the Cisco implementation of RIP sends triggered updates whenever a change is detected. Topology changes also trigger immediate updates in IGRP routers, regardless of the update timer. Without triggered updates, RIP and IGRP will not perform to their full efficiency because triggered updates will allow for faster convergence, which also will reduce the likelihood of routing loops.

When a router receives a routing update that includes changes to an entry, it updates its routing table to reflect the new route. The metric value for the path is increased by one, and the source interface of the update is indicated as the next hop in the route. RIP routers maintain only the best route to a destination; however, RIP routers can maintain multiple routes to the same destination if those routes have the same metric.

After updating its routing table due to a configuration change, the router immediately begins transmitting routing updates to inform other network routers of the change. These updates are sent independently of the regularly scheduled updates that RIP routers forward. If the update is sent out to an interface on a different major network than the receiving interface, then RIP advertises only the classful network or major class network address. In other words, subnetted information is not summarized to the major network address if the update is sent out an interface that is on the same major network. Classful routing protocols such as RIP do not send the subnet mask with the routing update.

To enable RIP, use the commands in Table 7-1, beginning in global configuration mode.

Table 7-1 Commands to Enable RIP

Command	Purpose
Router(config)#**router rip**	Enables a RIP routing process, which then switches to the router configuration mode
Router(config-router)#**network** *network-number*	Associates a network with a RIP routing process

The following commands show the process of enabling RIP and specifying directly connected networks.

```
BHM(config)#router rip
! selects RIP as the routing protocol
BHM(config-router)#network 1.0.0.0
! specifies a directly connected network)
BHM(config-router)#network 2.0.0.0
! specifies a directly connected network
```

The Cisco router interfaces that are connected to networks 1.0.0.0 and 2.0.0.0 send and receive RIP updates. These routing updates enable the router to learn the network topology from neighboring routers also running RIP.

Only the classful or major network address is used with the RIP **network** command. If one or more interfaces are subnetted, only a single **network** command with the classful network address is used. If a subnetted address is used, the IOS converts it to the classful address, which can be seen with **show running-config**.

 Lab 7.2.2 Configuring RIP

In this lab, you set up an IP addressing scheme using Class C networks and configure RIP on all routers.

Using the ip classless Command

Sometimes, a router receives packets destined for an unknown subnet of a network that has directly connected subnets. To forward these packets to the best supernet route possible, use the **ip classless** global configuration command. The **ip classless** command is enabled by default in Cisco IOS Software Release 11.3 and later. To disable this feature, use the no form of this command.

When this feature is disabled and a packet is being sent to a subnet of a network that has no network default route, the router discards the packet. Figure 7-10 illustrates this principle. If the host sends a packet to 128.20.4.1 and no network default route exists, the router discards the packet.

IP classless affects only the operation of the forwarding processes in IOS. IP classless does not affect the way the routing table is built. This degree of impact is the essence of classful routing. If part of a major network is known and the destination subnet toward which the packet is destined is unknown, the packet is dropped.

Figure 7-10 No IP Classless Routing

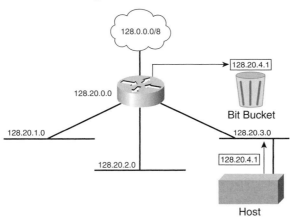

The most confusing aspect of this rule is that the router uses the default route only if the major network destination does not exist in the routing table. By default, a router assumes that all subnets of a directly connected network are present in the routing table. If a packet is received with an unknown destination address within an unknown subnet of an attached network, the router assumes that the subnet does not exist. Therefore, the router drops the packet, even if a default route exists. Configuring **ip classless** on the router resolves this problem by instructing the router to ignore the classful boundaries of the networks in its routing table and simply route to the default route, as Figure 7-11 demonstrates.

Figure 7-11 IP Classless

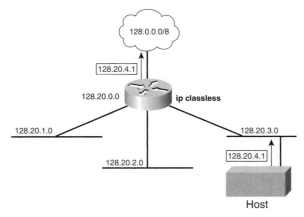

Common RIP Configuration Issues

RIP routers must rely on neighboring routers for network information. RIP uses a distance vector routing algorithm. All distance vector routing protocols have problems that result in slow convergence.

Some of these issues include routing loops and counting to infinity. These problems both result in inconsistencies due to routing update messages with outdated routes being propagated around the internetwork.

To reduce routing loops and counting to infinity, RIP uses the following methods:

- Split horizon
- Poison reverse
- Holddown timer
- Triggered updates

Some of these methods might require some configuration, while others do not require or rarely require configuration.

RIP permits a maximum hop count of 15. Any destination greater than 15 hops away is tagged as unreachable. The maximum hop count for RIP greatly restricts its use in large internetworks, but prevents a problem called count to infinity from causing endless network routing loops.

The split horizon rule is based on the fact that it is usually not useful to send information about a route back in the direction from which the route came. In some network configurations, it might be necessary to disable split horizon. It is disabled on a per-interface basis.

To disable **split horizon**, use the following command:

```
Router(config-if)# no ip split-horizon
```

The holddown timer is another mechanism that might need some changes. Holddown timers help prevent counting to infinity but also increase convergence time. The default holddown for RIP is 180 seconds. This holddown prevents any inferior route from being updated, but might also prevent a valid alternative route from being installed. The holddown timer can be decreased to speed up convergence, but take such action with caution. The ideal solution is to set the timer just longer than the longest possible update time for the internetwork. In Figure 7-12, the loop consists of four routers. With each router having an update time of 30 seconds, the longest loop possible is 120 seconds. Therefore, the holddown timer should be set to slightly more than 120 seconds.

Figure 7-12 Holddown Timers

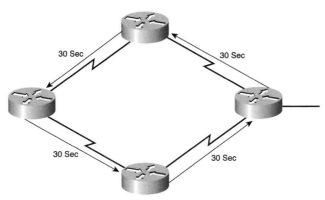

To change the holddown timer, use the **timers basic** *update invalid holddown flush* [*sleep-time*] command, where the arguments are specified in seconds. For example, to change the update for IGRP to 30 seconds, you also must change the other timers, as demonstrated in the following command line.

```
Router(config-router)#timers basic 30 90 100 300
```

One additional item that affects convergence and can be configured is the update interval. By default, Cisco IOS Software runs IP RIP updates every 30 seconds. This time can be reconfigured for longer intervals to conserve bandwidth or for a shorter interval to decrease convergence time.

As discussed earlier in this chapter, another issue with routing protocols is the unwanted advertisement of routing updates out a particular interface. When a **network** command is issued, RIP sends advertisements out all interfaces within that network address range. To control the set of interfaces that exchanges routing updates, the network administrator can disable the sending of routing updates on specified interfaces by configuring the **passive-interface** command. RIP will continue to listen for RIP updates on that interface, but it will not send any RIP updates.

Because RIP is a broadcast protocol, the network administrator might have to configure RIP to exchange routing information in a nonbroadcast network such as Frame Relay. In this type of network, RIP needs to be informed of other neighboring RIP routers. To define a neighboring router with which to exchange routing information, use the following **neighbor** command:

```
Router(config-router)#neighbor ip address
```

By default, the software receives RIP-1 and RIP-2 packets, but sends only RIP-1 packets. The network administrator can configure the router to receive and send only RIP-1 packets or to send only RIP-2 packets. To configure the router to send and receive packets from only one version, use the commands in the router configuration mode as specified in Table 7-2.

Table 7-2 Specifying the RIP Version

Command	Purpose
(config-router)#**version {1 | 2 }**	Configures the software to receive and send only RIPv1 or RIPv2 packets.
(config-if)#**ip rip send version 1**	Configures an interface to send only RIPv1 packets.
(config-if)#**ip rip send version 2**	Configures an interface to send only RIPv2 packets.
(config-if)#**ip rip send version 1 2**	Configures an interface to send only RIPv1 or RIPv2 packets.

To control how packets received from an interface are processed, use the following commands described in Table 7-3.

Table 7-3 Controlling Packets

Command	Purpose
(config-if)#**ip rip receive version 1**	Configures an interface to accept only RIPv1 packets.
(config-if)#**ip rip receive version 2**	Configures an interface to accept only RIPv2 packets.
(config-if)#**ip rip receive version 1 2**	Configures an interface to accept either RIPv1 or RIPv2 packets.

Verifying RIP Configuration

Several commands can be used to verify that RIP is properly configured. Two of the most commonly used commands are **show ip route** and **show ip protocols**.

The **show ip protocols** command outputs information about all the IP routing protocols configured on the router, as demonstrated in Example 7-1. This output can be used to verify most, if not all, of the RIP configuration. Some of the most common configuration items to verify are the following:

- That RIP is configured
- That the correct interfaces are sending and receiving RIP updates
- That the correct RIP version is being sent and received
- That the router is advertising the correct networks

Example 7-1 show ip protocols *Command Output*

```
GAD# show ip protocols
Routing Protocol is "rip"
! Line above verifies that RIP is configured
  Sending updates every 30 seconds, next due in 5 seconds
  Invalid after 180 seconds, hold down 180, flushed after 240
  Outgoing update filter list for all interfaces is
  Incoming update filter list for all interfaces is
  Redistributing: rip
  Default version control: send version 1, receive any version
! Line above verifies the RIP version
    Interface         Send  Recv  Triggered RIP  Key-chain
! Line above verifies RIP interfaces
    FastEthernet0/0  1     1 2
    Serial0/0        1     1 2
  Routing for Networks:
    192.168.1.0
    192.168.2.0
! Lines above verify networks being advertised
  Routing Information Sources:
    Gateway         Distance      Last Update
    192.168.2.2         120       00:00:11
  Distance: (default is 120)
```

The **show ip route** command can be used to verify that the routes received by RIP are being installed in the routing table, as Example 7-2 shows. Examine the output of the command and look for RIP routes, signified by "R." Remember that the network takes some time to converge, so the routes might not appear immediately.

Example 7-2 show ip route *Command Output*

```
GAD# show ip route
Codes: C - connected, S - static, I - IGRP, R - RIP, M - mobile, B - BGP
       D - EIGRP, EX - EIGRP external, O - OSPF, IA - OSPF inter area
       N1 - OSPF NSSA external type 1, N2 - OSPF NSSA external type 2
       E1 - OSPF external type 1, E2 - OSPF external type 2, E - EGP
       i - IS-IS, L1 - IS-IS level-1, L2 - IS-IS level-2, ia - IS-IS inter area
       * - candidate default, U - per-user static route, o - ODR
```

continues

Example 7-2 show ip route *Command Output (Continued)*

```
        P - periodic downloaded static route


Gateway of last resort is not set


C    192.168.1.0/24 is directly connected, FastEthernet0/0
C    192.168.2.0/24 is directly connected, Serial0/0
R    192.168.3.0/24 [120/1] via 192.168.2.2, 00:00:07, Serial0/0
! line above verifies RIP routes received
```

The last entry, beginning with the letter *R*, indicates that network 192.168.3.0 was learned from RIP and it can be reached via adjacent router (next hop) interface 192.168.2.2, which is remotely attached to this router's Serial 0/0 interface.

Additional commands you can use to check RIP configuration are as follows:

- **show interface** *interface*
- **show ip interface** *interface*
- **show running-config**

These commands are useful when it is necessary to find out information about a particular interface. Using the **show interface** command displays all information about an interface, including whether it is up or down and what type of protocol, IP address, or encapsulation type might be configured on the interface. Basically, these commands provide an administrator with all the configuration information that is available about a particular interface. The **show running-config** command, however, is used to show the current configuration on the router and all its interfaces. Recall that a Cisco router runs each protocol separately from other protocols. For this reason including the **ip** in the **show ip interface** command is necessary to list specifically just IP information regarding the specific interface.

Troubleshooting RIP Update Issues

Most of the RIP configuration errors involve an incorrect **network** statement, discontinuous subnets, or split horizon. The primary tool for finding RIP update issues is the **debug ip rip** command.

The **debug ip rip** command displays RIP routing updates as they are sent and received. Figure 7-13 and Example 7-3 demonstrate a router using **debug ip rip** and receiving an update.

Figure 7-13 RIP Network for Debugging

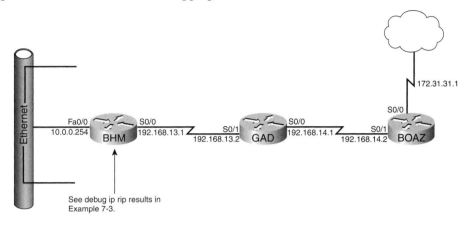

Example 7-3 debug ip rip *Output*

```
BHM# debug ip rip
RIP event debugging is on
BHM#
00:45:36 RIP:received v1 update from 192.168.13.2 on Serial0/0
00:45:36     192.168.14.0 in 1 hop
00:45:36     172.31.0.0 in 2 hops
00:45:36     172.29.0.0 in 15 hops
00:45:36 RIP sending v1 update to 255.255.255.255 via Serial0/0 (192.168.13.1)
00:45:36     network 10.0.0.0, metric 1
00:45:36 RIP sending v1 update to 255.255.255.255 via FastEthernet0/0
 (10.0.0.254)
00:45:36     network 192.168.13.0 metric 1
00:45:33     network 192.168.14.0 metric 2
00:45:33     network 172.31.0.0 metric 3
00:45:36     network 172.29.0.0 metric 16
```

The router sends update information out the two RIP interfaces. The output shows the router is using RIPv1 and broadcasts the update (address 255.255.255.255). The number in parentheses represents the source address encapsulated into the IP header of the RIP update.

You can look for several problems in the **debug ip rip** output. A couple of the problems that you can diagnose are discontiguous subnetworks or duplicate networks. A symptom of these problems is a routing protocol's advertising a network route with a metric that is less than the metric received for that network.

Example 7-4 shows the output of the **debug ip rip** command.

Example 7-4 **debug ip rip** *Command Output*

```
BMH# debug ip rip
RIP event debugging is on
BHM#
7w2d: RIP: received v1 update from 192.168.13.2 on serial0/0
7w2d:        192.168.14.0 1 hop
7w2d:        172.31.0.0 in 2 hops
7w2d:    RIP: sending v1 update to 255.255.255.255 via Serial0/0 (192.168.13.1)
7w2d:        network 172.31.0.0 metric 1
7w2d:    RIP: sending v1 update to 255.255.255.255 via FastEthernet0/0
  (10.0.0.254)
7w2d:        192.168.13.0 metric 1
7w2d:        192.168.14.0 metric 2
```

Additionally, you can use the following commands to troubleshoot RIP:

- **show ip rip database**—Used to display the contents of the private database when triggered extensions to RIP are enabled.

- **show ip protocols** {**summary**}—Used to display IP routing protocol information.

- **show ip route**—Used to show the IP routing table on the router.

- **debug ip rip** {**events**}—Used to display the RIP information the router is processing across the prompt for an administrator to see.

- **show ip interface brief**—Lists a summary of an interface's IP information and status in privileged EXEC mode. The **brief** parameter is an option that displays a brief summary of IP status and configuration.

All of these commands provide information that can be helpful when troubleshooting a router.

 Lab 7.2.6   Troubleshooting RIP

In this lab, you set up an IP addressing scheme using Class B networks and configure RIP on the routers. You observe routing activity using the **debug ip rip** command and examine routes using the **show ip route** command.

Preventing Routing Updates Through an Interface

Using the **passive-interface** command can prevent routers from sending routing updates through a router interface. Keeping routing update messages from being sent through a router interface prevents other systems on that network from learning about routes dynamically. As illustrated in Figure 7-14, Router E uses the **passive-interface** command to keep routing updates from being sent:

```
RouterE(config-router)# passive-interface Fa0/0
```

Figure 7-14 Defining a Passive Interface

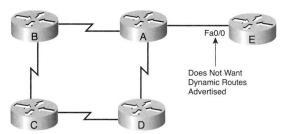

For RIP and IGRP, the **passive-interface** command stops the router from sending updates to a particular neighbor, but the router continues to accept and utilize routing updates from that neighbor. Keeping routing update messages from being sent through a router interface prevents other systems on the interface from learning about routes dynamically.

Lab 7.2.7 Preventing Routing Updates Through an Interface

In this lab, you prevent routing updates through an interface to regulate advertised routes and observe the results. You use the **passive-interface** command and add a default route.

Load Balancing with RIP

Load balancing is a concept that allows a router to take advantage of multiple best paths to a given destination. These paths are derived either statically or with a dynamic protocol such as RIP.

RIP is capable of load balancing over as many as six equal-cost paths using the **maximum-paths** *num-paths* router command. Load balancing over four paths is the default. RIP performs what is referred to as *round robin* load balancing, which means that RIP takes turns forwarding packets over the parallel paths. The default for most interfaces is Fast Switching, using the interface command **ip route-cache**. Load balancing is distributed according to the destination IP address. Given two paths to the same network, all packets for one destination IP address will travel over the first path, all packets for a second destination will travel over the second path, all packets for the third destination will again travel over the first path, and so on, for a given flow of packets. The **no ip route-cache** command must be used to enable process switching to see the load balancing. This is discussed in more detail later in this chapter.

Figure 7-15 shows an example of RIP routes with four equal-cost paths. The router starts with an interface pointer to the interface connected to Router 1. Then the interface pointer cycles through the interfaces and routes in a deterministic fashion, such as 1-2-3-4-1-2-3-4-1, and so on. Because the metric for RIP is hop count, no regard is given to the speed of the links. Therefore, the 56-kbps path handles as much traffic between the two networks as the 155-Mbps path when process switching is enabled on the interface.

Figure 7-15 Load Balancing RIP

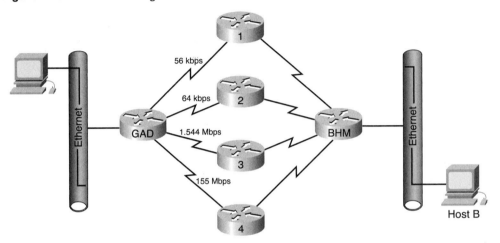

Equal-cost routes can usually be found by using the **show ip route** command. Example 7-5 is a display of the output for **show ip route** to a particular subnet with multiple routes.

Example 7-5 *Verifying Equal-Cost Routes via* **show ip route** *Command Output*

```
RouterC# show ip route 192.168.2.0
Routing entry for 192.168.2.0/24
  Known via "rip", distance 120, metric 1
  Redistributing via rip
  Last update from 192.168.4.2 on FastEthernet0/0, 00:00:18 ago
  Routing Descriptor Blocks:
    192.168.4.1, from 192.168.4.1, 00:02:45 ago, via FastEthernet0/0
      Route metric is 1, traffic share count is 1
  * 192.168.4.2, from 192.168.4.2, 00:00:18 ago, via FastEthernet0/0
      Route metric is 1, traffic share count is 1
```

Notice there are two routing descriptor blocks. Each block is one route. Also, an asterisk (*) is next to one of the block entries. This asterisk corresponds to the active route that is used for new traffic.

Load Balancing Across Multiple Paths

Load balancing describes the capability of a router to transmit packets to a destination IP address over equal-cost multiple paths. Load balancing is a concept that allows a router to take advantage of multiple paths to a given destination. The paths are derived either statically or with dynamic protocols, such as RIP, Enhanced IGRP (EIGRP), Open Shortest Path First (OSPF), and IGRP. Figure 7-16 shows an example of load balancing.

Figure 7-16 Load Balancing

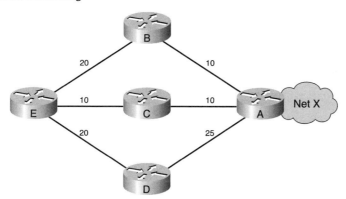

When a router learns of multiple routes to a specific network through multiple routing processes or routing protocols, it installs the route with the lowest administrative distance into the routing table. Sometimes, the router must choose from many routes provided by the same routing process with the same administrative distance. In this case, the router chooses the path with the lowest cost or metric to the destination. Each routing process calculates its cost differently, and the costs might need to be manually configured to achieve load balancing.

If the router receives and installs multiple paths with the same administrative distance and cost to a destination, load balancing can occur. Cisco IOS Software imposes a six equal-cost routes limit on the routing table, but some Interior Gateway Protocols (IGPs) set their own limitations. For example, EIGRP allows up to four equal-cost routes.

By default, most IP routing protocols install a maximum of four parallel routes in a routing table. Static routes always install six routes. The exception is the exterior routing protocol Border Gateway Protocol (BGP), which by default allows only one path to a destination.

The number of maximum paths ranges from one to six paths. To change the maximum number of parallel paths allowed in a routing table, use the following command while in router configuration mode:

```
Router(config-router)#maximum-paths maximum
```

IGRP and EIGRP allow for multiple, unequal cost paths to a given network. IGRP and EIGRP can load balance up to six unequal links. RIP networks must have the same hop count to load balance, whereas IGRP uses bandwidth to determine how to load balance.

In Figure 7-16, there are three ways to access Network X:

- E to B to A with a metric of 30
- E to C to A with a metric of 20
- E to D to A with a metric of 45

Router E chooses the second path, E to C to A with a metric of 20, which is a lower cost than 30 and 45. If two or more of the paths had the same metric, load balancing could occur.

When routing IP, Cisco IOS Software offers two methods of load balancing:

- Per-packet load balancing
- Per-destination load balancing

If process switching is enabled, the router alternates paths on a per-packet basis. If Fast Switching is enabled, only one of the alternate routes is cached for the destination address, so all packets in the packet stream bound for a specific host take the same path. Packets bound for a different host on the same network might use an alternate route, in which case traffic is load balanced on a per-destination basis.

Video and Animation   Administrative Distance

Administrative distance is used by routers to select the best route for a data packet. In this video, default administrative distances for static and various routing protocols are presented. You see how a router chooses which route a packet takes in a network using multiple protocols based on their administrative distances.

Lab 7.2.9   Load Balancing Across Multiple Paths

In this lab, you configure load balancing across multiple paths with RIP, and then you observe the load balancing process.

Integrating Static Routes with RIP

Static routes are user-defined routes that force packets to take a specified path to their destination. Static routes become very important if Cisco IOS Software cannot build a route to a particular destination. They are also useful for specifying a "gateway of last resort," which all packets without a more specific route are sent through.

A router running RIP can receive a default network address through an update from another router running RIP. Another option is for the router to generate the default network itself.

The static routes can be removed using the **no ip route** global configuration command. The administrator can override a dynamic route with static routing information using administrative distance values. Each dynamic routing protocol has a default administrative distance, which allows the static route to act as a backup for the dynamic route in the event that it fails.

Static routes that point to an interface are not advertised via RIP. For administrative distance purposes only, static routes that point to an interface are considered to be connected, but they do not lose their static nature. If a static route is assigned to an interface that is not one of the networks defined in a **network** command, no dynamic routing protocols advertise the route unless a **redistribute static** command is specified for these protocols.

When an interface goes down, all static routes through that interface are removed from the IP routing table. Additionally, when the software can no longer find a valid intermediate address for the address specified as the forwarding address for a router in a static route, the static route is removed from the IP routing table.

A static route is one that is specifically entered by an administrator so that the router specifically knows the route to a destination. A dynamic route is one that is learned by the router using the various routing protocol standards. In this case, it is not guaranteed that the router knows the route to the intended destination.

To configure a static route, use the following command in global configuration mode:

```
Router(config)#ip route prefix mask {address | interface} [distance]
```

In Figure 7-17, a floating static route is configured in the GAD router to take the place of the RIP route in the event that the RIP route fails.

Figure 7-17 RIP with Floating Static Routes

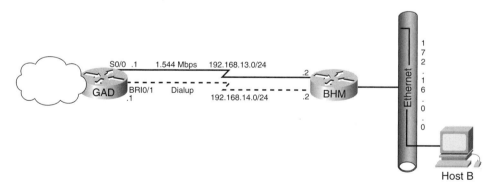

Example 7-6 shows the floating static route being added with an administrative distance of 130. The floating static route is configured by declaring an administrative distance (130), which is greater than the administrative distance (AD) of RIP (120). A router chooses the best route based on AD. A router always chooses a manually configured static route over a dynamically learned route because the static route always has a lower AD. Static routes have an AD of 1 by default. By configuring the floating static route with an AD of 130, the router chooses the dynamically learned RIP route with the lower AD of 120. Again, the router uses the floating static route if the dynamically learned RIP route fails.

Keep in mind, that after the static route to network 172.16.0.0 through 192.168.14.2 is entered, the routing table does not show it. Only the dynamic route learned through RIP is present. This is because the administrative distance (AD) of 130 is higher for the floating static route, and unless the RIP route through S0/0 goes down, the static route is not installed in the routing table.

Example 7-6 *Floating Static Route*

```
GAD# configure terminal
GAD(config)# ip route 172.16.0.0 255.255.0.0 192.168.14.2 130
GAD(config)# ^z
GAD# show ip route
Codes: C - connected, S - static, I - IGRP, R - RIP, M - mobile, B - BGP
       D - EIGRP, EX - EIGRP external, O - OSPF, IA - OSPF inter area
       N1 - OSPF NSSA external type 1, N2 - OSPF NSSA external type 2
       E1 - OSPF external type 1, E2 - OSPF external type 2, E - EGP
       i - IS-IS, L1 - IS-IS level-1, L2 - IS-IS level-2, ia - IS-IS inter area
       * - candidate default, U - per-user static route, o - ODR
       P - periodic downloaded static route


Gateway of last resort is not set


C    192.168.13.0/24 is directly connected, Serial0/0
C    192.168.14.0/24 is directly connected, BRI0/1
R    172.16.0.0/16 [120/1] via 192.168.13.2, 00:00:24, Serial0/0
```

Notice that the static route is treated like a dynamic route because the AD of the RIP route (120) is lower than the AD of the backup floating static route (130). It starts with an *R* instead of an *S* because the **redistribute static** command is configured on the GAD router. Recall that when configuring a floating static route or a static route, the **redistribute static** command redistributes the static routes, so if the primary RIP route fails, the other routers begin to see the remote networks advertised from the GAD router.

IGRP

Like RIP, *Interior Gateway Routing Protocol (IGRP)* is a distance vector routing protocol. Unlike RIP, IGRP is a Cisco-proprietary protocol rather than a standards-based protocol. While remaining very simple to implement, IGRP is a more complex routing protocol than RIP, and it is able to use a number of factors to determine the best route to a destination network. This section introduces IGRP configuration and troubleshooting as well as the following IGRP topics:

- IGRP features
- IGRP metrics
- IGRP routes
- IGRP stability features
- Configuring IGRP
- Migrating RIP to IGRP
- Verifying IGRP configuration
- Troubleshooting IGRP

IGRP Features

IGRP is a distance vector IGP. Distance vector routing protocols mathematically compare routes by measuring distances. This measurement is known as the distance vector. Routers using distance vector protocols must send all or a portion of their routing table in a routing update message at regular intervals to each of their neighboring routers. As routing information proliferates through the network, routers can perform the following functions, among others:

- Identify new destinations
- Learn of failures

IGRP is a distance vector routing protocol developed by Cisco. IGRP sends routing updates at 90-second intervals, advertising networks for a particular autonomous system. Key design characteristics of IGRP are as follows:

- The versatility to automatically handle indefinite, complex topologies
- The flexibility needed to segment with different bandwidth and delay characteristics
- Scalability for functioning in very large networks

NOTE

Several sources incorrectly include MTU as a metric used by IGRP and EIGRP. MTU has never been used as a routing metric for either of these routing protocols.

By default, the IGRP routing protocol uses bandwidth and delay as metrics. Additionally, IGRP can be configured to use a combination of variables to determine a composite metric. Those variables include

- Bandwidth
- Delay
- Reliability
- Load

Interactive Media Activity   Checkbox: RIP Versus IGRP

After completing this activity, you will understand RIP and IGRP.

Video and Animation   IGRP Overview

In this video, you learn how IGRP routers route traffic.

IGRP Metrics

The **show ip protocols** command displays parameters, filters, and network information concerning the routing protocols in use on the router. You need this information to define the value of the K1–K5 metrics and provide information concerning the maximum hop count to calculate the composite metric for IGRP, which is figured as follows:

Metric = [K1 · Bandwidth + (K2 · Bandwidth)/(256 – Load) + K3 · Delay] · [K5/(Reliability + K4)]

The metric K1 represents bandwidth, and the metric K3 represents delay. By default, the values of the metrics K1 and K3 are set to 1, while K2, K4, and K5 are set to 0.

The default constant values are K1 = K3 = 1 and K2 = K4 = K5 = 0. If K5 = 0, the [K5/(reliability + K4)] term is not used. So, given the default values for K1 through K5, the composite metric calculation used by IGRP reduces to

Metric = Bandwidth + Delay.

The K values in these formulas are constants that can be defined using the following router configuration command:

```
metric weights tos k1 k2 k3 k4 k5
```

To find the bandwidth, find the smallest of all the bandwidths from outgoing interfaces and divide 10,000,000 by that number. (The bandwidth is scaled by 10,000,000 in kilobits per second.) To find the delay, add all the delays from the outgoing interfaces and divide this number by 10. (The delay is in tens of microseconds.) Remember, the path with the smallest metric is the best path.

This composite metric is more accurate than RIP's hop count metric when choosing a path to a destination. The path that has the smallest metric value is the best route.

IGRP's metric includes the following components:

- **Bandwidth**—The lowest bandwidth value in the path
- **Delay**—The cumulative interface delay along the path
- **Reliability**—The reliability on the link toward the destination as determined by the exchange of keepalives
- **Load**—The load on a link toward the destination based on bits per second

IGRP uses a composite metric, which is calculated as a function of bandwidth, delay, load, and reliability. By default, only the bandwidth and delay characteristics are considered; the other parameters are considered only if enabled via configuration. Delay and bandwidth are not measured values, but are set via the **delay** and **bandwidth** interface commands. The **show ip route** command in Example 7-7 shows the IGRP metric values in brackets. The first number represents the administrative distance, and the second number is the calculated metric value. A link with a higher bandwidth has a lower metric, and a route with a lower cumulative delay has a lower metric.

Example 7-7 **show ip route** *Command Output Reveals IGRP Metric Values*

```
RouterA# show ip route
Codes: C - connected, S - static, I - IGRP, R - RIP, M - mobile, B - BGP
       D - EIGRP, EX - EIGRP external, O - OSPF, IA - OSPF inter area
       N1 - OSPF NSSA external type 1, N2 - OSPF NSSA external type 2
       E1 - OSPF external type 1, E2 - OSPF external type 2, E - EGP
       i - IS-IS, L1 - IS-IS level-1, L2 - IS-IS level-2, ia - IS-IS inter area
       * - candidate default, U - per-user static route, o - ODR
       P - periodic downloaded static route


Gateway of last resort is not set

C    192.168.1.0/24 is directly connected, FastEthernet0/0
C    192.168.2.0/24 is directly connected, Serial0/0
I    192.168.3.0/24 [100/80135] via 192.168.2.2, 00:00:30, Serial0/0
```

IGRP Routes

IGRP advertises three types of routes:

- *Interior routes* are routes between subnets of a network attached to a router interface. If the network attached to a router is not subnetted, IGRP does not advertise interior routes.

NOTE

Today, IGRP is showing its age; it lacks support for variable- length subnet masks (VLSMs). Rather than develop an IGRP version 2 to correct this problem, Cisco has built upon IGRP's legacy of success with Enhanced IGRP (EIGRP).

- *System routes* are routes to networks within an autonomous system. Cisco IOS Software derives system routes from directly connected network interfaces and system route information provided by other IGRP-speaking routers or access servers. System routes do not include subnet information.

- *Exterior routes* are routes to networks outside the autonomous system that are considered when identifying a gateway of last resort. Cisco IOS Software chooses a gateway of last resort from the list of exterior routes that IGRP provides. The software uses the gateway (router) of last resort if a better route is not found and the destination is not a connected network. If the autonomous system has more than one connection to an external network, different routers can choose different exterior routers as the gateway of last resort.

IGRP Stability Features

IGRP has a number of features that are designed to enhance its stability, such as

- Holddowns
- Split horizon with poison reverse
- Poison reverse updates

Holddowns are used to prevent regular update messages from inappropriately reinstating a route that might not be up. When a router goes down, neighboring routers detect this status via the lack of regularly scheduled update messages.

Split horizon is derived from the premise that it is usually not useful to send information about a route back in the direction from which it came. The split horizon rule helps prevent routing loops.

Split horizon prevents routing loops between adjacent routers, but *poison reverse updates* are necessary to defeat larger routing loops. Generally speaking, increases in routing metrics indicate routing loops. Poison reverse updates then are sent to remove the route and place it in holddown. With IGRP, poison reverse updates are sent only if a route metric has increased by a factor of 1.1.

IGRP also maintains a number of timers and variables containing time intervals that include the following:

- *Update timer*—Specifies how frequently routing update messages are sent. The IGRP default for this variable is 90 seconds.

- *Invalid timer*—Specifies how long a router waits in the absence of routing-update messages about a specific route before declaring that route invalid. The IGRP default for this variable is three times the update period.

- *Hold-time timer*—Specifies the amount of time for which information about poorer routes is ignored. The IGRP default for this variable is three times the update timer period plus 10 seconds.

■ *Flush timer*—Indicates how much time passes before a route is flushed from the routing table. The IGRP default is seven times the routing update timer.

Example 7-8 shows the output from the **show ip protocols** command. Notice the line that indicates the IGRP is running and its metric values.

Example 7-8 *IGRP Routing Statistics*

```
RouterB# show ip protocols
Routing Protocol is "igrp 101"
  Sending updates every 90 seconds, next due in 51 seconds
  Invalid after 270 seconds, hold down 280, flushed after 630
  Outgoing update filter list for all interfaces is
  Incoming update filter list for all interfaces is
  Default networks flagged in outgoing updates
  Default networks accepted from incoming updates
  IGRP metric weight K1=1, K2=0, K3=1, K4=0, K5=0
  IGRP maximum hopcount 100
  IGRP maximum metric variance 1
  Redistributing: igrp 101
  Routing for Networks:
    192.168.2.0
    192.168.3.0
  Routing Information Sources:
    Gateway         Distance      Last Update
    192.168.2.1          100      00:00:54
  Distance: (default is 100)
```

Configuring IGRP

To configure the IGRP routing process, use the **router igrp** global configuration command:

```
RouterA(config)# router igrp as-number
```

To shut down an IGRP routing process, use the **no** form of this command.

```
RouterA(config)# no router igrp as-number
```

The autonomous system number is one that identifies the IGRP process. This is not a true autonomous system number, but a process-id. This number does not have to be a real AS number assigned by ARIN, or a number in the private AS range. It is significant only within the IGRP routing domain, and needs to be the same on all routers that want to share IGRP routing information. It is also used to tag the routing information.

To specify a list of networks for IGRP routing processes, use the **network** router configuration command:

```
RouterA(config)# router igrp 101
RouterA(config-router)# network 192.168.1.0
```

To remove an entry, use the **no** form of the command:

```
RouterA(config)# no router igrp 101
RouterA(config-router)# no network 192.168.1.0
```

Example 7-9 demonstrates how to configure IGRP using AS 101 on RouterA and RouterB.

Example 7-9 *Configuring IGRP*

```
RouterA(config)# router igrp 101
RouterA(config-router)# network 192.168.1.0
RouterA(config-router)# network 192.168.2.0
RouterB(config)# router igrp 101
RouterB(config-router)# network 192.168.2.0
RouterB(config-router)# network 192.168.3.0
```

As with RIP, with IGRP only the classful or major network address is used with the IGRP **network** command. If one or more interfaces are subnetted, only a single **network** command with the classful network address is used. If a subnetted address is used, IOS converts it to the classful address, which can be seen with **show running-config**.

Lab 7.3.5 Configuring IGRP

In this lab, you set up an IP addressing scheme using Class C networks, and you configure IGRP on all routers.

Migrating RIP to IGRP

With the creation of IGRP in the early 1980s, Cisco Systems was the first company to solve the problems associated with using RIP to route datagrams between interior routers. IGRP determines the best path through the internetwork by examining the bandwidth and delay of the networks between routers. IGRP converges faster than RIP, thereby avoiding the routing loops caused by disagreement over the next routing hop to be taken. In addition, IGRP does not share the hop count limitation of RIP. As a result of this and other improvements over RIP, IGRP enabled many large, complex, topologically diverse internetworks to be deployed.

These are the steps to follow to convert from RIP to IGRP.

Step 1 Enter **show ip route** to verify that RIP is the routing protocol on the routers to be converted, as shown in Examples 7-10 and 7-11.

Example 7-10 *Verifying Existing Routing Protocol for RouterA*

```
RouterA# show ip route
Codes: C - connected, S - static, I - IGRP, R - RIP, M - mobile, B - BGP
       D - EIGRP, EX - EIGRP external, O - OSPF, IA - OSPF inter area
       N1 - OSPF NSSA external type 1, N2 - OSPF NSSA external type 2
       E1 - OSPF external type 1, E2 - OSPF external type 2, E - EGP
       i - IS-IS, L1 - IS-IS level-1, L2 - IS-IS level-2, ia - IS-IS inter area
       * - candidate default, U - per-user static route, o - ODR
       P - periodic downloaded static route

Gateway of last resort is not set

C    192.168.1.0/24 is directly connected, Loopback0
C    192.168.2.0/24 is directly connected, Serial0/0
R    192.168.3.0/24 [120/1] via 192.168.2.2, 00:01:09, Serial0/0
```

Example 7-11 *Verifying Existing Routing Protocol for RouterB*

```
RouterB# show ip route
Codes: C - connected, S - static, I - IGRP, R - RIP, M - mobile, B - BGP
       D - EIGRP, EX - EIGRP external, O - OSPF, IA - OSPF inter area
       N1 - OSPF NSSA external type 1, N2 - OSPF NSSA external type 2
       E1 - OSPF external type 1, E2 - OSPF external type 2, E - EGP
       i - IS-IS, L1 - IS-IS level-1, L2 - IS-IS level-2, ia - IS-IS inter area
       * - candidate default, U - per-user static route, o - ODR
       P - periodic downloaded static route

Gateway of last resort is not set

R    192.168.1.0/24 [120/1] via 192.168.2.1, 00:00:28, Serial0/0
C    192.168.2.0/24 is directly connected, Serial0/0
C    192.168.3.0/24 is directly connected, FastEthernet0/0
```

Step 2   Configure IGRP on RouterA and RouterB, as shown in Example 7-12.

Example 7-12 *Configuring IGRP on RouterA and RouterB*

```
RouterA#configure terminal
RouterA(config)#router igrp 101
```

continues

Example 7-12   *Configuring IGRP on RouterA and RouterB (Continued)*

```
RouterA(config-router)#network 192.168.1.0
RouterA(config-router)#network 192.168.2.0
RouterB#configure terminal
RouterB(config)#router igrp 101
RouterB(config-router)#network 192.168.2.0
RouterB(config-router)#network 192.168.3.0
```

Step 3   Enter **show ip protocols** on RouterA and RouterB.

Step 4   Enter **show ip route** on RouterA and RouterB to verify the change has been made.

Lab 7.3.6   Default Routing with RIP and IGRP

In this lab, you configure a default route and use RIP to propagate this default information to other routers. When you have this configuration working, you must migrate the network from RIP to IGRP and configure default routing to work with that protocol as well.

Verifying IGRP Configuration

To verify that IGRP has been configured properly, enter the **show ip route** command and look for IGRP routes signified by an I.

Additional commands for checking IGRP configuration are as follows:

- **show interface** *interface*—Verifies that the Ethernet interface is properly configured.
- **show running-config**—Verifies that IGRP is enabled on the router.
- **show running-config interface** *interface*—Verifies that the proper IP address has been used.
- **show running-config | begin interface** *interface*—Verifies that IGRP is running on the router's interfaces starting at a specific interface.
- **show running-config | begin igrp**—Verifies that IGRP is enabled on the router.
- **show ip protocols**—Verifies that IGRP is enabled on the router.

To verify that the Ethernet interface is properly configured, enter the s**how interface fa0/0** command. Example 7-13 illustrates the output.

Example 7-13 show interface *Command Output*

```
RouterA# show interface fa0/0
FastEthernet0/0 is up, line protocol is up
  Hardware is AmdFE, address is 0009.7c89.5620 (bia 0009.7c89.5620)
  Internet address is 192.168.1.1/24
--- Output Omitted ---
```

To see if IGRP is enabled on the router, use the commands demonstrated in Example 7-14.

Example 7-14 show ip protocols and show running-config *Command Output*

```
RouterA# show ip protocols
Routing Protocol is "igrp 101"
---Output Omitted ---


RouterA# show running-config | begin igrp
router igrp 101
 network 192.168.1.0
 network 192.168.2.0
!
--- Output Omitted ---
```

To check for proper IP addresses, use the command demonstrated in Example 7-15.

Example 7-15 show running-config interface *Command Output*

```
RouterA# show running-config interface fa0/0
Building configuration...


Current configuration:
!
interface FastEthernet0/0
 ip address 192.168.1.1 255.255.255.0
 no ip directed-broadcast
end
```

Example 7-16 illustrates the output from the **show ip route** command and displays the routes available via this router's interfaces.

Example 7-16 **show ip route** *Command Output*

```
RouterA# show ip route
Codes: C - connected, S - static, I - IGRP, R - RIP, M - mobile, B - BGP
       D - EIGRP, EX - EIGRP external, O - OSPF, IA - OSPF inter area
       N1 - OSPF NSSA external type 1, N2 - OSPF NSSA external type 2
       E1 - OSPF external type 1, E2 - OSPF external type 2, E - EGP
       i - IS-IS, L1 - IS-IS level-1, L2 - IS-IS level-2, ia - IS-IS inter area
       * - candidate default, U - per-user static route, o - ODR
       P - periodic downloaded static route


Gateway of last resort is not set


C    192.168.1.0/24 is directly connected, Loopback0
C    192.168.2.0/24 is directly connected, Serial0/0
I    192.168.3.0/24 [100/80135] via 192.168.2.2, 00:01:00, Serial0/0
```

Troubleshooting IGRP

Most IGRP configuration errors involve a mistyped network statement, discontiguous subnets, or an incorrect autonomous system number.

The following commands are useful when troubleshooting IGRP:

- **show ip protocols**—Used to display IP routing protocol information in summary form. This command is also used to check for bad routing information.

- **show ip route**—Used to show the IP routing table on the router.

- **debug ip igrp events**—Displays information about summary IGRP routing that is running on the network.

- **debug ip igrp transactions**—Shows message requests from neighbor routers asking for an update and the broadcasts sent from the originating router towards that neighbor router.

- **ping**—A utility used to determine whether a specific IP address is accessible.

- **traceroute**—A utility that traces a packet from your computer to an Internet host, showing how many hops the packet requires to reach the host and how long each hop takes.

Example 7-17 illustrates output from a **debug ip igrp events** command.

Example 7-17 **debug ip igrp events** *Command Output*

```
RouterA# debug ip igrp events
IGRP event debugging is on

00:21:38: IGRP: sending update to 255.255.255.255 via FastEthernet0/0 (192.168.1
  .1)
00:21:38: IGRP: Update contains 0 interior, 2 system, and 0 exterior routes.
00:21:38: IGRP: Total routes in update: 2
00:21:38: IGRP: sending update to 255.255.255.255 via Serial0/0 (192.168.2.1)
00:21:38: IGRP: Update contains 0 interior, 1 system, and 0 exterior routes.
00:21:38: IGRP: Total routes in update: 1
```

Example 7-18 illustrates output from a **debug ip igrp transactions** command.

Example 7-18 **debug ip igrp transactions** *Command Output*

```
RouterA# debug ip igrp transactions
IGRP protocol debugging is on

00:22:17: IGRP: received update from 192.168.2.2 on Serial0/0
00:22:17:       network 192.168.3.0, metric 80135 (neighbor 110)
00:23:07: IGRP: sending update to 255.255.255.255 via FastEthernet0/0 (192.168.1
  .1)
00:23:07:       network 192.168.2.0, metric=80125
00:23:07:       network 192.168.3.0, metric=80135
00:23:07: IGRP: sending update to 255.255.255.255 via Serial0/0 (192.168.2.1)
00:23:07:       network 192.168.1.0, metric=110
```

If it is discovered that the wrong AS number is being used, correcting it as in Example 7-19 results in the corrected output.

Example 7-19 **debug ip igrp transactions**

```
RouterA(config)# no router igrp 102
RouterA(config)# router igrp 101
RouterA(config-router)# network 192.168.1.0
RouterA(config-router)# network 192.168.2.0
```

continues

Example 7-19 **debug ip igrp transactions** *(Continued)*

```
00:27:50: IGRP: broadcasting request on FastEthernet0/0
00:27:50: IGRP: sending update to 255.255.255.255 via FastEthernet0/0
  (192.168.1.1)
00:27:51: IGRP: Update contains 0 interior, 0 system, and 0 exterior routes.
00:27:51: IGRP: Total routes in update: 0 - suppressing null
00:28:01: IGRP: sending update to 255.255.255.255 via FastEthernet0/0
  (192.168.1.1)
00:28:01:        network 192.168.2.0, metric=80125
00:28:01:        network 192.168.3.0, metric=80135
00:28:01: IGRP: Update contains 0 interior, 2 system, and 0 exterior routes.
00:28:01: IGRP: Total routes in update: 2
00:28:01: IGRP: sending update to 255.255.255.255 via Serial0/0 (192.168.2.1)
00:28:01:        network 192.168.1.0, metric=110
00:28:01: IGRP: Update contains 0 interior, 1 system, and 0 exterior routes.
00:28:01: IGRP: Total routes in update: 1
```

 Lab 7.3.8 Unequal-Cost Load Balancing with IGRP

In this lab, you configure and tune IGRP for unequal-cost load balancing and observe load balancing using **debug** commands.

Summary

In this chapter, you learned the following:

- Routing information is maintained through updates as the topology changes in a network.

- Routing loops occur in a network from alternate routes, slow convergence, and inconsistent routing updates.

- Defining a maximum can be achieved to prevent count to infinity.

- Three methods of preventing routing loops: split horizon, triggered updated, and hold-down timers.

- Route poisoning is used by various distance vector protocols to overcome large routing loops and offer information about when a subnet or network is not accessible.

- To configure routing protocols: RIP and IGRP.

- To use the **ip classless** command.

- To troubleshoot routing protocols: RIP and IGRP.

- To verify routing protocols: RIP and IGRP.

- To configure default routes.

To supplement what you learned in this chapter, refer to the chapter-specific Videos and Interactive Media Activities on the CD-ROM accompanying this book.

Key Terms

adjacent neighbors   Two directly connected routers that participate in the exchange of routing information are said to be *adjacent*.

convergence   The speed and capability of a group of internetworking devices running a specific routing protocol to agree on the topology of an internetwork after a change in that topology.

count to infinity   A problem that can occur in routing algorithms that are slow to converge in which routers continuously increment the hop count to particular networks. Typically, some arbitrary hop-count limit is imposed to prevent this problem.

exterior routes   Routes to networks outside the autonomous system that are considered when identifying a gateway of last resort.

flush timer   Indicates how much time passes before a route is flushed from the routing table. The IGRP default is seven times the routing update timer.

holddowns   Prevent regular update messages from inappropriately reinstating a route that might not be up.

hold-time timer   Specifies the amount of time for which information about better routes is ignored. The IGRP default for this variable is 3 times the update timer period plus 10 seconds.

Interior Gateway Routing Protocol (IGRP)   An IGP developed by Cisco to address the problems associated with routing in large, heterogeneous networks. *Compare with* EIGRP. *See also* IGP, OSPF, and RIP.

interior routes   Routes between subnets of a network attached to a router interface. If the network attached to a router is not subnetted, IGRP does not advertise interior routes.

invalid timer   Specifies how long a router waits in the absence of routing-update messages about a specific route before declaring that route invalid. The IGRP default for this variable is three times the update period.

poison reverse updates   Updates that are necessary to defeat larger routing loops. Generally speaking, increases in routing metrics indicate routing loops. Poison reverse updates are then sent to remove the route and place it in holddown.

Routing Information Protocol (RIP)   An IGP supplied with UNIX BSD systems. The most common IGP in the Internet. RIP uses hop count as a routing metric.

routing metric   A method by which a routing algorithm determines that one route is better than another. This information is stored in routing tables and sent in routing updates. Metrics include bandwidth, communication cost, delay, hop count, load, MTU, path cost, and reliability. Sometimes referred to simply as a metric.

routing table   A table stored in a router or some other internetworking device that keeps track of routes to particular network destinations and, in some cases, metrics associated with those routes.

routing update   A message sent from a router to indicate network reachability and associated cost information. Routing updates are typically sent at regular intervals and after a change in network topology. *Compare with* Flash update.

split horizon   A routing technique in which information about routes is prevented from exiting the router interface through which that information was received. Split-horizon updates are useful in preventing routing loops.

system routes   Routes to networks within an autonomous system. Cisco IOS Software derives system routes from directly connected network interfaces and system route information provided by other IGRP-speaking routers or access servers. System routes do not include subnet information.

triggered update   A triggered update is an update that is sent without waiting for the update timer to expire.

update timer   Specifies how frequently routing update messages are sent. The IGRP default for this variable is 90 seconds.

Check Your Understanding

Complete all the review questions to test your understanding of the topics and concepts in this chapter. Answers are listed in Appendix B, "Check Your Understanding Answer Key."

1. What kind of entries does a router initially refer to?

   A. Entries about networks or subnets that are directly connected

   B. Entries that it has learned about from the Cisco IOS Software

   C. Entries whose IP address and mask information are known

   D. Entries that it has learned about from other routers

2. Which of the following best describes a static route?

   A. A routing table entry that is used to direct frames for which a next hop is not explicitly listed in the routing table

   B. A route that is explicitly configured and entered into the routing table and that takes precedence over routes chosen by dynamic routing protocols

   C. A route that adjusts automatically to network topology or traffic changes

   D. A route that adjusts involuntarily to direct frames within a network topology

3. Which of the following best describes a default route?

   A. A 0.0.0.0/0 routing table entry that is used to direct frames for which a next hop is not explicitly listed in the routing table

   B. A route that is explicitly configured and entered into the routing table

   C. A route that adjusts automatically to network topology or traffic changes

   D. A route that adjusts involuntarily to direct frames within a network topology

4. What are exterior routing protocols used for?

   A. To transmit between nodes on a network

   B. To deliver information within a single autonomous system

   C. To communicate between autonomous systems

   D. To set up a compatibility infrastructure between networks

5. What are interior routing protocols used for?

   A. They are used to set up a compatibility infrastructure between networks.

   B. They are used to communicate between autonomous systems.

   C. They are used to transmit between nodes on a network.

   D. They are used within a single autonomous system.

6. Which of the following is a global task?

    A. Addressing IP network numbers by specifying subnet values

    B. Enabling a routing protocol such as RIP or IGRP

    C. Assigning network/subnet addresses and the appropriate subnet mask

    D. Setting up a routing metric to find the best path to each network

7. What metric does RIP use to determine the best path for a message to travel on?

    A. Bandwidth

    B. Hop count

    C. Varies with each message

    D. Administrative distance

8. You suspect that one of the routers connected to your network is sending bad routing information. What command can you use to check?

    A. router(config)# **show ip route**

    B. router# **show ip route**

    C. router> **show ip protocol**

    D. router(config-router)# **show ip protocol**

9. Why would you display the IP routing table?

    A. To set the router update schedule

    B. To identify destination network addresses and next-hop pairs

    C. To trace where datagrams are coming from

    D. To set the parameters and filters for the router

10. If you want to learn which routing protocol a router was configured with, what command structure should you use?

    A. router> **show router protocol**

    B. router(config)> **show ip protocol**

    C. router(config)# **show router protocol**

    D. router> **show ip protocol**

11. In the following command, what does the last number stand for?
Router (config)# **ip route 2.0.0.0 255.0.0.0 1.0.0.2 5**

    A. The number of hops

    B. The number of routes to the destination

    C. The administrative distance

    D. The destination's reference number in the routing table

12. An administrative distance of 15 indicates which of the following?

    A. The IP address is static.

    B. The IP address is dynamic.

    C. The routing information source is relatively trustworthy.

    D. The routing information source is relatively untrustworthy.

13. If you just added a new LAN to your internetwork and you want to manually add the network to your routing table, what command structure would you use?

    A. router (config)> **ip route 2.0.0.0 255.0.0.0 via 1.0.0.2**

    B. router (config)# **ip route 2.0.0.0 255.0.0.0 1.0.0.2**

    C. router (config)# **ip route 2.0.0.0 via 1.0.0.2**

    D. router (config)# **ip route 2.0.0.0 1.0.0.2 using 255.0.0.0**

CHAPTER 8

TCP/IP Suite Error and Control Messages

Objectives

Upon completion of this chapter, you should be able to answer the following questions:

- What are the important uses of ICMP?

- What are some of the ICMP error message types and how are they identified?

- What are potential causes of specific ICMP error messages and how are they identified?

- What are some of the kinds of ICMP control messages used in networks today?

- What are some of the possible events that can cause ICMP control messages?

Additional Topics of Interest

In addition to the core objective areas, this chapter introduces you to the following topics of interest to networkers:

- ICMP message delivery

- Echo messages

- Miscellaneous error reporting

- Introduction to control messages

- ICMP redirect and change requests

- Clock synchronization and transit time estimation

- Information requests and reply message formats

- Address mask requests

- Router discovery messages

- Router solicitation messages

- Congestion and flow control messages

Key Terms

The following is a list of key terms introduced in this chapter. For your reference, a definition for each term can be found at the end of this chapter.

Internet Control Message Protocol (ICMP)   page 750

Transmission Control Protocol/Internet Protocol (TCP/IP)   page 750

datagram   page 751

ping   page 755

unicast   page 766

broadcast   page 766

multicast   page 767

Now that you have learned about the router configuration process, it is time to learn about Transmission Control Protocol/Internet Protocol (TCP/IP) suite error and control messages. In this chapter, you learn how the Internet Control Message Protocol (ICMP) provides control and message functions. In addition, you learn about potential causes of ICMP error messages and how to identify them.

Please be sure to look at this chapter's associated Videos that you will find on the CD-ROM accompanying this book. These CD elements are designed to supplement the material and reinforce the concepts introduced in this chapter.

Overview of TCP/IP Error Messages

The function of IP is to facilitate network communication between hosts. The design of IP allows for the addressing of hosts and networks. This distinguishes IP from nonroutable protocols that can address individual hosts but that are not designed to make distinctions between networks. IP acceptance is so widespread that, in addition to being the protocol used for data delivery over the Internet, it has become the default internal protocol for small LANs that do not necessarily require routing capabilities.

The limitation of IP is that it is a best-effort delivery system. IP has no mechanism to ensure that the data is delivered regardless of any problems encountered on the network. Data might fail to reach its destination for a variety of reasons, such as hardware failure, improper configuration, or incorrect routing information. If an intermediary device such as a router fails, or if a destination device is disconnected from the network, data cannot be delivered. This is why applications that use IP are typically faster: They don't have the error control or reliable mechanism that TCP has. To help identify these failures, IP uses the *Internet Control Message Protocol (ICMP)*. ICMP notifies the sender of the data that an error occurred in the delivery process.

The following sections review the different types of ICMP error messages and the forms they take. Knowledge of ICMP error messages and an understanding of the potential causes of these messages are essential parts of network troubleshooting.

Internet Control Message Protocol (ICMP)

ICMP is the component of the *Transmission Control Protocol/Internet Protocol (TCP/IP)* protocol stack that addresses IP's failure to ensure data delivery. ICMP does not overcome the unreliability limitation that exists in IP. ICMP simply sends error messages to the sender of the data, indicating that problems occurred with data delivery. Figure 8-1 shows where ICMP resides within the TCP/IP model.

Figure 8-1 ICMP and the TCP/IP Model

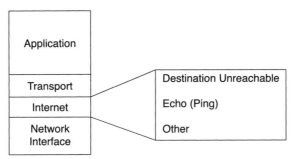

This section covers the various facets of ICMP, including ICMP message delivery, error reporting and correction, and ways of detecting and handling reachability issues.

Error Reporting and Error Correction

ICMP is an error-reporting protocol for IP. When datagram delivery errors occur, ICMP reports these errors to the sender of the datagram. For example, Workstation 1 in Figure 8-2 is sending a datagram to Workstation 6. When the corresponding interface on Router C goes down, Router C uses ICMP to send a message back to Workstation 1 indicating that the datagram could not be delivered. ICMP does not correct the encountered network problem.

In the example from Figure 8-2, ICMP does not attempt to correct the problem with the interface on Router C that is preventing datagram delivery. The only capability of ICMP is to report the errors back to Workstation 1.

Router C will not notify the intermediary devices of the delivery failure. Therefore, Router C will not send ICMP messages to Router A and Router B or to the originating device. Router C also does not know what path the *datagram* has taken to arrive there. Datagrams contain only source and destination IP addresses; they do not contain information about all the intermediary devices. The reporting device has only the sender's IP address with which to communicate. Although Routers A and B are not notified directly, they might become aware of the down interface on Router C. However, disseminating this information to neighbor routers is not the function of ICMP. Instead, ICMP reports on the status of the delivered packet to the sender; its function is not to propagate information about network changes.

Figure 8-2 Error Reporting Being Updated

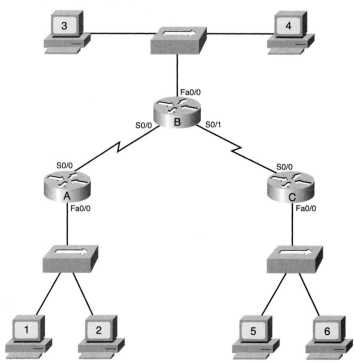

ICMP Message Delivery

ICMP messages are delivered using the IP protocol. ICMP messages are encapsulated into datagrams in the same way that any other data is delivered using IP. Table 8-1 displays the encapsulation of an ICMP packet within the IP packet datagram data area. The frame header can be from a LAN protocol, such as Ethernet, or a WAN protocol, such as HDLC.

Table 8-1 ICMP Encapsulation

Frame header	IP datagram header	ICMP header	ICMP data
Frame header	IP datagram header	IP datagram data area	
Frame header	Frame data area		

Data is encapsulated within a datagram when it reaches the network layer. From there, the datagram and its encapsulated data are encapsulated further into a frame at the data link layer. ICMP messages have their own header information. However, this information, along with the ICMP data, is encapsulated just as any other data is within the datagram. ICMP messages are transmitted in the same way as any other data. Therefore, ICMP messages are subject to the same delivery failures. This creates a scenario in which error reports could generate more error reports, causing increased congestion on an already ailing network. For this reason, errors created by ICMP messages do not generate their own ICMP messages. Therefore, it is possible for a datagram delivery error to occur but never be reported back to the sender of the data.

Unreachable Networks

Network communication depends on certain basic conditions:

- The TCP/IP protocol stack must be properly configured in the sending and receiving devices. This includes the installation of TCP/IP and proper configuration of the IP address and the subnet mask. A default gateway also must be configured if datagrams are to travel outside the local network.

- Intermediary devices must be in place to route the datagram from the source device and its network to the destination network. Routers serve this function.

- A router must have the TCP/IP protocol properly configured on its interfaces, and it must use an appropriate routing protocol or static routes.

If these conditions are not met, network communication cannot take place. For example, the sending device might address the datagram to a nonexistent IP address or to a destination device that is disconnected from its network. Routers also can be points of failure if a connecting interface is down or if the router does not have the information necessary to find the destination network. If a destination network is not accessible, it is said to be an *unreachable network*.

Destination unreachable messages include the following:

- **Network unreachable**—This message usually implies routing or addressing failures.

- **Host unreachable**—This message usually implies delivery failures, such as a wrong subnet mask.

- **Protocol unreachable**—This message usually implies that the destination does not support the upper-layer protocol specified in the packet.

- **Port unreachable**—This message usually implies that the TCP port (socket) is not available.

Figure 8-3 shows a router receiving a packet that it cannot deliver to its ultimate destination. The packet might be undeliverable because there is no known route to the destination. Because there is no known route, the router sends an ICMP host unreachable message to the source.

Figure 8-3 ICMP Host Unreachable

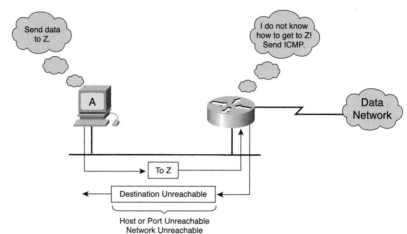

Using ping to Test Destination Reachability

The ICMP protocol can be used to test the availability of a particular destination. Figure 8-4 shows ICMP being used to issue an echo request message to the destination device. When the destination device receives the ICMP echo request, it formulates an echo reply message to send back to the source of the echo request. If the sender receives the echo reply, this confirms that the destination device can be reached using the IP protocol.

Figure 8-4 Echo Request

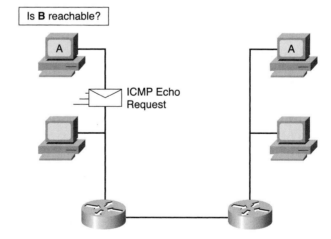

The echo request message typically is initiated using the *ping* command, as demonstrated in Example 8-1. In this example, the command is used with the IP address of the destination device. Example 8-1 and Figure 8-5 show a successful ping or echo request/reply.

Figure 8-5 ICMP ping

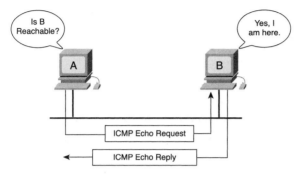

Example 8-1 *Echo Request Initiated by* **ping**

```
C:\> ping 198.133.219.25


Pinging 198.133.219.25 with 32 bytes of data:


Reply from 198.133.219.25: bytes=32 time=30ms TTL=247
Reply from 198.133.219.25: bytes=32 time=20ms TTL=247
Reply from 198.133.219.25: bytes=32 time=20ms TTL=247
Reply from 198.133.219.25: bytes=32 time=20ms TTL=247


Ping statistics for 198.133.219.25:
    Packets: Sent = 4, Received = 4, Lost = 0 (0% loss),
Approximate round trip times in milli-seconds:
    Minimum = 20ms, Maximum =  30ms, Average =  22ms


C:\>
```

More Information: Using **ping** with Destination Device DNS Name, **ping** Success and Failure, and **ping** Return Codes

The **ping** command also can be used as demonstrated in Example 8-2, using the DNS name of the destination device (assuming that DNS is available).

> **More Information: Using ping with Destination Device DNS Name, ping Success and Failure, and ping Return Codes (Continued)**

Example 8-2 *Using* **ping** *with Destination Device DNS Name*

```
C:\> ping www.cisco.com

Pinging www.cisco.com [198.133.219.25] with 32 bytes of data:

Reply from 198.133.219.25: bytes=32 time=30ms TTL=247
Reply from 198.133.219.25: bytes=32 time=20ms TTL=247
Reply from 198.133.219.25: bytes=32 time=20ms TTL=247
Reply from 198.133.219.25: bytes=32 time=20ms TTL=247

Ping statistics for 198.133.219.25:
    Packets: Sent = 4, Received = 4, Lost = 0 (0% loss),
Approximate round trip times in milli-seconds:
    Minimum = 20ms, Maximum =  30ms, Average =  22ms

C:\>
```

In these workstation examples, the **ping** command issues four echo requests and receives four echo replies confirming IP connectivity between the two devices. The output generated by the router **ping** command is somewhat different than the workstation **ping** command. Example 8-3 shows a successful and unsuccessful ping from RouterA to RouterB (IP address 192.168.100.100). The exclamation marks (!) indicate a successful ping, and the periods (.) indicate failure. Table 8-2 shows Cisco ping return codes generated when pinging between Cisco devices.

Example 8-3 *Router* **ping** *Examples: Success and Failure*

```
RouterA# ping 192.168.100.100

Type escape sequence to abort.

Sending 5, 100byte ICMP Echoes to 192.168.100.100, timeout is 2 seconds:
!!!!!

Success rate is 100 percent (5/5), round-trip min/avg/max =  36/36/36 ms

RouterA# ping 192.168.100.100

Type escape sequence to abort.
Sending 5, 100byte ICMP Echoes to 192.168.100.100, timeout is 2 seconds:
. . . . .

Success rate is 0 percent (0/5)
```

More Information: Using **ping** with Destination Device DNS Name, **ping** Success and Failure, and **ping** Return Codes (Continued)		

Table 8-2 Cisco **ping** Return Codes

Code	Meaning	Possible Cause(s)
!	Each exclamation point indicates receipt of an ICMP echo reply.	The ping completed successfully.
.	Each period indicates that the network server timed out while waiting for a reply.	This message can indicate many problems: • The ping was blocked by an access list or firewall. • A router along the path did not have a route to the destination and did not send an ICMP destination unreachable message. • A physical connectivity problem occurred somewhere along the path.
U	An ICMP unreachable message was received.	A router along the path did not have a route to the destination address.
C	An ICMP source quench message was received.	A device along the path—possibly the destination—might be receiving too much traffic; check input queues.
&	An ICMP time exceeded message was received.	A routing loop might have occurred.

Video and Animation   Ping (ICMP)

In this video, you learn how routers can test connectivity using the **ping** command.

Detecting Excessively Long Routes

Several problem situations can occur in network communication. In one situation, a datagram travels in a circle or loop, never reaching its destination. In another situation, no path exists between the source and the destination that conforms to the limitations of the routing protocol. An example of the first situation arises when two routers continually route a datagram back and forth. In this scenario, each router operates with the understanding that the other router should be the next hop to the destination. One potential cause of this problem is faulty routing information. Routing protocols can also have limits on the distance that a packet is allowed to travel. When there are several routers involved, a routing loop is created. In a routing loop, a router sends the datagram to the next hop router and thinks the next hop router will route the datagram to the correct destination. The next hop router then routes the datagram to the next router in the loop until it cycles back to the router on which it originated, thus creating the routing loop. An example of a situation in which no path exists between the source and the destination that conforms to the limitations of the routing protocol is with RIP. RIP has a hop limit of 15, which simply means that the packet is allowed to pass through only 15 routers. If more than 15 routers are present in the routing path, the packet will not reach the destination.

In each of these cases, an excessively long route exists. Whether the actual path includes too many hops or a circular routing path exists, the packet eventually will reach the end of its life. When a packet reaches the end of its life, it has reached its Time-To-Live (TTL). The TTL is a field in the IP packet, shown in Figure 8-6. It has a value that is set by the operating system of the host. For example, Windows XP sets the TTL to 128 by default, whereas some Linux operating systems set the TTL to 64. Each time a router receives that packet, the TTL is decremented by one. If the TTL reaches zero, the router discards the packet. ICMP uses a time exceeded message to notify the source device that the TTL has been exceeded.

Figure 8-6 TTL Field in the IP Packet

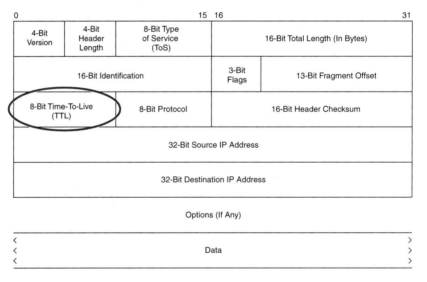

Video and Animation   TTL (ICMP)

In this video, you learn how routers use the Time-To-Live (TTL) field to determine whether to drop the packet.

Echo Messages

As with any type of packet, ICMP messages have special formats. Each ICMP message type shown in Table 8-3 has its own unique characteristics. However, all ICMP message formats start with the following three fields:

- Type
- Code
- Checksum

The Type field indicates the type of ICMP message being sent. The Code field includes further information that is specific to the message type. The Checksum field, as in other types of packets, verifies the integrity of the data.

Table 8-3 ICMP Message Types

ICMP	Message Types
0	Echo reply
3	Destination unreachable
4	Source quench
5	Redirect/change request
8	Echo request
9	Router advertisement
10	Router selection
11	Time exceeded
12	Parameter problem
13	Timestamp request
14	Timestamp reply
15	Information request
16	Information reply
17	Address mask request
18	Address mask reply

Figure 8-7 shows the message format for the ICMP echo request and echo reply messages. The relevant type and code numbers are shown for each message type. The Identifier and Sequence Number fields are unique to the echo request and echo reply messages. The Identifier and Sequence fields are used to match the echo replies to the corresponding echo request. The Data field contains additional information that might be a part of the echo reply or echo request message.

Figure 8-7 Message Format for Echo Request and Echo Reply

0	8	16	31
Type (0 or 8)	Code (0)	Checksum	
Identifier		Sequence Number	
Optional Data			
...			

Destination Unreachable Message

Datagrams cannot always be forwarded to their destinations, as shown in Figure 8-8. Hardware failures, improper protocol configuration, down interfaces, and incorrect routing information are some of the reasons why successful delivery might not be possible. In these cases, ICMP delivers back to the sender a destination unreachable message indicating that the datagram could not be properly forwarded.

Figure 8-8 Destination Unreachable Message

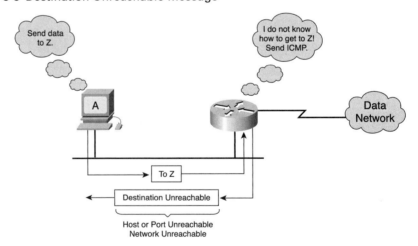

Figure 8-9 shows an ICMP destination unreachable message header. The value of 3 in the Type field indicates that it is a destination unreachable message. The Code value indicates the reason why the packet could not be delivered. The Code value is 0, indicating that the network was unreachable. Table 8-4 displays Code values and description.

Figure 8-9 Destination Unreachable Message Format

0	8	16	31

Type (3)	Code (0-5)	Checksum
Unused (Must be Zero)		
Internet Header + First 64 Bits of Datagram		
...		

Table 8-4 Code Values and Description

Code Value	Description
0	Network unreachable
1	Host unreachable
2	Protocol unreachable
3	Port unreachable
4	Fragmentation needed and DF set
5	Source route failed
6	Destination network unknown
7	Destination host unknown
8	Source host isolated
9	Communication with data network administratively prohibited
10	Communication with data host administratively prohibited
11	Network unreachable for type of service
12	Host unreachable for type of service

A destination unreachable message also might be sent when packet fragmentation is required to forward a packet. Fragmentation is usually necessary when a datagram is forwarded from a Token Ring network to an Ethernet network. If the datagram does not allow fragmentation, the packet cannot be forwarded. Therefore, a destination unreachable message is sent. Destination unreachable messages also can be generated if IP-related services such as FTP or web services are unavailable. To effectively troubleshoot an IP network, it is necessary to understand the various causes of ICMP destination unreachable messages.

Video and Animation   ICMP Destination Unreachable

In this video, you learn how routers send ICMP messages to unreachable destinations.

Miscellaneous Error Reporting

Devices that process datagrams might not be capable of forwarding a datagram due to an error in the header parameter. This error does not relate to the state of the destination host or network, but it still prevents the datagram from being processed and delivered. Due to this prevention, the datagram is discarded. In this case, an ICMP Type 12 parameter problem message is sent to the source of the datagram. Figure 8-10 shows the parameter problem message header.

The parameter problem message includes the Pointer field in the header. When the Code value is 0, the Pointer field indicates the octet of the datagram that produced the error.

Figure 8-10 Parameter Problem Message Format

0	8	16	31
Type (12)	Code (0-2)	Checksum	
Pointer		Unused (Must be Zero)	
Internet Header + First 64 Bits of Datagram			
...			

Overview of TCP/IP Suite Control Messages

The Internet Control Message Protocol (ICMP) is an integral part of the TCP/IP protocol suite. In fact, all IP implementations must include ICMP support. The reasons for this are simple. First, because IP does not guarantee delivery, it has no inherent method to inform hosts when errors occur. IP also has no built-in method to provide informational or control messages to hosts. ICMP performs these functions for IP.

Introduction to Control Messages

Unlike error messages, control messages are not the result of lost packets or error conditions that occur during packet transmission. Instead, control messages inform hosts of conditions such as network congestion or the existence of a better gateway to a remote network. ICMP control messages are encapsulated within an IP datagram. ICMP uses IP datagrams to traverse multiple networks.

ICMP uses multiple types of control messages; Table 8-3 listed some of the most common. Many of these control messages are discussed in the following sections.

ICMP Redirect/Change Requests

A common ICMP control message is the ICMP redirect/change request. This type of message can be initiated only by a gateway. All hosts that communicate with multiple IP networks must be configured with a default gateway. This default gateway is the address of a router port connected to the same network as the host. Figure 8-11 displays a host connected to a router that has access to the Internet.

After Host B is configured with the IP address of FastEthernet 0/0 as its default gateway, Host B uses that IP address to reach any network that is not directly connected. Normally, Host B connects to only a single gateway. However, in some circumstances, a host connects to a segment that has two or more directly connected routers. In this case, the host's default gateway might need to use a redirect/change request to inform the host of the best path to a certain network.

Figure 8-11 Redirect Request

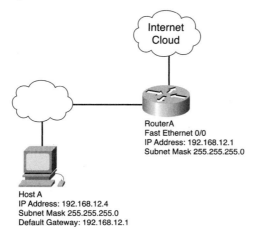

Default gateways send ICMP redirects/change requests only if the following conditions are met:

- The interface on which the packet comes into the router is the same interface on which the packet gets routed out.

- The subnet/network of the source IP address is the same subnet/network of the next-hop IP address of the routed packet.

- The datagram is not source-routed (that is, it is not routed from the place from which the data is taken).

- The route for the redirect is not another ICMP redirect or a default route.

- The router is configured to send redirects. By default, Cisco routers send ICMP redirects. The interface subcommand **no ip redirects** disables ICMP redirects.

The ICMP redirect/change request uses the format shown in Figure 8-12. The request has an ICMP Type code of 5. In addition, the request has a Code value of 0, 1, 2, or 3. The meanings of these code values with their required actions are shown in Table 8-5.

Figure 8-12 Redirect Request Message Format

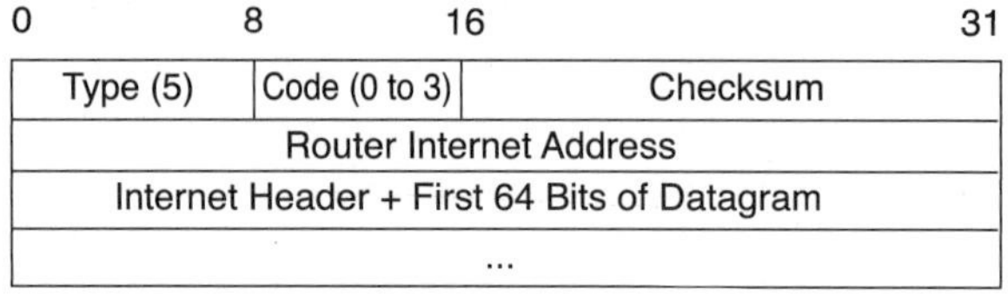

```
0               8               16                              31
┌───────────────┬───────────────┬───────────────────────────────┐
│   Type (5)    │ Code (0 to 3) │          Checksum             │
├───────────────┴───────────────┴───────────────────────────────┤
│                  Router Internet Address                       │
├────────────────────────────────────────────────────────────────┤
│          Internet Header + First 64 Bits of Datagram           │
├────────────────────────────────────────────────────────────────┤
│                              ...                               │
└────────────────────────────────────────────────────────────────┘
```

Table 8-5 Code Value with Required Action

Code Value	Required Action
0	Redirect datagrams for the network
1	Redirect datagrams for the host
2	Redirect datagrams for the type of service and the network
3	Redirect datagrams for the type of service and the host

The receiver of the redirect should use the gateway Internet address in the ICMP redirect as the router IP address when forwarding packets for a particular network. In the example shown in Figure 8-10, the ICMP redirect sent from Router A to Host B would have a gateway Internet address of 192.168.12.2, which is the IP address of Router B.

Clock Synchronization and Transit Time Estimation

The TCP/IP protocol suite allows systems to connect to one another over vast distances through multiple networks. Each individual network provides clock synchronization in its own way. This can result in problems when hosts on different networks try to communicate using software that requires time synchronization. The ICMP timestamp message type is designed to help reduce this problem.

The ICMP timestamp request message allows a host to ask for a remote host's current time. The remote host uses an ICMP timestamp reply message to respond to the request. Figure 8-13 shows the format for an ICMP timestamp request or reply.

Figure 8-13 Timestamp Request

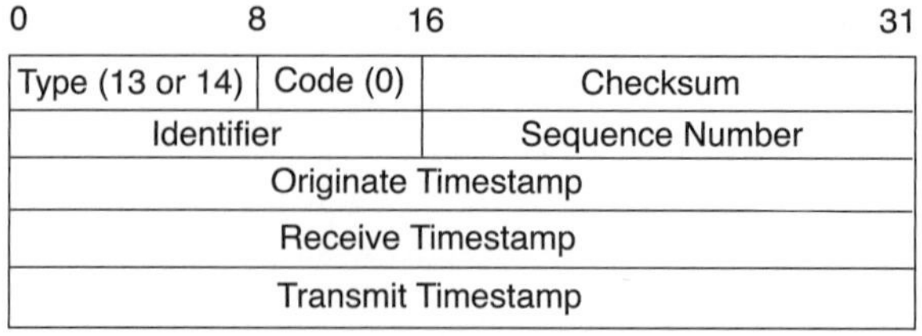

```
0               8               16                              31
┌───────────────┬───────────────┬───────────────────────────────┐
│ Type (13 or 14)│   Code (0)   │          Checksum             │
├───────────────┴───────────────┼───────────────────────────────┤
│          Identifier           │       Sequence Number         │
├────────────────────────────────────────────────────────────────┤
│                    Originate Timestamp                         │
├────────────────────────────────────────────────────────────────┤
│                     Receive Timestamp                         │
├────────────────────────────────────────────────────────────────┤
│                     Transmit Timestamp                        │
└────────────────────────────────────────────────────────────────┘
```

The Type field on an ICMP timestamp message can be either 13 for a timestamp request or 14 for a timestamp reply. The Code field value is always set to 0 because no additional parameters are available. The ICMP timestamp request contains an originate timestamp, which specifies the time on the requesting host just before the timestamp request was sent. The receive timestamp is the time that the destination host received the ICMP timestamp request. The transmit timestamp is filled in just before the ICMP timestamp reply is returned. Originate, receive, and transmit timestamps are computed in milliseconds elapsed since midnight Universal Time (UT).

All ICMP timestamp reply messages contain the originate, receive, and transit timestamps. Using these three timestamps, the host can estimate transmit time across the network by subtracting the originate time from the transmit time. It can also determine transmit time in the return direction by subtracting the transmit time from the current time. By subtracting the originate time from the transit time, the host can try to guess its transit time. However, this is only a guess because the true transit time can vary widely, depending on traffic and congestion on the network. Also, using these three timestamps, the host that originated the ICMP timestamp request can estimate the local time of the remote computer.

ICMP timestamp messages provide a simple way of estimating time on a remote host and the total network transit time. However, this is not the best way to obtain this information. Instead, protocols such as the Network Time Protocol (NTP), at the higher layers of the TCP/IP protocol stack, perform clock synchronization in a more reliable manner.

Information Requests and Reply Message Formats

The ICMP information requests and reply messages originally were intended to enable a host to determine the number of the network that it occupied. Figure 8-14 shows the format for an ICMP information request and reply message.

Figure 8-14 Information Request and Reply Message Format

0	8	16	31
Type (15 or 16)	Code (0)	Checksum	
Identifier		Sequence Number	

Two type codes are available in this message. Type 15 code signifies an information request message. Type 16 code identifies an information reply message. This particular ICMP message type is considered obsolete. Other protocols, such as BOOTP, Reverse Address Resolution Protocol (RARP), and Dynamic Host Configuration Protocol (DHCP), now are used to allow hosts to obtain their network numbers to which they are attached.

Address Mask Requests

When a network administrator uses the process of subnetting to divide a major IP address into multiple subnets, a new subnet mask is created. This new subnet mask is crucial in identifying network, subnet, and host bits in an IP address. If a host does not know the subnet mask, it might send an address mask request to the local router. If the address of the router is known, this request can be sent as *unicast*. If the address is not known, this request is sent using *broadcast*. When the router receives the request, it responds with an address mask reply. This address mask reply identifies the correct subnet mask. For example, assume that a host is located within a Class B network and has an IP address of 172.16.5.3. This host does not know the subnet mask, so it broadcasts an address mask request:

```
Source address        172.16.5.3
Destination address   255.255.255.255
Protocol              ICMP = 1
Type                  Address Mask Request = AM1
Code                  0
Mask                  0
```

This broadcast is received by 168.5.5.1, the local router. That router responds with the address mask reply:

```
Source address         172.16.5.1
Destination address   172.16.5.3
Protocol              ICMP = 1
Type                  Address Mask Reply = AM2
Code                  0
Mask                  255.255.255.0
```

Figure 8-15 shows the frame format for the address mask request. Table 8-6 lists the ICMP address mask request messages. Notice that the same frame format is used for both the address mask request and the reply. However, an ICMP Type number of 17 is assigned to the request, and 18 is assigned to the reply.

Figure 8-15 Address Mask Requests

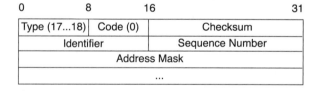

Table 8-6 ICMP Address Mask Request Messages

ICMP Field	Description
Type 17	Address mask request message.
Type 18	Address mask reply message.
Code 0	Address mask request message.
Code 0	Address mask reply message.
Checksum	For computing the checksum, the Checksum field should be 0. The checksum might be replaced in the future.
Identifier	An identifier to aid in matching requests and replies. It can be 0.
Sequence Number	A sequence number to aid in matching requests and replies. It can be 0.
Address Mask	A 32-bit mask. A gateway that received an address mask request should return it with the Address Mask field set to the 32-bit mask of the bits that identify the subnet and network for the subnet on which the request was received. If the requesting host does not know its own IP address, it can leave the source field 0; the reply then should be broadcast. However, this approach should be avoided if at all possible because it increases the superfluous broadcast lead on the network. Even when the replies are broadcast, there is no need to match requests with replies because there is only one possible address mask for a subnet. The Identifier and Sequence Number fields can be ignored. Type AM1 can be received from a gateway or host. Type AM2 can be received from a gateway, or a host acting in lieu of a gateway.

Router Discovery Message

The host can learn the available routers through the process of router discovery when the host has not been manually configured with a default gateway. This process begins with the host sending a *multicast* router-solicitation message to all routers, using the address 224.0.0.2. Figure 8-16 shows the ICMP router-solicitation message. This router solicitation also can be sent using broadcast to include routers that might not be configured for multicasting. RFC 1812 indicates that routers should be capable of supporting the router-discovery process for all the networks that are directly connected. However, this support is not always the case. If a router-solicitation message is sent to a router that does not support the discovery process, the solicitation will go unanswered.

Figure 8-16 Router-Discovery Message

0	8	16 31
Type (9)	Code (0)	Checksum
Number of Addresses	Address Entry Size	Lifetime
Router Address 1		
Preference Level 1		
Router Address 2		
Preference Level 2		

When a router that supports the discovery process receives the router-solicitation message, a router advertisement is sent in return. Table 8-7 provides an explanation for each field of the frame format.

Table 8-7 Router Frame Format

ICMP Field	Description
Type	9 (router advertisement).
Code	0.
Checksum	For computing the checksum, the Checksum field should be 0.
Number of Addresses	The number of router addresses advertised in this message.
Address Entry Size	The number of 32-bit words of information per each router address. This is 2 in the version of the protocol described here.
Lifetime	The maximum number of seconds that the router addresses are considered valid.
Router Addresses	The sending router IP address(es). The number of the address interface from which this message is sent.
Preference Level	Preference Level[i], i = 1..Num Addrs The preference level of each Router Address[i] as a default router address, relative to other router addresses on the same subnet. A signed, twos-complement value; higher values mean more preferable.

Router Solicitation Message

A host generates an ICMP router-solicitation message in response to a missing default gateway. This message is sent using multicast. This message is the first step in the router-discovery process. A local router responds with a router advertisement identifying the default gateway for the local host.

Figure 8-17 identifies the frame format, and Table 8-8 gives an explanation of each field.

Figure 8-17 Router Solicitation Message Frame Format

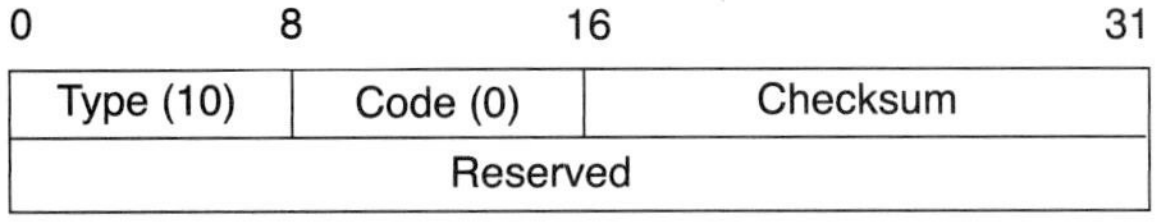

Table 8-8 Router Solicitation Message Frame Field Descriptions

ICMP Field	Description
Type	10.
Code	0.
Checksum	The 16-bit ones complement of the ones-complement sum of the ICMP message, starting with the ICMP type. For computing the checksum, the Checksum field should be 0.
Reserved	32 bits, set as 0; ignored on reception.

Congestion and Flow Control Messages

If multiple computers try to access the same receiver, the receiver can be overcome with traffic. Congestion also can occur when traffic from a high-speed LAN reaches a slower WAN connection. Congestion on the network or the receiver causes dropped packets, which results in a loss of data. To reduce the amount of data lost, ICMP messages must be sent to the source of the congestion. This type of ICMP message is called a *source quench message*. The source quench message notifies the sender of the congestion and asks the sender to reduce the rate at which it is transmitting packets. In most cases, congestion subsides after a short period of time. The source slowly increases the transmission rate as long as no other source quench messages are received. Most Cisco routers do not send source quench messages by default. This is because the source quench message might, in itself, add to the network congestion.

ICMP source quench messages might be used effectively in a small office, home office (SOHO). One such SOHO could consist of four computers networked together using Category 5 cable and Internet connection sharing (ICS) over a 56-kbps modem. It is easy to see that the 10-Mbps bandwidth of the SOHO LAN easily could overwhelm the available 56-kbps bandwidth of the WAN link. This could result in data loss and retransmissions. With

ICMP messaging, the host acting as the gateway in the ICS can request that the other hosts reduce their transmission rates to a manageable level. Reducing the transmission rates prevents continued data loss.

Summary

These key points were discussed in this chapter:

- IP is a best-effort delivery method that uses ICMP messages to alert the sender that the data did not reach its destination.
- ICMP echo request and echo reply messages enable the network administrator to test IP connectivity to aid in the troubleshooting process.
- ICMP messages are transmitted using the IP protocol, so their delivery is unreliable.
- ICMP packets have their own special header information, starting with a Type field and a Code field.
- Functions of ICMP control messages.
- ICMP redirect/change request messages.
- ICMP clock synchronization and transit time estimation messages.
- ICMP information request and reply messages.
- ICMP address mask request and reply messages.
- ICMP router-discovery message.
- ICMP router-solicitation message.
- ICMP congestion and flow-control messages.

To supplement all that you have learned in this chapter, refer to the chapter-specific Videos on the CD-ROM accompanying this book.

Key Terms

broadcast   Data packets that are sent to all nodes on a network.

datagram   In IP networks, packets often are called datagrams.

Internet Control Message Protocol (ICMP)   Network layer Internet Protocol that reports errors and provides other information relevant to IP packet processing. It is documented in RFC 792.

Multicast   Single packets copied by the network and sent to a specific subset of network addresses.

ping (Packet Internet Groper)   ICMP echo message and its reply. Often used in IP networks to test the reachability of a network device.

Transmission Control Protocol/Internet Protocol (TCP/IP)   Common name for the suite of protocols developed by the U.S. Department of Defense in the 1970s to support the construction of worldwide internetworks. TCP and IP are the two best-known protocols in the suite.

unicast   Message sent to a single network destination

Check Your Understanding

Complete all the review questions to test your understanding of the topics and concepts in this chapter. Answers are listed in Appendix B, "Check Your Understanding Answer Key."

1. ICMP is an error-reporting protocol for IP. True or false?

   A. True

   B. False

2. What does ICMP stand for?

   A. Internal Control Message Protocol

   B. Internet Control Message Portal

   C. Internal Control Message Protocol

   D. Internet Control Message Protocol

3. ICMP messages are encapsulated as data in datagrams in the same way that any other data is delivered using IP. True or false?

   A. True

   B. False

4. A default gateway must be configured if datagrams are to travel outside the local network. True or false?

   A. True

   B. False

5. What does TTL stand for?

   A. Time-To-List

   B. Time-To-Live

   C. Terminal-To-Live

   D. Terminal-To-List

CHAPTER 9

Basic Router Troubleshooting

Objectives

Upon completion of this chapter, you should be able to answer the following questions:

- What are some methods of performing basic network testing?

- What are some methods used to examine the routing table?

- How is the **ping** command used to perform basic network connectivity tests?

- How is the **telnet** command used to verify the application layer software between source and destination hosts?

- What are some methods of troubleshooting by testing OSI layers?

- How is the **show interfaces** command used to confirm Layer 1 and Layer 2 problems?

- How are the **show ip route** and **show ip protocol** commands used to identify routing issues?

- How is the **show cdp** command used to verify Layer 2 connectivity?

- How is the **traceroute** command used to identify the path that a packet takes between networks?

- How is the **show controller serial** command used to ensure that the proper cable is attached?

- How are the basic **debug** commands used to show router activity?

Key Terms

The following is a list of key terms introduced in this chapter. For your reference, a definition for each term can be found at the end of this chapter.

network interface card (NIC)   page 786

ping   page 788

Telnet   page 790

keepalive   page 792

traceroute   page 796

This chapter provides an overview of network testing and emphasizes the necessity of using a structured approach to troubleshooting. This chapter also describes the fundamentals of troubleshooting routers.

Please be sure to look at this chapter's associated Interactive Media Activities and Video that you will find on the CD-ROM accompanying this book. These CD elements are designed to supplement the material and reinforce the concepts introduced in this chapter.

Examining the Routing Table

A router might learn about routes to destination networks using a dynamic routing protocol. It might learn about routes when a network administrator configures static routes. The router very likely uses a combination of dynamic and static routing to discover routing information. Whatever the method used for route discovery, when a router determines that a route is the best path to a destination, it installs the route in its routing table. This section describes methods for examining and interpreting the contents of the routing table and covers the following topics:

- The **show ip route** command
- Determining the gateway of last resort
- Determining the route source and destination address
- Determining route administrative distance
- Determining route metric
- Determining route next hop
- Determining last route updates
- Observing multiple paths to destination

The show ip route Command

One of a router's primary functions is to determine the best path to a given destination. A router learns paths, also called routes, from an administrator's configuration or from other routers via routing protocols. They store this routing information in "routing tables" using onboard random-access memory (RAM). A routing table contains a list of the best available routes that routers use to make packet forwarding decisions.

The **show ip route** command displays the contents of the IP routing table. This table contains entries for all known networks and subnetworks, as well as a code that indicates how that information was learned. The additional keywords that can be used with the **show ip route** command are as follows:

- **connected**—Used to show the IP routing table on the router

- **network**—Gives detailed routing information about the specified network

- **rip**—Used to show the IP routing table information related to RIP on the router

- **igrp**—Used to show the IP routing table information related to IGRP on the router

- **static**—Used to show the static IP routing table information on the router

A routing table maps network prefixes to an outbound interface. When RTA receives a packet destined for 192.168.4.46, it looks for the prefix 192.168.4.0/24 in its table. RTA then forwards the packet out an interface (Ethernet0) based on the routing table entry. If RTA receives a packet destined for 10.3.21.5, it sends that packet out Serial 0/0. All routes in the routing table must be resolved to an exit interface. In other words, for any routes using next-hop IP addresses, the router must conduct a second lookup in the routing table on the next-hop IP address to find its directly connected network—its exit interface.

Additionally, RTA drops any packet destined for a network that is not listed in the routing table. To forward to other destinations, the routing table for RTA has to include more routes. These new routes can be added via one of two methods:

- **Static routing**—An administrator manually defines routes to one or more destination networks.

- **Dynamic routing**—Routers follow rules defined by a routing protocol to exchange routing information and independently select the best path.

Administratively defined routes are said to be *static* because they do not change until a network administrator manually programs the changes. Routes learned from other routers are *dynamic* because they can change automatically as neighboring routers update each other with new information. Each method has fundamental advantages and disadvantages.

Lab 9.1.1   Using **show ip route** to Examine Routing Tables

In this lab, you configure RIP and IGRP on routers and then examine the impact on the routing table of multiple routing protocols using the **show ip route** command.

Video   Routing Table

In this video, you learn how a router builds a routing table.

Determining the Gateway of Last Resort

It is not feasible, or even desirable, for a router to maintain routes to every possible destination. Instead, routers keep a default route, or a gateway of last resort. Default routes are used when the router is unable to match a destination network with a more specific entry in the routing table. The router uses the default route to hand off to another router, the gateway of last resort, in an effort to forward the packet.

A key scalability feature is that default routes keep routing tables as small as possible. They make it possible for routers to forward packets destined to any Internet host without having to maintain a table entry for every Internet network. The default route, in many cases, points to the ISP's network. Default routes can be statically entered by an administrator or dynamically learned via a routing protocol.

Default routing begins with the administrator. Before routers can dynamically exchange information, an administrator must configure at least one router with a default route. An administrator can use two very different commands to statically configure default routes:

```
ip route 0.0.0.0 0.0.0.0
ip default-network.
```

The **ip default-network** command establishes a default route in networks using dynamic routing protocols. This command is typically used for IGRP and EIGRP when propagating a default candidate route using one of these routing protocols.

The global command **ip default-network 195.16.11.0** defines the Class C network 195.16.11.0 as the destination path for packets that have no routing table entries. For every network configured with **ip default-network**, if a router has a route to the network, that route is flagged as a candidate for the default route. This command informs only other routers to use this network to forward packets toward when a more specific match does not exist in the routing table. However, the router that has this command configured must have a specific route to the packet's destination address network or a static default route using the **ip route 0.0.0.0 0.0.0.0** command.

Creating an **ip route** to 0.0.0.0/0 is another way to configure a default route:

```
Router(config)# ip route 0.0.0.0 0.0.0.0 [address | interface]
```

This command is commonly used with RIP, EIGRP, and OSPF dynamic routing protocols, along with the **default-information originate** command to propagate this default route to other routers.

After configuring a default route and/or default network, the command **show ip route** shows the following:

```
Gateway of last resort is 172.16.1.2 to network 0.0.0.0
```

If router RTY does not have the network in the routing table, it sends the packet to 172.16.1.2.

 Lab 9.1.2   Gateway of Last Resort

In this lab, you configure RIP routing and add default routes (gateways) to the routers. You remove RIP and the default routes, then configure IGRP routing, and add default routes (gateways) to the routers again.

Determining the Route Source and Destination

For traffic going through a network cloud, path determination occurs at the network layer. The path determination function enables a router to evaluate the available paths to a destination and to establish the preferred handling of a packet. Routing services use network topology information when evaluating network paths. This information can be configured by the network administrator or collected through dynamic processes running in the network.

The network layer provides best-effort, end-to-end packet delivery across interconnected networks. The network layer uses the IP routing table to send packets from the source network to the destination network. After the router determines which path to use, it takes the packet from one interface and forwards it to another interface or port that reflects the best path to the packet's destination.

Determining L2 and L3 Addresses

While network layer (Layer 3) addresses, also known as MAC addresses, are used to get packets from source to destination, it is important to understand that a different type of address is used to get packets from one router to the next. For a packet to get from the source to the destination, both Layer 2 and Layer 3 addresses are used.

The Layer 3 address is used to route the packet from the source network to the destination network. The source and destination IP addresses remain the same. The MAC address (Layer 2) changes at each hop or router. A data link layer address is necessary because the source host must have a way of addressing the next-hop router to which the packets are being forwarded. Also, when the packet is delivered to the intended host on a LAN, the router sends it directly to the host's MAC address.

 Interactive Media Activity   Drag and Drop: L2 and L3 Address

In this activity, you will be able to identify L2 and L3 addresses.

Determining the Route Administrative Distance

One of the intriguing aspects of Cisco routers, especially for those new to routing, is how the router chooses which route is the best among those presented by routing protocols, manual configuration, and various other means.

As each routing process receives updates and other information, it chooses the best path to any given destination and attempts to add this path to the routing table.

The router decides whether or not to add the routes presented by the routing processes based on the administrative distance of the route in question. If a path has the lowest administrative distance to a particular destination, it is added in the routing table; if not, then the route is rejected. Table 9-1 lists the default values for protocols supported by Cisco IOS Software.

Table 9-1 Default Administrative Distances

Route Type	Administrative Distance
Connected	0
Static	1
EIGRP summary route	5
external Border Gateway Protocol (eBGP)	20
EIGRP (internal)	90
IGRP	100
OSPF	110
IS-IS	115
RIP	120
EIGRP (external)	170
internal Border Gateway Protocol (iBGP)	200

Determining the Route Metric

Routing protocols use metrics to determine the best route to a destination. The metric is a value that measures the desirability of a route. Some routing protocols use only one factor to calculate a metric; for example, RIP-1 uses hop count as the only factor to determine the metric of a route. Other protocols base their metric on hop count, bandwidth, delay, load, reliability, and cost. Table 9-2 lists and describes each metric. After routes are chosen based on the best administrative distance, routes are then evaluated for the best metric. Routing protocols use metrics to determine the best route to a destination within a group of routes that all have the same administrative distance.

Table 9-2 Route Metrics

Metric	Description
Hop count	The number of routers that must be traversed to reach a destination. The path with the lowest hop count is preferred.
Bandwidth	The link speed. The path with the greatest bandwidth is preferred.
Delay	The amount of time it takes for a packet to travel a link. The path with the least delay is preferred.

Table 9-2 Route Metrics (Continued)

Metric	Description
Load	The amount of activity on a link. On Cisco routers, the value can typically range anywhere between 1 and 255, where 1 represents a link with the least load and 255 a link with the most load. Paths with the smallest load are preferred.
Reliability	The error rate on a link. On Cisco routers, the value can typically range anywhere between 1 and 255, with 255 representing a link with the highest reliability. Paths with the greatest reliability are preferred.
Cost	An administratively defined metric. Least-cost paths are preferred.

Each routing algorithm interprets what is best in its own way. The algorithm generates a number, called the metric value, for each path through the network. Typically, the smaller the metric number, the better the path.

Factors such as bandwidth and delay are static, in that they remain the same for each interface until the router is reconfigured or the network is redesigned. Factors such as load and reliability are dynamic, meaning that they are calculated for each interface in real time by the router.

The more factors that make up a metric, the greater the flexibility to tailor network operations to meet specific needs. By default, IGRP uses two static factors to calculate a metric value: bandwidth and delay. These two factors can be configured manually, allowing precise control over what routes a router chooses. IGRP can also be configured to include load and reliability, two dynamic factors in the metric calculation. By using dynamic factors, IGRP routers can make decisions based on current conditions. Thus, if a link becomes heavily loaded or unreliable, IGRP increases the metric of routes using that link. Alternate routes might present a lower metric than the downgraded route and are used instead.

IGRP calculates the metric by adding the weighted values of different characteristics of the link to the network in question. These values (bandwidth, bandwidth divided by load, and delay) are weighted with the constants K1, K2, and K3.

> Metric= K1 * Bandwidth + (K2 * Bandwidth)/256 - load) + K3 * Delay

The default constant values are K1=K3=1 and K2=0 so:

If K5 = 0, the [K5/(reliability + K4)] term is not used. Given the default values for K1 through K5, the composite metric calculation used by IGRP reduces to Metric = Bandwidth + Delay.

Interactive Media Activity Drag and Drop: Route Metric

In this activity, you will be able to understand route metric.

Determining the Route Next Hop

Routing algorithms fill routing tables with a variety of information. Destination/next hop associations tell a router that a particular destination can be reached optimally by sending the packet to a particular router representing the "next hop" on the way to the final destination.

When a router receives an incoming packet, it checks the destination address and attempts to associate this address with a next hop.

Determining the Last Routing Update

A network administrator can use the following commands to find the last route update:

- **show ip route**—Used to display the IP routing table on the router.

- **show ip route** *address*—Provides detailed routing information about the specified network.

- **show ip protocols**—Used to display IP routing protocol information.

- **show ip rip database**—Displays the contents of the RIP private database when triggered extensions to RIP are enabled.

The default update time for RIP is 30 seconds and for IGRP is 90 seconds.

Example 9-1 shows the output for the command **show ip route**.

Example 9-1 **show ip route** *Command Output*

```
rt1# show ip route
Codes: C - connected, S - static, I - IGRP, R - RIP, M - mobile, B - BGP
       D - EIGRP, EX - EIGRP external, O - OSPF, IA - OSPF inter area
       N1 - OSPF NSSA external type 1, N2 - OSPF NSSA external type 2
       E1 - OSPF external type 1, E2 - OSPF external type 2, E - EGP
       i - IS-IS, L1 - IS-IS level-1, L2 - IS-IS level-2, ia - IS-IS inter area
       * - candidate default, U - per-user static route, o - ODR
       P - periodic downloaded static route


Gateway of last resort is not set


R    200.200.200.0/24 [120/1] via 192.168.10.2, 00:00:14, Serial0/0
C    192.168.10.0/24 is directly connected, Serial0/0
C    192.168.0.0/24 is directly connected, Loopback0
```

Rt1 has received a RIP update for the network 200.200.200.0 from 192.168.10.2. RIP updates every 30 seconds, and the shaded area is the amount of time since the last update.

Example 9-2 shows the output for the command **show ip route 200.200.200.0**.

Example 9-2 show ip route 200.200.200.0 *Command Output*

```
rt1# show ip route 200.200.200.0
Routing entry for 200.200.200.0/24
  Known via "rip", distance 120, metric 1
  Redistributing via rip
  Last update from 192.168.10.2 on Serial0/0, 00:00:11 ago
  Routing Descriptor Blocks:
  * 192.168.10.2, from 192.168.10.2, 00:00:11 ago, via Serial0/0
      Route metric is 1, traffic share count is 1
Rt1 has received a RIP update for the network 200.200.200.0 from 192.168.10.2.
RIP updates every 30 seconds and the last update was 11 seconds ago.
```

Example 9-3 shows the output for the command **show ip protocols.**

Example 9-3 show ip protocols *Command Output*

```
rt1# show ip protocols
Routing Protocol is "rip"
  Sending updates every 30 seconds, next due in 9 seconds
  Invalid after 180 seconds, hold down 180, flushed after 240
  Outgoing update filter list for all interfaces is
  Incoming update filter list for all interfaces is
  Redistributing: rip
  Default version control: send version 1, receive any version
    Interface        Send  Recv  Triggered RIP  Key-chain
    Serial0/0         1     1 2
    Loopback0         1     1 2
  Routing for Networks:
    192.168.0.0
    192.168.10.0
  Routing Information Sources:
    Gateway          Distance      Last Update
    192.168.10.2          120      00:00:03
  Distance: (default is 120)
```

Example 9-4 shows the output for the command **show ip rip database.**

Example 9-4 **show ip rip database** *Command Output*

```
rt1# show ip rip database
192.168.0.0/24     auto-summary
192.168.0.0/24     directly connected, Loopback0
192.168.10.0/24    auto-summary
192.168.10.0/24    directly connected, Serial0/0
200.200.200.0/24   auto-summary
200.200.200.0/24
[1] via 192.168.10.2, 00:00:20, Serial0/0
```

The highlighted area in the command output shows the last update was received 20 seconds ago.

Lab 9.1.8   Last Route Update

In this lab, you gather information about routing updates and routing protocols to determine the most recent routing table updates.

Observing Multiple Paths to Destination

Some routing protocols support multiple paths to the same destination. Unlike single path algorithms, these multipath algorithms permit traffic over multiple lines, provide better throughput, and are more reliable.

Network Testing

Basic testing of a network should proceed in sequence from one OSI reference model layer to the next, as shown in Figure 9-1.

Figure 9-1 Testing Utilities and the OSI Reference Model

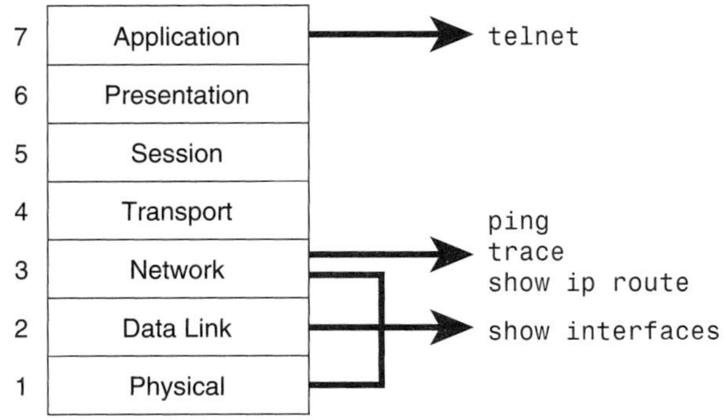

Introduction to Network Testing

Begin with Layer 1 of the OSI model and work up to Layer 7, if necessary. Beginning with Layer 1, look for simple problems such as power cords unplugged at the wall.

Layer 2 issues can include improperly configured serial or Ethernet interfaces, improper clock rate settings on serial interfaces, or network interface card (NIC) problems.

The most common problems that occur on IP networks result from errors in the addressing scheme, which are Layer 3 issues.

The various problems that can occur at all the layers of the OSI model are covered in detail later in this chapter. It is important to test the address configuration before continuing with further configuration steps.

Each test presented in this section focuses on network operations at a specific layer of the OSI model.

Using a Structured Approach to Troubleshooting

Troubleshooting is a process that helps a user to find problems on a network. An orderly process to troubleshooting should be used, based on the networking standards set in place by an administration. Documentation is a very important part of the troubleshooting process. The flowchart in Figure 9-2 shows a recommended logical sequence for troubleshooting network problems.

Figure 9-2 Troubleshooting Methodology

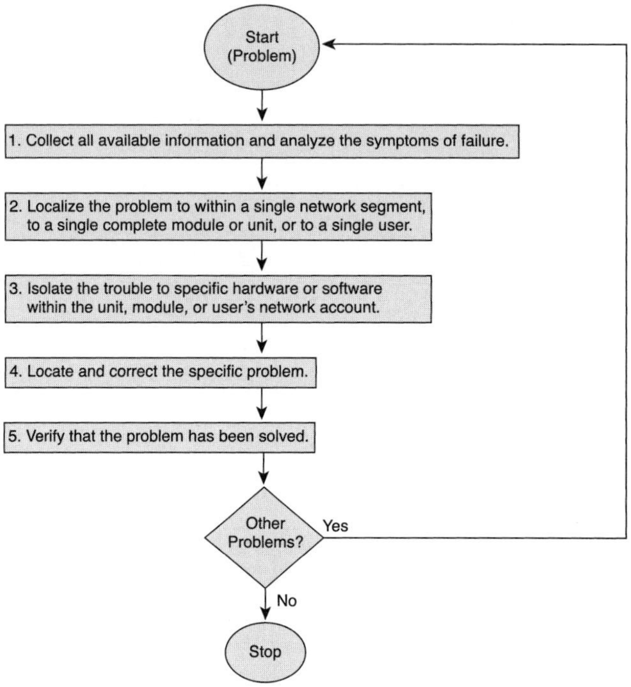

Figure 9-3 shows one approach to troubleshooting network problems.

With a structured approach, members of the network know what each member has completed to solve a problem. If a variety of ideas are used without any organization, the problem solving becomes chaotic. Without a structured approach, very few problems are solved.

The flowcharts in Figure 9-2 and Figure 9-3 are not the only methods of troubleshooting; however, the orderly process is very important to ensure that a network runs smoothly and efficiently.

Figure 9-3 OSI Layer Troubleshooting

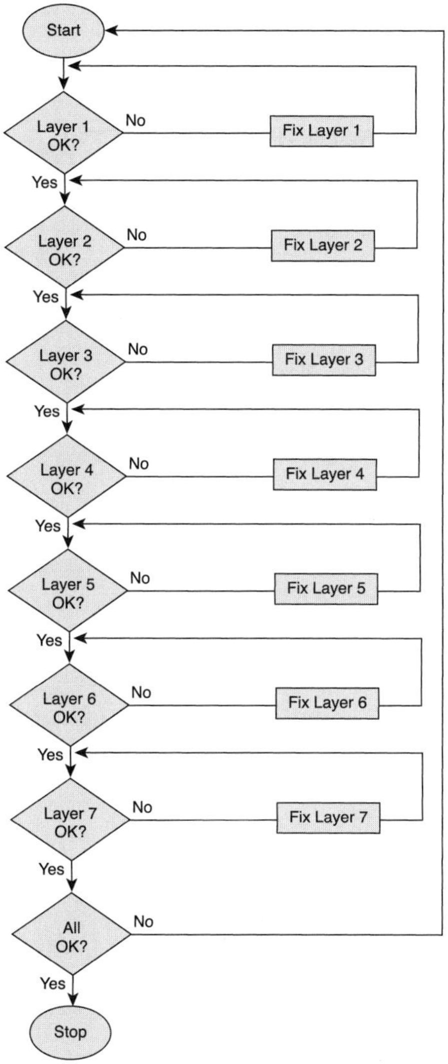

Testing by OSI Layers

Testing should begin with Layer 1 of the OSI model and work to Layer 7, if necessary.

Layer 1 (physical layer) errors can include the following:

- Broken cables
- Disconnected cables
- Cables connected to the wrong ports

- Intermittent cable connection

- Wrong cables used for the task at hand (must use rollovers, crossover cables, and straight-through cables correctly)

- Transceiver problems

- Data communications equipment (DCE) cable problems

- Data terminal equipment (DTE) cable problems

- Devices turned off

After exhausting all Layer 1 problems as possibilities for a network problem, the next step is to investigate Layer 2 problem possibilities.

Layer 2 errors can include the following:

- Improperly configured serial interfaces

- Improperly configured Ethernet interfaces

- Improper encapsulation set (High-Level Data Link Control [HDLC] is default for serial interfaces)

- Improper clock rate settings on serial interfaces

- *Network interface card (NIC)* problems

After exhausting all Layer 2 problems as possibilities for a network problem, the next step is to investigate Layer 3 problem possibilities.

Layer 3 errors can include the following:

- Routing protocol not enabled

- Wrong routing protocol enabled

- Routing protocol incorrectly configured

- Incorrect IP addresses

- Incorrect subnet masks

- Incorrect default gateway

If errors or problems related to connectivity appear on the network, testing through the layers using connectivity tools, such as **ping** or **telnet**, should be the first step in determining the point in the network where the packet gets dropped. The **ping** command can be used at Layer 3 to test connectivity. At Layer 7, the **telnet** command can be used to verify the application layer software between source and destination stations. Both of these commands are discussed in detail later in this chapter.

Interactive Media Activity   Matching: Testing with the OSI Layers

In this activity, you will be able to understand the OSI layers.

Layer 1 Troubleshooting Using Indicators

Indicators are useful tools for troubleshooting. Most interfaces or NICs have indicator lights that show whether there is a valid connection. This light usually is referred to as the *link light*. The interface also might have lights to indicate whether traffic is being sent (TX) or received (RX). If the interface has indicator lights that do not show a valid connection, check for faulty or incorrect cabling. If cabling is correct, power off the device and reset the interface card.

Many indicators are considered Layer 1 problems in a network, including the following:

- Broken cables
- Disconnected cables
- Cables connected to the wrong ports
- Intermittent cable connection
- Wrong cables used for the task at hand
- Transceiver problems
- Devices turned off

A faulty or incorrect cable could result in a link light indicating a bad connection or no link.

Check to make sure that all cables are connected to the appropriate ports. Make sure that all cross-connects are patched properly to the correct location using the appropriate cable and method. Verify that all switch or hub ports are set in the correct VLAN or collision domain, and have appropriate options set for Spanning Tree and other considerations.

Verify that the proper cable is being used. If a direct connection exists between two end systems—for example, between a PC and a router or between two switches—a special crossover cable might be required. Verify that the cable from the source interface is connected properly and is in good condition. If it does not seem to be a good connection, reset the cable and ensure that the connection is secure. Try replacing the cable with a known working cable. If the cable connects to a wall jack, use a cable tester to ensure that the jack is wired properly.

Also check any transceiver in use to ensure that it is the correct type and is properly connected and configured. If replacing the cable does not resolve the problem, try replacing the transceiver, if one is being used.

Before you run diagnostics or attempt complex troubleshooting, always check to make sure that the device is powered on. Some problems result from the simplest of errors.

Layer 3 Troubleshooting Using ping

The *ping* utility is used to test network connectivity. To aid in diagnosing basic network connectivity, many network protocols support an echo protocol, which is used to test whether protocol packets are being routed. The **ping** command sends a packet to the destination host and then waits for a reply packet from that host. Results from this echo protocol can help evaluate the path-to-host reliability, delays over the path, and whether the host can be reached or is functioning. The ping output displays the minimum, average, and maximum times that it takes for a ping packet to find a specified system and return. **ping** uses the Internet Control Message Protocol (ICMP) to verify the hardware connection and the logical address of the network layer. This is a basic testing mechanism.

For the network in Figure 9-4, the ping target 172.16.1.5 responded successfully to all five datagrams sent, as shown in Example 9-5.

Figure 9-4 Network for Testing with ping

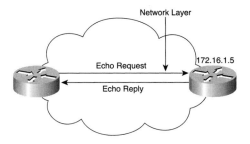

Example 9-5 **ping** *Results for Target 172.16.1.5*

```
Router> ping 172.16.1.5
Type escape sequence to abort
Sending 5, 100 byte ICMP Echos to 172.16.1.5,
timeout is 2 seconds:
!!!!!
Success rate is 100 percent,
round-trip min/avg/max - 1/3/4 ms
Router>
```

The exclamation points (!) indicate each successful echo. If any periods (.) instead of exclamations are received on a display, the application on the router timed out waiting for a given packet echo from the ping target. The **ping** command can be used to diagnose basic network connectivity.

ping tests network connections by sending ICMP echo requests to a target host and waiting for replies. When testing a connection, **ping** tracks the number of packets sent, the number of replies received, the percentage of packets lost, and the amount of time required for the packets to reach the destination and for replies to be received. This information enables users to verify whether their workstations can communicate with other hosts, and they can determine whether any information was lost.

The **ping** command can be initiated from both user EXEC mode and privileged EXEC mode. The **ping** command can be used to confirm basic network connectivity on AppleTalk, ISO Connectionless Network Service (CLNS), IP, Novell, Apollo, VINES, DECnet, or XNS networks.

ICMP uses messages to accomplish various tasks. Table 9-3 shows a list of ICMP message types.

Table 9-3 CMP Message Types

Message	Purpose
Destination unreachable	This tells the source host that there is a problem delivering a packet.
Time exceeded	The time that it takes a packet to be delivered has been too long, and the packet has been discarded.
Source quench	The source is sending data faster than it can be forwarded. This message requests that the sender slow down.
Redirect	The router sending this message has received some packet for which another router would have had a better route. The message tells the sender to use the better route.
Echo	This is used by the **ping** command to verify connectivity.
Parameter problem	This is used to identify a parameter that is incorrect.
Timestamp	This is used to measure round-trip time to particular hosts.
Address mask request/reply	This is used to inquire about and learn the correct subnet mask to be used.
Router advertisement and selection	This is used to allow hosts to dynamically learn the IP addresses of the routers attached to the subnet.

The extended command mode of the **ping** command permits users to specify the supported IP header options. This allows the router to perform a more extensive range of test options. To enter ping extended command mode, type the **ping** command with no options in privileged mode and press Enter. You are prompted for some basic options as well as the Extended Commands option. Enter yes at the Extended commands prompt to specify various extended ping options. An extended ping works the same way as a regular ping, but it supports the manipulation of some different parameters, such as packet size and frequency.

It is a good idea to use the **ping** command when the network is functioning properly, to see how the command works under normal conditions and so that you have something to compare against when troubleshooting.

Layer 7 Troubleshooting Using Telnet

Telnet is a virtual terminal protocol that is part of the TCP/IP protocol suite. Telnet allows the verification of the application layer software between source and destination stations. This is the most complete test mechanism available. Telnet allows connections to be made to remote devices, to gather information and run commands and applications.

Telnet is the most complete testing tool because it uses IP at the network layer and TCP at the transport layer to create a session with a remote host. If Telnet is successful, IP connectivity must be good.

The **telnet** command provides a virtual terminal so that administrators can use Telnet operations to connect with other network devices (such as routers and switches) running TCP/IP. If a router can be remotely accessed using Telnet, at least one TCP/IP application can reach the remote router. A successful Telnet connection indicates that the upper-layer application and the services of lower layers are functioning properly. Figure 9-5 illustrates a Telnet connection.

Figure 9-5 Using Telnet

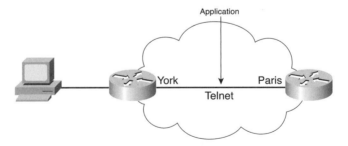

If an administrator can Telnet to one router but not to another router, the Telnet failure likely is caused by specific addressing, naming, or access permission problems. These problems can exist on the administrator's router or on the router that failed as a Telnet target.

If the Telnet to a particular server fails from one host, try connecting from a router and several other devices. Also try using **ping** as a more basic test. If you can ping the host, but cannot achieve a login prompt when trying to Telnet, check the following:

- Can a reverse DNS lookup on the client's address be found? Many Telnet servers do not allow connections from IP addresses that have no DNS entry. This is a common problem for DHCP-assigned addresses in which the administrator has not added DNS entries for the DHCP pools.

- A Telnet application might not be capable of negotiating the appropriate options and, therefore, will not connect. On a Cisco router, this negotiation process can be viewed using **debug telnet**. Look for error messages or an invalid IP or DNS address, which would indicate this problem.

- It is possible that Telnet is disabled or has been moved to a port other than 23 on the destination server. Recall that port 23 is the default port for Telnet.

Lab 9.2.6   Troubleshooting Using **ping** and **telnet**

In this lab, you use knowledge of OSI Layers 1, 2, and 3 to diagnose network configuration errors while using the **ping** and **telnet** utilities.

Troubleshooting Router Issues Overview

Routing problems are among the most common and difficult for network administrators to diagnose. Identifying and solving routing problems may not be simple, but many tools exist that can make the task easier. This section introduces several of the most important of these tools and provides practice in their use.

Troubleshooting Layer 1 Using show interfaces

Cisco IOS Software contains numerous commands for troubleshooting. The **show** command used to check the status and statistics of the interfaces is the **show interfaces** command. The **show interfaces** command without arguments returns status and statistics on all the router ports. The **show interfaces** *interface name* returns the status and statistics of only the named port. To view the status of Serial 0/0, use the **show interfaces serial 0/0** command. To view the status of FastEthernet 0/0, use **show interfaces fa0/0**.

The **show interfaces** command displays the status of two important portions of the interfaces. These can be related to the Layer 1 and the Layer 2 functions:

- **Physical (hardware) portion**—The hardware includes cables, connectors, and interfaces showing the condition of the physical connection between the devices.

■ **Logical (software) portion**—The software status shows the state of messages such as *keepalives*, control information, and user information that are passed between adjacent devices. This relates to the condition of a data link layer protocol passed between two connected neighboring router interfaces.

These important elements can be demonstrated by an example of a serial port on a modular router. The **show interfaces serial 0/0** command displays the line and data-link protocol status of serial port one, as shown in Example 9-6.

Example 9-6 **show interfaces serial** *Command Output*

```
Cougars# show interfaces serial 0
Serial0 is up, line protocol is up
  Hardware is HD64570
  MTU 1500 bytes, BW 1544 Kbit, DLY 20000 usec,
      reliability 255/255, txload 1/255, rxload 1/255
  Encapsulation HDLC, loopback not set
  Keepalive set (10 sec)
  Last input never, output never, output hang never
  Last clearing of "show interface" counters 00:02:57
  Input queue: 0/75/0/0 (size/max/drops/flushes); Total output drops: 0
  Queueing strategy: weighted fair
  Output queue: 0/1000/64/0 (size/max total/threshold/drops)
      Conversations  0/0/256 (active/max active/max total)
      Reserved Conversations 0/0 (allocated/max allocated)
      Available Bandwidth 1158 kilobits/sec
  5 minute input rate 0 bits/sec, 0 packets/sec
  5 minute output rate 0 bits/sec, 0 packets/sec
      0 packets input, 0 bytes, 0 no buffer
      Received 0 broadcasts, 0 runts, 0 giants, 0 throttles
      0 input errors, 0 CRC, 0 frame, 0 overrun, 0 ignored, 0 abort
      0 packets output, 0 bytes, 0 underruns
      0 output errors, 0 collisions, 8 interface resets
      0 output buffer failures, 0 output buffers swapped out
      0 carrier transitions
      DCD=up  DSR=up  DTR=up  RTS=up  CTS=up
```

The first parameter (Serial0 is up) refers to the hardware layer and essentially reflects whether the interface is receiving the carrier detect signal from the other end (DCE). If the line is down, a problem with the cabling might exist in a back-to-back connection, with one end being "administratively down." If the interface is administratively down, it has been disabled manually in the configuration.

The **show interfaces serial** command also provides information to help diagnose other Layer 1 issues that are not as easy to determine.

The following problems can be caused by an increasing number of carrier transitions counts on a serial link:

- Line interruptions from the service provider network
- Faulty switch, DSU, or router hardware

If an increasing number of input errors appear in the **show interfaces serial 0/0** output, there are several possible sources of those errors. Some common problems related to Layer 1 are as follows:

- Faulty telephone company equipment
- Noisy serial line
- Incorrect cable or cable length
- Damaged cable or connection
- Defective CSU or DSU
- Defective router hardware

Another area to examine is the number of interface resets. Interface resets are the result of too many missed keepalives. Layer 1 problems also could be caused by the following:

- Bad phone line causing CD transitions
- Possible hardware problem at the CSU, DSU, or switch

The number of errors should be interpreted relative to the amount of traffic that the router has processed and the length of time that the statistics have been captured. The router tracks statistics that provide information about the interface. The statistics reflect router operation since it was started or since the last time the counters were cleared, as shown in Example 9-7.

Example 9-7 *Statistics Accumulation*

```
Cougars# show interfaces serial 0
Serial0 is up, line protocol is up
  Hardware is HD64570
  MTU 1500 bytes, BW 1544 Kbit, DLY 20000 usec,
     reliability 255/255, txload 1/255, rxload 1/255
  Encapsulation HDLC, loopback not set
  Keepalive set (10 sec)
  Last input never, output never, output hang never
  Last clearing of "show interface" counters 00:02:57
```

If the **show interfaces** output shows the last clearing of the counters as never, use the **show version** command to determine how long the router has been functional, as shown in Example 9-8.

Example 9-8 *Router Uptime*

```
Cougars# show version
Cisco Internetwork Operating System Software
IOS (tm) 2600 Software (C2600-BNSY-L), Version 12.2(6h), RELEASE SOFTWARE (fc1)
Copyright (c) 1986-2002 by cisco Systems, Inc.
Compiled Mon 26-Aug-02 23:23 by kellythw
Image text-base: 0x0303ED8C, data-base: 0x00001000


ROM: System Bootstrap, Version 11.0(10c), SOFTWARE
BOOTLDR: 3000 Bootstrap Software (IGS-BOOT-R), Version 11.0(10c), RELEASE SOFTWA
RE (fc1)


Cougars uptime is 14 minutes
```

Use the **clear counters** privileged EXEC command, as shown in Example 9-9, to reset the counters to 0. These counters always should be cleared after an interface problem has been corrected. Starting from 0 gives a better picture of the current status of the network and helps verify that the issue has been corrected.

Example 9-9 **clear counters** *Command*

```
Cougars# clear counters
Clear "show interface" counters on all interfaces [confirm]yes
Cougars#
00:17:24: %CLEAR-5-COUNTERS: Clear counter on all interfaces by console
Cougars#
```

Troubleshooting Layer 2 Using show interfaces

The **show interfaces** command is one of the most important tools to discover Layer 1 and Layer 2 problems with the router. The first output parameter, or line, refers to the physical layer. The second parameter, or protocol, indicates whether Cisco IOS Software processes that control the line protocol consider the interface usable. This is determined by whether keepalives are successfully received. If the interface misses three consecutive keepalives, the line protocol is marked as down.

If the line is down, the protocol also must be down because there would be no usable media for the protocol. This occurs when the interface is down because of a hardware issue or if it is "administratively down" because of a configuration issue.

If the interface is up and the line protocol is down, a Layer 2 problem exists. The following list contains some possible causes:

- No keepalives
- No clock rate
- Mismatch in encapsulation type
- Interface is shutdown
- Authentication failed

These problems can be determined when the **show interfaces** command has been entered and a line appears stating, "Interface is up and the line protocol is down." Using the **clockrate** command or the **encapsulation** command, verify that there is no mismatch between interfaces.

The **show interfaces** command should be used after configuring a serial interface to verify the changes and to verify that the interface is operational.

Troubleshooting Using show cdp

Cisco Discovery Protocol (CDP) advertises device information to its direct neighbors, including MAC and IP addresses and outgoing interfaces.

The output from the **show cdp neighbors** command displays information about directly connected Cisco device neighbors, as demonstrated in Example 9-10.

Example 9-10 **show cdp neighbors** *Command Output*

```
routerA# show cdp neighbors
Capability Codes:
R - Router, T - Trans Bridge,
B - Source Route Bridge,
S - Switch, H - Host, I - IGMP


Device ID     Local Interface     Holdtime     Capability     Platform Port     ID
routerB       Eth 0               151          R              2501      Eth     0
routerB       Ser 0               165          R              2501      Ser     0
```

This information is useful for debugging connectivity issues. If a cabling problem is suspected, enable the interfaces with the **no shutdown** command and then execute the **show cdp**

neighbors detail command, as shown in Example 9-11, before any other configuration. The command displays specific device detail such as the active interfaces, the port ID, and the device.

Example 9-11 **show cdp neighbors detail** *Command*

```
routerA# show cdp neighbors detail
Device ID: routerB
Entry address(es):
   IP address: 198.92.68.18
Platform: 2501, Capabilities: Router
Interface: Ethernet0, Port ID (outgoing port): Ethernet0
Holdtime: 143 sec
```

If the physical layer is functioning properly, all other directly connected Cisco devices should be displayed. If a known device does not show up, there is probably a Layer 1 issue.

One area of concern with CDP is security. The amount of information that CDP provides is so extensive that it can be a potential security risk. For security reasons, CDP should be configured only on links between Cisco devices and should be disabled on user ports or links that are not managed locally.

Troubleshooting Using traceroute

The **traceroute** command is used to discover the routes that packets take when traveling to their destinations. The **traceroute** command, which is often referred to as the **trace** command in reference materials, is the ideal tool for finding where data is being sent in a network. **traceroute** also can be used to test the network layer, or Layer 3, on a hop-by-hop basis and to provide performance benchmarks.

The output of the **traceroute** command generates a list of hops that successfully were reached, as shown in Example 9-12. If the data successfully reaches the intended destination, then the output indicates every router that the datagram passes through. This output can be captured and used for future troubleshooting of the internetwork.

Example 9-12 **traceroute** *Command Output*

```
Cougars> traceroute 168.71.8.2
traceroute to pc-b.cisco.com (168.71.8.2), 30 hops max, 40 byte packets
 1   routerb (168.71.6.3)   3 ms   3 ms   3 ms
 2   *   *   *
 3   *   *   *
 4   *   *   *
```

Example 9-12 **traceroute** *Command Output (Continued)*

```
  5   *    *    *
Cougars>
```

traceroute output also indicates the specific hop at which the failure is occurring. For each router in the path, a line of output is generated on the terminal indicating the IP address of the interface that the data entered. If an asterisk (*) appears, the packet failed. You can isolate the problem area by obtaining the last good hop from the **traceroute** output and comparing it to a diagram of the internetwork.

traceroute also provides information indicating the relative performance of links. The round-trip time (RTT) is the time required to send an echo packet and get a response, as shown in Example 9-12. In this example, each of the three packets sent has an RTT of 3 milliseconds (ms). This is useful for an approximate idea of the delay on the link. These figures are not precise enough to be used for an accurate performance evaluation; however, this output can be captured and used for future performance troubleshooting of the internetwork.

The device receiving the **traceroute** also must know how to send the reply back to the source of the **traceroute**. For the **traceroute** or **ping** data to successfully make the round trips between routers, there must be known routes in both directions. A failed response is not always an indication of a problem because ICMP messages could be rate-limited or filtered at the host site. This is especially true across the Internet.

traceroute sends out a sequence of User Datagram Protocol (UDP) datagrams from the router to an invalid port address on the remote host. For the first sequence of three datagrams sent, a Time-To-Live (TTL) field value is set to 1. The TTL value of 1 causes the datagram to time out at the first router in the path. This router then responds with an ICMP time exceeded message (TEM) indicating that the datagram has expired.

Three more UDP messages now are sent, each with the TTL value set to 2. This causes the second router to return ICMP TEMs. This process continues until the packets actually reach the other destination or the maximum TTL has been reached. The default maximum TTL for **traceroute** is 30.

Because these datagrams are trying to access an invalid port at the destination host, ICMP port unreachable messages are returned instead of ICMP TEMs. This indicates an unreachable port and signals the **traceroute** program, terminating the process.

Lab 9.3.4 Troubleshooting Using **traceroute**

In this lab, you learn how to use the **traceroute** or **tracert** command to verify that the network layer between source, destination, and each router along the way is working properly.

Troubleshooting Routing Issues Using show ip route and show ip protocols

The **show ip protocols** and **show ip route** commands display information about routing protocols and the routing table. The output from these commands can be used to verify the routing protocol configuration.

The **show ip route** command is perhaps the single most important command for troubleshooting routing issues. This command displays the contents of the IP routing table. The output in Example 9-13 shows the entries for all known networks and subnetworks and how the information was obtained.

Example 9-13 show ip route *Command Output*

```
Cougars> show ip route
Codes: C - connected, S - static, R - RIP, M - mobile, B - BGP
D - EIGRP, EX - EIGRP external, O - OSPF, IA - OSPF inter area
E1 - OSPF external type 1, E2 - OSPF external type 2, E - EGP
i - IS-IS, L1 - IS-IS level 1, L2 - IS-IS level 2
* - candidate default


Gateway of last resort is not set

     144.253.0.0 is subnetted (mask is 255.255.255.0), 1 subnets
C    144.253.100.0 is directly connected. Ethernet1
R    153.50.0.0 [120/1] via 183.8.128.12, 00:00:09, Ethernet0
     183.8.0.0 is subnetted (mask is 255.255.255.128), 4 subnets
R       183.8.0.128 [120/1] via 183.8.128.130.00, 00:00:17, Serial0
                     [120/1] via 183.8.64.130, 00:00:17, Serial1
C    183.8.128.0 is directly connected, Ethernet0
C    183.8.64.128 is directly connected, Serial1
C    183.8.128.128 is directly connected, Ethernet0
```

If there is a problem reaching a host in a particular network, the output of the **show ip route** command can be used to verify that the router has a route to that network.

If the output of the **show ip route** command does not show the expected learned routes or shows no learned routes, the problem is possibly that routing information is not being exchanged. In this case, use **show ip protocols** commands, as shown in Example 9-14, on the router to check for a routing protocol configuration error.

Example 9-14 show ip protocols *Command Output*

```
Router> show ip protocols
Routing Protocol is rip
Sending updates every 30 seconds, next due in 13 seconds
Invalid after 180 seconds, hold down 180, flushed after 240
Outgoing update filter list for all interface is not set
Incoming update filter list for all interface is not set
Redistributing: rip
Routing for Networks:
183.8.0.0
144.253.0.0
Routing Information Sources:
Gateway          Distance      Last Update
183.8.128.12        120          0:00:14
183.8.64.130        120          0:00:19
183.8.128.130       120          0:00:03
Distance: (default is 120)
```

The **show ip protocols** command displays values about IP routing protocol information on the entire router. This command can be used to confirm which protocols are configured, which networks are being advertised, which interfaces are sending updates, and the sources of routing updates. The **show ip protocols** output also displays the routing parameters about timers, filters, and other information related to the routing protocol. When multiple routing protocols are configured, the information about each protocol is listed in a separate section.

The **show ip protocols** command output can be used to diagnose many routing issues, such as identifying a router that is suspected of delivering bad router information. The command output also can be used to confirm that the expected protocols, advertised networks, and routing neighbors are present. As with any troubleshooting process, identifying the problem is difficult, if not impossible, if there is no documentation indicating the expected results.

Lab 9.3.5   Troubleshooting Routing Issues with **show ip route** and **show ip protocols**

In this lab, you use the **show ip route** and **show ip protocols** commands to diagnose a routing configuration problem.

Troubleshooting Using show controllers

Router configuration and troubleshooting frequently are done remotely. Therefore, it is not possible to physically inspect the router connections. The **show controllers serial** command, shown in Example 9-15, is used to determine the type of cable connected without inspecting the cables.

Example 9-15 **show controllers serial** *Command Output*

```
Cougars# show controllers serial 0/0
QUICC Serial unit 0
idb at 0x20A31A8, driver data structure at 0x20A4C60
SCC Registers:
General [GSMR]=0x2:0x00000030, Protocol-specific [PSMR]=0x0
Events [SCCE]=0x0000, Mask [SCCM]=0x001F, Status [SCCS]=0x0006
Transmit on Demand [TODR]=0x0, Data Sync [DSR]=0x7E7E
Interrupt Registers:
… output omitted …
DTE V.35 serial cable attached.
--- output omitted ---
```

Being able to determine the type of cable that the controller detects is useful for finding a serial interface with no cable, the wrong type of cable, or a defective cable.

The **show controllers serial 0/0** command queries the integrated circuit, or chip, that controls the serial interfaces and displays information about the physical interface. This output varies among controller chips. Even within a router type, different controller chips can be used.

Regardless of the controller type, the **show controllers serial** command produces a tremendous amount of output. Other than the cable type, most of this output is internal technical detail regarding the controller chip status. Without specific knowledge of the integrated circuit, this information is not useful.

Introduction to debug

The **debug** commands assist in the isolation of protocol and configuration problems. The **debug** command is used to display dynamic data and events. Because the **show** commands display only static information, they provide a historical picture of the router operation. The **debug** command output provides more insight into the current events of the router. These events include traffic on an interface, error messages generated by nodes on the network, protocol-specific diagnostic packets, and other useful troubleshooting data. Example 9-16 shows sample output from the **debug ip rip** command.

Example 9-16 debug ip rip *Command Output*

```
Router# debug ip rip
RIP Protocol debugging is on
Router#
RIP:     received update from 183.8.128.130 on Serial0
183.8.0.128 in 1 hops
183.8.64.128 in 1 hops
0.0.0.0 in 16 hops (inaccessible)
RIP:     received update from 183.8.64.140 on Serial1
183.8.0.128 in 1 hops
183.9.128.128 in 1 hops
0.0.0.0 in 16 hops (inaccessible)
RIP:     received update from 183.8.128.130 on Serial0
183.8.0.128 in 1 hops
183.8.64.128 in 1 hops
0.0.0.0 in 16 hops (inaccessible)
RIP:     sending update to 255.255.255.255 via Ethernet0 (183.8.128.2)
subnet 183.8.0.128, metric 2
subnet 183.8.64.128, metric 1
subnet 183.8.128.128, metric 1
default 0.0.0.0, metric 16
network 144.253.0.0, metric 1
RIP:     sending update to 255.255.255.255 via Ethernet1 (144.253.100.202)
default 0.0.0.0, metric 16
network 153.50.0.0, metric 2
network 183.8.0.0, metric 1
```

The highlighted material in Example 9-16 shows that RIP debugging has been turned on and shows which routes, networks, and interfaces are accessible and inaccessible.

Lab 9.3.7   Troubleshooting Routing Issues with **debug**

In this lab, you learn how to use a systematic OSI troubleshooting process to diagnose routing problems.

CAUTION

The **debug all** command, in particular, should be used sparingly because it can disrupt router operations.

Summary

In this chapter, you learned the following:

- Network testing should be utilized to keep a network running smoothly and efficiently. It should be tested layer by layer.

- You should use a structured approach to troubleshooting.

- **ping** and **telnet** are two commands that are helpful in troubleshooting network problems.

- The **traceroute** command can be used to determine the status of links between routers.

- The different **show** commands help to confirm Layer 1 and Layer 2 problems.

- The **show ip route** and **show ip protocols** commands help to identify routing issues.

- Basic **debug** commands help to discover information about router activity.

To supplement all that you've learned in this chapter, refer to the chapter-specific Video and Interactive Media Activities on the CD-ROM accompanying this book.

Key Terms

keepalive   Message sent by one network device to inform another network device that the virtual circuit between the two is still active.

network interface card (NIC)   Board that provides network communication capabilities to and from a computer system.

ping   Packet Internet groper. ICMP echo message and its reply. Used in IP networks to test the reachability of a network device.

Telnet   Standard terminal-emulation protcol in the TCP/IP protocol suite. Telnet is used for remote terminal connection, enabling users to log in to remote systems and use resources as if they were connected to a local system.

traceroute   Program available on many systems that traces the path that a packet takes to a destination. It is used mostly to debug routing problems between hosts.

Check Your Understanding

Complete all the review questions to test your understanding of the topics and concepts in this chapter. Answers are listed in Appendix B, "Check Your Understanding Answer Key."

1. When a technician performs basic testing of a network, which of the following is true?

   A. The technician should proceed in sequence from one OSI reference model layer to the next.

   B. The technician should proceed with any desired OSI layer.

   C. The technician should proceed with the management level.

   D. The technician should test for OSI reference model layer issues in a random fashion.

2. What approach should a technician start with when he/she troubleshoots a network?

   A. The technician should start with a structured approach.

   B. The technician should start with an approach of his choice.

   C. The technician should start with any approach.

   D. The technician should start with a hit-and-miss approach.

3. When a technician troubleshoots a problem on a network, which layer of the OSI model should he/she begin with?

   A. Begin with Layer 1.

   B. Begin with Layer 2.

   C. Begin with Layer 3.

   D. Begin with Layer 4.

4. If a technician wants to test network connectivity, which basic command should be used?

   A. telnet

   B. ping

   C. debug

   D. traceroute

5. When a network administrator wants to verify the application layer software between source and destination stations, which of the following commands should be used?

   A. ping

   B. telnet

   C. debug

   D. traceroute

6. You suspect that one of the routers connected to your network is sending bad routing information, what command can you use to check?

   A. router(config)# **show ip route**

   B. router# **show ip route**

   C. router> **show ip protocols**

   D. router(config-router)# **show ip protocol**

7. Why would you display the IP routing table?

   A. To set the router update schedule

   B. To identify destination network addresses and next-hop pairs

   C. To trace where datagrams are coming from

   D. To set the parameters and filters for the router

8. If you wanted to see RIP routing updates as they are sent and received, what command structure would you use?

   A. router# **show ip rip**

   B. router# **debug ip protocols**

   C. router# **debug ip rip**

   D. router# **show ip rip update**

9. Complete the following sentence. The dynamic output of the **debug** command comes at a performance cost, which produces _____ processor overhead.

   A. High

   B. Low

   C. Medium

   D. Maximum

10. By default, the router sends the **debug** output and system messages to what?

   A. The console

   B. The switch

   C. The PC

   D. The user

11. The **telnet** command provides what type of terminal?

   A. Register

   B. Virtual

   C. Cisco IOS Software

   D. Command

12. What does ICMP stand for?

   A. Internet Control Message Parameter

   B. Internal Control Message Protocol

   C. Internet Control Message Protocol

   D. Internet Control Message Performance

13. Most interfaces or NICs have what type of lights that show whether there is a valid connection?

   A. Indicator

   B. Catalyst

   C. Responsive

   D. Inactive

14. Telnet is used at what layer of the OSI reference model?

   A. Layer 1

   B. Layer 5

   C. Layer 6

   D. Layer 7

15. If the routing protocol is not enabled or the IP address cannot be determined, at which layer of the OSI model should an administrator begin to look?

   A. Layer 1

   B. Layer 2

   C. Layer 3

   D. Layer 4

Objectives

Upon completion of this chapter, you should be able to answer the following questions:

- What is positive acknowledgment and retransmission (PAR) and how does it relate to TCP?

- How does TCP relate to multiple conversations between hosts?

Additional Topics of Interest

The following topics, already covered in the CCNA 1 chapters, are also important topics of concern to networkers and should be covered if these concepts were not mastered in the CCNA 1 course:

- What are the ports that are used for services and clients?

- What are the well-known ports?

- What is the relationship between MAC addresses, IP addresses, and port numbers?

- What are the primary functions of TCP?

- What is TCP synchronization and flow control?

- What are the primary processes and operation of the User Datagram Protocol (UDP)?

- What are the common port numbers and what are they used for?

Key Terms

The following is a list of key terms introduced in this chapter. For your reference, a definition for each term can be found at the end of this chapter.

Transmission Control Protocol (TCP)   page 811

User Datagram Protocol (UDP)   page 811

denial of service (DoS)   page 816

flow control   page 817

windowing   page 817

well-known ports   page 826

Address Resolution Protocol (ARP)   page 829

Reverse Address Resolution Protocol (RARP)   page 829

In this chapter, you learn about TCP/IP operation to ensure communication across any set of interconnected networks. In addition, you learn about the TCP/IP protocol stack components, such as protocols to support file transfer, e-mail, remote login, and other applications. You learn about reliable and unreliable transport layer protocols and about connectionless datagram (packet) delivery at the network layer. Finally, you learn how ARP and RARP work.

Please be sure to look at the Interactive Media Activities associated with this chapter that you will find on the CD-ROM accompanying this book. These CD elements are designed to supplement the material and reinforce the concepts introduced in this chapter.

More Information: The TCP/IP Protocol Suite

The TCP/IP suite of protocols was developed as part of the research done by the Defense Advanced Research Projects Agency (DARPA). It was originally developed to provide communication within DARPA. Later, TCP/IP was included with the Berkeley Software Distribution of UNIX. Now, TCP/IP is the de facto standard for internetwork communications and serves as the transport protocol stack for the Internet, enabling millions of computers to communicate globally. This chapter focuses on TCP/IP for several reasons:

- TCP/IP is a universally available protocol that you likely use at work.

- TCP/IP is a useful reference for understanding other protocols because it includes elements that are representative of other protocols.

- TCP/IP is important because the router uses it as a configuration tool.

The function of the TCP/IP protocol stack is to transfer information from one network device to another. In doing so, it closely maps the OSI reference model in the lower layers and supports all standard physical and data link protocols (see Figure 10-1).

Figure 10-1 Four Layer Model of TCP/IP

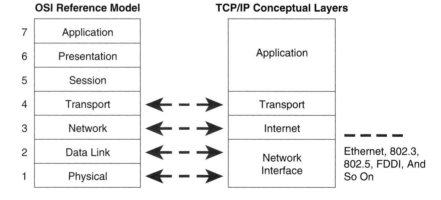

More Information: The TCP/IP Protocol Suite (Continued)

The OSI layers most closely related to TCP/IP are Layer 7 (application layer), Layer 4 (transport layer), and Layer 3 (network layer). Included in these layers are various types of protocols with a variety of purposes/functions, all of which are related to the transfer of information. The TCP/IP layers map quite well to the OSI model: TCP (at the transport or host-to-host layer) maps to the OSI transport layer, and the Internet layer maps to the OSI network layer.

TCP/IP enables communication among any set of interconnected networks and is equally well suited for both LAN and WAN communication. TCP/IP includes not only Layer 3 and 4 specifications (such as IP and TCP), but also specifications to support such common applications as e-mail, remote login, terminal emulation, and file transfer.

TCP/IP Protocol Stack and the Application Layer

The application layer of the TCP/IP or Internet protocols combines the functionality found in the OSI session, presentation, and application layers. TCP/IP has protocols to support file transfer, e-mail, and remote login, including the following (see Figure 10-2):

- **Domain Name System (DNS)** is a system used on the Internet for translating names of domains and their publicly advertised network nodes into IP addresses.

  This translation is considered to be transport layer functionality because it provides services to the layer above (application layer) and receives services from the layer below (Internetwork layer).

- **Windows Internet Naming Service (WINS)** is a Microsoft-developed standard for Microsoft Windows NT that automatically associates NT workstations with Internet domain names.

- **HOSTS** is a file created by network administrators and maintained on servers. The file is used to provide static mappings between IP addresses and computer names.

- **Post Office Protocol (POP3)** is an Internet standard for storing e-mail on a mail server until you can access it and download it to your computer. It enables users to receive mail from their inboxes using various levels of security.

- **Simple Mail Transfer Protocol (SMTP)** governs the transmission of e-mail over computer networks. It does not provide support for transmission of data other than plain text.

- **Simple Network Management Protocol (SNMP)** is a protocol that provides a means to monitor and control network devices and to manage configurations, statistics collection, performance, and security.

- **File Transfer Protocol (FTP)** is a reliable, connection-oriented service that uses TCP to transfer files between systems that support FTP. It supports bidirectional binary file and ASCII file transfers.

More Information: The TCP/IP Protocol Suite (Continued)

- **Trivial File Transfer Protocol (TFTP)** is a connectionless service that uses UDP. TFTP is used on the router to transfer configuration files and IOS images, and to transfer files between systems that support TFTP. It is useful in some LANs because it operates faster than FTP in a stable environment.

- **Hypertext Transfer Protocol (HTTP)** is the Internet standard that supports the exchange of information on the World Wide Web as well as on internal networks. It supports many different file types, including text, graphics, sound, and video. It defines the process by which web browsers originate requests for information to send to web servers.

Figure 10-2 Application Layer Protocols

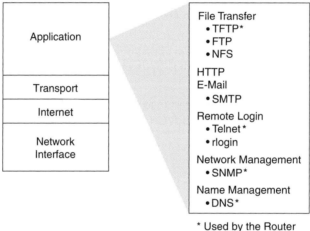

* Used by the Router

The following list provides an overview of some troubleshooting protocols:

- **Telnet** is a standard terminal emulation protocol used by clients to make remote terminal connections to Telnet server services. It enables users to remotely connect to routers to enter configuration commands.

- **Packet Internet Groper (ping)** determines whether a computer is reachable. **ping** uses the Internet Control Message Protocol (ICMP) echo request and reply messages.

- The **traceroute** program is available on many systems and is similar to **ping**, except that **traceroute** provides more information than **ping**. traceroute traces the path that a packet takes to a destination and is used to debug routing problems.

More Information: The TCP/IP Protocol Suite (Continued)

You also need to be familiar with a few Windows-based utilities:

- **NBSTAT**—A utility used to troubleshoot NetBIOS name resolution and used to view and remove entries from the name cache.

- **NETSTAT**—A utility that provides information about TCP/IP statistics; it can be used to provide information about the status of TCP/IP connections and summaries of ICMP, TCP, and UDP.

- **ipconfig/winipcfg**—Utilities used to view current network settings for all network interface cards (NICs) on a device; they can be used to view the MAC address, IP address, subnet mask, and gateway, as well as DNS and Dynamic Host Configuration Protocol (DHCP) information.

TCP/IP Protocol Stack and the Transport Layer

This section introduces the *Transmission Control Protocol (TCP)*, a Layer 4 protocol in the TCP/IP suite. TCP is a reliable, connection-oriented protocol that helps ensure reliable data delivery through the use of synchronization, windowing and window size, sequencing numbers, and acknowledgements (ACK).

The transport layer enables a user's device to segment data from several upper-layer applications for placement on the same Layer 4 data stream and enables a receiving device to reassemble the upper-layer application segments. The Layer 4 data stream is a logical connection, or virtual circuit, between the endpoints of a network; it provides transport services from a source host to a destination host. This service is sometimes referred to as an *end-to-end service*. The transport layer also provides two protocols (see Figure 10-3):

- **TCP**—A connection-oriented, reliable protocol that provides flow control by providing sliding windows and offers reliability by providing sequence numbers and acknowledgments. TCP resends anything that is not acknowledged and supplies a virtual circuit between end-user applications. The advantage of TCP is that it provides guaranteed delivery of segments.

- *User Datagram Protocol (UDP)*—A connectionless and unreliable protocol that is responsible for transmitting messages but provides no software checking for segment delivery. The advantage that UDP provides is speed. Because UDP provides no acknowledgments, less control traffic is sent across the network, making the transfer faster.

More Information: The TCP/IP Protocol Suite (Continued)

Figure 10-3 Transport Layer Protocols

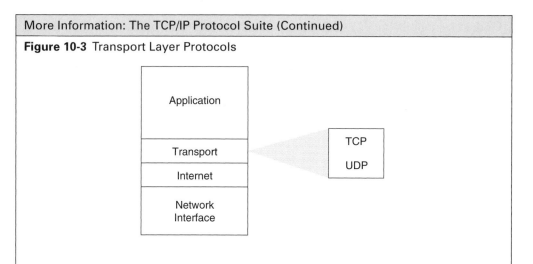

TCP and UDP Segment Format

TCP is known as a connection-oriented protocol. Connection-oriented means that the end stations are aware of each other and constantly communicate about the connection. A classic example of a non-technical connection-oriented communication is a telephone conversation between two people. A good example of a connectionless conversation is the U.S. postal service where, once you place the letter in the mail, you hope that the mailing process gets the package delivered. Figure 10-4 illustrates the TCP segment header format, the field definitions of which are described in the following list.

Figure 10-4 TCP Segment Format

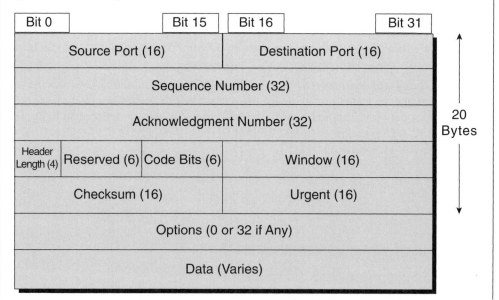

More Information: The TCP/IP Protocol Suite (Continued)

- **Source port**—The number of the source (port) for this segment.

- **Destination port**—The number of the destination (port) for this segment.

- **Sequence number**—The number used to ensure correct sequencing of the arriving data. It is the first byte of data that this segment represents.

- **Acknowledgment number**—The sequence number plus one, of the last byte of data that was successfully received.

- **Header length**—The number of 32-bit words in the header.

- **Reserved**—Set to 0.

- **Code bits**—The control functions (for example, setup and termination of a session).

- **Window**—The number of bytes that the sender is willing to accept.

- **Checksum**—The calculated checksum of the header and data fields.

- **Urgent**—Indicator of the end of the urgent data.

- **Options**—One currently defined: maximum TCP segment size.

- **Data**—Upper-layer protocol data.

When using UDP, application layer protocols must provide for reliability if it is necessary. UDP uses no windowing or acknowledgments. It is designed for applications that do not need to put sequences of segments together. Figure 10-5 shows the UDP header.

Figure 10-5 UDP Header Format

Source Port (16)	Destination Port (16)	Length (16)	Checksum (16)	Data (Variable)

TCP Operation

Routers use the IP address information in an IP packet header to determine which interface the packet should be switched to move to its destination. Because IP does not provide services to help ensure the packet actually reaches the destination, it is described as an unreliable, connectionless protocol that uses best-effort delivery. If packets are dropped in route, arrive in the wrong order, or are transmitted faster than the receiver can accept them, IP alone cannot correct the problem. To address these problems, IP relies on the Transmission Control Protocol (TCP).

TCP Operation

IP addresses allow for the routing of packets between networks. However, IP makes no guarantees about delivery. The transport layer is responsible for the reliable transport and regulation of data flow from source to destination. This reliability is accomplished by using sliding windows, sequencing numbers, and a synchronization process that ensures each host is ready and willing to communicate, as shown in Figure 10-6.

Figure 10-6 TCP Operation

To understand reliability and flow control, think of two people engaged in a conversation. First, they meet and maybe shake hands to acknowledge to each other that a conversation is about to take place and information is about to be sent. While they are talking and exchanging information, if a word or phrase is inaudible or unreachable to the other person, one person might simply ask the person to repeat their words (for reliability) so he or she can catch the words (flow control). The transport layer, Layer 4 of the OSI model, provides these services to Layer 3 via TCP.

Synchronization or 3-Way Handshake

TCP is a connection-oriented protocol. Prior to data transmission, the two communicating hosts go through a synchronization process to establish a virtual connection. This synchronization process ensures that both sides are ready for data transmission and enables the devices to determine the initial sequence numbers (ISNs). This process is known as a *three-way handshake*.

Synchronization is accomplished by exchanging packets carrying the ISNs and a control bit called SYN, which stands for *synchronize*. (Packets carrying the SYN bit are also called SYNs.) Successful connection requires a suitable mechanism for choosing an initial sequence and a slightly involved handshake to exchange the ISNs. Synchronization requires that each side send its own ISN and receive a confirmation and ISN from the other side of the connection.

Each side must receive the other side's ISN and send a confirming acknowledgment (ACK) in a specific order. A three-way handshake uses the following three-step process to establish a virtual connection (or circuit) between the two devices:

1. Host A initiates a connection by sending a SYN packet indicating its initial sequence number of x in the code field of the header set to indicate a connection request. This bit is set in the code field of the TCP header.

2. Host B receives the packet, records the sequence number of x, replies with an acknowledgment of x + 1, and includes its own initial sequence number of y. The acknowledgment number of x + 1 means Host B has received all octets up to and including x and Host A is expecting x + 1 next.

3. The initiating host, Host A, responds with a simple acknowledgement (ACK) of y + 1 (the sequence number of the second host + 1), indicating it received the previous ACK, which finalizes the connection process.

Figure 10-7 illustrates the three-way handshake/open connection. Both ends of a connection are synchronized with a three-way handshake/open connection sequence.

Figure 10-7 Three-Way Handshake

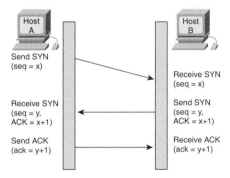

It is important to understand that sequence numbers are a part of initiating communication between the two devices. Sequence numbers act as reference starting numbers between the two devices. The sequence numbers give each host a way to ACK the SYN, so that the receiver knows the sender is responding to the proper connection request because a host can request and receive multiple TCP connections simultaneously.

A three-way handshake is necessary because TCPs might use different mechanisms for picking the ISN. The receiver of the first SYN has no way of knowing if the segment was an old delayed one unless it remembers the last sequence number used on the connection, which is not always possible. So, it must ask the sender to verify this SYN. At this point, either side can begin communicating and either side can break the communication because TCP is a peer-to-peer (balanced) communication method.

 Interactive Media Activity   Drag and Drop: TCP Synchronization

After completing this activity, you will understand TCP synchronization.

Denial-of-Service Attacks

Denial-of-service (DoS) attacks are designed to deny services to legitimate hosts attempting to establish connections. DoS attacks are a common method that hackers utilize to halt system response. One type of DoS is known as SYN flooding, which occurs during the three-way handshake synchronization process utilized by TCP.

During the three-way handshake, the initiating host sends a SYN packet. The SYN packet includes the source IP address and the destination IP address, just like any other packet. The recipient uses this source and destination address information to send the SYN/ACK packet back to the initiating device.

In a DoS attack, the hacker initiates a synchronization but falsifies the source IP address. The receiving device replies to a nonexistent, unreachable IP address and then is placed on hold while waiting to receive the final ACK from the initiator. The waiting request is placed in a connection queue or a holding area in memory. This waiting state requires the attacked device to commit system resources, such as memory, to the waiting process until the connection timer times out. Hackers flood the attacked host with these false SYN requests, utilizing all of its connection resources to respond and wait for bogus connections, preventing it from responding to legitimate connection requests.

To defend against these attacks, administrators can decrease the connection timeout period and increase the connection queue size. Also, software is available that can detect these types of attacks and initiate defensive measures. Figure 10-8 shows a DoS attack during synchronization.

Windowing and Window Size

In many instances, the amount of data that needs to be transmitted is too large to be sent in a single data segment. When this occurs, the data must be broken into smaller pieces to allow for proper data transmission. TCP is responsible for breaking data into segments. This process is similar to feeding a child. Because most small children cannot eat extremely large bites, the person feeding them often cuts their food into smaller pieces that their mouths can accommodate. Additionally, receiving machines might not be able to receive data as quickly as the source can send data. Sometimes discrepancy exists because the receiving device is busy with other tasks; other times the sender is simply a stronger device.

Figure 10-8 DoS Attack/SYN Flooding with no ACK

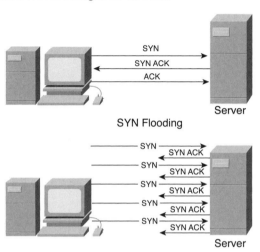

After the data is segmented, it must be transmitted to the destination device. One of the services provided by TCP is *flow control*, which regulates how much data is sent during a given transmission period. The process of flow control is known as *windowing*.

Window size determines the amount of data that can be transmitted at one time before receiving an acknowledgment from the destination. After a host transmits the window-sized number of bytes, the host must receive an acknowledgment that the data has been received before it can send any more messages. For example, with a window size of 1, each individual segment must be acknowledged before the next segment can be sent, as shown in Figure 10-9.

TCP uses a sliding window when determining transmission size. Sliding window algorithms are a method of flow control for network data transfers that use the receiver's window size, as shown in Figure 10-10. The sender computes its usable window, which is how much data it can immediately send. Over time, this sliding window moves to the right, as the receiver acknowledges data. The receiver sends acknowledgements as its TCP receives buffer empties.

Figure 10-9 Window Size of 1

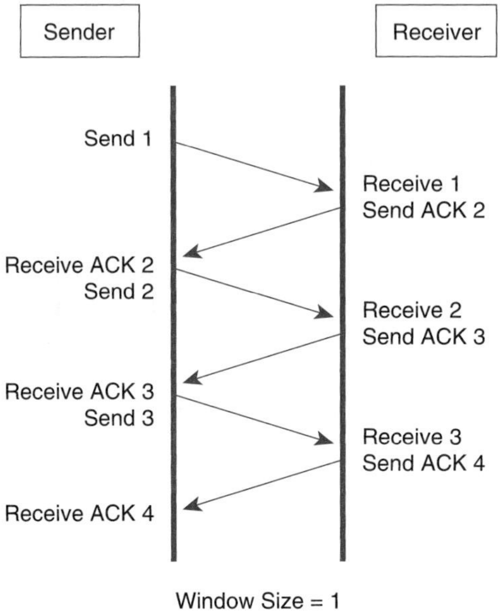

Window Size = 1

The sliding window process works as follows, shown in Figure 10-11:

1. Host B gives Host A a window size of 6 (octets or bytes).

2. Host A begins by sending octets to Host B—octets 1, 2, and 3—and slides its window over showing it has sent those 3 octets.

3. Host A will *not* increase its usable window size by three until it receives an ACKnowledgement from Host B that it has received some or all of the octets.

4. Host B, not waiting for all the 6 octets to arrive, after receiving the third octet, sends an expectational ACKnowledgement of "4" to Host A.

5. Host A does not have to wait for an acknowledgement from Host B to continue to send data, not until the window size reaches 6. Therefore, it sends octets 4 and 5, as shown in Figure 10-12.

6. Host A receives the acknowledgement of ACK 4 and can now *slide* its window over to equal six octets, three octets sent ACKed plus three octets, which can be sent as soon as possible.

Figure 10-10 Larger Window Size

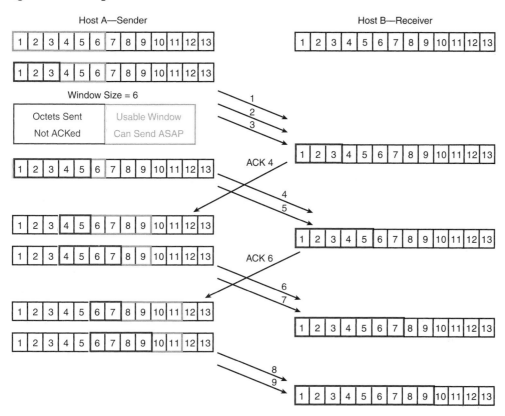

Figure 10-11 Sliding Windows

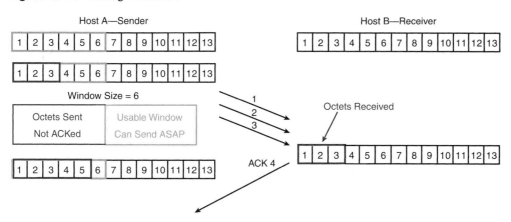

Figure 10-12 Sliding Windows

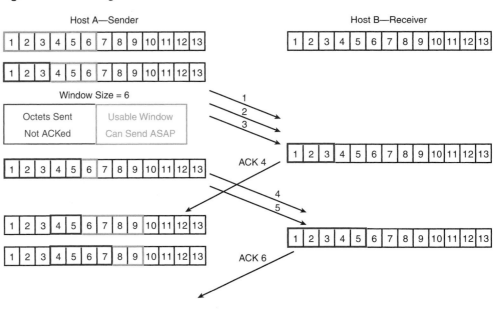

   Interactive Media Activity   Matching: Windowing

After completing this activity, you will understand windowing.

Sequencing Numbers

TCP breaks data into segments. The data segments are then transported from sender to receiver. Data transportation follows the synchronization process and the negotiation of a window size that dictates the number of bytes that can be transmitted at once. The data segments being transmitted must be reassembled once all of the data is received. No guarantee exists that the data will arrive in the order that it was transmitted, so TCP addresses this problem by using sequence numbers. TCP applies sequence numbers to the data segments it is transmitting so that the receiver will be able to properly reassemble the bytes in their original order. Sequencing numbers, shown in Figure 10-13, indicate to the destination device the correct order in which to put the bytes when they are received.

These sequencing numbers also act as reference numbers so that the receiver knows if it has received all of the data and can identify the missing data pieces to the sender so it can retransmit the missing data. This feature offers increased efficiency because the sender is required to retransmit only the missing segments instead of retransmitting the entire set of data.

Figure 10-13 Sequence Acknowledgment Numbers

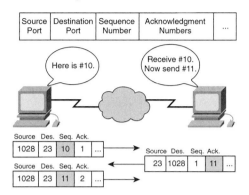

Each TCP segment is numbered before transmission. Figure 10-4 from earlier in the chapter showed the TCP segment format. Notice that the Sequence number portion follows the Destination port in the segment format. At the receiving station, TCP uses the sequence numbers to reassemble the segments into a complete message. If a sequence number is missing in the series, that segment is retransmitted.

Positive Acknowledgments (ACK)

Acknowledgment is a common step in the synchronization process, sliding windows, and the sequencing of data. In a TCP segment, the Sequence number field is followed by the Acknowledgment field. This field is where ACKs and SYNs are indicated.

One problem with the unreliable IP protocol is that no verification method exists in it for determining that data segments actually reached their destination. Therefore, data segments might be forwarded with no knowledge as to whether or not they were actually received. TCP utilizes positive acknowledgement and retransmission to control data flow and confirm data delivery.

Positive acknowledgment and retransmission (PAR) is a common technique many protocols use to provide reliability. With PAR, the source sends a packet, starts a timer, and waits for an acknowledgment before sending the next packet. If the timer expires before the source receives an acknowledgment, the source retransmits the packet and restarts the timer. TCP uses expectant acknowledgments in which the acknowledgment number refers to the next octet that is expected.

Windowing is a flow control mechanism. During windowing, the source device is required to receive an acknowledgment from the destination after transmitting a certain amount of data. With a window size of 3, the source device can send 3 bytes to the destination. It must then wait for an acknowledgment. If the destination receives the three bytes, it sends an acknowledgment to the source device, which can now transmit three more bytes. If the destination does not receive the three bytes, due to overflowing buffers or some other reason, it does not send an acknowledgment. If the source does not receive an acknowledgment, it knows that the bytes must be retransmitted and that the transmission rate should be slowed.

Lab 10.1.6 Multiple Active Host Sessions

In this activity, you enable HTTP services on a router and observe multiple HTTP and Telnet sessions on a single host using the **netstat** command.

UDP Operation

The TCP/IP protocol stack contains many different protocols, and each protocol is designed to perform a specific task. IP provides Layer 3 connectionless transport through an internetwork. TCP enables connection-oriented, reliable transmission of packets at Layer 4 of the OSI model. UDP provides connectionless, nonguaranteed transmission of packets at Layer 4 of the OSI model.

Both TCP and UDP use IP as their underlying Layer 3 protocol. In addition, TCP and UDP are used by various application layer protocols. TCP provides services for applications such as FTP, HTTP, SMTP, and DNS. UDP is the transport layer protocol used by DNS, TFTP, SNMP, and DHCP. Figure 10-14 illustrates the relationship between TCP/IP application, transport, and network layer protocols. Notice that DNS can operate with TCP or UDP. This is the case with many application layer protocols.

Figure 10-14 TCP/IP Application, Transport, and Network Layer Protocols

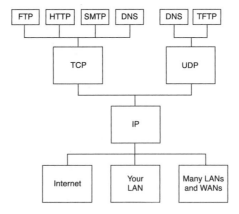

TCP must be used when applications need to guarantee that a packet arrives intact, in sequence, and unduplicated. However, the overhead associated with ensuring delivery of the packet is sometimes a problem when using TCP. Not all applications need to guarantee delivery of the data packet, and therefore, some use the faster, connectionless delivery mechanism offered by UDP. The UDP standard, described in RFC 768, is a simple protocol that exchanges segments without acknowledgments or guaranteed delivery. As an example, TFTP can be used to transfer a configuration file or a Cisco IOS Software image from a TFTP server to a router on an Ethernet network. TFTP uses the efficient UDP transport protocol because the quality of physical connections is usually very good and the acknowledgement and retransmission capabilities of TCP are not necessary. When transferring an IOS image or configuration file using TFTP, the router calculates a checksum at the end of the transfer to ensure the entire file is received uncorrupted. If the file is corrupted, the transfer process has to be started over manually.

UDP does not use windowing or acknowledgments. Therefore, application layer protocols provide error detection. UDP is designed for applications that do not need to put sequences of segments together.

Figure 10-5 earlier in this chapter displayed the UDP segment format. The Source Port field is an optional field, used only if information needs to return to the sending host. The Destination Port field specifies the application to which UDP must pass the protocol. A DNS request from a host to a DNS server has a Destination Port field of 53, the UDP port number for DNS. The Length field identifies the number of octets in the UDP segment. The UDP checksum is optional, but should be used to ensure that the data has not been damaged during transmission. For transport across the network, UDP is encapsulated within the IP packet.

After a UDP segment arrives at the destination IP address, a mechanism must exist that allows the receiving host to determine the destination application of the segment. Ports are used for this purpose. If a host is running both TFTP and DNS services, it must be able to determine what service the arriving UDP segments need. The Destination Port field in the UDP header determines the application to which a UDP segment is delivered.

Overview of Transport Layer Ports

Transport layer ports are 16-bit numbers used to identify the connection end points on either side of the connecting devices. A particular network connection is then identified by a four-part (source address, source port, destination address, destination port) sequence. In principle, this scheme allows for unique UDP connections between any two hosts. UDP is still connectionless and unreliable. To support connection-oriented applications that require reliable, in-sequence data streams, TCP is used. Like UDP, TCP also uses ports to identify connection end points.

Multiple Conversations Between Hosts

At any given moment, thousands of packets providing hundreds of different services are traveling through a modern network. In many cases, servers provide several different services simultaneously, which causes unique problems for the addressing of packets. For example, if a server is running both SMTP and World Wide Web services, a client cannot construct a packet destined for the IP address of the server just using TCP because both SMTP and the World Wide Web services use TCP as their transport layer protocol. A port number must be associated with the conversation between hosts to ensure that the packet reaches the appropriate service on the server. Without a way to distinguish between different conversations, the client is unable to send an e-mail and browse a web page at the same time using one server. A method to separate transport layer conversations must be used.

Hosts running TCP/IP associate ports at the transport layer with certain applications. Port numbers are used to keep track of different conversations that cross the network at the same time. Port numbers are necessary when a host is communicating with a server running multiple services. Both TCP and UDP use port, or socket, numbers to pass information to the upper layers. Figure 10-15 shows an example of TCP and UDP port numbers.

Figure 10-15 TCP and UDP Port Numbers

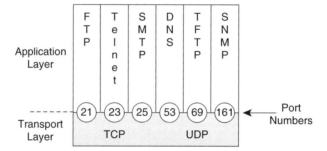

Application software developers have agreed to use the well-known port numbers that are defined in RFC 1700. For example, any conversation bound for the FTP application uses the standard port number 21. Conversations that do not involve applications with well-known port numbers are assigned port numbers that have been randomly selected from within a specific range. These port numbers are used as source and destination addresses in the TCP segment. Table 10-1 lists the reserved TCP and UDP port numbers.

Table 10-1 Reserved TCP and UDP Port Numbers

Decimal	Keyword	Description
0	-	Reserved
1–4	-	Unassigned
5	rje	Remote job entry (RJE)
7	echo	Echo
9	discard	Discard
11	users	Active users
13	daytime	Daytime
15	netstat	Who is up or netstat
17	quote	Quote of the day
19	chargen	Character generator
20	ftp-data	FTP (data)
21	ftp	FTP
23	telnet	Terminal connection
25	smtp	SMTP
37	time	Time of day
39	rlp	Resource Location Protocol
42	nameserver	Host name server
43	nickname	Who is
53	domain	DNS
67	bootps	Bootstrap protocol server
68	bootpc	Bootstrap protocol client
69	tftp	TFTP

continues

Table 10-1 Reserved TCP and UDP Port Numbers (Continued)

Decimal	Keyword	Description
75	-	Any private dial-out service
77	-	Any private RJE Service
79	finger	Finger
80	HTTP	Hypertext Transfer Protocol
123	ntp	Network Time Protocol (NTP)
133159	-	Unassigned
160223	-	Reserved
224241	-	Unassigned
242255	-	Unassigned

Port numbers have the following assigned ranges:

- The well-known ports are ports 0 through 1023
- The registered ports are ports 1024 through 49151
- The dynamic and/or private ports are 49152 through 65535

End systems use port numbers to select proper applications. As shown in Figure 10-16, the originating source port number (1028) is dynamically assigned by the source host. Usually, this port number is larger than 1023. The Internet Assigned Numbers Authority (IANA) controls port numbers in the range of 0 to 1023.

Ports for Services

Services running on hosts must have a port number assigned to them for communication to occur. A remote host attempting to connect to a service expects that service to run on certain transport layer protocols at particular ports. Some ports, defined in RFC 1700, are known as the *well-known ports*. These ports are reserved in both TCP and UDP.

These well-known ports can identify applications that run above the transport layer protocols. For example, a server running the FTP service forwards TCP connections using ports 20 and 21 from clients to its FTP application. This way, the server can determine exactly what service a client is requesting. TCP and UDP use port numbers to determine the correct service to forward service requests to.

Figure 10-16 Source and Destination Ports

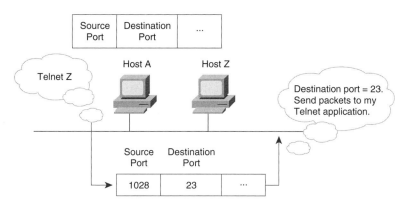

Ports for Clients

Whenever a client connects to a service on a server, a source and destination port must be specified. TCP and UDP segments contain fields for source and destination ports. Destination ports, or ports for services, are normally defined using the well-known ports. Source ports, those set by the client, are determined dynamically.

In general, a client determines the source port by randomly assigning a number above 1023. For instance, a client attempting to communicate with a web server uses TCP and assigns the destination port as 80 and the source port as 1045. When the packet arrives at the server, it passes up to the transport layer and eventually to the World Wide Web service, which operates at port 80. The World Wide Web server responds to the client's request with a segment that uses port 80 as the source and port 1045 as the destination. In this way, clients and servers use ports to distinguish what process the segment is associated with. If a client has two browser sessions open to two different web servers, the destination port is 80 for both sessions. However, the source port is a different number for each session (for example, 1045 and 1048). This difference allows the client to keep track of the two different conversations.

Port Numbering and Well-Known Port Numbers

Port numbers are represented by 2 bytes in the header of a TCP or UDP segment. This 16-bit value can result in port numbers ranging from 0 to 65,535. These port numbers are divided into three different categories:

- Well-known ports
- Registered ports
- Dynamic or private ports

The first 1023 ports are well-known ports. As previously discussed, these ports are used for well-known network services such as FTP, Telnet, DNS, or HTTP. Registered ports range from 1024 to 49151 and identify services such as Cisco-Net-Mgmt and Calendar Access Protocol. Finally, ports between 49152 and 65535 are defined as dynamic or private ports.

Example of Multiple Sessions Between Hosts

Port numbers are used to track multiple sessions that can occur between hosts. A port number and a network address combine to form a socket. A pair of sockets, one on each host, forms a unique connection or virtual circuit. For example, a host can have a Telnet connection through port 23, while simultaneously surfing the net through port 80. The IP address and the MAC address are the same because the packets are coming from the same host. However, the port numbers are different because they are different protocols and, thus, different sockets.

 Lab 10.2.5 Well-Known Port Numbers and Multiple Sessions

In this lab, you observe the well-known port numbers of multiple sessions on a single host using the **netstat** command.

Comparison of MAC Addresses, IP Addresses, and Port Numbers

MAC addresses, IP addresses, and port numbers are often confusing, but this confusion can be avoided if the addresses are explained in reference to the OSI reference model. Port numbers are located at the transport layer and are serviced by the network layer. The network layer assigns the logical address, or IP. It is then serviced by the data link layer, which assigns the physical address, or MAC.

A good analogy can be made with a normal letter. The address on a letter consists of a name, street, city, and state. These can be compared to the port, MAC, and IP address used for network data. The name on the envelope is equivalent to a port number, the street address is the MAC, and the city and state make up the IP address. Multiple letters can be mailed to the same street address, city, and state; however, they contain different names on the letters. For instance, two letters can be mailed to the same house with one addressed to John Doe and the other to Jane Doe. This is analogous to multiple sessions with different port numbers.

More Information: TCP/IP and the Internet Layer

Internet Protocol (IP) is the Layer 3 protocol responsible for the addressing scheme that allows packets to be properly routed over intranets and the Internet to their destinations. Routers use the IP address information in an IP packet header to determine which interface the packet should be switched to in order to reach its destination. IP does not provide any services to ensure that the packet reaches its destination. IP is described as an unreliable, connectionless protocol. Packets might be dropped in route, arrive in the wrong order, or be transmitted faster than the receiver can accept them. IP has no means of overcoming these and other delivery issues.

The Internet layer of the TCP/IP stack corresponds to the network layer of the OSI model. The network layer is responsible for getting packets through a network using software addressing.

As shown in Figure 10-17, several protocols operate at the TCP/IP Internet layer, corresponding to the OSI network layer:

- **IP**—Provides addressing and connectionless, best-effort delivery routing of datagrams, is not concerned with the content of the datagrams, and looks for a way to move the datagrams to their destination
- **ICMP**—Provides control and messaging capabilities
- *Address Resolution Protocol (ARP)*—Determines the data link layer (MAC) addresses for known IP addresses
- *Reverse Address Resolution Protocol (RARP)*—Determines network addresses when data link layer addresses are known

Figure 10-17 OSI Network Layer

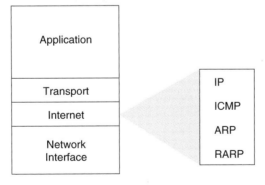

More Information: TCP/IP and the Internet Layer (Continued)

How ARP Works

ARP is used to resolve or map a known IP address to a MAC sublayer address. This mapping allows for communication because the data link hardware will not accept a frame unless the MAC address in the frame matches the hardware MAC address (or it is a broadcast MAC address). To determine a destination MAC address for a datagram, a table called the ARP cache is checked. Every host on a TCP/IP network (routers, workstations, servers, and so on) maintains an ARP cache. If the address is not in the table, ARP sends a broadcast that is received by every station on the network, looking for the destination station. The term *local ARP* describes the search for an address when the requesting host and the destination host share the same medium or wire. Before issuing the ARP, the 172.16.3.1 host uses its own IP address and subnet mask to determine what network it is on, as shown in Figure 10-18. In this case, this determines that the nodes are on the same subnet.

Figure 10-18 OSI Network Layer

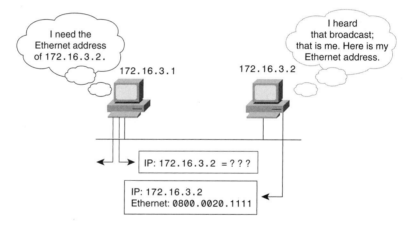

RARP is a TCP/IP protocol that permits a physical address, such as an Ethernet address, to be translated into an IP address. Consequently, this protocol is the opposite of ARP. Hosts such as diskless workstations often know only their hardware interface addresses, or MAC address, when booted, but not their IP addresses. They must discover their IP addresses from an external source. Usually, a RARP server using the RARP protocol can resolve this situation.

Summary

In this chapter, you learned the following:

- TCP is a connection-oriented transport layer protocol that provides necessary quality-of-service processes to the unreliable IP protocol.

- TCP provides reliability, flow control, and virtual connection services.

- TCP utilizes a three-way handshake to establish synchronized communication between hosts.

- Sliding windows allow for dynamic data flow control.

- Sequence numbers ensure proper data reassembly by the receiving host.

- UDP is a connectionless transport layer protocol.

- UDP and TCP use ports to distinguish upper-layer applications.

To supplement all that you've learned in this chapter, refer to the chapter-specific Interactive Media Activities on the CD-ROM accompanying this book.

Key Terms

Address Resolution Protocol (ARP)   Internet protocol used to map an IP address to a MAC address.

denial of service (DoS)   Type of attack on a network that is designed to bring the network to its knees by flooding it with useless traffic.

flow control   The process of adjusting the flow of data from one device to another to ensure that the receiving device can handle all of the incoming data.

Reverse Address Resolution Protocol (RARP)   Protocol in the TCP/IP stack that provides a method for finding IP addresses based on MAC addresses.

Transmission Control Protocol (TCP)   Connection-oriented transport layer protocol that provides reliable full-duplex data transmission. TCP is part of the TCP/IP protocol stack.

User Datagram Protocol (UDP)   Connectionless transport layer protocol in the TCP/IP protocol stack. UDP is a simple protocol that exchanges datagrams without acknowledgments or guaranteed delivery, requiring that error processing and retransmission be handled by other protocols.

well-known ports   These ports are defined in RFC 1700 and are reserved in both TCP and UDP. These well-known ports can identify applications that run above the transport layer protocols.

windowing   Manages the flow. The recipient reports to the sender what size window in terms of octets it's able to accept at this time. The sender then sends that many octets to the receiving host.

Check Your Understanding

Complete all the review questions to test your understanding of the topics and concepts in this chapter. Answers are listed in Appendix B, "Check Your Understanding Answer Key."

1. Which of the following best describes TCP/IP?

   A. It is a suite of protocols that can be used to communicate across any set of interconnected networks.

   B. It is a suite of protocols that allows LANs to connect into WANs.

   C. It is a suite of protocols that allows for data transmission across a multitude of networks.

   D. It is a suite of protocols that allows different devices to be shared by interconnected networks.

2. Which of the following is one of the protocols found at the transport layer?

    A. UCP

    B. UDP

    C. TDP

    D. TDC

3. What is the purpose of port numbers?

    A. They keep track of different conversations crossing the network at the same time.

    B. Source systems use them to keep a session organized and to select the proper application.

    C. End systems use them to dynamically assign end users to a particular session, depending on their application use.

    D. Source systems generate them to predict destination addresses.

4. Which of the following best describes UDP?

    A. A protocol that acknowledges flawed or intact datagrams

    B. A protocol that detects errors and requests retransmissions from the source

    C. A protocol that processes datagrams and requests retransmissions when necessary

    D. A protocol that exchanges datagrams without acknowledgments or guaranteed delivery

5. Which of the following TCP/IP layers includes file transfer, e-mail, remote login, and network management?

    A. Transport

    B. Application

    C. Internet

    D. Network

6. Why is sequence numbering in the TCP three-way handshake/open connections used?

    A. To ensure that lost data can be recovered if problems occur later

    B. To determine how much data the receiving station can accept at one time

    C. To provide efficient use of bandwidth by users

    D. To change binary ping responses into information in the upper layers

7. What does a TCP sliding window do?

   A. It makes the window larger so that more data can come through at once, which results in more efficient use of bandwidth.

   B. The window size slides to each section of the datagram to receive data, which results in more efficient use of bandwidth.

   C. It is a method of flow control for network data transfers using the receiver's window size.

   D. It limits the incoming data so that each segment must be sent one by one, which is an inefficient use of bandwidth.

8. UDP segments use what protocols to provide reliability?

   A. Network layer protocols

   B. Application layer protocols

   C. Internet protocols

   D. Transmission Control Protocols

9. Which of the following best describes window size?

   A. The maximum size of the window that software can have and still process data rapidly

   B. The number of bytes that can be transmitted while awaiting an acknowledgment

   C. The size of the window, in picas, that must be set ahead of time so that data can be sent

   D. The size of the window opening on a monitor, which is not always equal to the monitor size

10. What is the function of ARP?

    A. It completes research for a Layer 3 destination address.

    B. It is used to map a known IP address to an unknown MAC address.

    C. It is used to map an unknown IP address to a known MAC address.

    D. It sends a broadcast message looking for the router IP address.

CHAPTER 11

Access Control Lists (ACLs)

Objectives

Upon completion of this chapter, you should be able to answer the following questions:

- What are some of the uses and/or purposes of ACLs?

- How do ACLs provide security and/or control to a network?

- How do you determine which wildcard mask should be used?

- What is the difference between standard ACLs, extended ACLs, and named ACLs, and what are some of the scenarios in which each one might be used?

Additional Topics of Interest

In addition to the core objective areas, this chapter introduces you to the following topic of interest to networkers:

- In what ways do ACLs relate to firewall architecture?

Key Terms

The following is a list of key terms introduced in this chapter. For your reference, a definition for each term can be found at the end of this chapter.

access control lists (ACLs)   page 836

queuing   page 838

bit bucket   page 841

standard ACL   page 849

extended ACL   page 852

named ACLs   page 860

firewall   page 865

exterior router   page 865

interior router   page 865

border routers   page 865

In this chapter, you learn about using standard and extended access control lists (ACLs) as a means to control network traffic and how ACLs are used as part of a security solution.

In addition, this chapter includes tips, considerations, recommendations, and general guidelines on how to use ACLs, and includes the commands and configurations needed to create ACLs. Finally, this chapter provides examples of standard and extended ACLs and shows how to apply ACLs to router interfaces.

Please be sure to look at this chapter's associated Videos and Interactive Media Activities that you will find on the CD-ROM accompanying this book. These CD elements are designed to supplement the material and reinforce the concepts introduced in this chapter.

Access Control List Fundamentals

NOTE

ACLs consume CPU resources in the router because every packet has to be evaluated, increasing the number of processes used.

Network administrators must be capable of denying unwanted access to the network while allowing appropriate access. Although security tools such as passwords, callback equipment, and physical security devices are helpful, they often lack the flexibility of basic traffic filtering and the specific controls that most administrators prefer. For example, a network administrator might want to allow users access to the Internet but might not want external users Telnetting into the LAN.

Routers provide basic traffic-filtering capabilities, such as blocking Internet traffic, with *access control lists (ACLs)*. An ACL is a sequential collection of permit or deny statements that apply to addresses or upper-layer protocols.

Throughout the discussion of ACLs in this chapter, it is important to keep in mind that ACL statements belong to the same ACL and have the same ACL number. For example, consider the following bulleted list:

- Access Control List 1
    - ACL 1 Statement
    - ACL 1 Statement
    - ACL 1 Statement
    - ACL 1 Statement
- Access Control List 2
    - ACL 2 Statement
    - ACL 2 Statement
    - ACL 2 Statement
    - ACL 2 Statement
    - ACL 2 Statement

- Access Control List 3

    — ACL 3 Statement

    — ACL 3 Statement

    — ACL 3 Statement

The ACL statements for a particular ACL have the same number and are part of the same ACL.

It is important to configure ACLs correctly and to know where to place ACLs on the network. ACLs serve multiple purposes in a network. Common ACL functions include the following:

- Filtering packets internally

- Protecting the internal network from illegal Internet access

- Restricting access to virtual terminal ports

ACLs are lists of instructions that you apply to a router's interface. These lists tell the router what kinds of packets to accept and what kinds of packets to deny. Acceptance and denial can be based on certain specifications, such as source address, destination address, and TCP/UDP port number.

ACLs enable you to manage traffic and scan specific packets by applying the ACL to a router interface. Any traffic going through the interface is tested against certain conditions that are part of the ACL.

ACLs can be created for all routed network protocols, such as Internet Protocol (IP) and Internetwork Packet Exchange (IPX), to filter packets as the packets pass through a router. ACLs can be configured at the router to control access to a network or subnet.

ACLs filter network traffic by controlling whether routed packets are forwarded or blocked at the router's interfaces. The router examines each packet to determine whether to forward or drop it, based on the conditions specified in the ACL. ACL conditions could be the source address of the traffic, the destination address of the traffic, the upper-layer protocol, the port, or applications.

ACLs must be defined on a per-protocol basis. In other words, you must define an ACL for every protocol enabled on an interface if you want to control traffic flow for *that* protocol on *that* interface. (Note that some protocols refer to ACLs as *filter*s.) For example, if your router interface were configured for IP, AppleTalk, and IPX, you would need to define at least three ACLs. As shown in Figure 11-1, ACLs can be used as a tool for network control by adding the flexibility to filter the packets that flow in or out of router interfaces. This is accomplished by establishing a numbering range or scheme for each protocol's ACL. You learn more about the ACL numbers later in this chapter.

Figure 11-1 ACL Example

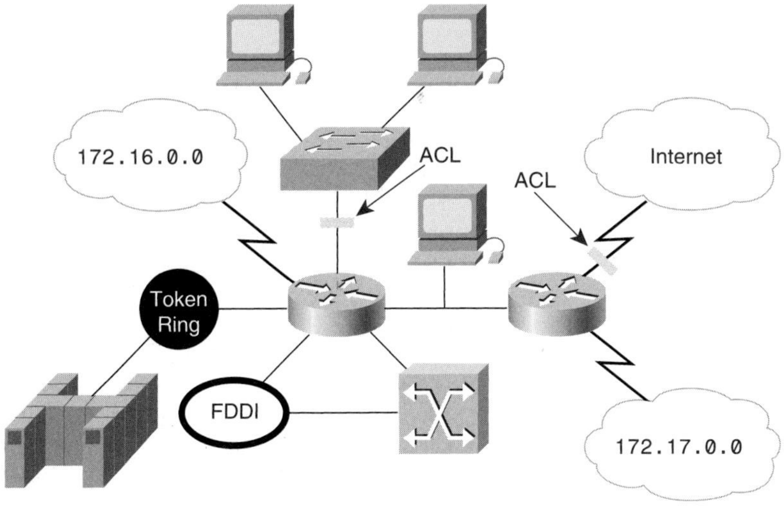

Introduction to ACLs

NOTE

The rule of thumb is one ACL per interface per direction per protocol.

Many reasons exist for creating ACLs. ACLs can be used to do the following:

- Limit network traffic and increase network performance. For example, ACLs can designate certain packets to be processed by a router before other traffic, on the basis of a protocol. This is referred to as *queuing*. Queuing ensures that routers will not process packets that are not needed. As a result, queuing limits network traffic and reduces network congestion.

- Provide traffic flow control. For example, ACLs can restrict or reduce the contents of routing updates. These restrictions are used to limit information about specific networks from propagating through the network.

- Provide a basic level of security for network access. ACLs can allow one host to access a part of your network and prevent another host from accessing the same area. In Figure 11-2, Host A is allowed to access the Human Resources network, and Host B is prevented from accessing the Human Resources network. If you do not configure ACLs on your router, all packets passing through the router could be allowed onto all parts of the network.

- Decide which type of traffic is forwarded or blocked at the router interface. For example, you can permit e-mail traffic to be routed, but at the same time block all Telnet traffic.

Figure 11-2 Limiting Network Traffic

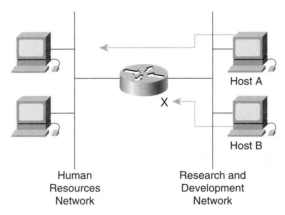

Human
Resources
Network

Host A

Host B

X

Research and
Development
Network

More Information: Creating an ACL: Why Order Matters

Order matters when creating an ACL. As traffic enters or exits a router's interface, where an ACL is applied, Cisco IOS Software compares the packet against the rules defined in the ACL. Statements are evaluated in the order they were entered into the ACL by the network administrator. The packet is compared, one at a time in sequence, until a match is found. After a match is found, the action specified in the line matching the traffic in question is taken. No more conditions are checked.

For example, if a condition statement permitting all traffic is created, statements added later will never be checked. If additional statements are required or if statements must be changed, you must delete the ACL and re-create it with the new statements. It is a good idea to use a PC text editor to create and modify ACLs and then send them to the router via Trivial File Transfer Protocol (TFTP) or HyperTerminal text file transfer.

When an ACL is created, new lines are added to the end of the ACL. Individual lines cannot be deleted. Only entire ACLs can be deleted.

Using ACLs

You can create an ACL for each protocol that you want to filter for each router interface. For some protocols, you create one ACL to filter inbound traffic and one ACL to filter outbound traffic.

After an ACL statement checks a packet for a match, the packet can be denied or permitted to use an interface in the access group. Cisco IOS Software ACLs check the packet and upper-layer headers, as shown in Figure 11-3.

More Information: Creating an ACL: Why Order Matters (Continued)

Figure 11-3 Checking the Packet and Upper-Layer Headers

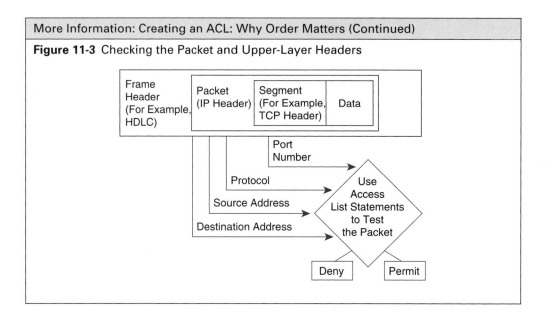

 Video and Animation Access Control List Overview

ACLs provide basic traffic control. In this video, you learn the reasons for applying ACLs and the steps required for configuring ACLs. You will be able to identify the two types of ACLs, standard and extended, and when each should be used.

How ACLs Work

An ACL is a group of statements that define how packets do the following:

- Enter inbound router interfaces
- Relay through the router
- Exit outbound router interfaces

As shown in Figure 11-4, the beginning of the communication process is the same, whether ACLs are used or not. As a packet enters an interface, the router checks to see whether the packet is routable. Now the router checks whether the inbound interface has an ACL. If one exists, the packet is tested against the conditions in the list. If the packet is allowed, it then is checked against routing table entries to determine the destination interface. ACLs filter not packets that originate in the router itself, but packets from other sources.

Next, the router checks whether the outbound interface has an ACL. If it does not, the packet can be sent to the outbound interface directly; for example, if it will use E0, which has no ACLs, the packet uses E0 directly.

ACL statements operate in a sequential, logical order. If a condition match is true, the packet is permitted or denied and the rest of the ACL statements are not checked. If all the ACL statements are unmatched, an implicit **deny any** statement is imposed. Even though you will not see the **deny any** as the last line of an ACL, it is there by default. In Figure 11-5, if by matching the first test a packet is denied access to the destination, it is discarded and dropped into the *bit bucket.* It is not exposed to any ACL tests that follow. If the packet does not match the conditions of the first test, it drops to the next statement in the ACL.

Figure 11-4 How ACLs Work

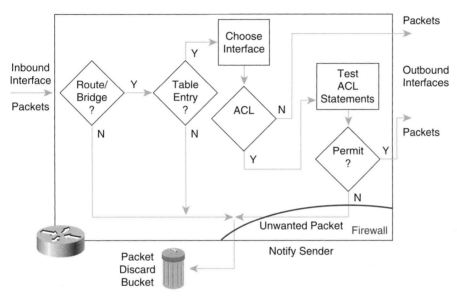

ACLs enable you to control what clients can access on your network. Conditions in an ACL file can do the following:

- Screen out certain hosts to either allow or deny access to part of your network

- Grant or deny users permission to access only certain types of applications, such as FTP or HTTP

Creating ACLs

ACLs are created in the global configuration mode. There are many different types of ACLs including standard, extended, IPX, AppleTalk, and others. When configuring ACLs on a router, each ACL must be uniquely identified by assigning a number to it. This number identifies the type of access list created and must fall within the specific range of numbers that is valid for that type of list.

Figure 11-5 ACL Test Matching and Implicit deny any

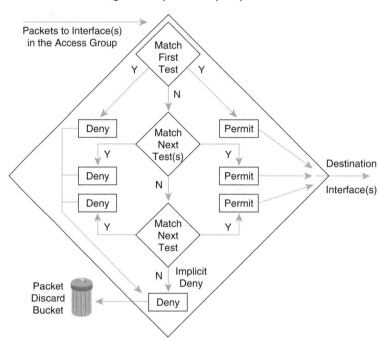

After the proper command mode is entered and the list type number is decided upon, the user enters the access list statements using the keyword **access-list**, followed by the proper parameters, as shown later in Example 11-1. Creating the access list is the first half of using it on a router. The second half of the process is assigning it to the proper interface.

ACLs are assigned to one or more interfaces and can filter inbound traffic or outbound traffic by using the **access-group** command, as shown in Example 11-1. The **access-group** command is issued in the interface configuration mode. When assigning an ACL to an interface, inbound or outbound placement should be specified. The filter direction can be set to check packets that travel into or out of an interface. When determining if the ACL is addressing inbound or outbound traffic, the network administrator needs to look at the interfaces from inside the router. This is a very important concept. Traffic coming in from an interface is filtered by an inbound access list and traffic going out an interface is filtered by the outbound access list. After creating a numbered ACL, it must be assigned to an interface. To alter an ACL that contains numbered ACL statements, all the statements in the numbered ACL must be deleted using the command **no access-list** *list-number*.

In practice, ACL commands can be lengthy character strings. Key tasks covered in this section for creating ACLs include the following:

- You create ACLs by using global configuration mode.

- Specifying an ACL number from 1 to 99 defines a standard ACL for IP and instructs the router to accept standard ACL statements.

- Specifying an ACL number from 100 to 199 defines an extended ACL for IP and instructs the router to accept extended ACL statements.

- You must carefully select and logically order the ACL. Permitted IP protocols must be specified; all other protocols should be denied unless required.

- You need to select which protocols to check; any other protocols are not checked. Later in the procedure, you can specify an optional destination port for more precision.

- You apply an ACL to an interface.

In practice, ACL commands can be lengthy character strings. Key tasks for creating ACLs are covered in this section. Although each protocol has its own set of specific tasks and rules that are required to provide traffic filtering, in general, most protocols require two basic steps:

Step 1   Create an ACL definition.

Step 2   Apply the ACL to an interface.

ACLs are assigned to one or more interfaces and can filter inbound traffic or outbound traffic, depending on the configuration and how they are applied. Outbound ACLs generally are more efficient than inbound and, therefore, are preferred. A router with an inbound ACL must check every packet to see whether it matches the ACL condition before switching the packet to an outbound interface.

Assigning a Unique Number to Each ACL

When configuring ACLs on a router, you can identify each ACL with a unique number. When you use a number to identify an ACL, the number must be within the specific range of numbers that is valid for the protocol. Example 11-1 defines ACLs 1 and 2 and applies the ACLs to interface Ethernet 0.

Example 11-1 *Assigning ACLs to an Interface*

```
Router(config)#access-list 1 permit 5.6.0.0 0.0.255.255
Router(config)#access-list 1 deny 7.9.0.0 0.0.255.255
!
Router(config)#access-list 2 permit 1.2.3.4 0.0.255.255
Router(config)#access-list 2 deny 1.2.0.0 0.0.255.255
!
Router(config)#interface ethernet 0
Router(config-if)#ip address 1.1.1.1 255.0.0.0
!
Router(config-if)#ip access-group 1 in
Router(config-if)#ip access-group 2 out
```

Table 11-1 lists valid protocol ACL numbers.

Table 11-1 Protocols, ACLs, and Their Corresponding Numbers

Protocol	Range
IP	1 to 99, 1300–1399
Extended IP	100 to 199, 2000–2699
AppleTalk	600 to 699
IPX	800 to 899
Extended IPX	900 to 999
IPX Service Advertising Protocol	1000 to 1099

Interactive Media Activity   Drag and Drop: Creating ACLs

After completing this activity, you will be able to create ACLs.

The Function of a Wildcard Mask

A *wildcard mask* is a 32-bit quantity that is divided into four octets, with each octet containing 8 bits. A wildcard mask bit of 0 means "check the corresponding bit value," and a wildcard mask bit of 1 means "do not check (ignore) that corresponding bit value" (see Figure 11-6).

Figure 11-6 Wildcard Mask Bit Matching

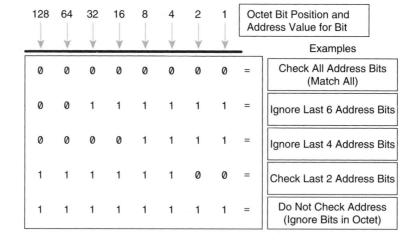

A wildcard mask is paired with an IP address, similar to how a subnet mask is paired with an IP address. Wildcard mask bits use the numbers 1 and 0 to identify how to treat the corresponding IP address bits.

ACLs use wildcard masking to identify a single address or multiple addresses for permit or deny tests. The term *wildcard masking* is a nickname for the ACL mask bit–matching process and comes from of an analogy of a wildcard that matches any other card in a poker game.

Although both are 32-bit quantities, wildcard masks and IP subnet masks operate differently. Recall that the 0s and 1s in a subnet mask determine the network, subnet, and host portions of the corresponding IP address. The 0s and 1s in a wildcard, as just noted, determine whether the corresponding bits in the IP address should be checked or ignored for ACL purposes.

As you have learned, the 0 and 1 bits in an ACL wildcard mask cause the ACL to either check or ignore the corresponding bits in the IP address. Figure 11-7 demonstrates how this wildcard masking process is applied.

Suppose that you want to test an IP address for subnets that will be permitted or denied. Assume that the IP address is a Class B address (that is, the first two octets are the network number) with 8 bits of subnetting (the third octet is for subnets).

You want to use IP wildcard mask bits to permit all packets from any host in the 172.30.16.0 to 172.30.31.0 subnets. Figure 11-7 shows an example of how to use the wildcard mask to do this.

Figure 11-7 Wildcard Mask Example

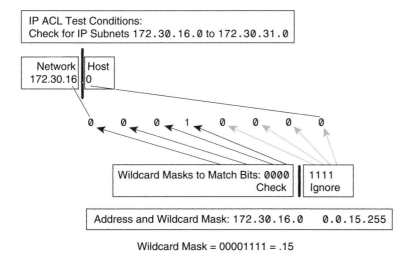

To begin, the wildcard mask checks the first two octets (172.30), using corresponding 0 bits in the wildcard mask.

Because there is no interest in individual host addresses (a valid host ID does not have .0 at the end of the address), the wildcard mask ignores the final octet, using corresponding 1 bits in the wildcard mask.

In the third octet, the wildcard mask is 15 (00001111), and the IP address is 16 (00010000). The first four 0s in the wildcard mask tell the router to match the first 4 bits of the IP address (0001). Because the last 4 bits are ignored, all numbers in the range of 16 (00010000) to 31 (00011111) will match because they begin in the pattern 0001.

For the final (least-significant) 4 bits in this octet, the wildcard mask ignores the value because in these positions, the address value can be binary 0 or binary 1, and the corresponding wildcard bits are 1s. In this example, the wildcard mask tells the router to match the first 4 bits of the IP address. The remaining 4 bits are ignored altogether. Therefore, the address 172.30.16.0 with the wildcard mask 0.0.15.255 matches subnets 172.30.16.0 to 172.30.31.0. The wildcard mask does not match any other subnets.

Using the Wildcard **any**

Working with decimal representations of binary wildcard mask bits can be tedious. For the most common uses of wildcard masking, you can use abbreviations. These abbreviations reduce the amount of typing you need to do when configuring address test conditions. One such example is the wildcard **any**. For example, assume that you want to specify that any destination address will be permitted in an ACL test. To indicate any IP address, you would enter 0.0.0.0, as shown in Figure 11-8; then, to indicate that the ACL should ignore (that is, allow without checking) any value, the corresponding wildcard mask bits for this address would be all 1s (that is, 255.255.255.255).

Figure 11-8 Wildcard **any**

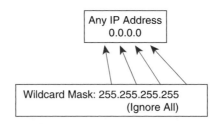

You can use the abbreviation of **any** to communicate this same test condition on Cisco IOS Software. Instead of typing 0.0.0.0 255.255.255.255, you can use the word **any** by itself as the keyword.

For example, instead of using this:

```
Router(config)#access-list 1 permit 0.0.0.0 255.255.255.255
```

You can use this:

```
Router(config)#access-list 1 permit any
```

Using the Wildcard **host**

A second common condition in which Cisco IOS Software permits an abbreviation in the ACL wildcard mask arises when you want to match all the bits of an entire IP host address. For example, suppose that you want to specify that a unique host IP address will be permitted in an ACL test. To indicate a host IP address, you would enter the full address (for example, 172.30.16.29, as shown in Figure 11-9). Then, to indicate that the ACL should check all the bits in the address, the corresponding wildcard mask bits for this address would be all 0s (that is, 0.0.0.0).

Figure 11-9 Wildcard **host**

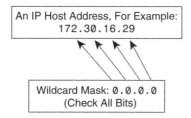

You can use the abbreviation of **host** to communicate this same test condition on Cisco IOS Software. In the example, instead of typing 172.30.16.29 0.0.0.0, you can use the word **host** in front of the address.

For example, instead of using this:

```
Router(config)#access-list 1 permit 172.30.16.29 0.0.0.0
```

You can use this:

```
Router(config)#access-list 1 permit host 172.30.16.29
```

Verifying ACLs

The **show ip interface** command displays IP interface information and indicates whether any ACLs are set. Example 11-2 shows the output of the **show ip interface** command. As you can see in rows 9 and 10 in Example 11-2, ACL 10 is set to the outgoing traffic on interface Ethernet 0. There is no ACL set to inbound traffic.

Example 11-2 **show ip interface** *Command Output*

```
Router> show ip interface
Ethernet0 is up, line protocol is up
Internet address is 192.54.22.2, subnet mask is 255.255.255.0
Broadcast address is 255.255.255.255
Address determined by nonvolatile memory
MTU is 1500 bytes
Helper address is 192.52.71.4
Secondary address 131.192.115.2, subnet mask 255.255.255.0
Outgoing ACL 10 is set
Inbound ACL is not set
Proxy ARP is enabled
Security level is default
Split horizon is enabled
ICMP redirects are always sent
ICMP unreachables are never sent
ICMP mask replies are never sent
IP fast switching is enabled
Gateway Discovery is disabled
IP accounting is disabled
TCP/IP header compression is disabled
Probe proxy name replies are disabled
Router>
```

The **show access-lists** command displays the contents of all ACLs. By entering the ACL name or number as an option for this command, you can see a specific list.

Access Control Lists

Routers provide basic traffic-filtering capabilities, such as blocking Internet traffic, with access control lists (ACLs). An ACL is a sequential list of **permit** or **deny** statements that apply to addresses or upper-layer protocols. This section introduces standard and extended ACLs as a means to control network traffic. It also discusses how ACLs are used as part of a security solution.

Standard ACLs

A *standard ACL* checks the source address of routed IP packets and compares it against the statements defining the ACL, as demonstrated in Figure 11-10.

Figure 11-10 Standard ACL Operations

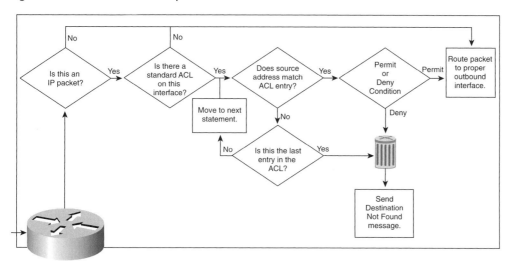

Standard ACLs either permit or deny access for an entire protocol suite (such as IP), based on the network, subnet, and host addresses. For example, packets coming in interface E0 or Fa0/0 are checked for their source addresses and protocols and then are compared against the ACL. When a match is found, that action (permit or deny) is performed. Packets matching **permit** statements in the ACL then are routed through the router to an output interface. Packets matching **deny** statements in the ACL are discarded (dropped) at the incoming interface.

The following is the full syntax of the standard ACL command:

```
Router(config)# access-list access-list-number {deny I permit I remark} source
  [source-wildcard] [log]
```

The **remark** keyword makes the access list easier to understand. Each remark is limited to 100 characters.

For example, it is not immediately clear what the purpose of the following entry is:

```
access-list 1 permit 171.69.2.88
```

It is much easier to read a remark about the entry to understand its effect, as follows:

```
access-list 1 remark permit only Howard workstation through access-list 1 permit
  171.69.2.88.
```

The **no** form of this command is used to remove a standard ACL. The following is the syntax for the **no** form of this command:

```
Router(config)# no access-list access-list-number
```

Table 11-2 shows descriptions of the parameters used in this syntax.

Table 11-2 Standard ACL Parameters

Parameter	Description
access-list-number	Number of an access list. This is a decimal number from 1 to 99 or from 1300 to 1999.
deny	Denies access if the conditions are matched.
permit	Permits access if the conditions are matched.
remark	Makes the access list easier to understand and scan.
source	Number of the network or host from which the packet is being sent. There are two alternative ways to specify the source: <ul><li>Use a 32-bit quantity in four-part dotted-decimal format.</li><li>Use the **any** keyword as an abbreviation for a *source* and *source-wildcard* of 0.0.0.0 255.255.255.255.</li></ul>
source-wildcard	(Optional) Wildcard bits to be applied to the source. There are two alternative ways to specify the source wildcard: <ul><li>Use a 32-bit quantity in four-part dotted-decimal format. Place 1s in the bit positions you want to ignore.</li><li>Use the **any** keyword as an abbreviation for a source and *source-wildcard* value of 0.0.0.0 255.255.255.255.</li></ul>
log	(Optional) Causes an informational logging message about the packet that matches the entry to be sent to the console. (The level of messages logged to the console is controlled by the **logging console** command.) The message includes the access list number, whether the packet was permitted or denied, the source address, and the number of packets. The message is generated for the first packet that matches and then at five-minute intervals, including the number of packets permitted or denied in the previous five-minute interval.

Table 11-2 Standard ACL Parameters (Continued)

Parameter	Description
log	Use the **ip access-list log-update** command to generate the logging messages to appear when the number of matches reaches a configurable threshold (instead of waiting for a five-minute interval). To learn more about the **ip access-list log-update** command, you can check the following resource at Cisco for more information: www.cisco.com/univercd/cc/td/doc/product/ software/ios120/ 12cgcr/cbkixol.htm. The logging facility might drop some logging message packets if there are too many to be handled or if there is more than one logging message to be handled in one second. This behavior prevents the router from crashing because of too many logging packets. Therefore, the logging facility should not be used as a billing tool or an accurate source of the number of matches to an access list.

The standard version of the **access-list** global configuration command defines a standard ACL with a number ranging from 1 to 99. Example 11-3 shows four ACL statements, all of which belong to access list 2; although this combination is not likely, it illustrates how several different statement can work. Also remember that if a packet does not match any of these tests, there is an implicit (unseen) **deny any** at end of the ACL.

Example 11-3 *Standard ACL Statements*

```
access-list 2 deny 172.16.1.1
access-list 2 permit 172.16.1.0 0.0.0.255
access-list 2 deny 172.16.1.1 0.0.255.255
access-list 2 permit 172.16.1.1 0.255.255.255
```

In the first ACL statement, notice that there is no wildcard mask. In situations like this, when no wildcard mask is shown, the default mask is used, which is 0.0.0.0. This statement denies the IP address 172.16.1.1.

The second statement permits the specific host 172.16.1.0 or any host from the 172.16.1.0 subnet.

The third statement denies any host from the 172.16.0.0 network, and the fourth statement permits any host from any network starting with 172.

The **ip access-group** command links an existing ACL to an interface. It is necessary to enter interface configuration mode first to access the desired interface (for example, s0/0). The format of the command is as follows:

```
Router(config-if)#ip access-group access-list-number {in | out}
```

Lab 11.2.1a Configuring Standard Access Lists

In this lab, you configure and apply a standard ACL to permit or deny specific traffic.

Lab 11.2.1b Standard ACLs

In this lab, you plan, configure, and apply a standard ACL to permit or deny specific traffic and test the ACL to determine whether the desired results were achieved.

Extended ACLs

An *extended ACL* is used more often than a standard ACL because an extended ACL provides a greater range of flexibility and control. Extended ACLs check the source and destination IP addresses and also can check for protocols and TCP or UDP port numbers. Figure 11-11 illustrates the decision process that a router uses to evaluate packets against extended ACLs.

Figure 11-11 Extended ACL Operations

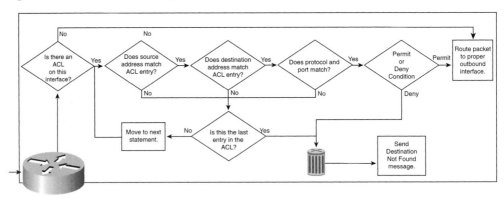

Access can be permitted or denied based on where a packet originated, its destination, the protocol type, the port addresses, and application. An extended ACL can allow e-mail traffic from Fa0/0 to specific S0/0 destinations while denying file transfers and web browsing. When packets are discarded, some protocols send an echo packet to the sender, which states that the destination was unreachable.

Extended ACLs have more granularity in terms of control and packet manipulation than standard ACLs. Whereas standard ACLs can prevent or deny only an entire protocol suite, extended ACL gives you the capability to "nitpick" which protocol in the suite you want to deny or allow. For example, allow HTTP but not FTP.

The following is the full syntax of the extended ACL command:

```
Router(config)# access-list access-list-number [dynamic dynamic-name
  [timeout  minutes]] {deny | permit} protocol source source-wildcard
  destination destination-wildcard [precedence precedence] [tos tos]
  [log | log-input] [time-range time-range-name] [fragments]
```

The **no** form of this command is used to remove a standard ACL. The following is the syntax for the **no** form of this command:

```
Router(config)# no access-list access-list-number
```

The syntax for extended ACL statements can get very long and often wraps in the terminal window. Many additional options are available in extended ACLs, as documented in Table 11-3.

Table 11-3 Extended ACL Parameters

Parameter	Description
access-list-number	Number of an access list. This is a decimal number from 100 to 199 or from 2000 to 2699.
dynamic *dynamic-name*	(Optional) Identifies this ACL as a dynamic ACL. Refer to lock-and-key access documented in the "Configuring Lock-and-Key Security (Dynamic Access Lists)" chapter in the *Cisco IOS Security Configuration Guide.*
timeout *minutes*	(Optional) Specifies the absolute length of time, in minutes, that a temporary access list entry can remain in a dynamic access list. The default is an infinite length of time and allows an entry to remain permanently. Refer to lock-and-key access documented in the "Configuring Lock-and-Key Security (Dynamic Access Lists)" chapter in the *Cisco IOS Security Configuration Guide.*
deny	Denies access if the conditions are matched.
permit	Permits access if the conditions are matched.
remark	Makes the access list easier to understand and scan.

continues

Table 11-3 Extended ACL Parameters (Continued)

Parameter	Description
protocol	Name or number of an Internet protocol. It can be one of the keywords **eigrp**, **gre**, **icmp**, **igmp**, **igrp**, **ip**, **ipinip**, **nos**, **ospf**, **pim**, **tcp**, or **udp**, or an integer in the range from 0 to 255 representing an Internet protocol number. To match any Internet protocol (including ICMP, TCP, and UDP), use the **ip** keyword. Some protocols allow further qualifiers.
source	Number of the network or host from which the packet is being sent. There are three alternative ways to specify the source: Use a 32-bit quantity in four-part dotted-decimal format. Use the any keyword as an abbreviation for a *source* and *source-wildcard* of 0.0.0.0 255.255.255.255. Use host source as an abbreviation for a source and *source-wildcard* of *source* 0.0.0.0.
source-wildcard	Wildcard bits to be applied to the source. Each wildcard bit 0 indicates the corresponding bit position in the source. Each wildcard bit set to 1 indicates that both a 0 bit and a 1 bit in the corresponding position of the IP address of the packet will be considered a match to this access list entry. There are three alternative ways to specify the source wildcard: ■ Use a 32-bit quantity in four-part dotted-decimal format. Place 1s in the bit positions that you want to ignore. ■ Use the **any** keyword as an abbreviation for a *source* and *source-wildcard* of 0.0.0.0 255.255.255.255. ■ Use host source as an abbreviation for a *source* and *source-wildcard* of source 0.0.0.0. Wildcard bits set to 1 need not be contiguous in the *source* wildcard. For example, a *source* wildcard of 0.255.0.64 would be valid.
destination	Number of the network or host to which the packet is being sent. There are three alternative ways to specify the destination: ■ Use a 32-bit quantity in four-part dotted-decimal format. ■ Use the **any** keyword as an abbreviation for the *destination* and *destination-wildcard* of 0.0.0.0 255.255.255.255. ■ Use host destination as an abbreviation for a *destination* and *destination-wildcard* of destination 0.0.0.0.

Table 11-3 Extended ACL Parameters (Continued)

Parameter	Description
destination-wildcard	Wildcard bits to be applied to the destination. There are three alternative ways to specify the destination wildcard: ■ Use a 32-bit quantity in four-part dotted-decimal format. Place 1s in the bit positions that you want to ignore. ■ Use the **any** keyword as an abbreviation for a *destination* and *destination-wildcard* of 0.0.0.0 255.255.255.255. ■ Use host destination as an abbreviation for a *destination* and *destination-wildcard* of destination 0.0.0.0.
precedence *precedence*	(Optional) Packets can be filtered by precedence level, as specified by a number from 0 to 7. This is used by the quality of service (QoS) mechanism.
tos *tos*	(Optional) Packets can be filtered by type of service level, as specified by a number from 0 to 15. This is used by the QoS mechanism.
log	(Optional) Causes an informational logging message about the packet that matches the entry to be sent to the console. (The level of messages logged to the console is controlled by the **logging console** command.)
log	The message includes the access list number, whether the packet was permitted or denied; the protocol, whether it was TCP, UDP, ICMP, or a number; and, if appropriate, the source and destination addresses and source and destination port numbers. By default, the message is generated for the first packet that matches and then at five-minute intervals, including the number of packets permitted or denied in the previous five-minute interval. Use the **ip access-list log-update** command to generate logging messages when the number of matches reaches a configurable threshold (instead of waiting for a five-minute interval). See the **ip access-list log- update command** for more information. The logging facility might drop some logging message packets if there are too many to be handled or if there is more than one logging message to be handled in one second. This behavior prevents the router from crashing because of too many logging packets. Therefore, the logging facility should not be used as a billing tool or an accurate source of the number of matches to an access list.

continues

Table 11-3 Extended ACL Parameters (Continued)

Parameter	Description
log-input	(Optional) Includes the input interface and source MAC address or VC in the logging output.
time-range time-range-name	(Optional) Name of the time range that applies to this statement. The name of the time range and its restrictions are specified by the **time-range** command.
icmp-type	(Optional) ICMP packets can be filtered by ICMP message type. The type is a number from 0 to 255.
icmp-code	(Optional) ICMP packets that are filtered by ICMP message type also can be filtered by the ICMP message code. The code is a number from 0 to 255.
icmp-message	(Optional) ICMP packets can be filtered by an ICMP message type name or ICMP message type and code name.
igmp-type	(Optional) IGMP packets can be filtered by IGMP message type or message name. A message type is a number from 0 to 15.
operator	(Optional) Compares source or destination ports. Possible operands include lt (less than), gt (greater than), eq (equal), neq (not equal), and range (inclusive range).
	If the operator is positioned after the *source* and *source-wildcard*, it must match the source port.
	If the operator is positioned after the *destination* and *destination-wildcard*, it must match the destination port.
	The range operator requires two port numbers. All other operators require one port number.
port	(Optional) Indicates the decimal number or name of a TCP or UDP port. A port number is a number from 0 to 65,535. TCP port names can be used only when filtering TCP. UDP port names can be used only when filtering UDP.
	TCP port names can be used only when filtering TCP. UDP port names can be used only when filtering UDP.

Table 11-3 Extended ACL Parameters (Continued)

Parameter	Description
established	(Optional) For the TCP protocol only: Indicates an established connection. A match occurs if the TCP datagram has the ACK, FIN, PSH, RST, SYN, or URG control bits set. The nonmatching case is that of the initial TCP datagram to form a connection.
fragments	(Optional) This ACL entry applies to noninitial fragments of packets; the fragment is either permitted or denied accordingly.

For a single ACL, multiple statements can be configured. Each of these statements must contain the same *access-list-number* to relate the statements to the same ACL, as in Example 11-3. There can be as many condition statements as necessary. These condition statements are limited only by the available router memory. The more statements there are, the more difficult it will be to comprehend and manage the ACL. The three statements in Example 11-4 combine to permit **telnet**, **ftp**, and **ftp-data** from any host on the 172.16.6.0 subnetwork to any other network.

Example 11-4 *Extended ACL Statements*

```
access-list 114 permit tcp 172.16.6.0 0.0.0.255 any eq telnet
access-list 114 permit tcp 172.16.6.0 0.0.0.255 any eq ftp
access-list 114 permit tcp 172.16.6.0 0.0.0.255 any eq ftp-data
```

Extended ACLs are very versatile and, as such, provide different options and arguments based on the protocol used. Therefore, syntax will differ based on which of these protocols are in use. These protocols are listed here:

- Internet Control Message Protocol (ICMP)
- Internet Group Message Protocol (IGMP)
- Transmission Control Protocol (TCP)
- User Datagram Protocol (UDP)

The sections that follow describe the syntax variation of extended ACLs based on the protocol used.

> ### More Information: Configuring Extended ACLs for ICMP
>
> ACLs for ICMP use the following syntax:
>
> ```
> access-list access-list-number [dynamic dynamic-name [timeout minutes]] {deny |
>   permit} icmp source source-wildcard destination destination-wildcard [icmp-type
>   [icmp-code] | icmp-message] [precedence precedence] [tos tos] [log | log-input]
>   [time-range time-range-name] [fragments]
> ```
>
> #### Configuring Extended ACLs for IGMP
>
> ACLs for IGMP use the following syntax:
>
> ```
> access-list access-list-number [dynamic dynamic-name [timeout minutes]] {deny |
>   permit} igmp source source-wildcard destination destination-wildcard [igmp-type]
>   [precedence precedence] [tos tos] [log | log-input] [time-range time-range-name]
>   [fragments]
> ```
>
> #### Configuring Extended ACLs for TCP
>
> ACLs for TCP use the following syntax:
>
> ```
> access-list access-list-number [dynamic dynamic-name [timeout minutes]] {deny |
>   permit} tcp source source-wildcard [operator [port]] destination destination-
>   wildcard [operator [port]] [established] [precedence precedence] [tos tos] [log |
>   log-input] [time-range time-range-name] [fragments]
> ```
>
> #### Configuring Extended ACLs for UDP
>
> ACLs for UDP use the following syntax:
>
> ```
> access-list access-list-number [dynamic dynamic-name [timeout minutes]] {deny |
>   permit} udp source source-wildcard [operator [port]] destination destination-
>   wildcard [operator [port]] [precedence precedence] [tos tos] [log | log-input]
>   [time-range time-range-name] [fragments]
> ```
>
> #### Extended ACL Defaults
>
> An extended ACL defaults to a list that denies everything. An extended ACL is terminated by an implicit **deny** statement.
>
> At the end of the extended ACL statement, additional precision is gained from a field that specifies the optional TCP or UDP port number. Figure 11-12 illustrates this concept.
>
> **Figure 11-12** Transport/Application Port Numbers
>
>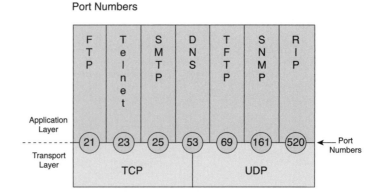

> **More Information: Configuring Extended ACLs for ICMP (Continued)**
>
> Table 11-4 lists some of the more common reserved UDP and TCP port numbers.
>
> **Table 11-4** Some Reserved TCP/UDP Numbers
>
> | Decimal | Keyword | Description |
> |---------|---------|-------------|
> | 0 | | Reserved |
> | 1 to 4 | | Unassigned |
> | 5 | RJE | Remote job entry |
> | 7 | ECHO | Echo |
> | 9 | DISCARD | Discard |
> | 11 | USERS | Active users |
> | 13 | DAYTIME | Daytime |
> | 15 | NETSTAT | Who is up, or NETSTAT |
> | 17 | QUOTE | Quote of the day |
> | 19 | CHARGEN | Character generator |
> | 20 | FTP-DATA | File Transfer Protocol (data) |
> | 21 | FTP | File Transfer Protocol |
> | 23 | TELNET | Terminal connection |
> | 25 | SMTP | Simple Mail Transfer Protocol |
> | 53 | DOMAIN | Domain Name Server (DNS) |
> | 69 | TFTP | Trivial File Transfer Protocol |
> | 80 | HTTP | Hypertext Transfer Protocol (WWW) |
>
> The **ip access-group** command links an existing extended ACL to an interface. Only one ACL per interface, per direction, per protocol is allowed, as emphasized in Figure 11-13. The format of the command is as follows:
>
> ```
> Router(config-if)# ip access-group access-list number {in | out}
> ```

More Information: Configuring Extended ACLs for ICMP (Continued)
Figure 11-13 ACL Rules  One List, Per Port, Per Direction, Per Protocol

 Lab 11.2.2a   Configuring Extended Access Lists

In this lab, you plan, configure, and apply an extended ACL to permit or deny specific traffic and test the ACL to determine whether the desired results were achieved.

 Lab 11.2.2b   Simple Extended Access Lists

In this lab, you configure and apply extended access lists to filter network to network, host to network, and network to host traffic.

Named ACLs

IP *named ACLs* were introduced in Cisco IOS Software Release 11.2, which allowed standard and extended ACLs to be given names instead of numbers. The advantages that a named access list provides are as follows:

- Intuitively identifies an ACL using an alpha or alphanumeric name

- Eliminates the limit of 99 standard and 100 extended ACLs

- Enables administrators to modify ACLs without having to delete and then reconfigure them

A named ACL is created with the **ip access-list** command. The named ACL syntax is as follows:

```
ip access-list {extended | standard} name
```

This places the user in ACL configuration mode:

```
Router(config-std-nacl)#
```

or

```
Router(config-ext-nacl)#
```

In these modes, you can specify one or more conditions for permitting or denying access to a packet. Depending on the mode, the available options are as follows:

```
Router(config-std-nacl)#permit | deny {source [source-wildcard] | any} [log]
Router(config-ext-nacl)#permit | deny protocol source source-wildcard [operator
  [port]] destination destination-wildcard [operator [port]] [established]
  [precedence precedence] [tos tos] [log] [time-range time-range-name]
```

The **permit** or **deny** operand tells the router what action to take when a packet has met the other criteria specified in the ACL—that is, whether to forward or drop the packet.

Example 11-5 demonstrates applying a named ACL.

Example 11-5 *Named ACL Statements*

```
! Named ACL created:
Rt(config)# ip access-list extended server-access
Rt(config-ext-nacl)# permit tcp any host 131.108.101.99 eq smtp
Rt(config-ext-nacl)# permit tcp any host 131.108.101.99 eq domain
Rt(config-ext-nacl)# deny ip any any log
Rt(config-ext-nacl)# ^Z
! Named ACL Applied:
Rt(config)# interface fastethernet0/0
Rt(config-if)# ip access-group server-access out
Rt(config-if)# ^Z
```

In Example 11-5, the access list is given the name server-access. This access list then is applied to interface Fast Ethernet 0/0. This access list enables users to access the mail and DNS server only; all other requests are denied.

A named ACL allows for the deletion of statements, but statements can be inserted only at the end of a list, as demonstrated in Example 11-6.

Example 11-6 *Named ACL Statements*

```
router# configure terminal
  Enter configuration commands, one per line.
  router(config)# ip access-list extended test
  router(config-ext-nacl)# permit ip host 2.2.2.2 host 3.3.3.3
  router(config-ext-nacl)# permit tcp host 1.1.1.1 host 5.5.5.5 eq www
  router(config-ext-nacl)# permit icmp any any
  router(config-ext-nacl)# permit udp host 6.6.6.6 10.10.10.0 0.0.0.255 eq domain
  router(config-ext-nacl)# ^Z
```

continues

Example 11-6 *Named ACL Statements (Continued)*

```
1d00h: %SYS-5-CONFIG_I: Configured from console by consoles-1
router# show access-list
Extended IP access list test
    permit ip host 2.2.2.2 host 3.3.3.3
    permit tcp host 1.1.1.1 host 5.5.5.5 eq www
    permit icmp any any
    permit udp host 6.6.6.6 10.10.10.0 0.0.0.255 eq domain

router# configure terminal
Enter configuration commands, one per line. End with CNTL/Z.
router(config)# ip access-list extended test
!--- The following command deletes a named ACL entry.
router(config-ext-nacl)# no permit icmp any any
!--- The following command adds a named ACL entry.
router(config-ext-nacl)# permit gre host 4.4.4.4 host 8.8.8.8
router(config-ext-nacl)# ^Z
1d00h: %SYS-5-CONFIG_I: Configured from console by consoles-1

router# show access-list
Extended IP access list test
    permit ip host 2.2.2.2 host 3.3.3.3
    permit tcp host 1.1.1.1 host 5.5.5.5 eq www
    permit udp host 6.6.6.6 10.10.10.0 0.0.0.255 eq domain
    permit gre host 4.4.4.4 host 8.8.8.8
```

Consider the following before implementing named ACLs:

- Named ACLs are not compatible with Cisco IOS Software releases prior to Release 11.2.

- The same name cannot be used for multiple ACLs. For example, it is not permissible to specify both a standard and an extended ACL named George.

The series of commands shown in Example 11-7 first create a standard ACL named Internet-filter and an extended ACL named marketing_group. The commands then access interface e0/5, assign an IP address, and then apply both ACLs to an interface (Ethernet 0/5).

Example 11-7 *Named ACL Creation*

```
. . .
ip access-list standard Internetfilter
permit 1.2.3.4
deny any
ip access-list extended marketing_group
permit tcp any 171.69.0.0 0.255.255.255 eq telnet
deny tcp any any
deny udp any 171.69.0.0 0.255.255.255 lt 1024
deny ip any log
ip interface Ethernet0/5
ip address 2.0.5.1 255.255.255.0
ip access-group Internetfilter out
ip access-group marketing_group in
```

Lab 11.2.3a Configuring a Named Access List

In this lab, you create a named ACL to permit or deny specific traffic and test the ACL to determine if the desired results were achieved.

Lab 11.2.3b Simple DMZ Extended Access Lists

In this lab, you use extended access lists to create a simple demilitarized zone (DMZ).

Lab 11.2.3c Multiple Access Lists Functions (Challenge Lab)

In this lab, you configure and apply an extended access control list to control Internet traffic using one or more routers.

Lab 11.2.6 vty Restriction

In this lab, you use the **access-class** and **line** commands to control Telnet access to the router.

Placing ACLs

CAUTION

ACL operation can slow the router in performing its routing tasks. The router has to read more of the packet and compare more parameters before it even gets to the routing operations.

ACLs control traffic by filtering packets and eliminating unwanted traffic on a network. An important consideration when implementing ACLs is where the access list is placed. When placed in the proper location, ACLs not only filter traffic, but they also can make the entire network operate more efficiently. For filtering traffic, the ACL should be placed where it has the greatest impact on increasing network efficiency.

Refer to Figure 11-14. Suppose that the enterprise policy wants to deny Telnet or FTP traffic on Router A access to the switched Ethernet LAN on the Fa0/0 port of Router D. At the same time, other traffic must be permitted. This policy can be implemented several ways. The recommended approach uses an extended ACL, specifying both source and destination addresses. If this extended ACL is placed in Router A, packets will not cross the Ethernet of Router A or the serial interfaces of Routers B and C, and will not enter Router D. This will reduce traffic on the network links between Routers A and D. Traffic with different source and destination addresses still will be permitted.

Figure 11-14 Placing ACLs

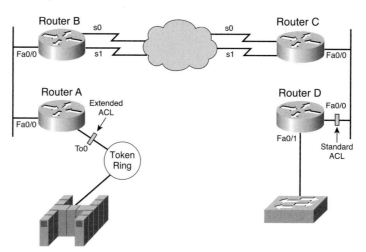

The general rule is to put the extended ACLs as close to the source of the denied traffic as possible. Standard ACLs do not specify destination addresses, so they should be placed as close to the destination as possible. For example, a standard ACL would be placed on Fa0/0 of Router D to prevent traffic from Router A.

 Interactive Media Activity   Point and Click: ACL Placement

After completing this activity, you will be able to place ACLs.

Firewalls

A *firewall* is a computer or networking device that exists between the user and the outside world to protect the internal network from intruders. In most circumstances, intruders come from the global Internet and the thousands of remote networks that it interconnects. Typically, a network firewall consists of several different machines that work together to prevent unwanted and illegal access. Figure 11-15 shows a simple firewall architecture.

Figure 11-15 Firewall Architecture

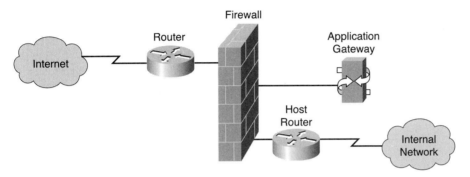

In firewall architecture, the router that is connected to the Internet is referred to as the *exterior router*. It forces all incoming traffic to pass through the application gateway. The router that is connected to the internal network is the *interior router*. The interior router accepts packets only from the application gateway. The gateway controls the delivery of network-based services both to and from the internal network. For example, the firewall might allow only certain users to communicate with the Internet, or permit only certain applications to establish connections between an interior and exterior host. If the only application that is permitted is mail, then only mail packets will be allowed through the router. This protects the application gateway and avoids overwhelming it with unauthorized packets.

Using ACLs with Firewalls

ACLs should be used in firewall routers, which often are positioned between the internal network and an external network, such as the Internet. The firewall router provides a point of isolation so that the rest of the internal network structure is not affected. You also can use ACLs on a router positioned between two parts of the network, to control traffic entering or exiting a specific part of the internal network.

To provide the security benefits of ACLs, you should, at a minimum, configure ACLs on *border routers*, which are routers situated on the boundaries of the network, and are also known as *firewall routers*. This provides basic security from the outside network, or from a less controlled area of the network, into a more private area of the network.

On these border routers, ACLs can be created for each network protocol configured on the router interfaces. You can configure ACLs so that inbound traffic, outbound traffic, or both are filtered on an interface.

Restricting Virtual Terminal Access

Standard and extended ACLs apply to packets traveling through a router. They are not designed to block packets that originate within the router. By default, an outbound Telnet-extended ACL does not prevent router-initiated Telnet sessions.

In addition to physical ports or interfaces on the router, such as Fa0/0 and S0/0, there are virtual ports. These virtual ports are called vty lines. There are five vty lines, which are numbered 0 through 4, as shown in Figure 11-16. For security purposes, users can be denied or permitted virtual terminal access to the router, but denied access to destinations from that router. For example, an administrator can configure the ACL to allow terminal access to the router for management or troubleshooting purposes, while at the same time restricting access beyond this router.

Figure 11-16 Restricting vty Access with ACLs

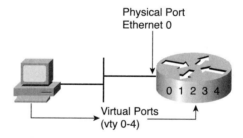

Restricting vty access is not commonly used as a traffic control mechanism; instead, it is for increasing network security. vty access is accomplished using the Telnet protocol to make a nonphysical connection to the router. As a result, there is only one type of vty ACL. Identical restrictions should be placed on all vty lines because it is impossible to control which line a user will connect on.

Whereas a vty ACL is created the same way as on an interface, applying the vty ACL to a terminal line requires using the **access-class** command instead of the **access-group** command. Example 11-8 demonstrates creating and applying a virtual terminal access list.

Example 11-8 *Restricting vty Access with ACLs*

```
! Creating the standard list:
Rt1(config)# access-list 2 permit 172.16.1.0 0.0.0.255
Rt1(config)# access-list 2 permit 172.16.2.0 0.0.0.255
```

Example 11-8 *Restricting vty Access with ACLs (Continued)*

```
Rt1(config)# access-list 2 deny any
! Applying the access list:
Rt1(config)# line vty 0 4
Rt1(config)# login
Rt1(config)# password secret
Rt1(config)# access-class 2 in
```

Keep the following considerations in mind when configuring access lists on vty lines:

- A name or number can be used when controlling access to an interface.

- Only numbered access lists can be applied to virtual lines.

- Identical restrictions should be set on all the virtual terminal lines because a user can attempt to connect to any of them.

Summary

This chapter presented an overview of the following key points:

- The two main types of ACLs are standard and extended.

- Named ACLs allow access lists to be identified by name instead of number.

- ACLs can be configured for all routed network protocols.

- ACLs typically are used in firewall routers, which often are positioned between the internal network and an external network such as the Internet.

- ACLs also can restrict virtual terminal access to the router.

- ACLs perform several functions within a Cisco router, including implementing security/access procedures.

- ACLs are used to control and manage traffic.

- For some protocols, you can apply up to two ACLs to an interface: one inbound ACL and one outbound ACL.

- With ACLs, after a packet is checked for a match with the ACL statement, it can be denied or permitted the use of an associated interface.

- Wildcard mask bits use the numbers 1 and 0 to determine how to treat the corresponding IP address bits.

To supplement what you learned in this chapter, refer to the chapter-specific Videos and Interactive Media Activities on the CD-ROM accompanying this book.

Key Terms

access control list (ACL)   A means of controlling or limiting network traffic that compares different criteria to a defined rule set.

bit bucket   The destination of discarded bits (dropped packets), as determined by the router.

border router   A router situated at the edges or end of the network boundary, which provides basic security from the outside network or from a less controlled area of the network into a more private area of the network.

extended ACL   Compares source IP address, destination IP address, TCP/UDP port number, and other criteria to the rules defining an extended ACL.

exterior router   In firewall architecture, the router that is connected to the Internet is referred to as the exterior router. It forces all incoming traffic to pass through the application gateway.

firewall   One or more network devices, such as routers or access servers, designated as a buffer between any connected public networks and a private network. A firewall router uses access control lists and other methods to ensure the security of the private network.

interior router   The router that is connected to the internal network. The interior router accepts packets only from the application gateway. The gateway controls the delivery of network-based services both to and from the internal network.

named ACL   ACL that allows standard and extended ACLs to be given names.

queuing   A process by which ACLs can designate certain packets to be processed by a router before other traffic, on the basis of some configurable parameter such as specifying a protocol.

standard ACL   ACL that compares source IP addresses to the rules defining a standard ACL.

Check Your Understanding

Complete all the review questions to test your understanding of the topics and concepts in this chapter. Answers are listed in Appendix B, "Check Your Understanding Answer Key."

1. Common ACL functions include filtering packets internally, protecting the internal network from illegal Internet access, and restricting access to virtual terminal ports. True or false?

   A. True

   B. False

2. ACL is an acronym for:

 A. Accessibility control list

 B. Accountability control list

 C. Assessment control list

 D. Access control list

3. Which type of ACL works by comparing the source IP address against the ACL rules?

 A. Extended

 B. Named

 C. Standard

 D. Router

4. Which type of ACL works by comparing the source IP address, destination IP address, or other parameters against the ACL rules?

 A. Extended

 B. Named

 C. Standard

 D. Router

5. Which type of ACL uses names instead of numbers to distinguish ACLs.

 A. Extended

 B. Named

 C. Standard

 D. Router

6. As a general rule, ACLs should be placed where in the network?

 A. In the Internet

 B. In the core

 C. Closest to the traffic to be controlled

 D. None of the above

7. What command is used to apply an ACL to a vty port?

 A. **access-group**

 B. **ip access-class**

 C. **ip access-group**

 D. **access-class**

8. Which of the following commands would you use to find out whether any ACLs are set on an interface?

   A. **show running-config**

   B. **show ip protocols**

   C. **show ip interface**

   D. **show ip network**

9. If you want to permit traffic based on its addressing or protocol type, you would use which of the following commands?

   A. Router #**access-list** *access-list number* {**permit | deny**} {*test conditions*}

   B. Router (config)#**access-list** *access-list number* {**permit | deny**} {*test conditions*}

   C. Router (config-if)#**access-list** *access-list number* {**permit | deny**} {*test conditions*}

   D. None of the above

10. Standard IP access lists permit or deny routing of a packet based on the IP address that it originates from and the protocol suite that it is destined for. True or false?

    A. True

    B. False

11. Access lists impact network security based on which of the following factors?

    A. The data content of the packets

    B. The destination subnet/host/network for the packets

    C. The source subnet/host/network of the packets

    D. The type of the network they are routed through

12. What type of networking device would be needed to implement access lists to increase network security?

    A. Hub

    B. Router

    C. Bridge

    D. Switch

13. What does the following access list allow? **access-list 1 permit 204.211.19.162 0.0.0.0**

    A. "Deny my network only."

    B. "Permit a specific host."

    C. "Permit only my network."

    D. None of the above.

Structured Cabling

Objectives

Upon completion of this appendix, you will be able to

- Understand the roots of structured cabling

- Adhere to structured cabling standards when designing and performing installations

- Recognize subsystems of structured cabling, including demarcation points, telecommunications and equipment rooms including roles such as, MC, IC, and HC

- Recognize the special requirements of cabling in the work area

- Express familiarity with standards organizations such as Telecommunications Industry Association (TIA), the Electronic Industries Association (EIA) TIA/EIA, and the European Committee for Electrotechnical Standardization (CENELEC), as well as world-level organizations such as the International Organization for Standardization (ISO)

- Perform low-voltage telecommunications work with attention to safety, and be safe around electricity

- Understand basic points of ladder safety and the importance or proper attire for cabling work

- Have a familiarity with the basic specialized hand tools of the installer's craft, as well as with basic telecom test and measurement equipment

- Understand which cabling tasks accompany which phase of a typical project

- Understand the basic business processes that lead to successful cabling organization

Key Terms

The following is a list of key terms introduced in this appendix. For your reference, a definition for each term can be found at the end of this appendix.

This appendix covers the following topics:

- Structured cabling systems, standards, and codes

- Safety

- Tools of the trade

- The installation process

- The finish phase

- The cabling business

- Case study

Be sure to look at this appendix's associated Interactive Media Activities, which you will find on the CD-ROM accompanying this book. These CD elements are designed to supplement the material and reinforce the concepts introduced in this chapter.

Structured Cabling Systems, Standards, and Codes

Structured cabling systems (SCS) refer to telecommunications wiring built in a standardized, approved manner, starting at the *demarcation point*, working through the various *equipment rooms*, and continuing to the *work area*. The issue of scalability also is addressed.

Items of importance that students should be aware of include these:

- Rules of structured cabling

- Subsystems of structured cabling

- Scalability

- Demarcation point

- Telecommunications and equipment rooms

- Work areas

- MC, IC, and HC

- Telecommunications Industry Association (TIA) and Electronic Industries Association (EIA)

- European Committee for Electrotechnical Standardization (CENELEC)

- International Organization for Standardization (ISO)

- U.S. codes

- Evolution of standards

Rules of Structured Cabling for LANs

Structured cabling is a systematic approach to cabling. It is a method for creating an organized cabling system that can be easily understood by installers, network administrators, and any other technicians that deal with cables.

The following three rules help ensure that the structured cabling design projects are both effective and efficient:

- **Look for a complete connectivity solution**—An optimal solution for network connectivity includes all the systems that are designed to connect, route, manage, and identify structured cabling systems. A standards-based implementation will help to make sure that both current and future technologies can be supported. Following standards makes sure that the project will deliver performance and reliability over the long term.

- **Plan for future growth**—The number of circuits installed should meet these future requirements as well. Category 5e, Category 6, and fiber-optic solutions should be considered where feasible to ensure that future needs will be met. It should be possible to plan a physical layer installation that works for ten or more years.

- **Maintain freedom of choice in vendors**—Even though a closed and proprietary system may be less expensive initially, this could end up being much more costly over the long term. A non-standard system from a single vendor may make it more difficult to make moves, adds, and changes at a later time.

More Information: The Rules of Structured Cabling
For more information on the rules of structured cabling, visit www.panduit.com and search for the document "Rules of Structured Cabling."

Subsystems of Structured Cabling

Seven subsystems are associated with the structured cabling system (see Figure A-1). Each subsystem performs certain functions to provide voice and data services throughout the cable plant.

- The demarcation point (demarc) within the entrance facility (EF) in the equipment room
- The *telecommunications room (TR)*
- *Backbone* cabling, also known as vertical cabling
- Distribution cabling, also known as horizontal cabling
- The work area
- Equipment room (ER)
- Administration

Figure A-1 Subsystems of Structured Cabling

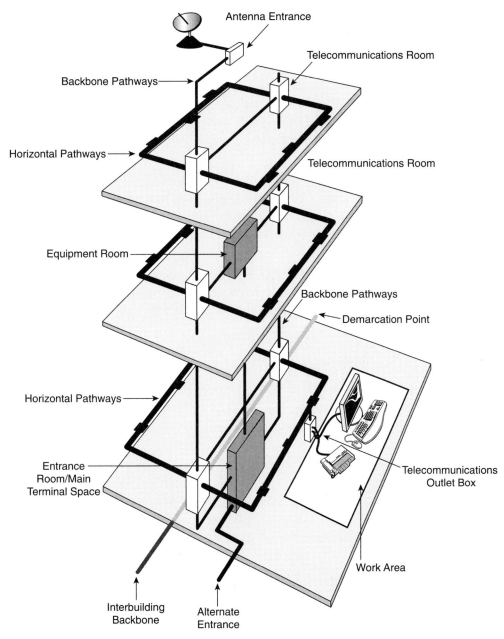

The *demarc* is where the outside service provider cables connect to the customer's cables in the facility.

Backbone cabling is the feeder cables that are routed from the demarc to the equipment rooms and then on to the telecommunications rooms throughout the facility. Horizontal cabling distributes cables from the telecommunication rooms to the work areas. The telecommunications rooms are where connections take place to provide a transition between the backbone cabling and horizontal cabling.

These subsystems make structured cabling, by nature, a distributed architecture with management capabilities that are limited to the active equipment (PCs, switches, hubs, etc.). Designing a structured cabling infrastructure that properly routes, protects, identifies and terminates the copper or fiber media is absolutely critical for network performance and future upgrade.

Scalability

A LAN that can accommodate future growth in size is referred to as being scalable. It is important to plan ahead when estimating the number of cable runs and cable drops in a work area. It is always easier to ignore extra installed cables than to not have them when they are required.

In addition to pulling extra cables in the backbone area for future growth, it is also common practice to pull an extra cable to each workstation or desktop for future use. This protects against pairs that might fail during installation and also provides for expansion.

Backbone Scalability

To determine how much extra copper cabling to pull, first determine the number of runs that are needed now and then add some extra, about 20 percent.

One way to obtain this reserve capability is to use fiber-optic cabling and equipment as part of the building backbone cabling. Updating the termination equipment (by inserting faster lasers and drivers, for example) can accommodate fiber growth.

Work Area Scalability

Although it might be obvious that each work area needs one cable for voice and one for data, other devices might need a connection to either the voice system or the data system. Network printers, fax machines, laptops, or another user in the work area all can require their own network cable drops.

When the cables are in place, use multiport wall plates over the jacks. Many types of configurations are possible for either walls or partition walls. In addition, use jacks that are color-coded to make it easier to identify types of circuits. Administration standards require that every circuit should be clearly labeled to assist in connections and troubleshooting.

A new technology that is becoming popular is *Voice over Internet Protocol (VoIP)*. This technology allows special telephones to use data networks instead of telephone wiring. A great advantage to this technology is the capability to avoid costly long-distance charges by using this service over existing network connections. Other devices, such as printers and computers, can be plugged into the IP phone. The IP phone thus becomes a hub or switch for the work area. Even if these types of connections are planned, enough cables should be installed to allow for growth. Especially consider that IP telephony and IP video traffic may share the network cables in the future.

To accommodate the changing needs of users in offices, it is recommended to provide at least one spare cable to the work area outlet. Offices might change from single-user to multiuser spaces. In these cases, a work area can become inefficient if only one set of communication cables were pulled. Assume that every work area could accommodate multiple users in the future (see Figure A-2).

Demarcation Point

The demarcation point (demarc), provides the point at which outdoor cabling interfaces with the intrabuilding backbone cabling (See Figure A-3). It represents the boundary between the service provider's responsibility and that of the customer. In many buildings, this is near the point of presence (POP) for other utilities, such as electricity and water.

Figure A-2 Allow for Growth

The service provider is responsible for everything from the demarc to the service provider's facility. Everything from the demarc into the building is the customer's responsibility.

The local telephone carrier typically is required to terminate cabling within 15m (49.2 ft.) of building penetration and to provide primary voltage protection. This usually is installed and provided by the service provider.

Figure A-3 Demarcation Point

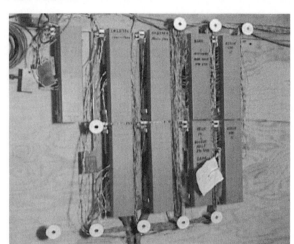

The *Telecommunications Industry Association (TIA)* and Electronic Industries Association (EIA) develop and publish standards for many industries, including the cabling industry. To ensure that the cabling installation is safe, is installed correctly, and retains performance ratings, these standards always should be followed when performing any voice or data cabling installation or maintenance.

TIA/EIA-569-A specifies the standards for the demarc space. The standards for the structure and size of the demarc space are based on the size of the building. In buildings larger than 2000 usable square meters, a locked, dedicated, and enclosed room is recommended.

The following are general guidelines when setting up a demarcation point space:

- Allow $1m^2$ of plywood wall mount for each $20m^2$ ($215.3 \; ft^2$) area of floor space.

- The surfaces where the distribution hardware is mounted must be covered with fire-rated plywood or plywood that is painted with two coats of fire-retardant paint.

- Either the plywood or the covers for the termination equipment should be colored orange to indicate the point of demarcation.

Telecommunications and Equipment Rooms

After the cable enters the building through the demarc, it travels to the entrance facility (EF), which is usually in the equipment room (ER). The equipment room is the center of the voice and data network. An equipment room is essentially a large telecommunications room that may house the main distribution frame, network servers, routers, switches, the telephone PBX, secondary voltage protection, satellite receivers, modulators, high-speed Internet equipment, and so on. The design aspects of the equipment room are specified in the TIA/EIA-569-A standard.

In larger facilities, the equipment room may feed one or more telecommunications rooms (TR) which are distributed throughout the building (see Figure A-4).

A wiring hub and patch panel in a TR may be mounted to a wall with a hinged wall bracket, a distribution rack (see Figure A-5), or a full equipment cabinet.

Figure A-4 Telecommunications Room

Figure A-5 Panduit Distribution Rack

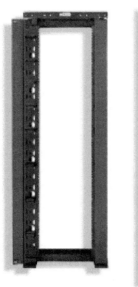
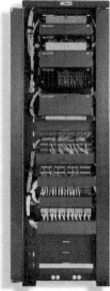

- If the choice is a hinged wall bracket, the bracket must be attached to the plywood panel that covers the underlying wall surface. The purpose of the hinge is to allow the assembly to swing out so that workers and repairmen easily can access the back side of the wall. Care must be taken, however, to allow 48 cm (18.9 in.) for the panel to swing out from the wall.

- If you are using a distribution rack, it must have a minimum of 1 meter (3 feet) of workspace clearance in the front and rear of the rack. A 55.9-cm (22-in.) floor plate, used to mount the distribution rack, provides stability and determines the minimum distance for its final position.

- If the *patch panel*, hub, and other equipment are mounted in a full equipment cabinet, they require at least 76.2 cm (28.6 in.) of clearance in front, for the door to swing open. Typically, such equipment cabinets are 1.8m high · .74m wide · .66m deep (5.9 ft. · 2.4 ft. · 216.5 ft.).

Equipment must be placed in equipment racks with care. Considerations include whether the equipment uses electricity, cable routing, cable management, and ease of use. For example, a patch panel would not be placed high on a rack if a significant number of changes were to take place after the systems were installed. Convenience of use is a large consideration when planning the equipment layout.

Scalability is also a consideration in an equipment layout because future growth should be accommodated. Space should be left on a rack for future patch panels, or floor space should be left for future rack installations in an initial layout.

Proper installation of equipment racks and patch panels in the TR allows easy changes and modifications to the cabling installation in the future. This is important when considering the design and layout of the work areas.

Work Areas

The area serviced by an individual telecommunications room is called a work area. In most cases, a work area occupies one floor or part of one floor of a building (see Figure A-6).

The maximum distance for a cable from the termination point in the TR to the termination at the work area outlet must not exceed 90 meters (295 ft). This 90-meter maximum horizontal cabling distance is referred to as the permanent link. Each work area must have at least two cables, one for data and the other for voice. As previously discussed, accommodations for other services and future expansion must also be considered.

This distance must be reduced because cables usually cannot be strung across the floor; they usually ride in wiring-management devices such as trays, baskets, ladders, and raceways. These devices route the paths of the wires above workspaces, often in the *plenum* areas above suspended ceilings. This means that the height of the ceiling times two (once up to the wiring management device and once back down) must be subtracted from the proposed work area radius.

Figure A-6 Work Areas

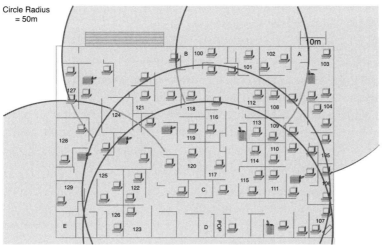

In addition, ANSI/TIA/EIA-568-B specifies that there can be 5m (16.4 ft.) of patch cord to interconnect equipment patch panels, and 5m of cable from the cable termination point on the wall to the telephone or computer. This additional maximum of 10 meters of patch cords added to the permanent link is referred to as the horizontal channel. The maximum distance for a channel is 100 meters—the 90-meter maximum permanent link plus 10 meters maximum of patch cords.

Finally, the routes that the cables actually take might not be straight to the destination. Wiring-management devices can be costly, and the location of heating, ventilation, and air-conditioning equipment; power transformers; and lighting equipment can dictate paths that add length. This further decreases the radius of the work area. Typically, when everything is taken into account, the actual radius might be closer to 60 to 70m (196.9 to 229.7 ft.) than 100m (328.1 ft.); 50m (164 ft.) commonly is used as a work-area radius for design purposes.

Servicing the Work Area

Patching is done when connectivity changes are needed often or are foreseen. It is much easier to patch cable from the work area outlet to a new position in the TR than it is to remove terminated wires from connected hardware and reterminate them to another circuit. Patch cords also are used to connect networking equipment to the cross-connects in a TR. Patch cords are limited by the TIA/EIA-568-B.1 standard to 5m (16.4 ft.).

A uniform wiring plan must be used throughout a patch panel system. All jacks and patch panels should be wired using the same wiring plan. If the T568A wiring plan is used for the information outlets or jacks, T568A patch panels should be used. The same is true for the T568B wiring plan.

Patch panels can be for unshielded twisted-pair (UTP), shielded twisted-pair (STP), or fiber-optic connections. The most common patch panels are for UTP. These patch panels use RJ-45 jacks; patch cords with RJ-45 plugs connect to these ports.

In most facilities, there is no provision to keep authorized maintenance personnel from installing unauthorized patches or installing an unauthorized hub into a circuit. There is an emerging family of automated patch panels, however, which can provide extensive network monitoring in addition to simplifying the provisioning of moves, adds, and changes. These patch panels normally provide an indicator lamp over any patch cord that needs to be removed, and then once the cord is released, provide a second light over the jack to which they should be re-affixed. In this way, the system can automatically guide a relatively unskilled employee through moves, adds, and changes.

The same mechanism that detects when the operator has moved a given jack works also to detect when a jack has been pulled. An unauthorized resetting of a patch can trigger an event in the system log, and if need be, trigger an alarm. For example, if a half-dozen wires to the work area suddenly show up as being open, and it is 2:30 A.M., this is an event worth looking into, because theft may be occurring.

Types of Patch Cables

Patch cables (see Figure A-7) come in a variety of wiring schemes. The most common, the straight-through cable, has the same wiring scheme on both ends of the cable. In other words, pin 1 on one end is connected to pin 1 on the other end. Pin 2 on one end corresponds to pin 2 on the other, and so on. These types of cables connect PCs to a network hub.

Figure A-7 UTP Patch Cable

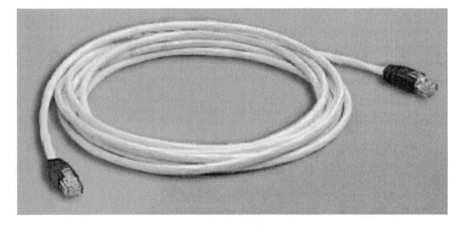

When connecting a communications device to a network hub, a crossover cable usually is used. Crossover cables use the T568A wiring plan on one end and T568B on the other.

 Lab A-1 Examination of Termination Types

In this lab, you review the T568A, T568B, and RJ-45 USOC wiring standards, and you learn to terminate the ends of a Category 5e cable.

Cable Management

Cable-management devices are used for routing cables and providing a neat and orderly path for the cables and to assure minimum bend radius is maintained. Cable management also eases cable additions and modification to the wiring system. Many options for cable management exist in the TR. Cable baskets can be used when an easy, lightweight installation is needed. Ladder racks often are used when heavy loads of bundled cable need to be supported. Different types of conduits can be used to run cable inside walls, ceilings, and floors, or when they need to be shielded from external conditions. Cable management systems are used vertically and horizontally on telecommunications racks to distribute cable in a neat and orderly fashion (see Figure A-8).

Figure A-8 Panduit Rack-Mounted Vertical and Horizontal Cable Management System

MC, IC, and HC

Most networks have more than one TR for various reasons. First of all, a medium or large network usually is spread over many floors or buildings. A TR is needed for each floor of each building (see Figure A-9). Second, media can carry a signal only so far before the signal starts to degrade or attenuate. Therefore, TRs are located at defined distances throughout the LAN to provide interconnects and cross-connects to hubs and switches to assure desired network performance. These TRs house equipment, such as repeaters, hubs, bridges, or switches, that are needed to regenerate the signals.

Figure A-9 MC, HC, and IC Planning

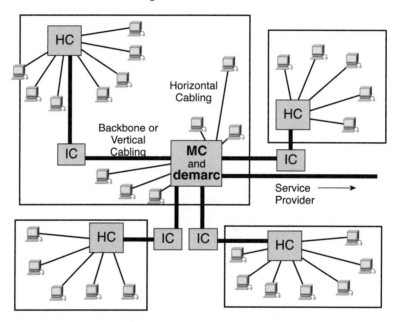

Not all TRs are equal. The primary TR, called the *main cross-connect (MC)*, is the center of the network. This is where all the wiring originates and where most of the equipment is housed. The *intermediate cross-connect (IC)* is connected to the MC and can house the equipment for a building on a campus. The *horizontal cross-connect (HC)* provides the cross-connect between the backbone and horizontal cables on a single floor of a building.

Main Cross-Connect

The MC is the main concentration point of an entire building or campus. In effect, the MC is the primary TR. It is the room that controls the rest of the TRs (the ICs and HCs) in a building or campus. In some networks, it is the place where the inside cable plant meets the outside world's connectivity (the demarc).

All ICs or HCs are connected to the MC in a star topology. Backbone cabling, or *vertical cabling*, is used to connect those ICs and HCs located on other floors. Where the entire network is confined to a single multistory building, the MC usually is located on one of the middle floors of the building, even though the demarc might be located in an entrance facility on the first floor or in the basement.

For networks that comprise multiple buildings, one building typically houses the MC. Each individual building typically has its own version of the MC, called the intermediate cross-connect (IC), which connects all the HCs within the building. The IC allows the extension of backbone cabling from the MC to each HC because this interconnection point does not degrade the communication signals. Only one MC can exist for the entire structured cabling installation. The MC feeds the ICs, and each IC feeds multiple HCs. There can be only one IC between the MC and any HC.

The backbone cabling (red lines in the figure) runs from the MC to each of the ICs. The ICs are located in each of the campus buildings, and the HCs serve work areas. Horizontal cabling, running from the HCs to the work areas, is represented by the black lines.

Horizontal Cross-Connect

The horizontal cross-connect (HC) is the TR closest to the work areas. Like all copper cross-connects, the HC is typically a patch panel or punch-down block, and possibly networking devices such as repeaters, hubs, or switches. It can be a rack mounted in a room or in a cabinet. Because a typical horizontal cable system includes multiple cable runs to each workstation, it can represent the largest concentration of cable in the building infrastructure. A building with a 1000 workstations easily can contain a horizontal cable system consisting of 2000 to 3000 individual cable runs.

Horizontal cabling includes the copper or optical fiber networking media that is used in the area that extends from the wiring closet to a workstation (see Figure A-10). Horizontal cabling includes the networking medium that runs along a horizontal pathway to the telecommunications outlet or connector in the work area, and the patch cords or jumpers in the HC.

Figure A-10   Horizontal Cabling and Symbols

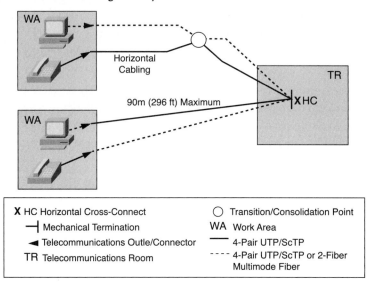

X HC Horizontal Cross-Connect	○ Transition/Consolidation Point
─┤ Mechanical Termination	**WA** Work Area
◄ Telecommunications Outle/Connector	── 4-Pair UTP/ScTP
TR Telecommunications Room	---- 4-Pair UTP/ScTP or 2-Fiber Multimode Fiber

Lab A-2   Terminating a Category 5e Cable on a Category 5e Patch Panel

In this lab, you terminate a Category 5e cable on a Category 5e patch panel and learn the proper use of a 110 punch-down tool as well as a cable stripper.

Backbone Cabling

Any cabling installed between the MC and another TR is known as backbone cabling. The difference between horizontal and backbone cabling is clearly defined in the standards. Backbone cabling is also referred to as vertical cabling. It consists of the backbone cables, intermediate and main cross-connects, mechanical terminations, and patch cords or jumpers used for backbone-to-backbone cross-connection. Backbone cabling includes the following:

- TRs on the same floor (MC to IC, IC to HC)

- Vertical connection (risers) between TRs on different floors (MC to IC)

- Cables between TR and demarcation point

- Cables between buildings (interbuilding) in a multibuilding campus

The maximum distances for cabling runs vary from one type of cable to another. For backbone cabling, the maximum distance for cabling runs also can be affected by how the backbone cabling is to be used. To understand what this means, assume that a decision has been made to use single-mode fiber-optic cable for the backbone cabling. If the networking media were to be used to connect the HC to the MC, then the maximum distance for the backbone cabling run would be 3000m (9842.5 ft).

At times, the maximum distance of 3000m (9842.5 ft) for the backbone cabling run must be split between two sections, as when the backbone cabling is to be used to connect the HC to an IC and the IC to the MC. When this occurs, the maximum distance for the backbone cabling run between the HC and the IC is 300m (984 ft). The maximum distance for the backbone cabling run between the IC and the MC is 2700m (8855 ft).

Fiber-Optic Backbone

Fiber optics are an extremely effective means of moving backbone traffic. This is because optical fibers are impervious to electrical noise and radio frequency interference. Fiber also does not conduct currents that can cause ground loops. Fiber-optic systems also have high bandwidth and can work at high speeds. This means that a fiber-optic backbone with certain characteristics that is installed today can be upgraded in the future to even greater performance when the terminal equipment is available. This can make fiber optic very cost-effective.

Fiber has an additional advantage when used as a backbone medium: It can go much farther than copper. Multimode optical fiber used as a backbone can support lengths of up to 2000m. Single-mode fiber-optic cables can go up to 3000m. Although optical fiber, especially single-mode fiber, can carry signals much farther than this (60 to 70 miles is feasible, depending on terminal equipment), these longer distances are considered to be out of the scope of LAN standards.

MUTOAs and Consolidation Points

Raised floors and dropped ceilings also can hold patch panels. These typically are used to house consolidation points or *multiuser telecommunications outlet assemblies (MUTOAs)*.

Additional specifications for horizontal cabling in work areas with moveable furniture and partitions have been included in TIA/EIA-568-B.1. Horizontal cabling methodologies are specified for "open-office" environments by means of MUTOAs and consolidation points (see Figure A-11). These methodologies are intended to provide increased flexibility and economy for installations with open-office workspaces that require frequent reconfiguration.

Rather than replacing the entire horizontal cabling system feeding these areas, a CP or MUTOA can be located close to the open-office area and eliminate the need to replace the cabling all the way back to the TR whenever the furniture is rearranged. The cabling only needs to be replaced between the new work area outlets and the CP or MUTOA. The longer distance of cabling back to the TR remains permanent.

A MUTOA is a device that enables users to move and add devices and to make changes in modular furniture settings without rerunning the cable. *Patch cords* can be routed directly from a MUTOA to work-area equipment (see Figure A-12). A MUTOA location must be accessible and permanent, and it cannot be mounted in ceiling spaces or under access flooring. Similarly, it cannot be mounted in furniture unless that furniture is secured permanently to the building structure.

Figure A-11 Typical MUTOA Installation

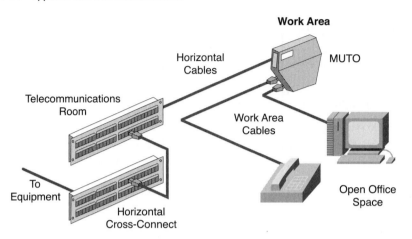

Figure A-12 Typical Consolidation Point Installation

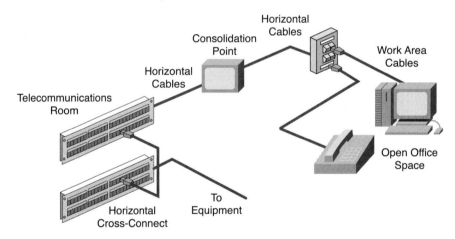

When using MUTOAs, the TIA/EIA-568-B.1 standard specifies the following:

- At least one MUTOA is needed for each furniture cluster.

- A maximum of 12 work areas can be used for each MUTOA.

- Patch cords at work areas shall be labeled on both ends with unique identifiers.

- The maximum patch cord length is 22m (72.2 ft.).

Consolidation points (CP) provide limited area connection access. Typically, a permanent, flush, wall-mounted, ceiling-mounted, or support column-mounted panel serves modular furniture work areas. The panels must be unobstructed and fully accessible without moving fixtures, equipment, or heavy furniture. Consolidation points differ from MUTOAs, in that workstations and other work-area equipment do not plug into the CP like they do with the MUTOA. Workstations plug into an outlet that then is connected to the CP.

The TIA/EIA-569 standard specifies the following:

- At least one CP for each furniture cluster

- A maximum of 12 work areas for each CP

- A maximum patch cord length of 5m (16.4 ft.)

For both consolidation points and MUTOAs, TIA/EIA 568-B.1 recommends a separation of at least 15m (49 ft) equipment between the TR and the CP or MUTOA. This is to avoid problems dealing with crosstalk and return loss.

Structured Cabling Standards and Codes

Standards are sets of rules or procedures that are either widely used or officially specified, and that serve as the gauge or model of excellence. Standards can take many forms. They can be specified by a single vendor or can be industry standards that support multivendor interoperability:

- Standardized media and layout descriptions for both backbone and horizontal cabling

- Standard connection interfaces for the physical connection of equipment

- Consistent and uniform design that follows a system plan and basic design principles

Numerous companies, organizations, and even government bodies regulate and specify the cables in use. In addition to these organizations, local, state, county, and national government agencies issue specifications, requirements, and codes.

The power of standards is this: The network that is built to standards should work well with, or interoperate with, other standard network devices. The long-term performance and investment value of many network cabling systems have been severely diminished by installers who do not know or follow mandatory and voluntary standards.

It is important to understand that these standards constantly are being reviewed and periodically updated to reflect new technologies and the ever-increasing requirements of voice and data networks. Just as new technologies are added to the standards, others are dropped or phased out. In many cases, a network might include technologies that are no longer a part of the current standard or that are being eliminated. Typically, this does not require an immediate changeover, but these older, slower technologies eventually are replaced in favor of faster ones.

Standards often are developed by or at the direction of international organizations that try to reach some form of universal standard. Organizations such as the IEEE, ISO, and IEC are all examples of international standards bodies. These international standards organizations are composed of members from many nations, each of which has its own standards-making process.

In many countries, the national codes become the model for state/provincial agencies as well as municipalities and other governmental units to incorporate into their laws and ordinances. The enforcement then moves to the most local authority. Always check with local authorities to determine what codes are enforced. For the most part, local codes take precedence over national codes, which take precedence over international codes.

Telecommunications Industry Association and Electronic Industries Alliances

NOTE

For more information on TIA and EIA, visit www.tiaonline.org and www.eia.org.

The Telecommunications Industry Association (TIA) and the Electronic Industries Alliance (EIA) are trade associations that jointly develop and publish a series of standards covering areas of structured voice and data wiring for LANs (see Figure A-13).

Both the TIA and the EIA are accredited by the American National Standards Institute (ANSI, section 6.2.7) to develop voluntary industry standards for a wide variety of telecommunications products. This means that many standards often are labeled ANSI/ TIA/EIA. The various committees and subcommittees of TIA/EIA develop standards for fiber optics, user premises equipment, network equipment, wireless communications, and satellite communications.

Although there are many standards and supplements, the following are used most frequently by cable installers (see Figure A-14).

Figure A-13 TIA/EIA Standards for Buildings

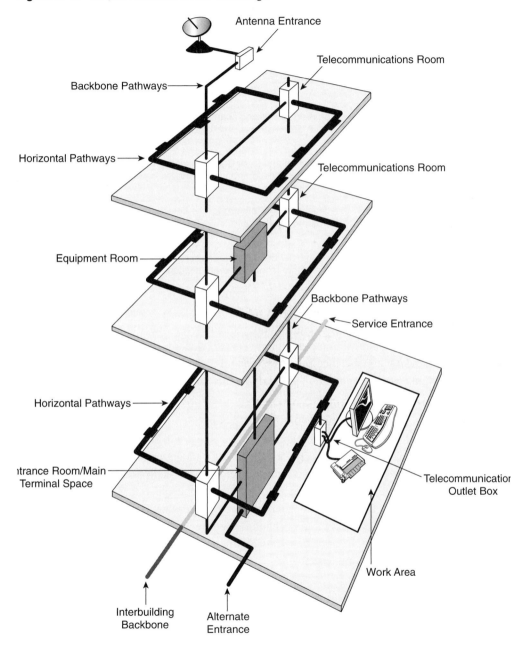

Figure A-14 TIA/EIA Structured Cabling Standards

- TIA/EIA 568-A is the Commercial Building Standard for Telecommunications Wiring. The standard specifies minimum requirements for telecommunications cabling, recommended topology and distance limits, media and connecting hardware performance specifications, and connector and pin assignments.

- TIA/EIA-568-B is the Cabling Standard. This standard specifies the component and transmission requirements for media. TIA/EIA-568-B.1 specifies a generic telecommunications cabling system for commercial buildings that will support a multiproduct, multivendor environment. TIA/EIA-568-B.1.1 is an addendum that applies to four-pair unshielded twisted-pair (UTP) and four-pair screened twisted-pair (ScTP) patch cables bend radius. TIA/EIA-568-B.2 specifies cabling components, transmission, system models, and the measurement procedures needed for verification of twisted-pair cabling. TIA/EIA 568-B.2.1 is an addendum about requirements for Category 6 cabling. TIA/EIA-568-B.3 specifies the component and transmission requirements for an optical fiber cabling system.

- TIA/EIA 569-A is the Commercial Building Standard for Telecommunications Pathways and Spaces. The standard specifies design and construction practices within and between buildings that are in support of telecommunications media and equipment.

- TIA/EIA-606-A is the Administration Standard for the Telecommunications Infrastructure of Commercial Buildings, including cable labeling standards. The standard specifies that each hardware termination unit must have some kind of unique identifier. This standard also outlines the requirements for record keeping and maintaining documentation for administering the network.

- TIA/EIA-607-A is the standard for Commercial Building Grounding and Bonding Requirements for Telecommunications. It supports a multivendor, multiproduct environment, as well as the grounding practices for various systems that might be installed on customer premises. The standard specifies the exact interface points between the building grounding systems and the telecommunications equipment grounding configuration, and specifies building grounding configurations needed to support this equipment.

European Committee for Electrotechnical Standardization

CENELEC is known in English as the European Committee for Electrotechnical Standardization. It was set up in 1973 as a nonprofit organization under Belgian law. CENELEC develops electrotechnical standards for most of Europe; it works with 35,000 technical experts from 19 European countries to publish standards for the European market. It has been officially recognized as the European standards organization by the European Commission in Directive 83/189/EEC. Many CENELEC cabling standards mirror ISO cabling standards, with minor changes.

NOTE

For more information on CENELEC, visit www.cenelec.org.

Although CENELEC and the International Electrotechnical Commission (IEC) operate at two different levels, their actions have a strong mutual impact because they are the most important standardization bodies in the electrotechnical field in Europe. Cooperation between CENELEC and the IEC is described in what is known as the Dresden Agreement, approved and signed by both partners in that German city in 1996. This agreement was intended to expedite the publication and common adoption of international standards and accelerate the standards preparation process in response to market demands. This agreement also was intended to ensure rational use of available resources. Therefore, full technical consideration of the content of the standard preferably should take place at the international level.

International Organization for Standardization

The International Organization for Standardization (ISO) is an international organization composed of national standards bodies from more than 140 countries. For example, the American National Standards Institute (ANSI) is a member of the ISO. The ISO is a nongovernmental organization established to promote the development of standardization and related activities. The ISO's work results in international agreements, which are published as international standards.

NOTE

For more information on the ISO, visit www.iso.org/iso/en/ISOOnline.frontpage.

The ISO has defined a number of important computer standards, the most significant of which is perhaps the Open Systems Interconnection (OSI) model, a standardized architecture for designing networks.

U.S. Codes

NOTE

The Americans with Disabilities Act (ADA) has led to several important changes in new construction, alterations, and renovations regarding networking and telecommunications. Depending on the use of the facility, these changes might be mandatory, and fines can be assessed for failure to comply.

For some networking projects, a permit is required to ensure that the work is being done properly. Contact local zoning departments for information on permit requirements.

To obtain copies of local or state building codes, contact the building official for the local jurisdiction. All of the basic building codes—CABO, ICBO, BOCA, SBCCI, ICC, and so on—that are adopted throughout the United States can be purchased from the International Conference of Building Officials (ICBO).

It is common for codes requiring local inspection and enforcement to be incorporated into state or provincial governments, and then possibly down to city and county enforcement units. Building codes, fire codes, and electrical codes are examples. Like occupational safety, these were originally local issues, but disparity of standards and often lack of enforcement has led to national standards. When adopted by state or local authorities and enforced to appropriate levels, these standards then are turned over to the lower-level authorities for implementation.

Note that violating these codes often can be expensive in both penalties and delayed project costs.

Some codes are enforced variously by city, county, or state agencies. This means that a project within the city would be handled by the appropriate city agencies, while those outside the city would be covered by county agencies. For instance, fire codes can be enforced by the county building permit department in some communities but by the local fire department in others.

NOTE

Most countries have similar systems of codes. Knowledge of these local codes is important if you are planning to do a project that crosses national boundaries.

Although local entities inspect and enforce the codes, they often do not write them. Standards-making organizations frequently do that for them. For instance, the National Electrical Code is written to sound like a legal ordinance. This makes it possible for local governments to adopt the code by vote. This might not happen regularly, and the government might fall behind. Always know which version of the NEC is in force for your area.

Evolution of Standards

As network bandwidth has increased from 10 Mbps to 1000 Mbps and beyond, it has created new demands on cabling. Older types of cable are often inadequate for use in the faster modern networks. For this reason, the types of cabling used changes over time, and the standards reflect this. The following are the standards for TIA/EIA 568-B.2:

- For twisted-pair cables, only 100-ohm Category 3, 5e, and 6 cables are recognized. Category 5 cable no longer is recommended for new installations and has been moved from the body of the standard into an appendix. Category 5e or greater is now the recommended cable for 100-ohm twisted-pair cable.

■ The Category 6 standard specifies performance parameters that ensure that products meeting the standard are component-compliant, backward-compatible, and interoperable between vendors.

■ When terminating Category 5e and higher cables, the pairs shall not be untwisted more than 13 mm (0.5 in) from the point of termination. The minimum bend radius for UTP horizontal cabling remains four times the cable diameter. The minimum bend radius for UTP patch cable is now equal to the cable diameter because it contains stranded wires and thus is more flexible than solid-core copper cables used in horizontal cabling.

The acceptable length of patch cords in the telecommunications room has changed from 6m to 5m (19.7 ft. to 16.4 ft.) at maximum. The acceptable length of a jumper cable in the work area has changed from 3m to 5m (9.8 ft. to 16.4 ft.) at maximum. The horizontal segment distance remains at 90m (295.3 ft.). If a MUTOA is used, the work-area jumper can be increased in length if the horizontal length is decreased a corresponding amount to keep the total link segment length not longer than 100m (328.1 ft) (see Figure A-15).

The use of a MUTOA or consolidation point also mandates a separation of at least 15 meters (49 ft) between the TR and the MUTOA or consolidation point in order to limit problems with crosstalk and return loss.

Figure A-15 Changes to Horizontal Cabling Standards

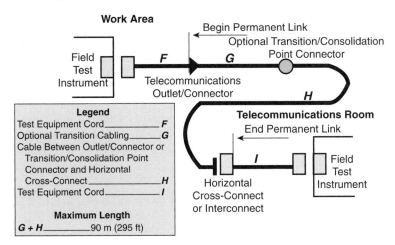

All patch cords and cross-connect jumpers formerly were required to use stranded cable to provide the flexibility needed to survive repeated connection and reconnection. The wording around this topic now has been changed from *shall* to *should* regarding stranded conductors. This allows solid conductor cord designs.

Patch cords are critical elements in the network system. Language regarding the onsite manufacture of patch cords and jumpers still allows these cables to be created, but it now is strongly encouraged that network designers purchase cables that are premade and have been tested.

Category 6 and Category 7 are the newest copper cables available. Because Category 6 cable is used more frequently, it is important for cable installers to understand its benefits.

The significant difference between Category 5e and Category 6 is the means used to maintain the spacing between the pairs inside the cables. Some Category 6 cables use a physical divider down the center of the cable. Others have a unique sheath that locks the pairs into position. Still other Category 6 cables use a foil screen that overwraps the pairs in the cable. The latter type of cable often is called screened twisted-pair cable, or ScTP.

To achieve even greater performance than Category 6, Category 7 cables that are available use a fully shielded construction that limits crosstalk among all pairs. Each pair is enveloped within a foil wrap, and an overall braided sheath surrounds the four foil-wrapped pairs. A drain wire might be provided in future cables to facilitate grounding.

Standards for the structured cabling will continue to evolve. The focus will be on supporting the new technologies that are converging on the data network, such as the following:

- IP telephony and wireless utilizing a power signal in the transmission to provide power to the IP phones or access points

- Storage area networking utilizing 10 GB Ethernet transmission

- Metro Ethernet "last mile" solutions that require optimizing bandwidth and distance requirements

The standard for Power over Ethernet (PoE) is under development and will be available in the near future. PoE embeds a power signal on cables used for Ethernet transmissions. This power signal is used to free IP phones and wireless access points from the need for connection to AC power outlets, simplifying deployment and reducing costs.

Safety

Safety is an important concept containing information that often is overlooked in coverage of low-voltage telecommunications wiring. Students not accustomed to working in the physical workplace will benefit from labs and training. Other important safety topics include these:

- Safety codes and standards for the United States

- Safety around electricity

- Lab and workplace safety practices

- Personal safety equipment

Safety Codes and Standards for the United States

Most nations have rules designed to protect workers against hazardous conditions. In the United States, the organization charged with worker safety and health is the *Occupational Safety and Health Administration (OSHA)*. Since the agency was created in 1971, workplace fatalities have been cut in half and occupational injury and illness rates have declined 40 percent. At the same time, U.S. employment has nearly doubled from 56 million workers at 3.5 million worksites to 105 million workers at nearly 6.9 million sites.

It is OSHA's responsibility to protect workers by enforcing U.S. labor laws. Technically, OSHA is not an agency related to building code or building permits. However, OSHA inspectors have the power to impose heavy fines and to shut down a job site if they find serious safety violations. Anyone who works on or is responsible for a construction site or business facility needs to be familiar with OSHA regulations. The organization offers safety information, statistics, and publications on its website.

NOTE

For more information on OSHA, visit www.osha.gov.

MSDS

A *material safety data sheet (MSDS)* is a document that contains information on the use, storage, and handling of a hazardous material. It provides detailed information on the potential health effects of exposure and how to work safely with the material. It tells what the hazards of the material are, how to use it safely, what to expect if the recommendations are not followed, what to do if accidents occur, how to recognize symptoms of overexposure, and what to do if such incidents occur.

Underwriters Laboratories, Inc.

Underwriters Laboratories, Inc. (UL), is an independent, nonprofit product safety testing and certification organization. UL has tested products for public safety for more than a century. The UL focuses on safety standards but has expanded its certification program to evaluate twisted-pair LAN cables for performance according to IBM and Telecommunications Industry Association/Electronic Industries Alliance (TIA/EIA) performance specifications, as well as National Electrical Code (NEC) safety specifications. The UL also established a program to mark shielded and unshielded twisted-pair LAN cables, which should simplify the complex task of making sure that the materials used in the installation are up to specification. Listing by UL denotes initial testing and periodic retesting to ensure continuing conformance to standards.

NOTE

For more information on the Underwriters Laboratories, Inc., visit www.ul.com.

The UL tests and evaluates samples of cable and then, after granting a UL listing, conducts follow-up tests and inspections. This independent testing and follow-through make the UL markings valuable symbols to buyers.

The UL LAN Certification Program addresses not only safety, but also performance. Companies whose cables earn these UL markings display them on the outer jacket (Level I, LVL I, or LEV I, for example).

National Electrical Code

NOTE

For more information on the National Fire Protection Association (NFPA), visit www.nfpa.org/Home/index.asp.

The purpose of the *National Electrical Code (NEC)* is to safeguard persons and property from hazards arising from the use of electricity. This code is sponsored by the *National Fire Protection Association (NFPA)* under the auspices of the *American National Standards Institute (ANSI)*. The code is revised every three years.

Several organizations, including the UL, have established standards for flame and smoke that apply to network cables laid inside buildings. However, the NEC contains the codes most widely supported by local licensing and inspection officials.

NEC Type Codes

NEC type codes are listed in catalogs of cables and supplies. These codes classify specific categories of products for specific uses, as shown in Table A-1.

Table A-1 NEC Cable Type Codes

Type of Cable	Description
OFC (fiber optic)	Contains metal conductors inserted for strength.
OFN (fiber optic)	Contains no metal.
CMP (communication plenum)	Passed tests showing limited spread of flame and low smoke. Plenum cable typically is coated with a special jacket material such as Teflon. The letter *P* in this code defines a plenum as a channel or ductwork fabricated for handling air.
CMR (communications riser)	The letter *R* shows that the cable has passed similar but slightly different tests for the spread of flame and production of smoke, compared to CMP cable. For example, riser cable is tested for its burning properties in a vertical position. According to the code, you must use cable rated for riser service when the cable penetrates a floor and a ceiling. Riser cables typically have a polyvinyl chloride (PVC) outer jacket.

Generally, interior network cables are listed in the category of type CM for communications or type MP for multipurpose. Some companies choose to run their cables through the testing process as remote-control or power-limited circuit cables CL2 or CL3 (Class 2 or Class 3) general tests instead of through the CM or CP tests, but the flame and smoke criteria is generally the same for all tests. The differences between these markings concern the amount of electrical power that could run through the cable in the worst case. MP cable is subjected to tests that assume the most power-handling capability, with CM, CL3, and CL2 going through tests with decreasing levels of power handling.

Safety Around Electricity

In addition to learning about the industry's safety organizations, the cable installer should learn about basic safety principles that will be used every day on the job and that are also necessary for the curriculum labs. Because many hazards exist when installing cable, the installer should be prepared for all situations so that accidents or injuries can be prevented.

High Voltage

Cable installers work with wiring designed for low-voltage systems. The voltage applied to a data cable would be hardly noticeable to most people. However, the voltage of network devices that data cables plug into can range from 100V to 240V (in North America). If a circuit failure allowed the voltage to become accessible, it could give the installer a dangerous shock—and it could be fatal. In addition, it is not unheard of for a low-voltage installer inadvertently to skin the insulation off existing high-voltage wiring and contact voltage that way.

Do not become complacent about the hazards of high-voltage wiring nearby just because most of the work deals with low voltage. If someone suddenly comes in contact with high voltage, that person might find it difficult to control his or her muscles or might not have the ability to pull away.

Lightning and High-Voltage Danger

High voltage is not limited to power lines; lightning is another source of high voltage. Because lightning can be fatal and also can damage network equipment, care must be taken to prevent it from entering the network cabling.

The following precautions should be taken to avoid personal injury and damage to network equipment from lightning and electrical shorts:

- All outside wiring must be equipped with properly grounded and registered signal circuit protectors at the point that they enter the building, known as the entrance point. These protectors must be installed in compliance with local telephone company requirements and applicable codes. Telephone wire pairs should not be used without authorization. If authorization is obtained, do not remove or modify telephone circuit protectors or grounding wires.

- Never run wiring between structures without proper protection. In fact, protection from lighting effects is probably one of the biggest advantages to using fiber optics between buildings.

- Avoid wiring in or near damp locations.

- Never install or connect copper wiring during electrical storms. Improperly protected copper wiring can carry a fatal lightning surge for many miles.

High-Voltage Safety Test

Voltage is invisible. Its effects are seen in tools that run, equipment that operates, or the unpleasant experience of getting shocked.

When working with anything that plugs into the wall for power, it is a safety best practice to check for voltages on surfaces and devices before coming in contact with them. Using a known reliable voltage-measurement device such as a *multimeter* or voltage detector, take measurements immediately before starting work. Measure again whenever work is resumed the following day or after a break on any job; someone might have made changes. Recheck the measurements again when finished.

Some forms of electricity cannot be predicted. Lightning and static electricity fall into this category. Never install or connect copper wiring during electrical storms; copper wiring can carry a fatal lightning surge for many miles. This is particularly an issue with external wiring that is strung between buildings or underground wiring. Equip all outside wiring with properly grounded and approved signal circuit protectors. These protectors must be installed in compliance with the local codes, which, in most cases, align with national codes.

Grounding

Grounding works by providing a direct path to the earth for any voltages that come in contact with it. Equipment designers purposely isolate the circuits in equipment from the *chassis*—that is, the box where the circuits are mounted. Any voltage that leaks from the equipment to its chassis should not stay in the chassis. Grounding equipment conducts any stray voltage to the earth without hurting that equipment. Without a proper path to the ground, stray voltages use another path to the ground, such as a person's body.

The grounding electrode is the metal rod that is buried in the ground near the entrance point of the building—that is, the place where electricity enters a building. How the ground system connects to the earth is often another matter. For years, cold-water pipes, which enter the building from the underground water mains, were considered good grounds. Large structural members, such as I-beams and girders, were also acceptable. Although these might provide an adequate path to the ground, most local codes now require a dedicated grounding system, such as installed grounding conductors connecting equipment to grounding electrodes.

Be aware of the grounding system in the lab and on each job site. Verify that the grounding system actually works. It is not uncommon to find that grounding was improperly done or never was installed in the first place. A more common situation occurs when an installer takes a few shortcuts and accomplishes a technically adequate ground, but in a nonstandard way. Later, changes to other parts of the network or to the building itself might destroy or eliminate the nonstandard grounding system, leaving equipment and people at risk.

Bonding

Bonding involves providing a means for various wiring fixtures to interconnect with the grounding system (see Figure A-16). It can be thought of as an extension of ground wiring. A device such as a switch or a router might have a bonding strap between its case and a ground circuit to ensure a good connection.

Figure A-16 Bonding

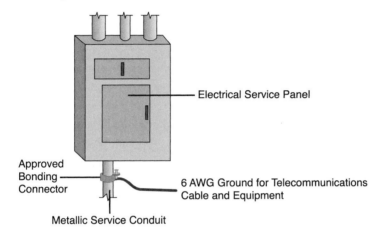

Properly installed bonding and grounding will accomplish the following:

- Minimize electrical surge (spike) effects
- Maintain the integrity of the electrical grounding plant
- Provide a safer and more effective path to ground

Telecommunications bonds typically are used in the following ways:

- Entrance facilities
- Equipment rooms
- Telecommunications rooms

Grounding and Bonding Standards

The National Electrical Code contains much information on grounding and bonding. The TIA/EIA standard on grounding and bonding, TIA/EIA-607-A, "Commercial Building Grounding and Bonding Requirements for Telecommunications," extends grounding and bonding into the telecommunications structured cabling system. TIA/EIA-607-A specifies the exact interface points between the grounding system of a building and the telecommunication equipment grounding configuration. It supports a multivendor, multiproduct environment for the grounding practices for various systems that may be installed on customer premises. It also specifies the necessary grounding and bonding configurations needed in the building to support this equipment.

Lab and Workplace Safety Practices

Although cable installation is generally a safe profession, there are plenty of opportunities for being injured. Many injuries are caused when installers come in contact with stray sources of voltage, called foreign voltages, such as lightning, static electricity, or other types of voltages caused by installation faults or induction currents that somehow find themselves onto network cables.

When working in walls, ceilings, or attics, the first thing that should be done is to turn off power to all circuits that might pass through those work areas. If it is not clear which wires pass through the section of the building being worked in, a good rule to follow is to shut off all power. Never touch power cables. Even if all power to the area has been shut off, there is no way to know whether circuits are still "live."

Most countries have one or more agencies that develop and administer safety standards. Some of these are designed to ensure public safety; others are designed to protect the worker. Those that protect the worker usually cover laboratory safety, general workplace safety, compliance with environmental regulations, and hazardous waste disposal.

Workplace Safety

The following are guidelines for keeping a workplace safe:

- Before beginning work, learn the locations of all fire extinguishers in the area. A small extinguishable fire can get out of control if no one is able to locate an extinguisher quickly.

- Always find out in advance what the local codes are. Some building codes might prohibit drilling or cutting holes in certain areas, such as firewalls or ceilings. The site administrator or facility engineer will be able to help determine which areas are off-limits.

- When installing cable between floors, use a riser-rated cable. Riser cable is covered with a flame-retardant fluorinated ethylene propylene (FEP) jacket and, therefore, will not allow flames from one floor to use the cable to reach another floor.

- Outdoor cables typically have a polyethylene jacket (PVC). Polyethylene burns readily and gives off dangerous gases. NEC codes state that polyethylene building entrance cables cannot be exposed more than 15m (approximately 49 ft.) into a building. If greater distances are required, the cable must be in metallic conduits.

- Consult the building's maintenance engineer to find out whether there is asbestos, lead, or PCB in the working areas. If so, follow all government regulations in dealing with that material. These materials are called hazardous for a reason. No one's health should be risked by working unprotected in these areas.

- Finally, if cable must be routed through spaces where air is circulated, be sure to use a fire-rated cable (plenum-rated). The most common plenum cables are jacketed with Teflon or Halar. Plenum-grade cable does not give off poisonous gases when it burns, like regular cables, which have a polyvinyl chloride (PVC) jacket.

Ladder Safety

Ladders come in many sizes and shapes to be used for many specific purposes. They can be made of wood, aluminum, or fiberglass, and are designed for either light or industrial use. The two types that are the most common are straight ladders and stepladders. Regardless of the type or construction, be sure that the ladder has a label certifying that it complies with specifications of the American National Standards Institute (ANSI) and that Underwriters Laboratories (UL) lists it as passing its standards.

- Select the right ladder for the job. Be sure that the ladder is long enough to work from comfortably and is sturdy enough to withstand repeated use. Fiberglass ladders most commonly are used in cable installation. Although aluminum ladders are lighter, they are less stable and never should be used around electricity. When working near electricity, only fiberglass ladders should be used.

- Inspect the ladder first. Any ladder can develop a problem that can render it unsafe. Inspect ladders for loose or damaged rungs, steps, rails, or braces. Make certain the spreaders on stepladders can be locked in place and that the ladder has safety feet that will provide more stability and reduce the chances of the ladder slipping while working. Never use a ladder that is defective.

- Stepladders should be fully opened with the hinges locked. Straight ladders should be placed at a 4:1 ratio. This means that the base of the ladder should be 0.25m (10 in.) away from the wall or other vertical surface for every 1m (3 ft.) of height to the point of support. If possible, secure a straight ladder as close to the point of support as possible, to prevent shifting. Ladders always should be placed on a solid, level surface.

- Never climb higher than the second step from the top on a stepladder, or the third from the top on a straight ladder.

- Cordon off the work area with appropriate markers, such as traffic cones or caution tape. Post signs so that people are aware of the ladder. Lock or block any nearby door that might swing toward the ladder if it opens.

Fiber-Optic Safety

Because fiber-optic cable contains glass, it is important to take appropriate precautions. The scrap material is sharp and must be disposed of properly. As with any glass product, when broken, it can cut or can splinter into tiny slivers that can get lodged in the skin.

These rules should be followed to avoid injury when working with fiber optics:

- Always wear safety glasses with side shields.

- Place a mat or piece of adhesive on the table so that all glass shards that fall are more easily identified.

- Do not touch eyes while working with fiber-optic systems until hands have been cleansed thoroughly. Similarly, do not handle contact lenses until hands have been washed thoroughly.

- Put all cut fiber pieces in a safe place and dispose of them properly.

- If some of the material gets on clothing, use a piece of adhesive or masking tape to remove it. Use tape to remove shards from fingers and hands.

- No food or beverages in the work area should be allowed.

- Do not look directly into the end of fiber cables. Some laser-driven devices could cause irreversible damage to the eye.

Fire Extinguisher Use

CAUTION

If someone catches on fire, remember the tip, "Stop, Drop, and Roll":

- Stop, do not run. Fire spreads quickly if a burning person starts running.

- Drop to the floor.

- Roll on the floor to extinguish the flames.

Never attempt to fight a fire without knowing how to use a fire extinguisher. Read instructions beforehand and check the valve. In the United States, regulations state that fire extinguishers used in commercial buildings must be checked at regular intervals and replaced if they're not in good working order.

Fire extinguishers have labels that identify which kinds of fires they are designed to fight. In the United States, these are called ratings. Four different types of fires have been classified in the United States:

- Class A fires involve ordinary materials, such as burning paper, lumber, cardboard, plastics, and so on.

- Class B fires involve flammable or combustible liquids, such as gasoline, kerosene, and common organic solvents used in the laboratory.

- Class C fires involve energized electrical equipment, such as appliances, switches, panel boxes, power tools, hot plates, and most other electronic devices. Water is a particularly dangerous extinguishing medium for Class C fires because of the risk of electrical shock.

- Class D fires involve combustible metals, such as magnesium, titanium, potassium, and sodium. These materials burn at high temperatures and react violently with water, air, and other chemicals.

Personal Safety Equipment

Determine before you enter the workplace that you will work safely that day. Part of having a safe work attitude involves choosing to wear proper work attire. Wearing protective clothing or gear can prevent an injury or make an injury less severe.

When working with power tools, for instance, it is important to protect eyes from flying debris and ears from deafening noises. If goggles and earplugs are not used, eyesight or hearing could be damaged permanently.

Work Clothes

Long trousers and sleeves help protect the arms and legs from cuts, scratches, and other hazards. Avoid wearing excessively loose or baggy clothing because it might catch on a protruding object or get caught in power tools.

Wear shoes that are appropriate for the job. Sturdy, fully enclosed shoes should be worn. They should be able to protect the soles of the feet from sharp objects on the floor. Thick-soled shoes are best when working around nails, scrap metal, and other materials that could puncture the soles of regular athletic shoes. Steel-toed shoes can protect toes when a heavy object is dropped on the shoes. Also make sure that the soles have traction to prevent slipping.

Eye Protection

Eyes are much easier to protect than to repair, so safety glasses should be worn when cutting, drilling, sawing, or working in a crawl space (see Figure A-17). With some cable-termination processes, as materials are cut, prepped, and discarded, there are opportunities for small particles to become airborne. While working with fiber optics, the glass fibers, adhesives, and solvents can come in contact with the eyes. Also, small particles or chemicals might get on the hands and accidentally be rubbed into the eyes. Therefore, glasses also protect the eyes from contaminated hands. It is a good idea to wear safety glasses any time when working in a crawl space or above a dropped ceiling. If something falls from above, the eyes will be protected. Many job sites require safety glasses at all times.

Figure A-17 Eye Protection

Eye protection should be worn in all labs. Before starting any lab exercise, review the safety instructions and safety equipment needed.

Hard Hat Use

As with all safety equipment, a hard hat protects the user from injury. Hard hats might be required at job sites, especially those involving construction. Many employers supply hard hats; others require installers to buy their own. The furnished hard hats might be of a company color or might be equipped with company logos to identify the wearer as belonging to a certain organization. Even if you are purchasing a hard hat for personal use, do not adorn it without obtaining permission from the employer. In addition, OSHA does not allow stickers on hard hats because they could hide cracks.

Periodically check the hard hat for cracks. A cracked hat might fail to protect a head. For hard hats to provide effective protection, they must be adjusted properly. Take the time to adjust the internal straps to make sure that they function and ensure that the hat fits snugly and is comfortable. Hard hats are required when working on top of a ladder and often are required when working in new-construction environments.

Tools of the Trade

As with any craft, tools of the trade are often what makes the difference between a hard job with mediocre results and a simple job with outstanding results. Students should get hands-on experience with several of the tools used by low-voltage cabling installers to have professional results.

Students should become versed in the following technologies:

- Stripping and cutting tools
- Termination tools
- Diagnostic tools
- Installation support tools

Stripping and Cutting Tools

Stripping tools are used to cut the cable jacket and insulation of the wires. The Panduit UTP cable-stripping tool (see Figure A-18) is used to remove the outer jacket from four-pair cables. It also can be used for most coaxial cable. The tool features an adjustable cutting blade to accommodate cables with different jacket thicknesses. The cable is inserted into the tool, and then the tool is twisted around the cable. The blade cuts through the outer jacket only, allowing the installer to simply pull the jacket off the cable to expose the twisted pairs.

Figure A-18 Panduit UTP Cable-Stripping Tool

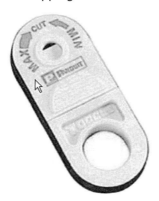

The electrician's scissors and cable knife set (see Figure A-19) also can be used for removing cable jackets. The knife is used for removing the jacket from large cables, such as those that enter the building from the telco or ISP. This knife is sharp, so care should be taken when using this tool. It is recommended that gloves be worn when working with it, preferably gloves that will resist injuring the hand if the knife slips.

The scissors can be used to cut individual wires, remove the outer jacket of smaller cables, and remove the insulation on individual wires. Not visible in the figure, the scissors features two different-size notches on the back of the blade that will strip insulation on wire sizes from 22- to 26-gauge.

Figure A-19 Electrician's Scissors and Cable Knife

Termination Tools

Termination tools are designed to cut and terminate specific types of cable. The multipair termination tool (see Figure A-20) is designed to terminate and cut UTP cable and seat connecting blocks. This tool features an ergonomically designed handle that helps reduce fatigue when trimming wire or seating connecting blocks to the wiring base. Additionally, it has the following features:

- Terminates five pairs at a time
- Terminates wires on both the cable side and the cross-connect side of connecting blocks
- Has replacement cutting blades available
- Can be used in the cut or noncut position
- Clearly displays CUT designation for proper orientation during termination
- Includes a reliable impact mechanism
- Has an ergonomically designed rubber handle with a ribbed edge that provides a no-slip grip

The impact punchdown tool (see Figure A-21) has interchangeable blades so that it can terminate wires on 66 and 110 hardware. Unlike the multipair termination tool, this tool terminates only one wire at a time. The reversible blades have a punch-and-cut function on one side and a punch-only function on the other.

Figure A-20 Panduit Multipair Impact Tool

Figure A-21 Panduit Impact Tool

 Lab A-3   Tool Usage and Safety

In this lab, you learn to identify, examine, and use the tools that are used in cable installations.

Diagnostic Tools

It is sometimes necessary to access individual wires inside a telecommunications outlet or jack. The modular adapter, or banjo, is used to provide access to these wires (see Figure A-22). A common line cord is plugged into the adapters and then into the jack. The technician can use an ohmmeter or other test devices without having to disassemble the jack. Banjos come in three-pair and four-pair configurations.

Figure A-22 Modular Adapter (Banjo)

To locate metal pipes, wood studs or joists, or other hidden structure components behind a wall or under a floor, use wood and metal sensors. This should be done before drilling for any cabling project. A deep-scanning metal sensor can find metal studs, conduit, copper piping, electrical lines, rebar, telephone lines, cable lines, nails, and other metal objects. This tool usually can scan through up to 15 cm (about 6 in.) of a nonmetallic surface, such as concrete, stucco, wood, or vinyl siding. It identifies both the location and the depth of piping or rebar.

Another type of sensor is a stud sensor (see Figure A-23). This sensor locates wooden studs and joists behind walls. This tool helps the installer make informed decisions on the best location to drill or saw when installing outlets or raceways. The stud and rebar sensor also detects metal and even can find rebar embedded in up to 100 cm of concrete. All the modes detect AC wires to alert the installer, to prevent drilling or nailing into a live electrical wire.

Figure A-23 Stud Sensor

Installation Support Tools

A cable installer also will find other tools useful. A measuring wheel is used to estimate the length of a cable run (see Figure A-24). The wheel has a counter mounted on the side. An installer simply rolls the wheel down the intended path of the cable. When the end is reached, the counter indicates the distance.

Cable installers also need tools and materials for cleaning up the job site. Brooms, dust pans, and vacuums make the cleanup process go quickly. Cleanup is one of the final but important steps in completing a cabling project. A shop vacuum is designed for industrial or heavy-use jobs.

Figure A-24 Measuring Wheel

Fish Tape

One device specifically designed to make the retrieval of wires inside a wall a quick and easy process is fish tape (see Figure A-25). Fish tape can be run through walls or conduits. After running the fish tape to its intended destination of some convenient partway point, secure the cable to be pulled to the end of the fish tape. Retrieve by pulling and winding. The desired cable will come with it.

For cabling work, a fiberglass fish tape is safer than a steel one. Also, most seasoned cable installers pull a string along with their cables. This provides a convenient way to pull extra cables later.

Figure A-25 Fish Tape

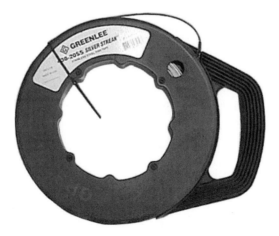

Cable Tree

During the rough-in phase, *cable trees*, jacks, and rollers are used to support cable reels to make laying the cable faster and easier, and to prevent injuries. A cable tree supports a number of small reels of cable (see Figure A-26). This enables the cable installer to pull multiple cables simultaneously. Because all cables terminate at the telecommunications room, a cable tree would be set up in the staging area. After cable is pulled to a jack location, the other end is cut from the reel and pulled into the telecommunications room.

Figure A-26 Cable Tree

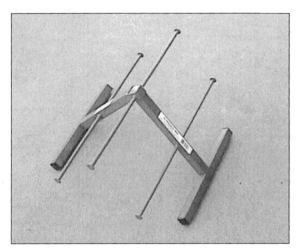

Cable jacks and reel rollers are designed for large reels that hold backbone cable. Because large reels are often too large and heavy to lift by hand, cable jacks provide the leverage that enable two people to raise them. After they are raised, the jacks allow the reel to rotate freely and safely during the pulling process.

Reel rollers also are used to support large cable reels. Rollers come in sets of two, each used to support one side of the reel. Rollers mounted on bearings allow the reel to be turned easily. When pulling from a reel roller, one installer generally is stationed at the reel, to assist in the turning of it.

Bullwheels

Bullwheels, in particular, normally are used to make the first or last turn in the path, but they can be used to make an offset or turn in the center of the run.

A bullwheel is a large-diameter pulley that is used in a mechanical cable-pulling process. Bullwheels seldom are used when pulling cable by hand. The bullwheel itself generally is made of aluminum, is at least 0.3m (about 1 ft.) in diameter, and is supported on some type of bearing on its frame. The bullwheel differs from a pulley, in that it often has two shackles for attachment to fixed points. It also can be removed from its frame so that it can be put into a cable run from the middle of the cable.

Pulleys

Pulleys are used on long, open cable runs to support cables and prevent them from dragging on surfaces that could damage the cable sheath. They also are used on surfaces that could be damaged by pulling cable across them. Pulleys are used in straight cable runs to support the weight of the cable and reduce pulling friction. Pulleys also can assist with minor offsets in the cable run (see Figure A-27).

Pulleys are used when pulling by hand or when using a cable puller or winch. When turns in the run exceed 45°, use bullwheels instead.

Pulleys are used for both multiple network cable runs and heavy backbone cable runs. Although lightweight pulleys can be used for network cable runs, heavy-duty pulleys should be used for backbone cables. Backbone cable pulleys have a larger frame, and the pulley wheel is a larger diameter.

Figure A-27   Cable Pull Using a Bullwheel and Pulleys

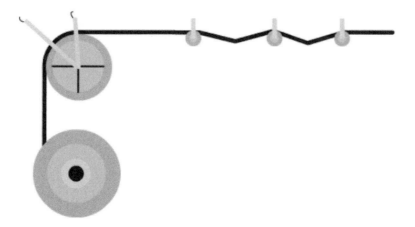

Wire Mesh or Kellem Grips

Wire mesh or Kellem grips are attached to the end of the cable so that a pulling rope can be tied to the end of the cable (see Figure A-28). The grip is slid over the end of the cable, and the last 15 cm (about 6 in.) are taped tightly with good-quality vinyl electrical tape. As tension is placed on the cable, the grip draws tighter around the sheath of the cable. These grips are designed for single-cable use only; they generally are not to be used with a bundle of network distribution cables. These grips come in various sizes to accommodate different cable sizes.

Kellem grips are also available in a split version, for where the end of the cable might not be accessible. These versions are used to pull additional slack in the middle of a cable run. Split grips also are used to support large backbone cables in a riser installation—that is, when cables are pulled between floors. To attach these split Kellem grips, the grip is opened and placed around the cable. A special rod then is threaded through the wire mesh.

Figure A-28 Wire Mesh or Kellem Grip

Installation Process

The installation process contains the many elements of an installation, starting from the rough-in phase, in which the cables first are pulled into place. Riser cables are treated, as are the fire stops used where a wire passes through a fire-rated wall. Copper terminations are covered, as are wall adapters and other fixtures.

Topics that will be treated here include these:

- Rough-in phase

- Vertical cable installation

- Fire-stops

- Termination of copper media

- The trimout phase

Four phases cover all aspects of a cabling project: rough-in, trimout, finish, and customer support. The characteristics of each are as follows:

- **Rough-in phase**—In the rough-in phase, all of the cables are installed in the ceilings, walls, floor ducts, and risers.

- **Trimout phase**—The principal tasks during this phase are cable management and termination of the wires.

■ **Finish phase**—The principle tasks during the finish phase are performing cable testing, troubleshooting, and certification.

■ **Customer support phase**—The final phase of the project focuses on satisfying the customer. In this phase, a walkthrough of the network is done with the customer, and the customer is presented with formal test results and other documentation, such as as-built drawings. The customer then can sign off on the project if satisfied. Afterward, the cable installation company provides ongoing support to the customer if there are problems with the installation.

Rough-In Phase

The rough-in phase involves pulling the cable from a work area called the staging area to individual rooms or work areas. The staging area is generally an area just outside the telecommunications room. Each cable is labeled on both ends so that it can be identified. In the work area, enough cable is pulled so that there is plenty to work with when terminating. If the cable is to be run behind a wall, it is pulled out at the termination end so that it is ready for termination in the next phase.

In most cases, a new construction environment is less challenging than a remodeling project because there are fewer obstructions. Special planning usually is not required in this environment because structures that will support cables and terminals generally are built as needed. However, coordination with other trades on the job site is essential. Other workers must be aware of data cable locations so that they can avoid damage to the newly installed cables.

The staging area is where the cable installation operation is based. This area generally is situated near the telecommunications room, where one end of every cable is terminated. Proper setup of equipment saves time during the cable-pulling process. Different types of cable runs require a different setup. Network distribution cabling normally requires a setup of multiple small cable reels. Backbone cabling, on the other hand, generally requires setting up a single large reel of cable.

 Lab A-4   Identification of Cables

In this lab, you learn to identify the different types of cables used in CCNA 1 and CCNA 2.

Horizontal Cable Installation

Horizontal cable is cable that travels between the HC and the work-area outlet. The cable can travel either horizontally or vertically. When installing horizontal cable, it is important to follow these guidelines:

■ Cables always should run parallel to walls.

■ Cables never should be placed diagonally across a ceiling.

- When selecting the path for cabling, select the most direct path with the fewest number of turns.

- Do not have cables lying directly on top of ceiling tiles.

After the backbone cabling has been installed, the horizontal network-distribution cable must be installed. Horizontal cables provide users and devices with network connectivity from the backbone cabling. Generally, this type of distribution cable is from workstations back to the TRs, where it is interconnected to the backbone cabling.

Horizontal Cable Installation in Conduits

Installing horizontal cables in conduits requires similar setups and procedures as installing cables in an open ceiling. Pulleys are not needed for temporary support because the cables are supported within the conduits. Although the initial staging is the same, some special techniques and concerns must be considered when pulling cable in conduits.

The conduit must be large enough to handle all the cables that are being pulled. Conduits never should be filled to more than 40 percent of their capacity. Charts are available that give the maximum cable fill or size for specific conduits. Next, the length of the run and the number of 90° bends in the conduit must be considered. Generally accepted practices are that conduit runs will be no longer than 30m (98 ft.) without a pull box, and a run of conduit shall have no more than two 90° bends. Large cable pulls require long radius conduits for the bends. The standard radius for a 10-cm (4-in.) conduit is 60 cm (24 in.). This is not adequate for large communications distribution cables, such as those with at least 400 pairs. A minimum 90-cm (35-in.) radius conduit should be used in these larger pulls.

A specialized vacuum cleaner attachment can help with this (see Figure A-29). A special foam-rubber missile, sometimes called a mouse, can be inserted into the conduit, with a light pull string tied to the missile. When the missile is lubricated slightly with common household liquid detergent, a high-powered vacuum cleaner, like those for commercial use, can draw the missile (with string attached) through an entire conduit run. Special attachments for the vacuum also can allow the missile to be blown through the conduit. For particularly difficult runs, one vacuum can be set up to blow on one end and another can be set up to draw on the other. When the string has reached the other end of the conduit, it is used to pull a pull rope through the conduit. This, in turn, pulls the cable or cables.

Raceways

A *raceway* is a generic term for channels that contain cables in an installation. Raceways include common electrical conduits, specialized cable trays or ladder racks, in-floor duct systems, and plastic or metal surface-mounted raceways.

Surface-mounted raceways are used when there is no hidden path for the cable (see Figure A-30). Plastic surface-mounted raceways come in various sizes to accommodate any number of cables. These are much easier to install than metallic conduits and are considered much more attractive.

Figure A-29 Conduit Blowing System

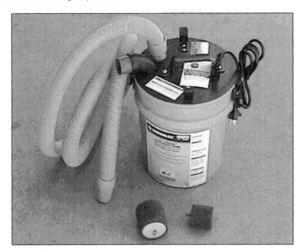

Figure A-30 Raceways

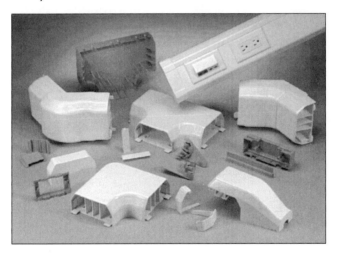

Pulling Cable to the Jacks

At the work-area end of the cables, the cable must be pulled to the jack or outlet location. If conduits are used to run behind the walls from the ceiling to the outlet boxes, a fish tape can be inserted into the outlet box at the end of the conduit and pushed up the conduit until it comes out into the open ceiling. The cable can be attached directly to the fish tape and then pulled down from the ceiling and out through the outlet box.

Some walls, such as concrete and brick walls, obviously do not have the cables run behind them. Surface-mounted raceways are used for these types of walls instead. Before cables are installed, the surface-mounted raceways should be secured to the wall following the manufacturer's recommendations. After cable has been pulled through to the outlets, the cable installers return to the telecommunications room to finish pulling the cable at that end.

Fastening Cable

The final step in the rough-in process is fastening the cables permanently. Many types of fasteners are available, such as J-hooks and hook and loop ties. Network cables never should be tied to electrical cables. Although this might appear to be the most practical approach, especially for individual cables or small bundles, it is a violation of the electrical code. Cables also should never be tied to water or sprinkler pipes.

Because high-performance network cables have a minimum bend radius that cannot exceed four times the diameter of the cable, fasteners should be selected that support the minimum bend radius (see Figure A-31). Fastener spacing might be defined in the job specifications. If no spacing is specified, fasteners should be placed at intervals no greater than every 1.5m (4.9 ft.).

Figure A-31   Panduit Hook and Loop Ties

If a cable tray or basket is installed in the ceiling, permanent fasteners are not needed.

Horizontal Cabling Precautions

Pulling cables can cause damage to the cable sheaths if care is not taken. Too much tension or making corners so tight they exceed the bend radius can decrease the ability of a cable to carry data. Installers stationed along the route of the pull should watch for snags and possible trouble spots before sheath damage can occur.

The following are several of the precautions that should be taken when pulling horizontal cabling:

- As the cable enters the conduit, it can become caught or get scuffed on the end of the conduit. Use a plastic conduit guard or shoe to avoid this type of sheath damage.

- Extremely hard pulls around a 90° turn can cause cables to flatten, even when using bullwheels and pulleys. If pulling tension is too great, shorten the length of the pull and do it in stages. Do not exceed 25 ft./lbs. of pull tension for twisted-pair cable, or 50 ft./lbs. for fiber.

- When pulling with a cable puller or winch, it is important to perform the pull in a single smooth action. When the pull has begun, if at all possible, continue the pull until complete. Stopping and starting can cause additional stress on the cable.

Mounting Jacks in Drywall

Safety Rules

Whenever working in walls, ceilings, or attics, the first thing to do is turn off power to all circuits that might pass through those work areas. If it is not clear whether wires pass through the section of the building you are working in, a good rule to follow is to shut off all power.

Before beginning work, learn the locations of all the fire extinguishers in the area.

Wear appropriate clothing. Long pants and sleeves help protect arms and legs. Do not wear excessively loose or baggy clothing because it could catch on something.

If working in a dropped-ceiling area, survey the area. Lift a few of the ceiling tiles and look around. This process will help you locate electrical conduits, air ducts, mechanical equipment, and anything that might cause problems later.

Protect your eyes with safety glasses when cutting or sawing. It is also a good idea to wear safety glasses when working in a crawl space or above a dropped ceiling. If something falls from above, or in the dark, your eyes will be protected.

Consult the maintenance engineer of the building to find out whether there is asbestos, lead, or PCBs where the work is being done. If so, follow all government regulations in dealing with that material.

Keep the work area orderly and neat. Do not leave tools lying in places where someone might trip over them. Use caution with tools that have long extension cords. They are easy to trip over.

To mount an RJ-45 jack in drywall, follow these steps:

1. Select a position for the jack that will be 30-45 cm (10–15 in) above the floor. Drill a small hole in the selected location. Check for any obstructions behind the hole by bending a piece of wire, inserting it into the hole, and rotating it in a circle. If the wire hits an obstruction, you must select a new location farther away from the first hole. Then, perform the procedure again until you find an unobstructed location.

2. Determine the size of the opening you need for the box that will hold the jack. Trace an outline of the template that was included with the box or bracket.

WARNING

Never, ever touch power cables. Even if you cut all power to the area you are working in, there is no way to know whether they are "live."

NOTE

When working in walls, ceilings, or attics, it is extremely important to turn off the power to all circuits that go to, or pass through, the work area. If it is unclear whether wires pass through the section of the building, a good rule to follow is to shut off all power.

3. Before cutting into the wall, use a carpenter's level to make sure the opening will be straight. Use a utility knife to cut the opening. Push the knife through the drywall, inside the template outline, until you have an opening large enough to accommodate the blade of either a keyhole saw or a drywall saw.

4. Insert the saw into the hole, and cut along the edge of the penciled outline. Continue cutting carefully along the line until you can pull out the piece of drywall. Make sure the box or bracket will fit the opening.

If you are using a box to flush-mount the jack, do not secure the box until you bring the cable to the opening.

Mounting Jacks in Plaster

It is more difficult to cut into a plaster wall than it is to cut into drywall. To achieve the best results, follow these steps:

1. Determine the appropriate location for the jack.

2. Use a hammer and chisel to remove the plaster from the wall so that the lath behind the plaster is exposed.

3. Use a utility knife to carefully trim plaster away from the lath.

4. Place the template against the lathwork so that it overlaps three strips of lath, equally, at the top and bottom of the opening. Trace an outline around the template. Use an electric saw to cut away the full lath strip that is exposed in the center of the opening.

5. Make several small cuts on the full strip, first on one side and then on the other. Continue to make these small cuts until you completely cut through the center lath.

CAUTION

Be careful when doing Step 5. If you attempt to cut all the way through one side before cutting into the other side, the saw will cause the lath to vibrate when you make the second cut. This vibration can cause the plaster around the opening to crack and separate from the lath.

Finish preparing the opening by removing the required portions of the lath strips at the top and bottom. Cut vertically along the sides of the hole, making several small cuts first on one side and then on the other, as before. Continue until the laths are notched evenly with the top and bottom of the hole. Now, cut a curve in the bottom piece of lath from the top-right corner to the bottom-left corner. Bottom out the curve so that it is flat just before it gets to the corner. Remove the lath that should fall free when the cut reaches the corner. Turn the saw around and cut flush along the bottom of the hole until you reach the opposite corner. The remaining lath should fall free. Repeat the process for the top piece of lath.

Mounting Jacks in Wood

To prepare wood for flush-mounting a jack, follow these steps:

1. Select the position where you want to place the box. Remember, if you place the RJ-45 jack on a wooden baseboard, avoid cutting the box opening into the bottom 5 cm (1.5 in) of the baseboard.

2. Use the box as a template, and trace around the outside. Drill a starter hole in each corner of the outline. Insert a keyhole saw, or jigsaw, into one of the holes and saw along the outline until you reach the next hole. Turn the saw and continue cutting until you can remove the piece of wood.

Flush-Mounting a Jack in a Wall

After preparing an opening in which to position the jack, place it in the wall. If using a box to mount the jack, hold the cable and feed it through one of the slots into the box. Then, push the box into the wall opening. Use the screws to secure the box to the wall's surface. As you tighten the screws, you will pull the box tighter to the wall.

If you are mounting the jack in a flat, low-voltage mounting bracket, sometimes called a "wallboard adapter" or "old work box," position it now. Place the bracket against the wall opening, the smooth side facing outward. Push the top and bottom flanges toward the back so that the bracket grips the wall. Then, push one side up and the other down to securely mount the bracket.

Pulling Cable to the Jacks

At the work-area end of the cables, you must pull the cable to the jack or outlet location. If conduits run behind the walls from the ceiling to the outlet boxes, you can insert a fish tape into the outlet box at the end of the conduit and push it up the conduit until it comes out into the open ceiling. You can attach the cable directly to the fish tape and then pull it down from the ceiling and out through the outlet box. (See Figure A-32.)

Figure A-32 Pulling Cable to the Jacks with a Fish Tape

If no conduits are in the walls, you can pull the cable behind the wall. First, cut a hole into the drywall at the location of the jack. You must take care to avoid making the hole too large. Drill another hole into the top plate of the wall. This hole should be 1-2 cm (.39-.79 in) in diameter. Push a fish tape down through the top hole and find it at the lower hole. Some installers use a weight and a string instead, which they drop down from the top hole and tie off so that it cannot accidentally drop down through the hole. At the bottom (outlet) hole, the installer can use a hook or a coat hanger to find the string.

Once you capture the end of the fish tape at the outlet location, tie a pull string to it. Then, pull the fish tape back up to the original location where the cables are tied to the pull string. Finally, pull the pull string down to the outlet location with the cables attached.

Some walls, like concrete or brick walls, will obviously not have the cables run behind them. These types of walls have surface-mounted raceways instead. Before you install cables, you should secure the surface-mounted raceways to the wall following the manufacturer's recommendations. After you pull the cable through to the outlets, you return to the telecommunications room to finish pulling the cable at that end.

Fishing Cable from Below a Wall

When running horizontal cabling in a building that has a basement, fish cable from there to the work areas on the first floor. Do this by following these steps:

1. Drill a 3.2 mm (1/8 in) hole, at an angle, through the floor next to a baseboard.

2. Push a coat hanger or stiff piece of wire into the hole to indicate the spot in the basement.

3. Go to the basement and locate the wire.

4. Use a tape measure to mark a spot under the area of the wall. This mark should be 57 mm from the hole.

5. Drill a new hole in this spot. This hole should be 19 mm in diameter. Unlike the first hole that you drilled at an angle, drill this hole straight up through the subfloor and wall plate.

6. Push the cable up through this second hole to the wall opening where you want to locate the work-area outlet.

7. Be sure to allow enough excess cable so that it can reach the floor and extend another 60-90 cm (2-3 feet).

Vertical Cable Installation

Pulling cables vertically is quite different from pulling cables horizontally. Vertical cable installation can include network-distribution cables and backbone cables. Although backbone cables can be pulled horizontally, they are considered part of the vertical distribution system. Network-distribution cables, on the other hand, are part of the horizontal distribution system.

Vertical installations generally are done in conduits, in conduit sleeves through the floors, or in slots cut through the floor. A rectangular opening in the floor is called a slot or a pipe chase. Risers are a series of holes in the floor, typically 10 cm (3.9 in.) in diameter, possibly with conduit sleeves installed (see Figure A-33). The conduit sleeves can protrude up to 10 cm (3.9 in.) above and below the floor. Not all risers are stacked perfectly above one another; sometimes they are offset, so riser alignment should be checked before the rough-in phase.

Figure A-33 Typical Riser

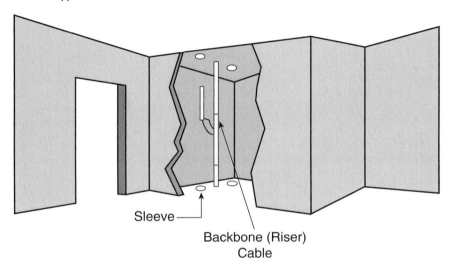

Vertical cable installation takes place either from an upper floor to a lower floor or from a lower floor to an upper floor. In most cases, pulling cables from an upper floor to a lower floor is easier because gravity assists in the effort, and mechanical aids such as winches or cable pullers generally are not needed. Because it is not always possible to bring large reels of cable to upper floors in a building, in some instances, vertical cables must be pulled from a lower floor. When pulling upwards, mechanical aids such as winches or cable pullers are generally not needed, but reel brakes are required to prevent a cable free fall.

Cable Winches

Vertical pulls require care when lowering cable so that the cable does not start paying off the reel too fast and falling out of control. A reel brake can help provide added tension.

For lifting cables, a cable winch often is employed (see Figure A-34). Because the equipment used for pulling cable can pose a danger for both cable installers and onlookers, only members of the cable installation crew should be in the area. Pulling large cables with a cable winch creates a great deal of tension on the pulling rope. If this rope were to snap, someone in the area could be injured. Experienced cable installers know that they should avoid being too close to the pull rope under tension.

Figure A-34 Capstan Winch

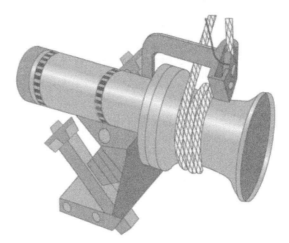

Cables can be ordered from the factory with a pulling eye installed, which is particularly useful for large, heavy pulls. If this is not possible, a Kellem grip can be used. Again, when the pull begins, it should be a slow steady pull. The pull should not be interrupted unless absolutely necessary. When the cable is pulled into place, the pull rope and winch hold it in place until it is fastened permanently between floors using strut systems, friction clamps, or Kellem grips secured with bolts (see Figure A-35).

Fastening Vertical Cables

One method for fastening vertical cables is to use a split wire-mesh grip, like a Kellem grip, and a large bolt that is 25 cm to 30 cm (9.8 in. to 11.8 in.) long. It is important that the grip size be appropriate for the bundle of cables. While the winch or the reel brake supports the cable, a split wire-mesh grip is installed at each floor, and the bolt is installed through the loops in the grip. The cable then is lowered gently until it is supported by the grips. This is a permanent installation.

Figure A-35 Split Kellem Grip Secured with a Through Bolt

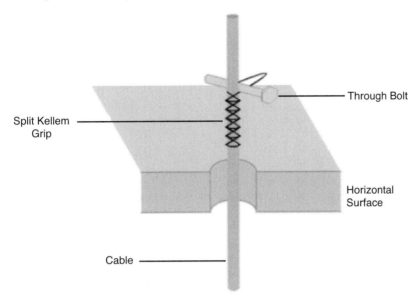

Cable Installation Tips

The following are tips for pulling cable:

- Whenever possible, the staging area should be close to the first 90° bend. It is much easier to pull cable around a bend when it first comes out of the box or off the reel than it is to pull it around a bend near the end of the pull. This is because the installer will be pulling the weight of all the cable pulled up to that point.

- Pulling lubricant should be used for long, difficult pulls to prevent damage to cables.

- Adjust the reel so that cable comes off the top of the reel instead of from beneath it.

- If a fish tape appears to be stuck in a conduit bend, rotate the fish tape a few turns while pushing.

- Pull an additional piece of pull string with the cable. This can be used as a pull string if additional cables are needed later, eliminating the need to use a fish tape through this space again.

- If cable must be coiled on the floor for a secondary pull, coil the cable in a figure-8 configuration to eliminate tangles when uncoiling. Use two safety cones or even buckets as guides for coiling the cable.

- Supporting cables vertically through multiple floors can be a challenge. Run a steel strand or messenger between the floors, and anchor it at both ends. Vertical cable runs can be tie-wrapped to this steel strand for vertical support.

Fire-Stops

The choice of cabling materials and how they are installed can greatly affect how a fire moves through a building, the type of smoke and gasses emitted, and the speed at which the smoke and flames spread. Using plenum-rated cables where required, minimizing penetrations through fire walls, and using proper fire-stopping when penetration is unavoidable can reduce and slow the spread of smoke and flames. It is usually smoke that kills, not flame.

Firewall

A *firewall* is constructed out of special materials and techniques that resist the movement of smoke and gasses from one area to another. Fire-rated walls also limit the spread of flames from the area where a fire originates into areas that are not affected directly. If an area does catch fire, a fire-rated wall slows the spread of flames to new areas. These measures can protect building occupants and firefighters from being exposed to toxic smoke, as well as give them extra time to evacuate the building.

Firewall Penetrations

Sometimes cables must pass through a firewall. This requires making a special opening called a penetration (see Figure A-36).

Figure A-36 Typical Firewall Penetration

Several construction materials are used to construct firewalls. The most common used is likely drywall or sheetrock. When applied floor to ceiling, each layer of this material can resist the spread of flame for roughly a half hour. Two overlapping layers provide protection for twice as long. Other common firewall materials include concrete blocks and poured concrete.

When cable is to be pulled through a firewall, a hole must be drilled through the firewall. This is called a penetration. Penetrations can go all the way through the firewall or can go through one side only. In this case, the penetration is called a membrane penetration.

After the hole is drilled, the penetration usually is sleeved. To do this, a small section of conduit is inserted in the hole. The conduit must be large enough to hold the cables, with extra room for additional cables in the future. This conduit also must protrude 0.3m (11.3 in.) on both sides of the wall. Cables then are pulled through the conduit. After the cables have been pulled through the conduit, the conduit must be sealed with an approved fire-stop material. This prevents fire from spreading from one section of a building to another through the hole in the firewall.

When cables are installed in an existing firewall penetration, the fire-stop material must be removed to clear space for the new cables. After the new cables have been pulled, the hole and conduits should be sealed with new fire-stop material.

Terminating Copper Media

Communications cables are color-coded to identify individual pairs. The color-coding is the same for all telecommunications cables in North America. The use of color codes ensures uniformity in identifying individual cable pairs. Each colored cable pair is associated with a specific number.

Four-pair Color Code

For most voice and data cabling, UTP cables are used. These cables have four pairs of twisted wires in each cable. The four-pair color code is as follows:

- **Pair 1**—White/blue
- **Pair 2**—White/orange
- **Pair 3**—White/green
- **Pair 4**—White/brown

Pair 1 always appears on positions, or pins, 4 and 5 on an eight-pin jack or plug. Pair 4 always appears on positions, or pins, 7 and 8 on an eight-pin jack or plug. The other pairs have different appearances depending upon the standard (either T568A or T568B) used for the wiring plan (see Figure A-37).

T568A or T568B always should be used for this wiring scheme. A new wiring scheme never should be created because each wire has a specific purpose. If the wiring is not correct, the devices on either end will not be capable of communicating or will experience severely degraded performance.

Figure A-37 TIA/EIA T568A and T568B Wiring Schemes

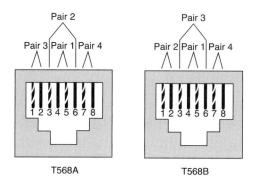

If the installation is in a new building, whether to use either T568A or T568B is likely to be dictated by contract. If the choice is left to the installers, use whatever scheme is most popular in the area. If there is existing wiring in the building that is either T568A or T568B, follow the existing scheme. Remember that every installer on the team must use the same wiring scheme.

Occasionally, there is some confusion over pair numbers and pin numbers. A pin is a specific location on a plug or a jack. The colored pairs are always the same. For example, pair 2 is always the white/orange pair. On an RJ-45 jack, however, pair 2 may connect to pins 3 and 6, or to pins 1 and 2, depending on whether T568A or T568B is used.

RJ-45 Plugs and Jacks

RJ-45 jacks are eight conductor jacks that are designed to accept either RJ-45 plugs or RJ-11 plugs (see Figure A-38). Jacks should be wired to the T568A or T568B standards.

Figure A-38 8P8C (RJ-45) Jack

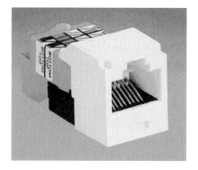

RJ-45 plugs have eight pins that will accommodate up to four pairs of wires. As with RJ-11 plugs and jacks, pair 1 always is terminated on the center pins—in this case, pins 4 and 5. Pair 4 (white/brown) always is terminated on pins 7 and 8. Pairs 2 and 3 might differ depending on the wiring plan. Using T568B, pair 2 (white/orange) terminates on pins 1 and 2. Pair 3 (white/green) terminates on pins 3 and 6. T568A reverses pairs 2 and 3 so that pair 2 terminates on pins 3 and 6, while pair 3 terminates on pins 1 and 2.

An RJ-45 jack terminates one end of the horizontal cable. The other end of the cable typically is terminated on a patch panel with a 110-style connector or a 110-style connecting block.

Lab A-5   Category 5e Outlet Termination

In this lab, you learn the proper safety procedures when using cabling tools, as well as how to use the T568B standard when terminating Category 5e cable on a modular jack at the modular patch panel.

110-Block

110-blocks are high-density termination blocks suitable for either voice or data applications (see Figure A-39). The insulation displacement connection provides a low-resistance gas-tight connection. 110-blocks come in many configurations. Blocks are designed to be stacked in different combinations to accommodate different size requirements. The 110 system includes wire-management troughs that also act as spacers between the blocks. 110-blocks can use a special multipunch tool that can punch down up to five pairs of wire at a time. Care must be taken to avoid using such a tool on patch panels that contain printed circuit boards, however, because the impact could damage the internal wiring.

Figure A-39   110-Block

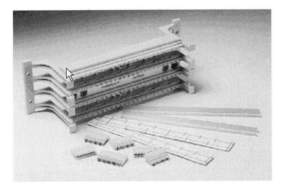

Lab A-6   Terminating Category 5e to a 110-Block

In this lab, you learn how to terminate Category 5e cable to a 110-type termination block, as well as how to properly use a 110 punchdown tool and a 110 multipunch tool.

The Trimout Phase

In the rough-in phase of cable installation, excess cable was left at both ends of the cable run. These coils of cable, which are used to take up slack and facilitate later changes, are known as service loops. Service loops are discouraged by EIA/TIA standards. It is not uncommon to have 1m (3 ft.) of ends hanging out of a wall jack at the finish of the rough-in stage. In the telecommunications room (TR), where hundreds of cables are terminated, it is not uncommon to have 2m to 3m (6 ft. to 10 ft.) of ends.

Although this practice appears to be wasteful, experienced installers know that an excess of cable provides more flexibility in cable routing and provides greater access to cables when toning (testing) individual cables. A common mistake of new installers is to cut the cable short. Remember, excess can always be cut off, but a short cable cannot be extended. If a cable is too short, the only alternative is to pull another cable, and this is a costly alternative in terms of labor and time.

If there is 1m (3 ft.) of cable coming out of the wall at the jack location, it is best to cut this back to about 25 cm (9.8 in.). A new label should be applied to the cable about 15 cm (5.9 in.) from the end. The jacket then should be stripped back about 5 cm to 7 cm (2 in. to 2.8 in.), exposing the individual twisted pairs. The completed jack termination should have no more that 1.5 cm (.6 in.) of unjacketed conductor exposed and no more than 1.5 cm (.6 in.) of untwist in the cable pairs. Excess conductor length should be cut off at the final termination (see Figure A-40).

The jack is terminated with approximately 15 cm to 20 cm (6 in. to 8 in.) of cable still protruding from the wall. This excess cable is coiled carefully into the wall or wall box when the jack is installed. This excess cable can be used to reterminate the jack at a later date or enable the removal of the faceplate and the addition of another jack to the outlet. At workstation terminations, it is common for the wires in the jack to lose contact with the pins because the patch cord to the work area often is pulled, kicked, or stretched by the workstation users.

Terminate or Punchdown

The termination of communications cables at a TR is referred to as punching down. Cables also are punched down on termination panels mounted on wall fields and at the rear of cross-connect panels.

Figure A-40 Cutting Cable to Length

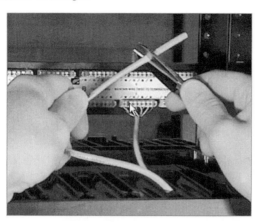

Wires are inserted into the appropriate locations on termination panels, and then the punch-down tool is placed over the wires. Depending on the type of termination hardware used, replaceable blades in the termination tool can be changed out to accommodate the termination type (see Figure A-41).

Figure A-41 Removable Termination Blade

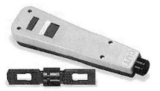

As pressure is exerted on the tool, spring tension increases to a point at which a firing-pin type mechanism releases the energy stored in the spring. The wire instantly is forced between two insulation-displacement connections, and excess wire is cut off in the same operation. The connection is referred to as insulation displacement because the insulation is pushed out of the way by the contacting points on the terminal.

Insulation-displacement connections provide a secure, gas-tight connection, which means that the actual connection is not exposed to the atmosphere because the displaced insulation presses tightly against the block. This is necessary to provide long-term, corrosion-free connections. Patch panels typically are used for data networks, as are 110-blocks, which also are used for voice applications.

Wire Management

Some termination systems come with a wire-management scheme built in. 110-blocks use plastic troughs and spacers between blocks. Troughs can be used both horizontally and vertically. Rack-mount installations incorporate a variety of wire-management features (see Figure A-42). Some use a combination of D-rings and troughs.

Figure A-42 Panduit Wire Management

When purchasing cable-management systems, consider the following:

- The system should protect the cable from pinching and should maintain the maximum bend radius.

- The system is scalable, so when more cables are needed, it can handle them.

- The system is flexible, so cables can come into it from all directions.

- The system offers a smooth transition to horizontal pathways so that cable is not damaged nor exceeds maximum bend radius.

- The system is durable, so it will last as long as the cables and equipment mounted on it.

Careful Labeling

Labeling is another important part of a structured cabling system. If cables are not labeled clearly on both ends, there can be confusion. TIA/EIA-606 specifies that each hardware termination unit must have some kind of unique identifier. This identifier must be marked on each termination hardware unit or on its label. When identifiers are used at the work area, station terminations must have a label on the faceplate, the housing, or the connector itself. Most Requests For Proposals and specifications require that labels be computer generated so that they are permanent, legible, and more professional in appearance.

Use labels that will remain understandable to someone who might work on the system many years in the future. Many network administrators incorporate room numbers in the label information. They assign letters to each cable that leads to a room. Some labeling systems, particularly those in very large networks, also incorporate color-coding.

To ensure that the labels do not rub off or get cut off (the end) later, mark the cable several times, approximately 60 cm (23.6 in.) apart, at the free end. After the cable is run, repeat the procedure at the box or spool end. To keep all cables tied securely together, use electrical tape. Bind the cable ends with the end of a pull string. Ensure that the pull string does not come loose by tying some half-hitch knots around the cables with the pull string before taping the ends. Do not skimp on the tape. If the string or cables pull out later, it could cost time and money.

After pulling the cable along the selected route, bring it into the TR. Allow enough cable for the ends to reach all the way to each jack location, plus enough excess or slack to reach the floor and extend another 60 cm to 90 cm (23.6 in. to 35.4 in.).

Go back to the spools of cable at the central point or TR. Use the labels on each spool as a reference, and then mark each cable with the appropriate room number and letter. Do not cut the cables unless they have a label. If each of these steps is followed, the networking media used for the horizontal cabling run should be labeled at both ends.

Finish Phase

The finish phase is the point at which installers test and, in some cases, certify their work. Testing makes certain that all the wires route to their appointed destinations. Certification is a statement of the quality of the wiring and connection.

Important aspects of the finish phase include these:

- Cable testing
- Time domain reflectometer (TDR)
- Cable certification and documentation
- Cutting over

Diagnostic tools are important in determining existing and potential problems or flaws in a network cabling installation.

Cable Testing

Cable testers are used to test cables for opens, shorts, split pairs, and other wiring problems. After the cable installer has terminated a cable, the cable should be plugged into the cable tester to verify that the termination was done correctly. If a wire accidentally was mapped to the wrong pin, the cable tester will indicate the wiring mistake. Similarly, it can test for problems with the cable, such as shorts or opens. A cable tester should be a part of every cable installer's toolbox. After the cable has been tested for continuity using these cable testers, the cables can be certified by using certification meters.

Testing is the most important step in the finish phase of cable installation. Testing verifies that all wires are working so that the customer does not find that there are problems later. It is better to catch a problem before it becomes a major issue.

Tests relating to cable function are found in TIA/EIA-568-B.1. Common things to test for include the following (see Figure A-43):

- **Opens**—Wires in cables fail to make a continuous path from end to end. This is usually the result of improper termination or breakage. Occasionally, it is because of faulty cable.

- **Shorts**—Wires in cables touch each other, shorting the circuit.

- **Split pairs**—Wires are mixed among pairs.

- **Wire-mapping errors**—Wires in a multipair cable do not terminate at the correct positions.

Figure A-43 Wiring Faults Caused by Improper Termination

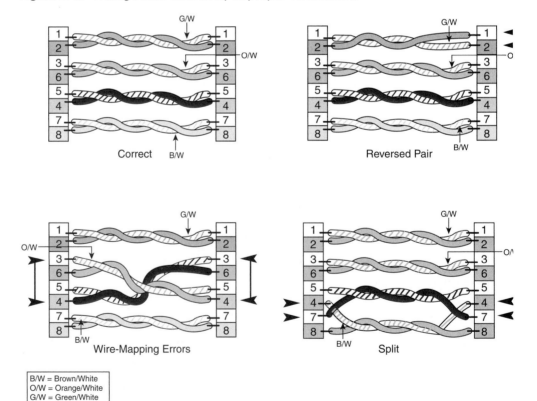

In most cases, simple functional testing for opens, shorts, split pairs, and wire-mapping errors are done from one end of the cable only.

Testing for Shorts

A short is formed when the two wires in a pair touch each other, providing an undesired shortcut in the flow of signal (see Figure A-44). This shortcut is a completion of the circuit before the voltage reaches the intended target.

Figure A-44 Wire Short

Short = Bare Cables Touch

To determine whether there is a short, measure the continuity or resistance between the wires. No continuity should be measured between them, and there should be an infinite amount of resistance between them. Make these measurements with an ohmmeter using a low-resistance scale. If a higher-resistance scale is used, the installer runs the risk of inadvertently measuring the installer's own body resistance when the wires are held to the probes. Some installers find it useful to create a small test fixture to avoid this problem. Many test probes can be fitted with slip-on alligator clips. They can hold one of the wires so that both leads are not touched at the same time.

Testing for Reversals

A reversal occurs when the tip (or ring) side of a pair is terminated on the ring (or tip) position at the opposite end of the wire (see Figure A-45).

To repair a reversed pair in a cable, the RJ-45 connector must be removed and the cable end with the pair reversal must be terminated again.

Testing for Split Pairs

Split pairs happen when wires are mixed among pairs (see Figure A-46). One way to test for splits is with an ohmmeter. First, test the pairs for shorts. If none is found, place a short across each pair. When it is tested with an ohmmeter, finding a short is the anticipated result. If an open is found, something is wrong. The pair is either split or open. A tone generator then can be used to determine which is the case. Higher-end testers detect split pairs by measuring *crosstalk* between pairs.

Figure A-45 Reversal

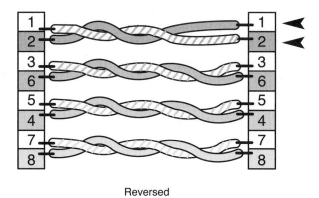

Reversed

Figure A-46 Split Pairs

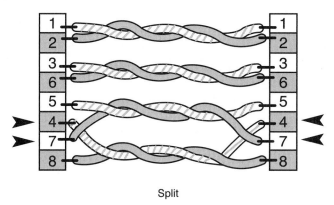

Split

A simple cable tester can be used to check for split pairs as well. This type of tester uses LEDs that immediately notify the installer if there is a problem with polarity or continuity.

To repair a split, one or both of the connectors must be removed and the cable end must be terminated again.

Time Domain Reflectometer

A *time domain reflectometer (TDR)* works by sending a pulse down the wire and then monitoring the electronic echoes that occur on the cable because of cable problems. TDRs determine whether there is a cable fault and, if so, whether it is an open or short; they also determine the distance from the meter to the fault. The signal is reflected back when it reaches the end of the cable, as well as anytime it encounters a defect in the cable along the way. The speed at which the signal travels is known as the nominal velocity of propagation. This is a known quantity for different cable types. When set, the tester knows how fast the signal travels and can measure the length of the cable by measuring the amount of time that it takes for the signal to be sent and reflected back. A TDR readout typically is calibrated in feet or meters. This is an extremely efficient means of locating cable problems, although the instrument must be adjusted properly and used with skill.

Cable Certification and Documentation

Testing is not the same as certification. Testing is for functionality—that is, it determines whether the wire can carry the signal from end to end. Certification, or performance testing, is a statement about cable performance. It answers these questions: How well does the signal travel down the cable? Is the signal free from interference? Is the signal of adequate strength at the other end of the cable?

Certification Tester

Certification goes beyond functionality testing. Performance testing also must be done. Structured cabling systems that adhere to installation standards are required to be certified. Certification meters perform all of the required performance tests to adhere to the ANSI/TIA/EIA-568-B standards (see Figure A-47). Some meters have an autotest function, so all required tests are performed with the touch of a single button. These tests include some or all of the following:

- Near-end crosstalk (NEXT)
- Wire map
- Impedance
- Length
- DC loop resistance
- Propagation delay
- Return loss
- Delay skew
- Attenuation
- Attenuation-to-crosstalk ratio.

These meters hold multiple test results in memory. Test results are downloaded to a computer so that a test report can be generated and presented to the customer. In addition to certification, these meters include diagnostic features that not only identify problems, but also actually show how far these problems are from the end of the cable being tested.

Figure A-47 Fluke Networks 4000 Cable Certification Meter

Performance testing usually takes place at a designated test frequency. The frequency is selected to exercise the cable at a speed that will be part of its intended operation. For example, Category 5e cable is tested at 100 MHz, and Category 6 cable is tested at 250 MHz. Performance testing is described in various addenda to TIA/EIA-568-B. Modern testing hardware and software can provide both text and graphic output. This allows ready comparisons as well as analysis at a glance.

 Lab A-7 Category 6 Jack Termination

In this lab, you learn how to practice proper safety procedures when using cabling tools as well as how to terminate a Category (CAT) 6 cable using proper techniques for high-bandwidth data cabling.

The cable certification process forms a baseline measurement for the cabling system. When the contract is established, the certification standard to which the resulting job must conform usually is included as part of the contract. The installation must meet or exceed the specifications for the wire grade that is being used. Detailed documentation showing that the cabling has reached these standards is submitted to the customer.

The certification procedure is an important step in completing a cabling job. It enables the installer to say unequivocally that at a certain day and time, the cables performed to certain specifications. Any later change in cable performance must be attributable to some cause, and it will be easier to figure out what that cause is if there is hard, fast evidence of the cables' condition at an earlier point. Different grades of cable require different minimum test results to be acceptable. Generally, the higher the cable category is, the tighter the manufacturing tolerances are, the higher the quality is, and the better the performance is.

Certification Tests

To pass certification, cables must meet or exceed the minimum test requirements for their grade. Actual test results that outperform the minimum are often encountered. The difference between the actual test results and the minimum test results is known as headroom. If the results show lots of headroom, less cable maintenance should be needed in the future, and the network should be more tolerant of poor-grade patch cords and equipment cables.

The commonly used specifications include these:

- **Specified frequency range**—Each cable is tested at a frequency range at which it is most likely to be used in daily service. The higher the grade is, the higher this range is.

- **Attenuation**—The amount of signal that a cable will absorb is a measure of its attenuation. The lower the attenuation is, the more perfect the conductors are and the higher quality the cable is.

- **Near-end crosstalk (NEXT)**—Near-end crosstalk occurs when signals from one pair interfere with another at the near end of the cable. Crosstalk can affect the capability of the cable to carry data. The amount of NEXT that a cable must be capable of tolerating is specified for each grade.

- **Power Sum NEXT**—In cables in which all the conductors are used (such as Gigabit Ethernet), the signals on one cable interfere with several pairs, not just one. Calculating the effect of these disturbances requires that the interactions of all pairs in the cable be taken into account. The power sum NEXT equation measurement does this.

- **ACR**—The attenuation-to-crosstalk ratio (ACR) is an indication of how much stronger the received signal is when compared to the NEXT or noise on the same cable. Sometimes this measurement is referred to as the signal-to-noise ratio (SNR). Be aware that SNR takes into account external interference as well.

- **Power sum ACR**—When all of the pairs in a cable are used, the interaction between the pairs becomes more complicated. This is because more wires are involved, meaning that there are more mutual interactions. The power sum equations help take this greater mutual disturbance into account.

- **Equal-level far-end crosstalk (ELFEXT)**—Equal-level far-end crosstalk is a calculated measurement of the amount of crosstalk that occurs at the far end of the wire. If this characteristic is high, it means that the cable is not carrying the signals well and that the ACR (signal-to-noise) ratio is not well controlled.

- **Power sum ELFEXT**—As with the other power sum measurements, interaction among multiple pairs in the same cable increase the complexity of equal-level far-end crosstalk characteristics. The power sum version of the measurements takes this into account.

- **Return loss**—Some of the signal traveling down a wire bounces off imperfections such as impedance mismatches in the wire. It can be reflected back toward the sender and can form a source of interference. This is called return loss.

- **Propagation delay**—The electrical properties of the cable can affect the speed at which signals travel through it. The value of this delay must be known to perform certain measurements, such as time domain reflectometry. Propagation delay for cable usually is specified as a maximum allowable amount of delay, in nanoseconds.

- **Delay skew**—Because each pair in a cable has a different number of twists, signals that enter the cable at the same time are bound to be slightly out of sync when they get to the far end. This lagging and leading of signals on adjacent pairs is called delay skew. This problem can be heightened by sloppy termination, in which the cables are asymmetric with respect to the connector pins. Finally, if there is a difference in propagation delay between the wires in a cable pair, it could affect the signal because of delay skew.

Link and Channel Testing

Two methods are used when testing: the channel test and the link test. The channel test goes truly end-to-end from the workstation or telephone to the device in the telecommunications room (TR). The channel test measures all of the cable and patch cords, including the line cord from the jack to the user equipment and the patch cord from the patch panel to the communications equipment. Alternatively, the link test tests only the cable from the wall back to the patch panel. There are two types of link tests, the basic link test and the permanent link test. The basic link test allows no connectors, but the point of measurement starts near the field tester and ends near the field tester remote unit at the other end of the link. The permanent link test excludes the cable portions of the field test units, but includes the mated connection where the cable is connected to the adapter cable at each end (see Figure A-48).

Figure A-48 Permanent Link Test

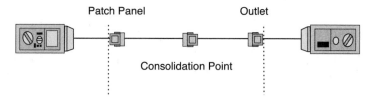

The permanent link test also allows for a consolidation point, which is desirable for open-office cabling installations and is therefore more practical.

The only accepted test is the permanent link test. The channel test officially has been eliminated by TIA/EIA-568-B.1.

Certification Tips

How test results are interpreted is just as important as detecting problems. The best way to learn how to interpret test results is to use test equipment on known good wires and circuits. This will give the installer a knowledge base of how to properly use test equipment and how the test results should appear when the circuits are functioning properly.

To gain experience with troubleshooting and problem identification, create cables with specific problems. Observe how testers react to these problems. Practice identifying these problems based on the results of testers by randomly choosing cables. It will be worth spending the time now to be efficient because the installer will want to be able to quickly determine what is wrong and fix it.

Professional Certification Documentation

Many cable certification tools include the capability to export results in a database format. This can be used in a personal computer to produce high-quality documents (see Figure A-49).

Figure A-49 Cable Certification Documentation

PASS	MAIN	SR	MAIN	SR
Worst Pair	36-45	36-45	36-45	12-45
ACR (dB)	18.2	71.7	15.2	16.5
Freq. (MHz)	214.5	3.5	250.0	248.0
Limit (dB)	8.2	61.8	4.8	4.8
Worst Pair	45	36	45	36
PSACR (dB)	16.0	13.2	13.0	13.2
Freq. (MHz)	250.0	240.0	248.5	250.0
Limit (dB)	5.7	2.0	2.2	2.0

PASS	MAIN	SR	MAIN	SR
Worst Pair	45	12	45	45
RL (dB)	17.4	26.0	17.4	20.2
Freq. (MHz)	244.0	7.3	244.0	174.0
Limit (dB)	10.1	21.0	10.1	11.5

Compliant Network Standards:

10BASE-T	100BASE-TX	100BASE-T4
1000BASE-T	ATM-25	ATM-51
ATM-155	100VG-AnyLan	TR-4
TR-16 Active	TR-16 Passive	

Installation software, generally provided with sophisticated certification testers, enables the contractor to present the test result to the customer in an orderly and presentable manner. The software eliminates the need for entering the results by hand into a spreadsheet. Software packages store test results as either pass or fail. When deficiencies are found and corrected, items are retested and presented to the customer. Customers generally want both an electronic copy of the test results as well as a paper copy.

Documentation must be accessible to be useful. Electronic delivery ensures that the results are always available to those who might need them. In addition, a paper set of both the as-built documents and the certification results should be provided to the customer, as well as retained in the installer's permanent records.

When a cabling system undergoes certification testing, the test results should be collected to create the as-built documents. Certification documentation can become important to an installer if there is a question about the quality or accuracy of the wiring job. It shows that on a certain date, the wires existed in a particular order and could carry signals at a particular quality. Changes over time that affect the cable's capability to move signals can be illustrated by comparing current tests to previous ones.

Because of unexpected obstacles, change orders, and last-minute equipment upgrades, there is a possibility that the network wiring system documentation that was used to construct a facility wiring system is not representative of the system that actually was constructed. Anytime someone is asked to make a modification to the wiring system, it is imperative to know what really is going on in the system. Otherwise, making changes could have unpredictable effects. As-built documents can help avoid this kind of trouble. Always create change documents before actually making any changes.

Cutting Over

Cutting over is the term used when transferring existing services to a new cable system or when installing new equipment on a newly installed cable system.

Cutover Guidelines

Good cutovers require careful planning, organization, and meticulous attention to detail. When cutting over, follow these guidelines to ensure success:

- Keep detailed records of the installation. Such records will verify that all cables have been installed and that they were installed in the correct location.

- Test every cable that is installed.

- Develop accurate cut sheets, charts of circuits, and the cable or circuit on which they operate. The installation supervisor normally develops cut sheets with information received by the customer.

- Schedule the cutover when it inconveniences the customer the least. Because cutovers usually require taking some systems offline, they often are scheduled late at night or on weekends.

Removing Abandoned Cable

When the National Electrical Code, edition 2002 or later, is used, all abandoned cables must be removed when certain criteria defined within the code is met. Currently, this is a decision that is made by the customer and the cable installation contractor regarding whether the cost involved in removing cables is justified. The customer and the contractor must be sure to adhere to local code. Always check with the local authority and discuss the details with the customer before beginning the retrofit.

Before removing any abandoned cable, verify that no live circuits are on the cable. This is accomplished by checking with the customer and then verifying with either a multimeter or a telephone test set. Care must be taken not to damage ceiling tiles or dropped ceiling-support members when removing abandoned cable.

The Cabling Business

The cabling business requires its share of attention, as does the business side of any other enterprise. Before cables can be installed, there must be a bid. Before there can be a bid, there must be a request for a proposal and walk-throughs to determine the precise scope of the work. Documentation both to describe the project and to show how it was actually built might be required. Licenses might be required to perform the work, as well as perhaps union membership. All projects must be performed in a timely manner, with minimal waste of time or materials. This is usually a job for project planning, using program-management applications.

Topics of particular importance in the cabling business field are these:

- Site survey
- Labor situations
- Contract revision and signing
- Project planning
- Final documentation

As with most jobs, a cable installer's appearance and demeanor can have an affect on how he is perceived by customers, bosses, and fellow employees. The choices that a cable installer makes on the job can affect whether he is promoted or even terminated. As an employee of a company, the cable installer represents that company on a job. His appearance and conduct reflects on the company. Therefore, you should always maintain a professional appearance and demeanor.

When working on a job, follow these guidelines:

- Respect the job site. Be careful not to cause damage or discard trash. Clean up all messes immediately if they affect another person, or clean them up at the end of the day.
- Come to the job site wearing clean, neat work clothes.
- Show up to a job at the agreed upon time. Punctuality is important.
- Be considerate of noise. If working on a retrofit project where business still is being conducted, avoid playing music, whistling, singing, or shouting.
- Treat customers, building occupants, co-workers, and bosses with respect.

Site Survey

The site survey, or project walk-through, is one of the most important events before preparing a cost estimate for the project. It gives the contractor the opportunity to see any issues that might impact the installation. Drawings and specifications supplied by the customer might not indicate problems or complications.

It is advisable to create a sketch of the project while conducting the walk-through. The sketch will be useful for identifying problem areas when it becomes time to actually perform the estimate.

A number of key questions should be asked on a site survey:

- Are there plenum ceiling areas?

- Is there a staging and storage area for materials?

- Are special work hours required?

- Are there special safety requirements? (This is particularly relevant in factory environments.)

- Which walls are firewalls?

- Is there asbestos in the building?

- Will the customer supply spare ceiling tiles in the event of breakage?

- Are there special labor issues to be considered?

Requirements Documents

The *blueprints*, which are scaled drawings, provide distance information required for determining the length of cable runs (see Figure A-50). Blueprints also should show service outlet locations and TRs. They will not always show available paths or routing information. Routing information generally is gathered through the site survey. Most structured wiring systems define a minimum of two four-pair cables per location, while many customers specify more. This information should be duplicated in the specifications for the project.

Counting outlet locations and measuring cable distances on a blueprint are referred to as doing take-offs. Doing take-offs requires a great degree of accuracy because this gives the material requirements for the bid. Automated measuring devices are available to help minimize the chance for error.

Installation Icons and Symbols

Standard icons and symbols are used on blueprints and schematics to identify cable runs, different types of raceways, and information about outlets and jacks (see Figure A-51). They provide a uniform method of graphically identifying requirements on a blueprint.

Figure A-50 Typical Building Blueprints

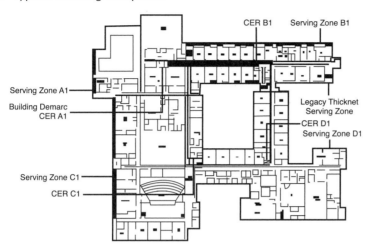

Figure A-51 Cabling Installation Icons

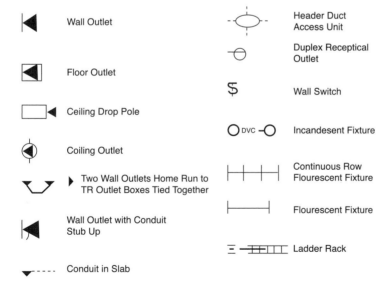

Drawing Types

Construction blueprints follow a standardized format. Drawings are grouped according to category. Drawings are labeled with a prefix that associates the drawings with the category. For example, all drawings that have to do with the electrical system are grouped together and have the prefix *E* for electrical. Architectural sections begin with *A*, plumbing begins with *P*, and so on. Telephone and data usually are grouped together and are represented on the *T* drawings, as follows:

- **T0**—Campus or site plans: exterior pathways and interbuilding backbones
- **T1**—Layout of complete building per floor: serving zone boundaries, backbone, and horizontal pathways
- **T2**—Serving zone drawings: drop locations and cable labels
- **T3**—Communication equipment rooms: plan views of racks and elevations of walls
- **T4**—Typical detail drawings: faceplate labeling, fire-stops, and safety features
- **T5**—Schedules (cabling and equipment spreadsheets) for cutovers

There may be additional drawings, such as furniture plans. Furniture plans are found in either the A drawings or in a miscellaneous category.

Drawings that the estimator will require include the following:

- A site plan, to get an overview of the project
- Floor plans
- T drawings (telephone)
- E drawings (electrical), for reference
- Furniture plans to help determine outlet placement
- A drawings (architectural), for assistance with available pathways

Design documents provide a narrative describing the project. This might include a description of the functionality of the cabling system to be installed. It might include a statement such as "the system must support 1000BASE-T (Gigabit Ethernet on twisted pair)."

Design documents also usually include trade jargon and acronyms unique to an industry or the system to be installed. The estimator should have a good understanding of all terms in the design document. Glossaries of terms and acronyms are available. The Building Industry Consultants Service International (BICSI) website includes a glossary of such terms and acronyms.

Design documents specify the requirements of the system and the types of materials to be used. Information on the number of cables required per information outlet or jack is supplied in the design document. Design documents also describe testing specifications and labeling specifications and formats.

Schematic Diagrams

Schematic drawings are not to scale. They are used to depict connectivity—that is, the way things are connected. A typical schematic shows the main TR or main cross-connect (MC) and the intermediate cross-connect (IC). It shows the type and size of cables between these points. It generally does not detail the actual terminations at these locations, and it does not show individual cable runs to information outlets or jacks. It shows cable runs to specific pieces of equipment, such as servers or other major components that are used in the project.

Labor Situations

Every cable-installation company must deal with labor issues. Some of these issues can cause problems with unions. The installation company must be aware of the rules and regulations that cover things such as unions and licensing.

Unions

Some projects require the use of union labor. Unions are organizations that represent workers. Although the use of union labor is more common on new-construction projects, it is not limited to new construction. The use of union labor might be part of the contract. If the customer clearly states that union labor must be used, the contractor must use union labor.

Other labor situations dictate the job classification and the work that is allowed. In a union environment, supervisors normally are not allowed to perform installation work of any kind. Likewise, cable installers are not allowed to install raceway. Sometimes, cable installers can install raceway up to a certain size or a certain length; an electrician must install anything beyond that. These rules are defined by a union agreement and often are determined by an agreement between unions of different trades.

Contractor's Licenses

Not all countries or even all states require contractors to be licensed. In the United States, contractor license rules vary from state to state. Some states require the contractor show that he is licensed by displaying the license number on all advertising, business cards, and letterhead. Contractors that operate without a license in a place where a license is required can be fined for doing so. They also can lose certain rights, such as the right to file a lien, if the customer does not pay for services rendered.

The requirements for a contractor to become licensed include technical knowledge, business knowledge, and knowledge of the labor laws of the state. It is the contractor's responsibility to know whether he must be licensed in a particular state or country.

Contract Revision and Signing

When all the negotiations are complete, the contract must be revised to reflect the changes that both parties agreed to. Both parties still must review the contract in detail. Contract negotiation is a verbal event in which both parties must ensure that their intentions accurately are represented in the written document. Changes to the contract that occur as the project progresses often are addressed in amendments to the contract. Amendments are agreed to by both parties and signed by both parties.

Responsible and authorized parties from the customer's organization and the contractor's organization must sign the contract before it is a valid agreement. When both parties have signed the contract, the commitment is made. No materials should be ordered and no work should commence before the contract is signed.

Common documents, such as change orders, can be created in advance as a template and simply filled in with the correct information. These templates can be taken along to the project site and filled out during the initial meeting or at the different walk-throughs.

Any changes to a project after it has been started should be made by written change order only. No changes to the original plan should be started by verbal instructions only; the contractor should have change order forms. The project manager should have these forms on the job site. Change orders that result in extra work should include the cost of the extra labor and materials, whenever possible. If this is not possible, the change order should include a statement that the customer agrees to pay for extra work.

Project Planning

The planning phase of a project actually begins after a project is awarded and before a formal contract is signed. Bidding and estimating information is assembled, special requirements are noted, resource allocations are made, and a final review of the RFP takes place to make sure that all the components will be addressed.

The following are all steps that should be taken in this planning phase:

Step 1   The first step in planning a cabling project is selecting the project manager or supervisor.

Step 2   Crews must be selected based on the size of the project, number of hours for completion, skills required, and time allowed for completion.

Step 3   Subcontractors must be identified and scheduled.

Step 4   Material delivery schedules must be made.

Step 5   Provisions for waste disposal must be made.

Suppliers

The estimator normally selects suppliers on the basis of cost, delivery, and service. The estimator uses the following questions to determine the total cost of material:

- Does the supplier's pricing include shipping?

- Does the supplier have a history of delivering goods at the time promised?

- What is the supplier's policy on returned goods?

- Can the supplier provide cut sheets and engineering drawings in a timely manner?

- Can the supplier provide technical advice and support?

Ordering Materials

After the contract is signed, written purchase orders should be used to order materials from suppliers. Purchase orders should include the description of the material, the manufacturer's part number, quantity, price, delivery date, and delivery location.

Generally, the lowest-cost supplier that can provide the specified cable and equipment in the quantities that are required is the supplier to select. Shipping costs must be considered when evaluating the lowest cost. Supplier pricing should include a guarantee that the pricing will be firm for a specified period of time. Generally, suppliers guarantee pricing for at least 30 days. The supervisor or lead contractor must take care that no unapproved substitutions are made in an effort to reduce cost.

Final Documentation

Providing as-built drawings to the customer is one of the most important parts of completing a cabling project. The drawings show cable routes, termination points, and cable types as they actually were installed. In most cases, some cables are not installed as originally planned because obstructions or problems were encountered. Typical changes include adding or deleting cable runs or outlets, or routing cables by a different path. The as-built drawings give the customer a diagram of the work that actually was performed (see Figure A-52).

Figure A-52 As-Built Drawings

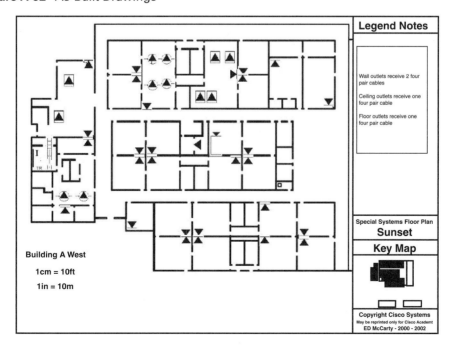

As-built drawings are not created until all cables are placed, all jacks are installed, and all cables are terminated. Drawing can begin while final testing is taking place, but assurances must be made that no changes or additional work is done that is not reflected accurately in the drawings.

Floor plans, furniture plans, or T drawings usually are used as the basis for as-built drawings. The contractor is not required to redraw the building plans for the as-built drawings. The contractor draws all cable runs, terminations, and outlets, and supplies all labeling information as it was installed.

The punch list is the checklist that the customer provides the contractor with when the contractor considers the project complete (see Figure A-53).

Figure A-53 Typical Punch List

Punch List

A punch list is a record of all items within a project that the contractor must correct or complete to the satisfaction of the homeowner before the job is considered finalized.

Prior to the project closeout and final payments, homeowner and contractor or architect should jointly conduct a project walk-through to observe all items that need correcting or completing.

All parties understand that when the homeowner agrees that the punch list details itemized below have been completed to his or her satisfaction, the project is entirely complete and all outstanding payments are due to the contractor and/or architect.

Punch List Items	Date	Approved

The punch list is a list containing items that were not completed (missing outlets or cable runs, for example), items that were completed unsatisfactorily (cables not fastened to ladder racks or outlets that do not work, for example), or cleanup items (debris left in corridor, for example) that the customer requires corrected before approval for final payment. The punch list can take the form of the customer's final acceptance of the project. When the items on the punch list are completed to the customer's satisfaction, payment is expected.

Case Study: FARB Software Development, Ltd.: Network Design and Implementation

Lab exercises give you the opportunity to practice the manual skills portion of structured cabling installation. The case study is designed to give you a hands-on opportunity to participate in the design of a structured cabling system for a fictitious software-development company that is occupying a new three-story building and requires it to be built out.

Overview

To complete this case study, you should be able to

- Gather information for the preinstallation process and lay plans for the installation process

- Create documentation as would be required for creating a real network

- Comply with TIA, EIA, and electrical standards

Using this supplement, as well as having mastered the CCNA 3 curriculum, will prepare you to complete many tasks related to real-world network creation. These objectives are spelled out within this case study in a letter from Cheryl Farb, president of FARB Software Development, Ltd., who, for this case study, is serving as the client company.

The following are some review items that will help you to focus on the case study.

General Design Process Framework

Network design is best done by following a framework. Determining where the wires go requires knowledge of the structure of the networks. You will need to know where the users are and what their applications are before you can begin to sketch out a viable network. A Layer 1 LAN logical and physical topology must be developed. This development includes the type of cable and the physical (wiring) topology that are selected, as well as the physical placement of infrastructure connection points on the network.

A Layer 2 segmentation plan must be overlaid on the previously created Layer 1 topology. This layer plan includes devices added to the topology to improve its efficiency and functionality. Examples of these devices might be switches and bridges. This layer also includes the use of technologies such as microsegmentation, virtual LANs (VLANs), and the Spanning Tree Protocol (STP), to add efficiency and reliability.

A Layer 3 hierarchical plan then is overlaid on both of the previous two layers. This plan includes adding Layer 3 devices that will provide intranetwork and internetwork functionality to the network, as well as creating a network address plan. Layer 3 is where routing and firewalls are implemented, imposing a logical structure on the network. They also can be used for segmentation of both collision and broadcast domains.

An extension of the Layer 3 plan might be considered a Layer 4 plan. This plan could be laid over the first three; it moves strictly to software and controls access and availability of the network. It involves access lists and firewall configuration. Although a complete network design keeps moving up the OSI model, it is beyond the focus of this project.

This design focuses on Ethernet, IP, Layer 1, Layer 2, and Layer 3, which is the focus of this curriculum. The design process logically flows up the layers of the OSI model.

That said, it is important to remind ourselves of one of the purposes of structured cabling. The cabling system must be able to withstand change and growth over its life of service. Odds are good that most companies will be in different quarters by the time their structured cabling system is worn out. This means that care must be taken to not follow the current network layout so closely that the cables are not good for any other organization that may follow. An appropriate structured cabling system may be said to fit the network today, but accommodate easily the network of tomorrow.

The most important—and, many times, the most neglected—part of network design and operation is the documentation. The main focus of this project is the documentation of the network design. Documentation for this project should include wiring maps, addressing schemes, any brainstormed ideas, problem-solving matrices, and any other notes made while making these determinations.

Predesign Process

Before a network can be designed, the data needed to design the network must be gathered. For a network to be effective and serve the needs of its users, this data should be gathered according to a systematic series of preplanned steps. These steps provide a guide to completely discover the data needed to create the network.

The first step in the process is to gather information about the organization. This information should include the following:

- Organization history and current status
- Projected growth
- Operating policies and management procedures
- Building diagrams (blueprints)
- Existing network diagrams and documentation
- Office systems and procedures
- Viewpoints of the people who will be using the LAN

In the information packet that follows this section, you will find communications from the president outlining FARB Software Development, Ltd. This document exists at FARB Software Development LTD.doc.

In this letter, Farb indicates her specific requirements for this project.

The second step is to make a detailed analysis and assessment of the current and projected requirements gathered in the first step. This step identifies and defines issues or problems that need to be addressed (for example, a remote room in the building might not have network access). It also provides information about future network expansion needs, access, and security.

The third step is to identify the resources and constraints of the organization. Organization resources that can affect the implementation of a new LAN system fall into the categories of hardware, software, and human resources. If this were a network expansion or upgrade, existing computer hardware and software would have to be documented. Identification and definition of those projected needs also must be done. The answers to some of these questions also will help determine how much training will be required and how many people will be needed to support the LAN. The questions asked should include the following:

- What are the financial resources of the organization?

- How are these resources currently linked and shared?

- How many people will be using the network?

- What are the computer skill levels of the network users?

- What are the attitudes toward computers and computer applications?

Following these steps, documenting the information in the framework of a formal report will help estimate costs and develop a budget for the implementation of a LAN.

Design Methodology and Deliverables

With the material that has been presented to this point, a strong foundation and understanding should have been developed for the concepts of a layered communications model. Using the OSI model as the framework, an understanding of the functions and devices that support operations at those layers also should have been gained.

To perform this case study, material related to the physical design and installation of a network must be learned. As was presented in previous material, rules and standards govern how a network is designed and built. These rules and standards must be learned before the actual case study can be performed.

Students completing this lesson should be able to

- Develop a Layer 1 and 2 topology

- Gather information for both the preprocess and the process

- Create documentation during the course of the process

- Comply with TIA, EIA, and electrical standards

Note that this aligns with Farb's requests for her company's project.

Standards Organizations

When designing and building networks, it is necessary to ensure compliance with all applicable fire codes, building codes, and safety standards. Perhaps the most important part of the network-design process is designing according to the EIA/TIA and ISO/IEC industry standards. The focus in this curriculum is on the standards for networking media that have been developed and issued by the following groups:

- **ISO**—International Organization for Standardization (not an acronym—see glossary)
- **IEEE**—Institute of Electrical and Electronics Engineers
- **UL**—Underwriters Laboratories
- **EIA**—Electronic Industries Alliance
- **TIA**—Telecommunications Industry Association

The latter two organizations jointly issue a list of standards called the TIA/EIA standards. In addition to these organizations, local, state, county, and national government agencies issue specifications and requirements that can impact the type of cabling that can be used in a local-area network.

It is also important to understand that these standards are being reviewed constantly and are updated periodically to reflect new technologies and the ever-increasing requirements of voice and data networks. Just as new technologies are added to the standards, others are dropped or phased out. In many cases, a network might include technologies that are no longer a part of the current standard or that are being eliminated. Typically, this does not require an immediate changeover, but these older, slower technologies eventually are replaced in favor of faster ones.

Standards Definitions

The primary standards that will affect layer design have been created by the TIA/EIA. The Telecommunications Industry Association (TIA) and the Electronic Industries Alliance (EIA) are trade associations that jointly develop and publish a series of standards covering structured voice and data wiring for LANs. These industry standards evolved after the U.S. telephone industry deregulation in 1984, which transferred responsibility for on-premises cabling to the building owner. Before that, AT&T used proprietary cables and systems.

Both the TIA and the EIA are accredited by the American National Standards Institute (ANSI, section 6.2.7) to develop voluntary industry standards for a wide variety of telecommunications products. This means that many standards often are labeled ANSI/TIA/EIA. The various committees and subcommittees of TIA/EIA develop standards for fiber optics, user premises equipment, network equipment, wireless communications, and satellite communications.

TIA/EIA 568-A is the Commercial Building Standard for Telecommunications Wiring. The standard specifies minimum requirements for telecommunications cabling, recommended topology and distance limits, media and connecting hardware performance specifications, and connector and pin assignments. Several supplements cover some of the newer, faster copper media. This standard has been replaced by TIA/EIA-568-B.

TIA/EIA-568-B is the Cabling Standard. This standard specifies the component and transmission requirements for media. TIA/EIA-568-B.1 specifies a generic telecommunications cabling system for commercial buildings that will support a multiproduct, multivendor environment. TIA/EIA-568-B.1.1 is an addendum that applies to four-pair unshielded twisted-pair (UTP) and four-pair screened twisted-pair (ScTP) patch cables' bend radius. TIA/EIA-568-B.2 specifies cabling components, transmission, system models, and the measurement procedures needed for verification of twisted-pair cabling. TIA/EIA-568-B.3 specifies the component and transmission requirements for an optical-fiber cabling system.

TIA/EIA 569-A is the Commercial Building Standard for Telecommunications Pathways and Spaces. The standard specifies design and construction practices within and between buildings that are in support of telecommunications media and equipment. Specific standards are given for rooms or areas and pathways into and through which telecommunications equipment and media are installed.

TIA/EIA-606 is the Administration Standard for the Telecommunications Infrastructure of Commercial Buildings, including cable-labeling standards. The standard specifies that each hardware-termination unit must have some kind of unique identifier. This identifier must be marked on each termination hardware unit or on its label. When identifiers are used at the work area, station terminations must have a label on the faceplate, the housing, or the connector itself. All labels must meet legibility, defacement, and adhesion requirements, as specified in UL969.

TIA/EIA-607 is the standard for Commercial Building Grounding and Bonding Requirements for Telecommunications. It supports a multivendor, multiproduct environment, as well as the grounding practices for various systems that might be installed on customer premises. The standard specifies the exact interface points between the building grounding systems and the telecommunications equipment grounding configuration, and specifies building grounding configurations needed to support this equipment.

More Information: TIA/EIA Standards Codes

For more information on the various TIA/EIA standards codes, visit http://www.tiaonline.org/.

Electrical Safety

Generally, electrical current follows the path of least resistance. Because metals such as copper provide little resistance, they frequently are used as conductors for electrical current. Materials such as glass, rubber, and plastic provide more resistance and do not make good electrical conductors. Instead, these materials frequently are used as insulators. They are used to insulate conductors to prevent shock, fires, and short circuits.

Many different shapes of electrical outlets exist throughout the world. Two of the three connection points provide the power circuit. The third connector protects people and equipment from shocks and short circuits. This connector is called the safety ground connection. In electrical equipment where this is used, the safety ground wire is connected to any exposed metal part of the equipment. If there is a wiring fault inside of the device, the ground connection protects people from exposure to hazardous voltages.

An accidental connection between the hot wire and the chassis is an example of a wiring fault that could occur in a network device. If such a fault were to occur, the safety ground wire connected to the device would serve as a low-resistance path to the earth ground. The safety ground connection provides a lower-resistance path than the human body, thus reducing the risk of shock or electrocution.

When properly installed, the low-resistance path, provided by the safety ground wire, offers sufficiently low resistance and current carrying capacity to prevent the buildup of hazardously high voltages. The circuit links directly to the hot connection to the earth.

Telecommunications Room Requirements

Layer 1 design is the largest component of the total network design. It involves the implementation of the preliminary designs gathered in the preprocess phase of the network design to create the structured cabling system. This includes, but is not limited to, creating the logical topology, creating the wiring map, selecting wiring closets, and selecting cable. This design must conform to the appropriate standards organization's rules for design.

Students completing this lesson should be able to

- List location and design requirements for telecommunications rooms

- Explain cable-management design and specification

- List considerations for selecting and installing equipment racks

- Explain key environmental, safety, and power considerations in telecommunications room location, design, and installation

Work-Area Cabling

Work-area cabling extends from the telecommunications outlet in a room to the user workstation. Work-area cabling is designed to be simple to interconnect so that it can be moved or changed relatively easily. Each work area serves a maximum of $10m^2$ of usable floor space.

Work-area equipment includes the following components:

- Workstation equipment, such as computers, data terminals, telephones, fax machines, and printers

- Cables, such as patch cables, modular cords, PC adapter cables, and fiber jumpers

- Adapters external to the telecommunications outlet

The TIA/EIA-568-B standard requires a minimum of two telecommunication outlets for each individual work area. The first outlet must be a four-pair, 100 Ω unshielded twisted-pair (UTP) or screened twisted-pair (ScTP) cable and connector. Category 5e is recommended for this outlet. The standard allows three choices for the second outlet:

- Four-pair, 100 Ω UTP or ScTP cable and connector (Category 5e recommended)

- Two-fiber 62.5/125 μm or 50/125 μm optical fiber and connector

- 150 Ω shielded twisted-pair (STP) cable and connector (not recommended for new installations)

Network Applications at FARB

Estimating the amount of traffic that the network will carry requires you to understand the nature of the traffic. Database transfers seem to take a lot of bandwidth, as does videoconferencing. Web applications are often gentle on bandwidth, with the exception of streaming audio and video applications.

The IT staff at FARB has accumulated a list of software applications frequently used by the staff. This is broken out by which group of users uses which application.

 You can find the information about FARB and software requirement list in the Case Study Materials section on the CD-ROM that accompanies this book.

Where Does It All Go?

FARB has not progressed in its planning to the point that you have been told which users get what seats, nor even which department gets which area of the building. You have been handed some fairly developed blueprints from which to begin your efforts. They are entirely adequate for locating the telecommunications rooms in the project.

 You can find these drawings for desk assignments, plumbing and HVAC, rooms, and electric telephone and lighting, along with the building plan legend, roof cross-section end view and side view, in the Case Study Materials section on the CD-ROM that accompanies this book.

As is often the case, not all the information that you need is on any one drawing. Furthermore, some of the drawings seem to be not useful to your requirements. Nevertheless, they are a good start toward designing a network to meet FARB's requirements.

Note that there is no indication of where the TRs should go, with the exception of the entrance facility, marked Point of Presence, on the ground floor. There is no indication of which areas of the building are to be occupied by which department. Consult the teacher or lab instructor for this information.

The following section contains hints that should help students work out some of these issues.

Structured Cabling Case Study Hints

This case study will give you experience in practicing your networking and cabling skills. As you work through the study, your goal is to design the network layout for FARB Software Development, Ltd. You will reach this goal by performing several tasks involved in understanding the request for information and in deriving that information from the drawings.

Four layers of documentation are involved:

1. A file that specifies President Cheryl Farb's idea for the network facility in the proposed new FARB building.

2. A requirements document that has been worked up by the internal IP staff, of which you are a part. This lists what must be connected where.

3. Several sets of drawings of each of the four floors of the building.

4. Some detail drawings to give you some idea of the methods of construction to be used. This will help you make decisions about cable routing.

Take your time as you work through this case study. You will find that much of the value will come from trying several different approaches. Discussion with class members and teammates might help solidify your understanding of the important topics that this case study brings forward.

Instructions:

Locate the letter to the internal support team from President Cheryl Farb. This document shows ten items on which your ideas and input are requested. The last part of the letter includes a forecast of the company growth.

Here are the ten items (some of them have several steps):

1. Recommendations of network equipment

2. Recommendations of network cabling

3. Any construction requirements

4. Network equipment locations

5. A wiring plan that includes the following:

    — A horizontal and vertical logical layout

    — A horizontal and vertical physical cabling layout

    — A cabling plan for the server room

    — Layouts of all MDFs and IDFs

    — Work-area cable outlet identification plan

6. Security and fire-prevention recommendations for server room, MDF, and IDFs

7. Electrical protection for equipment

8. An IP addressing scheme for all devices on the network

9. A cost projection for the implementation of the network, including the following:

— Equipment purchase costs

— Cabling and testing costs

— Equipment installation costs

— Training and support costs

10. A timeline for the implementation of the network

Following is a study guide that contains hints to help you complete these tasks.

Hints

You can find the answers to these questions at the conclusion of Appendix B, "Check Your Understanding Answer Key."

Recommendations for network equipment

Look at page 1 of FloorPlan1-Desk-Assignments-building floor1 (ground floor)

Work through the following questions:

What is the purpose of this floor?

What door will workers move freight through?

What doors will visitors come in?

Where are visitors most likely to go after they sign in?

Where would you consider using wireless technology?

If your department someday is tasked with wiring IP security cameras, what areas would you want to keep under surveillance?

From where does the telephone company serve this building?

What kind of lock should it have?

Would the POP be a good place for the servers?

If it is determined that the server room must exist separate from the POP, what considerations should guide its location?

Could you install the risers in the POP?

Where might you install the risers?

The horizontal cabling always should go parallel to walls. Getting to Room 1.2 while staying parallel to walls makes a cable run of how many meters? Is this useable?

Floor 2

Floor 2 is dense with offices. It also contains the bottom floor of an auditorium. Not only would the auditorium be a possible candidate for wireless, but it also might affect the routing of wires because it extends several floors in height.

Where might you put the telecommunications room on Floor 2? You might consider using two of them.

Floor 3

Floor 3 has large unplanned spaces in Rooms 3.1 and 3.2. If you place the telecommunications room in Room 3.10, how can you serve these spaces, especially the far side of Room 3.2?

Floor 4

You notice a large deck on Floor 4, as well as a banquet area with a piano. What would you need to provide network connectivity to this area?

Where will you put the TR?

You are now prepared to go to work. Count up the number of desks that would be served by each of these telecommunications rooms. Multiply by two outlets per desk. Divide this number by 16, round up as required, and order that many 16-port switches. That is your first item for the network equipment list.

You will need rack frames to support those switches. Order two frames per room to start.

Order patch panels to cover the number of specified lines. Remember that there is a certain amount of network equipment, such as, switches and routers that must fit in these TRs. To calculate accurate totals, consider entering this information into a spreadsheet.

Network Cabling

You determined how many work-area outlets you needed for each TR in Step 1. Use cabling of a high grade, Category 5e or greater. Using a ruler, map out the routes for these runs and then pick off the dimensions. Add them all up, round up to the nearest 1000, add 1000, and then divide by 1000. This is how much cable (1000-foot boxes) you need.

It is important to pull cable efficiently. Avoid trying to get by with too few boxes or reels, or else it may be necessary to duplicate runs. Pulling new cable over existing cables may result in damaging the cable that was pulled earlier.

There is a trick here. Look at the drawings called FloorPlan2-Plumbing-and-HVAC-building floor4. This shows the water and air-conditioning duct work. Notice that there is both supply and return air. The ceiling is not a plenum ceiling. You can specify a cable that is not plenum or riser-rated. This will result in considerable savings.

Construction Requirements

You determined that you needed risers between each floor. This requires coring and requires that the bottom floor will pass through the mechanical space. This will require conduit.

You also modified some rooms on the fourth floor by adding the TR.

Next Steps

You now are prepared to work your way through most of the rest of the case study. Have fun. Relax. Remember that the thinking and planning and false starts and discussion with teammates is where the true value of this exercise lies.

Summary

The standards are written in a way that will promote performance. Following standards also tends to unify the methods of construction and installation. For instance, the point at which a telecommunications utility enters the premises almost always is referred to as an entrance facility (EF). The point at which responsibility for the lines and equipment transfers from the network provider to the user is called the point of demarcation, or the demarcation point. The EF and the demarc usually are installed in a room created for that purpose, called a telecommunications room (TR). A TR can have one of several functions. A main cross-connect (MC) distributes the signals to one or more intermediate cross-connects (IC). These, in turn, pass the signal to one or more horizontal cross-connects (HC), which deliver the signal to the area near the end user, called the work area.

Work must be performed in a way that does not injure workers, the public, or the environment. Often this requires marking off the work area with signs or cones to warn passersby. Also, ladder safety is an important practice. Ensure that ladders are in good condition, with no loose or broken portions. When deploying a straight ladder, secure it, if possible, near the point where it contacts a structure. If possible, have someone guard the base of the ladder, and by all means make sure that no one can open a door and knock you off of it. In the case of a stepladder, make sure that the feet firmly contact the ground and that the spreaders are fully extended and latched. Do not use a stepladder as a straight one. Never stand on the very top of any ladder.

Cabling and wiring require tools adapted to the craft, and installers are well advised to use them and not get by with substitutes. Stripping tools take the insulation off pieces of wire, often in multiple levels to accommodate installing connectors. Cutting tools cut off pieces of wire, often in a way that does not compress the inside of the wires. A termination tool is used to affix a connector to a prepared cable end. These basic tools should be part of every installer's kit, but perhaps more important are tools for diagnosis. A cable tester gives an indication that every pair is going to the correct place and that each wire is going to the correct terminal.

As the cables are pulled into place, it is important to keep in mind that firewalls must not be penetrated unless the equipment is available to restore them to their original condition. The fire-stopping tools and materials that do this vary but generally consist of materials that are certified to resist the spread of smoke and flame. Following the rough-in phase, cable is routed, terminated, and set into patch panels and cover plates in the trimout and finish phases. The finish phase is also the time during which cables are tested or certified. Certification consists of passing specialized signals through a cable to determine whether the amounts of frequency-specific attenuation and headroom are within tolerance. Certification results usually are presented to the building owner as part of the cabling plant documentation.

There are no cabling jobs to be had if bids are not won, and accurate bidding requires a thorough site survey and careful estimating. Labor regulations and union restrictions might affect the timing of a project and should be taken into account. The external factors of each job can greatly affect the amount of profitability that is expected.

The study presented in this material involves using a company's written requirements and a set of blueprints to develop the necessary plan, estimates, and documentation for a network installation in a four-story office/warehouse complex.

To supplement all that you have learned in this appendix, refer to the chapter-specific Videos and Interactive Media Activities on the CD-ROM that accompanies this book.

Key Terms

American National Standards Institute (ANSI)   A voluntary organization composed of corporate, government, and other members that coordinates standards-related activities, approves U.S. standards, and develops positions for the United States in international standards organizations. ANSI helps develop international and U.S. standards relating to, among other things, communications and networking.

backbone   A pathway or cable that runs between telecommunications rooms (TRs) and buildings.

blueprint   An architectural plan or technical drawing that provides details of a construction project or an existing structure.

bullwheel   A large-diameter pulley that is used in a mechanical cable-pulling process.

cable tree   A device that supports a number of small reels of cable. This enables the cable installer to pull multiple runs of cable simultaneously.

Comité Europe en de Normalisation Electrotechnique CENELEC)   European Committee for Electrotechnical Standardization.

crosstalk   The signal from a transmitting pair being coupled to the receiving pair or other pairs in the cable. Crosstalk occurs most frequently near the transmitters in a circuit.

demarc   The point at which the service provider's cable interfaces with the building distribution cabling.

demarcation point   Usually the point at which the access provider's facilities stop and the customer-owned structured cabling begins.

equipment room   Space for equipment. Also can be used as a telecommunications room.

horizontal cross-connect (HC)   Area where patch panels or punchdown blocks are used to connect cables from work areas to the MC. The HC can be a telecommunications room, a cabinet, or a floor or ceiling installation.

intermediate cross-connect (IC)   The connection point between a backbone cable that extends from the MC to the HC.

main cross-connect (MC)   The cross-connect that normally is located in the primary telecommunications room or the equipment room.

material safety data sheet (MSDS)   A document that contains information on the use, storage, and handling of a hazardous material. It provides detailed information on the potential health effects of exposure and how to work safely with the material.

multimeter   A testing tool used to ensure that no voltage is on the telecommunications line. Most of these devices can measure AC/DC voltage, current, resistance, diode, continuity, and transistor.

multiuser telecommunications outlet assembly (MUTOA)   A device that holds multiple outlets for use in work areas where modular furniture is used. Computers and telephones are plugged directly into the MUTOA.

National Electrical Code (NEC)   A document prepared by the National Fire Protection Association (NFPA), which is considered to be the blueprint for electrical safety throughout the world. The NEC focuses on the proper installation of electrical systems and equipment to protect people and property from the potential dangers of electricity.

National Fire Protection Association (NFPA)   An organization that develops, publishes, and disseminates more than 300 consensus codes and standards intended to minimize the possibility and effects of fire and other risks. Virtually every building, process, service, design, and installation in society today is affected by NFPA documents.

Occupational Safety and Health Administration (OSHA)   A branch of the U.S. Department of Labor that assures the safety and health of America's workers by setting and enforcing standards; providing training, outreach, and education; establishing partnerships; and encouraging continual improvement in workplace safety and health.

patch cable   A cable with a connector on each end, used to transfer signals from one piece of network equipment to another.

patch cord   A length of cable used to connect links at the cross-connect.

patch panel   A device used to interconnect data networking or voice systems to the physical cable network. The rear of the patch panel has network cables that are punched down. The front of the patch panel has a factory-terminated interface of some type.

plenum   An open ceiling that acts as an air-return duct for heating, ventilation, and air-conditioning systems.

raceway   Channels that contain cables in an installation. Raceways include common electrical conduit, specialized cable trays or ladder racks, in-floor duct systems, and plastic or metal surface-mounted raceways.

structured cabling   A uniform cabling system with standards that define the actual cable, cabling distances, type of cable, and type of terminating devices.

structured cabling system (SCS)   Integrated cable plans that include the connectors, wiring, distribution centers, and installation techniques developed by specific companies.

Telecommunications Industry Association (TIA)   An organization that develops standards relating to telecommunications technologies. Together, the TIA and the Electronic Industries Alliance (EIA) have formalized standards, such as EIA/TIA-232, for the electrical characteristics of data transmission.

telecommunications room (TR)   The area within a building that houses the telecommunications cabling system equipment.

time domain reflectometer (TDR)   A device that can measure the lengths of cables that are installed and locate faults. It does these tasks by sending a signal down a cable and then measuring the amount of time that it takes for that signal to return.

vertical cabling   Backbone cables, intermediate and main cross-connects, mechanical terminations, and patch cords or jumpers used for backbone-to-backbone cross-connections.

work area   A space where computers, telephones, and other network equipment is used.

Check Your Understanding
Answer Key

This appendix contains the answers to the Check Your Understanding review questions that appear at the end of each chapter.

CCNA 1

Chapter 1

1. D

2. B

3. A

4. B

5. D

6. C

7.

Bit	The smallest unit of data in a computer
Byte	A unit of measure that describes the size of a data file, the amount of space on a disk or another storage medium, or the amount of data being transferred over a network
kbps	A standard measurement of the rate at which data is transferred over a network connection
MHz	A unit of frequency; the rate of change in the state or cycle in a sound wave, alternating current, or another cyclical waveform

8. C

9. B

10. C

11. A

12. A

13. D

Chapter 2

1. C
2. C
3. B
4. C
5. B
6. A, B, D
7. A
8. C
9. D
10. B
11. B
12. B
13. B
14. D
15. D
16. B
17. B
18. D
19. B
20. B
21. D
22. C
23. B
24. C
25. D

Chapter 3

1. C
2. D
3. D

4. D

5. D

6. B

7. C

8. C

9. C

10. B, C

11. A

12. D

Chapter 4

1. D

2. A

3. A

4. C, E, F

5. A, B, E

6. C

7. C

8. D

9. D

10.

A. Near-end crosstalk	Crosstalk signal measured from the same end of the link
B. Far-end crosstalk	Crosstalk occuring further away from the transmitter
C. Power sum near-end crosstalk	Measures the cumulative effect of NEXT
D. Attenuation	Decrease in signal amplitude over the length of a link
E. Insertion loss	Combination of impedance discontinuities on a communications link and signal attenuation
F. Wire map	Ensures that no open or short circuits exist in the cable

Chapter 5

1. C
2. C
3. C
4. A
5. B
6. B
7. D
8. B
9. D
10. A
11. B
12. C
13. B

Chapter 6

1. B
2. B
3. B
4. B
5. C
6. B
7. C
8. A
9. D
10. C
11. A
12. B
13. D
14. C

Chapter 7

1. B

2. C

3. C

4. C

5. C, D

6. D

7. C

8. C

9. A

10. D

Chapter 8

1. D

2. B

3. D

4. Store-and-forward, cut-through, and fragment-free

5. B

6. D

7. C

8. A, B, D

9. A

10. B

11. A

12. C

13. B

Chapter 9

1. C
2. D
3. D
4. C
5. A
6. D
7. A
8. C
9. D
10. D
11. A
12. B
13. A
14. A
15. C
16. D
17. B

Chapter 10

1. B
2. B
3. A
4. B
5. C
6. A
7. D
8. B
9. A
10. B
11. B

12. B

13. C

14. B

15. D

16. C

17. C

18. C

19. B

20. A

21. A

Chapter 11

1. A

2. B

3. D

4. A

5. A

6. B

7. D

8. D

9. C

10. C

11. B

12. A

13. A, B

14. C

15. B

16. D

17. A

18. B

19. A

20. D

21. B

22. D

23. A

24. A

CCNA 2

Chapter 1

1. A

2. A

3. B

4. D

5. D

6. C

7. D

8. D

9. D

10. D

11. D

12. D

13. C

14. A

15. D

16. A

17. D

18. A

Chapter 2

1. B

2. C

3.

BAUD	9600
DATA BITS	8
PARITY	None
STOP BITS	1
FLOW CONTROL	None

4. A

5. A

6.

Ctrl + a	Moves to the beginning of the command line
Ctrl + b	Moves back one character
Ctrl + e	Moves to the end of the command line
Ctrl + f	Moves forward one character
Esc + b	Moves back one word
Esc + f	Moves forward one word
Ctrl + z	Moves out of configuration mode

7.

Tab	Completes the entry
Ctrl + p	Recalls the last command
Ctrl + n	Recalls the most recent command
show history	Shows the command buffer
terminal history size #	Sets the command buffer size
terminal editing	Enables advanced editing
terminal no editing	Disables advanced editing features

8. A

9. C

10. B

11. A

12. D

13. D

14. A

15. A

16. B

Chapter 3

1. B

2. C

3. C

4. A

5. A

6. B

7. B

8. D

9. B

10. A

11. A

12. A

13. A

14. A

15. B

Chapter 4

1. C

2. A

3. A, C

4. D

5. A

6. A

7. D

8. A

9. C

10. A

11. D

Chapter 5

1. A

2. C

3. B

4. C

5. D

6. B

7. C

8. A

9. D

10. D

11. A

12. A

13. D

14. B

Chapter 6

1. C

2. B

3. A

4. A

5. A

6. A

7. D

8. A

9. A

10. A

11. D

12. C

Chapter 7

1. A

2. B

3. A

4. C

5. D

6. B

7. B

8. C

9. B

10. D

11. C

12. C

13. B

Chapter 8

1. A

2. D

3. A

4. A

5. B

Chapter 9

1. A
2. A
3. A
4. B
5. B
6. C
7. B
8. C
9. A
10. A
11. B
12. C
13. A
14. D
15. C

Chapter 10

1. A
2. B
3. A
4. D
5. B
6. A
7. C
8. B
9. B
10. C

Chapter 11

1. A
2. D
3. C
4. A
5. B
6. C
7. D
8. C
9. B
10. A
11. C
12. B
13. B

Answers to Hints in Appendix A

What is the purpose of this floor?

Answer: Warehouse, reception area

What door will workers move freight through?

Answer: The large garage doors at the rear of the building

What doors will visitors come in?

Answer: Front doors off lobby that has reception station in it.

Where are visitors most likely to go after they sign in?

Answer: The conference room adjacent to the reception area

Where would you consider using wireless technology?

Answer: Guests could log on to the Internet via wireless in the reception and conference areas. Warehouse staff could use wireless for inventory.

If your department someday is tasked with wiring IP security cameras, what areas would you want to keep under surveillance?

Answer: The two secure storage areas, the rear walkthrough door, and the reception area

From where does the telephone company serve this building?

Answer: There is a point of presence [POP] next to the mechanical room.

What kind of lock should it have?

Answer: A good one that can be opened from the inside

Would the POP be a good place for the servers?

Answer: Possibly—it is certainly big enough and is close to the elevators, for easy access.

If it is determined that the server room must exist separate from the POP, what considerations should guide its location?

Answer: The location should be in a TR and should be on a middle floor.

Could you install the risers in the POP?

Answer: No. Check the floor above, and you will see that it has a conference room in that position.

Where might you install the risers?

Answer: There is a small hallway adjacent to each stairway. Check that out.

The horizontal cabling always should go parallel to walls. Getting to Room 1.2 while staying parallel to walls makes a cable run of how many meters? Is this useable?

Answer: The distance is about 94 meters. This is barely enough to make the run, go down the walls, and join a work-area connector. The designer must decide whether to cheat a little bit or to take advantage of the wireless system that is installed for the warehouse or conference room. This would present a security hassle but would solve a major problem.

Where might you put the telecommunications room on Floor 2? You might consider using two of them.

Answer: Room 2.31 because it offers ceiling access to Room 3.10 above and to the mechanical room below. You might need to add one at Room 2.7 to accommodate the offices against that wall.

Floor 3 has large unplanned spaces in Rooms 3.1 and 3.2. If you place the telecommunications room in Room 3.10, how can you serve these spaces, especially the far side of Room 3.2?

Answer: Wireless is a good solution for now. Then when the rooms are built out, put a second telecommunications room in either of them.

You notice a large deck on Floor 4, as well as a banquet area with a piano. What would you need to provide network connectivity to this area?

Answer: You would need only one TR and some wireless to serve this area.

Where will you put the TR?

Answer: This is tough. Room 4.5 seems to be an office. However, Room 4.8 is blank. Also, there is a hallway with an exterior door shown next to the staircase by Room 4.10. Because this is the fourth floor, you suspect an error. Furthermore, Room 4.10 is shown with a door facing into a stairwell. Chances are, you could mention these apparent errors and at the same time request that a TR be installed between Rooms 4.4 and 4.5.

Glossary of Key Terms

10BASE5   10-Mbps baseband Ethernet specification using standard (thick) 50-ohm baseband coaxial cable. 10BASE5, which is part of the IEEE 802.3 baseband physical layer specification, has a distance limit of 500m (1640 ft.) per segment.

10BASE-T   10-Mbps baseband Ethernet specification using two pairs of twisted-pair cabling (Category 3, 4, or 5): one pair for transmitting data and the other for receiving data. 10BASE-T, which is part of the IEEE 802.3 specification, has a distance limit of approximately 100m (328 ft.) per segment.

10-Gb Ethernet   Built on the Ethernet technology used in most of today's LANs, 10-Gb Ethernet is described as a technology that offers a more efficient and less expensive approach to moving data on backbone connections between networks, while also providing a consistent technology end to end. Ethernet now can step up to offering data speeds at 10 Gbps.

100BASE-FX   100-Mbps baseband Fast Ethernet specification using two strands of multimode fiber-optic cable per link. To guarantee proper signal timing, a 100BASE-FX link cannot exceed 400m (1312 ft.) in length. It is based on the IEEE 802.3 standard.

100BASE-TX   100-Mbps baseband Fast Ethernet specification using two pairs of either UTP or STP wiring. The first pair of wires is used to receive data; the second is used to transmit. To guarantee proper signal timing, a 100BASE-TX segment cannot exceed 100m (328 ft.) in length. It is based on the IEEE 802.3 standard.

10BASE2   10-Mbps baseband Ethernet specification using 50-ohm thin coaxial cable. 10BASE2, which is part of the IEEE 802.3 specification, has a distance limit of 185m (606 ft.) per segment.

1000BASE-LX   1000-Mbps baseband Gigabit Ethernet specification using a long wavelength for a long-haul, fiber-optic cable for a maximum length of 10,000m (32808.4 ft.).

1000BASE-SX   1000-Mbps baseband Gigabit Ethernet specification using a short laser wavelength on multimode fiber-optic cable for a maximum length of 550m (1804.5 ft.).

1000BASE-T   1000-Mbps baseband Gigabit Ethernet specification using four pairs of Category 5 UTP cable for a maximum length of 100m (328 ft.).

4D-PAM5   The symbol-encoding method used in 1000BASE-T. The four-dimensional (4D) quinary symbols received from the 8B1Q4 data encoding are transmitted using five voltage levels (PAM5). Four symbols are transmitted in parallel each symbol period.

8B1Q4   For IEEE 802.3, the data-encoding technique used by 1000BASE-T when converting GMII data (8B-8 bits) to four quinary symbols (Q4) that are transmitted during one clock (1Q4).

acknowledgment   Notification sent from one network device to another to acknowledge that some event (for example, receipt of a message) occurred. Sometimes abbreviated ACK.

ACL (access control list)   A means of controlling or limiting network traffic that compares different criteria to a defined rule set.

active hub   Must be plugged into an electrical outlet because it needs power to amplify the incoming signal before passing it out to the other ports.

Address Resolution Protocol (ARP)   Internet protocol used to map an IP address to a MAC address.

adjacent neighbors   Two directly connected routers that participate in the exchange of routing information are said to be *adjacent.*

administrative distance   A rating that shows trustworthiness of a routing information source. This value is shown as a numeric value between 0 and 255. The higher the value is, the lower the trustworthiness rating is.

algorithm   A well-defined rule or process for arriving at a solution to a problem. In networking, algorithms are commonly used to determine the best route for traffic from a particular source to a particular destination.

alien crosstalk   When crosstalk is caused by a signal from outside the cable.

alignment error   A message that does not end on an octet boundary.

AM (amplitude modulation)   Modulates the height of the carrier wave.

American National Standards Institute (ANSI) A voluntary organization composed of corporate, government, and other members that coordinates standards-related activities, approves U.S. standards, and develops positions for the United States in international standards organizations. ANSI helps develop

international and U.S. standards relating to, among other things, communications and networking.

amplitude   The amplitude of an electrical signal represents its height, but it is measured in volts instead of meters.

analog bandwidth   Typically refers to the frequency range of an analog electronic system. Analog bandwidth can be used to describe the range of frequencies transmitted by a radio station or an electronic amplifier.

angle of incidence   The angle at which the ray hits the glass surface.

angle of reflection   The angle between the reflected ray and the normal.

application   Interprets the data and displays the information in a comprehensible format as the last part of an Internet connection. Applications work with protocols to send and receive data across the Internet.

application layer   Layer 7 of the OSI reference model. This layer provides services to application processes (such as e-mail, file transfer, and terminal emulation) that are outside the OSI reference model. The application layer identifies and establishes the availability of intended communication partners (and the resources required to connect with them), synchronizes cooperating applications, and establishes agreement on procedures for error recovery and control of data integrity.

ASCII (American Standard Code for Information Interchange)   An 8-bit code (7 bits plus parity) for character representation.

attenuation   The decrease in signal amplitude over the length of a link.

AUI (attachment unit interface) The 15-pin physical connector interface between a computer's NIC and Ethernet cable.

autonomous system A network or set of networks that are under the administrative control of a single entity, such as the Cisco.com domain.

backbone The part of a network that acts as the primary path for traffic that is most often sourced from, and destined for, other networks.

backoff The retransmission delay enforced when a collision occurs.

backplane A large circuit board that contains sockets for expansion cards.

balanced hybrid routing protocol Routing protocols that utilize elements of distance vector and link-state routing protocols.

bandwidth The amount of information that can flow through a network connection in a given period of time.

binary A number system characterized by 1s and 0s (1 = on, and 0 = off).

bit The smallest unit of data in a computer. A bit equals 1 or 0. It is the binary format in which data is processed, stored, and transmitted by computers. In a computer, bits are represented by on/off switches or the presence or absence of electrical charges, light pulses, or radio waves.

bit bucket The destination of discarded bits (dropped packets), as determined by the router.

blueprint An architectural plan or technical drawing that provides details of a construction project or an existing structure.

Boolean logic In computer operation with binary values, Boolean logic can describe electromagnetically charged memory locations or circuit states that are either charged (1 or true) or not charged (0 or false). The computer can use an AND gate or an OR gate operation to obtain a result that can be used for further processing.

bootstrap The protocol used by a network node to determine the IP address of its Ethernet interfaces to affect network booting.

border router A router situated at the edges or end of the network boundary, which provides basic security from the outside network or from a less controlled area of the network into a more private area of the network.

bridge A Layer 2 device designed to create two or more LAN segments, each of which is a separate collision domain.

bridge protocol data unit (BPDU) Spanning Tree Protocol hello packet that is sent out at configurable intervals to exchange information among bridges in the network.

broadcast A data packets that is sent to all nodes on a network. Broadcasts are identified by a broadcast address.

broadcast address Used to broadcast packets to all the devices on a network.

broadcast domain A set of all devices that receive broadcast frames originating from any device within the set. Broadcast domains are typically bounded by routers (or, in a switched network, by VLANs) because routers do not forward broadcast frames.

bullwheel A large-diameter pulley that is used in a mechanical cable-pulling process.

bus   A collection of circuits through which data is transmitted from one part of a computer to another.

bus topology   Commonly called a linear bus, this topology connects all the devices with a single cable. This cable proceeds from one computer to the next like a bus line going through a city.

byte   A unit of measure that describes the size of a data file, the amount of space on a disk or another storage medium, or the amount of data being sent over a network. 1 byte equals 8 bits of data.

cable tree   A device that supports a number of small reels of cable. This enables the cable installer to pull multiple runs of cable simultaneously.

CD-ROM drive   An optical drive that can read information from a CD-ROM.

cell-switched services   Provide a dedicated-connection switching technology that organizes digital data into cell units and transmits them over a physical medium using digital signal technology.

central processing unit (CPU)   The computer's "brain," where most of the calculations take place.

circuit switching   A WAN switching method in which a dedicated physical circuit through a carrier network is established, maintained, and terminated for each communication session. ISDN is an example of a circuit-switched WAN technology.

Cisco Discovery Protocol (CDP)   Used to obtain information about neighboring devices, such as the types of devices connected, the router interfaces they are connected to, the interfaces used to make the connections, and the model numbers of the devices.

Cisco Internetwork Operating System (IOS) Software   Software stored as an image file in Flash memory on the router that, when loaded into RAM, provides the operating system that runs the router.

Class A address   Designed to support extremely large networks. A Class A IP address uses only the first octet to indicate the network address. The remaining three octets enumerate host addresses.

Class B address   Designed to support the needs of moderate- to large-sized networks. A Class B IP address uses two of the four octets to indicate the network address. The other two octets specify host addresses.

Class C address   The most commonly used of the original address classes. This address space was intended to support a lot of small networks.

Class D address   Created to enable multicasting in an IP address.

Class E address   The IETF reserves these addresses for its own research. Therefore, no Class E addresses have been released for use on the Internet.

classless interdomain routing (CIDR)   A technique supported by BGP and based on route aggregation. CIDR allows routers to group routes to cut down on the quantity of routing information carried by the core routers. With CIDR, several IP networks appear to networks outside the group as a single, larger entity.

coaxial cable   A cable consisting of a hollow outer cylindrical conductor that surrounds a single inner wire conductor.

collision   In Ethernet, the result of two nodes transmitting simultaneously. The frames from each device impact and are damaged when they meet on the physical medium.

collision domain   In Ethernet, the network area within which frames that have collided are propagated. Repeaters and hubs propagate collisions; LAN switches, bridges, and routers do not.

Comité Europe en de Normalisation Electrotechnique CENELEC)   European Committee for Electrotechnical Standardization.

command-line interface (CLI)   An interface that enables the user to interact with the operating system by entering commands and optional arguments.

connectionless   Data transfer without the existence of a virtual circuit.

connection-oriented   Data transfer that requires the establishment of a virtual circuit.

contention   Occurs when there is competition for resources, such as when two or more nodes try to send frames simultaneously.

convergence   The speed and capability of a group of internetworking devices running a specific routing protocol to agree on the topology of an internetwork after a change in that topology.

count to infinity   A problem that can occur in routing algorithms that are slow to converge in which routers continuously increment the hop count to particular networks. Typically, some arbitrary hop-count limit is imposed to prevent this problem.

crossover cable   A cable that crosses the critical pair to properly align transmit and receive signals on the device with line connections.

crosstalk   The transmission of signals from one wire pair to nearby pairs. Adjacent wire pairs in the cable act like antennas generating a weaker but similar electrical signal onto the nearby wire pairs. This crosstalk causes interference with data that might be present on the adjacent wires.

CSMA/CD (carrier sense multiple access collision detect)   A media-access mechanism wherein devices ready to transmit data first check the channel for a carrier. If no carrier is sensed for a specific period of time, a device can transmit. If two devices transmit at once, a collision occurs and is detected by all colliding devices. This collision subsequently delays retransmissions from those devices for some random length of time. CSMA/CD access is used by Ethernet and IEEE 802.3.

cut-through switching   A packet-switching approach that streams data through a switch so that the leading edge of a packet exits the switch at the output port before the packet finishes entering the input port. A device using cut-through packet switching reads, processes, and forwards packets as soon as the destination address is looked up and the outgoing port is determined. *See also* store-and-forward switching.

data center   A globally coordinated network of devices designed to accelerate the delivery of information over the Internet infrastructure.

data link layer   Layer 2 of the OSI reference model. Provides transit of data across a physical link. The data link layer is concerned with physical addressing, network topology, line discipline, error notification, ordered delivery of frames, and flow control.

datagram   A logical grouping of information sent as a network layer unit over a transmission medium without prior establishment of a virtual circuit. IP datagrams are the primary information units in the Internet. The terms *cell, frame, message, packet,* and *segment* also describe logical information groupings at various layers of the OSI reference model and in various technology circles.

daughter card   Similar to an expansion board, but it accesses the motherboard components (memory and CPU) directly instead of sending data through the slower expansion bus.

DCE (data circuit-terminating equipment)   Devices and connections of a communications network that comprise the network end of the user-to-network interface. The DCE provides a physical connection to the network, forwards traffic, and provides a clocking signal used to synchronize data transmission between DCE and DTE devices. Modems and interface cards are examples of DCE.

debug   A command used to find and remove errors (bugs) from a program or design.

decibel   An important way of describing networking signals as a unit that measures the loss or gain of the power of a wave. Decibels are usually negative numbers representing a loss in power as the wave travels, but can also be positive values representing a gain in power if the signal is amplified.

de-encapsulation   Unwrapping data in a particular protocol header.

delay skew   The propagation delays of different wire pairs in a single cable can differ slightly because of differences in the number of twists and electrical properties of each wire pair. Delay skew is the delay difference between pairs.

demarc   The point at which the service provider's cable interfaces with the building distribution cabling.

demarcation point   Usually the point at which the access provider's facilities stop and the customer-owned structured cabling begins.

denial of service (DoS)   Type of attack on a network that is designed to bring the network to its knees by flooding it with useless traffic.

digital bandwidth   Measures how much information can flow from one place to another in a given amount of time.

dispersion   The broadening of light signals along the length of the fiber.

distance vector routing protocol   A class of routing algorithms that iterate on the number of hops in a route to find a shortest-path spanning tree. Distance vector routing algorithms call for each router to send its entire routing table in each update, but only to its neighbors. Distance vector routing algorithms can be prone to routing loops but are computationally simpler than link-state routing algorithms. Also called a Bellman-Ford routing algorithm.

DNS (Domain Name System)   The system used in the Internet for translating names of network nodes into addresses.

dotted-decimal format   In this notation, each IP address is written as four parts separated by periods, or dots.

dotted-decimal notation   A syntactic representation for a 32-bit integer that consists of four 8-bit numbers written in base 10 with periods (dots) separating them. Used to represent IP addresses on the Internet, as in 192.67.67.20.

DSSS (direct-sequence spread spectrum) A technology in which transmissions are more reliable because each bit (1 or 0) is represented by a string of 1s and 0s, called a chipping sequence.

DTE (data terminal equipment) Device at the user end of a user-network interface that serves as a data source, destination, or both. DTE connects to a data network through a DCE device (for example, a modem) and typically uses clocking signals generated by the DCE. DTE includes such devices as computers, protocol translators, and multiplexers.

dynamic routing Routing that adjusts automatically to network topology or traffic changes. Also called adaptive routing. Requires that a routing protocol be run between routers.

EIA (Electronic Industries Association) A group that specifies electrical transmission standards. The EIA and TIA have developed numerous well-known communication standards.

ELFEXT (equal-level far-end crosstalk) A test that measures FEXT.

EMI (electromagnetic interference) An electromagnetic field that has the potential to disrupt the operation of electronic components, devices, and systems in its vicinity.

EMI (electromagnetic interference) Noise from nearby sources such as motors and lights.

encapsulation Wrapping of data in a particular protocol header. For example, upper-layer data is wrapped in a specific Ethernet header before network transit. Also, when bridging dissimilar networks, the entire frame from one network simply can be placed behind the header used by the data link layer protocol of the other network.

encoding Process by which bits are represented by voltages.

Enhanced Interior Gateway Routing Protocol (EIGRP) Advanced version of IGRP developed by Cisco. Provides superior convergence properties and operating efficiency, and combines the advantages of link-state protocols with those of distance vector protocols.

equipment room Space for equipment. Also can be used as a telecommunications room.

Ethernet A baseband LAN specification invented by Xerox Corporation and developed jointly by Xerox, Intel, and Digital Equipment Corporation. Ethernet networks use CSMA/CD and run over a variety of cable types at 10, 100, and 1000 Mbps. Ethernet is similar to the IEEE 802.3 series of standards.

expansion slot An opening in a computer, usually on the motherboard, where an expansion card can be inserted to add new capabilities to the computer.

extended ACL Compares source IP address, destination IP address, TCP/UDP port number, and other criteria to the rules defining an extended ACL.

extended-star topology A network in which a star network is expanded to include an additional networking device that is connected to the main networking device.

Exterior Gateway Protocol (EGP) An Internet protocol used to exchange routing information between autonomous systems. Border Gateway Protocol (BGP) is the most common EGP.

exterior router In firewall architecture, the router that is connected to the Internet is referred to as the exterior router. It forces all incoming traffic to pass through the application gateway.

exterior routes   Routes to networks outside the autonomous system that are considered when identifying a gateway of last resort.

extranet   Intranet-based applications and services that employ extended, secure access to external users or enterprises.

Fast Ethernet   Any of a number of 100-Mbps Ethernet specifications. Fast Ethernet offers a speed increase 10 times that of the 10BASE-T Ethernet specification, while preserving such qualities as frame format, MAC mechanisms, and MTU. Such similarities allow the use of existing 10BASE-T applications and network-management tools on Fast Ethernet networks. Fast Ethernet is based on an extension to the IEEE 802.3 specification.

FDDI (Fiber Distributed Data Interface)   A LAN standard, defined by American National Standards Institute (ANSI) 3T9.5, specifying a 100-Mbps token-passing network using fiber-optic cable, with transmission distances of up to 2 km. FDDI uses a dual-ring architecture to provide redundancy.

FEXT (far-end crosstalk)   Crosstalk that occurs when signals on one twisted pair are coupled to another pair as they arrive at the far end of a multipair cable system.

FHSS (frequency-hopping spread spectrum)   A technology in which transmissions hop from one frequency to another in random patterns. This feature enables the transmissions to hop around narrowband interference, resulting in a clearer signal and higher reliability of the transmission.

fiber-optic cable   A physical medium capable of conducting modulated light transmission. Compared with other transmission media, fiber-optic cable is more expensive but is not susceptible to electromagnetic interference. Sometimes called optical fiber.

File Transfer Protocol (FTP)   An application protocol, part of the TCP/IP protocol suite, used to transfer files between network hosts.

firewall   One or more network devices, such as routers or access servers, designated as a buffer between any connected public networks and a private network. A firewall router uses access control lists and other methods to ensure the security of the private network.

Flash memory   A special type of EEPROM that can be erased and reprogrammed in blocks instead of one byte at a time. Many modern PCs have their BIOS stored on a Flash memory chip so that it can be updated easily, if necessary. Such a BIOS is sometimes called a Flash BIOS. Flash memory is also popular in modems because it enables the modem manufacturer to support new protocols as they become standardized.

flooding   A traffic-passing technique used by switches and bridges in which traffic received on an interface is sent out all that device's interfaces except the interface on which the information was received originally.

floppy disk drive   Reads and writes to floppy disks.

flow control   A technique for ensuring that a transmitting entity does not overwhelm a receiving entity with data. When the buffers on the receiving device are full, a message is sent to the sending device to suspend the transmission until the data in the buffers has been processed. In IBM networks, this technique is called pacing.

flush timer   Indicates how much time passes before a route is flushed from the routing table. The IGRP default is seven times the routing update timer.

FM (frequency modulation)   Modulates the frequency of the wave.

fragment-free switching   Switching that filters out collision fragments, which are the majority of packet errors, before forwarding begins.

frame   A logical grouping of information sent as a data link layer unit over a transmission medium.

frequency   The amount of time between each wave.

FTP (File Transfer Protocol)   An application protocol, part of the TCP/IP protocol stack, used for transferring files between network nodes. FTP is defined in RFC 959.

full duplex   The capability for simultaneous data transmission between a sending station and a receiving station.

full-mesh topology   Connects all devices (nodes) to each other for redundancy and fault tolerance.

GB (gigabyte)   Approximately 1 billion bytes. Sometimes called a "gig." Hard drive capacity on most PCs is typically measured in GB.

GBIC (Gigabit Interface Converter)   A hot-swappable input/output device that plugs into a Gigabit Ethernet port.

Gbps (gigabits per second)   One billion bits per second. A standard measurement of the amount of data transferred over a network connection. 10G or 10 Gigabit Ethernet operates at 10 Gbps.

ghost   Fluke Networks coined this new term to mean energy (noise) detected on the cable that appears to be a frame but that lacks a valid SFD. To qualify as a ghost, this "frame" must be at least 72 octets long (including preamble); otherwise, it is classified as a remote collision.

Gigabit Ethernet   Standard for a high-speed Ethernet, approved by the IEEE 802.3z standards committee in 1996.

global configuration mode   Used for one-line commands and commands that make global changes to the router configuration.

half duplex   A capability for data transmission in only one direction at a time between a sending station and a receiving station.

hard disk drive   Reads and writes data on a hard disk. The primary storage device in the computer.

header   Control information placed before data when encapsulating that data for network transmission.

hertz   The unit of measure for the frequency of an electrical signal in the number of complete cycles per second.

hierarchical topology   Created similarly to an extended-star topology. The primary difference is that it does not use a central node. Instead, it uses a trunk node from which it branches to other nodes.

holddowns   Prevent regular update messages from inappropriately reinstating a route that might not be up.

hold-time timer   Specifies the amount of time for which information about better routes is ignored. The IGRP default for this variable is 3 times the update timer period plus 10 seconds.

hop   The passage of a data packet from one network node, typically a router, to another.

hop count   A routing metric used to measure the distance between a source and a destination. RIP uses hop count as its sole metric.

horizontal cross-connect (HC)   Area where patch panels or punchdown blocks are used to connect cables from work areas to the MC. The HC can be a telecommunications room, a cabinet, or a floor or ceiling installation.

HTML (Hypertext Markup Language)   A simple hypertext document formatting language that uses tags to indicate how a given part of a document should be interpreted by a viewing application, such as a web browser.

HTTP (Hypertext Transfer Protocol)   The protocol used by web browsers and web servers to transfer files, such as text and graphics files.

hub   A common connection point for devices in a network. Hubs commonly connect segments of a LAN. A hub contains multiple ports. When a packet arrives at one port, it is copied to the other ports so that all the segments of the LAN can see all the packets.

hyperlink   A computer program command that points to other HTML files on a web server or other places on the same documents. Provides shortcuts to other web pages and files.

IEEE (Institute of Electrical and Electronic Engineers)   A professional organization whose activities include the development of communications and network standards. IEEE LAN standards are the predominant LAN standards.

IEEE 802.2   An IEEE LAN protocol that specifies an implementation of the LLC sublayer of the data link layer. IEEE 802.2 handles errors, framing, flow control, and the network layer (Layer 3) service interface.

IEEE 802.3   An IEEE LAN protocol that specifies an implementation of the physical layer and the MAC sublayer of the data link layer. IEEE 802.3 uses CSMA/CD access at a variety of speeds over a variety of physical media. Extensions to the IEEE 802.3 standard specify implementations for Fast Ethernet. Physical variations of the original IEEE 802.3 specification include 10BASE2, 10BASE5, 10BASE-F, 10BASE-T, and 10BROAD36. Physical variations for Fast Ethernet include 100BASE-TX and 100BASE-FX.

impedance   The resistance to the movement of electrons in an AC circuit.

insertion loss   The combination of the effects of signal attenuation and impedance discontinuities on a communications link.

intelligent hub   Sometimes called "smart hubs." These devices basically function as active hubs, but also include a microprocessor chip and diagnostic capabilities. They are more expensive than active hubs, but are useful in troubleshooting situations.

interface   Connection between two systems or devices. In routing terminology, a network connection.

Interior Gateway Protocol (IGP)   An Internet protocol used to exchange routing information within an autonomous system. Examples of common Internet IGPs are IGRP, OSPF, and RIP.

Interior Gateway Routing Protocol (IGRP)   An IGP developed by Cisco to address the problems associated with routing in large, heterogeneous networks.

interior router   The router that is connected to the internal network. The interior router accepts packets only from the application gateway. The gateway controls the delivery of network-based services both to and from the internal network.

interior routes   Routes between subnets of a network attached to a router interface. If the network attached to a router is not subnetted, IGRP does not advertise interior routes.

intermediate cross-connect (IC) The connection point between a backbone cable that extends from the MC to the HC.

Internet The largest global internetwork, connecting tens of thousands of networks worldwide and having a culture that focuses on research and standardization based on real-life use.

Internet Control Message Protocol (ICMP) Network layer Internet Protocol that reports errors and provides other information relevant to IP packet processing. It is documented in RFC 792.

Internet Protocol (IP) A network layer protocol in the TCP/IP protocol suite offering a connectionless internetwork service.

intranet A common LAN configuration. Intranets are designed to be accessed by users who have access privileges to an organization's internal LAN.

invalid timer Specifies how long a router waits in the absence of routing-update messages about a specific route before declaring that route invalid. The IGRP default for this variable is three times the update period.

IP address A 32-bit address assigned to hosts using TCP/IP. An IP address belongs to one of five classes (A, B, C, D, or E) and is written as four octets separated by periods (that is, dotted-decimal format). Each address consists of a network number, an optional subnetwork number, and a host number. The network and subnetwork numbers together are used for routing, and the host number is used to address an individual host within the network or subnetwork. A subnet mask is used to extract network and subnetwork information from the IP address. CIDR provides a new way to represent IP addresses and subnet masks. Also called an *Internet address*.

IP address class A 32-bit IP address is broken into a network part and a host part. A bit or bit sequence at the start of each address determines the address's class.

IP Version 6 (IPv6) The replacement for the current version of IP (Version 4). IPv6 includes support for flow ID in the packet header, which can be used to identify flows. Formerly called IPng (IP next generation).

jabber Defined several places in the 802.3 standard as being a transmission of at least 20,000 to 50,000 bit-times in duration. However, most diagnostic tools report jabber whenever a detected transmission exceeds the maximum legal frame size—which is considerably smaller than 20,000 to 50,000 bit-times.

jitter The slight movement of a transmission signal in time or phase that can introduce errors and loss of synchronization. More jitter will be encountered with longer cables, cables with higher attenuation, and signals at higher data rates

Kb (kilobit) Approximately 1000 bits.

KB (kilobyte) Approximately 1000 bytes (1024 bytes exactly).

kbps (kilobits per second) One thousand bits per second. A standard measurement of the amount of data transferred over a network connection.

kBps (kilobytes per second) One thousand bytes per second. A standard measurement of the amount of data transferred over a network connection.

keepalive Message sent by one network device to inform another network device that the virtual circuit between the two is still active.

keyboard port Connects a keyboard to a PC.

latency   Delay between the time when a device receives a frame and the time when that frame is forwarded out the destination port.

light-emitting diode (LED)   Semiconductor device that emits light produced by converting electrical energy. Status lights on hardware devices are typically LEDs.

link-state advertisements (LSAs)   Small packets of routing information that are sent between routers.

link-state routing protocol   A routing algorithm in which each router broadcasts or multicasts information regarding the cost of reaching each of its neighbors to all nodes in the internetwork. Link-state algorithms create a consistent view of the network and are therefore not prone to routing loops. However, they achieve this at the cost of relatively greater computational difficultly and more widespread traffic than do distance vector routing algorithms.

LLC (Logical Link Control)   The higher of the two data link layer sublayers defined by the IEEE. The LLC sublayer handles error control, flow control, framing, and MAC-sublayer addressing. The most prevalent LLC protocol is IEEE 802.2, which includes both connectionless and connection-oriented variants.

load sharing   When dynamic routing protocols direct traffic from the same session over different paths in a network for better performance.

local-area network (LAN)   A high-speed, low-error data network covering a relatively small geographic area (up to a few thousand meters). LANs connect workstations, peripherals, terminals, and other devices in a single building or another geographically limited area.

logarithms   Equals the exponent that a given number has to be raised to in order to generate a certain value.

logical connection   Uses standards called protocols.

long frame   A frame that is longer than the maximum legal size and that takes into consideration whether the frame was tagged.

MAC (Media Access Control)   The lower of the two sublayers of the data link layer defined by the IEEE. The MAC sublayer handles access to shared media, such as whether token passing or contention will be used. See also *LLC*.

MAC address   A standardized data link layer address that is required for every device that connects to a LAN. Other devices in the network use these addresses to locate specific devices in the network and to create and update routing tables and data structures. MAC addresses are 6 bytes long and are controlled by the IEEE. Also known as a hardware address, a MAC-layer address, or a physical address.

main cross-connect (MC)   The cross-connect that normally is located in the primary telecommunications room or the equipment room.

Manchester encoding   Digital encoding scheme, used by IEEE 802.3 and Ethernet, in which a mid–bit-time transition is used for clocking; a 1 is denoted by a high level during the first half of the bit time.

material safety data sheet (MSDS)   A document that contains information on the use, storage, and handling of a hazardous material. It provides detailed information on the potential health effects of exposure and how to work safely with the material.

Mb (megabit)   Approximately 1 million bits.

MB (megabyte)   Approximately 1 million bytes (1,048,576 bytes exactly). A megabyte is sometimes called a "meg." The amount of RAM in most PCs is typically measured in MB. Large files are typically some number of MB in size.

Mbps (megabits per second)   One million bits per second. A standard measurement of the amount of data transferred over a network connection. Basic Ethernet operates at 10 Mbps.

MBps (megabytes per second)   One million bytes per second. A standard measurement of the amount of data transferred over a network connection.

media   The plural of medium. Media refers to various physical environments through which transmission signals pass. Common network media include twisted-pair, coaxial, fiber-optic cable, and the atmosphere (through which microwave, laser, and infrared transmission occurs).

Media Access Control (MAC)   A hardware address that uniquely identifies each node of a network. This address controls data communication for the host on the network.

memory chips   RAM chips on memory cards plug into the motherboard.

metric   An algorithm that generates a number for each path through the network. Typically, the smaller the metric number is, the better the path is.

metropolitan-area network (MAN)   A network that spans a metropolitan area. Generally, a MAN spans a larger geographic area than a LAN but a smaller geographic area than a WAN.

microprocessor   A silicon chip that contains a CPU.

microsegmentation   Allows the creation of private or dedicated segments—one host per segment. Each host receives instant access to the full bandwidth and does not have to compete for available bandwidth with other hosts.

modal dispersion   When multiple modes of light propagating through fiber travel different distances, depending on their entry angles, which causes them to arrive at the destination (receiving end of the cable) at slightly different times.

modem   Device that converts digital and analog signals. At the source, a modem converts digital signals to a form suitable for transmission over analog communication facilities. At the destination, the analog signals are returned to their digital form. Modems allow data to be transmitted over voice-grade telephone lines. The term *modem* is also used to describe various digital devices such as CSU/DSUs and ISDN terminal adapters.

motherboard   A computer's main circuit board.

mouse port   Connects a mouse to a PC.

MTU (Maximum Transmission Unit)   The maximum packet size, in bytes, that a particular interface can handle.

multicast   Single packets copied by the network and sent to a specific subset of network addresses.

multicast address   A unique network address that directs packets that have that destination address to predefined groups of IP addresses.

multimeter   A testing tool used to ensure that no voltage is on the telecommunications line. Most of these devices can measure AC/DC voltage, current, resistance, diode, continuity, and transistor.

multimode A type of fiber-optic cable that transmits more than one light path.

multiuser telecommunications outlet assembly (MUTOA) A device that holds multiple outlets for use in work areas where modular furniture is used. Computers and telephones are plugged directly into the MUTOA.

named ACL ACL that allows standard and extended ACLs to be given names.

narrowband interference Noise that only affects small ranges of frequencies.

National Electrical Code (NEC) A document prepared by the National Fire Protection Association (NFPA), which is considered to be the blueprint for electrical safety throughout the world. The NEC focuses on the proper installation of electrical systems and equipment to protect people and property from the potential dangers of electricity.

National Fire Protection Association (NFPA) An organization that develops, publishes, and disseminates more than 300 consensus codes and standards intended to minimize the possibility and effects of fire and other risks. Virtually every building, process, service, design, and installation in society today is affected by NFPA documents.

NetBIOS Extended User Interface (NetBEUI) An enhanced version of the NetBIOS protocol used by network operating systems such as LAN Manager, LAN Server, Windows for Workgroups, and Windows NT. NetBEUI formalizes the transport frame and adds functions. NetBEUI implements the OSI LLC2 protocol.

network access layer The layer that is concerned with all the issues that an IP packet requires to make a physical link to the network medium.

network interface card (NIC) A printed circuit board that fits into the expansion slot of a bus on a computer motherboard. Also can be a peripheral device.

network layer Layer 3 of the OSI reference model. This layer provides connectivity and path selection between two end systems. The network layer is the layer at which routing occurs.

NEXT (near-end crosstalk) Computed as the ratio in voltage amplitude between the test signal and the crosstalk signal when measured from the same end of the link.

noise As related to communications, noise refers to undesirable signals. Noise can originate from natural and technological sources and is added to the data signals in communications systems.

nonvolatile random-access memory (NVRAM) RAM that retains its contents when a unit is powered off.

NRZ (nonreturn to zero) Signals that maintain constant voltage levels with no signal transitions (no return to a 0V level) during a bit interval.

NRZI (nonreturn to zero inverted) Signal that maintains constant voltage levels with no signal transitions (no return to a 0V level). It interprets the presence of data at the beginning of a bit interval as a signal transition and interprets the absence of data as no transition.

Occupational Safety and Health Administration (OSHA) A branch of the U.S. Department of Labor that assures the safety and health of America's workers by setting and enforcing standards; providing training, outreach, and education; establishing partnerships; and encouraging continual improvement in workplace safety and health.

octet   Eight bits. In networking, the term *octet* often is used (rather than byte) because some machine architectures employ bytes that are not 8 bits long.

Open System Interconnection (OSI) reference model
A network architectural model developed by the ISO. This model consists of seven layers, each of which specifies particular network functions, such as addressing, flow control, error control, encapsulation, and reliable message transfer. The OSI reference model is used universally as a method for teaching and understanding network functionality.

oscilloscope   An important electronic device used to view electrical signals such as voltage waves and pulses.

OUI (organizationally unique identifier)   Three octets assigned by the IEEE in a block of 48-bit LAN addresses.

packet   A logical grouping of information that includes a header containing control information and (usually) user data. Packets most often refer to network layer units of data. The terms *datagram, frame, message,* and *segment* also describe logical information groupings at various layers of the OSI reference model and in various technology circles.

packet-switched services   Routes small units of data called packets through a network based on the destination address contained within each packet.

parallel port   An interface that can transfer more than 1 bit simultaneously. It connects external devices, such as printers.

partial-mesh topology   At least one device maintains multiple connections to others without being fully meshed. A partial-mesh topology still provides redundancy by having several alternative routes.

patch cable   A cable with a connector on each end, used to transfer signals from one piece of network equipment to another.

patch cord   A length of cable used to connect links at the cross-connect.

patch panel   A device used to interconnect data networking or voice systems to the physical cable network. The rear of the patch panel has network cables that are punched down. The front of the patch panel has a factory-terminated interface of some type.

patch panel   An assembly of pin locations and ports that can be mounted on a rack or wall bracket in the wiring closet. Patch panels act like switchboards that connect workstations' cables to each other and to the outside.

peer-to-peer communication   A form of communication in which each layer of the OSI model at the source must communicate with its peer layer at the destination.

peer-to-peer network   Networked computers act as equal partners, or peers, to each other. As peers, each computer can take on the client function or the server function.

Personal Computer Memory Card International Association (PCMCIA)   An organization that has developed a standard for small credit card-sized devices called PCMCIA cards (or PC cards). Originally designed to add memory to portable computers, the PCMCIA standard has been expanded several times and is now suitable for many types of devices.

physical connection   A connection to a network that is made by connecting a specialized expansion card, such as a modem or NIC, from a PC with a cable to a network.

physical layer   Layer 1 of the OSI reference model. The physical layer defines the electrical, mechanical, procedural, and functional specifications for activating, maintaining, and deactivating the physical link between end systems.

ping (Packet Internet Groper)   ICMP echo message and its reply. Often used in IP networks to test the reachability of a network device.

plenum   An open ceiling that acts as an air-return duct for heating, ventilation, and air-conditioning systems.

plug-in   Software or a program that can easily be installed and used as part of a web browser.

PM (phase modulation)   Modulates the polarity (phase) of the wave.

poison reverse updates   Updates that are necessary to defeat larger routing loops. Generally speaking, increases in routing metrics indicate routing loops. Poison reverse updates are then sent to remove the route and place it in holddown.

port   In IP terminology, an upper-layer process that receives information from lower layers. Ports are numbered, and many are associated with a specific process. For example, SMTP is associated with port 25. A port number of this type is called a well-known port or address.

power cord   Connects an electrical device to an electrical outlet to provide power to the device.

power-on self-test (POST)   Set of hardware diagnostics that runs on a hardware device when that device is powered up.

power supply   Supplies power to a computer.

presentation layer   Layer 6 of the OSI reference model. This layer ensures that information sent by the application layer of one system can be read by the application layer of another.

printed circuit board (PCB)   A thin plate on which chips (integrated circuits) and other electronic components are placed.

privileged mode   Used for copying and managing entire configuration files.

propagation delay   A simple measurement of how long it takes for a signal to travel along the cable being tested.

protocol   A formal description of a set of rules and conventions that govern how devices on a network exchange information.

protocol stack   A set of related communications protocols that operate together and, as a group, address communication at some or all of the seven layers of the OSI reference model. Not every protocol stack covers each layer of the model, and often a single protocol in the stack addresses a number of layers at once. TCP/IP is a typical protocol stack.

PSELFEXT (power sum equal-level far-end crosstalk)   The combined effect of ELFEXT from all wire pairs.

PSNEXT (power sum near-end crosstalk)   Measures the cumulative effect of NEXT from all wire pairs in the cable.

pulse   Determines the value of the data being transmitted. If a disturbance is deliberately caused and involves a fixed, predictable duration, it is called a pulse.

queuing   A process by which ACLs can designate certain packets to be processed by a router before other traffic, on the basis of some configurable parameter such as specifying a protocol.

raceway   Channels that contain cables in an installation. Raceways include common electrical conduit, specialized cable trays or ladder racks, in-floor duct systems, and plastic or metal surface-mounted raceways.

random-access memory (RAM)   Also known as read-write memory. Can have new data written to it as well as stored data read from it.

range error   A frame that had a legal-size value in the Length field but that did not match the actual number of octets counted in the Data field of the received frame.

read-only memory (ROM)   A type of computer memory in which data has been prerecorded.

reflection   The photons of light striking a surface and leaving that surface in an equal but opposite direction.

refraction   The change in direction of a beam of light when it enters another medium.

remote copy protocol (RCP)   Protocol that allows users to copy files to and from a file system residing on a remote host or server on the network.

repeater   A networking device that exists at Layer 1, the physical layer, of the OSI reference model. The purpose of a repeater is to regenerate and retime network signals at the bit level, allowing them to travel a longer distance on the medium.

resistance   The property of a material that resists electron movement.

Reverse Address Resolution Protocol (RARP)   Protocol in the TCP/IP stack that provides a method for finding IP addresses based on MAC addresses.

RFI (radio frequency interference)   The noise on wires caused by radio signals.

ring topology   A topology in which hosts are connected in the form of a ring or circle. Unlike the physical bus topology, the ring topology has no beginning or end that needs to be terminated.

RJ-45   A connector commonly used for finishing a twisted-pair cable

routed protocol   Any network protocol that provides enough information in its network layer address to allow a packet to be forwarded from one host to another host based on the addressing scheme.

router   A network layer device that uses one or more metrics to determine the optimal path along which network traffic should be forwarded. Routers forward packets from one network to another based on network layer information contained in routing updates. Occasionally called a *gateway* (although this definition of *gateway* is becoming increasingly outdated).

routing   The process of finding a path to a destination host. Routing is very complex in large networks because of the many potential intermediate destinations that a packet might traverse before reaching its destination host.

Routing Information Protocol (RIP)   An IGP supplied with UNIX BSD systems. The most common IGP in the Internet. RIP uses hop count as a routing metric.

routing metric   A method by which a routing algorithm determines that one route is better than another. This information is stored in routing tables and is sent in routing updates. Metrics include bandwidth, communication cost, delay, hop count, load, MTU, path cost, and reliability. Sometimes simply called a *metric*.

routing protocol   A protocol that accomplishes routing through the implementation of a specific routing algorithm. Examples of routing protocols are IGRP, OSPF, and RIP.

routing table   A table stored in a router or some other internetworking device that keeps track of routes to particular network destinations and, in some cases, metrics associated with those routes.

routing update   A message sent from a router to indicate network reachability and associated cost information. Routing updates are typically sent at regular intervals and after a change in network topology. Compare with Flash update.

segment   In the TCP specification, a logical information group at transport layers of the OSI reference model.

serial port   Can be used for serial communication in which only 1 bit is transmitted at a time.

session layer   Layer 5 of the OSI reference model. This layer establishes, manages, and terminates sessions between applications and manages data exchange between presentation layer entities.

shortest path first (SPF) algorithm   A calculation performed on the database resulting in the SPF tree.

Simple Network Management Protocol (SNMP) Network management protocol used almost exclusively in TCP/IP networks. SNMP provides a means to monitor and control network devices, and to manage configurations, statistics collection, performance, and security.

simplex   The capability for transmission in only one direction between a sending station and a receiving station. Broadcast television is an example of a simplex technology.

sine waves   Graphs of mathematical functions of many natural occurrences that change regularly over time, such as the distance from the earth to the sun, the distance from the ground while riding a Ferris wheel, and the time of day that the sun rises.

single-mode   An optical fiber that has only one mode of light transmission. Contrast with multimode.

SNMP (Simple Network Management Protocol)   A network-management protocol used almost exclusively in TCP/IP networks. SNMP provides a means of monitoring and controlling network devices and managing configurations, statistics collection, performance, and security.

SNR (signal-to-noise ratio)   The ratio of useable signal being transmitted to the undesired signal (noise). It is a measure of transmission quality. The ratio of good data (signal) to bad (noise) on a line, expressed in decibels (dB).

sound card   An expansion board that handles all sound functions.

spectrum analyzer   An electronic device that creates graphs for frequency-domain analysis. Engineers also use frequency-domain analysis to study signals.

split horizon   A routing technique in which information about routes is prevented from exiting the router interface through which that information was received. Split-horizon updates are useful in preventing routing loops.

square waves   Graphs that do not continuously vary with time. The values remain the same for some time, then suddenly change, then remain the same, and then suddenly return to the initial value.

SS (spread spectrum)   A modulation technique developed in the 1940s that spreads a transmission signal over a broad band of radio frequencies. The term spread spectrum describes a modulation technique that sacrifices bandwidth to gain signal-to-noise performance.

standard   A set of rules or procedures that are either widely used or officially specified.

standard ACL   ACL that compares source IP addresses to the rules defining a standard ACL.

star topology   The most commonly used physical topology in Ethernet LANs. The star topology is made up of a central connection point that is a device such as a hub, switch, or router, where all the cabling segments meet.

static routing   The process of manually defining and configuring the routes.

storage-area network (SAN)   A dedicated, high-performance network that moves data between servers and storage resources.

store-and-forward switching   A packet-switching technique in which frames are processed completely before being forwarded out the appropriate port. This processing includes calculating the CRC and checking the destination address. In addition, frames must be stored temporarily until network resources (such as an unused link) are available to forward the message.

STP (shielded twisted-pair)   A two-pair wiring medium used in a variety of network implementations. STP cabling has a layer of shielded insulation to reduce EMI.

STP (Spanning Tree Protocol)   Bridge protocol that uses the spanning tree algorithm, enabling a learning bridge to dynamically work around loops in a network topology by creating a spanning tree. Bridge exchange BPDU messages with other bridges to detect loops and then remove the loops by shutting down selected bridge interfaces.

straight-through cable   A cable that maintains the pin connection all the way through the cable. Thus, the wire connected to pin 1 is the same on both ends of the cable.

structured cabling   A uniform cabling system with standards that define the actual cable, cabling distances, type of cable, and type of terminating devices.

structured cabling system (SCS)   Integrated cable plans that include the connectors, wiring, distribution centers, and installation techniques developed by specific companies.

stub network   An OSPF area that carries a default route, intra-area routes, and inter-area routes, but that does not carry external routes.

subnet address   A portion of an IP address that is specified as the subnetwork by the subnet mask.

subnet mask   A 32-bit address mask used in IP to indicate the bits of an IP address that are used for the subnet address. Sometimes simply called a *mask*.

subnetting   The method of dividing full network address classes into smaller pieces. This has prevented complete IP address exhaustion.

subnetwork
1. In IP networks, a network sharing a particular subnet address. Subnetworks are networks arbitrarily segmented by a network administrator to provide a multilevel, hierarchical routing structure while shielding the subnetwork from the addressing complexity of attached networks. Sometimes called a *subnet*.

2. In OSI networks, a collection of ESs and ISs under the control of a single administrative domain and using a single network access protocol.

Subnetwork Access Protocol (SNAP)   Internet protocol that operates between a network entity in the subnetwork and a network entity in the end system. SNAP specifies a standard method of encapsulating IP datagrams and ARP messages on IEEE networks. The SNAP entity in the end system makes use of the services of the subnetwork and performs three key functions: data transfer, connection management, and QoS selection.

subnetwork mask   A 32-bit address mask used in IP to indicate the bits of an IP address that are being used for the subnet address.

switch   A device that connects LAN segments, uses a table of MAC addresses to determine the segment on which a frame needs to be transmitted, and reduces traffic. Switches operate at much higher speeds than bridges.

system routes   Routes to networks within an autonomous system. Cisco IOS Software derives system routes from directly connected network interfaces and system route information provided by other IGRP-speaking routers or access servers. System routes do not include subnet information.

system unit   The main component of a PC system.

TB (terabyte)   Approximately 1 trillion bytes. Hard drive capacity on some high-end computers is measured in TB.

Tbps (terabits per second)   One trillion bits per second. A standard measurement of the amount of data transferred over a network connection. Some high-speed core Internet routers and switches operate at more than Tbps.

TCP (Transmission Control Protocol)   A connection-oriented transport-layer protocol that provides reliable full-duplex data transmission. TCP is part of the TCP/IP protocol stack.

Telecommunications Industry Association (TIA)   An organization that develops standards relating to telecommunications technologies. Together, the TIA and the Electronic Industries Alliance (EIA) have formalized standards, such as EIA/TIA-232, for the electrical characteristics of data transmission.

telecommunications room (TR)   The area within a building that houses the telecommunications cabling system equipment.

Telnet   A standard terminal emulation protocol in the TCP/IP protocol stack. Telnet is used for remote terminal connection, enabling users to log in to remote systems and use resources as if they were connected to a local system. Telnet is defined in RFC 854.

TFTP (Trivial File Transfer Protocol)   A simplified version of FTP that allows files to be transferred from one computer to another over a network.

Thicknet   An early form of coaxial cable using 10BASE5 for networking. Thicknet was once desirable because it could carry signals up to 500 meters.

Thinnet   A simple, thin, coaxial network cable for the 10BASE2 system. Thinnet can carry a signal only 185 meters, but was much easier to work with than thicknet.

three-way handshake   A sequence of messages exchanged between two or more network devices to ensure transmission synchronization before sending user data.

throughput   The rate of information arriving at or passing through a particular point in a network system.

TIA (Telecommunications Industry Association)   A standards association that publishes standards for telecommunications.

TIA/EIA-568-B standard   Specifies ten tests that a copper cable must pass if it is used for modern, high-speed Ethernet LANs.

time domain reflectometer (TDR)   A device that can measure the lengths of cables that are installed and locate faults. It does these tasks by sending a signal down a cable and then measuring the amount of time that it takes for that signal to return.

token passing   An access method by which network devices access the physical medium in an orderly fashion based on possession of a small frame called a token.

Token Ring   A token-passing LAN developed and supported by IBM. Token Ring runs at 4 or 16 Mbps over a ring topology.

topological database   A collection of information gathered from LSAs.

traceroute   Program available on many systems that traces the path a packet takes to a destination. It is used mostly to debug routing problems between hosts.

trailer   Controls information appended to data when encapsulating the data for network transmission.

Transmission Control Protocol/Internet Protocol (TCP/IP)   A common name for the suite of protocols developed by the U.S. DoD in the 1970s to support the construction of worldwide internetworks. TCP and IP are the two best-known protocols in the suite.

transport layer   Layer 4 of the OSI reference model. This layer is responsible for reliable network communication between end nodes. The transport layer provides mechanisms to establish, maintain, and terminate virtual circuits, transport fault detection and recovery, and information flow control.

triggered update   A triggered update is an update that is sent without waiting for the update timer to expire.

Trivial File Transfer Protocol (TFTP)   Simplified version of FTP that allows files to be transferred from one computer to another over a network, usually without the use of client authentication (for example, username and password).

Type Length Values (TLVs)   Blocks of information embedded in CDP advertisements.

unicast   Message sent to a single network destination

universal serial bus (USB) port   Lets peripheral devices such as mice, modems, keyboards, scanners, and printers be plugged in and unplugged without resetting the system.

update timer   Specifies how frequently routing update messages are sent. The IGRP default for this variable is 90 seconds.

uptime   The amount of time that the device is functional and in service relative to the users' requirements for its availability.

User Datagram Protocol (UDP)   Connectionless transport layer protocol in the TCP/IP protocol stack. UDP is a simple protocol that exchanges datagrams without acknowledgments or guaranteed delivery, requiring that error processing and retransmission be handled by other protocols.

UTP (unshielded twisted-pair)   A four-pair wire medium used in a variety of networks.

vertical cabling   Backbone cables, intermediate and main cross-connects, mechanical terminations, and patch cords or jumpers used for backbone-to-backbone cross-connections.

video card   A board that plugs into a PC to give it display capabilities.

virtual private network (VPN)   A private network constructed within a public network infrastructure such as the global Internet.

WAN (wide-area network)   A data communications network spanning a large geographic area, such as a state, province, or country. WANs often use transmission facilities provided by common carriers, for example, telephone companies.

wave   Energy traveling from one place to another.

wavelength   The length of a wave measured from any point on one wave to the corresponding point on the next wave. The wavelength of light is usually measured in nanometers (nm).

WDM (wavelength-division multiplexing)   Multiple optical wavelengths can share the same transmission fiber. The spectrum occupied by each channel must be separated adequately from the other.

web browser   A graphical user interface (GUI)-based hypertext client application, such as Internet Explorer or Netscape Navigator, used to access hypertext documents and other services located on remote servers throughout the WWW and the Internet.

well-known ports   These ports are defined in RFC 1700 and are reserved in both TCP and UDP. These well-known ports can identify applications that run above the transport layer protocols.

WEP (wired equivalent privacy)   A security mechanism, defined within the 802.11 standard, that is designed to protect the over-the-air transmission between wireless LAN APs and NICs.

white noise   Noise that affects all transmission frequencies equally.

windowing   A flow-control mechanism requiring that the source device receive an acknowledgment from the destination after transmitting a certain amount of data.

work area   A space where computers, telephones, and other network equipment is used.

Index

B

X–Z